High Performance Parallelism Pearls

Multicore and Many-core Programming Approaches

Volume Two

High Performance Parallelism Pearls

Multicore and Many-core Programming Approaches

Volume Two

James Reinders

Jim Jeffers

Intel Corporation, United States

AMSTERDAM • BOSTON • HEIDELBERG • LONDON
NEW YORK • OXFORD • PARIS • SAN DIEGO
SAN FRANCISCO • SINGAPORE • SYDNEY • TOKYO
Morgan Kaufmann is an imprint of Elsevier

Acquiring Editor: *Todd Green*
Editorial Project Manager: *Lindsay Lawrence*
Project Manager: *Mohana Natarajan*
Designer: *Maria Inês Cruz*

Cover Background: Photo of the COSMOS@DiRAC SGI UV2000 based Supercomputer manufactured by SGI, Inc and operated by the Stephen Hawking Centre for Theoretical Cosmology, University of Cambridge. Photo courtesy of Philip Mynott.

Cover Foreground: 3D visualization of statistical fluctuations in the Cosmic Microwave Background, the remnant of the first measurable light after the Big Bang. CMB data is from the Planck satellite and is the topic of Chapter 10 providing insights into new physics and how the universe evolved. Visualization rendered with Intel's OSPRay ray tracing open source software by Gregory P. Johnson and Timothy Rowley, Intel Corporation.

Morgan Kaufmann is an imprint of Elsevier
225 Wyman Street, Waltham, MA 02451, USA

Notices
Knowledge and best practice in this field are constantly changing. As new research and experience broaden our understanding, changes in research methods, professional practices, or medical treatment may become necessary.

Practitioners and researchers must always rely on their own experience and knowledge in evaluating and using any information, methods, compounds, or experiments described herein. In using such information or methods they should be mindful of their own safety and the safety of others, including parties for whom they have a professional responsibility.

To the fullest extent of the law, neither the Publisher nor the authors, contributors, or editors, assume any liability for any injury and/or damage to persons or property as a matter of products liability, negligence or otherwise, or from any use or operation of any methods, products, instructions, or ideas contained in the material herein.

British Library Cataloguing-in-Publication Data
A catalogue record for this book is available from the British Library

Library of Congress Cataloging-in-Publication Data
A catalog record for this book is available from the Library of Congress

ISBN: 978-0-12-803819-2

For information on all Morgan Kaufmann publications
visit our website at http://store.elsevier.com/

Contents

Contributors

Jefferson Amstutz
SURVICE Engineering, USA

Jefferson is a Software Engineer in the Applied Technology Operation of SURVICE Engineering Company. His work leverages advances in massively parallel computing architectures to solve a variety of physics-based simulation problems in domains such as ballistic vulnerability analysis, radio-frequency propagation, and soft-body simulation.

Cedric Andreolli
Intel Corporation, France

Cédric is an Application Engineer in the Energy team where he helps optimize customer applications running on Intel platforms for the Oil and Gas industry.

Meenakshi Arunachalam
Intel Corporation, USA

Meena is a Performance Architect working on performance analysis and modeling of workloads on Intel Xeon and Intel Xeon Phi products. She works on projections and modeling of key workloads and industry benchmarks. She builds insights using her models and tools including microarchitecture analyses and optimizing application performance as seen by the user.

Gaurav Bansal
Intel Corporation, USA

Gaurav is an HPC Software Applications Engineer in the Software and Services Group. His focus is on enabling and modernizing applications in the manufacturing vertical, such as computational fluid dynamics and structural analysis, including advantage of the Intel's current and future generation multicore and many-core platforms.

Martin Berzins
SCI Institute & School of Computing, University of Utah, USA

Martin is a Professor of Computer Science in the School of Computing and the Scientific Computing and Imaging Institute at the University of Utah. His broad research interests include parallel software for use on modern heterogeneous computer architectures.

Paul Besl
Intel Corporation, USA

Paul works in the Software and Services Group with a focus on CAE applications used by manufacturing organizations. Paul is also chair of the SPEC Graphics Workstation Performance Group.

Ashraf Bhuiyan
Intel Corporation, USA

Ashraf is a Software Engineer, specializing in code optimization, and has helped projects including Amber utilize parallelism. Prior to Intel, he worked on NSF funded projects as a multicore optimization expert.

Stephen Blair-Chappell
Intel Corporation, United Kingdom

Stephen is a Technical Consulting Engineer at Intel, and has worked in the Compiler team for the last 15 years. Stephens provides consulting and training to the Intel Parallel Computing Centers in EMEA. Stephen is an author of the book *Parallel Programming with Intel Parallel Studio XE*.

Leonardo Borges
Intel Corporation, USA

Leo is a Senior Staff Engineer and has been engaged with the Intel Many Integrated Core program from its early days. He specializes in HPC applying his background in numerical analysis and in developing parallel numerical math libraries. Leo is focused on optimization work related to the Oil and Gas industry.

James P. Briggs
University of Cambridge, UK

James is a Parallel Programmer at the COSMOS IPCC at the Stephen Hawking Centre for Theoretical Cosmology at the University of Cambridge. He works with scientists to modernize and optimize cosmology codes for modern and future architectures. His interests are in computational astrophysics and parallel and high-performance computing.

Mikhail Brinskiy
Intel Corporation, Russia

Mikhail is a Software Development Engineer working in the Software and Services Group with focus on the Intel MPI Library development. Mikhail has a strong background on numerical modeling for applied physics.

Michal Brylinski
Department of Biological Sciences, Louisiana State
University, USA

Michal runs a Computational Systems Biology Lab, where most of the projects lie at the intersection of structural biology, bioinformatics, and high-performance computing. He is actively involved in the design and development of novel algorithms and codes for drug discovery and repositioning. He is highly interested in the application of massively parallel hardware accelerators in structural bioinformatics, functional genomics, cheminformatics, and pharmacogenomics. He also teaches courses on computational biology, biophysics, physical chemistry, and molecular dynamics.

Vlad Calina
Intel Corporation, Romania

Vlad is a Software Engineer at Intel working on performance analysis and characterization of HPC applications. He focuses on the impact that various architectural features like vectorization and prefetching have on application performance.

James Dinan
Intel Corporation, USA

James is a Software Architect working in the area of High-Performance Computing. He has served on the MPI Forum for several years and was a contributor to the MPI 3.0 specification. Jim was previously the James Wallace Givens postdoctoral fellow at Argonne National Laboratory. His research interests include parallel programming models, high-performance fabrics, scalable runtime systems, distributed algorithms, scientific computing, and computer architecture.

Jussi Enkovaara
CSC, Finland

Jussi is a Senior Application Scientist in High-Performance Computing support at CSC and a docent of computational physics in Aalto University, Finland. Among others, he is interested in numerical methods for electronic structure simulations and utilizing Python in the context of high-performance computing. He is one of the key developers of the density-functional-theory-based software package GPAW.

Rob Farber
TechEnablement.com, USA

Rob is a Consultant with an extensive background in HPC and a long history of working with national laboratories and corporations engaged in HPC optimization work. Rob has authored/edited several books on GPU programming and is the CEO/Publisher of TechEnablement.com.

Julia Fedorova
Intel Corporation, Russia

Julia is a Principal Engineer in the Software and Services Group where she works on performance profiling and analysis tools including Intel VTune Amplifier XE. Recently, she has been focusing on GPU compute analysis. She loves the challenge of optimizing software and improving the tools they develop through this experience.

Wei P. Feinstein
Louisiana State University, USA

Wei works in the HPC group assisting researchers from different disciplines to efficiently utilize computer cluster resources. She is also a computational biologist interested in developing algorithms for computational biophysics with applications in drug discovery. She develops high-performance parallel and heterogeneous codes to boost the performance of applications in biology. In addition, Wei co-leads the TESC (Technologies for Extreme Scale Computing) team, where a group of interdisciplinary graduate students at LSU collaborate to improve the performance of various domain science projects using hardware accelerators.

Evan Felix
Pacific Northwest National Laboratory (PNNL), USA

Evan is a Research Scientist and HPC Engineer in the Environmental Molecular Sciences Laboratory, a Department of Energy (DOE) users facility at PNNL. He is a senior member of the team that runs the Molecular Science Computing Facility, which provides supercomputing resources and archive capabilities for researchers at PNNL, and at universities and laboratories around the world. This team has deployed systems that have ranked highly on the top500.org supercomputer list, and maintains a multi-petabyte data archive. He works on numerous open-source projects, many of which are used to maintain, monitor, and deploy supercomputing systems.

James R. Fergusson
University of Cambridge, UK

James is a Lecturer in the Department of Applied Mathematics and Theoretical Physics. His work mainly concerns connecting theoretical models of the very early universe with observational data. He is a member of the Planck satellite mission and has done extensive work in the field of non-Gaussianity, producing the strongest available constraints on non-standard models of inflation.

Evgeny Fiksman
Intel Corporation, USA

Evgeny works with customers to help optimize their financial applications. He previously worked on the implementation of OpenCL runtime for Intel processors and Intel Xeon Phi coprocessors, and has background in optimization of video enhancement algorithms for $\times 86$ platforms. Prior to joining Intel, he lead development of a naval team training simulator.

Indraneil Gokhale
Intel Corporation, USA

Indraneil is a Software Architect at Intel with emphasis on post- and presilicon performance analysis and optimization of HPC workloads on Intel Xeon Phi coprocessors. He focuses on optimizations using parallelism, vectorization, and key architectural features for performance. Indraneil participates in delivering transformative methods and tools to expose new insights for the MIC program. His research areas include VLSI, Computer Architecture.

Christiaan Gribble
SURVICE Engineering, USA

Christiaan is a Principal Research Scientist and the Team Lead for High-Performance Computing in the Applied Technology Operation of SURVICE Engineering Company. His research explores the synthesis of interactive visualization and high-performance computing, focusing on algorithms, architectures, and systems for predictive rendering and visual simulation applications.

Diana Guttman
Pennsylvania State University, USA

Diana is a Graduate Student in the Microsystems Design Lab at Penn State. Her research focuses on architecture-aware software optimizations for multicores.

Tom Henderson
NOAA Earth System Research Laboratory, USA

Tom Henderson is a Software Engineer at NOAA's Global Systems Division where he provides high-performance computing expertise to numerical weather prediction model development efforts. He served on the MPI-1 Forum and current research focuses on accelerator architectures.

John Holmen
SCI Institute & School of Computing, University of Utah, USA

John is pursuing a Ph.D. in Computing (Scientific Computing Track) at the University of Utah. His research focuses on exploiting the Intel MIC Architecture to help improve the performance and scalability of the Uintah Computational Framework, specifically to run on current and emerging MIC-based hybrid supercomputer architectures.

Allen H.-L. Huang
University of Wisconsin-Madison, USA

Allen is affiliated with the Space Science and Engineering Center at the University of Wisconsin-Madison. He is an SPIE Fellow, a member of the Committee on Earth Study of the National Academies, and a member of the International Radiation Commission. His research interests include remote sensing and high-performance computing.

Bormin Huang
University of Wisconsin-Madison, USA

Bormin is the Director of the Intel Parallel Computing Center at the University of Wisconsin-Madison. He is also affiliated with the Space Science and Engineering Center at the University of Wisconsin-Madison. He is an SPIE Fellow and an NVIDIA CUDA Fellow. His research interests include remote sensing and high-performance computing.

Alan Humphrey
SCI Institute & School of Computing, University of Utah, USA

Alan is a Software Developer at the Scientific Computing and Imaging Institute and a Ph.D. candidate in Computer Science at the University of Utah. His research focuses on improving the performance and scalability of the Uintah Computational Framework, specifically to run on current and emerging hybrid supercomputer architectures.

Juha Jäykkä
University of Cambridge, UK

Juha currently manages the COSMOS IPCC and the COSMOS supercomputers at the Stephen Hawking Centre for Theoretical Cosmology. His research interests lie in theoretical physics and in enabling scientists get the most out of their HPC systems using portable, sustainable, efficient, and optimized software. He has previously worked on mathematical physics, classical field theories, and large-scale HPC simulations.

Jim Jeffers
Intel Corporation, USA

Jim is a Principal Engineer and Engineering Manager in the Technical Computing Group. Jim coedited the first volume of High Performance Parallelism Pearls (Morgan Kaufmann, 2014) and coauthored Intel Xeon Phi Coprocessor High Performance Programming (Morgan Kaufmann, 2013). Jim currently leads Intel's technical computing visualization team.

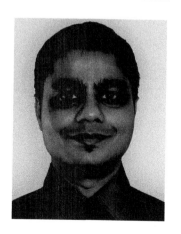

Ashish Jha
Intel Corporation, USA

Ashish is a Senior Software Architect in the Software and Services Group. He works on Hardware Software Co-Design focusing on new Instruction Set Architecture pathfinding and High-Performance Computing performance optimizations integrating the newest Intel processor capabilities.

Bálint Joó
U.S. DOE Thomas Jefferson National Accelerator Facility, USA

Balint is a Computational Scientist at Jefferson Lab specializing in algorithms and software for lattice QCD calculations. His research interests include Linear Solvers, Monte Carlo methods, extreme scale computing, and optimizing lattice QCD codes for new high-performance computing architectures.

Dhiraj D. Kalamkar
Intel Corporation, India

Dhiraj is a Research Scientist in the Parallel Computing Laboratory. His research interests include parallel computer architecture, GPGPU architectures, hardware-specific power and performance optimizations, Hardware-enabled platform security. He is currently working on analyzing and optimizing various workloads for Intel Xeon, Gen and MIC architectures.

Mahmut Taylan Kandemir
Pennsylvania State University, USA

Mahmut is a Professor in the Computer Science and Engineering Department at Penn State. His research focuses on computer architecture, compiler support for multicore/manycore systems, and high-performance storage systems.

Rahul Khanna
Intel Corporation, USA

Rahul is a Platform Architect and Principal Engineer involved in development of energy-efficient algorithms. Rahul has worked on server system software technologies including platform automation, power/thermal optimization techniques, reliability, optimization, and predictive methodologies. He is the co-inventor of the Intel IBIST methodology for High-Speed interconnect testing. He has 33 patents. His research interests include machine-learning-based power/thermal optimization algorithms, narrow-channel high-speed wireless interconnects, and information retrieval in dense sensor networks. Rahul is a member of IEEE and the recipient of three Intel Achievement Awards. He is the author of upcoming book *A Vision for Platform Autonomy: Robust Frameworks for Systems*.

Taylor Kidd
Intel Corporation, USA

Taylor is a Software Engineer; he leads a team of other engineers that generates collateral and address customer issues relating to the Intel Xeon Phi coprocessor and its technology. Currently, Taylor writes technical articles in a variety of areas, but is mostly focused on application energy consumption and policy.

Jeongnim Kim
Intel Corporation, USA

Jeongnim is a Senior HPC Application Engineer in the Technical Computing Group focusing on parallel application development and optimization. She has extensive experience in developing numerical algorithms and materials applications on large-scale parallel platforms.

Michael Klemm
Intel Corporation, Germany

Michael works in the Software and Services Group with a focus on High-Performance and Throughput Computing. Michael is the project lead for the development of pyMIC. Michael is an Intel representative to the OpenMP Language Committee and leads the efforts to develop error handling features for OpenMP.

Shuo Li
Intel Corporation, USA

Shuo works in the Software and Service Group as a Software Performance Engineer covering financial service industry. He works closely with developers of financial software and helps them achieve higher performance in their applications. His main interest is parallel programming and application software performance.

Yongchao Liu
Georgia Institute of Technology, USA

Yognchao is Research Scientist II at the Georgia Institute of Technology. His research interests focus on parallel and distributed algorithm design for bioinformatics, heterogeneous computing with accelerators, specifically CUDA-enabled GPUs and Intel Xeon Phi coprocessors, and high-performance computing on big data. He has released a set of software tools, the majority of which are open-source, associated with his paper publications.

Belinda Liviero
Intel Corporation, USA

Belinda leads the Platform Launch and Scale Engineering team in the Software and Services group, focused on enabling ISV developers across Intel technologies (Servers, Storage, Networks, Desktops, and Mobile platforms).

Mark Lubin
Intel Corporation, USA

Mark works in the Software and Services Group with a focus on High-Performance Computing. Prior to joining Intel, Mark did his postdoctoral research at UCSD, where he developed computer models and software for parallel computers.

Luke Mason
STFC Daresbury Laboratory, UK

Luke works, at the Hartree centre, porting scientific codes to the Intel Xeon Phi coprocessor. Concurrent with the completion of this book, he completed a PhD in Smoothed Particle Hydrodynamics for high velocity impact and plastic deformation of metals. That's parallelism!

Zakhar A. Matveev
Intel Corporation, Russia

Zakhar is a Software Architect of Intel Parallel Studio. He focuses on software requirements, design, and implementation for "Vector Advisor". Before joining Intel, he had been working with TV broadcast automation software domain and embedded software/hardware co-design. His professional interests focus on HPC systems optimization, parallel programming, computer graphics (PhD), software design and usability.

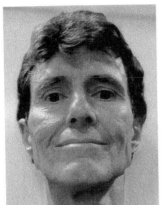

Lawrence Meadows
Intel Corporation, USA

Larry has worked on compilers, tools, and applications software for HPC since 1982. He was a founding member of The Portland Group and has worked at Intel since 2004.

John Michalakes
NOAA National Centers for Environmental Prediction, USA

John is a Scientific Programmer/Analyst in the NOAA National Centers for Environmental Prediction. He was lead software developer for the Weather Research and Forecast (WRF) Model software at the National Center for Atmospheric Research.

Jarno Mielikainen
University of Wisconsin-Madison, USA

Jarno is the Deputy Director of the Intel Parallel Computing Center at the University of Wisconsin-Madison. He is also affiliated with the Space Science and Engineering Center at the University of Wisconsin-Madison. His primary research interests include high-performance computing and data compression algorithms.

Ravi A. Murty
Intel Corporation, USA

Ravi leads the software architecture for Knights Landing and is responsible for delivering key software components and performance tuning for the Intel Manycore Platform Software Stack (MPSS) for HPC. He has previously contributed to other projects including Infiniband, Wireless Networking, Graphics and OS driver development.

Perri Needham
San Diego Supercomputing Center, USA

Perri is an NSF funded postdoctoral research associate working on advanced molecular dynamics simulations. Her specific focus is on GPU-accelerated molecular dynamics as well as Intel funded work to explore the use of Intel Many Integrated Core technologies to accelerate molecular dynamics within the AMBER software package.

Chris J. Newburn
Intel Corporation, USA

CJ serves as an HPC architect, focused on Intel's Xeon Phi product family. He focuses on hardware and software co-design and has over 75 patents. Performance analysis and tuning have always figured prominently in his development and production readiness work. He is delighted to have worked on some high volume products that his Mom uses.

Matthias Noack
Zuse Institute Berlin, Germany

Matthias is a part of the Scalable Algorithms group at Zuse Institute Berlin (ZIB). His interests include parallel programming models, heterogeneous architectures, and scientific computing. He focuses on Heterogeneous Active Messages for efficient offloading and programming methods for vectorization.

Enda O'Brien
Irish Centre for High-End Computing, Ireland

Enda works in the weather and climate group at ICHEC, at the interface between meteorology and high-performance computing. His focus is on optimizing the performance (especially parallel performance) of weather models, particularly on novel computer architectures. He has experience both as a research meteorologist (University of Miami) and HPC applications expert (DEC/Compaq/Hewlett-Packard).

Klaus-Dieter Oertel
Intel Corporation, Germany

Klaus-Dieter is a Senior Technical Consultant for HPC in the Software and Services Group. He belongs to the first generation of parallelization experts in Germany and worked on all kinds of supercomputers. Klaus-Dieter supports several Intel Parallel Computing Centers in their code modernization efforts targeting parallelism on all system levels from processes, over threads, to vectors.

Simon J. Pennycook
Intel Corporation, UK

John is an Application Engineer focused on enabling developers to fully utilize the current generation of Intel Xeon Phi coprocessors. His previous research focused on the optimization of scientific applications for a wide range of different microarchitectures and hardware platforms, as well as the issues surrounding performance portability.

Dmitry Prohorov
Intel Corporation, Russia

Dmitry is an Engineering Manager in the Software and Services Group. Dmitry works on performance and threading analysis tools. He manages data processing and visualization team developing Intel VTune Amplifier XE performance and power profiler and leads HPC-related product definition.

Narayan Ranganathan
Intel Corporation, USA

Narayan is a Platform Software Architect in the Datacenter Group (DCG) working on technology intercepts for the next generation of Intel server platforms and software optimizations for the same. He holds two patents and is a previous recipient of an Intel achievement award (IAA).

George M. Raskulinec
Intel Corporation, USA

George work in the Financial Services team focusing on customer code optimization. He previously developed computer telephony libraries.

James Reinders
Intel Corporation, USA

James promotes increased use of parallel programming throughout the industry. His projects have included both the world's first TeraFLOP/s supercomputer (ASCI Red) and the world's first TeraFLOP/s microprocessor (Intel Xeon Phi coprocessor). James coedited the first volume of High Performance Parallelism Pearls (Morgan Kaufmann, 2014) and coauthored Intel Xeon Phi Coprocessor High Performance Programming as well as several other books related to high-performance programming. James has received an Intel Achievement Award (IAA).

Bertil Schmidt
Johannes Gutenberg University Mainz, Germany

Bertil is a Professor of Computer Science at the University of Mainz, where he leads the HPC group. His research group has designed a variety of algorithms and tools for Bioinformatics and Computational Science mainly focusing on the analysis of large-scale sequence and short read datasets.

Michael Seaton
STFC Daresbury Laboratory, UK

Michael has been a Computational Scientist at STFC Daresbury Laboratory since 2009. He is the lead developer of DL_MESO and an active contributor to DL_POLY_4. His research focuses on mesoscale modeling techniques, their implementation for high-performance computing architecture, and their applications in multiscale modelling problems.

Edward P. Shellard
University of Cambridge, UK

Paul is a Professor of Cosmology and Director of the Stephen Hawking Centre for Theoretical Cosmology at the Department of Applied Mathematics and Theoretical Physics in the University of Cambridge. His primary research interest lies in advancing the confrontation between theories of the early universe and observational cosmology, for which the latest HPC technologies are an essential tool.

Mikhail Smelyanskiy
Intel Corporation, USA

Mikhail is a Principal Engineer at the Parallel Computing Laboratory. His focus is on design, implementation, and analysis of parallel algorithms and workloads for current and future generation parallel processor systems. His research interests include medical imaging, computational finance, and fundamental high-performance compute kernels.

Paulo Souza
Petrobras, Brazil

Paulo has a Computer Engineering background and works as an HPC Consultant and Researcher. He has been working for 12 years with seismic imaging on HPC clusters and multiple architecture optimizations. His work with GPGPUs started in 2006 porting seismic imaging applications to CUDA with great performance gains in production workloads.

Dan Stanzione
Texas Advanced Computing Center (TACC), USA

Dan is the Executive Director of TACC, which is located at the University of Texas at Austin. He served as a deputy director since June 2009 and assumed the new post mid-2014. He is the principal investigator (PI) for several leading projects. He is the PI of the upcoming Wrangler system, a supercomputer designed specifically for data-focused applications. He served for 6 years as the co-director of the iPlant Collaborative, a large-scale NSF life sciences cyberinfrastructure. Dan was a co-principal investigator for TACC's Ranger and Lonestar supercomputers. Dan previously served as the founding director of the Fulton High Performance Computing Initiative at Arizona State University and served as an American Association for the Advancement of Science Policy Fellow in the NSF's Division of Graduate Education.

Philippe Thierry
Intel Corporation, France

Philippe leads the Intel Energy Engineering Team supporting end users and software vendors in the energy sector. His work includes profiling and tuning of HPC applications for current and future platforms as well as for super-computer definition with respect to the applications behaviors. His research activity is devoted to performance extrapolation and application characterization and modeling toward exascale computing.

Prashanth Thinakaran
Pennsylvania State University, USA

Prashanth is a PhD candidate in Computer Science and Engineering department. He is a member of the High Performance Computing Laboratory. His research interests are in the areas of systems software and parallel programming. His work focuses on improving the application performance on cloud and data centers through several system level optimizations.

Karthikeyan Vaidyanathan
Intel Corporation, India

Karthikeyan is a Research Scientist in the Parallel Computing Labs. His research interests include high-performance computing, high-speed interconnects, storage, and performance optimizations in parallel computer architecture. He is currently working on analyzing and optimizing communication performance of various workloads for Intel Xeon and Xeon Phi architectures.

Sergei Vinogradov
Intel Corporation, Russia

Sergei is a Software Developer in the Software and Service Group working on performance profiling tools and threading runtime libraries. Sergei prototyped and promoted several new features to Intel VTune Amplifier XE and Intel. He is working to prototype new features for heterogeneous computations in the Intel Threading Building Blocks (TBB) library.

Ross C. Walker
University of California San Diego, USA

Ross serves as an Associate Research Professor at the San Diego Supercomputer Center (SDSC) at the University of California, San Diego (UCSD), as an Adjunct Associate Professor of Chemistry and Biochemistry at UCSD, an NVIDIA Fellow, Director of the SDSC Intel Parallel Computing Center of Excellence and as biosciences lead of the Scientific Applications Computing group at the SDSC. He is a principal developer of the AMBER Molecular Dynamics code and has extensive experience in developing and teaching classical and QM/MM molecular dynamics techniques.

Florian Wende
Zuse Institute Berlin, Germany

Florian is a part of the Scalable Algorithms workgroup, in the Distributed Algorithms and Supercomputing department. He is interested in accelerator and many-core computing with application in Computer Science and Computational Physics. His focus is on load balancing of irregular parallel computations and on close-to-hardware code optimization.

Freddie Witherden
Imperial College London, UK

Freddie is a PhD candidate in the Department of Aeronautics at Imperial College London. His primary focus is on the efficient implementation of high-order accurate schemes for computational fluid dynamics (CFD). He is also the lead author of PyFR; a Python framework for high-order CFD on many-core platforms.

Praveen Yedlapalli
Pennsylvania State University, USA

Praveen is a PhD student in Computer Science and Engineering department at the Pennsylvania State University. He is a member of Microsystems Design Laboratory. Praveen's research interests are in the areas of computer architecture and compilers. His work focuses on improving the processor-memory interface for a broad range of systems ranging from mobile platforms to high-performance chip multiprocessors.

Acknowledgments

It has been our good fortune to work with the incredible contributors to this book. We are indebted to them for sharing their expertise. Their names are listed at the start of their chapters to which they contributed, and you can learn more about them and see their pictures in the "Contributor" section earlier in this book. We hope you find the pearls within each chapter that we have seen in working with these wonderful contributors.

Thank you to Dan Stanzione for his support and encouragement over the years, and offering his thoughts in the Foreword.

Thank you to Mike Greenfield, Ron Green, Elizabeth Schneider, David Mackay, Claude Wright, Jim Cownie, Lisa Smith, Sayantan Sur, Terry Wilmarth, Dave Poulsen, Martin Corden, Rob Farber, Steve Lionel, Arch Robison, Andrey Churbanov, Dick Kaiser, and Joe Curley for helping us even if they do not know why we imposed on their kindness to tap their expertise to help with the book. We were also blessed with the support and encouragement of some special managers in Intel including Nathan Schultz, Herb Hinstorff, Bob Burroughs, Sanjiv Shah, Charlie Wuischpard, Raj Hazra, and Diane Bryant.

James Reinders thanks his wife Susan Meredith for her love and support that were felt throughout the process of working on this book. James also thanks his daughter Katie and son Andrew for their wonderful and positive support. Finally, my coauthor and friend, Jim Jeffers, who worries from time to time that he is falling behind simultaneous with me thinking exactly the same thing. I do not think a better partnership for editing a book could exist, perhaps that is why this is our third book together. Thank you Jim.

Jim Jeffers has a special thank you to his wife Laura for her continued support and encouragement. Jim also thanks his children (including spouses), Tim, Patrick, Colleen, Sarah, Jon, and his very special grand-daughter Hannah for keeping him both grounded and incredibly proud. Many thanks to my coauthor and good friend, James Reinders, for his perseverance, good humor (most of the time!), and incredible organization (aka herding cats) without which our books would take years (if ever) to finish instead of months. I still don't understand how he magically gets me to work on another one even when I say "not this time."

We appreciate the hard work by the entire Morgan Kaufmann team including the three people we worked with directly: Todd Green, Lindsay Lawrence, and Mohan a Natarajan.

Numerous colleagues offered information, advice, and vision. We are sure that there are more than a few people who we have failed to mention who have positively impacted this book project. We thank all those who helped and we apologize for all who helped us and were not mentioned here.

Thank you all,
Jim Jeffers and James Reinders

Foreword

I am very honored and pleased to be asked to write this foreword, and very eager to see this new volume in the "Pearls" series about multicore and many-core programming. The growth we see today in many-core processors was probably inevitable. While it is easy to say that in hindsight, it does in some small way validate a rather large bet my team at the Texas Advanced Computing Center (TACC) and our colleagues at Intel made half a decade ago.

MAKING A BET ON MANY-CORE

In late 2010, the National Science Foundation (NSF) in the United States was about to put out a call for proposals to fund the next flagship supercomputer in its TeraGrid program, which in one form or another has provided computing power to scientific researchers at U.S. universities since the mid-1980s. It was an especially critical competition for TACC, as our previous system awarded through this program, Ranger, would be reaching its end of life when this new competition came to fruition. Ranger had been remarkably successful, supporting thousands of researchers who ran several million jobs over the life of the system, and across an incredible diversity of engineering and scientific research problems.

In some ways, this success created a bit of a quandary for both us and for the NSF. We had a large and diverse user community that relied upon our systems for their day-to-day research progress. We had a burgeoning new community of researchers who were addressing new challenges related to data-intensive computing (the "big data" wave was beginning to build). And we had fundamental changes in the computing industry—core count was exploding, and for the first time, we were likely to propose a system with a lower clock rate than systems we had built the previous year. This trend seemed likely to continue and would unleash enormous pressure on the scientific software ecosystem.

Faced with the challenge of balancing the needs of a large existing community, a new emerging community, and a shifting technology landscape, the NSF released a rather unique solicitation. The proposer was to present a system that would spend 80% of the investment on a "production" resource and the remaining 20% on an "innovative component" to address the fast changing landscape. The solicitation in turn created a unique challenge for us; how best to respond in a way that would continue to serve our broad mission, yet innovate in a way to move the scientific community forward.

And so, the risk we chose to take was to embrace, with Intel, the path to many-core. Nearly two and a half years before the Intel® Xeon Phi™ coprocessor would come to market (indeed, before there was any such name as "Xeon Phi"), we chose to build a system whose production component would revolve around the Intel® Xeon® processor, and clustering technology with which we had been so successful, and that we would add to *every* node in the system an Intel Xeon Phi coprocessor. We chose to take this approach because we knew we not only needed to replace the system we had, but we needed to get our *entire* user community ready for the many-core future. So, this new system would have nodes that had both the familiar incremental progress toward many-core in the Intel Xeon processors, but also a *sneak peak* at the future of processors with many more cores, more thread-level parallelism, and lower clock rates. This was a leap for us, for Intel, and our chosen system vendor Dell; to be successful, this new system would not just have a "Xeon Phi" experiment (on a much more aggressive schedule than the original plan to reach the market), but this many-core processor would have to function in every node of a system in production around the clock. Fortunately for us, Intel and Dell agreed with our vision that an investment in making this technology available as widely as possible was the right approach. Even more fortunate for us, the NSF review team agreed, and our proposal was selected for funding!

2013 STAMPEDE—INTEL MANY-CORE SYSTEM – A FIRST

This proposal resulted in the Stampede system, which was deployed in January 2013, and 2 years later still ranks as the seventh largest system in the world. Stampede supports well in excess of 2000 research projects and is in constant high demand. Even on weekends and holidays, there is always a long list of jobs waiting to run.

We felt the risk in pitching a many-core processor as the "innovative component" on Stampede was a safe bet, because it had become clear to us that we are entering the area of ubiquitous parallelism at all levels of systems—while we have all felt this was coming for a long time, it can no longer be ignored. Massive parallelism is no longer simply a phenomenon for the scientific community either. It has spread past the High-Performance Computing world, to the world at large; now enterprise and desktop computing is becoming as much concerned with many-core parallel computing techniques for performance as the science and engineering community.

HPC JOURNEY AND REVELATION

For me, the path to many-core has become a personal journey through my career as well. When I started in HPC, not called HPC at the time, another era was ending—for a long time, there was a notion that higher performance could be achieved by improving the design of a single CPU functional unit pipeline. The RISC versus CISC and superpipelining wars were raging, gallium arsenide and other materials were being discussed to build even faster chips; Moore's law was charging along, allowing us all to ride process improvements to "free" performance in the form of clock-rate improvements, whether we were right about our architectural choices or not.

I began in HPC as the cold war had ended, and the cost of custom silicon was becoming prohibitive for supercomputing. Fortunately, I had the right PhD advisor (Walt Ligon at Clemson University), who met some folks who had this crazy idea of Linux-based commodity clusters (in what came to be known as the "Beowulf" project at NASA Goddard Space Flight Center). We deployed the "Grendel" cluster at Clemson with 16 processors, and the "big-iron" approach began to crack. MPI came along about the same time and the rest is well-documented history; Linux clusters rose and much of big-iron supercomputing fell.

Silicon process improvement continued, giving us higher clock rates and better architectures. Sitting at a computer architecture conference in 1998, watching the 15th consecutive paper on how some crazy architecture trick had increased CPU performance by 3% at the expense of tens of thousands of transistors, I had the revelation (probably a couple of years after everyone else in the room) that multi-core nodes in clusters were inevitable, and I should get on board. Moore's law (though there were forecasts it was ending then too) was going to keep producing smaller transistors, and the only reasonable thing to do with them was to simply create more functional units. Power constraints were going to guarantee that clock rates would stop rising. So, without faster clocks, and without architecture tricks to make one thread go faster, we were going to have more parallelism on every chip and every node, and the only remaining debate was how these parallel units would be organized—thick cores versus thin cores, long vectors versus short vectors—parallelism at the node level was coming.

Another realization came along with that—if chips were going to get a lot more parallel, software was going to have to change with it. A large amount of parallelism at the chip level was going to mean increasing shared memory parallelism, so MPI alone would not likely suffice forever. The chips would change, that much was clear; but the software ecosystem is much more diffuse and fragmented; how would it be able to follow the trend? The good news is the community knows a lot about code tuning and parallelism. Little of what has happened with chips in recent years involves a radical new concept; it is a matter of proportion and scale. Vectors have gotten longer, but vectorization is not new. We have more hardware threads per chip, but threading is not new. More cores share a cache, but cache coherency and cache tuning are not new. What has changed is the balance and focus. For 20 years, most coders could successfully ignore vectorization, but no longer.

STAMPEDE USERS DISCOVER: IT'S PARALLEL PROGRAMMING

Which brings us back to Stampede. One of the most fascinating aspects of the project has been to watch the user community begin to adapt and to understand the demands of many-core processors to deliver good performance. Unlike every other technology we have deployed, we started with this one "at scale." Almost none of our users had development systems prior to Stampede—when they got access to that system, it was their very first exposure to Intel Xeon Phi programming and all the learning had to happen "on the fly." Two years later, more than 1200 of the users of the system have run a production job using the Xeon Phi. We are seeing more and more applications that can use the Xeon Phi, and even more encouragingly, we are seeing code improvements in general—developers are tuning their codes for Xeon Phi, and learning that good parallel code is simply good parallel code, and the changes made are benefiting code performance on the conventional Intel Xeon processors and other platforms as well.

THIS BOOK IS TIMELY AND IMPORTANT

This is what makes this book so timely and important. Modern processors are many-core, and will become moreso, that trend is simply not going away. Users and developers are flocking to these platforms. What we need to do to use them is not revolutionary, simply to make good use of techniques that have been known for a long time. But those techniques need to be used much more widely, with different emphasis, and at different scales. We don't need new theories, we need to take the theory we have and build a new practice of programming. That's what this book is here to do; to share as a community how theory is turning into practice and changing the way we code. From Grendel to Stampede, I've seen the community move performance forward by a factor of 10 million in 20 years. If we keep using and sharing what we have learned from this, I look forward to the next 10 million time improvement in the next 20 years.

Dan Stanzione
Executive Director
Texas Advanced Computing Center
The University of Texas at Austin

Preface

Welcome to our second "pearls" book, a collection of real-world parallel programming examples and techniques that are both timely and timeless. This book draws on 73 authors who share how their parallel programming, inspired by the highly parallel Intel® Xeon Phi™ coprocessors, unlocks processor performance as well as performance on the coprocessor.

This book is not about multicore programming alone or many-core programming alone, it is about parallel programming. That is possible because the Intel Xeon Phi coprocessor shares the same programming models, programming languages and tools with processor programming. The coprocessor does have the challenges of living across a PCIe bus from the processor, which limits its memory capacity and introduces latencies in moving data to and from the coprocessor. That, it turns out, will disappear with the next Intel Xeon Phi product codenamed Knights Landing which will come in the form of a stand-alone Intel Architecture processor as well as a coprocessor on a card. Most lessons in this Pearls book, and the prior Pearls book, are equally important for Knights Landing as they are for the original Intel Xeon Phi coprocessor.

The only real challenge in programming Intel Xeon Phi products long term is indeed parallel programming. The same challenge, the same techniques, as an Intel Xeon processor-based system (or any other processor for that matter). That is what makes these "pearls" books so important. We can never have too many good lessons from which to learn, especially when experts from around the world write them.

INSPIRED BY 61 CORES: A NEW ERA IN PROGRAMMING

In the first "pearls" book, we remarked on our experiencing the awakening that the Intel Xeon Phi coprocessor has brought to parallel programming. The experience continues and is related time and time again in the chapters of this book. We keep seeing this: programming for the Intel Xeon Phi coprocessor heightens awareness in the need for scaling, vectorization and increasing temporal locality of reference—exactly the keys to parallel programming. And, once we address those keys to effective parallel programming, we find that we have a parallel program that makes Intel Xeon Phi coprocessors *and* processors optimized for higher performance.

This book shows techniques that have proven effective in unlocking performance through parallel programming in a manner that brings permanent goodness to an application. By accelerating multicore processors and the compatible many-core devices that we know as Intel Xeon Phi products, with the same code changes, we truly find an evolutionary path to parallelism that will preserve investments in such parallel programming.

While we thank the contributing authors with the "Contribution" pages dedicated to them, we cannot thank them enough. The authors of the chapters found inside this book spent precious time away from their influential work to explain their work so we might all learn from their successes. We hope you enjoy and benefit from their shared efforts, and we hope you discover value in the "pearls" that they have shared as we continue to further usher in this new era of parallel computing.

Jim Jeffers and James Reinders
Intel Corporation
August 2015

INTRODUCTION

James Reinders, Jim Jeffers

Intel Corporation, USA

It has become well known that programming for the Intel Xeon Phi coprocessor heightens awareness of the need for scaling, vectorization, and increasing temporal locality of reference—exactly the keys to parallel programming. Once these keys to effective parallel programming are addressed, the result is a parallel program that makes Intel® Xeon Phi™ coprocessors *and* multicore processors optimized for higher performance. That represents a highly compelling preservation of investment when focus is given to modifying code in a portable and performance portable manner. Unsurprisingly, that means the chapters in this book use C, C++, and Fortran with standard parallel programming models including OpenMP, MPI, TBB, and OpenCL. We see that optimizations improve applications both on processors, such as Intel® Xeon® processors, and Intel Xeon Phi products.

We are not supposed to have a favorite chapter, especially since 73 amazing experts contributed to this second Pearls book. They share compelling lessons in effective parallel programming through both specific application optimizations, and their illustration of key techniques...and we can learn from every one of them. However, we cannot avoid feeling a little like the characters on Big Bang Theory (a popular television show) who get excited by the mere mention of Stephen Hawking. Now, to be very clear, Stephen Hawking did not work on this book. At least, not to our knowledge.

APPLICATIONS AND TECHNIQUES

The programming topics that receive the most discussion in this book are OpenMP and vectorization, followed closely by MPI. However, there are many more topics which get serious attention including nested parallelism, latency optimizations, prefetching, Python, OpenCL, offloading, stream programming, making code thread-safe, and power savings.

This book does not have distinct sections, but you will find that the first half of the book consists of chapters that dive deeply into optimizing a single application and dealing with the work that is needed to optimize that application for parallelism. The second half of the book switches to chapters that dive into a technique or approach, and illustrate it with a number of different examples.

In all the chapters, the examples were selected for their educational content, applicability, and success. You can download codes and try them yourself! Examples demonstrate successful approaches to parallel programming that have application with both processors and coprocessors. Not all the examples scale well enough to make an Intel Xeon Phi coprocessor run faster than a processor. This is reality we all face in programming, and it reinforces something we should never be bashful in pointing out: a common programming model matters a great deal. The programming is not making a choice on what will run better; it focuses on parallel programming and can use either multicore or many-core products. The techniques utilized almost always apply to both processors and coprocessors. Some chapters utilize nonportable techniques and explain why. The most common use of nonportable programming you will see in this book is focused targeting to 512-bit SIMD, a feature that arrived in Intel Xeon Phi coprocessors before appearing in processors. The strong benefits of common programming emerge over and over in real-life examples, including those in this book.

SIMD AND VECTORIZATION

Many chapters make code changes in their applications to utilize SIMD capabilities of processors and coprocessors, including Chapters 2–4, 8. There are three additional vectorization focused chapters tackling key techniques or tools that you may find indispensible. The concept of an SIMD function is covered in Chapter 22. SIMD functions allow a program written to operate on scalar (one at a time) data to be vectorized by the appropriate use of OpenMP SIMD directives. A tool to help analyze your vectorization opportunities and give advice is the subject of Chapter 23. An increasingly popular library approach to parallel vector programming, called OpenVec, is covered in Chapter 24.

We do have a really cool chapter that begins with "The best current explanation of how our universe began is with a period of rapid exponential expansion, termed inflation. This created the large, mostly empty, universe that we observe today. The principle piece of evidence for this comes from......the Cosmic Microwave Background (CMB), a microwave frequency background radiation, thought to have been left over from the big bang..."

Who would not be excited by that?

In an attempt to avoid accusations that we have a favorite chapter...... we buried "Cosmic Microwave Background Analysis: Nested Parallelism In Practice" *in the middle of the book so it is as far as possible from the cover which features the Cosmos supercomputer that theoretical physicists at the University of Cambridge use. The same book cover that has an OSPRay rendered visualization from the Modal program that they optimize in their chapter (and yes, they do work with Dr. Hawking — but we still are not saying he actually worked on the book!).*

OpenMP AND NESTED PARALLELISM

Many chapters make code changes in their applications to harness task or thread level parallelism with OpenMP. Chapter 17 drives home the meaning and value of being more "coarse-grained" in order to scale well. The challenges of making legacy code thread-safe are discussed in some detail in Chapter 5, including discussions of choices that did not work.

Two chapters advocate nested parallelism in OpenMP, and use it to get significant performance gains: Chapters 10 and 18. Exploiting multilevel parallelism deserves consideration even if rejected in the past. OpenMP nesting is turned off by default by most implementations, and is generally consider unsafe by typical users due to concerns of oversubscription and the resulting poor application performance. Proper considerations of how to express and use nested parallelism can have a profound impact on performance.

LATENCY OPTIMIZATIONS

Certain applications are more focused on latency than the traditional concern in HPC on throughput. Chapter 7 gives us a definitive look that specific optimizations that are the most critical in achieving low latency.

PYTHON

Python code can offload to an Intel Xeon Phi coprocessor using the pyMIC module. Chapter 14 shows examples of such offloading.

STREAMS

Heterogeneous systems can be programmed with "streams" as demonstrated in Chapter 15. The hStreams library is illustrated with some problems from the field of linear algebra, endeavoring to show the speed and flexibility of hStreams on both processors and coprocessors.

RAY TRACING

Chapter 12 discusses high-performance ray-based radio frequency simulation and visualization using the open source, high-performance Embree and OSPRay ray tracing libraries.

TUNING PREFETCHING

Chapter 21 shows that prefetching effectiveness, and therefore applications performance, can be enhanced through the use of the superior knowledge of the programmer. It is known that prefetching is extremely important for good performance on in-order architectures like the Intel Xeon Phi coprocessor, however the authors surprised even themselves by being able to expose techniques which show value on out-of-order cores as well. Often simply tuning the compiler prefetching distance is an easy way for application developers to get better performance without having to rewrite their code. In some cases, the more labor-intensive method of adding intrinsics for prefetching may be worthwhile.

MPI SHARED MEMORY

Chapter 16 discusses an interprocess, shared memory extension, which was added in MPI 3.0 standard, and how it can be used to perform communication efficiency and memory footprint optimization. A simple 1-D ring "hello world" example is shown and then extended for several node runs.

USING EVERY LAST CORE

Chapter 13 measures the effects of application usage of the "reserved" core on an Intel Xeon Phi co-processor through an examination of multiple thread placement strategies. This chapter also extends discussion on less conventional thread management techniques when using a centralized scheduler model, and look at the interoperability of MPI and PThreads.

OpenCL VS. OpenMP

Two chapters explore solving the same problems in OpenCL and OpenMP: Chapters 19 and 20. These are educational in understanding both OpenCL and OpenMP.

POWER ANALYSIS FOR NODES AND CLUSTERS

Chapter 25 builds on basic principles from the first Pearls book. The chapter first examines how a developer can make simple nonalgorithmic application changes, such as thread distribution, in concert with power measurements, which can significantly change the application's performance per watt. The chapter also takes a look at how administrators and developers can use big data techniques like waterfall plots to examine profiling information across cluster environments, and their potential impact on data center performance.

Perhaps we can easily deny it is our favorite chapter because it does not feature Fortran. Even Thinglings are taught "Fortran... the Greatest of the Programming Languages!" *[Simpsons (another popular television program), season 26, episode 10:* "The Man Who Came to Be Dinner"]*. Obviously we favor chapters with Fortran, including Chapters 2, 3, 5, 6, 17, and 22.*

THE FUTURE OF MANY-CORE

We can expect multiple generations of Intel Xeon Phi devices beyond the first prototype code named *Knights* Ferry and the original coprocessor product code named *Knights Corner* including the second-generation product, code named *Knights Landing,* and the third generation product, code named *Knights Hill.*

The best way to prepare for the future is to be truly "inspired by 61 cores." Tuning for today's Intel Xeon Phi product is the best way to be sure an application is on track to make good use of future generations.

The techniques in this book focus on a common programming model shared with all processors. This means that the core lessons throughout apply to today's Intel Xeon processors, and today's Intel Xeon Phi products, and apply forward to future Intel Xeon Phi products.

The parallel programming challenges are scaling (multithreading), use of SIMD (vectorization) and locality of reference (data layout and use). These are recurring topics throughout both Pearls books.

We can logically conclude that the future for many-core is bright. We hope the 'pearls' in this book provide guidance and motivation for modernizing your applications for the high levels of parallel programming available today.

DOWNLOADS

The key concepts in each chapter are highlighted with important code segments listed in the chapters. In addition, the examples are available for download from our website http://lotsofcores.com and often also from project web sites. The "For More Information" sections at the end of each chapter will steer you to the places to find the code.

We really cannot have a favorite. Not just because everyone worked so hard on these great chapters! We have no favorite because we really enjoy all of these chapters. And, we hope you do as well!

Instructors, and all who create presentations, can appreciate the value in being able to download all figures, diagrams and photos used in this book from http://lotsofcores.com. Please reuse them to help teach and explain parallel programming to more software developers! We appreciate being mentioned when you attribute the source of figures but otherwise we place no onerous conditions on their reuse.

FOR MORE INFORMATION

Additional reading worth considering includes:

- Downloads associated with this book: http://lotsofcores.com.
- Website sponsored by Intel dedicated to parallel programming: http://go-parallel.com.
- Intel website for information on the Intel Xeon Phi products: http://intel.com/xeonphi.
- Intel website for information on programming the Intel Xeon Phi products: http://intel.com/software/mic.
- Intel Xeon Phi Users Group website: https://www.ixpug.org.
- Advanced Vector Instructions information: http://software.intel.com/avx.

NUMERICAL WEATHER PREDICTION OPTIMIZATION

2

Tom Henderson*, John Michalakes[†], Indraneil Gokhale[‡], Ashish Jha[‡]

National Oceanic and Atmospheric Administration (NOAA)/Earth Systems Research Laboratory, in Affiliation with the Colorado State University's Cooperative Institute for Research in the Atmosphere, USA* NOAA National Centers for Environmental Prediction, USA[†] Intel Corporation, USA[‡]

NUMERICAL WEATHER PREDICTION: BACKGROUND AND MOTIVATION

Weather affects everyone's life every day. Accurate weather forecasts have a large impact on economic activity, especially in cases of extreme weather events such as hurricanes, tornadoes, and severe winter storms. Numerical weather prediction (NWP) models are the basis for all modern weather forecasts. Since the inception of NWP in the mid 1950s, forecast skill has steadily improved as new and more powerful computers have allowed increases in model fidelity and accuracy. Figure 2.1 illustrates how forecast skill and compute power have increased during the past six decades. With global NWP models at sub-10 km resolution already able to make efficient use of hundreds of thousands of traditional CPU cores, there is much interest in applying Intel® Many Integrated Core (Intel® MIC) architecture to further reduce model execution times and improve energy efficiency.

Modern NWP models are typically separated into two major components: a dynamical core (dynamics) and a set of physical parameterizations (physics). The dynamics is concerned with simulating large-scale flow in the atmosphere. The physical parameterizations approximate sub-grid scale processes that cannot be directly simulated with existing compute resources.

A "microphysics" scheme is an important and costly physical parameterization that simulates processes in the atmosphere that cause precipitation of rain, snow, and graupel. Distributed as part of the widely used Weather Research and Forecast (WRF) model, the WRF Single Moment 6-class Microphysics (WSM6) scheme is used by a wide variety of research and operational NWP models including, the Global/Regional Integrated Modeling System (GRIMS), the Nonhydrostatic Icosahedral Model (NIM), and the Model for Prediction Across Scale (MPAS). This chapter describes efforts to improve performance of the WSM6 via a variety of techniques including threading, vectorization, array alignment, improving data locality, and optional use of compile-time constants for loop and array index bounds. We include code examples to illustrate each technique along with its performance benefits on Intel® Xeon® processors and Intel® Xeon Phi™ coprocessors. Use of tools such as Intel® Thread Inspector to speed the performance tuning process is also described.

Finally, code changes for performance tuning must take into account cultural aspects of the application domain in order to be accepted. In NWP, codes are primarily written in Fortran and the majority of code contributors are domain experts who have limited experience with parallelization and

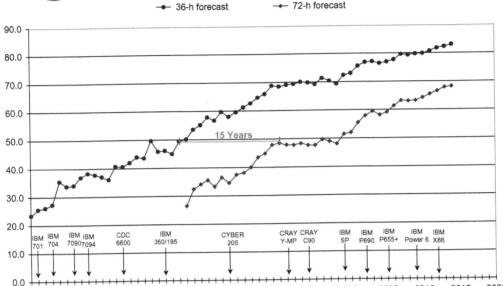

FIGURE 2.1

This plot illustrates increases in NWP forecast skill score over time. Installations of new computers at the National Weather Service's National Centers for Environmental Prediction (NCEP) are shown at the bottom. Increases in forecast skill are well correlated with increases in computing power.

performance tuning. A relatively small number of software engineers support NWP development efforts. Therefore, wholesale change of large NWP codes to different languages or significantly different programming models is not cost effective. NWP codes are large and often evolve rapidly, especially prior to operational implementation. Maintenance of multiple versions of a code optimized for different compute platforms is prohibitively expensive. Performance-portability of a single-source code is a key requirement for NWP. Intel MIC architecture's ability to be programmed within the same overarching software environment as the Intel Xeon processor family is a good match for the NWP single-source requirement.

WSM6 IN THE NIM

Performance of any NWP physics package is best evaluated in the context of a dynamical core. For our tests of WSM6, we use the NIM dynamical core. NIM is a recently developed research dynamical core designed for high-resolution global NWP simulations. Here, high resolution means grid spacing that is

FIGURE 2.2

The Nonhydrostatic Icosahedral Model (NIM) uses an icosahedral grid as shown above. Except for 12 pentagons, all grid cells are hexagons. Compared to other commonly used discretizations of the sphere, this grid minimizes variation in grid cell spacing across the globe allowing model time step to be maximized.

smaller than 10 km. NIM uses an icosahedral grid that minimizes variation in grid cell sizes when mapped to the globe, as illustrated in Figure 2.2. Since its inception, NIM has been a close collaboration involving NWP domain experts and HPC software engineers. NIM supports serial, MPI, OpenMP, and hybrid MPI+OpenMP build options and has been ported to all major HPC system architectures and software stacks.

NIM dynamics computations are performed in single-precision. NIM dynamics arrays are organized with all model columns addressed via a single horizontal dimension, "ipn." Neighboring columns are located via look-up table. To avoid costs of indirect addressing in the look-up table, the vertical "k" index over each column appears innermost. MPI parallelism is achieved by distributing subsets of model columns across MPI tasks. Dynamically allocated memory maintains global index space on each MPI task and run-time specification of model configuration options (MPI tasks, OpenMP threads, etc.) is preferred wherever possible.

The NIM dynamics is a single-source code that performs well on Intel and AMD CPUs, NVIDIA GPUs, and Intel MIC architecture. The NIM dynamics also exhibits good strong scaling at high resolution. NIM scales from 10,000 cores to 240,000 cores with 96% parallel efficiency on Oak Ridge National Laboratory's Titan supercomputer at 3 km global resolution. WSM6, it is the most expensive physical parameterization in NIM, consuming 18% of total run time. So WSM6 is a logical first target for exploring performance tuning of physics parameterizations on processors and coprocessors.

In contrast to the NIM dynamics, WSM6 computations are performed in double-precision and, for the majority of computations, arrays are stored with the "i" dimension innermost. Due to the differences in storage order and precision, transposition between dynamics arrays and physics arrays is required.

Fortunately, dynamics and physics share a relatively small set of arrays so transposition costs are small (total costs for all physics packages are less than 3% of total run time).

Compared to NIM dynamics, WSM6 computations are somewhat more complex. Some loops contain data-dependent branches that reduce the efficiency of vectorized code. Some computations require calls to intrinsic transcendental functions (e.g., log, power, exponential). Also, some dynamic load imbalance occurs due to uneven distribution of precipitation types across the globe. To avoid excessively skewing performance results due to load imbalance, test runs involve multiple time steps of the dynamical core. To ensure representativeness of our performance results, we repeated many of our experiments using three different input datasets consisting of both real and idealized initial conditions.

Finally, some computations in WSM6 have "k" as the innermost dimension. This "single-column" part of the WSM6 code handles complex data-dependent vertical iterations that start and end at different levels of each column. With significant effort, it is possible to refactor these inner "k" loops to instead have "i" innermost. We will examine tradeoffs related to this refactoring later.

A sample program containing only the WSM6 source code, a simple driver that calls it once, and input and output datasets is downloadable from lotsofcores.com. Code snippets in this chapter are cross-referenced to the sample code whenever possible. All line numbers in this chapter refer to sample code source file src/kernel/wsm6_kernel.F90 unless otherwise noted.

SHARED-MEMORY PARALLELISM AND CONTROLLING HORIZONTAL VECTOR LENGTH

In NIM, physics packages are threaded by adding OpenMP directives around a single column loop from which all physics packages are called. This approach requires that all code in the entire physics (of which WSM6 is a component) be thread-safe. Unfortunately, some physics packages were not thread-safe. Finding every race condition and performance bug would have been very time consuming and tedious. Fortunately, Intel Inspector largely automates the task of identifying and correcting threading errors. All threading issues were found and fixed in less than 1 week saving us at least 2 weeks of additional laborious and error-prone manual effort.

Our next step was to control vector length by replacing the physics column loop with a loop over "chunks" of columns. Chunk width (number of columns in each chunk) can then be adjusted to tune performance. This technique has been used in many other NWP and climate models such as the Community Atmosphere Model, Integrated Forecast System, and in previous work on WSM5. Since WRF physics routines such as WSM6 already have arrays organized with (i,k,j) ordering, we can use the "i" dimension to loop over a single chunk, "k" to loop over the vertical dimension, and "j" to loop over the chunks. (Recall that in Fortran, the leftmost index is innermost.)

A disadvantage of organizing columns into chunks arises when the total number of columns on each MPI task is not evenly divisible by the chunk width. Since different MPI tasks will almost always be responsible for slightly different numbers of columns, the last "chunk" will nearly always contain unused columns on at least one MPI task. The extra computations are negligible but we must avoid floating-point exceptions from operations on uninitialized data in these unused columns. An "if" mask could be added to every "i" loop but this would require extensive code modifications and could also impede vectorization. Instead, we simply copy the last valid model column into any "empty" columns in the last chunk during the transposition from dynamics-to-physics, as illustrated in Figure 2.3. The extra columns are simply

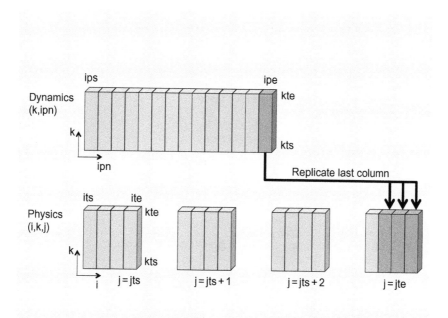

FIGURE 2.3

Replication of the last dynamics column avoids adding "if" blocks around every "i" loop inside the physics. In this example, "chunk width" = 4.

discarded during the transposition from physics back to dynamics. In practice, each MPI task typically computes hundreds to thousands of columns so the cost of a few redundant computations is far outweighed by the performance benefit of avoiding conditionals in vectorized loops.

Another benefit of the column replication approach is that code changes are limited to the code that transposes between physics and dynamics. Relatively simple changes are sufficient to handle the replication and discarding of columns as shown in Figure 2.4. In the snippet, the "j" loop over number of chunks is threaded via OpenMP. The first "i" loop iterates over the current chunk ("j") and translates to the horizontal dynamics "ipn" index (which iterates over all dynamics model columns). On each MPI task, dynamics columns are numbered "ips,ipe," while columns in each physics "chunk" are numbered "its,ite." For both dynamics and physics, vertical levels in each column are numbered "kts,kte." The expression `ipn=min(ij+i+ips-1,ipe)` ensures that any "empty" columns in the last chunk will contain a copy of the last valid dynamics column. This is the only line that had to be modified in the dynamics-to-physics transposition. After this, the physics driver is called. It calls all physics packages including WSM6 and is responsible for all computations in chunk "j." After the physics driver returns, the second "i" loop transposes back from physics-to-dynamics. The "ipn=ij+i+ips-1" index computation and immediately following "if" statement are all that was needed to implement the physics-to-dynamics transposition.

```
!$OMP PARALLEL DO PRIVATE ( ij,i,k,j,ipn ) &
!$OMP SCHEDULE(runtime)
   do j = jts,jte
      ij = (j-1)*CHUNK
      ! transpose from dynamics to physics
      do i = its,ite
         ipn = min(ij+i+ips-1,ipe)
         do k = kts,kte
            u_phy(i,k,j) = u_dyn(k,ipn)
            ! transpose other arrays...
         end do   ! k loop
      end do   ! i loop
      ! physics computations on chunk "j", including WSM6
      call nim_mpas_physics_driver(...)
      ! transpose from physics to dynamics
      do i = its,ite
         ipn = ij+i+ips-1
         if ((ips<=ipn).and.(ipn<=ipe)) then
            do k = kts,kte
               su_dyn(k,ipn) = tend_u_phy(i,k,j)*r_dyn(k,ipn)
               ! transpose other arrays...
            enddo   ! k loop
         endif
      enddo   ! i loop
   enddo   ! j loop
```

FIGURE 2.4

Code to transpose between dynamics and physics data structures. Code additions needed to handle replication of the last dynamics column are highlighted. This code does not appear in the sample code because NIM dynamics is not included.

ARRAY ALIGNMENT

Alignment of arrays in memory is key to good vector performance on the first generation of Intel Xeon Phi coprocessors. Unaligned arrays can generate inefficient scalar instructions to handle array elements at the beginning and end of each array. The Intel compiler option "-align array64byte" can be used to ensure that every array begins on a vector boundary. In a perfect world, this would be sufficient to ensure that all arrays are really aligned. However, the Intel compiler requires additional assistance in some cases to recognize that some arrays are really aligned. Use of the Intel compiler options "-qopt-report-phase=loop,vec -qopt-report=4" will cause the compiler to complain whenever it is not convinced that an array is really aligned. We use this information to identify opportunities to insert Intel-specific compiler directives "ASSUME_ALIGNED" and "VECTOR ALIGNED" as shown in Figure 2.5. Here the "ASSUME_ALIGNED" directive is used to tell the Intel compiler that the arrays listed are aligned on 64-byte boundaries (e.g., "worka:64"). The "VECTOR_ALIGNED" directive tells the compiler that all the arrays in the immediately following loop are aligned. Note that this optimization is best combined with optional compile-time constants for memory and loop bounds as described below. Telling the compiler that arrays are aligned when they are not will lead to incorrect results or

```
#ifdef ALIGN_OK
!DIR$ ASSUME_ALIGNED den:64,denqrs:64,qrs:64
#endif
        do k = kte, kts, -1
#ifdef ALIGN_OK
!DIR$ VECTOR_ALIGNED
#endif
          do i = its, ite
            denqrs(i,k,1) = den(i,k)*qrs(i,k,1)
            denqrs(i,k,2) = den(i,k)*qrs(i,k,2)
            denqrs(i,k,3) = den(i,k)*qrs(i,k,3)
          enddo
        enddo
```

FIGURE 2.5

Code with Intel-specific alignment directives added. Note use of cpp token "ALIGN_OK" to disable directives for build configurations where arrays are not really aligned. This loop can be found in the sample code at line 470.

segfaults. To avoid incorrect alignment, we introduce cpp token "ALIGN_OK" which is only defined when compile-time constants are used (see below).

LOOP RESTRUCTURING

Data locality is a key to good performance on all modern CPU and fine-grained architectures. In many cases, loop fusion can be used to demote temporary arrays to arrays of lower rank (or even to scalars). In other cases, loop fusion can improve cache reuse by allowing multiple computations that use the same array values to iterate through those values only once.

However, WSM6 contained a few large extremely complex loops that inhibited vectorization. These loops contain very intricately interwoven conditional blocks with multiple layers of data-dependent "if-else" constructs. Despite their good locality, these loops were simply too complicated for the vectorizer to understand and manual loop splitting was required. We were guided by compiler optimization reports when making these changes. See Figure 2.6 for a simplified example of one of these loops. This code computes changes in mass of cloud water, cloud ice, rain, snow, and graupel due to melting and freezing and adjusts temperatures in response to these changes. For brevity, complex inline computations are abbreviated as function calls (e.g., "rain_freeze()"). This snippet would normally be good for data locality since scalars "del2" and "del3" are reused for many different computations. Since the compiler could not vectorize this loop, even with directives added, we manually split the loop. This required promotion of scalars "del2" and "del3" to arrays as shown in Figure 2.7.

COMPILE-TIME CONSTANTS FOR LOOP AND ARRAY BOUNDS

Some modern Fortran compilers (including the Intel and Cray compilers) are able to generate more efficient code when loop lengths and bounds of array dimensions are known at compile time. Ideally, a compiler would generate the fastest possible code and branch around it if alignment, loop lengths,

```
REAL :: rain(its:ite,kts:kte)
REAL :: snow(its:ite,kts:kte)
! similar for water, ice, graupel, etc.
REAL :: del2,del3
do k = kts, kte
!DIR$ VECTOR ALIGNED
  do i = its, ite
    del2=0.;   del3=0.
    if(rain(i,k).lt.qmin.and.snow(i,k).lt.qmin) del2=1.
    if(rain(i,k).lt.qmin) del3=1.
    ! if temperature is below freezing
    if(t(i,k).le.t0c) then
      rain(i,k) = rain_freeze(rain,snow,...,del2,del3)
      snow(i,k) = snow_freeze(rain,snow,...,del2,del3)
      ! similar for water, ice, graupel, etc.
    else
      rain(i,k) = rain_liq(rain,snow,...,del2,del3)
      snow(i,k) = snow_liq(rain,snow,...,del2,del3)
      ! similar for water, ice, graupel, etc.
    endif
  enddo
enddo
```

FIGURE 2.6

The ifort compiler could not vectorize this loop due to complexity. Normally, the use of scalars del2 and del3 would be ideal since they are reused by many following computations. This original loop does not appear in the sample code.

and memory bounds were not "perfect." In practice, the complexity of the conditionals that would have to be evaluated before every invocation of a loop would slow down code enough to overwhelm performance benefits in many cases. So user-supplied compile-time information yields performance improvements. Unfortunately, statically declaring array bounds is impractical because modern NWP codes such as NIM allow users to conduct successive runs on different numbers of MPI tasks without the need for recompilation. Run-time specification of array bounds satisfies this requirement while greatly simplifying the MPI-parallel code. On the other hand, for performance-critical operational weather forecasts, a single configuration and MPI task count of the model may be run many thousands of times; in these cases, defining array dimensions statically at compile time to achieve best performance is desirable, given the burden of recompilation is insignificant. Judicious use of information hiding can give the best of both worlds by optionally exposing only inner dimensions as compile-time constants.

The code snippets in Figures 2.8 and 2.9 illustrate this approach. Physics state array "t" is declared as allocatable in module "state_arrays." Sizes of each array dimension are declared in separate module "array_sizes." Sizes of the outer dimensions are declared as variables and determined at run time. Use of cpp macro "_CHUNKSIZE_" allows the size of the innermost dimension, "chunksize," to be determined at build time (i.e., when _CHUNKSIZE_ is defined) or at run time. A switch is added to the build automation to optionally set _CHUNKSIZE_ to a user-specified value (i.e., "-D_CHUNKSIZE_=8).

Using both of the above modules, subroutine "allocate_state" sets the outer two dimensions at run time, sets chunksize at run time when _CHUNKSIZE_ is not defined, and allocates "t." At some point

```
! same array declarations for rain, snow, etc.
! del2, del3 promoted from scalars to arrays
REAL :: del2(its:ite,kts:kte)
REAL :: del3(its:ite,kts:kte)
do k = kts, kte
!DIR$ VECTOR ALIGNED
  do i = its, ite
    del2(i,k)=0.;  del3(i,k)=0.
    if(rain(i,k).lt.qmin.and.snow(i,k).lt.qmin)
del2(i,k)=1.
    if(rain(i,k).lt.qmin) del3(i,k)=1.
  enddo
enddo
do k = kts, kte
!DIR$ VECTOR ALIGNED
  do i = its, ite
    ! if temperature is below freezing
    if(t(i,k).le.t0c) then
      rain(i,k) = rain_freeze(rain,snow,...,del2,del3)
    else
      rain(i,k) = rain_liq(rain,snow,...,del2,del3)
    endif
  enddo
enddo
! similar for snow, water, ice, graupel, etc.
```

FIGURE 2.7

After loops were split, the compiler was able to vectorize. Note that loop splitting forced promotion of del2 and del3 to higher rank, reducing data locality. These loops can be found in the sample code beginning at line 1038. Note that variable names have been shortened (e.g., "delta2" → "del2") and code blocks have been abbreviated as function calls in the figure.

```
module state_arrays
  real, allocatable :: t(:,:,:)    ! (i,k,j)
end module state_arrays

module array_sizes
  integer :: nlevels     ! vertical (k) size
  integer :: numchunks   ! number of chunks (j)
#ifdef _CHUNKSIZE_
  ! chunk size is a compile-time constant
  integer, parameter :: chunksize = _CHUNKSIZE_
#else
  ! chunk size is set at run time prior to allocations
  integer :: chunksize
#endif
end module array_sizes
```

FIGURE 2.8

Modules used to implement optional compile-time constant loop and array bounds without sacrificing the flexibility of allocatable arrays. This code can be found in the sample code beginning at line 3450, in somewhat simplified form.

```
subroutine allocate_state
  use module state_arrays
  use module array_sizes
  ! set number of vertical levels and number of chunks at
run time
  nlevels = …
  numchunks = …
#ifndef _CHUNKSIZE_
  ! set chunksize at run time
  chunksize = …
#endif
  allocate(t(chunksize,nlevels,numchunks))
end subroutine allocate_state

subroutine wsm6(t,…)
  use module array_sizes
  real,intent(inout) :: t(chunk,nlevels,numchunks)
  integer :: i,k,j
  do j=1,numchunks
    do k=1,nlevels
      do i=1,numchunks
        t(i,k,j) = ...
      enddo
    enddo
  enddo
end subroutine wsm6
```

FIGURE 2.9

Optional compile-time constant loop and array bounds in subroutines. Since the compiler cannot see the original allocatable declaration of array "t," it must use the dummy argument declaration. Thus, the compiler sees a compile-time constant for the size of the inner dimension of "t" and for the length of the "i" loop in the wsm6 subroutine. This code does not appear in the sample code because it uses a somewhat simpler and less flexible approach.

during each model time step, the wsm6 subroutine is called (not shown) and passed "t" as its first argument. All three array dimensions appear in the dummy argument declaration for "t." Since the compiler cannot see the original declaration of actual argument "t" in module state_arrays, it cannot know that "t" was actually allocated. Therefore, it will see both the size of innermost dimension of "t" and the length of any "i" loops as being compile-time constants inside the wsm6 subroutine. This has significant performance benefit as described below.

The "chunksize" compile-time switch allows a great deal of performance tuning flexibility within a single-source code. For NVIDIA GPUs, setting "chunksize" to be a multiple of streaming multiprocessor size (32) yields the most efficient code. For processors and coprocessors with cores that support vector instructions, such as Intel® Advanced Vector Extensions, it is usually best to set chunksize equal to vector length, as will be seen below.

WSM6 also performs some expensive computations inside "single-column" loops that have "k" innermost. These loops consume about 20% of the execution time. Initially, we were concerned that the cost of transposing between "i-inside" arrays to "k-on-inside" vectors for every model column would be inefficient. Therefore, we refactored these complex loops to push "i" innermost, closely following the approach used by Michalakes for WSM5. We also examined leaving the "k" loops as-is and instead adding the capability of making the "k" loops and dimension compile-time constants. We added separate build automation to optionally set the size of the "k" dimension at build time. Since there are no "chunks" in the "k" dimension, our only options are to set the size to the number of vertical levels in the model or to leave it as a run-time-specified variable. Switches to toggle "compile-time-i" and "compile-time-k" are independent to ease experimentation with these optimization options. Figures 2.10 and 2.11 illustrate how each type of loop appears to the compiler when both switches are turned on at compile time.

Simplified examples of the WSM6 "single-column" loops in their original "k-inside" form and refactored "i-inside" form are shown as code snippets in Figures 2.12 and 2.13. The snippets have been greatly simplified for brevity. The transpositions in the "k-inside" code are not shown and the promotions of many "k" vectors to (i,k) arrays in the "i-inside" code are omitted.

The "i-inside" version allows the same fine control of vector length via "chunksize" as the other WSM6 loops. Most importantly, chunksize can be adjusted to match vector length, which yields the best performance for vector capable processing cores such as the processor and the coprocessor as shown in the results section below. This advantage is lost in the k-inside code. When "k" loop lengths are made compile-time constants, the "k" loop length must match the number of vertical levels in the model. In practice, this is significantly larger than the vector length (and may not be evenly divisible by it).

However, as the code snippets illustrate, the price for the more flexible vector length in the "i-inside" code is introduction of vector mask (lmask) and a missed opportunity to skip a large amount of computation. For example, the "cycle" statement following the comment "skip if no precipitation in this column" allows the "k-inside" code to completely skip all computations for a column that contains no precipitation. In the "i-inside" code, computations can be skipped only if every column in the chunk has no precipitation (see the "alldry" if statement in Figure 2.13). This is possible, but relatively rare.

```
real :: a1(its:ite,kts:kte),a2(its:ite,kts:kte)
real :: x(kts:kte),y(kts:kte)
! i-inside loop
do k=kts,kte
  do i=its,ite
    a1(i,k) = a2(i,k) + ...
  enddo
enddo
! k-inside loop
do k=kts,kte
  x(k) = x(k) + y(k) * ...
enddo
```

FIGURE 2.10

Sample declarations and loops prior to application of optional compile-time constants by build automation. An example of an i-inside loop can be found in the sample code at line 291. A k-inside loop can be found at line 1492.

```
real :: a1(1:8,1:32),a2(1:8,1:32)
real :: x(1:32),y(1:32)
! i-inside loop
do k=1,32
  do i=1,8
    a1(i,k) = a2(i,k) + ...
  enddo
enddo
! k-inside loop
do k=1,32
  x(k) = x(k) + y(k) * ...
enddo
```

FIGURE 2.11

Code from Figure 2.10 as seen by the compiler after application of optional compile-time constants by build automation. In this example, chunksize ("i")=8 and number of vertical levels ("k")=32. Transformed loops with literal constants can be seen in file src/kernel/wsm6_kernel_kcmd.f90 after building the sample code. Note that literal constants are shown here for clarity and to illustrate the simplified build mechanism used by the sample code. Build automation for the complete NIM model uses Fortran parameters instead.

```
real    :: qq(kts:kte,its:ite)
i_loop : do i=its,ite
    ! skip if no precipitation in this column
    if(sum(qq(kts:kte,i)).le.0.0) cycle i_loop
    intp : do k=kts,kte
      qq(k,i) = ...
      ! lots of computation
    enddo intp
enddo i_loop
```

FIGURE 2.12

About 20% of WSM6 computations occur in "k-inside" code. A simplified example is shown here to illustrate difficulties in transforming the code to "i-inside." The "k-inside" code is included in the sample code and is built when default build-time settings are used. This simplified example is extracted from subroutine nislfv_rain_plm() which appears at line 1579.

Usually, some columns have precipitation while others do not, so coding the "i-inside" version with logical mask "lmask" means performing many unnecessary computations that are discarded. The WSM6 code is much more complex than this example and requires cascading nests of masks in the i-inside code. In practice, the inefficiency introduced by these vector masks outweighs the benefits of flexible inner loop lengths as shown in the results section below. Therefore, in these tests the compile-time coded k-inside version yielded superior performance.

With all of the aforementioned optimizations in-place, it is possible to use Intel compiler warning messages to identify and improve optimization where the compiler is unable to make decisions automatically. Compiler warning messages about "unaligned access," "PARTIAL LOOP," "REMAINDER LOOP," and "PEEL LOOP" guide us to spots where additional directives may be needed or where our optimizations are not fully implemented.

```
real    :: qq(its:ite,kts:kte)
real    :: allold(its:ite)
logical :: lmask(its:ite)
allold(its:ite) = 0.0
do k=kts,kte
  allold(its:ite) = allold(its:ite) + qq(its:ite,k)
enddo
! skip if no precipitation in every column
alldry: if (maxval(allold).gt.0.0) then
  lmask = allold .gt. 0.0
  intp: do k=kts,kte
    do i=its,ite
      if (lmask(i) then
        qq(i,k) = ...
        ! lots of computation
      endif
    enddo
  enddo intp
endif alldry
```

FIGURE 2.13

Code from Figure 2.12 transformed into "i-inside" form. Vector mask "lmask" must be introduced and the opportunity to completely skip a column that lacks precipitation is missed. The "i-inside" code is included in the sample code and can be swapped in via a build-time switch. This simplified example is extracted from subroutine nislfv_rain_plm_ii() which appears at line 2238.

Note that all of the above optimizations must be in place before the full benefits of compile-time constants become apparent. All of the compiler complaints must be addressed via directives or loop restructuring. Compiler flags must be correct. And the innermost bounds of every declaration and loop visible to the compiler must be a compile-time constant.

PERFORMANCE IMPROVEMENTS

Performance was evaluated by measuring execution time for WSM6 during a 225-km resolution NIM test case. This configuration uses 32 vertical levels and runs through 72 model time steps (900 s of simulated time). A 225-km NIM model has 10,242 model columns. This is an interesting small test case because very high-resolution model runs typically have similar numbers of columns assigned to each node.

Thread-safe timers are placed immediately before and after the call to the top-level WSM6 subroutine inside the single OpenMP loop that contains all physics calls. Execution time of the slowest thread is reported. Due to run-to-run variability of slowest thread execution times on some machines, at least 10 separate runs were made for each case and the minimum times are reported.

We performed experiments on the following Intel Xeon processor and Intel Xeon Phi coprocessor nodes: "SNB" (Sandybridge, Intel Xeon E5-2670 processor, 2.6 GHz, 2 sockets, 16 cores), "IVB-EP" (Ivybridge, Intel Xeon E5-2697v2, 2.7 GHz, 2 sockets, 24 cores), "HSW-EP" (Haswell, Intel Xeon

Device	Threads	Chunk Width	Time (seconds)
KNC	240	8	13.2
SNB	32	4	9.4
IVB-EP	48	4	4.7

FIGURE 2.14

WSM6 "baseline" run times prior to performance improvements. OpenMP "chunking" is included (or nodes cannot be fully utilized). Units of chunk width are double-precision (64-bit) words.

E5-2697v3, 2.6 GHz, 2 sockets, 28 cores), and "KNC" (Knights Corner, Intel Xeon Phi 7120A coprocessor, 1 socket, 60 cores, 1.2 GHz). Figure 2.14 shows execution times on three node types for "baseline" code prior to optimization. The baseline code contains the single OpenMP loop around model physics (performance results without OpenMP are not informative since most of a node is idle). Figure 2.15 shows execution times for each node type with all of the above optimizations included. For both sets of results, chunk width was adjusted to match vector length (four double-precision words for the processors or eight for the coprocessor). And thread count was adjusted to fully utilize the cores (two threads per core for the processors, four for the coprocessors).

We also ran the experiments with reduced thread count to see if resource contention between threads might be slowing down execution when cores are fully populated with threads. Results are shown in Figure 2.16. For WSM6, it is clear that the best performance is achieved at maximum thread count (two per core for processors, four per core for coprocessors).

Tests were repeated for the coprocessor and Intel Xeon E5-v2 EP using different chunk widths. Results are shown in Figure 2.17. Performance is best when chunksize matches vector length for both

Device	Threads	Chunk Width	Time (seconds)
SNB	32	4	7.5
KNC	240	8	8.7
IVB-EP	48	4	3.4
HSW-EP	56	4	2.6

FIGURE 2.15

WSM6 "best" run times with all performance improvements. Units of chunk width are double-precision (64-bit) words.

Device	Maximum Threads	25%	50%	75%	100%
KNC	240	14.9	10.5	8.7	8.7
IVB-EP	48	8.5	4.4	3.8	3.4

FIGURE 2.16

Variation of WSM6 run times (in seconds) with thread count. Thread count are expressed as a fraction of maximum number of threads available on each device. WSM6 performs best when each device is fully utilized. Note that 100% utilization corresponds to the "best" times in Figure 2.15.

Device	2 DP Words	4 DP Words	8 DP Words	16 DP Words	32 DP Words
KNC	—	—	8.7	8.8	10.1
IVB-EP	3.8	3.4	3.5	3.7	3.7

FIGURE 2.17

Variation of WSM6 run times (in seconds) with chunksize. Run times are minimized when chunksizes match vector length (i.e., times match the "best" times from Figure 2.15). Performance falls off quickly as chunksize is increased beyond vector length on Xeon Phi. Here, "DP" refers to "double-precision" (64-bit) words.

processors and the coprocessor. Note that performance gets worse as chunksize increases, especially beyond twice the vector length on the coprocessor.

Since performance falls off as chunksize increases, we expected the "i-inside" version of WSM6 to perform better than the "k-inside" version. Figure 2.18 shows that our expectation was incorrect. Although the technique of pushing a horizontal index down into single-column (k-innermost) code has proven beneficial for other physics packages such as shortwave radiation (recent work by Michalakes), in the case of WSM6, the slowdown incurred by the need to introduce complex and sparse masks in the "i" dimension overwhelmed the benefit of matching chunksize to vector length.

We also looked at the effect of compile-time constants in both the "i" and "k" dimensions. Starting with optimum chunksize in the "i" dimension, use of compile-time constants for each dimension were turned off as shown in Figure 2.19. For WSM6, we see that use of compile-time constants improves

Device	Threads	Time with k-inside	Time with i-inside
KNC	240	8.7	9.5
IVB-EP	48	3.4	4.3

FIGURE 2.18

Effect of refactoring to change WSM6 single-column (k-inside) code to "i-inside" code. The "i-inside" times used chunk width that matched vector lengths. Performance gain from matching ideal chunk width was overwhelmed by masking complexity making the "i-inside" code slower. Note that "k-inside" times match the "best" times from Figure 2.15.

Device	No compile-time constants	Time with constant k	Time with constant i and k
KNC	12.5	11.6	8.7
IVB-EP	4.4	4.1	3.4

FIGURE 2.19

Effect of compile-time constants on WSM6 execution time. This optimization improved performance when applied to loops with both "i" and "k" as inner dimensions (and matches "best" times from Figure 2.15). The sample code contains build-time options that allow each of these cases to be built and run, as described in the "For More Information" section.

performance by about 30% on Intel Xeon E5-v2 EP and 40% on the coprocessor. Since observing this result with WSM6, we have applied the technique to a long-wave radiation package and observed similar performance improvements on Intel Xeon processors using both the Intel and Cray Fortran compilers. Also, we have applied the technique to the entire NIM dynamical core and seen an 8% speedup on Intel Xeon processors.

It is clear that some kinds of code benefit more than others from compile-time constants. The WSM6 and long-wave radiation packages are very similar in terms of computational intensity and calls to transcendental math functions, but differ due to all loops in the radiation package having k-innermost. The NIM dynamics also has all loops with k-innermost, but it has lower compute intensity and no calls to transcendental functions. So compute intensity appears to be the most relevant difference between the physics packages that significantly benefit from compile-time constants and the NIM dynamics, which does not. Compile-time constants allow the compiler to generate aligned vector instructions that reduce instruction latency. This speeds up compute-intensive code more than memory-intensive code. In addition, the use of "unaligned" instructions on "aligned" memory incurs no performance penalty on Intel Xeon processors, but significantly slows the Intel Xeon Phi coprocessor. Thus, the use of compile-time constants benefits the coprocessor more than the processor.

In general, NWP has low computational intensity (the number of arithmetic operations per access to memory from last-level cache): often less than 1 and almost never greater than 2. Therefore, we assume that the upper bound for an NWP code's performance is memory bandwidth (as opposed to computation). Even so, NWP physics packages studied to date such as microphysics and radiation invariably fall short of this limit. The optimizations discussed above target factors behind the code's failure to saturate memory bandwidth: memory access latency, pipeline stalls around complex instructions, and otherwise insufficient instruction- and/or thread-level parallelism.

SUMMARY

NWP has an insatiable appetite for faster computers. As CPU clock rates have stalled, development focus has shifted to exploitation of fine-grained parallelism on emerging many-core and GPGPU architectures. Flexible optimization techniques such as those described in this chapter benefit Intel Xeon processors, Intel Xeon Phi coprocessors, other CPUs, and GPGPUs. Because these techniques are minimally intrusive, many have already been incorporated into NWP model code bases. As new "accelerator" architectures such as Intel Xeon Phi products and NVIDIA GPU have emerged to challenge traditional CPUs, the CPUs themselves have adapted to better exploit fine-grained parallelism. For WSM6, coprocessors and GPGPU are competitive with older "Sandy Bridge" Intel Xeon processors. But recently, the Intel Xeon processors have caught up and passed the accelerators with "Ivy Bridge" Intel Xeon E5 v2 and "Haswell" Intel Xeon E5 v3 processors clearly beating coprocessors and GPGPU. We are hopeful that future GPUs and the upcoming Intel Xeon Phi many-core processors codenamed Knights Landing will once again be competitive with high-end processors. But whether a clear "winner" emerges or the architectures simply merge in the future, flexible software approaches that expose and exploit fine-grained parallelism have already paid off and will continue to provide benefit in the NWP domain.

FOR MORE INFORMATION

Sample Code:

A stand-alone sample program and datasets for a single-step execution of WSM6 can be found at lotsofcores.com. The sample code allows most of the optimizations discussed in this chapter to be independently toggled on/off via build-time switches. Independently switchable optimizations include "k-inside" versus "i-inside" code sections, use of compile-time constants for "i" loops and array declarations, use of compile-time constants for "k" loops and array declarations, and selection of i-loop "chunk" size. The number of threads can be optionally undersubscribed at run time. Please see the README file that accompanies the sample code for details.

- Community Atmosphere Model: http://www.cesm.ucar.edu/models/atm-cam/.
- Collins, W.D., et al., 2004. Description of the NCAR Community Atmosphere Model (CAM3). Technical Report NCAR/TN-464+STR, National Center for Atmospheric Research, Boulder, CO, 226 pp.
- GRIMS: https://www.grims-model.org/start.jsp.
- Hong, S.-Y., Park, H., Cheong, H.-B., Kim, J.-E.E., Koo, M.-S., Jang, J., Ham, S., Hwang, S.-O., Park, B.-K., Chang, E.-C., Li, H., 2013. The global/regional integreated model system (GRIMs). Asia-Pacific J. Atmos. Sci. 49, 219-243. DOI:10.1007/s13143-013-0023-0.
- Integrated Forecast System: http://old.ecmwf.int/research/ifsdocs/.
- Untch, A., Hortal, M., 2004. A finite-element scheme for the vertical discretization of the semi-Lagrangian version of the ECMWF forecast model. Q. J. R. Meteorol. Soc. 130, 1505-1530.
- Barros, S.R.M., Dent, D., Isaksen, L., Robinson, G., Mozdzynski, G., Wollenweber, F., 1995. The IFS Model: A parallel production weather code, Parallel Comput. 21, 1621-1638.
- MPAS: http://mpas-dev.github.io.
- Skamarock, W.C., Klemp, J.B., Duda, M., Fowler, L.D., Park, S.-H., Ringler, T., 2012. A multiscale nonhydrostatic atmospheric model using centroidal voronoi tesselations and C-grid staggering. Mon. Weather Rev. 140(9), 3090-3105. DOI:10.1175/MWR-D-11-00215.1.
- NIM: http://esrl.noaa.gov/gsd/nim/.
- WRF: http://www.wrf-model.org/index.php.
- Skamarock, W.C., Klemp, J.B., Dudhia, J., Gill, D.O., Barker, D. M., Wang, W., Powers, J.G., 2005. A description of the Advanced Research WRF Version 2. NCAR Tech Notes-468+STR.
- WSM6: Hong, S.-Y., Lim, J.-O., 2006. The WRF single-moment 6-class micro- physics scheme (WSM6). J. Korean Meteor. Soc. 42, 129-151.
- Xeon Phi and GPU acceleration of WSM5: Michalakes, J., Vachharajani, M., 2008. GPU acceleration of numerical weather prediction. Parallel Process. Lett. 18, 531. DOI: 10.1142/S0129626408003557, https://www2.cisl.ucar.edu/sites/default/files/michalakes_5.pdf.

WRF GODDARD MICROPHYSICS SCHEME OPTIMIZATION

Jarno Mielikainen, Bormin Huang, Allen H.-L. Huang
University of Wisconsin-Madison, USA

THE MOTIVATION AND BACKGROUND

The Weather Research and Forecasting (WRF) model is an open-source Numerical Weather Prediction model. It is suitable for simulating weather phenomena with spatial resolution ranging from meters to thousands of kilometers. WRF is the most widely used community weather forecast and research model in the world. Both operational forecasters and atmospheric researchers are using it in 153 countries. The WRF has an extensible design. Therefore, it is possible to add physics, chemistry, hydrology models, and other features to it. In the real-world scenarios, WRF is initialized with boundary conditions and topography using measured observations. This flexibility allows WRF to be used in a wide variety of areas including tropical storm prediction, simulation of wildfire, air-quality modeling, prediction of regional climate, and storm-scale research.

There is an insatiable demand for computational power in weather forecasting models. Improving the computational performance of WRF will allow running more ensemble runs, doing runs at higher resolution, doing runs with smaller simulation time step, or running more complex models. All of these are desirable for a more accurate weather prediction, and they can be combined, and use of each increases the need for more computational performance.

Ensemble forecasting is an interesting component in this appetite for computational power. Weather forecasts are susceptible, sometime dramatically, to input variations. In order to gage susceptibility, a computer model is run a number of times from slightly different starting conditions. An ensemble forecast system is generally designed so that each member is equally likely, and the initial small differences in inputs should be consistent with uncertainties in the inputs (observations). Optimization can allow more ensemble runs to occur, which in turn allows a better estimation of forecast uncertainty and of which weather events may occur.

WRF uses OpenMP to distribute work between cores within a cluster node and message passing interface (MPI) to distribute work between nodes. Currently, the latest community release (WRFV3.6) runs natively on the Intel Xeon Phi coprocessor. Out of the several WRF physics components, the most time-consuming one is microphysics. Microphysics provides atmospheric heat and moisture tendencies. Microphysics includes explicitly resolved water vapor, cloud, and precipitation processes. Surface snowfall and rainfall are computed by microphysical schemes. Several bulk water microphysics schemes are available within the WRF, with different numbers of simulated hydrometeor classes and methods for estimating their size, fall speeds, distributions, and densities. In the WRF distribution, only WRF Single Moment 5-class (WSM5) cloud microphysics scheme code has been fully modernized to take full advantage of both the Intel Xeon Phi coprocessor and contemporary CPUs. The other modules are already auto-vectorized by the compiler. However, as we will see in this chapter, the speed of WRF code can be significantly improved by careful manual code optimization.

One of the most sophisticated microphysics schemes is the Goddard cloud microphysics scheme. In this chapter, we present results of optimizing the Goddard microphysics scheme. The code optimization techniques we present are also applicable to other physics components. Getting the maximum performance out of multicore Intel® Xeon® processors and many-core Intel Xeon Phi coprocessors will require optimizing legacy code. Those optimization techniques are discussed in this chapter. Furthermore, with the advent of unified AVX-512 vector extension instructions on Intel's future many-core products codenamed Knights Landing and future multicore Intel Xeon processors codenamed Skylake utilization of vector processing is becoming essential for peak performance on data parallel programs such as WRF.

Refer to the "For more information" at the end of this chapter for suggested readings to learn more about WRF, WSM5 optimizations, or a case study that analyzes the scalability trade-offs running one or more ranks of an MPI program on the coprocessor.

WRF GODDARD MICROPHYSICS SCHEME

We start with a quick overview of the theoretical background of WRF in general and specifically the Goddard microphysics scheme.

GODDARD MICROPHYSICS SCHEME

The WRF model contains two dynamic cores: the Nonhydrostatic Mesoscale Model core and the Advanced Research WRF core. A dynamic core contains a set of dynamic solvers that operates on a particular grid projection, grid staggering, and vertical coordinate system. The WRF model also contains several physics components, many of which can be used with both dynamic cores.

The WRF physics components are microphysics, cumulus parameterization, planetary boundary layer (PBL), land-surface/surface-layer model, and short-/longwave radiation. WRF physics components and their interactions are shown in Figure 3.1.

The microphysical processes simulated by the Goddard scheme are demonstrated in Figure 3.2 and explained in Figure 3.3. The scheme is a single-moment bulk cloud microphysics scheme, which updates seven variables (deviation of potential temperature, water vapor, and mixing ratio of five hydrometeors (cloud water, cloud ice, rain water, snow, graupel/hail)) in every time step using a prognostic equation saturation process and a microphysical interaction process.

BENCHMARK SETUP

To test the Goddard scheme, we used a CONtinental United States (CONUS) benchmark dataset for a 12 km resolution domain for 24 October 2001. A WRF domain is a geographic region of interest discretized into a two-dimensional grid parallel to the ground. Each grid point has multiple levels, which correspond to various vertical heights in the atmosphere. The size of the CONUS 12 km domain is 433×308 horizontal grid points with 35 vertical levels. As shown in Figure 3.4, the test problem is

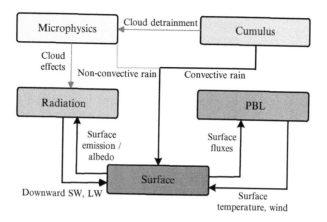

FIGURE 3.1

WRF physics components are microphysics, cumulus parametrization, planetary boundary layer (PBL), land-surface/surface-layer model, shortwave (SW), and longwave (LW) radiation.

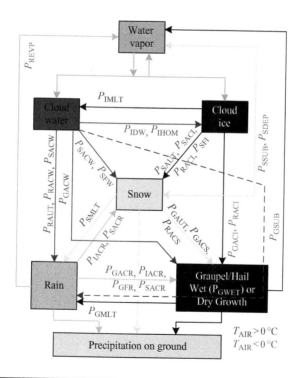

FIGURE 3.2

Cloud physics process simulated in the model with the snow field included. See Figure 3.3 for an explanation of the symbols.

P_{IDW}	depositional growth of cloud ice at the expense of cloud water
P_{IHOM}	homogeneous freezing of cloud water to form cloud ice
P_{IACR}	accretion of rain by cloud ice; produces snow or graupel depending on the amount of rain
P_{RACI}	accretion of cloud ice by rain; produces snow or graupel depending on the amount of rain
P_{RAUT}	auto-conversion of cloud water to form rain
P_{RACW}	accretion of cloud water by rain
P_{REVP}	evaporation of rain
P_{RACS}	accretion of snow by rain; produces graupel if rain or snow exceeds threshold
P_{SACW}	accretion of cloud water by snow. Also enhances snow melting
P_{SACR}	accretion of rain by snow. Produces graupel if rain or snow exceeds threshold; if not, produces snow. Also, the accreted water enhances snow melting
P_{SACI}	accretion of cloud ice by snow
P_{SAUT}	auto-conversion (aggregation) of cloud ice to form snow
P_{SFW}	Bergeron process (deposition and riming)—transfer of cloud water to form snow
P_{SFI}	transfer rate of cloud ice to snow through growth of Bergeron process embryos
P_{SDEP}	depositional growth of snow
P_{SSUB}	sublimation of snow
P_{SMLT}	melting of snow to form rain
P_{GAUT}	auto-conversion (aggregation) of snow to form graupel
P_{GFR}	probabilistic freezing of rain to form graupel
P_{GACW}	accretion of cloud water by graupel
P_{GACI}	accretion of cloud ice by graupel
P_{GACR}	accretion of rain by graupel
P_{GACS}	accretion of snow by graupel
P_{GSUB}	sublimation of graupel
P_{GMLT}	melting of graupel to form rain
P_{GWET}	wet growth of graupel

FIGURE 3.3

Microphysics processes.

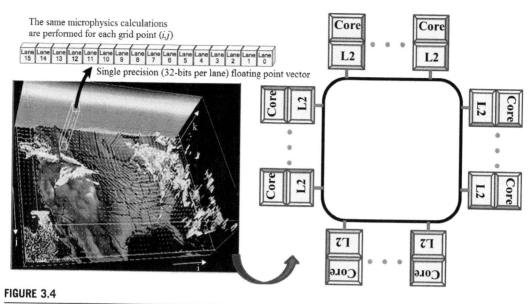

The same microphysics calculations
are performed for each grid point (i,j)

Single precision (32-bits per lane) floating point vector

FIGURE 3.4

Mapping of the CONUS 12 km domain onto an Intel Xeon Phi coprocessor thread domain, where the size of the CONUS domain is 433×308 horizontal grid points with 35 vertical levels.

a 12 km resolution 48-h forecast over the Continental U.S. capturing the development of a strong baroclinic cyclone and a frontal boundary that extends from north to south across the lower 48 states. Goddard microphysics computation is organized into a three-dimensional grid where the microphysical process computations in each column (k-dimension) are processed independently. Thus, there are two dimensions of parallelism (i- and j-dimensions) to work with. The total number of horizontal grid points is 133,364. An Intel Xeon Phi 7120P coprocessor core can process 16 grid points in parallel using its SIMD unit. Therefore, at least 3840 (16*60*4) grid points (i,j) are required to fully utilize all resources of 60 cores in the coprocessor when four threads are used per processor core. Thus, the test data will keep our test coprocessor fully utilized most of the time. However, at the end of the processing there is a tail effect when some of the cores are not fully utilized. With the test data, this will only happen after 34 full loads of 240×16 grid points have been processed. So, it is not an issue with the data. For a much smaller data size, this might become an issue. For example, if there were 250 grid points, 240 of those would be processed in parallel and when the remaining 10 points are processed most of the processor resources would be idle. Therefore, it is important to control the amount of data that is processed per processing unit or to have such a large amount of data such that the tail effect is either very small or nonexistent.

We used the Intel Fortran compiler, ifort, version 15.0.0 for compiling the Goddard source code for both Intel Xeon E5-2670 CPU and Intel Xeon Phi 7120P coprocessor. For CPU compilation, the following default WRF compiler options for ifort were used:

```
-O3 -openmp -w -ftz -fno-alias -auto -fp-model fast = 1
-no-prec-div -no-prec-sqrt -auto -align array64byte
```

For the coprocessor, the following compiler options from the WRF v3.6 distribution were used:

```
-mmic -auto -ftz -fno-alias -fimf-precision = low
-fimf-domain-exclusion = 15 -opt-assume-safe-padding
-opt-streaming-stores always -opt-streaming-cache-evict = 0
-mP2OPT_hlo _pref_use_outer_strategy = F -fp-model fast = 1
-no-prec-div -no-prec-sqrt -auto -align array64byte
```

Dynamic scheduling was used for OpenMP work sharing construct in a do-loop.

As can be seen from Figure 3.5, the microphysics is the most time-consuming physics component in WRF. The Goddard microphysics scheme has 2355 lines of code compared to over 60,000 lines of code in the ARW dynamics code. In total, the WRF consists of over half a million lines of code. Therefore, it makes sense to optimize the Goddard microphysics scheme first as this relatively small module can still give an overall speedup to the whole WRF. The processing times are an average of 10 execution runs. These processing times are measured running a stand-alone driver for the Goddard scheme. WRF uses 2D grid decomposition over the domain. The WRF computational domain is broken up into rectangular pieces are called tiles. Each tile is assigned to a thread for concurrent processing. A default domain decomposition of 4 east-west and 61 north-south tiles was used by the first version of Goddard code. The following optimizations we describe are cumulative, so that each optimization step always includes all previous optimization steps.

CODE OPTIMIZATION

Code validation was performed by checking that all code versions produced the same output values on a CPU. During code validation, precise math compiler options were used to force the compiler to strictly adhere to value-safe optimizations when implementing floating-point calculations. That disables optimizations that can change the result of floating-point calculations, which is required for strict ANSI conformance. These semantics ensure the reproducibility of floating-point computations including code vectorized or auto-parallelized by the compiler. However, this compiler options slows down the performance significantly. Therefore, the WRF does not use this compiler option as a default option.

This is in stark contrast to a situation when the default WRF compiler options are used, which tells the compiler to use more aggressive optimizations for floating-point calculations. These optimizations increase speed, but may affect the accuracy or reproducibility of floating-point computations.

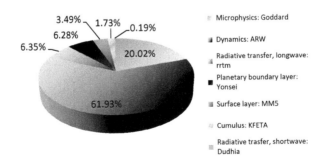

FIGURE 3.5

Intel Xeon Phi coprocessor processing times for the original WRF code as measured by Intel's profiling tool VTune.

```
16_X = (ite-its+1)/NUM_TILES_X+1
16_Y = (jte-jts+1)/NUM_TILES_Y+1


!$OMP PARALLEL DO &
!$OMP PRIVATE ( i, j, i_start, i_end, j_start, j_end) collapse(2)
   DO j = jts, jte, 16_Y
    DO i = its, ite, 16_X
     i_start = i
     i_end = min(i_start+(16_X-1),ite)
     j_start = j
     j_end = min(j_start+(16_Y-1),jte)

     CALL gsfcgce(        &
     ! ...                &
     )
     end do
   end do
 !$OMP END PARALLEL DO
```

FIGURE 3.6

Code listing—OpenMP code calling Goddard subroutine. Variables its and ite are lower and upper limits in east-west direction of the domain. Similarly, variables jts and jte define north-south domain limits. Thread private variables i_start, i_end, j_start, and j_end define the tile boundaries. This code is from file module_mp_gsfcgce. F, which is located in the directory WRFV3/phys in the source code of WRF.

We first experimented with different domain decompositions for OpenMP code in Figure 3.6, which calls the main subroutine. We got the best results when the domain was decomposed into 4×60 tiles, in east-west direction and north-south direction, respectively.

REMOVAL OF THE VERTICAL DIMENSION FROM TEMPORARY VARIABLES FOR A REDUCED MEMORY FOOTPRINT

The first optimization step was modifying the dimensions of some intermediate variables so that the k-dimension of that variable is removed. This process can be performed for variables that only require the use on one k-dimension value at a time. This optimization had the effect of reusing the cached data to increase computational intensity. An example of this process is shown in Figures 3.7 and 3.8, which shows the same code before and after optimization, respectively. In total, six variables were made

```
do k = kts, kte
        qrz(k)=qr(i,k,j)
        dzw(k)=dz8w(i,k,j)
     enddo
!  ...
fluxin=0.0
do k=max_q,min_q,-1
   fluxout=rhoz(k)*vtr(k)*qrz(k)
   flux=(fluxin-fluxout)/rhoz(k)/dzw(k)
   qrz(k)=qrz(k)+del_tv*flux
   qrz(k)=amax1(0.,qrz(k))
   qr(i,k,j)=qrz(k)
   fluxin=fluxout
   enddo
   if (min_q .eq. 1) then
      pptrain=pptrain+fluxin*del_tv
   else
      qrz(min_q-1)=qrz(min_q-1)+del_tv*   &
      fluxin/rhoz(min_q-1)/dzw(min_q-1)
      qr(i,min_q-1,j)=qrz(min_q-1)
   endif
```

FIGURE 3.7

Code listing—the original code with k-dimension intact for intermediate temporary variables. Two variables affected by optimization are in bold. This code is from file module_mp_gsfcgce.F, which is located in the directory WRFV3/phys in the source code of WRF.

scalars. Notice how scalar variables *dzw* and *qrz* need additional assignment statements in the optimized version. As a result, the processing time was reduced from 164.7 to 144.3 ms on the Intel Xeon Phi coprocessor and from 334.5 to 299.9 ms on the Intel Xeon processor.

COLLAPSE I- AND J-LOOPS INTO SMALLER CELLS FOR SMALLER FOOTPRINT PER THREAD

Vectorizing the main subroutine, saticel_s, was done in preparation for the next major optimization step. Vectorization refers to the process where a scalar implementation, which performs an operation one pair of operands at a time, is converted to a vector process, where a single instruction can refer to a

```
fluxin=0.0
do k=max_q,min_q,-1
   dzw=dz8w(i,k,j)
   qrz=qr(i,k,j)
   fluxout=rhoz(k)*vtr(k)*qrz
   flux=(fluxin-fluxout)/rhoz(k)/dzw
   qrz=qrz+del_tv*flux
   qrz=amax1(0.,qrz)
   qr(i,k,j)=qrz
   fluxin=fluxout
enddo
if (min_q .eq. 1) then
   pptrain=pptrain+fluxin*del_tv
else
   dzw=dz8w(i,min_q-1,j)
   qrz=qr(i,min_q-1,j)
   qrz=qrz+del_tv*   &
   fluxin/rhoz(min_q-1)/dzw
   qr(i,min_q-1,j)=qrz
endif
```

FIGURE 3.8

Code listing—optimized code with k-dimension intact for intermediate temporary variables. Two variables affected by optimization are in bold. This code is from file module_mp_gsfcgce.F, which is located in the directory WRFV3/phys in the source code of WRF.

many operand packed vector. This adds a form of parallelism to software in which one instruction or operation is applied to multiple pieces of data. The benefit is more efficient data processing and improved code performance. The Intel compiler build-log reports can be used to guide the code restructuring. Intel compiler option -vec-report (0 to 6) controls emission of the vectorization report. The most verbose is -vec-report 6, which outputs a detailed report from the vectorizer. The compiler reports what loops are auto-vectorized and the cause that prevents auto-vectorization. We used compiler report to remove a subroutine call to a diagnostic write subroutine, which prevented auto-vectorization of the loop in Figure 3.9.

Second issue preventing the compiler auto-vectorizing the loop was assumed dependency between two lines in the code. Those two lines accessing variable rp0 are shows in Figure 3.9. To solve this issue, split the i-loop nested inside j- and k-loops were into nine separate i-loops. This is illustrated

```
subroutine saticel_s()
    do j = jts,jte
    do k = kts,kte
    do i = its, ite
        !...

            rp0(i)=3.799052e3/p0(i,k)

!   ...

            if(qr(i).gt.0.0) then
                tair(i)=(pt(i)+tb0)*pi0(i)
                rtair(i)=1./(tair(i)-c358)
                qsw(i)=rp0(i)*exp(c172-c409*rtair(i))
!    ...
            if (alf+rn17c*tairc(i) .eq. 0.) then
                write(91,*) itimestep, i,j,k, alf, rn17c, tairc(i)
            endif
        !...
    end do
    end do
    end do
    end subroutine saticel_s
```

FIGURE 3.9

Code listing—the original non-vectorized code. This code is from file module_mp_gsfcgce.F, which is located in the directory WRFV3/phys in the source code of WRF.

in Figures 3.9 and 3.10. The loop consisted of 979 lines of code. We experimented with different loop fission options and ended up at nine separate innermost i-loops. An alternative solution would be to place a SIMD vectorization directive (!DIR$ SIMD) before the i-loop, which was not auto-vectorized by the compiler due to the suspected, but not real, existence of a vector dependence. On CPU, the SIMD directive solution was 11% slower than the multiple loop solution.

The original threading was done in a driver routine with each thread processing a tile of data out of the total 4×60 grid. In order to fit tile data better into cache memory, a new threading scheme was employed. This meant modifying the calling routine so that the new tile size is 16×1. Just like before, tiles are processed concurrently. However, unlike the original tiling scheme, the new scheme has to copy input data to vector-sized arrays of 16 elements. The copying of the data from one array to another array might seem unnecessary overhead. However, this provides several advantages along with a drawback. First, the new tiling scheme needs one index less than the original scheme to access the data in the new arrays. More importantly, the first dimension of the new arrays, which corresponds to east-west direction, is statically sized. This allows a compiler to perform some optimizations that overcomes the drawback of having to copy data between arrays in cases when the data is accessed multiple times. Furthermore, this strategy aligns the data to cache lines in memory. That alignment advantage will

```
subroutine saticel_s ()
   do j = jts,jte
   do k = kts,kte
   do i = its, ite
    !...
   end do
   do i = its, ite
    !...
   end do
   do i = its, ite
    !...
   end do
   do i = its, ite
    !...
   end do
   do i = its, ite
    !...
   end do
   do i = its, ite
    !...
   end do
   do i = its, ite
    !...
   end do
   do i = its, ite
    !...
   end do
   do i = its, ite
    !...
   end do
   end do
   end do
end subroutine saticel_s
```

FIGURE 3.10

Code listing—after loop-splitting, the code is vectorizable. This code is from file module_mp_gsfcgce.F, which is located in the directory WRFV3/phys in the source code of WRF.

be utilized again later in the chapter discussion using data alignment directives. Since each thread will process only 16 data elements, better data locality is achieved as more of the data can be accessed from the cache memories. In Figure 3.11, Goddard multithreaded code for this technique is shown. The processing time was reduced from 144.3 to 52.3 ms on the Intel Xeon Phi coprocessor and from 299.9 to 138.3 ms on the Intel Xeon CPU.

ADDITION OF VECTOR ALIGNMENT DIRECTIVES

Next, we added vector alignment directives before each i-loop so that the compiler can use a single aligned load instruction rather than the two-instruction unaligned load sequence. The data is known to be aligned in the memory because input data were copied to cells, which have a width of 16 data elements of 4 bytes each. Output data and local data use similar cells, which are also aligned. Therefore,

```
!$OMP PARALLEL DO &
!$OMP PRIVATE ( ic, j, ii, i, k ) &
!$OMP PRIVATE ( th1d, qv1d, ql1d, qr1d, qi1d, qs1d, &
!OMP qg1d, rho1d, pii1d, p1d & )
!$OMP SCHEDULE(dynamic,1)
   DO ip = 1,((1+(ite-its+1)/16)*16)*(jte-jts+1),16
      j = jts+(ip-1)/((1+(ite-its+1)/16)*16)
      IF ( j .ge. jts .and. j .le. jte ) THEN
         ii = its+mod((ip-1),((1+(ite-its+1)/16)*16))
         do k = kts, kte ! input variables
            DO ic=1,min(16,ite-ii+1)
               i = ii+ic -1
               th1d(ic,k)  = th(i,k,j)
               qv1d(ic,k)  = qv(i,k,j)
               ql1d(ic,k)  = ql(i,k,j)
               qr1d(ic,k)  = qr(i,k,j)
               qi1d(ic,k)  = qi(i,k,j)
               qs1d(ic,k)  = qs(i,k,j)
               qg1d(ic,k)  = qg(i,k,j)
               rho1d(ic,k) = rho(i,k,j)
               pii1d(ic,k) = pii(i,k,j)
               p1d(ic,k)   = p(i,k,j)
            ENDDO
         enddo
         IF ( min(16,ite-ii+1) .gt. 0 ) THEN
            ! If a row contains unprocessed cells
               call SATICEL_S(dt_in, ihail, itaobraun, &
                     ice2, istatmin, new_ice_sat, id, &
                     th1d, qv1d, ql1d, qr1d, qi1d, qs1d, &
                     qg1d, rho1d, pii1d, p1d, itimestep, &
                     kts,kte,kms,kme,min(16,ite-ii+1) )
            ENDIF
            do k = kts, kte ! output variables
               DO ic=1,min(16,ite-ii+1)
                  i = ii+ic -1
                  th(i,k,j) = th1d(ic,k)
                  qv(i,k,j) = qv1d(ic,k)
                  ql(i,k,j) = ql1d(ic,k)
                  qr(i,k,j) = qr1d(ic,k)
                  qi(i,k,j) = qi1d(ic,k)
                  qs(i,k,j) = qs1d(ic,k)
                  qg(i,k,j) = qg1d(ic,k)
               ENDDO
            enddo
         ENDIF
      ENDDO
```

FIGURE 3.11

Code listing—Fortran code for multi-threading using OpenMP. Input data are copied to vector-sized arrays of 16 elements. After computation, output data are copied to the original arrays for further processing by the other parts of WRF. This code is from file module_mp_gsfcgce.F, which is located in the directory WRFV3/phys in the source code of WRF.

the data alignment directives can be added before each loop in the source code. However, the data in the original arrays is not guaranteed to be aligned so we didn't add alignment directives into data copying loops described earlier. This had a bigger effect of the code running on the processor than on the co-processor. The processing time was reduced from 52.3 to 46.9 ms on the Intel Xeon Phi coprocessor and from 138.3 to 120.4 ms on the Intel Xeon processor.

SUMMARY OF THE CODE OPTIMIZATIONS

Figure 3.12 shows processing times for different optimization stages, which are summarized in Figure 3.13. The overall speedup from the code optimization on an Intel Xeon E5-2670 processor was 2.8× compared to 3.5× on the Intel Xeon Phi 7120P coprocessor. The fact that the same code optimizations also improved CPU performance indicates that using the single source code for both processor and coprocessor is a good strategy. This reduces development costs as any programming work done to modernize WRF for coprocessors will also likely improve performance on legacy proc-essors without requiring multiple code bases.

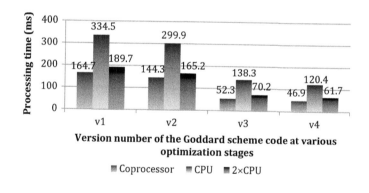

FIGURE 3.12

Processing times of Intel Xeon Phi 7120P coprocessor and Intel Xeon E5-2670 CPUs for the Goddard microphysics scheme.

Code version	Optimization description
V1	The original code
V2	The size of some temporary variables was reduced
V3	The memory footprint per thread was reduced
V4	Vector alignment directives were added before loops

FIGURE 3.13

Brief descriptions of the optimizations.

The results show that the scaling from a single CPU socket to a dual socket configuration is less than optimal due to memory (bandwidth) bound nature of the code. Code optimizations improved the CPU scaling from 1.76× to 1.95×. Furthermore, the relative performance increase from the code optimizations was higher for the coprocessors than processors. Thus, the performed optimizations are even more important on the coprocessor due to its larger speedup benefit from those optimizations.

ANALYSIS USING AN INSTRUCTION MIX REPORT

We used Intel Software Development Emulator to get a count of the number of executed instructions. Figure 3.14 shows the total number of instructions executed for both the original and optimized Goddard source code. Instruction counts are shown for AVX, AVX2, and AVX-512 (to be introduced in the many-core processor codenamed Knights Landing) instruction sets. Instruction count reduction for AVX-512 instruction set is quite small for the original code due to limited vectorization of the code. However, the optimized code has a lower instruction count because of the use of vector instructions instead of scalar instructions. Furthermore, AVX-512 offers significantly improved code vectorization capabilities as is evident from its low instruction count compared to AVX and AVX2 instruction counts on the optimized code.

VTune PERFORMANCE METRICS

In Figure 3.15, performance metrics for the original and optimized Goddard code on the Intel Xeon Phi coprocessor, as measured by the profiling tool, Intel® VTune™ Amplifier, are presented. The first metric, vectorization intensity, is a ratio between the total number of data elements processed by vector instructions and the total number of vector instructions. After the code was restructured to take a better advantage of vectorization, vectorization intensity was improved by a factor of 2×. In addition to vectorization improvement, memory access was also improved by code restructuring. L1 compute to data access ratio measures how many computations are performed on average for each piece of data loaded into the L1 cache. L1 compute to data access ratio was improved by over 1.48×. Furthermore, estimated latency impact was improved by 2.3×. This metric is an estimate of the average number of cycles takes to service L1 cache misses. So, it can be seen that data locality is improved as evident from the time to service L1 cache misses.

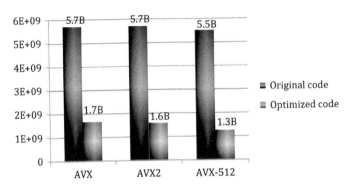

FIGURE 3.14

The total number of instruction executed on a CPU and on Intel Xeon Phi coprocessor.

Performance metric	Original Goddard code	Optimized Goddard code
Vectorization intensity	3.89	7.88
L1 compute to data access ratio	5.83	8.62
Estimated latency impact	222.28	98.18

FIGURE 3.15

Performance metrics for the original and optimized Goddard code on the Intel Xeon Phi coprocessor as measured by Intel's profiling tool VTune.

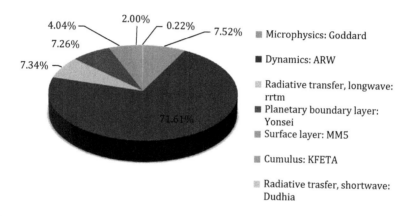

FIGURE 3.16

MIC processing times for the WRF after code optimizations measured by Intel's profiling tool VTune.

PERFORMANCE EFFECTS OF THE OPTIMIZATION OF GODDARD MICROPHYSICS SCHEME ON THE WRF

The optimized Goddard microphysics code was incorporated back into the WRF. Intel's VTune profiles measurements in Figure 3.16 show that after code optimizations, Goddard scheme takes only 7.6% of the total processing time and dynamics is even more dominant at 71.5% share of the total processing time. Thus, it is a natural candidate for further optimization of WRF. In addition, both radiative transfer and PBL are also two physics categories that warrant further optimization efforts as they both take over 7% of the total processing time.

SUMMARY

We have shown in this chapter that the Intel Xeon Phi coprocessor can be faster than a dual socket Intel Xeon processor system. However, to achieve that, both multi-threading and vectorization have to be utilized. Furthermore, code was optimized for frequent reuse of the cached data to increase computational intensity. Following these guidelines, the optimization of the WRF Goddard microphysics scheme was described in this chapter.

The results show that the optimizations improved performance of Intel Xeon Phi 7120P coprocessor by 4.7×. This speeds up the whole WRF by 1.15×. Furthermore, the optimizations improved performance on Intel Xeon E5-2670 processor by a factor of 3.3×. The optimizations that were performed were quite generic in nature. Those optimizations included vectorization of the code to better utilize vector units inside each CPU core. Furthermore, memory access was improved by optimizing the access to some of intermediate data arrays.

The generic nature of the performed optimizations means that the optimized code can be expected to run efficiently on future Intel many-core processors and on multicore CPUs. The next-generation Intel Xeon Phi products, codenamed Knights Landing (KNL), are not binary compatible with the first-generation coprocessors since AVX-512 SIMD instructions on KNL are encoded differently than the Initial Many-Core Instructions (Intel® IMCI) in the first generation. However, it is expected that the optimization that we have performed so far on the code will also run well on KNL. The future Intel Xeon platforms will also use the AVX-512 instruction encoding for vector instructions.

The Goddard microphysics scheme optimization work represents an initial step toward fully vectorizing WRF. As could be seen from the speedup figures, optimization of the code is essential for a good performance on the multicore processors and many-core coprocessors. Thus, we will also continue our work and optimize the other WRF modules.

ACKNOWLEDGMENTS

This work is supported by Intel Corporation, under Grant No. MSN171479, to establish the Intel Parallel Computing Center at the University of Wisconsin-Madison. The authors would like to thank Bob Burroughs and Michael Greenfield for their generous support.

FOR MORE INFORMATION

Here are some additional reading materials we recommend related to this chapter. A case study of WRF on the Intel® Xeon Phi™ coprocessor which analyzes the scalability trade-offs running one or more ranks of an MPI program on the coprocessor:

- Meadows, L., 2012. Experiments with WRF on Intel® Many integrated core (Intel@ MIC) architecture, OpenMP in a Heterogeneous World, 130-139.

To learn more about WSM5 optimization, see a presentation by Michalakes:

- Michalakes, J., 2013. Optimizing weather models for Intel Xeon Phi, Intel Theater Presentation SC '13, November 20.

To learn more about WRF, we encourage you to read:

- Skamarock, W.C., Klemp, J.B., Dudhia, J., Gill, D.O., Barker, D.M., Duda, M.G., Huang, X., Wang, W., and Powers, J.G., 2008. A description of the Advanced Research WRF Version3, NCAR Technical Note, TN-4475+STR, Boulder, Colorado, USA.

Download WRF source code, http://www2.mmm.ucar.edu/wrf/users/download.

Download the code from this, and other chapters, http://lotsofcores.com.

PAIRWISE DNA SEQUENCE ALIGNMENT OPTIMIZATION

Yongchao Liu*, Bertil Schmidt[†]

Georgia Institute of Technology, USA[*]
Johannes Gutenberg University Mainz, Germany[†]

As an optimal method for pairwise DNA sequence alignment, the Smith-Waterman (SW) algorithm is widely used. This algorithm is computationally demanding especially for long DNA sequences. In this chapter, we present a parallel implementation exploiting Intel® Xeon Phi™ coprocessors to accelerate the pairwise alignment of DNA sequences. We describe parallelization approaches in order to deeply explore the inherent parallelism within Intel Xeon Phi coprocessors. To achieve high speed, we explore two levels of parallelism within a single coprocessor and one more level of parallelism between multiple coprocessors. Within a single coprocessor, we exploit instruction-level parallelism within 512-bit single instruction multiple data (SIMD) instructions (vectorization) as well as thread-level parallelism over the many cores (multi-threading using OpenMP). Between coprocessors, we employ device-level parallelism in order to harness the compute power of clusters including Intel Xeon Phi coprocessors using MPI. Our code is written in C++ with a set of SIMD intrinsics, OpenMP, and MPI.

PAIRWISE SEQUENCE ALIGNMENT

Consider two DNA sequences $S1 = S1[1...m]$ and $S2 = S2[1...n]$ of length m and n, respectively, over the DNA alphabet $\sum = \{A, C, G, T\}$. We are interested in computing the score of an optimal local alignment of $S1$ and $S2$ according to a given scoring scheme. The scoring scheme considered here consists of a scoring function (also called a substitution matrix) sbt: $\sum \times \sum \rightarrow Z$, a gap opening penalty $go > 0$ and a gap extension penalty $ge \geq 0$. The SW algorithm calculates the optimal alignment score based on the concept of dynamic programming (DP) by means of computing a DP matrix (also called alignment matrix) based on the following recurrence relations for $1 \leq i \leq m$ and $1 \leq j \leq n$:

$$H[i,j] = \max\{0, E[i,j], F[i,j], H[i-1,j-1] + \text{sbt}(S1[i], S2[j])\}$$
$$E[i,j] = \max\{E[i-1,j], H[i-1,j] - go\} - ge$$
$$F[i,j] = \max\{F[i,j-1], H[i,j-1] - go\} - ge$$

The values $H[i, j]$, $E[i, j]$, and $F[i, j]$ represent the optimal local alignment score of the two prefixes $S1[1...i]$ and $S2[1...j]$ where the alignment ends with the letter $S1[i]$ aligned to the letter $S2[j]$, the letter $S1[i]$ aligned to a gap, and a gap aligned to the letter $S2[j]$, respectively. The recurrences are initialized as $H[i, 0] = H[0, j] = E[0, j] = F[i, 0] = 0$ for $0 \leq i \leq m$, and $0 \leq j \leq n$.

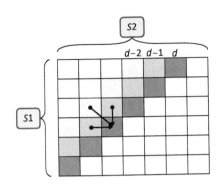

FIGURE 4.1

Data dependency in the SW algorithm.

In the DP matrix computation, each cell depends on its left, upper, and upper-left (diagonal) neighbors as depicted in Figure 4.1. This dependency also implies that all cells on the same minor diagonal can be computed in parallel, and the computation can be performed in the order of minor diagonal from the top-left corner to the bottom-right one in linear space. The optimal local alignment score, with respect to the given scoring scheme, corresponds to the maximum value in matrix H. The overall calculation has a quadratic computational complexity of $O(mn)$ and a linear space complexity of $O(m+n)$ and $O(\min(m, n))$ for the computation with and without optimal alignment retrieval, respectively. Note that in this chapter, we are only interested in computing the optimal local alignment score and not an actual alignment leading to this optimal score.

We assume that in the alignment matrix $S1$ is placed vertically and $S2$ horizontally and $m \leq n$ (see Figure 4.1). Considering the alignment matrix as a two-dimensional coordinate space on the Cartesian plane, we assume that the origin is the left-top corner, the horizontal coordinate x (corresponding to columns) increases from left to right, and the vertical coordinate y (corresponding to rows) increases from top to bottom. Hence, for a cell on diagonal $d(0 \leq d < m+n-1)$, the relationship between its coordinate (y, x), where x is the column index and y is the row index, and d can be expressed as $x+y=d$. We can see that the starting row index srow can be determined by computing the intersection point of a diagonal d with the line $y=0$ or $x=n-1$, and the ending row index erow can be determined by the intersection point of d with the line $y=m-1$ or $x=0$. Based on these observations, we compute srow and erow of diagonal d as $srow = \max(0, d-n+1)$ and $erow = \min(d, m-1)$. A corresponding calculation can also be made for the external diagonals in the tiled matrix (see Figure 4.2).

PARALLELIZATION ON A SINGLE COPROCESSOR

Our parallelization on a single coprocessor is based on the *scale-and-vectorize* approach. We first partition the DP matrix into tiles of size $\alpha \times \beta$ and distribute them over a team of threads using OpenMP. We call such a tile-based diagonal an *external diagonal*. The layout of the tiled DP matrix is shown in Figure 4.2. Our tiling scheme conceptually reorganizes the alignment matrix into a tiled DP matrix of size $R \times C$ with $R = \lceil m/\alpha \rceil$ and $C = \lceil n/\beta \rceil$. In the tiled alignment matrix, the computation of all tiles on an external diagonal d $(0 \leq d < R+C-1)$ can be performed independently. Within each tile, we can

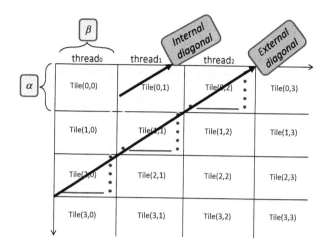

FIGURE 4.2

Layout of the tiled DP matrix.

therefore calculate cells on the same minor diagonal in parallel using vectorization based on instruction-level parallelism present in 512-bit SIMD vectors. We call the minor diagonals within tiles *internal diagonals*.

When enabling multi-threading, we configure the tiled alignment matrix to have $C = T$ (where T equals the number of threads) columns (and thus $\beta = \lceil n/T \rceil$) in order to trade-off the utilization both at the instruction level and the thread level. For vectorization, we split a 512-bit SIMD vector into 16 lanes with each lane occupying 32 bits. The number of vector lanes, denoted as V, is equal to 16 in our algorithm. In our implementation, we use $\alpha = V$ as default while allowing users to specify its value (must be a multiple of V) through a parameter.

MULTI-THREADING USING OpenMP

On any external diagonal D, T threads are computing all tiles on an external diagonal in parallel (see Figure 4.2). The threads need to be synchronized before moving to the next external diagonal. Each tile requires pairs of H and E values from its upper neighbor, pairs of H and F values from its left neighbor, and one H value from its upper-left neighbor. The necessary communication between threads is implemented as follows.

- *Vertical direction*: We allocate a global horizontal (GH) buffer of size $O(n)$ to store the upper H (H_{up}) and upper E (E_{up}) values for the whole alignment matrix. In this context, the term "global" indicates that the buffers are visible and shared by all threads in our OpenMP parallel regions. During the computation, a cell can access the required H_{up} and E_{up} values by its global column index (denoted as *globalCol*) in the alignment matrix. Within a tile, we read the H_{up} and E_{up} value pair from buffer GH to compute the first row, and then update the buffer with the newly computed H and E value pairs of all cells on the last row.

```
#pragma omp parallel firstprivate(GV,GD) default(shared)
for (d=0; d < R+C-1; ++d) {
        sExtRow = max(0,d-C+1);
        eExtRow = min(d,R-1);
        load the per-thread maximum score lmaxScore;
        #pragma omp barrier
        #pragma omp for schedule(static,1) nowait

        for (r=sExtRow; r <= eExtRow; ++r)
                compute all cells in tile(r,d-r);
        save lmaxScore to a global variable;
        swap the input and output of GV and GD;

}
reduce to get the optimal local alignment score;
```

FIGURE 4.3

Kernel for the multi-threaded computation (refer to function _swKernelShared() in AlignCoreTiling.cpp).

- *Horizontal direction*: We allocate C global vertical (GV) buffers of α elements each to store the α pairs of left $H(H_{\text{left}})$ and left $F(F_{\text{left}})$ values. Each column $c(0 \leq c < C)$ of the tiled alignment matrix has exactly one GV buffer. All of the GV buffers are communicated to by means of a (cyclic) buffered pipeline, where each tile on column c reads the H_{left} and F_{left} values from the cth GV buffer to compute the first column and writes the newly computed H and F values of all cells on the last column to the $(c+1)$th GV buffer.
- *Diagonal direction*: We allocate a one-element global diagonal (GD) buffer for each column c of the tiled alignment matrix, which stores the diagonal H (H_{diag}) required by the corresponding tile. All of the GD buffers are updated in the same manner as the GV buffer.

Figure 4.3 shows the coprocessor kernel for the computation over external diagonals. We synchronize all threads by means of a barrier, prior to entering the for-loop for the current diagonal computation. We remove the implicit barrier immediately following the loop using the *nowait* clause. In addition, one thread is assigned one tile at a time by a static scheduling policy (i.e., *schedule*(*static*, 1)). Our intention is that threads with consecutive IDs access consecutive vector-size elements along the diagonal. This scheduling policy, combined with the "balanced" affinity, enables the four threads resident within each core to have good data locality, thereby able to benefit from the L1/L2 cache hierarchy.

VECTORIZATION USING SIMD INTRINSICS

A tile is distributed to a thread and is then computed by means of SIMD vectorization. We segment a tile into α/V stripes with each stripe containing V rows, and finish the overall computation stripe-by-stripe from top to bottom. This striped computation is internal to each thread, and is used to force the vectorization efficiency within each thread by reducing the number of idle vector lanes and the number of instructions. Within a tile, the GH, GV, and GD buffers are multiplexed, and thus we do not need to allocate additional memory. To implement the data dependency relationship in SW algorithm, we use the following techniques.

- *Vertical direction*: A stripe loads the H_{up} and E_{up} values from buffer GH to compute its first row, and saves the newly computed H and E values of all cells on its last row to the buffer.
- *Horizontal direction*: The stripe loads H_{left} and F_{left} from the cth GV buffer to compute its first column, and stores the newly computed H and F values of all cells on its last column to the $(c+1)$th GV buffer.
- *Diagonal direction*: The stripe reads the H_{diag} value from the cth GD buffer for the computation, but saves the H_{up} corresponding to the last column to the $(c+1)$th GD buffer for the future use in the next diagonal.

Figure 4.4 shows an example of vectorized computation on internal diagonals with $V=4$, $\alpha=4$, and $\beta=10$, where the hatched cells appearing at both ends of a stripe mean that the corresponding vector lanes are idle. In the computation of a stripe, we move SIMD vectors from left to right in parallel with minor diagonals of the stripe.

If implementing a unified kernel for a stripe, we have to check for each minor diagonal of the stripe if a boundary cell lies on the last row or column. This would introduce branching instructions in the kernel. To avoid this undesirable branching we use the concept of *peeling*. Peeling removes the code for boundary conditions from the inner loop. We implement peeling by means of a three-step approach (see Figure 4.4), which uses separate kernels for the first V diagonals (Step 1), the middle diagonals (Step 2), and the last $V-1$ diagonals (Step 3).

To implement kernels, there are two general vectorization techniques: auto-vectorization (via compiler directives) and SIMD intrinsics. In our kernels, we have directly chosen to use SIMD intrinsics, without making the attempt to use auto-vectorization. This is because our prior experiences with auto-vectorization fell short in terms of runtime performance on the Intel Xeon Phi coprocessor, compared to SIMD intrinsics for our application, when we implemented an earlier program to accelerate bit-parallel approximate pattern matching.

Figure 4.5 shows the pseudocode of the kernel for Step 2 (Step 1 and Step 3 are similar). For each stripe, our code merely needs to load the corresponding V characters of $S1$ to a vector register once and can reuse the register until the completion of the stripe. We load V pairs of H_{left} and F_{left} values once to two vector registers. In the remaining computation, both H_{left} and F_{left} values can be completely stored and manipulated in vector registers. Furthermore, we load two integer values, i.e., H_{up} and E_{up}, from buffer GH to generate the H_{up} and E_{up} vector registers for the current diagonal. This generation can be realized by a vector push operation (implemented here by using *_mm512_alignr_epi32()*), which left-shifts the vector and replaces the least significant element with the corresponding integer value.

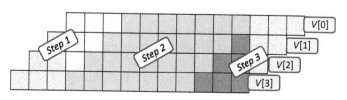

FIGURE 4.4

Vectorized computation for one stripe within a tile.

```
Compute the column index globalCol of the stripe in the
alignment matrix;
Compute the starting index startIndex of the GV buffer
for the stripe;
for (i=16; i < numTileCols; ++i, ++globalCol) {
        vHUp = _mm512_set1_epi32(GH[globalCol].h);
        vEUp = _mm512_set1_epi32(GH[globalCol].e);
        vEUp = _mm512_alignr_epi32(vE,vEUp,15);
        vHUp = _mm512_alignr_epi32(vH,vHUp,15);
        vE = _mm512_sub_epi32(vEUp,vGapExtend);
        vTmp = _mm512_sub_epi32(vHUp,vGapOE);
        vE = _mm512_max_epi32(vE,vTmp);
        vF = _mm512_sub_epi32(vF,vGapExtend);
        vTmp = _mm512_sub_epi32(vH,vGapOE);
        vF = _mm512_max_epi32(vF,vTmp);
        Compute the substitution score vSubScore;
        vH = _mm512_add_epi32(vHDiag, vSubScore);
        vTmp = _mm512_max_epi32(vE,vF);
        vH = _mm512_max_epi32(vH,vZero);
        vH = _mm512_max_epi32(vH,vTmp);
        lmaxScore = _mm512_max_epi32(lmaxScore,vH);
        vHDiag = vHUp;
        Save the H and E values for the cell on the last
        row of the stripe
    }
Save the H and F values for the cell on the last column
of the stripe;
```

FIGURE 4.5

Kernel for the vectorized computation of Step 2 (refer to function _swKernelShared() in AlignCoreTiling.cpp).

PARALLELIZATION ACROSS MULTIPLE COPROCESSORS USING MPI

Our distributed parallelization on a cluster of coprocessors is designed based on the MPI offload model, which launches MPI processes solely on the host CPUs and utilizes the offload capability within the process to offload some workload to the corresponding coprocessor. In this model, communications between coprocessors must be explicitly managed by the host via offload directives. The core idea of the distributed approach across multiple Intel Xeon Phi coprocessors is based on a second-level tiling. We further partition the alignment matrix into even bigger blocks of size $\alpha_{mpi} \times \beta_{mpi}$, reorganizing the matrix to have $R_{mpi} = \lceil m/\alpha_{mpi} \rceil$ rows and $C_{mpi} = \lceil n/\beta_{mpi} \rceil$ columns (see Figure 4.6).

We call the corresponding diagonals *block diagonals*. All blocks within such a diagonal are distributed over a network of coprocessors and one block is assigned to one coprocessor. Within any block, a variant of the aforementioned tiled approach is employed on a single coprocessor, which additionally processes intermediate data computed by other MPI processes. Similar to the tiled approach, the

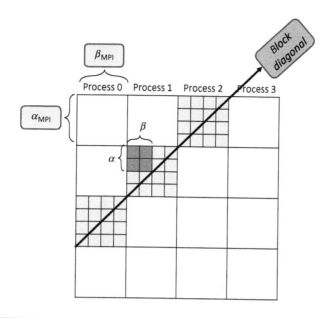

FIGURE 4.6

Layout of tiled DP matrix for multiple coprocessors.

distributed approach requires additional GH, GV, and GD buffers to store the block-level intermediate data distributed among MPI processes. Between diagonals we communicate both the block-level GV and GD buffers between MPI processes, and transfer the new data to the corresponding coprocessors by means of offloading. To improve communication efficiency, we use non-blocking communication routines (*MPI_Isend* and *MPI_Irecv*). In this way, we can initiate the communication between neighbors and then wait for their completion.

Figure 4.7 shows the pseudocode for the distributed computation, where we use $\beta_{mpi} = \lceil n/P \rceil$ (P is the number of coprocessors which is also equal to the number of MPI processes since our implementation requires a one-to-one correspondence between MPI processes and coprocessors) and $\alpha_{mpi} = 128$ K. We also employ the MPI offload model, which launches MPI processes solely on the host CPUs and utilizes the offload capability within the process to offload work to the coprocessor.

PERFORMANCE RESULTS

For our performance evaluation, we select six genome sequences with lengths ranging from 4.4 to 50 million base-pairs (see Figure 4.8), which are publicly available at the NCBI Nucleotide database. Run-times are measured on a compute node with two Intel E5-2670 8-core 2.60 GHz CPUs and 64 GB RAM running Linux. This compute node is further equipped with four Intel Xeon Phi coprocessors (B1PRQ-5110P/5120D). We use the Intel C++ compiler and OpenMPI to compile and link our algorithm. The environment variable *KMP_AFFINITY* is set to "balanced," since the "balanced" affinity more often gave us the best performance on the coprocessors through our evaluations.

```
Offload to transfer sequences S1 and S2;
Offload to allocate block-level GH, GV and GD buffers on
the coprocessor;
for (d = 0; d < Rmpi+Cmpi-1; ++d) {
        sMpiRow = max(0,d-Cmpi+1);
        eMpRow = min(d,Rmpi-1);
        sMpiCol = d-eMpiRow;
        eMpiCol = d-sMpiRow;
        currMpiCol = mpiRank;
        currMpiRow = d-currMpiCol;
        MPI_Barrier(MPI_COMM_WORLD);
        if (currMpiCol>=sMpiCol && currMpiCol<=eMpiCol) {
                #pragma offload target (mic: micIndex) in/out
                variable list{
                Invoke the Xeon Phi kernel;
                Calculate the local maximum score lmaxScore;
        }
        Communicate intermediate data using MPI_Isend and
        MPI_Irecv;
}
MPI_Reduce over lmaxScore to get overall optimal score;
```

FIGURE 4.7

Pseudocode of the MPI parallelization (refer to function _alignDistributed () in AlignCoreTiling.cpp).

Seq.	Length	Accession No.	Genome definition
S4.4	4,411,532	NC_000962.3	Mycobacterium tuberculosis H37Rv
S4.6	4,641,652	NC_000913.3	Escherichia coli K12 MG1655
S23	23,011,544	NT_033779.4	Drosophila melanogaster chr. 2L
S33	32,799,110	BA000046.3	Pan troglodytes DNA chr. 22
S42	42,034,648	NC_019481.1	Ovis aries breed Texel chr. 24
S50	50,073,674	NC_019478.1	Ovis aries breed Texel chr. 21

FIGURE 4.8

Information of the genome sequences used.

We first evaluate the scalability of the tiled approach with respect to a varying number of threads on a single coprocessor using the S4.4 and S4.6 sequence pair, where we start from $T=60$ threads and increment T until reaching 236 (equals to the value returned by *omp_get_num_procs()*). The speed gradually increases as T grows, albeit having some tiny fluctuations, and eventually reaches the maximum at $T=236$ (see Figure 4.9).

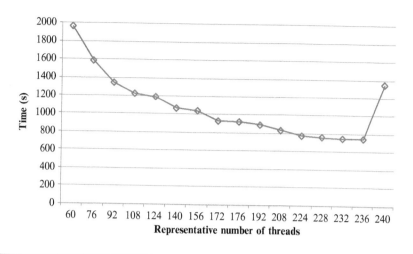

FIGURE 4.9

Parallel scalability in terms of some representative number of threads on a single coprocessor.

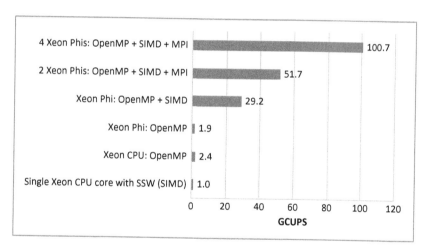

FIGURE 4.10

Performance comparisons in terms of GCUPS.

Figure 4.10 compares the performance achieved for computing the optimal pairwise alignment score of the S4.4 and S4.6 sequence pair in terms of billion cell updates per second (GCUPS). The comparison includes the performance of our OpenMP implementation without SIMD intrinsics on the Intel® Xeon processors using 16 threads and on a single Intel Xeon Phi coprocessor using 236 threads, our OpenMP implementation with SIMD intrinsics on a single coprocessor, and our OpenMP implementation with SIMD intrinsics and MPI on four coprocessors. It can be seen that using vectorization on a coprocessor improves the performance by a factor of 15.4 compared to the nonvectorized code. In some sense, this speedup also reflects the high efficiency of our SIMD vectorization.

Sequence Pairs	GCUPS			Speedup		Efficiency (%)	
	1 Phi	2 Phis	4 Phis	2 Phis	4 Phis	2 Phis	4 Phis
S4.4 vs. S4.6	29.2	51.7	100.7	1.8	3.4	88.4	86.2
S23 vs. S33	30.0	53.5	110.1	1.8	3.7	89.2	91.8
S23 vs. S42	30.0	53.9	110.6	1.8	3.7	89.7	92.1
S23 vs. S50	30.0	54.1	111.0	1.8	3.7	90.3	92.6
S33 vs. S42	30.1	54.0	111.4	1.8	3.7	89.8	92.6
S33 vs. S50	30.1	54.0	106.0	1.8	3.5	89.8	88.0
S42 vs. S50	30.0	54.1	111.4	1.8	3.7	90.1	92.7

FIGURE 4.11

Performance of our program on different numbers of coprocessors.

Meanwhile, the vectorized multi-threaded Intel Xeon Phi coprocessor implementation achieves a speedup of 12.2 compared to the nonvectorized multi-threaded host processor implementation. It needs to be noted that the nonvectorized coprocessor implementation uses the same OpenMP-based kernel code as the nonvectorized multi-threaded processor implementation.

Furthermore, using the smallest S4.4 and S4.6 sequence pair, good scalability in terms of the number of coprocessors (see Figure 4.11) is achieved with efficiencies of 88.4% and 86.2% for two and four coprocessors, respectively. For even longer input sequences (e.g., 50 million base-pairs) our code can further improve performance to up to 30.1 GCUPS on a single coprocessor and 111.4 GCUPS for four coprocessors (with an efficiency of 92.7%).

Finally, we have compared our vectorized multi-threaded MPI-based implementation to the SSW program (see Figure 4.10). SSW is a genomic sequence alignment algorithm optimized using Streaming SIMD Extensions 2 (SSE2) vector instructions coded using SSE2 intrinsics. For aligning the aforementioned S4.4 and S4.6 sequence pair, SSW achieves a performance of 1.02 GCUPS on a single CPU core. This means that using the same benchmarking sequences, our vectorized multi-threaded MPI-based implementation is able to achieve a speedup of 28.6 over SSW by using a single coprocessor, a speedup of 50.7 by using two coprocessors, and a speedup of 98.7 by using four coprocessors.

SUMMARY

We have presented a parallelized SW algorithm exploiting coprocessors to accelerate the pairwise alignment of long DNA sequences. We have exploited three levels of parallelism by means of OpenMP, SIMD intrinsics, and MPI. The OpenMP optimization applies to both the processor and coprocessor. Our choice of explicitly coding intrinsics for the 512-bit SIMD means that our vectorized implementations currently only run on the coprocessor. However, Knights Landing (the codename for the second-generation many-core Intel Xeon Phi product family) will include a standalone CPU, in addition to a coprocessor that must be paired with Intel Xeon CPUs. Knights Landing will also support Intel® AVX-512 instructions, enabling the intrinsic code compatibility with its predecessor. This means that our MPI-based vectorized implementations (using 512-bit SIMD vector instructions on the coprocessor) will run on Knights Landing after code recompilation.

Within a single coprocessor, we have used instruction-level parallelism within 512-bit SIMD instructions (vectorization) and thread-level parallelism over the many cores (multi-threading). Our vectorized code is implemented using three separate kernels to peel out unnecessary code for boundary conditions. Between coprocessors, we have used device-level parallelism to harness the power of clusters with coprocessors (distributed computing). The performance of our algorithm has been evaluated using DNA sequences of lengths ranging from 4.4 million to 50 million nucleotides. Our evaluation reveals that the implementation can achieve a stable performance for all tested sequences and can yield a performance of up to 30.1 GCUPS on a single coprocessor and up to 111.4 GCUPS on four coprocessors sharing the same host.

Currently, our implementation only computes the optimal local alignment score. An obvious extension of our work would be the calculation of an actual alignment leading to this optimal score. This could be done by storing the complete DP matrix and performing a *traceback* procedure. Unfortunately, the memory consumption of this approach is prohibitive, especially for very long DNA sequences (e.g., mammalian genomes can be billions of bases long), because the space complexity of the complete DP matrix is directly proportional to the product of the lengths of a sequence pair. Thus, the more challenging divide-and-conquer approach to calculating alignments in linear space would need to be employed. Mapping of this algorithm onto the Intel Xeon Phi coprocessor architecture is therefore part of our future work.

FOR MORE INFORMATION

Here are some additional reading materials that we recommend related to this chapter.

- General information about the Smith-Waterman algorithm: http://en.wikipedia.org/wiki/Smith-Waterman_algorithm.
- General information about Intel Xeon Phi coprocessor programming: Jeffers, J., Reinders, J., 2013. Intel Xeon Phi Coprocessor High-Performance Programming. Morgan Kaufmann, San Francisco, CA, USA.
- More details of our parallelization approach: Liu, Y., Tran, T., Lauenroth, F., Schmidt, B., 2014. SWAPHI-LS: Smith-Waterman algorithm on Xeon Phi coprocessors for long DNA sequences. 2014 IEEE International Conference on Cluster Computing, pp. 257-265.
- A GPU implementation of pairwise alignment with traceback: Sandes, E., de Melo, A., 2013. Retrieving Smith-Waterman alignments with optimizations for megabase biological sequences using GPU. IEEE Trans. Parallel Distrib. Syst. 24(5), 1009-1021.
- A Cell/BE implementation of pairwise alignment: Sarje, A., Aluru, S., 2009. Parallel genomic alignments on the cell broadband engine. IEEE Trans. Parallel Distrib. Syst. 20(11), 1600-1610.
- Smith-Waterman protein database search on Xeon Phi: Liu, Y., Schmidt, B., 2014. SWAPHI: Smith-Waterman protein database search on Xeon Phi coprocessors. 25th IEEE International Conference on Application-specific Systems, Architectures and Processors, pp. 184-185.
- The SSW program optimized using SSE2 vector instructions: Zhao, M., Lee, W.P., Garrison, E.P., Marth, G.T., 2013. SSW library: an SIMD Smith-Waterman C/C++ library for use in genomic applications. PLoS One 8, e82138.

- Another program we developed for which SIMD intrinsics showed to be more efficient than auto-vectoriztion with pragma directives: Tran, T.T., Schindel, S., Liu, Y., Schmidt, B., 2014. Bit-Parallel approximate pattern matching on the Xeon Phi coprocessor. 26th International Symposium on Computer Architecture and High Performance Computing, pp. 81-88.
- SWAPHI-LS is open source and the latest source code, as well as the manual, is available at http://swaphi-ls.sourceforge.net.
- Download the code from this, and other chapters, http://lotsofcores.com.

ACCELERATED STRUCTURAL BIOINFORMATICS FOR DRUG DISCOVERY

5

Wei P. Feinstein, Michal Brylinski

Louisiana State University, USA

Computer-aided design is one of the critical components of modern drug discovery. Drug development is routinely streamlined using computational approaches to improve hit identification and lead selection, to enhance bioavailability, and to reduce toxicity. In the last decade, a mounting body of genomic knowledge has been accumulated due to advancements in genome-sequencing technologies, presenting great opportunities for pharmaceutical research. However, new challenges also arose because processing this large volume of data demands unprecedented computing resources. On the other hand, the state-of-the-art heterogeneous systems currently deliver petaflops of peak performance to accelerate scientific discovery. In this chapter, we describe the development and benchmarking of a parallel version of *e*FindSite, a structural bioinformatics algorithm for the identification of drug-binding sites in proteins and molecular fingerprint-based virtual screening. Thorough code profiling reveals that structure alignment calculations in *e*FindSite consume approximately 90% of the wall-clock time. Parallelizing this portion of the code using pragma-based OpenMP enables the desired performance improvements, scaling well with the number of computing cores.

Compared to a serial version, the parallel code runs 11.8 and 10.1 times faster on the processor and the coprocessor, respectively; when both resources are utilized simultaneously, the speedup is 17.6. By comparing the serial and parallel versions of *e*FindSite, we show the OpenMP implementation of structure alignments for many-core devices. With minimal modifications, a complex, hybrid C++/Fortran77 code was successfully ported to a heterogeneous architecture yielding significant speedups. This demonstrates how modern drug discovery can be accelerated by parallel systems equipped with Intel® Xeon Phi™ coprocessors.

In this chapter, we show solutions to challenges in moving this code to parallelism that are lessons with wide applicability. For instance, we tackle porting extensive use of thread-unsafe common blocks in the Fortran77 code using OpenMP to make thread-private copies. We also enlarged stack sizes to avoid segmentation fault errors [ulimit -s]. Serial and parallel versions of *e*FindSite are freely available; please see "For more information" at the end of this chapter.

PARALLELISM ENABLES PROTEOME-SCALE STRUCTURAL BIOINFORMATICS

Advances in genome-sequencing technologies gave rise to the rapid accumulation of raw genomic data. Currently, one of the biggest challenges is to efficiently annotate this massive volume of biological sequences. Due to the prohibitively high costs associated with large-scale experiments, the most practical strategy is computation-based protein structure modeling followed by function inference, also known as structural bioinformatics. This approach routinely produces functional knowledge facilitating a wide range of research in biological sciences; for instance, cellular mechanisms can be investigated by constructing complex networks of molecular interactions at the level of complete proteomes. Systems-level research provides useful insights to support the development of new treatments for complex diseases, which often require a simultaneous targeting of multiple proteins. Consequently, polypharmacology that builds upon systems biology and drug discovery holds a great promise in modern medicine. Incorporating large biological datasets has become one of the central components in systems-level applications; however, significant challenges arise given the vast amount of data awaiting functional annotation. In order to achieve an acceptable time-to-completion in large projects, unprecedented computing power is needed.

In that regard, modern research-driven computer technology is shifting from the traditional single-thread to multiple-thread architectures in order to boost the computing power. Parallel high-performance computing (HPC) has become a key element in solving large-scale computational problems. For example, the Intel® Xeon Phi™ coprocessor featuring Intel® Many Integrated Cores (MIC) architecture offers massively parallel capabilities for a broad range of applications. The underlying x86 architecture supports common parallel programming models providing familiarity and flexibility in porting scientific codes. To take advantage of this unique architecture, we developed a parallel version of *e*FindSite for HPC systems equipped with Intel Xeon Phi coprocessors. *e*FindSite is a template-based modeling tool used in structural bioinformatics and drug discovery to accurately identify ligand-binding sites and binding residues across large datasets of protein targets. In most of the cases, we may expect the sequence similarity between a target protein and a template to be quite low, therefore, *e*FindSite was designed to make reliable predictions using only weakly homologous templates selected from the so-called "twilight zone" of sequence similarity. Consequently, its primary applications are genome-wide protein function annotation, drug design, and systems biology, which demand a sufficient computational throughput as well.

Briefly, *e*FindSite extracts ligand-binding knowledge from evolutionarily related templates stored in the Protein Data Bank (PDB), which are identified using highly sensitive protein threading and meta-threading techniques. Subsequently, ligand-bound templates are structurally aligned onto the target protein in order to detect putative binding pockets and residues. *e*FindSite predictions have a broad range of biological applications, such as molecular function inference, the reconstruction of biological networks and pathways, drug docking, and virtual screening. In the original version of *e*FindSite, template-to-target structure alignments are performed sequentially, thus many processor hours may be required to identify ligand-binding sites in a target protein. The slow modeling process complicates genome-wide applications that typically involve a considerable number of protein targets and large template libraries. In this chapter, we describe porting *e*FindSite to Intel Xeon Phi coprocessors and demonstrate the improved performance of the parallel code in detecting ligand-binding sites across large protein datasets. We show that executing *e*FindSite on computing nodes equipped with coprocessors greatly reduces the simulation time offering a feasible approach for genome-wide protein function annotation, structural bioinformatics, and drug discovery.

OVERVIEW OF *e*FindSite

How do drugs cure diseases? This is a complex question that can be simplified by focusing on the process of protein-ligand binding. In general, small ligand molecules, such as metabolites and drugs, bind to their protein targets at specific sites, often referred to as binding pockets. Ligand binding to proteins induces biological responses either as normal cellular functions or as therapeutic effects to restore homeostasis. On that account, the study of protein-ligand binding is of paramount importance in drug discovery. Since only ligand-free experimental structures and computationally constructed models are available for many pharmacologically relevant proteins, the detection of possible ligand-binding sites is typically the first step to infer and subsequently modulate their molecular functions. Currently, evolution/structure-based approaches for ligand-binding prediction are the most accurate and, consequently, the most widely used. Here, structural information extracted from evolutionarily weakly related proteins, called templates, is exhaustively exploited in order to identify ligand-binding sites and binding residues in target proteins that are linked to certain disease states. One example of an evolution/structure-based approach is *e*FindSite, a ligand-binding site prediction tool. It employs various state-of-the-art algorithms, such as meta-threading by *e*Thread to collect template proteins, clustering by Affinity Propagation to extract ligand information, and machine learning to further increase the accuracy of pocket detection. An important feature of *e*FindSite is an improved tolerance to structural imperfections in protein models, thus it is well suited to annotate large proteomic datasets. For a given target protein, *e*FindSite first conducts structural alignments between the target and each template from the ligand-bound template library. Next, it clusters the aligned structures into a set of discrete groups, which are subsequently ranked in order to predict putative ligand-binding pockets.

BENCHMARKING DATASET

All simulations in this study are performed using a benchmark dataset of protein-ligand complexes comprising proteins of different sizes and a varying number of associated ligand-bound templates. These proteins were selected from the original set of 3659 complexes used previously to develop and parameterize *e*FindSite to mimic a typical proteomic dataset. As shown in Figure 5.1, we first

		Number of templates			
		50-100	100-150	150-200	200-250
Target length (# residues)	200-300	50	50	50	50
	300-400	50	50	50	50
	400-500	34	32	23	12

FIGURE 5.1

Benchmarking dataset of 501 proteins.

defined 12 bins with an increasing number of amino acids in target proteins ranging from 200 to 500 as well as the number of associated templates varying from 50 to 250. Next, we randomly selected up to 50 proteins to populate each bin. The benchmarking dataset used in this project contains 501 proteins. For each protein, we use its experimental conformation as the target structure and weakly homologous templates identified by *e*Thread sharing less than 40% sequence identity with the target.

CODE PROFILING

Before converting the serial version of *e*FindSite to a parallel implementation, we conducted a thorough code profiling in order to figure out which portions of the code consume the most CPU cycles. According to the Pareto principle, also known as the 80/20 rule, most computer programs spend 80% of the wall time executing only 20% of the code. On that account, the single most important step prior to porting *e*FindSite to Intel Xeon Phi coprocessors was to identify a block of code that uses the majority of computing time. To conduct code profiling, we randomly selected one protein from each bin presented in Figure 5.1. Figure 5.2 shows the profiling outcome using gprof, a widely used performance analysis tool generating a function list based on the execution time. Four functions were identified as the most time-consuming: tmsearch, cal_tmscore, dp, and get_score taking 29%, 27%, 21%, and 15% of the entire execution time, respectively. Importantly, all these functions contribute to the calculation of structure alignments utilizing up to 92% of the computing time. Next, we measured the wall time by dividing *e*FindSite into three major steps, pre-alignment calculations, structure alignments, and post-alignment processing. As shown in Figure 5.2, structure alignments take 88% of the simulation time, which is consistent with the timings reported by gprof. These profiling results clearly point out at the template-to-target structure alignments as the most computationally expensive operations, thus parallelizing that this portion of the *e*FindSite code should result in the most cost-effective performance improvement in predicting ligand-binding sites.

In principle, there are three approaches to port serial codes to the coprocessor, native, offload, and symmetric modes. In the native mode, the entire code is first cross-compiled on the processor with the parallel regions marked by OpenMP pragmas, and then it is executed directly on the coprocessor. In contrast, the offload mechanism moves only portions of the code to the coprocessor for parallel

Method	Main functions	Time (%)
Gprof	tmsearch	29
	cal_tmscore	27
	dp	21
	get_score	15
Wall time	Pre-alignment	11
	Structure alignment	**88**

FIGURE 5.2

Profiling of *e*FindSite. Low-level function usage reported by gprof and the wall-clock time measured for the individual stages of *e*FindSite.

computation while leaving the rest of the serial code running on the processor. In the symmetric implementation, coprocessors are used independently as self-sufficient computing nodes often through an MPI protocol. We looked into the source code to determine which parallel mode would be optimal for *e*FindSite. We gave careful thought to several considerations. The framework of *e*FindSite is written in C++, whereas protein structure alignments are implemented in Fortran77. For each individual template-to-target structure alignment, the subroutine frtmalign is called from the main function. Figure 5.3 shows the detailed call graph generated by Doxygen, illustrating nested function calls by frtmalign and its subroutines. Transferring structure alignment computations to the coprocessor using Fortran-specific OpenMP pragmas would require the minimum code conversion. In addition, several pre- and post-alignment functions such as the Affinity Propagation clustering used to group template-bound ligands are available only as external libraries precompiled for Linux hosts. Moreover, according to the code profiling carried out previously, the total memory footprint of *e*FindSite grows with the target protein size and the number of associated templates to values that are prohibitively large considering the memory space available on the coprocessor. Therefore, we ruled out the native execution and decided to "offload" only the structure alignment portion to the coprocessor leaving the rest

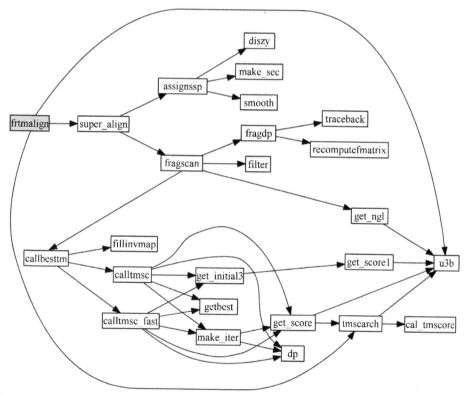

FIGURE 5.3

Call graph of subroutines for protein structure alignments. The top subroutine of frtmalign is called within the main function of *e*FindSite.

of the code, including pre- and post-alignment calculations, on the processor. In this chapter, we discuss the parallelization of *e*FindSite using the offload mode followed by the performance analysis against 501 target proteins.

PORTING *e*FindSite FOR COPROCESSOR OFFLOAD

The flowchart of the parallel version of *e*FindSite is shown in Figure 5.4. *e*FindSite takes a target protein structure and a ligand-bound template library as an input to identify ligand-binding sites. As a result, it produces a series of informative predictions, including putative ligand-binding sites and binding residues, structure alignments between the target and template proteins, and ligand molecular fingerprints for virtual screening. The workflow central to the binding site prediction breaks down into three stages. During the pre-alignment step, *e*FindSite extracts template information from the library and constructs global sequence alignments to the target; these computations are performed sequentially on the processor. Next, it structurally aligns each template onto the target; this section is well suited for parallel computing since individual alignments are fully independent of each other. The code profiling also identified this portion of the code as the most computing intense. Therefore, we decided to parallelize the structure alignment loop in order to perform the calculations using

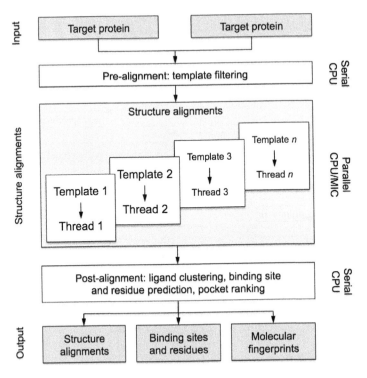

FIGURE 5.4

Workflow of *e*FindSite. Pre- and post-alignment calculations are performed using a single processor thread. Structure alignments are executed in parallel using multiple threads on the processor and/or coprocessor.

multiple processor and/or coprocessor threads. Figure 5.4 shows that each structure alignment is assigned to a unique hardware thread, so that different threads concurrently carry out calculations for different templates against the target protein. Once structure alignments are completed, the results are sent back to the processor, which clusters and ranks the identified binding pockets, and predicts the corresponding binding residues in the final post-alignment step.

In the following sections, we discuss some details of porting *e*FindSite to the coprocessor. Within the main function, structure alignments are executed inside a master loop iterating over the template library. The parallelization of structure alignments is implemented by executing each alignment concurrently using standard OpenMP pragmas as shown in Figure 5.5. The execution of a structure alignment starts when the wrapper function frtmalign is called within the main function, where the serial subroutine frtmalign implemented in Fortran77 is invoked to conduct the actual alignment calculation. We found that this portion of the code extensively uses common blocks making structure alignments thread-unsafe. To guarantee the thread safety, we marked all Fortran77 common blocks as private to threads using [!$omp threadprivate (/block_name/)], which is shown in Figure 5.6.

This implementation of *e*FindSite offloads portions of the code to the coprocessor, executes structure alignments on the coprocessor, and then transfers the results back to the processor to perform the final post-alignment calculations. Because the coprocessor has its own memory, the offload mode requires data transfer between the processor and coprocessor. *e*FindSite implements C++ classes to store and manipulate data associated with template proteins, such as atomic coordinates, amino acid residues, and sequences. To facilitate data transfer, we devoted extra work converting the original data structures into flat, bitwise copy-able data arrays before transferring them to the coprocessor as illustrated in Figure 5.7. We note that arrays containing the target protein and the template library are copied to the coprocessor only once, thus there is virtually no overhead from moving data back and forth. Each structure alignment

```
//loop through the library of template proteins to conduct structure alignments
std::multimap< int, Template *, greater<int> >::iterator tpl1;
//parallelize the loop
#pragma omp parallel for schedule(dynamic) private(tpl1)
for (tpl1 = template_set.begin(); tpl1 != template_set.end(); tpl1++ ){
        char template_seq[MAXPRO];
        int template_res[MAXPRO];
        double template_xyz[MAXPRO][3];
//assemble protein residue, sequence and coordinate from the template library
        int template_len = ((*tpl1).second)->getProteinResiduesTotal();
        strcpy(template_seq, (((*tpl1).second)->getProteinSequence()).c_str());
        for ( int t_i = 0; t_i < template_len; t_i++ ){
                template_res[t_i] = t_i + 1;
        }
        ((*tpl1).second)->getProteinCoordsCA(template_xyz);
        int t_score1, t_alig[MAXPRO];
        double t_score2, t_score3, t_score4, t_t[3], t_u[3][3];

// call structure alignment subroutine
        frtmalign_(&t_score1, &t_score2, &t_score3, &t_score4, &template_len,\
        &target_len, &template_seq, &target_seq, &t_alig, &template_res,\
        &target_res, &template_xyz, &target_xyz, &t_t, &t_u, &align_len);
}
```

FIGURE 5.5

OpenMP parallelization of the master loop performing structure alignments between the target protein and a set of ligand-bound templates.

```
      subroutine
      frtmalign(tm_score1,tm_score2,tm_score3,tm_score4,target_len,template_len,
     &          target_seq,template_seq,tm_align,target_res,template_res,
     &          target_xyz,template_xyz,tm_tt1,tm_uu1,align_length)

          parameter (maxres=1000)            ! no. of residues
          parameter (maxlen=2*maxres)        ! for alignment
          parameter (npr=2)                  ! no. of proteins to align
          double precision tm_score2,tm_score3,tm_score4,tm_xyz1a(0:2,0:maxres-1),
     &        template_xyz(0:2,0:maxres-1), tm_tt1(0:2),tm_uu1(0:2,0:2)
          integer tm_score1,target_len,template_len, align_length,
     &        tm_align(0:maxres-1), target_res(0:maxres-1),
     &        template_res(0:maxres-1)
          character*1 target_seq(0:maxres-1), template_seq(0:maxres-1)
          character*3 resa(maxres,npr),resn(maxres,0:1)
          character*1 seqa(maxres,npr),seqn(maxres,0:1)
          dimension invmap0(maxres),ires(maxres,0:1)
          dimension xtm1(maxres),ytm1(maxres),ztm1(maxres)
          dimension xtm2(maxres),ytm2(maxres),ztm2(maxres)
          dimension m1(maxres),m2(maxres)
          dimension xyz(3,maxres,npr),length(npr)
          common /coord/ xa(3,maxres,0:1)
          common /length/ nseq1,nseq2
          common /pdbinfo/ ires1(maxres,npr),resa,seqa
          common /secstr/ isec(maxres),jsec(maxres)      !secondary structure
          common /n1n2/ n1(maxres),n2(maxres)
          common /dinfo/ d8
          common /stru/xt(maxres),yt(maxres),zt(maxres),xb(maxres),yb(maxres),
     &        zb(maxres)
          // OpenMP pragma to mark thread private
          !$omp threadprivate(/coord/)
          !$omp threadprivate(/length/)
          !$omp threadprivate(/pdbinfo/)
          !$omp threadprivate(/secstr/)
          !$omp threadprivate(/n1n2/)
          !$omp threadprivate(/dinfo/)
          !$omp threadprivate(/stru/)

      cc  call other routines...

          end
```

FIGURE 5.6

Thread-safe implementation of common blocks in Fortran77.

executed on the coprocessor extracts data required for a given template from the transferred data block using an offset mechanism. In addition, we use compiler directives to mark the offload execution, as presented in Figure 5.8. Specifically, all Fortran77 subroutines and global variables for structure alignment calculations on the coprocessor are tagged with the offload attributes [!dir$ attributes offload:mic:: subroutine_name] and [!dir$ attributes offload:mic::variable_name], respectively. Moreover, when the OpenMP is invoked within the offloaded block, environment variables for the coprocessor are set using the "MIC_" prefix, i.e., [export MIC_OMP_NUM_THREADS=n]. Since the memory footprint for individual structure alignments in eFindSite is larger than the default OpenMP stack size, we increase it by using [export MIC_OMP_STACKSIZE=64M].

The Intel Xeon Phi coprocessor model SE10P features 61 cores and supports up to 240 parallel threads with the 61st core reserved for operating system, I/O operations, etc., when using offload. The physical distribution of threads over hardware cores is controlled by the thread affinity settings,

```
        int i_offset = 0;
        // flatten the data structure to data array
        for ( tpl1 = template_set.begin(); tpl1 != template_set.end(); tpl1++ ){
                template_len[i_offset] = ((*tpl1).second)->getProteinResiduesTotal();
                char t_seqt[MAXPRO];
                strcpy(t_seqt, (((*tpl1).second)->getProteinSequence()).c_str());
                for (int t_i=0;t_i<((*tpl1).second)->getProteinResiduesTotal();
                        t_i++ ){
                        template_seq[t_i+t_offset[i_offset]] = t_seqt[t_i];
                }

                for (int t_i=0;t_i<((*tpl1).second)->getProteinResiduesTotal();t_i++){
                        template_res[t_i+t_offset[i_offset]] = t_i + 1;
                }
                double *t_xyzt=new double [((*tpl1).second)->getProteinResiduesTotal()
                *3];
                ((*tpl1).second)->getProteinCoords1D(t_xyzt);
                for (int t_i 0;t_i<((*tpl1).second)->getProteinResiduesTotal()*3;t_i++)
                {
                        template_xyz[t_i+t_offset[i_offset]*3] = t_xyzt[t_i];
                }
                delete [] t_xyzt;
                i_offset++;
        }
        // offload to the coprocessor, data transfer
        #pragma offload target(mic) in(n_offset,t_offset,t_len1) \
                                    in(template_len:length(n_set)) \
                                    in(target_seq,target_res:length(n_tar)) \
                                    in(template_seq,template_res:length(n_off)) \
                                    in(target_xyz:length(n_tar*3)) \
                                    in(template_xyz:length(n_off*3)) \
                                    out(t_score1,t_score2,t_score3,\
                                        t_score4:length(n_set)) \
                                    out(t_alig:length(n_tar*n_set)) \
                                    out(t_rmat:length(n_set*12)){
        int tm_i;
        // parallelize the for loop
        #pragma omp parallel for schedule(dynamic) private(tm_i)
        for ( tm_i = 0; tm_i < n_offset; tm_i++ ){
                int o_score1;
                double o_score2, o_score3, o_score4;
                int target_o_len = target_len;
                int template_o_len = template_len[tm_i];
                char target_o_seq[MAXPRO];
                char template_o_seq[MAXPRO];
                int target_o_res[MAXPRO], template_o_res[MAXPRO];
                double target_o_xyz[MAXPRO][3], template_o_xyz[MAXPRO][3];
                for ( int t_i = 0; t_i < target_o_len; t_i++ ){
                        target_o_seq[t_i] = target_seq[t_i];
                        target_o_res[t_i] = target_res[t_i];
                        for ( int t_j = 0; t_j < 3; t_j++ ){
                                target_o_xyz[t_i][t_j] = target_xyz[t_i*3+t_j];
                        }
                }
                for (int t_i = 0; t_i < o_len2; t_i++ ){
                        template_o_seq[t_i] = template_seq[t_offset[tm_i]+t_i];
                        template_o_res[t_i] = template_res[t_offset[tm_i]+t_i];
                        for ( int t_j = 0; t_j < 3; t_j++ ){
                                mplate_o_xyz[t_i][t_j]=template_xyz[t_offset[tm_i]*3+t_i*3+t_j];
                        }
                }
        }
        int o_alig[MAXPRO];
        double o_t[3], o_u[3][3];

        frtmalign_(&o_score1, &o_score2, &o_score3, &o_score4, &tempalte_o_len, \
                   &target_o_len, &template_o_seq, &target_o_seq, &o_alig, \
                   &template_o_res, &target_o_res, &template_o_xyz, \
                   &target_o_xyz, &o_t, &o_u, &align_o_len );
}
//end of the parallel for loop
```

FIGURE 5.7

Data flattening and transfer for offloading structure alignments to the coprocessor.

```
c   Fr-TM-align converted into a subroutine

!dir$ attributes offload:mic::frtmalign

!dir$ attributes offload:mic::d8
!dir$ attributes offload:mic::xa
!dir$ attributes offload:mic::nseq1
!dir$ attributes offload:mic::nseq2
!dir$ attributes offload:mic::ires1
!dir$ attributes offload:mic::resa
!dir$ attributes offload:mic::seqa
!dir$ attributes offload:mic::isec
!dir$ attributes offload:mic::jsec
!dir$ attributes offload:mic::n1
!dir$ attributes offload:mic::n2
!dir$ attributes offload:mic::xt
!dir$ attributes offload:mic::yt
!dir$ attributes offload:mic::zt
!dir$ attributes offload:mic::xb
!dir$ attributes offload:mic::yb
!dir$ attributes offload:mic::zb

subroutine frtmalign(tm_score1,tm_score2,tm_score3,tm_score4,target_len,
     &        template_len,target_seq,template_seq,tm_align,target_res,
     &        template_res,target_xyz,template_xyz,tm_tt1,tm_uu1,align_length)
     .
     .
     .
end
```

FIGURE 5.8

Fortran77 subroutine frtmalign offloaded to the coprocessor.

which are typically set to either compact, balanced, or scatter modes. Since the affinity mode may have an impact on the parallel performance, we first benchmarked *e*FindSite using different Intel KMP affinity settings, [export MIC_KMP_AFFINITY=compact/scatter/balanced].

In order to analyze the performance of *e*FindSite, we first developed a reliable measure to quantify its computing speed. As shown in Figure 5.3, the subroutine u3b is a frequently called low-level function that calculates a root-mean-square deviation (RMSD) between two sets of atomic coordinates. We found that the total number of RMSD calculations correlates well with the total wall time and the structure alignment time; the corresponding Pearson correlation coefficients are as high as 0.963 and 0.960, respectively. Thus, we use the number of RMSD calculations per second to measure the *e*FindSite performance.

In Figure 5.9, we plot the performance of *e*FindSite with the structure alignment portion of the code offloaded to the coprocessor. Note that the pre- and post-alignment steps are sequentially executed on the processor. Because some proteins in the benchmark dataset have less than 50 templates, we only consider parallel execution using up to 24 threads per task in order to avoid idle threads. Encouragingly, increasing the number of threads on the coprocessor clearly improves the performance of *e*FindSite. The average performance is 4.27×10^4 and 2.30×10^5 RMSD calculations per second as the number of threads increases from 4 to 24. Considering structure alignment calculations alone, almost a perfect linear scaling is achieved (open circles in Figure 5.9). In contrast, the performance of *e*FindSite reaches a plateau when the total wall time is plotted (black circles in Figure 5.9). Here, the number of RMSD calculations per second improves from 3.98×10^4 for 4 threads to 1.76×10^5 for 24 threads, which can be explained by Amdahl's Law describing the relationship between the expected speedup of a parallel implementation relative to the serial algorithm. These performance measurements are carried out for the balanced and scatter thread affinity modes that maximize hardware utilization by evenly spreading

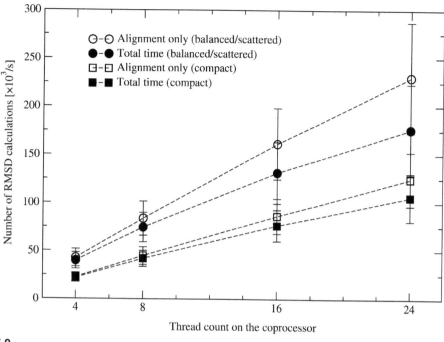

FIGURE 5.9

Performance of eFindSite using parallel coprocessor threads. The speed is measured by the number of RMSD calculations per second (mean±standard deviation) for 4, 8, 16, and 24 threads across the benchmarking dataset of 501 proteins. Solid and open symbols correspond to the total time and the time spent calculating structure alignments, respectively. Circles and squares show the performance using balanced/scatter and compact thread affinity, respectively.

threads across coprocessor cores. For the compact affinity setting placing four threads on a single core before moving to the next one, the rate of RMSD calculations increases from 2.27×10^4 to 1.25×10^5 for the alignment time (open squares in Figure 5.9), and from 2.19×10^4 to 1.06×10^5 for the total time (black squares in Figure 5.9). Although the balanced/scatter thread affinity yields an approximately 1.8 times higher performance per thread compared to the compact affinity mode, its advantage starts diminishing when the total number of threads on the coprocessor exceeds 120, and all affinity modes become essentially the same when the thread count reaches 240. In fact, a core-to-core performance comparison shows a slightly higher performance of the compact mode at 2.44×10^4 RMSD calculations per second compared to 2.38×10^4 for the balanced and scatter modes.

PARALLEL VERSION FOR A MULTICORE PROCESSOR

In addition to the Intel Xeon Phi coprocessor version of eFindSite, we also implemented a parallel code that can be executed on multicore processors. Similarly, we employed pragma-based OpenMP to parallelize structure alignment calculations with both pre- and post-alignment steps executed sequentially. We also increased the memory available to each thread to 64M using [export

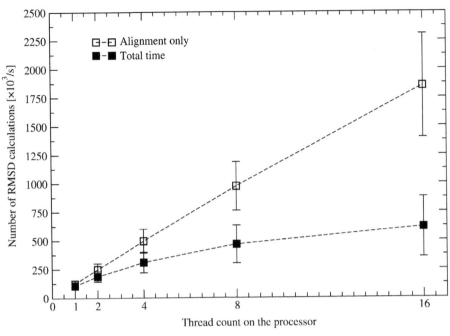

FIGURE 5.10

Performance of eFindSite using parallel processor threads. The speed is measured by the number of RMSD calculations per second (mean ± standard deviation) for 2, 4, 8, and 16 threads across the benchmarking dataset of 501 proteins. Solid triangles and open squares correspond to the total time and the time spent calculating structure alignments, respectively.

OMP_STACKSIZE=64M]. In Figure 5.10, we plot the performance of the multi-threaded version of eFind-Site on the Intel® Xeon® E5-2680 processor. Using the total simulation time, the serial (1 thread) and parallel (16 threads) versions have an average performance across the benchmarking dataset of 1.06×10^5 and 6.16×10^5 RMSD calculations per second, respectively. When considering the time spent calculating structure alignments, the average performance increases to 1.24×10^5 and 1.85×10^6 RMSD calculations per second. A good linear scaling is achieved with a speedup over the serial execution of 15 when 16 processor threads are utilized. The performance reaches a plateau at a speedup of 5.8 for the total wall time; we note that according to Amdahl's law, the maximum theoretical speedup of a code that is 90% parallelized using 16 threads is 6.4.

TASK-LEVEL SCHEDULING FOR PROCESSOR AND COPROCESSOR

Computing nodes equipped with Intel Xeon Phi coprocessor cards provide massively parallel capabilities through multicore processors and many-core coprocessors. Therefore, our ultimate goal was to develop a production code of eFindSite that takes full advantage of both resources. The production scheme for predicting ligand-binding sites across large datasets of proteins using *e*FindSite involves using both the processor and the coprocessor simultaneously. The processor executes the serial portion of the code, while structure alignments are offloaded to the coprocessor with the compact affinity mode to maximize the performance of *e*FindSite. At the same time, the processor also runs a parallel version of *e*FindSite as well, using relatively few threads. This way, we process multiple proteins concurrently by multiple parallel tasks executed simultaneously on both computing units.

We developed a job scheduler in Perl to launch up to 4 parallel tasks on the processor with 4 threads per task, and up to 10 parallel tasks on the coprocessor, each using 24 threads in the compact affinity mode. As shown in Figure 5.11, we first sort target proteins by a product of the residue count and the number of templates, which estimates the wall time required to complete the calculations. Because we

```
use Proc::Background;
my $n_mic = 10;           // 10 parallel jobs on a coprocessor
my $n_cpu = 4;            // four parallel jobs on a processor
my @lst3 = ();            // template protein list
foreach my $wlst2 ( sort { $lst2{$a} <=> $lst2{$b} } keys %lst2 ){
        push(@lst3, $wlst2);
}
while ( @lst3 ){
        # dispatching jobs to Xeon processor
        for ( my $xa = 0; $xa < $n_cpu; $xa++ ){
                # start a new process if the current is finished
                if ( @lst3 and !$j_cpu[$xa]->alive ){
                        #get an item from the top of the list (smaller template)
                        my $job = shift(@lst3);
                        printf("CPU%d <- %s ... %.1f%s\n", $xa, $job, \
                                (++$prg1/$nlst3)*100.0, '%');
                        $j_cpu[$xa]=Proc::Background->new("$ef_omp -s $job.pdb \
                                -t $job.ethread-fun -i $job.ss -e $job.prf -o $job- \
                                efindsite -b $foptb -x $foptx > $job.log 2>&1");
                        $c_cpu[$xa]++;
                        $l_cpu[$xa] += $lst2{$job};
                }
        }
        # offloading jobs to Xeon MIC jobs
        for ( my $xa = 0; $xa < $n_mic; $xa++ ){
                if ( @lst3 and !$j_mic[$xa]->alive ){
                        #get an item from the bottom of the list (larger template)
                        my $job = pop(@lst3);
                        my $kpt='export \
                                MIC_KMP_PLACE_THREADS=6c,4t,'.int($xa*6).'0';
                        printf("MIC%d <- %s ... %.1f%s\n", $xa, $job, \
                                (++$prg1/$nlst3)*100.0, '%');
                        $j_mic[$xa] = Proc::Background->new("$kpt ; $ef_mic -s \
                                $job.pdb -t $job.ethread-fun -i $job.ss -e $job.prf -o \
                                $job-efindsite -b $foptb -x $foptx > $job.log 2>&1");
                        $c_mic[$xa]++;
                        $l_mic[$xa] += $lst2{$job};
                }
        }
        sleep(2) if ( @lst3 );
}
```

FIGURE 5.11

Part of the task scheduler implemented in Perl dispatching four parallel tasks (4 threads per task) on the processor and 10 parallel tasks (10 threads per task) on the coprocessor.

use 24 threads per task on the coprocessor and 4 threads per task on the processor, we dispatch longer tasks to the coprocessor, whereas shorter jobs are executed on the processor. Running 4 parallel tasks on the processor and 10 parallel tasks on the coprocessor ensures that both resources are fully utilized. To avoid the oversubscription of coprocessor cores, the production code features an explicit mapping of parallel tasks to hardware threads at the compact thread affinity. Specifically, [export MIC_KMP_PLACE_THREADS=6c,4t,(i*6).'o'] defines the set of logical units assigned to each task, where 6c requests six cores, 4t starts four threads on each core, and (i*6).'o' is an offset of six cores between individual task. For example, when i=0, the first task runs on cores 0-5 with 4 threads per core totaling 24 threads, the next task sets i=1 to run on cores 6 through 11, and so forth. This way, the scheduler assigns different cores to different parallel tasks in order to conduct protein structure alignments at the maximum utilization of the accelerator hardware. Figure 5.12 lists partitioning details for the parallel execution for the benchmarking dataset using a computing node equipped with two 8-core Intel Xeon E5-2680 processors (8 threads, hyper-threading disabled) and one 61-core Intel Xeon Phi SE10P coprocessor (240 threads, compact thread affinity).

Hardware	Core range	Number of threads	Percentage of computations
Processor	1-4	4	12.2
	5-6	4	12.5
	7-11	4	12.7
	12-16	4	11.8
Coprocessor	1-6	24	5.1
	7-12	24	5.1
	13-18	24	5.1
	19-24	24	5.0
	25-30	24	5.3
	31-36	24	5.0
	37-42	24	4.7
	43-48	24	5.0
	49-54	24	5.4
	55-60	24	5.1
Processor	1-16	16	49.2
Coprocessor	1-60	240	50.8

FIGURE 5.12

Partitioning details for processing 501 benchmarking proteins using eFindSite simultaneously on the processor and coprocessor. The amount of computations is approximated by the product of the target protein length and the number of template structures.

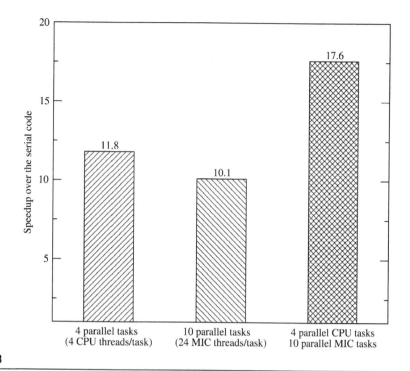

FIGURE 5.13

Speedups of the parallel versions of eFindSite over the serial code. Computations are performed using three parallel versions: multiple processor threads (4 tasks, each running on 4 threads), multiple coprocessor threads (10 tasks, each running on 24 threads), and multiple processor and coprocessor threads running simultaneously.

We processed the entire dataset of 501 proteins using task-level parallelism and measured the time-to-completion, defined as the total time required for the prediction of ligand-binding sites. Figure 5.13 compares the results for the serial version and three parallel processing schemes. The speedup over the serial version is 11.8, 10.1, and 17.6 for the parallel processing using the processor, the coprocessor, and both resources, respectively. Therefore, using the coprocessor in addition to the processor accelerates the prediction of binding sites across large protein datasets. We also monitored the utilization of computing resources to demonstrate that all hardware threads are utilized. Figure 5.14 shows that the average usage of the processor and the coprocessor during production simulations is 99.9% and 82.2%, respectively. The coprocessor threads periodically become idle while waiting for the processor to start the pre-alignment (reading input files, performing sequence alignments) and finish the post-alignment (pocket clustering and ranking) tasks resulting a relatively lower utilization of the coprocessor. On the other hand, the processor remains fully utilized not only facilitating tasks offloaded to the coprocessor but also performing eFindSite calculations by itself. Finally, we checked for the numerical correctness of the results. Different versions of eFindSite produce identical results, thus the parallelization of eFindSite using OpenMP and offloading to the Intel Xeon Phi coprocessor fully maintains the functionality of the original code with a great benefit of much shorter simulation times.

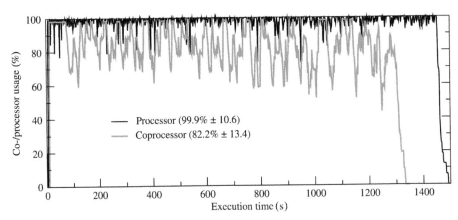

FIGURE 5.14

Resource utilization during the execution of the heterogeneous parallel version of eFindSite. Time courses of the percentage of processor usage (black line) are compared to that of the coprocessor (gray line).

CASE STUDY

Finally, we present a case study to illustrate binding pocket prediction using eFindSite. The target protein selected from the benchmarking dataset is human arginase I (PDB-ID: 3gn0, chain A), a binuclear manganese metalloenzyme hydrolyzing L-arginine. The abnormal activity of this protein is implicated in various disease states including erectile dysfunction, atherosclerosis, and cerebral malaria. eFindSite predicted a total of 10 pockets for this protein and assigned a confidence score of 91.9% to the top-ranked binding site. Figure 5.15 shows the crystal structure of this protein (transparent ribbons) with the top-ranked binding pocket predicted by eFindSite marked by a solid ball. The corresponding predicted binding residues are shown as a transparent gray surface. Two additional smaller balls mark the location of pockets at ranks 2 and 3. The prediction accuracy can be evaluated by revealing the location of a ligand α-difluoromethylornithine bound to the target protein in the experimental complex structure represented by solid sticks. We note that the ligand position was not part of the prediction procedure and it is used for validation purposes only. The distance between the predicted top-ranked binding site and the geometric center of the ligand is only 2.22 Å, demonstrating a high prediction accuracy of eFindSite. As a reliable tool for ligand-binding prediction, eFindSite is well suited for a broad range of applications ranging from protein function annotation to virtual screening and drug discovery.

SUMMARY

eFindSite is a ligand-binding site prediction software used in drug discovery and design. To meet the challenges of proteome-scale applications, we implemented a parallel version of eFindSite for processing large datasets using HPC systems equipped with Intel Xeon Phi coprocessors. This parallel version of eFindSite achieves 17.6 speedup over the serial code using both processor and coprocessor

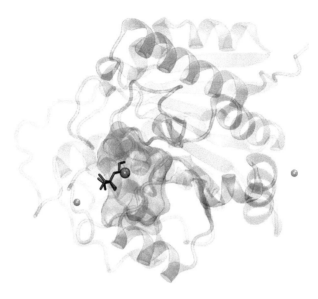

FIGURE 5.15

Ligand-binding pocket prediction for human arginase I using eFindSite. The crystal structure of the target protein and the binding ligand is displayed as transparent gray ribbons and solid black sticks, respectively. The top-ranked predicted binding site is shown as a solid ball representing the pocket center and a transparent molecular surface around the binding residues. Two smaller balls represent the centers of binding pockets predicted at ranks 2 and 3.

resources, which is considered significant when normalized by the cost of the hardware. The x86 coprocessor architecture allows for open-standard and portable parallel programming on both traditional processors as well as coprocessors. In particular, using OpenMP makes it relatively easy to parallelize portions of the code. eFindSite represents a typical scientific software written mostly by domain scientists, who contributed different components to the code using different programming languages and styles. From our porting experience, even fairly complex codes, such as the hybrid C++/Fortran77 source code of eFindSite, can be successfully ported to utilize both Intel Xeon processors and Intel Xeon Phi coprocessors together yielding speedups at minimal coding efforts.

The development of the parallel version of eFindSite was fairly straightforward; however, we would like to discuss a couple of problems encountered throughout this process. First, due to the extensive use of thread-unsafe common blocks in the Fortran77 code, we initially attempted to rewrite those subroutines to pass parameters explicitly instead of accessing common blocks. However, these efforts took a very long time and considering the "spaghetti-like" nature of the code with multiple access points to common blocks, we could not reproduce the correct results in a timely fashion. For that reason, we decided to use OpenMP pragmas to mark the global variables as thread-private in the original code. This method turned out to be very practical and time efficient in the process of developing a thread-safe parallel implementation. Another issue we ran into was related to the stack size. We found that the default stack size on some HPC systems is smaller than that set for eFindSite using OMP_STACKSIZE causing segmentation fault errors. Consequently, in addition to OpenMP pragmas, modifying the default system stack size using [ulimit -s] may be required.

Notwithstanding the 17-fold speedup, there is still room for improvements to fully benefit from wide single instruction, multiple data (SIMD) vectors featured by the coprocessor. For instance, a proper loop vectorization is critical to increase the overall performance. Vectorization reports collected for *e*FindSite show that the majority of loops taking the most execution time are indeed vectorized. However, other issues related to data dependency and alignment indicated in the reports need to be addressed by rearranging loops, data structure padding, improving register utilization, and data caching. Therefore, in addition to the parallelization of the remaining portions of the serial code, future directions of this project include a thorough code optimization to take better advantage of the Intel Xeon processor and Intel Xeon Phi coprocessor SIMD architectures. We plan to hand tune a relatively small portion of the kernel for RMSD calculations to further boost the parallel performance of *e*FindSite.

FOR MORE INFORMATION

- The source code for *e*FindSite can be found at www.brylinski.org/efindsite. This Web site also provides compilation and installation instructions, as well as a detailed tutorial on processing large datasets using heterogeneous computing platforms.
- Feinstein, W.P., Moreno, J., Jarrell, M., Brylinski, M., 2015. Accelerating the pace of protein functional annotation with Intel Xeon Phi coprocessors. IEEE Trans. Nanobiosci. DOI: 10.1109/TNB.2015.2403776.
- Brylinski, M., Feinstein, W.P., 2013. *e*FindSite: Improved prediction of ligand binding sites in protein models using meta-threading, machine learning and auxiliary ligands. J. Comput. Aided Mol. Des. 27, 551-567.
- Feinstein, W.P., Brylinski, M., 2014. *e*FindSite: Enhanced fingerprint-based virtual screening against predicted ligand binding sites in protein models. Mol. Inform. 33, 135-150.
- Download the code from this, and other chapters, http://lotsofcores.com.

AMBER PME MOLECULAR DYNAMICS OPTIMIZATION

6

Ashraf Bhuiyan*, Perri Needham[†], Ross C. Walker[†,‡]

Intel Corporation, USA[*] San Diego Supercomputing Center, USA[†]
University of California San Diego, USA[‡]

In this chapter, we show how the Amber Molecular Dynamics sotware (http://ambermd.org/) now uses message passing interface (MPI) at the cluster level, coupled with OpenMP and offload mode at the node level, to improve scaling for the PMEMD engine within the Amber software suite, with and without the use of coprocessors on the node. The observed performance gains include a $2.83\times$ speedup, over the original MPI-only code, when using four nodes (96 MPI tasks).

In the life science research arena, understanding the structural dynamics of large biological molecules, such as proteins, nucleic acids, and lipid bilayers, is crucial to understanding important biological pathways and mechanisms. Biologically significant structural changes that reveal the mechanisms for the underlying functionality of an enzyme often occur on the microsecond to millisecond timescale. Until recently, such timescales have typically been out of reach of classical molecular dynamics (MD) for most researchers who do not have access to significant computing resources. A key to improve the fidelity of MD simulations is increasing the rate at which conformational space can be explored. This not only makes it possible to study events that occur on longer timescales but also improves statistical convergence as well as providing a mechanism by which to more rapidly validate classical MD force fields.

In recent years, coprocessor (or accelerator) technologies have become prevalent in computational science offering an affordable solution to accelerating computational research. The Amber MD software package is a prime example of the successful use of coprocessor technology. The *pmemd* engine in Amber is a highly optimized MD simulation package capable of simulating explicitly or implicitly solvated molecular systems using multiple CPUs and/or Graphics Processing units with the Amber and CHARMM force fields. For more information please refer to the Amber 14 manual and Amber-related papers which are the first three items listed in Section "For more information" at the end of this chapter.

A more recent market addition is the Intel® Xeon Phi™ coprocessor based on the Intel® Many-Integrated Core (Intel® MIC) architecture. The first generation Intel Xeon Phi product, formerly code-named Knights Corner, offers up to 61 Intel $\times$86 cores running at 1.238 GHz (1.333 GHz turbo clock) with 16 GB of onboard memory providing up to 1.2 teraFLOPS of double-precision floating-point performance accessible via a PCI Express expansion card.

This chapter describes the Intel Xeon Phi coprocessor support added into Amber's *pmemd* MD engine targeting improved performance of explicit solvent (particle mesh Ewald—PME) MD simulations. While implicit solvent Generalized-Born MD simulations are also supported, they are not described in this chapter. Previous attempts at optimizing MD using coprocessors have relied on heavy code modification, SIMD vectorization, and Intel Threading Building Blocks (TBB). Previous attempts, published in the literature, have also frequently focused on implementation of a stripped down version of an MD algorithm where the long-range electrostatic contributions to the forces are neglected. For more information, please refer to the papers by Plotnikov and Sun in Section "For more information." The approach taken in this work avoids extensive code vectorization through major rewrites using assembly instructions or intrinsics since only a marginal performance improvement (~5%) was achieved in initial tests, and the assembly or intrinsic code would require extensive rewriting for each new Intel MIC architecture generation. The limited performance improvement seen from extensive explicit vectorization of the existing *pmemd* code is due to irregular memory access patterns within loops and addressing this comes at the expense of code maintainability and readability. Vectorization is important and is achieved by using the OpenMP *simd* directive. This avoids large algorithmic changes and instead focuses on maximizing flexibility, while still improving performance. The approach taken was to utilize the existing MPI framework to offload portions of the direct space sum calculation to the coprocessor and then further decompose the workload of each offloading MPI task using OpenMP threading, exposing fine-grain parallelism whilst minimizing the memory footprint and optimizing memory reuse. In this chapter, we discuss the theory of MD, performance improvements for the two most compute intensive parts of Amber, code optimization techniques, results achieved, and conclusions.

THEORY OF MD

MD simulation of biological systems, in its most widely used form, utilizes classical mechanics and a set of predetermined molecular mechanics force fields. These force fields have been parameterized from more accurate quantum mechanical data and/or fit to experimental observations, to evaluate the gradient of the potential energy of a given set of atomic coordinates as a function of time. This enables Newton's equations of motion, with a suitable integrator, to be used to propagate atomic positions through time. An MD time step is typically between 2 and 4 femtoseconds (fs) with such short time steps being needed to capture the fastest vibrational motions, but at the same time it is desirable to simulate microseconds or longer. This implies linear simulations requiring on the order of 10^9 integration steps.

In a typical MD simulation, the interaction of all the atoms present in the solvent (water+any additional ions) is discretely calculated along with the solute. Figure 6.1 formally describes the potential energy of a given configuration of atoms.

The summations involving bonds and angles are calculated with harmonic functions using force constants b_i and a_i and equilibrium bond distances $r_{i,eq}$ and angles $\theta_{i,eq}$. The third component in Figure 6.1 represents the dihedral energy and uses a truncated Fourier series comprising a torsional constant $V_{i,n}$ for each individual Fourier term n and phase shift $\gamma_{i,n}$. n typically runs from 1 to 4. These are the bonded terms in the potential energy function and are dependent on the covalent bonding in the structure being simulated. The nonbonded terms, the last two terms in Figure 6.1, describe the interaction of an atom with all other atoms in the system separated by more than 3 bonds (denoted by a prime). These are the van der Waals interactions, which are represented by a 12–6 Lennard-Jones

$$V_{\text{AMBER}} = \sum_{i}^{n_{\text{bonds}}} b_i (r_i - r_{i,\text{eq}})^2$$

$$+ \sum_{i}^{n_{\text{angles}}} a_i (\theta_i - \theta_{i,\text{eq}})^2$$

$$+ \sum_{i}^{n_{\text{dihedral}}} \sum_{n}^{n_{i,\text{max}}} \left(\frac{V_{i,n}}{2}\right) 2)[1 + \cos(n\phi_i - \gamma_{i,n})]$$

$$+ \sum_{i<j}^{n_{\text{atoms}}} {}' \left(\frac{A_{ij}}{r_{ij}^{12}} - \frac{B_{ij}}{r_{ij}^6}\right) + \sum_{i<j}^{n_{\text{atoms}}} {}' \left(\frac{q_i q_j}{4\pi\varepsilon_0 r_{ij}}\right)$$

FIGURE 6.1

The Amber potential energy equation.

potential using diatomic parameters A_{ij} and B_{ij}, and the Coulomb interactions calculated from atomic point charges q_i and q_j and the distance separating them r_{ij}. The Coulomb interaction is calculated using a mathematical approximation called the PME summation. This allows the Coulombic interactions to be separated into three fast converging parts: $V_{\text{direct}} + V_{\text{reciprocal}} + V_{\text{self}}$. Periodic boundary conditions are normally used in explicit solvent simulations such that particles leaving one edge of the simulation box re-enter on the opposite side. As the Lennard-Jones potential decays rapidly with distance this summation is typically truncated at distances greater than 8-12Å. The Coulomb summation is typically split into a matching direct part, truncated at the same distance as the Lennard-Jones equation, and represented by term 5 in Figure 6.1, and a separate reciprocal space sum that is calculated over the entire periodic system through the use of interpolation on a grid followed by a series of Fourier Transformations. The primes in terms 4 and 5 above imply that the summation is only carried out over atoms that are separated by three or more bonds, and that, for the case of exactly three bonds, the interaction is scaled by a force-field-dependent term. For a more detailed discussion of the full mathematical model used, the reader is referred to the papers by Solomon-Ferrer et al. and Needham et al., in Section "For more information."

The program flow of the Amber MD code is shown in Figure 6.2. The simulation time steps of the Amber MD simulation are configurable through the input file.

Analysis of the time spent on the various routines yields Figure 6.3, which shows the performance of the most computationally demanding portions of the MD equation. It can be seen that a natural choice to focus acceleration efforts on is the PME direct space sum (terms 4 and 5 in Figure 6.1), as this takes over 44% of the program's execution time. The calculation of the PME direct space sum relies on the neighbor list to identify atomic pairs that fall within the designated cutoff distance. This dependency of the PME direct space sum calculation on the neighbor list motivated the decision to also execute parts of the neighbor list build on the coprocessor. The decision came after investigation of the alternative, involving expensive data transfers between the host and the coprocessor ensuring PME direct space sum routine could access an up-to-date neighbor list, proved to be detrimental to performance.

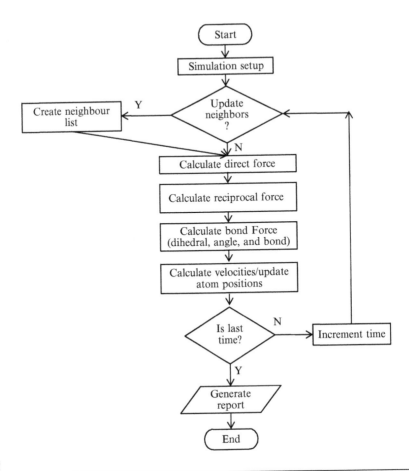

FIGURE 6.2

Program diagram showing the execution path of *pmemd* on each time step.

ACCELERATION OF NEIGHBOR LIST BUILDING USING THE COPROCESSOR

The neighbor list is executed across all the MPI tasks. The offloading MPI tasks concurrently execute the neighbor list on a processor and a coprocessor for their assigned atoms at a workload distribution ratio of 22:78 for a 12 core Intel® Xeon® processor. This ratio depends on the number of cores on the processor. The algorithm works by dividing the simulation space into buckets. The width of a bucket is roughly half the cutoff distance. This greatly reduces the computational effort in searching for neighboring atoms, as fewer neighboring buckets need to be found. The steps to accelerate and offload the neighbor list are:

(1) Offloading MPI tasks find their neighboring buckets on the host.
(2) The variables that are required to build the neighbor list for offloaded atoms are transferred to the coprocessors asynchronously.

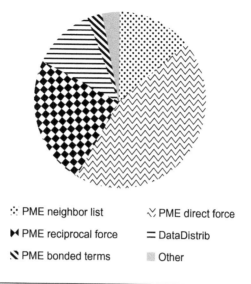

:·: PME neighbor list   ⋎ PME direct force

◂ PME reciprocal force   ═ DataDistrib

⩘ PME bonded terms   ▨ Other

FIGURE 6.3

Proportion of time spent in the main components of an Amber PMEMD simulation.

(3) Two separate neighbor lists are constructed concurrently: (a) host neighbor list and (b) coprocessor neighbor list. The coprocessor lists are private to the threads, following two strategies: (1) the lists reside on the hardware that the list is built on and (2) are never combined to a full neighbor list. These two strategies save substantial PCIe transfer and memory read/write time.

(4) Variables required by the host, such as the variables that hold a record of used atoms *img_used_lst* are asynchronously transferred from the coprocessor to the host.

(5) Host execution waits for the return signal from the coprocessor before continuing.

The coprocessor neighbor list is statically allocated giving each OpenMP thread a fixed number of memory locations for which to store neighboring atoms. The neighbor list is then reallocated if an atom's number of neighboring atoms grows beyond the memory allocated. This static memory allocation scheme keeps memory usage to a minimum (as only neighboring atoms whose PME direct space sum is to be computed on the coprocessor are stored) and reduces the amount of memory allocations (as the neighbor list for each atom might not grow each time it is built).

ACCELERATION OF DIRECT SPACE SUM USING THE COPROCESSOR

The PME direct space sum is executed on the host and coprocessor concurrently (Figure 6.4). The off-loading MPI tasks execute the following steps:

(1) Coprocessor variables are declared and global variables are copied to device memory locations.

(2) Variables that require updating every time the neighbor list is built are copied or reassigned to the coprocessor because it is more optimal than mapping data from host memory.

```
!dir$ offload begin mandatory signal(sig1) target (mic:0) &
in(flat_cit(0:cit_tbl_x_dim*cit_tbl_y_dim*cit_tbl_z_dim-1)  :  alloc_if(.false.)  free_if(.false.)
into(flat_cit_dev(:)))&
in(fraction(:,1:atm_cnt) : alloc_if(.false.) free_if(.false.) into(fraction_dev(:,:)))&
in(x_bkts(0    :    cit_tbl_x_dim_dev    *   3   -   1)   :   alloc_if(.false.)    free_if(.false.)
into(x_bkts_dev(:)))&
in(x_trans(0   :   cit_tbl_x_dim_dev   *   3   -   1)   :   alloc_if(.false.)    free_if(.false.)
into(x_trans_dev(:)))&
in(y_trans(0   :   cit_tbl_y_dim_dev   *   3   -   1)   :   alloc_if(.false.)    free_if(.false.)
into(y_trans_dev(:)))&
in(y_bkts(0    :   cit_tbl_y_dim_dev   *   3   -   1)   :   alloc_if(.false.)    free_if(.false.)
into(y_bkts_dev(:)))&
in(z_bkts(0    :   cit_tbl_z_dim_dev   *   2   -   1)   :   alloc_if(.false.)    free_if(.false.)
into(z_bkts_dev(:)))&
in(z_trans(0   :   cit_tbl_z_dim_dev   *   2   -   1)   :   alloc_if(.false.)    free_if(.false.)
into(z_trans_dev(:)))&
out(used_img_lst_thread_dev(1:atm_local) : alloc_if(.false.) free_if(.false.))
...............................
/*Offload code to build neighbor list for Xeon Phi*/
!dir$ end offload

...............................
/*Host code to build neighbor list for host/*
/*Synchronize Host and Xeon Phi*/
    !dir$ offload begin  mandatory target(mic:0) wait(sig1)
    !dir$ end offload
```

FIGURE 6.4

Code snippet of the parallel neighbor list build on both host and coprocessor. The complete code can be found in get_nb_list_offload() routine in nb_pairlist.F90 file of the Amber source code.

(3) Variables that are required on every time step are asynchronously transferred to the coprocessor allowing simultaneous execution on the host and coprocessor.

(4) Indexing code allows for identifying neighbors in the statically allocated coprocessor neighbor list.

(5) The force calculations start on the coprocessor using OpenMP threads spawned from offloading MPI ranks.

(6) Control is immediately passed back to the host allowing asynchronous computation of the PME direct space sum on the host and coprocessor.

(7) Each OpenMP thread has an individual copy of the array used to store the forces, as otherwise race conditions would occur. The use of locks to save memory was investigated and the results showed that even with the costly initialization and reduction of the multiple copies of the force array when using the private array approach, private arrays performed roughly 10-15% faster than the alternative lock approach.

(8) The PME direct space sum on the host uses a look-up table (LUT) to calculate the complementary error function, erfc. However, on the coprocessor the LUT created high memory access latency as a consequence of L2 cache misses. It causes poor performance when the coprocessor attempts to vectorize accesses. By calculating erfc on the fly, some of the latency is reduced (however, not all as some other arrays, i.e., the force and coordinate arrays, still have latency overheads due to irregular array accesses) which improves performance by a further 5%.

(9) Reduce the force arrays into a single force array once all OpenMP threads have finished.

(10) Host execution waits for the return signal from the coprocessor before continuing.

(11) The coprocessor force array is asynchronously copied back to the host and combined with the host force array.

ADDITIONAL OPTIMIZATIONS IN COPROCESSOR CODE

This section describes three key optimization techniques that have been applied to accelerate the coprocessor offload implementation in Amber 14.

REMOVING LOCKS WHENEVER POSSIBLE

In the original code snippet in Figure 6.5, the array index img_j defines a neighboring atom to the current atom being calculated. The updates to arrays indexed using img_j occur simultaneously as the loop is distributed across cores using an OpenMP loop. It is possible that multiple atoms have the same neighboring atom(s); therefore, img_j can be the same for multiple OpenMP threads resulting in a race condition.

To prevent this race condition, an OpenMP critical section was used in the original code. Since OpenMP critical sections of code are detrimental to performance, a work-around was found to avoid the critical section entirely, as shown in the optimized code. The *used_img_map()* array, and *used_img_cnt* variable are used to store values sequentially in the *used_img_lst()* array. Since two separate neighbor list is built for Host and Phi, two version of use_img_lst() and used_img_map() have been built; then, these two versions are combined to produce combined version of the two arrays. Later, both of these arrays are used in other routines. All of the functionality can be achieved by the simpler and lockless code as shown in the optimized code column. All OpenMP threads update this shared array, and same positions can be updated (placing 1) by multiple threads. The used_img_map() now contains "1"s in the position of img_j, which is an atom index. After used_img_map() array is built on the coprocessor, it is used with the host version of used_img_lst() and used_img_map() to build the combined version of used_img_lst() and used_img_map()._ The optimization is possible because *used_img_map()* is *single byte* type and 1's are stored on specific array positions. The optimized code can be found in get_nb_list_offload() routine inside the nb_pairlist.F90 file of the Amber source code.

EXCLUSION LIST OPTIMIZATION

In the original code as shown in Figure 6.6, on every time step the *excl_img_flags()* array (an array used in the neighbor list calculation) is initialized, allocated for each OpenMP thread and then reset back again after each bucket is searched.

Original Code	Optimized Code
/*Xeon Phi offload code*/	/*Xeon Phi offload code*/
OpenMP Do loop starts	OpenMP Do loop starts
....	....
!$omp critical	
if (used_img_map(img_j) .eq. 0) then	
used_img_map(img_j) = 1	
used_img_cnt = used_img_cnt + 1	
used_img_lst(used_img_cnt) = img_j	used_img_map(img_j) = 1
end if	
!$omp end critical	
....	....
OpenMP loop ends	OpenMP loop ends
....	....
/*Xeon Phi and Host version of used_img_map() are combined. Similarly two versions of used_img_lst() are combined for later use*/	/*Xeon Phi version of used_img_map() is used with used_img_map() and used_img_lst() to get combined version of used_img_lst() used_img_map() for later use*/

FIGURE 6.5

Code snippets to show the optimization of the assignment of neighboring atoms by removal of an omp critical section.

All of the tasks in the original code can be optimized by:

(1) allocating a larger array of size *atm_cnt * number of threads*, allowing one allocation of the array during system setup, removing the need to reallocate on each loop iteration
(2) One time initialization of the array in system setup
(3) using this larger array with proper indexing in the neighbor list code
(4) resetting only the positions of the larger array which have already been used. Thus, the array can be used again in the next time step.

With this optimization, we can save the time of resetting and allocating the array inside the OpenMP runtime in every time step; both of which are expensive. The optimized code can be found in get_nb_list_offload() routine inside nb_pairlist.F90 file.

REDUCE DATA TRANSFER AND COMPUTATION IN OFFLOAD CODE

In the original Amber MD code, as shown in Figure 6.7, each MPI rank allocates and uses the global atom list and force arrays. Thus, in the offload implementation, the global atom list and force arrays have to be transferred back and forth between the host and the coprocessor. However, since each MPI rank does not use the full list of atoms, an optimization is used to reduce data transfers and computation in the offloaded code. The ranges of atom indices are determined by finding the maximum and minimum indices of the used atoms before the direct space sum calculation.

This optimization is extended to other arrays where the full range of atoms (1 to atm_cnt) is not required. The optimized code can be found in get_nb_energy_offload() routine inside get_nb_energy_offload.i file.

The loop has been further optimized as shown in Figure 6.8. Fortran allows loop accesses to be indexed so that all the positions of the array are contiguous in memory to the compiler, which allows for memset to be issued in fewer clock cycles.

Original Code
/*inside neighbor list routine*/ /*Reset the array in each step*/ do i = atm_cnt excl_img_flags(i) = 0 end do OpenMP loop starts .... /*allocate arrays for each OpenMP threads*/ !$omp firstprivate(excl_img_flags_dev) ....   /*Reset excl_img_flags() back again after each bucket of atoms are searched for neighbors*/ do i = atm_mask_idx + 1, atm_mask_idx + atm_maskdata(atm_i)%cnt   excl_img_flags(offset_excl + atm_img_map(atm_mask(i))) = 0 end do .... OpenMP loop ends

FIGURE 6.6

Code snippets to show the optimization of the exclusion list calculation.

(Continued)

```
ptimized Code
/*inside an initial setup routine*/
do i = 1, atm_cnt*num_threads
   excl_img_flags_threaded(i) = 0
end do
/*inside neighbor list routine*/
OpenMP loop starts

    ..............

 do i = atm_mask_idx + 1, atm_mask_idx + atm_maskdata(atm_i)%cnt
    excl_img_flags_threaded(offset_excl + atm_img_map(atm_mask(i))) = 0
 end do

    ...........

 /*Reset excl_img_flags_threds() back again after each bucket is searched */
 do i = atm_mask_idx + 1, atm_mask_idx + atm_maskdata(atm_i)%cnt
    excl_img_flags(offset_excl + atm_img_map(atm_mask(i))) = 0
 end do

    .................
OpenMP loop ends
```

FIGURE 6.6,   Cont'd.

MODIFICATION OF LOAD BALANCE ALGORITHM

The work involved in calculating the forces on the atoms is distributed to the MPI tasks using the Amber load balancing scheme. The algorithm is modified so that the coprocessor gets an appropriate share of the load and runs concurrently with the processor, as shown below:

PME DIRECT SPACE SUM AND NEIGHBOR LIST WORK

All MPI tasks are assigned with PME direct space sum and neighbor list work. The load-balancer monitors the performance of each MPI task in calculating the PME direct space sum over 50–100 time steps and dynamically adjusts the amount of PME direct space sum and neighbor list work assigned to each MPI task accordingly. The neighbor list performance for each MPI task is not monitored as it is directly proportional to the performance of the PME direct space sum and so is automatically adjusted based on the PME direct space sum performance. At the start of a simulation, offloading MPIs outperform

Original Code
!dir$ offload begin mandatory signal(sig2) target (mic:0) &
out(img_frc_dev(:,1:atm_cnt): alloc_if(.false.) free_if(.false.)) &
in(img_crd(:,1:atm_cnt): alloc_if(.false.) free_if(.false.)
into(img_crd_dev(:,1:atm_cnt))) &
....
!dir$ end offload
....
do j = 1, atm_cnt
img_frc_thread(1:3,j)=0
end do
....

Optimized Code
!dir$ offload begin mandatory signal(sig2) target (mic:0) &
out(img_frc_dev(:,min:max): alloc_if(.false.) free_if(.false.))
in(img_crd(:, min:max): alloc_if(.false.) free_if(.false.)
into(img_crd_dev(:,min:max))) &
....
!dir$ end offload
....
do j = min, max
img_frc_thread(1;3,j)=0
end do
....

FIGURE 6.7

Code snippets to show the optimization of global atom list and force transfers between the processor and the coprocessor.

nonoffloading MPIs and so, as the simulation progresses, a larger proportion of the work is assigned to the offloading MPI tasks. The host:coprocessor workload ratio of 22:78 achieves optimal performance and was deduced by testing the performance at different ratios for a simulation of cellulose, as can be seen in Figure 6.9. The thread-based decomposition strategy used on the coprocessor ensures that all cores have as equal a workload as possible.

Original code	Optimized Code
do j = min, max	do j=min*3-2,max*3
img_frc_thread(1;3,j)=0	img_frc_thread(j,1)=0
end do	end do

FIGURE 6.8

Code snippet to show the optimization of the initialization of the force array to exhibit contiguous memory accesses.

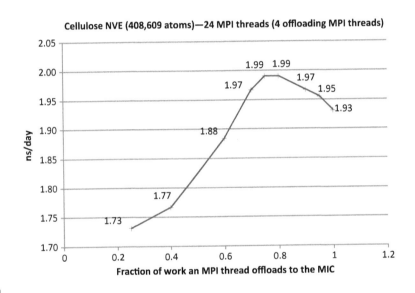

FIGURE 6.9

Performance of a cellulose simulation when varying the fraction of work offloaded to the coprocessor by each offloading MPI task. Hardware: 2 Intel Xeon E5 2697v2 processors (2 × 12 cores)+Intel Xeon Phi 7120P coprocessor (61 cores). MPI configuration: 24 MPI tasks launched on the host, 4 of which offload work to the coprocessor.

PME RECIPROCAL SPACE SUM WORK

Depending on the number of MPI tasks launched, either all or a fraction of the MPI tasks are given atoms for which to calculate the PME reciprocal space contribution. For example, a system of cellulose (408,609 atoms) distributes PME reciprocal space work to all MPI tasks; a smaller system would only distribute work to a fraction of the MPI tasks launched. However, as the PME reciprocal space sum is not offloaded to the coprocessor, offloading MPI tasks are restricted from being assigned PME recip-rocal space work. This is done to promote concurrent execution of the host and coprocessor as, if offloading MPIs were assigned PME reciprocal space work, execution of offloaded work on the co-processor would not be able to proceed until the PME reciprocal space work had been executed on the host, leaving the coprocessor idle. However, in the scenario where 10 or less MPI tasks are launched, all get assigned PME reciprocal space work. This is done as a safeguard. The load balancer takes into consideration the total number of ranks, the system size, direct space sum assignment, and the relative speed of the processing cores when assigning reciprocal space work to MPI tasks. We have introduced a new component *"offloading MPI not doing reciprocal space work"* in the already complicated load-balancing algorithm. Thus, a corner case can arise where only one MPI task will get all the reciprocal space work, or even worse, no MPI tasks get reciprocal space work. This situation can arise for low numbers of MPI tasks, such as 6 or lower, so a safety bar of 10 MPI tasks has been set for reciprocal space work assignment to offloading MPI tasks. The workload is then distributed evenly to the assigned MPI task(s).

BONDED FORCE WORK

A fraction of the MPI tasks launched are assigned bonded force work and the amount of work is dynamically assigned in a similar manner to the PME direct space sum and neighbor list work dependent on performance in previous time steps. As is the case with the PME reciprocal space sum, bonded work is restricted to nonoffloading MPI tasks only as, bonded force contributions are not calculated on the coprocessor and so asynchronous execution with the coprocessor can only occur when bonded force contributions are calculated using nonoffloading MPI ranks. Again, similar to the PME reciprocal space sum, if 10 MPI tasks or fewer are launched then bonded force work is assigned to offloading MPIs.

COMPILER OPTIMIZATION FLAGS

In Amber, the additional optimization flags (on top of original flags) for the coprocessor code are: -opt-streaming-cache-evict=0 -fimf-domain-exclusion=15 -align array64byte. In the get_nb_energy_ offload routine, some arrays are used only once, thus - opt-streaming-cache-evict=0 is used. It directs the compiler not to use any cache eviction instructions while using streaming stores. –fimf-domain-exclusion=15 specifies that domains such as infinities, extremes, nans, and denormals are excluded from accurate evaluation. This helps math functions run slightly faster. "-align array64byte" is a Fortran specific compiler flag that directs the compiler to align the array data. This helps improve data access performance.

RESULTS

The performance of the *pmemd* coprocessor offload algorithm was tested using a series of benchmarks designed to represent typical molecular systems that would be simulated in a real-world research project. The benchmark systems are: cellulose NVE (408,609)—a polysaccharide that provides the structure to plant cell walls; and satellite tobacco mosaic virus (stmv) (1,067,095 atoms)—a plant virus that worsens the symptoms of infection caused by the tobacco mosaic virus. Benchmarking was carried out on 2 Intel Xeon E5-2697 v2 processors (2×12 cores, 24 threads, 30 M Cache, 2.70 GHz) and 2 Intel Xeon E5-2697 v2 processors coupled to an Intel Xeon Phi 7120P coprocessor (61 cores, 240 threads). The Intel compiler version 14 update 1, Intel MPI version 4.1, MPSS version 3.2.3 and Flash version 2.1.02.0390 were used. The nondefault optimization flags used for FORTRAN source code were: -align array64byte -ip -O3 -no-prec-div -xHost -openmp -opt-streaming-cache-evict$=0$ -fimf-domain-exclusion$=15$ -fp-model fast$=2$; and for C/C++ source code were: -ip -O3 -no-prec-div -xHost -openmp -opt-streaming-cache-evict$=0$ -fimf-domain-exclusion$=15$ -fp-model fast $=2$. Details of the optimization flags used for tuning can be found in the compiler manual. All benchmark systems were parallelized with 24 MPI tasks.

All the benchmark runs used a 2 fs time step and hydrogen bonds were constrained using the SHAKE algorithm. All benchmark systems employed a direct space sum cutoff (cellulose (8 Å) and stmv (9 Å)) and periodic boundary conditions with long-range electrostatics computed using the PME method. Cellulose NVE was simulated for 2000 time steps and stmv was simulated for 1000 time steps. The input files used in the simulations are provided in the supporting documentation.

Figure 6.10 compares the performance in terms of speedup of nanosecond per day of the cellulose and stmv benchmarks when using 2 Intel Xeon E5-2697 v2 processors (2×12 cores) (codenamed Ivy Town or IVT) with default/tuned compilation and 2 Intel Xeon E5-2697 v2 processors (2×12 cores) plus Intel Xeon Phi 7120P coprocessor (61 cores) with tuned compilation. Tuned compilation, in this context, refers to the use of carefully tuned optimization flags (detailed above) as opposed to using the default optimization flags, which we refer to as default. As can be seen from the figure, using 2 Intel Xeon E5-2697 v2 processors and tuned compiler optimization flags provides a reasonable performance improvement, compared with using the default compiler optimization. Running the tuned offload algorithm on 2 Intel Xeon E5-2697 v2 processors plus an Intel Xeon Phi 7120P coprocessor gives a speedup of $1.43\times$ and $1.62\times$ for cellulose and stmv, respectively. A larger performance improvement is seen for stmv due to the larger system size, which allows for more computation per coprocessor core and so more opportunity for hiding data transfer latencies and coprocessor memory access latencies.

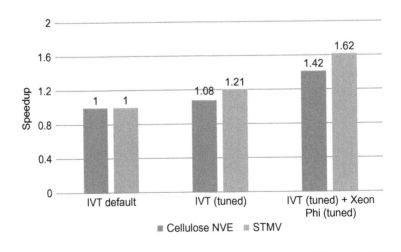

FIGURE 6.10

Speedup of Cellulose NVE (408,609 atoms) and STMV (1,067,095 atoms) showing original code, optimized code on two processors and then optimized code on two processors plus a coprocessor.

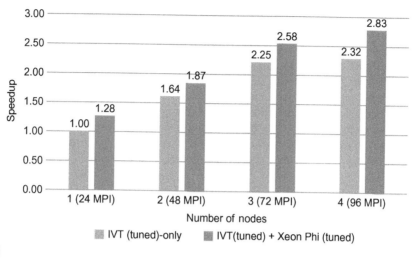

FIGURE 6.11

Speedup of Cellulose NVE (408,609 atoms) on two configurations using optimized code: two processors, two processors, and one coprocessor.

Figure 6.11 shows the speedup of the offload implementation when scaling across multiple nodes in comparison to using the parallel implementation of Amber's *pmemd* engine. Runs were carried out on two different platforms:

1. Processor-only platform whereby a node is comprised of two Intel Xeon E5 2697 processors (24 cores) on a dual socket platform (IVT).
2. Processor and coprocessor platform whereby the node is comprised of two Intel Xeon E5 2697 processors (24 cores) plus one Intel Xeon Phi 7120P coprocessor (61 cores) on a dual socket platform.

The total number of MPI tasks are shown in the X-axis for various numbers of nodes. For the offload runs, atom distribution was modified so, that in each node, only the middle 4 MPI ranks offload direct space sum work to the coprocessor. Each offloading MPI rank uses a quarter of the coprocessor's cores (15 cores). The same network switches (Single-Rail FDR Mellanox IB) are used for both platforms. The original Amber MD code does not scale well beyond about 96 MPI ranks because of all-to-all MPI communications used to distribute atom coordinates, force arrays, and FFT arrays. Thus performance results are only shown for up to 4 nodes (4 × 24 MPI ranks/node = 96 MPI ranks). As seen from the figure, the coprocessor offload code consistently out-performs the processor-only code. It also shows that the offload implementation has similar scaling to the processor-only code.

CONCLUSIONS

In this chapter, version 14 of the *pmemd* MD (MD) engine in the Amber MD software package was extended to support offloading to an Intel Xeon Phi coprocessor. Work involved the implementation of a two-fold decomposition strategy that employs spatial decomposition of the system using MPI followed by thread-based decomposition within offloading MPI tasks using OpenMP. The approach used was to have between 1 and 4 MPI tasks offload 78% of their PME direct space sum and neighbor list build workload to the coprocessor. Each offloading MPI task spawns OpenMP threads in a coprocessor partition to execute equally weighted portions of the workload. The results from the PME direct space sum are then passed back to the host and accumulated into the full force array.

Performance tests revealed that once the algorithm had been tuned with compiler optimization flags it performs 1.43× and 1.62× faster on processor+coprocessor platform when simulating systems of cellulose NVE (408K atoms) and a system of satellite tobacco mosaic virus (stmv, 1067K atoms), respectively, compared with running on processor-only platform. The multinode version of the offload code also scale similar to the processor-only code, but with higher performance. The 4 node processor+coprocessor offload code performs 2.83× of single node processor-only code. The theoretical double-precision peak performance of an Intel Xeon E5-2697v2 processor is 518.4 GFLOP/s. When coupled to an Intel Xeon Phi 7120P coprocessor a total of 1.7184 TFLOP/s of double precision performance is theoretically achievable, translating to a theoretical speedup of 3.3×. However, *pmemd MIC offload* sees an actual speedup of 1.62× for stmv, which is significantly lower. We believe that a lack of code vectorization, by the compiler, because of irregular loop structures and inefficient memory usage may be at the root of this gap. Resolving these issues seem to require significant code restructuring.

As mentioned earlier, this version of Amber uses MPI-only parallelism on the Host and OpenMP based parallelism on the coprocessor to exploit all the available cores and memory bandwidth. This also permits the Host and coprocessor runs to execute at the same time. However, as the Host MPI-only version does typically scale beyond a handful of nodes, a separate project is being undertaken in which a hybrid version of Amber (MPI+OpenMP) for the host is being implemented and optimized to improve cluster level scaling.

Future modifications to *pmemd coprocessor offload* will be aimed at finding solutions to these bottlenecks. One major change to the algorithm will be the implementation of a mixed precision model. This is thought to provide significant performance improvement by allowing double the number of simultaneous calculations by the SIMD vector units. Other future revisions will include improving the dynamic load-balancing scheme and adding to the amount of computation carried out on the Intel Xeon Phi coprocessor.

The resulting software modifications have been released as updates to the Amber 14 software suite and are automatically downloaded and applied during installation. The code is available as patch files on the Amber website (http://ambermd.org/bugfixes/14.0/update.5; http://ambermd.org/bugfixes/14.0/update.9).

FOR MORE INFORMATION

- Case, D.A., Babin, V., Berryman, J.T., Betz, R.M., Cai, Q., Cerutti, D.S., Cheatham III, T.E., Darden, T.A., Duke, R.E., Gohlke, H., Goetz, A.W., Gusarov, S., Homeyer, N., Janowski, P., Kaus, J., Kolossváry, I., Kovalenko, A., Lee, T.S., LeGrand, S., Luchko, T., Luo, R., Madej, B., Merz, K.M., Paesani, F., Roe, D.R., Roitberg, A., Sagui, C., Salomon-Ferrer, R., Seabra, G., Simmerling, C.L., Smith, W., Swails, J., Walker, R.C., Wang, J., Wolf, R.M., Wu, X., Kollman, P.A., 2014. Amber 14, University of California, San Francisco.

- Salomon-Ferrer, R., Case, D.A., Walker, R.C., 2013. An overview of the Amber biomolecular simulation package. WIREs Comput. Mol. Sci. 3 198-210.
- Goetz, A.W., Williamson, M.J., Xu, D., Poole, D., Le Grand, S., Walker, R.C., 2012. Routine microsecond molecular dynamics simulations with Amber—part I: generalized born. J. Chem. Theory Comput. 8 1542-1555.
- Plotnikov, M., 2014. GROMACS for Intel® Xeon Phi™ Coprocessor [accessed 2015 February]; Available from: https://software.intel.com/en-us/articles/gromacs-for-intel-xeon-phi-coprocessor.
- Sun, X., 2013. Molecular Dynamics Optimization on Intel® Many-Integrated Core Architecture (Intel® MIC) [accessed 2015 February]; Available from: https://software.intel.com/en-us/articles/molecular-dynamics-optimization-on-intel-many-integrated-core-architecture-intel-mic?language=en.
- Needham, P., Bhuiyan, A., Walker, R. Extension of the Amber Molecular Dynamics Software to Intel's Many-Integrated Core (MIC) Architecture. submitted and under review in J. Comput. Phys. Commun.
- User and Reference Guide for the Intel® Fortran Compiler 14.0. 2014 [accessed 2015 February]; Available from: https://software.intel.com/en-us/compiler_14.0_ug_f.
- Intel. Intel® MPI Library User's Guide for Linux* OS. 2014 [accessed 2015 February]; Available from: Intel® MPI Library User's Guide for Linux* OS.
- Intel. Intel® Manycore Platform Software Stack (MPSS). 2014 [accessed 2015 February]; Available from: https://software.intel.com/en-us/articles/intel-manycore-platform-software-stack-mpss.
- Download the code from this, and other chapters, http://lotsofcores.com.

LOW-LATENCY SOLUTIONS FOR FINANCIAL SERVICES APPLICATIONS

7

Ravi A. Murty

Technical Computing Group (TCG), Intel, USA

INTRODUCTION

While most high-performance computing (HPC) applications target sustained floating-point throughput and memory bandwidth, some applications, such as those used in the financial service industry (FSI), target low latency. This chapter explores techniques that demonstrate the applicability of the Intel® Xeon Phi™ coprocessor in latency-sensitive applications. In particular, it focuses on low-latency mechanisms to transfer data between the host and the coprocessor with the specific purpose of improving feed handlers used by financial services applications. While these techniques were useful in optimizing the feed handlers, they are also generically applicable to other "producer-consumer" type of applications that can take advantage of the large core count and high memory bandwidth available on current and future Intel Xeon Phi coprocessors. Additionally, some of the optimizations described in this chapter are generically applicable for many-core architectures running a general-purpose operating system (OS) such as Linux.

THE OPPORTUNITY

Financial exchanges provide information about the market via feed handlers that contain information about stocks and order details. With an increase in the number of symbols in a feed as well as the quantity of orders, there is a dramatic increase in the rate at which feed data need to be processed to make timely buy/sell decisions (see Figure 7.1). Additionally, exchanges such as NASDAQ and NYSE provide market data in a multitude of formats including multicast transmission and point-to-point over TCP/IP. The format of the data differs between exchanges and often between different feeds from the same exchange. The proprietary format of the feeds and their ever-changing nature has resulted in trading firms seeking commercial computing solutions instead of spending significant time and effort developing their own in-house feed handler.

Broadly speaking computing systems can be described as either general-purpose "off the shelf" or a custom "application specific" solution. A general-purpose "off the shelf" solution consists of a software application running on a general-purpose processor (e.g., Intel® Xeon® processors) and a standard operating system (OS) like Linux. In contrast, an example of a custom "application specific" solution consists of a Field Programmable Gate Array (FPGA) or an Application Specific Integrated Circuit

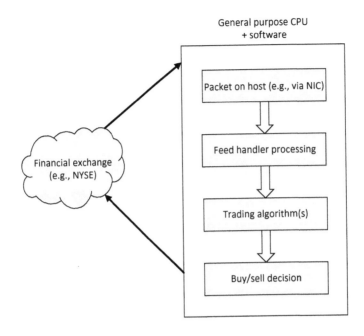

FIGURE 7.1

High-frequency trading overview.

(ASIC) in which data packets from the field handler are made available to processing elements with very low latency. The processing elements are able to process these packets with a fixed number of clock cycles (dependent on the type and size of the packet) in a very deterministic manner. However, as with any custom solution, a change in the feed-handling algorithm will dictate either a new ASIC, an expensive solution, or a custom reconfiguration of the FPGA requiring a specialized skill set and tools. This has made general-purpose solutions with software running on the processor attractive as long as certain latency guarantees can be made. General-purpose software and algorithms allow financial houses to more quickly build and customize feed handlers to handle data from different exchanges or in different formats.

An important aspect of any computing solution is the turnaround latency as well as the latency added by the commercial feed handler. This is especially crucial to high-frequency trading (HFT) firms since market data may be rendered worthless to end customers if there is an additional delay of even a few microseconds in the feed handlers. Typically, these feed handlers are limited to a small number of cores available to process data since a majority of the cores are used by the trading application itself. This results in an increase in latencies during the peak trading hours. The Intel Xeon Phi coprocessor with its large number of threads and general-purpose programming model offers a viable alternative to address this problem. A feed handler's performance is optimal when the threads are able to process the data at the same rate at which data are being received. We will see that providing a low-latency mechanism to transfer data between the host and the coprocessor will also be critical to optimize a feed handler application. The techniques described here could also be used to optimize other "producer-consumer" packet processing applications.

PACKET PROCESSING ARCHITECTURE

The Intel Xeon Phi coprocessor offers a general-purpose solution for a large class of *embarrassingly parallel* applications such as the HFT and feed-handling systems described above. It provides a powerful, general-purpose, computing platform consisting of:

- A large number of cache coherent cores and threads to handle many independent *streams* of work optimally
- Uniquely wide SIMD capability via 512 bit wide vectors instead of the narrower MMX, SSE, or AVX2 capabilities
- High performance support for instructions to perform reciprocals, square root and exponent operations which provide an ideal environment for Monte Carlo-related applications.
- A large amount of available memory bandwidth.
- An efficient, both from a bandwidth and latency perspective, communication pipe, the PCIe bus, between the host and all the attached coprocessors on the system.

This problem can be broken down into one involving *packet processing* as shown in Figure 7.2. One or more threads on the host receive packets over a socket connection from an external source, such as

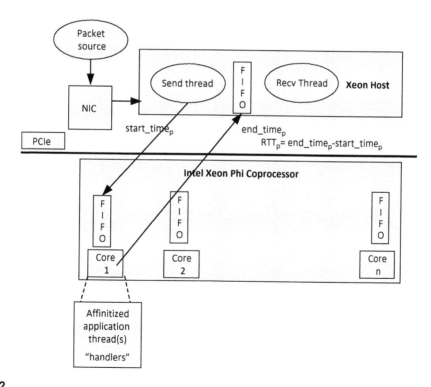

FIGURE 7.2

Generic packet processing application utilizing the coprocessor.

market data, through a standard network interface (NIC). The host threads queue up the packets, either in their entirety or just the relevant parts, into separate FIFOs for further processing. In the figure, the FIFOs reside in GDDR memory on the coprocessor and this choice is explained later in the chapter. An *affinitized* coprocessor-side thread, running on a core, processes each packet received on its FIFO in the order that it was received and runs the packet through a feed-handling algorithm. The result of the algorithm is then copied back into an FIFO, shown on the host in Figure 7.2, for further processing. The figure of merit for this architecture involves the average and worst-case latencies as measured by the *round trip time* (RTT) for every packet p. In the case of feed handlers, the worst-case latencies are expected at the beginning of the day when the exchange opens and at the end of the day just before the close of business. While it is expected that a burst of packets, consisting of back-to-back with little or no inter-packet gap, will lead to a backup and therefore an increase in RTT, the expectations from such a system is that the worst-case RTT is well bounded (no jitter) and preferably close to the average RTT. The rest of this chapter focuses on several optimization techniques to meet this requirement.

The sample code provides a simple packet processing application consisting of a client and a server (packet_processing/scif_connect_rbuf.cpp and packet_processing/scif_accept_rbuf.cpp, respectively). The optimizations described later in this chapter were used to optimize the packet processing sample application.

THE SYMMETRIC COMMUNICATION INTERFACE

The high-level architecture of the Intel® Manycore Platform Software Stack (Intel® MPSS) is shown in Figure 7.3 along with the Symmetric Communication Interface (SCIF) driver and library that application's link against in order to gain access to its services. SCIF provides efficient internode communication between two peer processes. A *node,* in this definition, is either the Intel Xeon processor or the Intel Xeon Phi coprocessor.

SCIF abstracts the details of communications over the PCIe bus and provides an interface that looks very similar to the Berkeley Sockets API. In this model, applications connect to each other (peer *endpoints*) and perform data transfer operations using the SCIF APIs. An important property of SCIF, as suggested by its name, is *symmetry*; SCIF drivers and libraries present the same interface on both sides of the PCIe bus. The process of establishing a connection is very similar to the sockets API, where one side listens (`scif_listen()`) for, and accepts (`scif_accept()`), incoming connections while the other side connects (`scif_connects()`) to the remote process.

As a starter, Figures 7.4 and 7.5 provide an example of a simple client/server application demonstrating the connection establishment process using SCIF.

Finally, SCIF provides several *classes* of APIs for:

- Connection management
- Messaging
- Memory Registration
- Remote Memory Access (for bulk transfer and low latency access)

The SCIF API set is quite small and most applications will use the entire set. The focus of this chapter is on APIs useful for low-latency data transfers between the host and coprocessor.

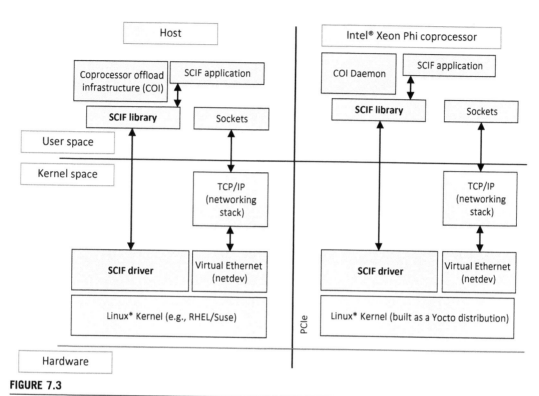

FIGURE 7.3

The Intel® Many-Core Platform Software Stack (Intel® MPSS) showing the SCIF driver and user mode library.

MEMORY REGISTRATION

Every process has a *virtual address space (VAS)*. Virtual addresses (VAs) in this space are backed by physical pages by the operating system when a thread of that process faults on a read or write access. SCIF introduces the concept of a *registered address space* (RAS). This address space is sparse and only specific ranges which have been registered, via `scif_register()`, by the application, called *registered windows or* just *windows,* can be accessed by the remote peer of the process after a connection has been established. Figure 7.6 shows the relationship between the physical, virtual and RAS for a process. A set of physical pages (P) backs a virtual range (V) that is referenced by the window offset (W) in the RAS. A point worth noting is that the physical and VAS on the host processor and all the coprocessors are only accessible by a locally running process. The RAS, however, allows a process to access the physical memory backing it in the context of a remote process.

Put another way, use of `scif_register()` marks a region of memory ready for remote access. It takes a page aligned VA and a length parameter (plus some flags) and returns an offset that represents the window in the RAS of the process. Optionally, the offset can be chosen by the application and provided as an input to `scif_register()` by specifying the `SCIF_MAP_FIXED` flag. The physical pages that

```
/* open end point */
if ((epd = scif_open()) == SCIF_OPEN_FAILED) {
    printf("scif_open failed with error %d\n", errno);
    exit(1);
}


/* bind end point to available port, generated
 * dynamically
 */
if ((conn_port = scif_bind(epd, 0)) < 0) {
    printf("scif_bind failed with error %d\n", errno);
    exit(1);

}
printf("bind success to port %d\n", conn_port);


/* initiate a connection to remote node, when
 * successful returns the peer portID. Re-tries
 * for 20 seconds and exits with error message
 */
__retry:
if (scif_connect(epd, &portID) < 0) {
        if ((errno == ECONNREFUSED) && (tries > 0)) {
            printf("connection to node %d failed : trial
%d\n", portID.node, tries);
                tries--;
                sleep(1);
                goto __retry;

        }
    printf("scif_connect failed with error %d\n", errno);
        exit(1);

}
printf("connect success\n");
```

FIGURE 7.4

The client side (in connection/scif_connect_register.c) of the SCIF connection showing the basic SCIF APIs for connection establishment.

```
/* open end pt */
if ((epd = scif_open()) == SCIF_OPEN_FAILED) {
    printf("scif_open failed with err %d\n", errno);
    exit(1);
}
/* bind end pt to specified port */
if ((conn_port = scif_bind(epd, PORT_NO)) < 0) {
    printf("scif_bind failed with error %d\n", errno);
    exit(1);
}
printf("bind success to port %d\n", conn_port);

/* marks an end pt as listening end pt and queues
 * up a maximum of BACKLOG no: of incoming connection
 * requests
 */
if (scif_listen(epd, BACKLOG) != 0) {
    printf("scif_listen failed with error %d\n", errno);
    exit(1);
}

/* accepts a conn request by creating a new end pt
 * that connects to peer
 */
 if (scif_accept(epd, &portID, &newepd,
SCIF_ACCEPT_SYNC) != 0) {
    printf("scif_accept failed with error %d\n", errno);
    exit(1);
}
printf("accept success\n");
```

FIGURE 7.5

The server side (in connection/scif_accept_register.c) of the SCIF connection showing the basic SCIF APIs for connection establishment.

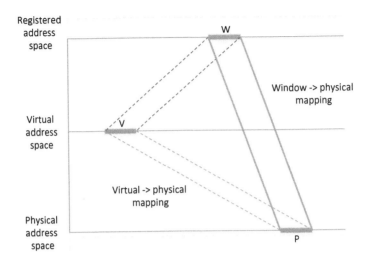

FIGURE 7.6

Registered address space and a window within it created by SCIF registration APIs.

back a window (see Figure 7.6) are *pinned* (locked) by the SCIF driver and cannot be swapped out by the OS or be reused for other purposes.

The window in the RAS of the remote peer of a local endpoint is called a *remote window* and every window (W) in the local RAS of a process is a remote window to its peer endpoint. Lastly, the pages represented by a window in an RAS are available for use in many of the SCIF APIs including scif_mmap() which is described below.

MAPPING REMOTE MEMORY VIA *scif_mmap()*

SCIF supports an API that enables a local process to map the exposed (via SCIF registration) physical memory of a remote peer process into its local VAS. Developers on Linux may recognize this as similar to the mmap() system call that allocates a VA in the VAS of the calling process.

Like mmap(), scif_mmap() allows the calling process (shown as Process X in Figure 7.7) to allocate a VA in its VAS. However, the physical pages that back the returned VA are in the physical address space of the peer endpoint of the connection, shown as Process Y in Figure 7.7. What this essentially means is that any load/store instructions to the memory page represented by Vx will read/write directly to the physical pages in the physical address space of process Y. It must be noted that Figure 7.7 is an extension of Figure 7.6 where the process Y "opened" a window in its RAS, passed on the offset of the window to process X thereby allowing process X to generate a mapping in its local VAS using in scif_mmap().

Note: Coprocessor memory is mapped *write combining* (WC) on the host and there are some implications of performing reads and writes to WC memory that need to be handled carefully as described later in this chapter.

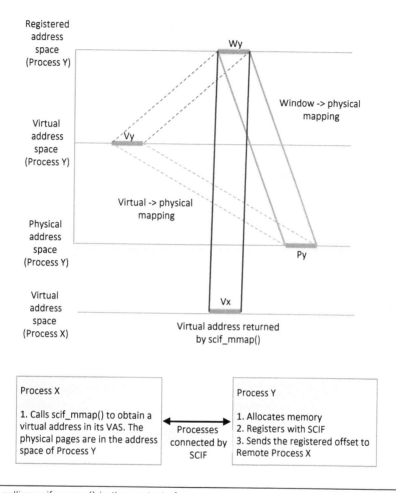

FIGURE 7.7

The effects of calling scif_mmap() in the context of a process.

OPTIMIZING PACKET PROCESSING ON THE COPROCESSOR

With the background provided so far, this section highlights a set of optimizations, including techniques to transfer data between the host and the coprocessor efficiently. For reference, the sample code in the packet_processing directory highlights all the optimizations described here.

OPTIMIZATION #1: THE RIGHT API FOR THE JOB

As an efficient communication infrastructure between the host and attached coprocessors, SCIF provides several methods to transfer data from one side to the other. However, the designer of the system must carefully consider the requirements of the system (bandwidth vs. latency) and use the right API for the job:

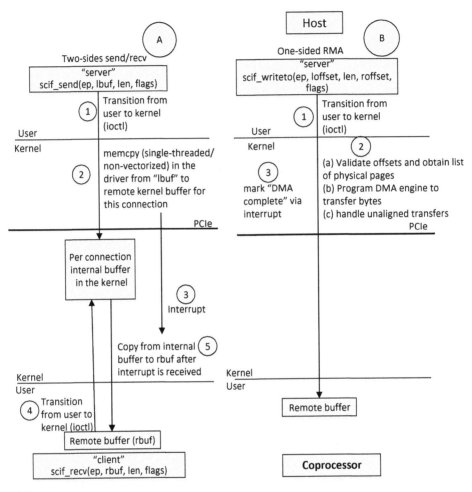

FIGURE 7.8

Comparison of send/receive and SCIF RMA APIs for data transfer.

- `scif_send` and `scif_recv`: These APIs are simple to use but are not meant to be very efficient. As shown by "A" in Figure 7.8, transferring data using these APIs involves ring transitions on both the send and receive sides, several memory copies as well as interrupts across PCIe.
- `scif_(v)writeto` and `scif_(v)readfrom`: These APIs use the DMA engines (see "B" in Figure 7.8) to transfer data from one end to the other. While they provide the highest bandwidth path and free up the CPU to do something else in the meantime, this method of transfer incurs the overhead of programming DMA descriptors (2) and handling interrupts (3). In addition, programming the DMA block of hardware is done in the kernel mode driver that involves a ring

transition (1). Thus, the use of the DMA APIs isn't the most optimal choice to transfer "small" buffers.

- `scif_mmap`: Using `scif_mmap()` as described earlier and in Figure 7.7, the host application can obtain a VA that maps a coprocessor allocated buffer into its own address space as shown by "C" in Figure 7.9. Then the application can copy, using a highly Vectorized version of Intel compiler provided *memcpy*, data from the host side local buffer to the coprocessor-side remote buffer very efficiently. This method completely bypasses the kernel providing the lowest latency path for "small" buffer transfers between two processes in the application (Figures 7.10 and 7.11 provide an example that demonstrates one such example).

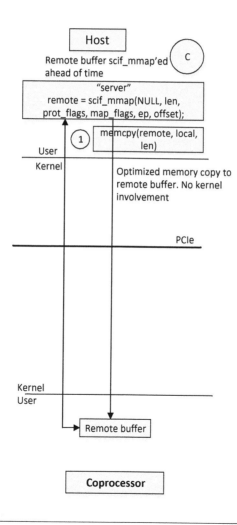

FIGURE 7.9

Data transfer using `scif_mmap()`.

```
/* Step1: get a pointer to the card side
 * (registered) memory. I'll reuse the offset I got
 * earlier
 */
printf("Getting pointer to buffer on card ... ");
remotep = scif_mmap(NULL, msg_size,
SCIF_PROT_READ|SCIF_PROT_WRITE, 0, epd, START_OFFSET);
if (remotep == SCIF_MMAP_FAILED) {
    printf("scif_mmap failed with error : %d\n",
get_curr_status());
    goto __end;
}
printf("Done\n");


/* Step2: write something to page 0 */
strcpy(remotep, "Hello Card, How are you?");


/* Step3: flip a flag on the card */
curr_addr = remotep + num_buf * PAGE_SIZE;


    __asm __volatile("sfence"::);


    /* "go" */
    *(volatile unsigned int *)curr_addr  = 0xC0DE;
```

FIGURE 7.10

Host-side of the application, using scif_mmap() (see mmap/scif_connect_rma_fence.c) to obtain a mapping to a buffer on the coprocessor.

OPTIMIZATION #2: BENEFIT FROM WRITE COMBINING (WC) MEMORY TYPE

scif_mmap() allows physical pages on the "other" side of the PCIe bus to be mapped into the page tables of the process calling it. It must be noted that when the process calling scif_mmap() is on the coprocessor, the physical pages (in host memory) are mapped as *uncached* or UC memory type. This means that a read (load) or a write (store) to host memory from a coprocessor core is an uncached operation which results in a PCIe transaction (read or write). This is not very efficient.

```
/* scif_register : marks a memory region for remote
 * access
 */
if ((buffer.offset = scif_register (newepd,
                                    buffer.self_addr,
                                    msg_size,
                                    START_OFFSET,
                                    SCIF_PROT_READ |
                                    SCIF_PROT_WRITE,
                                    SCIF_MAP_FIXED)) < 0) {
     printf("scif_register failed with error : %d\n",
get_curr_status());
        goto __end;
}
printf("Memory is registered, waiting for data now!");
...


/* Okay now we'll test the scif_mmap() capabilities
 * -- the "low latency" way of doing things
 */


/* wait for this to become "go" */
while (*(volatile unsigned int *)curr_addr != 0xC0DE);

printf("Flag transitioned to \"go\" \n");
printf("Host wrote: %s \n", (char *)buffer.self_addr);


/* card will now write something to page 1 */
strcpy((char *)buffer.self_addr + PAGE_SIZE, "I'm okay, How are
you doing, Host?");
```

FIGURE 7.11

Bypassing the kernel for low latency data transfers between host and attached coprocessor(s) (see mmap/scif_accept_rma_fence.c).

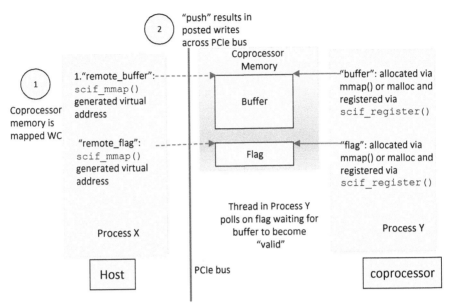

FIGURE 7.12

"Producer-Consumer" model of transferring data using scif_mmap() and memcpy().

Coprocessor memory, on the other hand, is mapped *write combining* or WC by the host. While reads from a host core is still an uncached operation, writes (stores) to WC memory type are not cached in the typical sense of the word cache (i.e., they don't go into the cache hierarchy). Instead they are stored in an internal buffer, called the *WC buffer*, in hopes of being able to combine multiple writes to adjacent regions of the WC buffer resulting in a larger, and more efficient, PCIe bus transaction. So while writes to the WC buffer get delayed for a bit, software can "flush" the WC buffer at any time via a *serializing instruction* such as *sfence, mfence,* or *cpuid*. The WC buffers also get flushed when software writes outside the address range of what is stored in the buffer (as it would do when executing memcpy).

By performing full cacheline writes (the size of the WC buffer) across PCIe, WC memory type offers advantages when memcpy is used to copy the contents of a buffer from host memory into a buffer in coprocessor memory (see (2) in Figure 7.12). There are some caveats that should be kept in mind when using WC memory type:

- WC memory is *weakly ordered*. What this means is that there is no guaranteed ordering of stored data at the destination. This is acceptable in situations such as the "producer-consumer" example where ordering is not important, as long as all the memories are transferred correctly, and a memcpy operation can be used to copy a buffer from host to coprocessor efficiently.
- Software needs to ensure that all writes to the "remote_buffer" (see Figure 7.12) are globally visible on the coprocessor before "remote_flag" is set. Software can enforce this with a serializing instruction such as sfence.

OPTIMIZATION #3: "PUSHING" VERSUS "PULLING" DATA

There are two ways of copying data between host memory and coprocessor memory:

- A thread on the host processor can initiate the copy operation (e.g., memcpy).
- A thread on the coprocessor can initiate the copy operation. This is usually the case when the coprocessor side of the application has finished processing the buffer that needs to be moved back up to the host for further processing or decision making.

Data are transferred over PCIe via read or write transaction layer packets or TLPs. Each TLP contains a header plus the data as payload. The size of the payload carried by a TLP depends on the size of the TLP (typically sizes include 64, 128, or 256 bytes). The *max payload size* in the PCIe configuration of the Intel Xeon Phi specifies how big the TLPs can get and this value should be set to 256 bytes.

A write operation from a CPU (host or coprocessor) translates into a PCIe write transaction called a *posted* write. A posted transaction is quick in that the initiator (CPU in the case of a memcpy) of the posted transaction does wait for a reply (or acknowledgment). A read operation, on the other hand, is a *nonposted* operation. Every read operation expects a response. What this implies for our simple producer-consumer example is that if the copy operation is initiated by the side that has the destination buffer, all the resulting PCIe transactions are non-posted reads. On the other hand, if the initiator is on the source side of the memcpy operation, all the transactions are posted writes—which are far more efficient. Therefore, it is more efficient to "push" data (source on local side, destination on remote side) compared to a "pull" for data as shown in Figure 7.12.

OPTIMIZATION #4: "SHADOW" POINTERS FOR EFFICIENT FIFO MANAGEMENT

Described by virtually any basic computer science textbook, an FIFO is a simple data structure to implement a queue. Data that are placed in the FIFO can be elements of a fixed size (e.g., a record) or just a simple byte stream. In either case, a set of pointers, head, and tail track the two ends of the queue as shown in Figure 7.13.

When used in the producer-consumer example, the producer *enqueues* work at the tail of the queue (think of people joining a line at the bank); while the consumer *dequeues* work from the head of the queue (the teller calls the next person at the head of the line). There are two important operations that need to be performed in this context:

- The producer needs to ensure that there is free space in the queue before adding more work into the queue. Therefore, the producer compares the head and tail pointer as shown in Figure 7.13.
- The consumer needs to ensure that there is valid work in the queue before dequeueing it for processing. So, the consumer compares the head and tail pointer to make sure that the queue is not empty.

In the packet processing architecture, the producer lives on the host. Therefore, the test to check for free space before enqueueing work consists of reading the head and tail pointers that live in coprocessor memory. As we have already seen, reading across the PCIe bus results in UC accesses to coprocessor memory that turn into (long latency) read transactions that are highly inefficient; especially for something as simple as a "full condition" check. However, this can be easily optimized using a more efficient implementation. In such an implementation, the producer would maintain shadow copies of the head

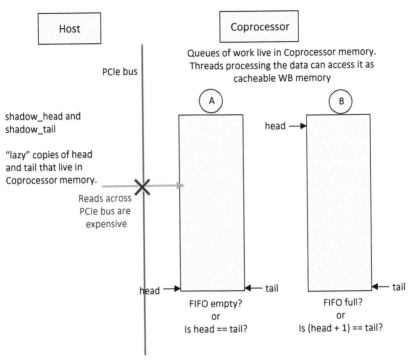

FIGURE 7.13

Better FIFO management using shadow pointers to detect full and empty conditions.

and tail (called "shadow_head" and "shadow_tail" on the Host side in Figure 7.13). The steps of the algorithm would then be:

- At initialization time, head, tail, shadow_head and shadow_tail all point to the same location in the FIFO (e.g., to the beginning of the queue).
- The producer (on the host) performs a full condition check before enqueueing (writing data across PCIe) something into the FIFO. However, instead of reading head and tail, shadow_head and shadow_tail are used as proxies. On the host, shadow_head and shadow_tail live in host memory and these accesses are simple memory accesses to cacheable *write back* (WB) memory. If there is space, data are written and shadow_tail is advanced locally on the host. Additionally, and this is important, a copy of shadow_tail is written (a PCIe posted transaction) to tail to ensure that the consumer "sees" new data in the FIFO.
- If/when the producer encounters a full condition, the values in shadow_head and shadow_tail are "refreshed" by reading the *real* values of head and tail. Assuming that a processing thread on the coprocessor core was in fact processing data by dequeueing elements or bytes, head has now advanced. The refresh operation causes shadow_head to get an accurate copy of head. While this is a UC read across the bus, it is performed less frequently resulting in slightly optimized code. Additionally reads are performed from the host side—a core with much higher single threaded performance!

OPTIMIZATION #5: TICKLESS KERNELS

The kernel (OS) running on the Intel Xeon Phi coprocessor is general-purpose Linux which is not a real-time operating system. Therefore, it does not provide any guarantees in terms of when threads are scheduled for execution. Application threads can be context switched out by other, higher priority threads or interrupted by a variety of interrupt sources. Historically, one guaranteed source of "interruptions" to application threads is the *periodic timer* interrupt. In addition to periodically interrupting the "currently running thread", the handler for the timer interrupt causes other side-effects to highly optimized applications that spend a lot of time prefetching data into the cache hierarchy to avoid long latency memory accesses. Examples of side effects include:

- Cache and TLB pollution—the interrupt handler in the kernel performs a number of activities such as RCU data structure updates, scheduling decision and updates process user/kernel statistics for profiling. This code execution pulls a lot of kernel data structures (in addition to kernel code in the instruction cache!) into the data cache hierarchy. Similarly the application specific TLBs are evicted and replaced with TLBs for pages of the kernel and its data structure.
- The timer interrupt wakes up kernel threads whose execution is delayed. These threads context switch into CPUs displacing the currently running application threads.

The cache and TLB pollution problem is especially impactful on an architecture like the Intel Xeon Phi coprocessor with its smaller L2 cache size (compared to Intel Xeon processors) and four hardware threads per core, each of which takes a timer interrupt at a different time (the interrupts are not synchronized in Linux) resulting in $4\times$ the number of timer interrupts per core every second. The net result for applications is unpredictable latencies and potential *jitter*.

For this reason, *tickless* kernels are of special importance to applications in both HPC and financial services (FSI). Recent Linux kernels support a mode called "full NOHZ" where the periodic timer tick, that we all are familiar with, has been reduced from 100 or 1000 times a second (depending on how HZ is configured) to one per second. This should not be confused with a feature Linux has had for a very long time called "idle tickless" where the kernel turns off the periodic timer tick when the "CPU" is idle, resulting in huge savings in power by allowing the CPU to go into deeper sleep states.

Starting with the 3.10 Linux kernel, "full NOHZ" enables a mode where the kernel turns down the tick rate when a single thread is running on a CPU. A running application is thus not interrupted as often (see "Previewing tickless support for Linux on the Intel® Xeon Phi coprocessor" in section "For more information" section at the end of this chapter). While a single thread on a CPU is not a common situation on a desktop, it is very common to see a dedicated application run on the entire processor chip in HPC and FSI systems. An example of where this helps is when threads need to come together to perform some kind of a collective operation (e.g., barrier) before moving to the next phase of the application. If one or more threads are interrupted unpredictably, the remaining (uninterrupted) threads progress to the barrier but waste time waiting (spinning) for the interrupted threads to join. This reduces overall scaling and performance of applications running on large HPC clusters.

In addition, for applications like the packet processing example discussed in this chapter, the periodic timer tick causes "spikes" and increases packet-processing latencies unpredictably; something that is unacceptable on a production system.

OPTIMIZATION #6: SINGLE THREAD AFFINITY AND CPU "ISOLATION"

In addition to using the tickless kernel as described above, two simple strategies to further mitigate the effects of "OS noise" are thread affinity and CPU isolation. Note that, in this discussion, the term "CPU" refers to an hardware thread or logical CPU that is seen as an independent unit of execution by the kernel.

Put simply, explicitly affinitizing application threads tell OS scheduler to stop moving them around. Why does is happen? In addition to performing the typical scheduler activities that we are familiar with—finding the highest priority threads to run and preempting a lower priority thread to "make room" for a higher priority thread that just became runnable—the scheduler tries to ensure that the overall system performance is maximized. One way to achieve this is to spread the load of *runnable* threads evenly across all available CPUs. This means that, in the ideal case, every CPU has the same number of runnable threads on its *run-queue* waiting to be scheduled and start execution. The thread scheduler keeps track of the load on every CPU in the system, migrating threads from heavily loaded CPUs to lightly loaded ones to smooth out the load. While this is nice for a general-purpose system (so no one CPU is idle while four threads share another CPU where each thread gets only 25% of CPU time there), systems where a single application is dedicated to run on a set of CPUs, as is the case in HPC or FSI, the OS can avoid scanning the CPU run queues looking for load balancing opportunities if it knew exactly where each application thread wanted to run. This is where thread affinity helps. Thread affinity provides a way for an application thread to tell the OS scheduler exactly where its threads can (and would like to) run. The scheduler in turn does not have to spend a lot of time load balancing the system because application threads are already where they need to be. It is obvious that migrating a thread, needed for load balancing, has other associated costs with it including the cost of context switching as well as cache/TLB misses because a migrated thread always starts with a cold cache and TLB! There are several mechanisms available on Linux and Intel runtimes, such as OMP, to define thread affinity. This includes *numactl* and KMP_AFFINITY, in addition to programmatic approaches via `sched_setaffinity()`.

Thread affinity also helps with another feature offered in newer Linux kernels called CPU *isolation*. This is a feature where the kernel running on a processor can be configured, via a kernel command line called *isolcpus*, to isolate a set of CPUs which basically means that the kernel scheduler avoids looking at them from a thread scheduling and load balancing perspective as described earlier. Since these CPUs are ignored, the only way to get on or off these isolated CPUs is via explicit thread affinity. Non-affinitized threads—both kernel and application threads—are kept out of running on the set of CPUs listed in the kernel command line (the set of isolated CPUs). By defining a set of isolated CPUs and by affinitizing application threads on the set of isolated CPUs—one application thread per CPU, all unwanted kernel threads and miscellaneous user mode applications, such as daemons for various purposes can be kept out providing a quiescent operating environment for applications.

OPTIMIZATION #7: MISCELLANEOUS OPTIMIZATIONS

Besides some of the optimizations described in this chapter, here are additional optimization considerations that should not be forgotten:

- Use the Intel C compiler with –O3 for optimization. One place where this matters is in the choice of memcpy that is used. When compiled with icc –O3, all memcpy calls in the application are replaced with a version of memcpy that is highly Vectorized and optimized for caching. This has a huge role to play considering that memcpy across the PCIe bus results in full cache line transactions.

- Disable power management options on both the Intel Xeon processor host and the Intel Xeon Phi Coprocessor. While power management allows the processor subsystems to go into *sleep states*, also called C-states, when it is not actively executing instructions (idle), there is an associated latency of both entering and exiting the lower power states from when it is operating *normal* (called C0) mode. In other words, while deeper sleep states (e.g., C6) result in larger power savings in a system, the latency of exiting such a deep state is higher and is detrimental to applications that are very sensitive to latency—think of what would happen if the threads on the coprocessor went idle for a period of time that was long enough for the processor to enter a deep sleep state and a packet arrived that required the thread to wake up and start running to process the packet. While most operating systems such as Linux enable power management by default, it is advisable to disable power management before running a latency sensitive application. On Linux this is easily done via a kernel command line called `intel_idle.max_cstate=0`

RESULTS

Using the optimizations described above, we transformed the sample code provided. We ran the sample code with two different payload sizes—50 bytes and 1500 bytes. Also, different values for "inter packet gap" were chosen—0, 10 and 100 μs'—defined as *publishing frequency*.

When the payload was ~50 bytes (as shown in Figure 7.14), the mean latencies were within the expected range (~10 μs) but the tails were quite high (~460 μs when publishing frequency was 10 μs). With 1500 byte payloads (as shown in Figure 7.15) even the mean latencies were in the

Publishing Frequency (μs)	Mean RTT (μs)	50%	70%	90%	99%	99.99%	100%
0	3870.08	3808	4046	4083	4122	4122	4387
10	11.15	11	11	12	13	374	460
100	10.83	11	11	12	12	59	309

FIGURE 7.14

Initial implementation (without optimizations) with 50 byte payload.

Publishing Frequency (μs)	Mean RTT (μs)	50%	70%	90%	99%	99.99%	100%
0	113,531	114,119	114,233	114,284	114,499	115,004	115,114
10	113,427	114,075	114,193	114,237	114,315	114,551	114,561
100	88,196	106,920	106,999	106,699	107,131	107,181	107,224

FIGURE 7.15

Initial implementation (without optimizations) with 1500 byte payload.

Publishing Frequency (µs)	Mean RTT (µs)	50%	70%	90%	99%	99.99%	100%
0	2538	2560	2568	2580			2588
10	3.85	4	4	4	5	21	46
100	3.84	4	4	4	5	19	34

FIGURE 7.16

Results after optimizing the code with 50 byte payload.

Publishing Frequency (µs)	Mean RTT (µs)	50%	70%	90%	99%	99.99%	100%
0	8808	8900			8938		9085
10	16.04	16	16	16	37	114	155
100	15.81	16	16	16	18	116	224

FIGURE 7.17

Results after optimizing the code with 1500 byte payload.

	Without Optimizations	With Optimizations
Mean RTT (µs)	113,427	16
100% (µs)	114,561	114

FIGURE 7.18

Performance comparison for interpacket gap of 10 µs and 1500 byte payload.

millisecond range (11.3 ms) and therefore completely unacceptable as a solution. While not shown here, other payload sizes resulted in similar issues.

By following a systematic approach involving tracing the "life of a packet" and applying the optimizations mentioned in this chapter (as shown in the sample code), the results shown in Figure 7.16 and Figure 7.17 were obtained. The optimizations result in dramatic improvements in performance especially in the 1500 byte payload case as shown in Figure 7.18.

CONCLUSIONS

The Intel Xeon Phi coprocessor provides a general-purpose programming environment for applications that benefit from having many independent threads of execution, wide vectors for data processing, large amounts of memory bandwidth and a PCIe interface that provides a high bandwidth and low-latency mechanism to share memory between the host and coprocessors in the system. Using the example of a packet processing engine this chapter presented several key optimization techniques that can significantly increase the performance of the application as well as help achieve the low-latency solution desired by the application. The optimizations include:

1. Ensure that the right API is being used for the application. Bandwidth sensitive applications benefit from using the DMA engine even though this involves a transition into the kernel. Latency sensitive applications, on the other hand, benefit from APIs that are able to avoid ring transitions and SCIF provides methods to implement such techniques.
2. Taking advantage of the fact that coprocessor memory is mapped write combining allows an application to effectively combine larger amounts of data before they are pushed across the PCIe bus resulting in higher protocol efficiency.
3. Conversion of PCIe read transactions into write transactions results in significant performance improvements because of the posted nature of the latter.
4. Avoiding expensive and unnecessary reads across the PCIe bus in the implementation of a FIFO for full and empty checks by shadowing the head and tail pointers provides additional benefits without any loss in correctness of the code.
5. Tickless kernels play a big role in reducing overall jitter and run-to-run variability in applications running on a general-purpose OS such as Linux. Avoiding constant interruptions from the OS, and the associated TLB and cache pollution, translate into additional application performance gains.
6. Thread affinity, via standard pthreads APIs or a runtime provided environment variable allow the placement of threads avoiding both oversubscription and load imbalance issues. It also keeps the kernel scheduler from having to load balance threads across the system resulting in lower kernel involvement.
7. Finally, use of several simple, yet effective, miscellaneous optimizations, such as the use of a compiler generated vectorized memcpy as well as careful consideration of power management can result in higher performance and lower latency impacts on an application.

FOR MORE INFORMATION

- Symmetric Communication InterFace (SCIF) User's guide in MPSS: https://software.intel.com/en-us/articles/intel-manycore-platform-software-stack-mpss.
- A discussion on the Symmetric Communication InterFace (SCIF) APIs—https://software.intel.com/de-de/forums/topic/393771.
- Section 11.3, Intel® 64 and IA-32 Architectures Software Developer's Manual, Combined volumes 1, 2A, 2B, 2C, 3A, 3B and 3C, January 2015.
- Write Combining Memory Implementation Guidelines http://download.intel.com/design/pentiumii/applnots/24442201.pdf.
- Previewing tickless support for Linux on the Intel® Xeon Phi Coprocessor: https://software.intel.com/en-us/articles/previewing-tickless-support-for-linux-on-the-intel-xeon-phi-coprocessor.
- Processor power management: https://people.cs.pitt.edu/~kirk/cs3150spring2010/ShiminChen.pptx.
- Download the code from this, and other chapters, http://lotsofcores.com.

PARALLEL NUMERICAL METHODS IN FINANCE

8

Shuo Li
Intel Corporation, USA

OVERVIEW

In the realm of scientific calculations, many problems are expressed using nonlinear equations. The same is true for quantitative finance problems such as computing implied volatility or computing the yield of fixed coupon bonds. There are several well-known numerical methods for solving nonlinear equations. The simplest of all is the bisection method and the most popular is Newton-Raphson method.

In this chapter, we utilize a slightly more complicated example, American option pricing, and develop a C/C++ program that use the Newton-Raphson method to find solutions to partial differential equations based on the Black-Scholes model. We demonstrate how the principles of high performance parallel computing can be applied to the numerical approximation in general and Newton-Raphson in Finance specifically.

The first part of this chapter focuses on the quantitative finance and numerical methods of this problem. We start by reviewing the challenges in pricing American options. Next, we derive the pricing equation for American options using approximation techniques. In the final section, we develop a C/C++ implementation of the Newton-Raphson method.

The second part of this chapter applies a systematic approach to the program we developed in the first part. We start by fine-tuning the numerical operations in the initial program to arrive at a *scalar-optimized* implementation. Next, we introduce SIMD parallelism. The *vector-optimized* version of the program is then derived. Next, we introduce thread and core parallelism. We will see how OpenMP 4.0 can be applied to the program to create *scalar parallel* and *vector parallel* programs.

Finally, we compare the performance of various versions of the program and demonstrate the benefit of several high-performance techniques and postulate how the same methodology can be applied to other types of numerical approximation to achieve superior performance results.

INTRODUCTION

In the prior Pearls book, Chapter 19, covered the Black-Scholes model and the Black-Scholes formula to price European options. Thereby, applying high-performance computing methods to achieve high performance on the European style option pricing algorithm. However, nearly all the options written on a wide variety of underlying financial products including stocks, commodities and foreign exchanges are the American style with an early exercise clause included into the contracts. Unlike the European style option pricing problems, there is no close-form solution for the American style option pricing problem. The pricing of American options has mainly focused on using the finite difference methods of Brennan and Schwartz, the binomial of Cox, Ross Rubinstein and trinomial of Tian. While these numerical methods are capable of producing accurate solutions to the American option pricing problems, they are also difficult to use and consume at least two orders of magnitude more computational resources. As a result, for the past 40 years, many talented financial mathematicians have been searching for newer and better numerical methods that can produce good enough results while being much more efficient computationally. In this chapter, we look at a successful effort pioneered by Barone-Adsi and Whaley to create a program that can exceed our expectations for high performance while producing acceptable numerical results.

PRICING EQUATION FOR AMERICAN OPTION

Consider an option on a stock providing a dividend yield equal to b. We will denote the difference between the American and European option prices by v. Because both the American and the European option prices satisfy the Black-Scholes differential equation, so does v. Therefore,

$$\frac{\partial v}{\partial t} + (r - b)S\frac{\partial v}{\partial S} + \frac{1}{2}\sigma^2 S^2 \frac{\partial^2 v}{\partial S^2} = rv$$

For convenience, we define

$$\tau = T - t$$

$$h(\tau) = 1 - e^{-rt}$$

$$\alpha = \frac{2r}{\sigma^2}, \ \beta = \frac{2(r - q)}{\sigma^2}$$

We also can write, without loss of generality,

$$v = h(\tau)g(S, h)$$

With appropriate substitutions and variable changes, this gives

$$S^2 \frac{\partial^2 g}{\partial S^2} + \beta S\frac{\partial g}{\partial S} - \frac{\alpha}{h}g - (1 - h)\alpha\frac{\partial g}{\partial h}g = 0$$

The approximation involves assuming that the final term on the left-hand side is zero, so that

$$S^2 \frac{\partial^2 g}{\partial S^2} + \beta S\frac{\partial g}{\partial S} - \frac{\alpha}{h}g = 0 \tag{8.1}$$

The ignored term is generally fairly small. When τ is large, $1 - h$ is close to zero; when τ is small, $\partial g/\partial h$ is close to zero.

The American call and put prices at time t will be denoted by $C(S,t)$ and $P(S,t)$, respectively, where S is the stock price, and the corresponding European call and put price will be denoted by $c(S,t)$ and $p(S,t)$. Equation (8.1) can be solved using standard techniques. After boundary conditions have been applied, it is found that

$$C(S, t) = \begin{cases} c(S, t) + A_2 \left(\frac{S}{S^*}\right)^{r^2} & \text{when } S < S^* \\ S - K, \text{when } S \geq S^* \end{cases}$$

The variable $S*$ is the critical price of the stock above which the option should be exercised. It is estimated by solving the equation:

$$S^* - K = c(S^*, t) + \left\{1 - e^{-b(T-t)} N[d1(S^*)]\right\} \frac{S^*}{\gamma_2}$$

iteratively. For a put option, the valuation formula is

$$P(S,t) = \begin{cases} p(S,t) + A_1 \left(\frac{S}{S^{**}}\right)^{\gamma^1}, & \text{when } S > S^{**} \\ K - S, & \text{when } S \leq S^{**} \end{cases}$$

The variable S^{**} is the critical price of the stock below which the option should be exercised. It is estimated by solving the equation:

$$K - S^{**} = p(S^{**}, t) - \left\{1 - e^{-b(T-t)} N[-d1(S^{**})]\right\} \frac{S^{**}}{\gamma_1}$$

iteratively. The other variables that have been used here are

$$\gamma 1 = \left[-(\beta - 1) - \sqrt{(\beta - 1)^2 + \frac{4\alpha}{h}}\right] / 2$$

$$\gamma 1 = \left[-(\beta - 1) + \sqrt{(\beta - 1)^2 + \frac{4\alpha}{h}}\right] / 2$$

$$A_1 = -\left(\frac{S^{**}}{\gamma_1}\right) \left\{1 - e^{-b(T-t)} N[-d_1(S^{**})]\right\}$$

$$A_2 = \left(\frac{S^{**}}{\gamma_1}\right) \left\{1 - e^{-b(T-t)} N[d_1(S^{**})]\right\}$$

$$d_1(S) = \frac{\ln(S/K) + (r - b + \sigma^2/2)(T - t)}{\sigma\sqrt{T - t}}$$

Options on stock indices, currencies, and futures contracts are analogous to options on a stock providing a constant dividend yield. Hence, the quadratic approximation approach can easily be applied to all of these types of options.

INITIAL C/C++ IMPLEMENTATION

To implement the above formula, we have to find the critical value $S*$ to satisfy the following equation:

$$S^* - X = c(S^*, T) + \frac{S^*}{q_2}\left(1 - e^{(b-r)(T-t)} N(d1(S^*))\right)$$

This is equivalent to using Newton-Raphson method to find the root of $g(S^*) = 0$ with:

$$g(S^*) = S^* - X - c(S^*, T) - \frac{S^*}{q_2}\left(1 - e^{(b-r)(T-t)} N(d1(S^*))\right) = 0$$

We can start by finding a first seed value S_0. The next estimates of S_i can be found by using the standard method:

$$S_{i+1} = S_i - \frac{g(x)}{g'(x)}$$

At each iteration, we need to evaluate $g(x)$ and its derivative $g'(x)$.

$$g(S) = S - X - c(S, T) - \frac{1}{q_2} S \left(1 - e^{(b-r)(T-t)} N(d1(S)) \right)$$

$$g'(S) = \left(1 - \frac{1}{q_2} \right) \left(1 - e^{(b-r)(T-t)} N(d1(S)) \right) + \frac{1}{q_2} \left(e^{(b-r)(T-t)} n(d1(S)) \right) \frac{1}{\sigma\sqrt{T-t}}$$

$c(S)$ is the European option value from Black-Scholes formula, $N(x)$ is the cumulative normal distribution function, and $n(x)$ is the normal distribution function.

Our initial C/C++ implementation of American option approximation using Newton-Raphson iteration looks like the code listed in Figure 8.1.

The first step in implementing an approximation algorithm is to ensure that the analytical formula is correctly represented in the source code and the iteration process converges, as it is supposed to be, to a rational value.

SCALAR OPTIMIZATION: YOUR BEST FIRST STEP

Before we start to vectorize or parallelize this program, we need to make sure that the initial implementation has reached the optimal performance. We need to make sure any inefficiency is removed before being replicated in other SIMD lanes or other processor cores.

Our observations on scalar optimization come from our understanding of the target platform and the software tools and libraries used in the build process. In our example, we want to optimize the program running on Intel® Xeon® Processors codenamed Haswell and Intel Xeon Phi™ Coprocessor codenamed Knights Corner (KNC) using the Intel compiler found in Intel Composer XE 2015. The objective is to optimize the code so that the program executable, built by the selected tools, reaches its peak performance on the targeted execution environment.

COMPILER INVOCATION SWITCHES

The Intel Compiler can be invoked in the same way GCC is invoked. However, the target-specific switches can be different. Microarchitecture specifications and accuracy in numeric operation are the two major variations.

Microarchitecture specification
Microarchitecture switches in GCC are implemented as target specifications (Figure 8.2).

Floating point numeric operation control
Both GCC and Intel Composer give you controls to select high speed or high accuracy or both for floating point numeric operations (Figure 8.3). The most important ones are reciprocal and FMA, or fused-multiplication and add.

```
float N(float d){
        const float       A1 = 0.31938153;
        const float       A2 = -0.356563782;
        const float       A3 = 1.781477937;
        const float       A4 = -1.821255978;
        const float       A5 = 1.330274429;
        const float RSQRT2PI=0.39894228040143267793994605993438;
        float K = 1.0 / (1.0 + 0.2316419 * fabs(d));
        float cnd = RSQRT2PI * exp(- 0.5 * d * d) *
            (K*(A1 + K * (A2 + K * (A3 + K * (A4 + K* A5)))));
        if(d > 0)
            cnd = 1.0 - cnd;
        return cnd;
}

float n(const float& z) {
        return (1.0/sqrt(2.0*PI))*exp(-0.5*z*z);
};

float bs_euro_call ( const float& S
                    const float& X,
                    const float& r,
                    const float& q,
                    const float& sigma,
                    const float& time) {
    float sigma_sqr = sigma*sigma;
    float time_sqrt = sqrt(time);
    float d1 = (log(S/X) +
                (r-q + 0.5*sigma_sqr)*time)/(sigma*time_sqrt);
    float d2 = d1-(sigma*time_sqrt);
    float call_price = S * exp(-q*time)* CND(d1) -
            X * exp(-r*time) * CND(d2);
    return call_price;
}
float ameri_call_approx_baw( const float& S,
                             const float& X,
                             const float& r,
                             const float& b,
                             const float& sigma,
                             const float& time)
{
    const float ACCURACY=1.0e-6;
```

FIGURE 8.1

Initial C/C++ implementation for American option approximation.

(continued)

```
float sigma_sqr = sigma*sigma;
float time_sqrt = sqrt(time);
float nn = 2.0*b/sigma_sqr;
float m = 2.0*r/sigma_sqr;
float K = 1.0-exp(-r*time);
float q2 = (-(nn-1)+sqrt(pow((nn-1),2.0)+(4*m/K)))*0.5;
float q2_inf =0.5*(-(nn-1) + sqrt(pow((nn-1),2.0)+4.0*m));
float S_star_inf = X / (1.0 - 1.0/q2_inf);
float h2=-(b*time+2.0*sigma*time_sqrt)*(X/(S_star_inf-X));
float S_seed = X + (S_star_inf-X)*(1.0-exp(h2));
int no_iterations=0;
float Si=S_seed;
float g=1;
float gprime=1.0;
while ( no_iterations++<100)
{
   float c  = euro_call_payout(Si,X,r,b,sigma,time);
   float d1 = (log(Si/X)+(b+0.5*sigma_sqr)*time)
/(sigma*time_sqrt);
       g=(1.0-1.0/q2)*Si-X-c+(1.0/q2)*Si*exp((b-
r)*time)*CND(d1);
         gprime=( 1.0-1.0/q2)*(1.0-exp((b-r)*time)*CND(d1))+
(1.0/q2)*exp((b-r)*time)*n(d1)*(1.0/(sigma*time_sqrt));
         Si=Si-(g/gprime);
   };
   float S_star = 0;
   if (fabs(g)>ACCURACY) {
     S_star = S_seed;
   }
   else {
     S_star = Si;
   };
   float C=0;
   float c  = euro_call_payout(S,X,r,b,sigma,time);
   if (S>=S_star) {
     C=S-X;
   }
   else {
      float d1 = (log(S_star/X)+(b+0.5*sigma_sqr)*time) /
  (sigma*time_sqrt);
        float A2 =  (1.0-exp((b-r)*time)*CND(d1))* (S_star/q2);
        C=c+A2*pow((S/S_star),q2);
   };
   return max(C,c);
};
```

FIGURE 8.1, Cont'd

Use ISA upto	GNU Compiler Collection	Intel Composer XE 2015
SSE4.2	-march=Nehalem	-xSSE4.2
AVX	-march=sandybridge	-xAVX
AVX2	-march=haswell	-xCORE_AVX2
AVX512	-march=AVX512F	-xCORE-AVX512

FIGURE 8.2

Microarchitecture/target specifications for GCC and Intel composer XE.

Instruction	GNU Compiler Collection	Intel Composer XE
Approximate divide	-mrecip=div	-no-prec-div
Approximate square root	-mrecip=sqrt	-no-prec-sqrt
FMA	-ffast-math	Default

FIGURE 8.3

Floating point numeric operation control for GCC and Intel composer XE.

TRANSCENDENTAL FUNCTIONS

Financial applications tend to use a lot of transcendental function calls. Managing transcendental function calls can result in big performance advantage. Function calls are expensive, if you can use the basic arithmetic operations to replace a function call, it will be optimal.

Identify special cases to avoid unnecessary function call

In general, function calls are expensive and should be avoided if possible. For example, function call *pow((nn-1), 2.0)* can be replaced by (nn-1)*(nn-1).

Use the correct parameter types

When you have to call a runtime library function, call it with the right parameter type. For example, use powf() instead of pow() in order to spare the compiler from issuing unnecessary but costly float point conversion instructions.

REUSE AS MUCH AS POSSIBLE AND REINVENT AS LITTLE AS POSSIBLE

When you have to call a function or use a constant that is not provided by the runtime library, try to find out if you can compose then from the existing functions or constants. Sometimes, knowing a little about the math behind functions can go a long way. For example, $N(x)$ is related to error function erf(x) via the following formula:

$$N(x) = \frac{1}{2} + \frac{1}{2} * \text{erf}\left(\frac{1}{\sqrt{2}}x\right)$$

Constants such as $\frac{1}{\sqrt{2}}$, $\frac{2}{\sqrt{\pi}}$, $\log_2(E)$, ln 2 are predefined in math.h which are used by both GCC and Intel Composer XE. Always reuse these constants, as listed in Figure 8.4, rather than recalculate them at runtime.

Symbol	Constant	Symbol	Constant
log2(e)	M_LOG2E	E	M_E
log10(e)	M_LOG10E	2/sqrt(π)	M_2_SQRTPI
ln(2)	M_LN2	sqrt(2)	M_SQRT2
ln(10)	M_LN10	1/sqrt(2)	M_SQRT1_2
Π	M_PI	Pi/2	M_PI_2
1/pi	M_1_PI		

FIGURE 8.4

Mathematical constants in math.h available from GCC and Intel composer XE.

```
const float rsqrtf2 = M_SQRT1_2;
float N(float d){
        return .5f + .5f *erff(rsqrtf2 * d);
}
```

FIGURE 8.5

Using optimized C/C++ runtime library with the Intel compiler.

Figure 8.5 shows the implementation of $N(x)$ using erf(x) function and predefined constants. Notice that constant data conversion happens at compile time, which does not affect runtime performance.

Next, we apply a little mathematical background, which can be very handy, in order to get more performance.

SUBEXPRESSION EVALUATION

If (1.0-1.0/q2) is used repeatedly, you may be tempted to evaluate q2 first. This may not be the optimal choice. This is because divide is expensive and if q2 only appears in the denominator, a better choice would be to calculate 1.0/q2 first and turn subsequent division into multiplication as shown in Figure 8.5.

Another example involves square root in the denominator. It turns out that reciprocal of square root is an instruction on our target. If all you need is square root to be a factor in denominator, use reciprocal of square root and a multiplication (Figure 8.6).

The optimized scalar version source listing in Figure 8.7 saves more than 35% of compute cycles compared to the initial version. The performance chart in Figure 8.8 shows the scalar optimization performance gain on Intel® Xeon® Processor v3.

```
float time_sqrt = sqrt(time);
float d1 = (log(S/X) + (r-q + 0.5*sigma_sqr)*time)/(sigma*time_sqrt);

float time_sqrt = rsqrt(time);
float d1 = ((log(S/X) + (r-q + 0.5*sigma_sqr)*time)/sigma)*rsqrt;
```

FIGURE 8.6

Calculate square root or reciprocal of square root.

```
float baw_scalaropt( const float S,
              const float X,
              const float r,
              const float b,
              const float sigma,
              const float time)
{
    float sigma_sqr = sigma*sigma;
    float time_sqrt = sqrtf(time);
    float nn_1 = 2.0f*b/sigma_sqr-1;
    float m = 2.0f*r/sigma_sqr;
    float K = 1.0f-expf(-r*time);
    float rq2 = 1/((-(nn_1)+sqrtf((nn_1)*(nn_1) +(4.f*m/K)))*0.5f);

    float rq2_inf = 1/(0.5f * ( -(nn_1) + sqrtf(nn_1*nn_1+4.0f*m)));
    float S_star_inf = X / (1.0f - rq2_inf);
    float h2 = -(b*time+2.0f*sigma*time_sqrt)*(X/(S_star_inf-X));
    float S_seed = X + (S_star_inf-X)*(1.0f-expf(h2));
    float cndd1 = 0;
    float Si=S_seed;
    float g=1.f;
    float gprime=1.0f;
    float expbr=expf((b-r)*time);
    for (int no_iterations =0; no_iterations<100; no_iterations++) {
        float c  = european_call_opt(Si,X,r,b,sigma,time);
        float d1 = (logf(Si/X)+
                   (b+0.5f*sigma_sqr)*time)/(sigma*time_sqrt);
        float cndd1=cnd_opt(d1);
        g=(1.0f-rq2)*Si-X-c+rq2*Si*expbr*cndd1;
        gprime=( 1.0f-rq2)*(1.0f-expbr*cndd1)+
               rq2*expbr*n_opt(d1)*(1.0f/(sigma*time_sqrt));
        Si=Si-(g/gprime);
    };
    float S_star = 0;
    if (fabs(g)>ACCURACY) {
            S_star = S_seed;
    }
    else {
        S_star = Si;
    };
    float C=0;
    float c  = european_call_opt(S,X,r,b,sigma,time);
    if (S>=S_star) {
        C=S-X;
    }
    else {
        float d1 = (logf(S_star/X)+
                   (b+0.5f*sigma_sqr)*time)/(sigma*time_sqrt);
        float A2 = (1.0f-expbr*cnd_opt(d1))* (S_star*rq2);
        C=c+A2*powf((S/S_star),1/rq2);
    };
    return (C>c)?C:c;
};
```

FIGURE 8.7

Scalar optimized implementation of approximation of pricing American call options.

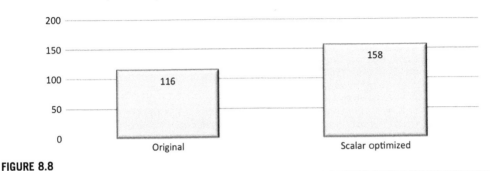

FIGURE 8.8

Scalar optimization impact on an Intel Xeon processor.

SIMD PARALLELISM—VECTORIZATION

Optimizations we have done so far are scalar in nature. Only one input value is fed into an operation and one result is produced after an operation. However, our target ISA (instruction set architecture) is capable of taking multiple data if they are packed in vector registers and operate them together and produce 2, 4, 8, or even 16 results at the same time. The process of packing scalar data into vector data and using vector instructions is called vectorization. Vectorization increases application performance because it can apply the same operation on multiple data and thus deliver multiple results simultaneously.

In this section, we show how to turn the scalar optimized the American option approximation routine baw_sclaropt() into a vector optimized routine. There are two ways to vectorize a scalar routine, manually and automatically. We will cover both in this section. First, we show how to manually or explicitly declare and handle the vector data using the Intel C/C++ compiler. The programming has to follow the vector syntax to ensure that the program produces the same results as its scalar counterpart. Second, we can also annotate the existing scalar program to ask for the vector version and the compiler will generate the vectorized counterpart automatically. In both methods, the programmer has to understand the vector syntax and ensure the final code is equivalent to the scalar version. The difference is that in the automatic method, the compiler handles tedious activities such as the loop trip count calculation based on vector length, remainder loop generation, etc.

DEFINE AND USE VECTOR DATA

Both GCC and the Intel Compiler support vector intrinsic syntax. For example, they both accept vector data type __m256. GCC added vector_size attribute to the basic C type, while Intel added a thin C++ wrapper to vector intrinsic data type. With these extensions, the programmer has the flexibility to handle the vector data either at the high-level C/C++ syntax or at the low-level intrinsic syntax or both. Figure 8.9 summarizes GCC and Intel Compiler's vector extension syntax.

	GNU Compiler Collection	Intel Parallel Composer
Include File	include <intrin.h>	include <immintrin.h>
Intrinsics	__m256 a;	__m256 a;
C/C++ Single	typedef float vsf __attribute__ ((vector_size (16)));	F32vec8 vsf;
C/C++ Double	typedef double vdf __attribute__ ((vector_size (16)));	F64vec4 vdf;

FIGURE 8.9

Vector intrinsic and vector extension in GCC and Intel composer XE 2015.

```
F32vec8 baw_vecopt(F32vec8 S, F32vec8 X,  F32vec8 r,
            F32vec8 b,   F32vec8 sigma,F32vec8 time);
```

FIGURE 8.10

Vector routine declaration using vector class in Intel composer XE 2015.

The rest of this section uses Intel vector class wherever possible when we declare and handle the vector data. Figure 8.10 shows the profile of our American pricing function with vector data types.

VECTOR ARITHMETIC OPERATIONS

One of the benefits of using C++ class syntax is that C/C++ operators, such as $+ - * /$, can easily be overloaded to operate on the vector class. Statements such as:

F32vec8 sigma_sqr = sigma*sigma; work because of C++ operator overloading. However, the vector syntax does not allow mixed scalar vector operation. You cannot write F32vec8 nn_1 = 2.0f*b/sigma_sqr − 1.0f. Nevertheless, the code in Figure 8.11 is perfectly fine.

One of the benefits of using vector classes is that this syntax allows you to mix your code with the intrinsic code if you don't find the operation you want. In this example, we explicitly use one of the swizzle instructions, vector blend for branch statement.

The benefit of using vector classes, as opposed to intrinsics, is that vector classes rely on the compiler to do instruction selection, while direct intrinsic usage shifts that responsibility to the programmer. Target-dependent instructions such as FMA can be generated automatically when using vector classes, and may have to be explicitly rewritten for each new target when intrinsics have been used.

```
F32vec8 twof = F32vec8(2.0f);
F32vec8 onef = F32vec8(1.0f);
F32vec8 nn_1 = twof*b/sigma_sqr - onef;
```

FIGURE 8.11

Simple arithmetic operation using vector class in Intel composer XE 2015.

VECTOR FUNCTION CALL

Function calls on vector data work because there are vector versions of that same function. There is no need to differentiate the function by its input data type because of the polymorphism on C++. Figure 8.12 shows the vector code for the initial setup for the Newton-Raphson iteration.

Any function you have to call that is not provided by the C/C++ runtime library will have to be written. Figure 8.13 is the vectorized version of general Black-Scholes European option with yield q on underlying financial asset.

BRANCH STATEMENTS

Branch statements break the vector execution model because they require different operation for different data elements. So far, our vector execution model applies the same operation to each data element. In our case, we have a few simple two-way IF-statements. In general, we have to evaluate the state changes on each branch of the IF statement and apply those changes to the vector data based on the IF conditions.

Figure 8.14 shows how a vectorized if-statement can be implemented using vector compare and the blend instructions.

The first statement is a vector comparison. It compares the corresponding data elements between the two vector input registers and sets a mask register that records the comparison result. The second statement first evaluates both branches of the statement as it prepares the first two parameters, and

```
F32vec8 twof = F32vec8(2.0f);
F32vec8 onef = F32vec8(1.0f);
F32vec8 sigma_sqr = sigma*sigma;
F32vec8 time_sqrt = sqrt(time);
F32vec8 nn_1 = twof*b/sigma_sqr - onef;
F32vec8 m = twof*r/sigma_sqr;
F32vec8 K = onef-exp(-r*time);
F32vec8 halff = F32vec8(0.5f);
F32vec8 fourf = F32vec8(4.0f);
F32vec8 rq2 = rcp((-(nn_1)+
                sqrt((nn_1)*(nn_1)+(fourf*m/K)))*halff);
F32vec8 rq2_inf = rcp(halff * (-(nn_1) +
                 sqrt(nn_1*nn_1,twof)+fourf*m)));
F32vec8 S_star_inf = X / (onef -rq2_inf );
F32vec8 h2 = -(b*time+twof*sigma*time_sqrt)*
                (X/(S_star_inf-X));
F32vec8 S_seed = X + (S_star_inf-X)*(onef-exp(h2));
int no_iterations=0;
F32vec8 Si=S_seed;
F32vec8 g=onef;
F32vec8 gprime=onef;
```

FIGURE 8.12

First few line of code for the routines using the Intel compiler.

```
__forceinline
F32vec8 N(F32vec8 x)
{
    return halff + halff*erf(rsqrtf2*x);
}

F32vec8 bs_call( F32vec8 S,
        F32vec8 X,
        F32vec8 r,
        F32vec8 q,
        F32vec8 sigma,
        F32vec8 time)
{
    F32vec8 sigma_sqr = sigma*sigma;
    F32vec8 time_sqrt = sqrt(time);
    F32vec8 d1 =(log(S/X)+(r-q+ halff*sigma_sqr)*time)/(sigma*time_sqrt);
    F32vec8 d2 = d1-(sigma*time_sqrt);
    F32vec8 call_price =S*exp(-q*time)* N(d1) - X * exp(-r*time) * N(d2);
    return call_price;
};
```

FIGURE 8.13

User-defined vector function using vector class from the Intel compiler.

```
        if (fabs(g)>ACCURACY)
        { S_star = S_seed; }
        else
        { S_star = Si; };

        __m256 solved = _mm256_cmp_ps(g, F32vec8(ACCURACY),
    _CMP_GT_OQ);
            S_star = _mm256_blendv_ps(Si, S_seed, solved);
```

FIGURE 8.14

First branch statement using vector class with the Intel compiler.

selectively applies either of them based on the comparison result. In general, the IF-statement reduces the efficiency of the vector code execution because both branches have to be evaluated to complete a vector branch statement. You can clearly see it in the second branch statement implemented in Figure 8.15.

Since d1 and A2 are used only to calculate C, it is harmless to do it outside the branch. The fact that both branches of the conditional statement end up executed makes it less efficient for vector programming. Theoretically, if every statement in a routine is a branch statement, the vector version could be slower than the scalar version. However, if there is only a small portion of the statements are branch statements, as is the case here, it still makes sense to vectorize the routine.

```
if (S>=S_star) {
      C=S-X;
}
else {
      float d1 = (log(S_star/X)+
                  (b+0.5*sigma_sqr)*time)/(sigma*time_sqrt);
      float A2 = (1.0-exp((b-r)*time)*CND(d1))* (S_star/q2);
      C=c+A2*pow((S/S_star),q2);
};

F32vec8 d1 = (log(S_star/X)+
                  (b+halff*sigma_sqr)*time)/(sigma*time_sqrt);
F32vec8 A2 = (onef-exp((b-r)*time)*N(d1))* (S_star*rq2);
C = _mm256_blendv_ps(S-X,
                  c+A2*pow((S/S_star), rcp(rq2)),
                  _mm256_cmp_ps(S, S_star, _CMP_LT_OQ));
```

FIGURE 8.15

Second branch statement using vector class with the Intel compiler.

```
#include <dvec.h>
    simd_max(a, b)
    simd_min(a, b)
```

FIGURE 8.16

Vertical simd operations as part of vector ISA in Intel composer XE 2015.

To minimize the branch statement impact, certain conditional execution capabilities have been built-in to the vector processing unit. For example, vertical operation to find maximum and minimum are part of vector instruction set. You can access them in C/C++ as they are listed in Figure 8.16. You can take advantage of them and reduce the branch statements in your code. The last line of the code in the vector source code actually takes advantage of this fact and avoids another branch.

Putting all together, we have a complete vector version of American call approximation in Figure 8.17.

CALLING THE VECTOR VERSION AND THE SCALAR VERSION OF THE PROGRAM

To find out how much performance gain we have achieved due to vectorization, we have to put both scalar optimized and vector version in a test program. To call the vector version, we have to prepare the input data in vector registers and take the result data from a vector register to a memory location. Loading to and storing from the vector registers are two subjects we have been avoiding. However, we cannot avoid it any more if we indeed intend to use both vector and scalar version and measure the performance.

```
F32vec8 baw_vecopt(F32vec8 S,
                 F32vec8 X,
                 F32vec8 r,
                 F32vec8 b,
                 F32vec8 sigma,
                 F32vec8 time)
{
    F32vec8 sigma_sqr = sigma*sigma;
    F32vec8 time_sqrt = sqrt(time);
    F32vec8 nn_1 = twof*b*rcp_nr(sigma_sqr) - onef;
    F32vec8 m = twof*r*rcp_nr(sigma_sqr);
    F32vec8 K = onef-exp(-r*time);
    F32vec8 rq2 = rcp_nr((-
(nn_1)+sqrt(nn_1*nn_1+(fourf*m*rcp_nr(K))))*halff);
    F32vec8 rq2_inf = rcp_nr(halff * ( -(nn_1) +
sqrt(nn_1*nn_1+fourf*m)));
    F32vec8 S_star_inf = X *rcp_nr(onef -rq2_inf );
    F32vec8 h2 = -
(b*time+twof*sigma*time_sqrt)*(X*rcp_nr(S_star_inf-X));
    F32vec8 S_seed = X + (S_star_inf-X)*(onef-exp(h2));

    int no_iterations=0;
    F32vec8 Si=S_seed;
    F32vec8 g=onef;
    F32vec8 gprime=onef;
    while ( no_iterations++<100) {
       F32vec8 c  = bs_call(Si,X,r,b,sigma,time);
       F32vec8 d1 =
(log(Si/X)+(b+halff*sigma_sqr)*time)/(sigma*time_sqrt);
       g=(onef-rq2)*Si-X-c+rq2*Si*exp((b-r)*time)*N(d1);
       gprime=( onef-rq2)*(onef-exp((b-r)*time)*N(d1))
           +rq2*exp((b-r)*time)*vn(d1)*(onef/(sigma*time_sqrt));
       Si=Si-(g/gprime);
    };
    F32vec8 S_star = F32vec8(0.0f);
    __m256 solved = _mm256_cmp_ps(abs(g), F32vec8(ACCURACY),
_CMP_GT_OQ);
    S_star = _mm256_blendv_ps(Si, S_seed, solved);
    F32vec8 C = F32vec8(0.0f);
    F32vec8 c  = bs_call(S,X,r,b,sigma,time);
    F32vec8 d1 =
(log(S_star*rcp_nr(X))+(b+halff*sigma_sqr)*time)*rcp_nr(sigma*time
_sqrt);
    F32vec8 A2 =   (onef-exp((b-r)*time)*N(d1))* (S_star*rq2);
    C = _mm256_blendv_ps(c+A2*pow((S/S_star), onef/rq2), S-X,
_mm256_cmp_ps(S, S_star, _CMP_GE_OQ));
    return simd_max(C,c);
}
```

FIGURE 8.17

The vector version of American call approximation.

Loading to and storing from vector registers

Option data normally sits in the main memory. For the scalar version, transferring the input value one data element a time should be OK. But for vector version, it would be too slow. At the C/C++ level, we can declare a vector register quantity and deference a memory address. The compiler generates the vector load and store for you. Assuming StockMem is the variable where current stock price is stored and ResultMem is the memory variable where the result you would expect. They are both aligned to 4-byte or 32-bit memory boundary. Source code in Figure 8.18 will result in correct vector load and store instructions.

Calling vector version of the program

Let's further assume that the stock price is stored in an array and layout in memory one next to another without any gap. So are the other input parameters. The output parameter is also laid out in the memory contiguously. The risk-free rate R is scalar, we can broadcast it to a vector data type so it can be used across all lanes.

We should expect the source code like Figure 8.19 to exercise the vector version of the American call option approximation program. The performance of vector version is compared with the original and scalar optimized version in Figure 8.20.

Comparing vector and scalar version

Let's use input arrays of size of 125.9 million elements, running one thread for scalar version and one thread for vector version. On Intel® Xeon® E5-2697 processor with two sockets and 14-cores per socket, at 2.6 GHz, the scalar version achieves 157.62 K options/s, the vector version achieves 560.536 K options/s as in Figure 8.20.

```
F32vec8 S = * (F32vec8*) &StockMem;
F32vec8 res = baw_vecopt (S,X,R,b,v,T);
* (F32vec8 *) & (ResultMem) = res;
```

FIGURE 8.18

Loading to and storing from vector registers.

```
for (int opt = 0; opt < OptPerThread; opt += 8)
{
        F32vec8 T = * (F32vec8*) &OptionYears[opt];
        F32vec8 S = * (F32vec8*) &StockPrice[opt];
        F32vec8 X = * (F32vec8*) &OptionStrike[opt];
        F32vec8 b = * (F32vec8*) &CostofCarry[opt];
        F32vec8 v = * (F32vec8*) &Volatility[opt];
        * (F32vec8 *) & (CallResult[opt]) = baw_vecopt (S,X,R,b,v,T);

}
```

FIGURE 8.19

Loading option input data into the vector register, call the approximation program and then same the result.

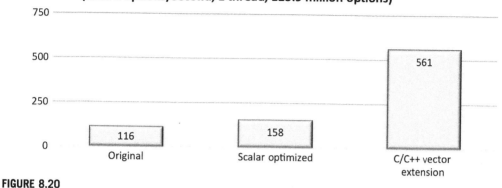

FIGURE 8.20

American option approximation gain on vectorization using C/C++ vector extensions on an Intel Xeon processor.

VECTORIZATION BY ANNOTATING THE SOURCE CODE: #PRAGMA SIMD

The code vectorization we achieve so far comes from explicit handling of SIMD data types. The programmer can choose either C/C++ vector extensions using high-level language constructs or just the processor intrinsic functions. The programmer has to express the underlying algorithm using the vector syntax that usually results in a rewrite of the original scalar program. The vector code generation is the direct result of using the vector constructs in the program.

An alternate way of achieving code vectorization is by annotation of the original scalar program with high-level language directives such as #pragma. The explicit vector programming is achieved by the programmer using #pragma SIMD directive for the portion of the code to be vectorized. The benefit of #pragma SIMD is that the program does not have to create another vector version of the same program. Neither is there a need to choose or even care about the instructions for the vector program. The compiler analyzes the serial program and the vector directives and generates vector code on programmer's behalf. In our example, the code annotation occurred at the caller for the scalar optimized routines, as in Figure 8.21.

To ensure the compiler can vectorize the code, the program has to tell the compiler what to do when a function call happens. The vectorizer inside the compiler has two choices. Either inline the function or find a version of the same function that takes the vector parameters. In our case, we inline the function call to baw_scalaropt and also to a few other functions that it calls that we defined. Runtime library functions such as expf(x), logf(x), and sqrtf(x) all have their counter parts with vector parameters.

Source listing in Figure 8.22 shows how custom defined functions and runtime functions are used in annotation based vector programming.

C/C++ VECTOR EXTENSION VERSUS #PRAGMA SIMD

In this section, we show two distinctive styles of explicit vector programming: C/C++ vector extensions and #pragma SIMD. Both result in SIMD instruction taking advantage of the vector processing unit in the modern microprocessors. But they are uniquely different. With the C/C++ vector extensions, you

```
sTime = second();
    #pragma vector nontemporal (CallResult)
    #pragma simd
    #pragma vector aligned
for (int opt = 0; opt < OptPerThread; opt++)
{

        float T = OptionYears[opt];
        float S = StockPrice[opt];
        float X = OptionStrike[opt];
        float b = CostofCarry[opt];
        float v = Volatility[opt];

        CallResult[opt] = baw_scalaropt(S,X,RISKFREE,b, v, T);
}
eTime = second();
printf("Completed pricing %7.5f million options in %7.5f seconds:\n",
        OPT_N/1e6, eTime-sTime);
printf(
"Scalar %s version runs at %7.5f Thousand options per second.\n",
        (ThreadNum > 1)?"parallel":"serial", OPT_N/(1e3*(eTime-sTime)));
```

FIGURE 8.21

Vectoriztion by annotating the scalar source code.

have to declare and handle the vector data yourself. You have to rewrite the existing scalar code using vector syntax. While the #pragma SIMD approach works with the scalar code, you don't have to rewrite new code, you just have to decorate the existing scalar code to tell the compiler vectorizer the certain actions you want while the scalar code is vectorized by the compiler. So, from productivity point of view, #pragma SIMD usually achieves higher productivity.

The second argument is the code generation. With the C/C++ vector extension, an intrinsic function is ultimate defined for each numerical operation, which limits the compiler's capability to optimize the instruction selection. This explains why #pragma SIMD can achieve slightly higher performance when it's obvious to the compiler what the program is trying to do. Figure 8.23 shows that, in our case, vector programming with #pragma SIMD can achieve higher performance.

In general, when you try to get your code to vectorize, annotate the code well so that the compiler knows what you are trying to do; apply #pragma SIMD to see if it vectorizes your code correctly. Use C/C++ vector extension for the code that the compiler cannot vectorize or it's impossible to annotate the programmer's intension.

THREAD PARALLELIZATION

Modern microprocessors, from the one in your cell phones to the one in big data centers, are all multi-core. This means that you have to create threads to get the processor cores fully working for you. On our Intel® Xeon® E5-2697 processor-based system, there are 28 cores and 56 threads. So far, our vectorized program can only create one thread and take advantage of not more than, most of the time less than, one

```
    __forceinline
float cnd_opt(float d){
  return 0.5f +0.5f*erff(float(M_SQRT1_2)*d);
}

    __forceinline
float n_opt(const float z) {
    return (1.0f/sqrtf(2.0f*PI))*expf(-0.5f*z*z);
};

    __forceinline
float european_call_opt( const float S,
              const float X,
              const float r,
              const float q,
              const float sigma,
              const float time)
{
    float sigma_sqr = sigma*sigma;
    float time_sqrt = sqrtf(time);
    float d1 = (logf(S/X) + (r-q + 0.5f*sigma_sqr)*time)/
               (sigma*time_sqrt);
    float d2 = d1-(sigma*time_sqrt);
    float call_price = S * expf(-q*time)* cnd_opt(d1) -
                      X * expf(-r*time) * cnd_opt(d2);
    return call_price;
};
    __forceinline
float baw_scalaropt( const float S,
              const float X,
              const float r,
              const float b,
              const float sigma,
              const float time){ . . .};
```

FIGURE 8.22

Custom function calls are inlined to enable compiler-based vectorization.

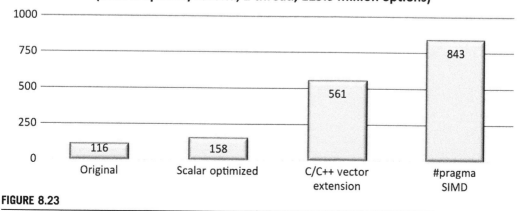

**American option approximation
gain using vector extension vs.# pragma SIMD
(unit: K options/second, 1 thread, 125.9 million options)**

Original	Scalar optimized	C/C++ vector extension	#pragma SIMD
116	158	561	843

FIGURE 8.23

#Pragma SIMD with performance advantage on an Intel Xeon processor.

core performance potential of the total system. To tap the performance offered by the rest of the cores, we have to create more threads and split the input parameters so that multiple threads can work simultaneously. In our example, we can split our total option data into 56 pieces and assignment each piece to a thread and have each thread work on a different set of input data. The number 56 matches the number of hardware threads on this system. We can use OpenMP to manage the creation and destroy process. However to ensure the multithreaded application works harmoniously, we have to pay attention to memory allocation and thread binding.

MEMORY ALLOCATION IN NUMA SYSTEM

In a serial application, since there is only one thread, memory allocations usually take place at the beginning of the program. As a result, the application usually gets a huge chunk of memory local to the core that executes your main program. In a two socket, two memory controller platform, this memory allocation model enables half of the threads to have fast local memory accesses and half of the threads to have more expensive remote memory access (i.e., across the socket interconnect, today known as QPI). In a multithreaded application, a better memory allocation model would be to create worker threads first before any memory application takes place. Another concern for memory allocation in a multithreaded application is the thread-safety of the allocation library and the scalability of the interface with the number of working threads. We can address both concerns by using Intel Threading Building Blocks (TBB) as we demonstrate in Figure 8.24.

```
#include <tbb/scalable_allocator.h>
#include <omp.h>
#pragma omp parallel
{
#ifdef _OPENMP
        threadID = omp_get_thread_num();
#else
        threadID = 0;
#endif
        float *Call =
                (float *)scalable_aligned_malloc(msize, ASIZE);
        float *Stock =
                (float *)scalable_aligned_malloc(msize, ASIZE);
        float *Strike =
                (float *)scalable_aligned_malloc(msize, ASIZE);
        ... ... ...

        scalable_aligned_free(Call);
        scalable_aligned_free(Stock);
        scalable_aligned_free(Strike);
}
```

FIGURE 8.24

Using OpenMP and TBB memory allocation to create worker thread and then allocate memory from the worker thread.

THREAD BINDING AND AFFINITY INTERFACE

Worker threads created by using OpenMP #pragma are user-level threads, which execute application code on behalf of the programmer. At execution time, the OpenMP runtime library will work with the host-operating system to secure a kernel schedulable entry also known as threads, or kernel threads. On Intel® Xeon® processor, each core has two kernel threads, while on Intel® Xeon Phi™ coprocessors, each core support has four kernel threads. The process of mapping user threads to kernel threads at the runtime is called thread binding. Thread binding is important because kernel threads from difference cores and sockets may share resources such as cache memory bandwidth, etc. The programmer can take advantage of these differences and specify a binding strategy that maximizes application performance.

In our example, for the dual-socket processor, we want to use both kernel threads a core supports and we want to use them in a way that memory bandwidth demand for the system is constant and will not vary during the course of program execution. In Figure 8.25, we demonstrate the code to accomplish this objective.

Figure 8.26 adds the 28-core 56-thread parallel performance to the previous comparison.

To measure the real performance, we just have to time the performance from the beginning to the end. Since each thread is doing exactly the same amount of work, we can safely measure the top-to-bottom time on the busiest thread. The source listing in Figure 8.27 is the way we measure the scalar parallel performance.

SCALE FROM MULTICORE TO MANY-CORE

As the last exercise, we take the vectorized and parallelized source program and rebuild them to run natively on Intel® Xeon Phi™ coprocessor codename KNC. Using the Intel Compiler, we just have to inform the compiler the target is the coprocessor by using –mmic instead of –xCORE-AVX2. For #pragma SIMD-based code, since there is no direct reference of any processor intrinsic functions, we don't even have to make any changes to the source code at all. To demonstrate that the compiler still made aggressive optimizations for execution on the coprocessor, we can compare the vectorized C runtime math function calls by looking at their compiler generated listing files.

icpc -c –S -xCORE_AVX2 -openmp -O3 -ipo -restrict -fimf-precision=low -fimf-domain-exclusion=31 -fno-alias -qopt-report=5 -o am_call_vp.s am_call.cpp

```
#ifdef _OPENMP
        kmp_set_defaults("KMP_AFFINITY=scatter, granularity=fine");
        int ThreadNum = omp_get_max_threads();
        omp_set_num_threads(ThreadNum);
#else
        int ThreadNum = 1;
#endif
```

FIGURE 8.25

Create one user thread for each kernel thread and put the adjacent user thread as far away as possible so that the resource demand to the system are constant.

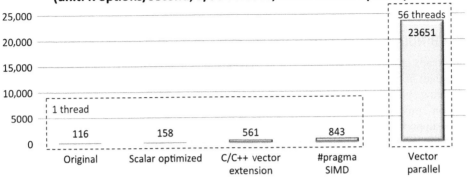

FIGURE 8.26

American option approximation gain on parallelization on an Intel Xeon processor.

```
#include <sys/time.h>
#include <time.h>

#pragma omp parallel
{
#ifdef _OPENMP
      threadID = omp_get_thread_num();
#else
      threadID = 0;
#endif
// allocate memory

// Read-in the input data
#pragma omp master
      sTime = second();

#pragma vector nontemporal (CallResult)
for (int opt = 0; opt < OptPerThread; opt++)
{
      float T = OptionYears[opt];
      float S = StockPrice[opt];
      float X = OptionStrike[opt];
      float b = CostofCarry[opt];
      float v = Volatility[opt];
      CallResult[opt] = baw_scalaropt(S,X,RISKFREE,b,v,T);
}

#pragma omp master
{
      eTime = second();
      printf(
      "Completed pricing %7.5f million options in %7.5f seconds:\n",
            OPT_N/1e6, eTime-sTime);
      printf(
      "Parallel version runs at %7.5f Thousand options per second.\n",
            OPT_N/(1e3*(eTime-sTime)));
      }
// de-allocate memory
}
```

FIGURE 8.27

Core parallelization using OpemMP4.0 for American options approximation.

icpc -c –S -xCORE_AVX2 -openmp -O3 -ipo -restrict -fimf-precision=low -fimf-domain-exclusion=31 -fno-alias -qopt-report=5 -o am_call_knc.s am_call.cpp

All vectorized runtime math functions start their name with __svml_, we can grep the pattern from these listing files. What you will see is four difference function calls resulting from using expf(x), logf(x), erff(x) powf(x) in the source code in –xCORE_AVX2 targeted listing file, while you will see 0 on –mmic targeted listing file. What happened to the vectorized math library function calls on the coprocessor? It turns out that the coprocessor has exp2(x) and log2(x) instructions. Calls to exp(x) and log(x) can easily be composed of exp2(x) and log2(x), so is the powf(x). As for erff(x), the Intel Compiler inlined its implementation so that its code sequence is dropped right into the source code for baw_scalaropt(). The rationale behind inline math functions is to avoid function call overhead. Figure 8.28 lists equivalences between Intel Xeon processor highest performance method and on an Intel Xeon Phi coprocessor.

You can aggressively inline as many runtime math function calls you want. However, the benefit will drop when your basic block reaches a certain size. You can run out of registers for the compiler to do other optimizations and you can increase instruction TLB misses at runtime. Function inlining is something you have to experiment with in your source code. In general, if you have a small tight loop, you usually can expect a performance pay off from function inlining. In our case, it pays off big. Figure 8.29 shows the three levels of optimization gains achieved on American option pricing algorithm on Intel Xeon and Xeon Phi™ processors. For the Intel Xeon Phi coprocessor runs, the transcendental functions and inlining single precision small vector math library (svml) calls allows the compiler to create code that is effectively all vectorized. Figure 8.30 shows the resulting strong performance on an Intel Xeon Phi coprocessor (the rightmost bar, the other bars are on a Intel Xeon processor code named Haswell).

4th Gen. Intel® Xeon Processor	Intel® Xeon Phi™ Coprocessor
__svml_expf8_ep	Use `vexp223ps` instruction and compose
__svml_logf8_ep	Use `vlog2ps` instruction and compose
__svml_erff8_ep	inline to avoid call overhead
__svml_powf8_ep	Compose of `vlog2ps` and `vexp223ps`

FIGURE 8.28

Math runtime function implementation on Intel® Xeon® and Intel® Xeon Phi™ products.

Methodology	Processor Gain Ratio	Coprocessor Gain Ratio
Scalar optimization	1.357	4.943
SIMD parallelism	5.350	15.812
Core parallelism	28.047	168.287

FIGURE 8.29

American option approximation gain on all three types of performance improvement.

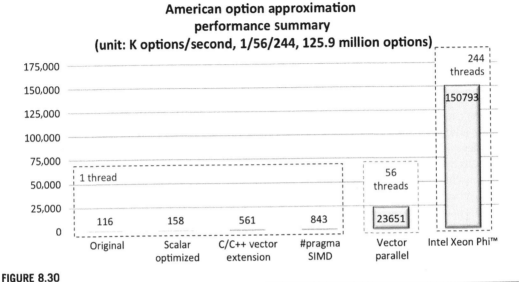

FIGURE 8.30

American option approximation results on Xeon processor (up to 56 threads on 28 cores), with final run on Intel Xeon Phi coprocessor (244 threads on 61 cores).

SUMMARY

In this chapter, we looked at how Newton-Raphson method can be used to approximate American call options. We have taken one example of such algorithm pioneered by Barone-Adsi and Whaley and applied processor specific optimizations and enabled SIMD and multicore parallel programming to achieve more than 200× gain on the same hardware: 28-core Intel Xeon E5-2697 processors. We also demonstrated that the same methodology and common toolset enables us to make easy transition from the multicore platform to many-core platform with zero source code changes and make even more impressive performance gains on Intel Xeon Phi 7210 coprocessors, the first generation Intel Xeon Phi product. This is possible because of the similarity between the Intel Xeon and Intel many-core products. The closeness of their ISAs enables a single set of development tools, which also makes the common source possible.

In the end, approximation methods such as Newton-Raphson technique have been widely used by financial mathematicians in derivative pricing, risk management and portfolio analysis. You can apply the same optimization framework and achieve impressive gains in other approximation based algorithms.

FOR MORE INFORMATION

- Barone-Adesi, G.,Whaley, R.E., 1987. Efficient analytic approximation of american option values. J. Finance 42, 301-320.

- Brennan, M.J., Schwartz, E.S., 1978. Finite difference methods and jump processes arising in the pricing of contingent claims: a synthesis. J. Finan. Quant. Anal. 13, 461-474.
- Cox, J.C., Ross, S., Rubinstein, M., 1979. Option pricing: a simplified approach. J. Finan. Econ. 7, 229-264.
- Tian, Y.S., 1993. A Modified lattice approach to option pricing. J. Futures Mark. 13 563-577.
- Meyerov, I., Sysoyev, A., Astafiev, N., Burylov, I. Performance Optimization of Black-Scholes Pricing High Performance Parallelism Pearls—Multicore and Many-core Programming Approaches, pp. 319-340 (Chapter 19).
- Download the code from this, and other chapters, http://lotsofcores.com.

WILSON DSLASH KERNEL FROM LATTICE QCD OPTIMIZATION

9

Bálint Joó*, Mikhail Smelyanskiy[†], Dhiraj D. Kalamkar[‡], Karthikeyan Vaidyanathan[‡]

U.S. Department of Energy, Thomas Jefferson National Accelerator Facility (Jefferson Lab), USA*
Parallel Computing Lab, Intel Corporation, California, USA[†] Parallel Computing Lab,
Intel Corporation, India[‡]

Quantum chromodynamics (QCD) is the theory of the strong nuclear force, one of the fundamental forces of nature making up the Standard Model of particle interactions. QCD is responsible for binding quarks together into protons and neutrons, which in turn make up the nuclei of atoms. Lattice quantum chromodynamics, (lattice QCD or LQCD) is a version of QCD suitable for use on computers. It is the only model independent approach for carrying out nonperturbative calculations in QCD, and it is used primarily in calculations for theoretical nuclear and high energy physics. Lattice QCD simulations of quarks and gluons were one of the original Grand Challenge problems in High Performance Computing, and lattice QCD codes are typically implemented early on new high performance computing systems. Lattice QCD calculations use significant proportions of supercomputer time in the United States and worldwide. As an example, in 2014 lattice QCD calculations were responsible for consuming 13% of the computer resources at the U.S. Department of Energy, National Energy Research Scientific Computing Center (NERSC).

In this chapter, we will explore a key kernel of LQCD calculations, known as the Wilson-Dslash kernel. This kernel is essentially a finite difference operator, similar in spirit to stencils. We will outline our optimizations of this operator for the Intel Xeon Phi coprocessor following the methods described first in our paper "Lattice QCD on Intel Xeon Phi coprocessors" (see the "For more information" section at the end of this chapter for the specific information). Our approach is to take the reader on a journey, starting from an existing production implementation of this operator which already features thread-level parallelism, and yet still does not achieve very high performance when deployed on the Intel Xeon Phi coprocessor. By comparing performances with a simple performance model, we will proceed to show how improving cache reuse and memory bandwidth utilization along with vectorization can improve the performance of this code by more than a factor of $8\times$ over the original implementation running on Intel Xeon Phi coprocessor. What is more, when we feed the optimizations back to regular Intel Xeon processors, we observe a $2.6\times$ performance improvement over the best configuration of the original code on that platform too.

Throughout the chapter we will make reference to the supplied Code package, which contains both our initial implementation of Wilson-Dslash as well as the optimized one, along with some dependency libraries. While we concentrate primarily on these two Dslash implementations and a code generator, the Code package features many directories which we set up to allow the code to be built in different configurations, utilizing different optimizations. Throughout the chapter we will always highlight the directory in the Code package where one should work in order to follow our discussion. We note up-front, that our work on the Intel Xeon Phi coprocessor architecture was done exclusively in *native-mode* rather than using heterogeneous, offload techniques. For build instructions in the Code package, we urge the reader to follow the supplied README file.

THE WILSON-DSLASH KERNEL

In this section, we will describe the Wilson-Dslash kernel and consider some of its computational properties. Before going into the nitty gritty let us say a few words about the LQCD setup. The idea is that instead of the usual continuum we represent four-dimensional space-time as a four-dimensional (hyper)cubic lattice. Each lattice point has coordinates $x = (n_x, n_y, n_z, n_t)$ where the components are just the coordinates in the usual X, Y, Z, and T directions. The quark fields are defined on the lattice sites and are known as *spinors*, denoted as $\psi(x)$. For current purposes $\psi(x)$ can be thought of as a set of complex numbers with two additional indices which are called "color" and "spin." So a quark field at site x is denoted $\psi_\alpha^a(x)$ with $a = \{0,1,2\}$ being the color indices, and $\alpha = \{0,1,2,3\}$ being the spin indices. In general, Latin indices will indicate color, and Greek-letter indices will indicate spin. In addition to the quark fields, one also has fields for the gluons known as *gauge fields*. These are ascribed to directed links between lattice points and for this reason they are often referred to as *gluon links* or *link matrices*. Typically they are denoted as $U_\mu^{ab}(x)$ where a and b are color indices again, but μ is a *direction* index. For $\mu = \{0,1,2,3\}$ we understand that $U_\mu^{ab}(x)$ is the gluon field on the link *emanating* from site x, in the forward direction in X, Y, Z, and T directions, respectively. As one can guess from the Latin indices, on each link U is a 3×3 complex matrix in *color*, with no spin index. Further, U is more than just a 3×3 matrix, it is also a member of the group $SU(3)$, which means that it is *unitary*, so that the Hermitian Conjugate of any given link matrix (the transpose of the matrix with each element complex conjugated) is its inverse: $(U^{a,b})^\dagger = (U^{b,a})^* = U^{-1}$ and each matrix has determinant $\det(U_\mu^{a,b}(x)) = 1$.

With these definitions in mind, we can write down the Wilson-Dslash operator D, acting on a quark spinor ψ as:

$$D_{\alpha,\beta}^{a,b}(x,y)\psi_\beta^b(y) = \sum_{\mu=0}^{3} U_\mu^{a,b}(x)P_{\alpha,\beta}^{-\mu}\psi_\beta^b(x+\hat{\mu}) + U^{\dagger\,a,b}(x-\hat{\mu})P_{\alpha,\beta}^{+\mu}\psi_\beta^b(x-\hat{\mu}),$$ (9.1)

where in the equation above, *repeated indices are summed over*, and the $P^{\pm\mu}$ are *projection matrices* acting on *spin indices*. We can also see that the operation is like a stencil: for each output point x, we use the spinors from the neighboring points in the forward and backward μ directions: $\psi(x+\hat{\mu})$ and $\psi(x-\hat{\mu})$; and the sum involves all four directions. Each spinor from a neighboring site is multiplied by the link connecting the central site to it. So $\psi(x+\hat{\mu})$ is multiplied by $U_\mu(x)$ and $\psi(x-\hat{\mu})$ is multiplied by $U^\dagger(x-\hat{\mu})$, which—because of the Hermitian conjugation—should be interpreted as the "inverse" of the link pointing from $x-\hat{\mu}$ to x, that is, the link pointing from x to $x-\hat{\mu}$.

The multiplication by the U links is done only for the color indices, and must be repeated for each of the four spin indices. It may help to think of the spinor as a four-component vector, where each component is itself a three-component complex vector (also known as a color-vector, or color 3-vector). Likewise, the multiplication by $P^{\pm\mu}$ is done only for spin-indices, and must be repeated for each of the three color indices of ψ. In this case, and when working with spin-indices, it may be helpful to consider the spinor as an object with three elements, each of which is a four-component vector (spin-vector).

One final trick to consider is due to the nature of the projectors: $P^{\pm\mu} = (1 \pm \gamma_\mu)$. The γ_μ are 4×4 complex matrices acting only on spins, and they are sparse. We choose them to be in a particular representation which we show below:

$$\gamma_0 = \begin{pmatrix} 0 & 0 & 0 & i \\ 0 & 0 & i & 0 \\ 0 & -i & 0 & 0 \\ -i & 0 & 0 & 0 \end{pmatrix} \quad \gamma_1 = \begin{pmatrix} 0 & 0 & 0 & -1 \\ 0 & 0 & 1 & 0 \\ 0 & 1 & 0 & 0 \\ -1 & 0 & 0 & 0 \end{pmatrix}$$

$$\gamma_2 = \begin{pmatrix} 0 & 0 & i & 0 \\ 0 & 0 & 0 & -i \\ -i & 0 & 0 & 0 \\ 0 & i & 0 & 0 \end{pmatrix} \quad \gamma_3 = \begin{pmatrix} 0 & 0 & 1 & 0 \\ 0 & 0 & 0 & 1 \\ 1 & 0 & 0 & 0 \\ 0 & 1 & 0 & 0 \end{pmatrix}$$

The projectors possess a particular property which we illustrate below for the case for P^{-0}. Let us consider the spinor ψ_α^a on a single site, for just one color component, say $a = 0$ for simplicity (and of course this is repeated for all color components). We can write $\psi_\alpha = (\psi_0, \psi_1, \psi_2, \psi_3)^T$. Then

$$P^{-0}\psi = \begin{pmatrix} 1 & 0 & 0 & -i \\ 0 & 1 & -i & 0 \\ 0 & i & 1 & 0 \\ i & 0 & 0 & 1 \end{pmatrix} \begin{pmatrix} \psi_0 \\ \psi_1 \\ \psi_2 \\ \psi_3 \end{pmatrix} = \begin{pmatrix} \psi_0 - i\psi_3 \\ \psi_1 - i\psi_2 \\ i\psi_1 + \psi_2 \\ i\psi_0 + \psi_3 \end{pmatrix} = \begin{pmatrix} h_0 \\ h_1 \\ -ih_1 \\ -ih_0 \end{pmatrix}, \tag{9.2}$$

where we defined $h_0 = \psi_0 - i\psi_3$ and $h_1 = \psi_1 - i\psi_2$. In other words, the lower two spin components of the result (to which we will refer as r_2 and r_3) are the same as the upper two, but multiplied by $-i$. This property is general, and applies to all of the projectors, although the details do vary with the projector in question. The action of finding the right h_0 and h_1 is known as *projection* and the placement into the lower components and the multiplies by i, etc. is called *reconstruction*. We show the details of how to perform these operations for all the projectors, with our particular choice of γ matrices in the table shown in Figure 9.1. The practical use of this property is that when we multiply the projected spinors by the U link matrices, we do not need to repeat the matrix multiplication for each of the four spin indices of ψ. Instead, we need to multiply only the two color vectors h_0 and h_1 resulting from the

$(\pm, \mu)$	h_0	h_1	r_2	r_3
$(-, 0)$	$\psi_0 - i\psi_3$	$\psi_1 - i\psi_2$	ih_1	ih_0
$(-, 1)$	$\psi_0 + \psi_3$	$\psi_1 - \psi_2$	$-h_1$	h_0
$(-, 2)$	$\psi_0 - i\psi_2$	$\psi_1 + i\psi_3$	ih_0	$-ih_1$
$(-, 3)$	$\psi_0 - \psi_2$	$\psi_1 - \psi_3$	$-h_0$	$-h_1$
$(+, 0)$	$\psi_0 + i\psi_3$	$\psi_1 + i\psi_2$	$-ih_1$	$-ih_0$
$(+, 1)$	$\psi_0 - \psi_3$	$\psi_1 + \psi_2$	h_1	$-h_0$
$(+, 2)$	$\psi_0 + i\psi_2$	$\psi_1 - i\psi_3$	$-ih_0$	ih_1
$(+, 3)$	$\psi_0 + \psi_2$	$\psi_1 + \psi_3$	h_0	h_1

FIGURE 9.1

How to compute h_1 and h_2 for the projectors $P^{\pm\mu}$, and how to reconstruct the lower spin components r_2 and r_3 of the projected result from h_1 and h_2.

projection of ψ with $P^{\pm\mu}$. These form the top two components to be accumulated in the result. We can recover the lower two components from them by the reconstruction step.

This leads us to the *pseudocode* for computing the application of the Wilson-Dslash operator to a lattice spinor shown in Figure 9.2. We assume that each array element holds complex numbers. We have a loop over the four dimensions and within each, we loop over the forward and backward

```
// Pseudocode for Wilson Dslash Operator
// array elements are assumed to be complex
// Input arrays: psi[x][color][spin]
//               U[x][mu][color][color]
//
// Output array: result[x][color][spin]
// Temporary arrays: h[color][2], and uh[color][2]
//
forall sites x {

  // Zero result for this site
  for(int spin=0; spin < 4; spin++) {
   for(int color=0; color < 3; color++) {
    result[x][color][spin] = 0;
    }
   }


  for(dim=0; dir < 4; dim++) {
    for(forw_back=0; forw_back < 2; forw_back++) {
       int neighbor;
       if ( forw_back == 0 ) {
         neighbor = forward_neighbor_index(x,dim);
      }
      else {
         neighbor = back_neighbor_index(x,dim);
      }

      for(int color=0; color<3; color++) {
        h[color][0] = project_h0(dim, forw_back, psi[neighbor][color]);
        h[color][1] = project_h1(dim, forw_back, psi[neighbor][color]);
      }

      if( forw_back == 0 ) {
        // Forward links: Multiply h by U
        uh[:][0] = mat_mult(U[dim][x], h[:][0]);
        uh[:][1] = mat_mult(U[dim][x], h[:][1]);
      }
      else {
        // Back links: Multiply h by U^\dagger
        uh[:][0] = mat_adj_mult(U[dim][neighbor], h[:][0]);
        uh[:][1] = mat_adj_mult(U[dim][neighbor], h[:][1]);
      }

      // Reconstruct bottom 2 indices and accumulate
      for(int color=0; color < 3; color++) {
        result[x][color][0] += uh[color][0];
        result[x][color][1] += uh[color][1];
        result[x][color][2] = reconstruct_r2(dim,forw_back,uh[color]);
        result[x][color][3] = reconstruct_r3(dim,forw_back,uh[color]);
      }
    } // forw_back loop
  } // loop over dim
} // loop over sites
```

FIGURE 9.2

Pseudocode for implementing the Wilson-Dslash operator.

directions. In each direction, we compute the projections h_0, h_1 for the neighboring site. Then, depending on whether they are the forward or backward neighbors, we multiply h_0 and h_1 either by U or $U^\dagger$ as appropriate to form uh_0 and uh_1. We accumulate uh_0 and uh_1 into the top two spin components of the result, and the appropriate reconstructions into the lower components of the result.

PERFORMANCE EXPECTATIONS

Let us now consider some basic performance expectations for this operation. First, we will work out the naive arithmetic intensity, in terms of the number of floating point operations (FLOP-s) needed versus the minimum useful amount of data movement. In this discussion, sign flips and multiplies by i which are basically just interchanging real and imaginary complex components and potentially flipping signs, will not be considered as floating point operations. We will also refer generically as *additions* to both additions and subtractions.

Each projection operation reads in all 4×3 (spin $\times$ color) components of a spinor, which corresponds to 12 complex numbers or 24 floating point numbers. Each projection operation of the spinor is 2 complex additions per color component, that is, 6 complex additions or 12 floating point additions.

We can consider the matrix-vector products as three complex scalar (dot) product operations. Each dot product is between a row of the matrix, and the vector with which it is multiplied. This has a floating point cost of three complex multiplies, and two complex additions. A complex multiply is made of six floating point operations. Hence, the dot product is $3 \times 6 + 4 = 22$ FLOP-s where the four comes from the two complex additions. The whole matrix vector operation is then $3 \times 22 = 66$ FLOP-s. For each neighbor, one needs to repeat this twice (for h_0 and h_1) which gives: 132 FLOP-s. In terms of memory traffic, one also needs to load the U matrix, which is $3 \times 3 = 9$ complex numbers or 18 real numbers.

While no FLOP-s are needed for the reconstruction, one does need to sum all the results. To sum the eight neighbors one needs seven spinor additions. Each of these is $4 \times 3 = 12$ complex additions, or 24 real additions. Finally, one needs to write out the result to memory, which involves saving 12 complex numbers or 24 floating point numbers.

In summary, the minimum memory traffic per output lattice site is

$$d = 8 \times 24 + 8 \times 18 + 24 = 360 \text{ floating point numbers,} \tag{9.3}$$

where the first term is for the eight neighbor spinors (read), the second term is for the eight link-matrices (read), and the last term is for the writing of the result. In single precision, this comes to $d_s = 4d = 1440$ bytes, in double it is $d_d = 8d = 2880$ bytes, where the factors for 4 and 8 are the sizes of `float` and `double` in bytes, respectively.

The arithmetic involved for the same site is:

$$F = 8 \times 12 + 8 \times 132 + 7 \times 24 = 1320 \text{ FLOP} - s, \tag{9.4}$$

where the three terms can be identified with the cost of eight projections, eight sets of matrix multiplies and the accumulation of the results as discussed before. This gives us a *naive arithmetic intensity* of $I_s = F/d_s = 0.92$ FLOP/byte in single precision or $I_d = F/d_d = 0.46$ FLOP/byte in double precision.

In practice, the Intel Xeon Phi coprocessor, can sustain about 150 GB/s of memory bandwidth and the 60 cores can provide approximately 2022 single precision GFLOPS. The practical single precision FLOP/byte balance point of the Intel Xeon Phi coprocessor model 5110P is thus approximately 13.5 FLOP/byte, while in double precision it is around 6.74 FLOP/byte.[1] Hence, this naive performance model predicts that for problems which do not fit into caches, Wilson-Dslash will always be memory bound on the Intel Xeon Phi coprocessor architecture.

REFINEMENTS TO THE MODEL

Up until now, we have not considered hardware in the above discussions, however, by taking into account some hardware features, we can arrive at a more sophisticated model. While the number of *useful* FLOPS remains unchanged, we can refine the memory traffic part of the calculation. In particular, Intel Xeon Phi coprocessors feature 32 kb of L1 cache and 512 kb of L2 data-cache per core. The L2 caches appear as a unified coherent cache to the programmer through a tag directory mechanism, while Intel Xeon processors have large unified L3 caches. One can then consider a more refined model which we present below:

$$F = \frac{1320}{\frac{8G}{B_r} + \frac{(8-R)S + rS}{B_r} + \frac{S}{B_w}}, \tag{9.5}$$

where now F is the performance in GFLOPS, G is the size of the gauge matrices in bytes, S is the size of the spinors in bytes, B_r and B_w are the read-bandwidth and write bandwidths in GB/s between the memory and the *lowest level of cache*, respectively, and R is the number of neighbors per site which are cached and can be re-used without main memory traffic. The factor r is in place to allow us to consider *read-for-write* when writing. If one can use *streaming stores* which bypass the cache on write, then we can set $r = 0$. If we need to read a piece of memory to cache before writing it we can set $r = 1$. This model assumes that the cache is infinitely faster than accessing main memory. While no explicit assumption is made about the size of the cache, one can in principle attempt to capture cache-size effects by tuning the reuse factor R.

We note that we assume no reuse for the gauge fields, since the Dslash typically operates on a checkerboarded lattice as shown in Figure 9.3. When processing a point of a given color (e.g., black), one needs the links pointing to it from its backward neighbor sites of the opposite color (red in this example), and the links pointing forward from the site in question. When processing the next point of the original color, we must remember that this is not an immediate neighbor of the first one, since checkerboarding does not allow two sites of the same color to be neighbors, and hence there must be at least one site of the other color between the two under consideration, which is the backward neighbor of the second site. The second site will use the links of this intermediate site instead of those of the first site.

Additional tricks—compression

Our naive performance indicates that the problem is memory bandwidth bound, with an arithmetic intensity of around 0.92 FLOP/byte in single precision. One way to increase the arithmetic intensity is to consider gauge field compression to reduce memory traffic (reduce the size of G), and using the

---

[1]The peak GDDR bandwidth is quoted as 320 GB/s; however, we have never been able to reach more than around 170 GB/s in practice, hence quoting the peak value seems excessive. We will stick with a nominal 150 GB/s in the remainder of the chapter.

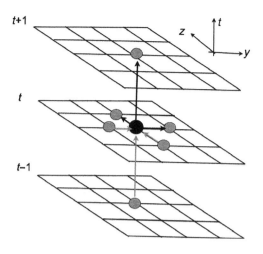

FIGURE 9.3

A graphical illustration of the Wilson-Dslash operator. Sites are checkerboarded. A given site needs its nearest neighbors (of opposite color). We have suppressed the X dimension in this figure. A site of a given color needs links of the same color emanating from it, and links of the opposite color from the backward neighbors ending on it.

essentially free FLOP-s provided by the node to perform decompression before use. This idea was explored in depth for GPU architectures in the QUDA library, and we sketch only the bare bones of it here.

Due to the $SU(3)$ nature of the gauge fields they have only eight real degrees of freedom: the coefficients of the eight $SU(3)$ generators. In principle, this means that instead of nine complex numbers, we can store the gauge fields as eight real numbers. However, re-constructing all nine complex numbers this way involves the use of some trigonometric functions.

A simpler approach is to consider two-row storage of the $SU(3)$ matrices. This idea has long been used to save space when writing gauge fields out to files, but was adapted as an on-the-fly bandwidth saving (de)compression technique (see the "For more information" section using "mixed precision solvers on GPUs"). The basic idea is to consider the rows of the matrix as row vectors:

$$\begin{pmatrix} a_0 & a_1 & a_2 \\ b_0 & b_1 & b_2 \\ c_0 & c_1 & c_2 \end{pmatrix} \quad \mathbf{a} = (a_0, a_1, a_2), \quad \mathbf{b} = (b_0, b_1, b_2), \quad \mathbf{c} = (c_0, c_1, c_2). \tag{9.6}$$

Then, if one has the first two rows: $\mathbf{a}$ and $\mathbf{b}$, both having been normalized to be of unit length, one can compute $\mathbf{c} = (\mathbf{a} \times \mathbf{b})^*$, that is, by taking the vector (cross) product of $\mathbf{a}$ and $\mathbf{b}$ and complex conjugating the elements of the result. This trick is quite simple, and reduces the size of the gauge links to 6 complex numbers, or 12 real numbers.

Now considering the formula in Eq. (9.5), we can compute the expected effects of neighbor spinor reuse, two-row compression and streaming stores. We make the simplifying assumption that $B_w = B_r$, and then can divide out the bandwidth, to get the arithmetic intensity. We show some results in the table shown in Figure 9.4. First, we note that even the naive arithmetic intensity of 0.92 FLOP/byte we computed initially, relies on not having read-for-write traffic when writing the output spinors, that is, it

R	Compress	Streaming Store	A/I (FLOP/Byte)
0	No	No	0.86
0	No	Yes	0.92
7	No	No	1.53
7	No	Yes	1.72
7	Yes	No	1.96
7	Yes	Yes	2.29

FIGURE 9.4

The expected effects of neighbor spinor reuse, compression, and streaming stores on the arithmetic intensity of Wilson-Dslash in single precision, with the simplifying assumption that $B_w = B_r$

needs streaming stores, without which the intensity drops to 0.86 FLOP/byte. Second, we see that by being able to reuse seven of our eight neighbor spinors, we can significantly improve in performance over the initial bound, to get an intensity between 1.53 and 1.72 FLOP/byte, depending on whether or not we use streaming stores. Finally, we see that we can benefit even further from gauge compression, to reach our highest predicted intensity of 2.29 FLOP/byte when cache reuse, streaming stores and compression are all present. We note when considering compression, we ignored the extra FLOP-s needed to perform the decompression, and counted only the *useful* FLOP-s.

FIRST IMPLEMENTATION AND PERFORMANCE

Before looking at the optimized implementation, let us take a look at a real-world implementation of Dslash which has been in production use for some years in the Chroma code. The package is called cpp_wilson_dslash and can be obtained from GitHub (see the "For more information" section). It is an offshoot of prior work by Chris McClendon. It is also in the included code bundle in the Code/Original/cpp_wilson_dslash directory. The package contains versions of the code for both single, and multinode versions of the Dslash operator, and we will focus our attention here on the single node, multithreaded version.

The code uses an "array of structures" (AoS) approach for the fields, keeping the internal indices of the spinors and gauge fields as local arrays as defined in include/cpp_dslash_types.h. We show the single precision versions of these types in Figure 9.5.

The structure of the GaugeMatrix (3 × 3 complex matrix) and of the FourSpinor (4 × 3 complex matrix) should be recognizable. The HalfSpinor type is the result of the projection, and because the code was targeted originally for Streaming SIMD Extensions (SSE), we have swapped the color and spin indices compared to the FourSpinor so that coupled with the two complex components they make up a group of four floats for SSE.

```
namespace Dslash32BitTypes {
  typedef float  FourSpinor[4][3][2];
  typedef float  HalfSpinor[3][2][2];
  typedef float  GaugeMatrix[3][3][2];
}
```

FIGURE 9.5

Single precision data types for the naive-Dslash operator.

```
// The operator is coded as a function-object
// res and psi are really FourSpinor* objects cast to float*
// u is a pointer to the gauge fields of which there are 4 per site
void Dslash<float>::operator() (float* res,
                                float* psi,
                                float *u, /* Gauge field suitably packed */
                                int isign, /* apply D or D^\dagger */
                                int cb) /* target checkerboard */
{
  if (isign == 1) {

    // Dispatch our DPsiPlus kernel to the threads
    CPlusPlusWilsonDslash::dispatchToThreads((void (*)(size_t, size_t, int,
        const void *))&DPsiPlus,
                                             (void*)psi,
                                             (void*)res,
                                             (void *)u,
                                             (void *)s,
                                             1-cb,
                                             s->totalVolCB());

  }
  // below would follow the D^\dagger case, very similar to the D
  // case, so we omit it for space
```

FIGURE 9.6

Dispatching the site loop for Dslash over available threads.

The code already features threading. Looking at Figure 9.6 from the file `lib/cpp_dslash_scalar_32bit.cc` we see that the first major step of the user called `operator()` method is a dispatch of a function to the available threads.

The OpenMP version of the `dispatchToThreads` function is found in the file `lib/dispatch_scalar_openmp.cc` and is also shown in Figure 9.7. An important point to note here is that the

```
void dispatchToThreads(void (*func)(size_t, size_t, int, const void *),
                       void* source,
                       void* result,
                       void *u,
                       void *s,
                       int cb,
                       int n_sites)
{
  ThreadWorkerArgs a;
   int threads_num,myId,low,high;

  a.psi = source; a.res = result; a.u = u; a.cb = cb; a.s = s;

#pragma omp parallel shared(func, n_sites, a)                          \
  private(threads_num, myId, low, high) default(none)
    {

      threads_num = omp_get_num_threads();
      myId = omp_get_thread_num();
      low = n_sites * myId/threads_num;
      high = n_sites * (myId+1)/threads_num;
      (*func)(low, high, myId, &a);
  }
}
```

FIGURE 9.7

The OpenMP thread dispatch in the naive code.

dispatcher tries to split the total work (n_sites) into chunks. Each chunk is specified by a beginning (low) site and a last (high) site. As we will see when looking at the function DPsiPlus, each thread then traverses its own chunk in lexicographic order. We illustrate this schematically in Figure 9.8, with boxes around groups of sites representing the chunk belonging to a single thread, and arrows between the sites representing the order of traversal.

The main compute kernels are the routines DPsiPlus for Wilson-Dslash and DPsiMinus for its Hermitian conjugate. We show a snippet of DPsiPlus in Figure 9.9. We deleted some of the details, to fit it into the figure, but as usual the full source is available in the Code package in the cpp_dslash_scalar_32bit.cc file in the lib/ subdirectory. The structure should be straightforward though. After unwrapping the arguments from the input ptr pointer, we enter a site loop from the low to the high index. We work out our "site" (thissite) from the current index in the lattice, and first find our forward and backward neighbors from the ShiftTable object s using the forwardNeighbor and backwardNeighbor methods, in direction 0. We set the input spinor pointer sp1 to the forward neighbor, the gauge pointer up1 to the gauge field, and we invoke dslash_plus_dir0_forward which performs the projection, multiplies, and reconstructs and accumulates into half spinors r12_1 and r34_1. We then go through all the directions until we get to the last one, where we call dslash_plus_dir3_backward_add_store and store the result at pointer *sn1. The various utility functions, such as dslash_plus_dir3_backward_add_store can be found in the include directory in the cpp_dslash_scalar_32bit_c.h source file as functions to be inlined. There is also a version which has the functionality coded with SSE intrinsics in cpp_dslash_scalar_32bit_sse.h.

Finally, there are testing and timing routines in the tests/ subdirectory. A test routine in the testDslashFull.cc function will test the Dslash operator against a slower variant coded in the QDP++ framework. This test is run from the code t_dslash.cc, whereas a straightforward timing harness, which executes Dslash in a loop and times the execution is in the timeDslash.cc file, that is called by the time_dslash.cc main-program. For both of these tests, one can choose the lattice volume and the number of timing iterations in the file testvol.h. For a many-core device like Intel Xeon Phi coprocessor, a reasonable lattice size is $32 \times 32 \times 32 \times 64$ sites, which we will use throughout.

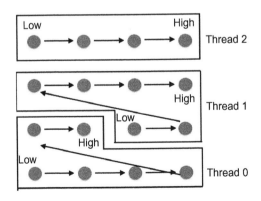

FIGURE 9.8

A schematic illustration of splitting lattice between three threads in the naive code. Within the chunks belonging to the individual threads the traversal is lexicographic.

```
void DPsiPlus(size_t lo, size_t hi, int id, const void *ptr)
{
  const ThreadWorkerArgs *a
    = (const ThreadWorkerArgs*)ptr;  /* Cast the (void *) to an (
      ThreadWorkerArgs*) */

  // Unwrapping of params deleted for space
  // please see source code...
  ...

  for (int ix1 = low; ix1 < high; ix1++)  {
    int thissite = s->siteTable( ix1 );
    int fsite = s->forwardNeighbor(ix1,0);
    int bsite = s->backwardNeighbor(ix1,0);

    /***************************** direction +0 ******************/
    /* ...(1-isign*gamma(0)) psi(x + \hat{0}) */
    sp1 = &psi[ fsite  ];
    up1 = &(gauge_field[ix1][0]);
    dslash_plus_dir0_forward(*sp1, *up1, r12_1, r34_1);

    sm1 = &psi[ bsite ];
    um1 = &(gauge_field[bsite][0]);
    dslash_plus_dir0_backward_add(*sm1, *um1, r12_1, r34_1);

    ... // Deleted branches in other directions for space

    // Last direction...
    sm1 = &psi[bsite];
    um1 = &(gauge_field[bsite][3]);
    sn1 = &res[ix1];  /*we always walk across the result
      lexicographically */

    dslash_plus_dir3_backward_add_store(*sm1, *um1, r12_1, r34_1, *sn1);
  } // for loop
} // function
```

FIGURE 9.9

The site loop in the `DPsiPlus` function, as executed by each thread.

In terms of timing benchmarks, we typically set the iterations so that the test will run for a couple of seconds which can typically be achieved with about 400-500 iterations. However, for purposes of performance measurement in VTune, we often use a smaller number of iterations, for example, 10 or 50.

RUNNING THE NAIVE CODE ON INTEL XEON PHI COPROCESSOR

We ran the correctness and timing tests with the above lattice size on 59 cores (to stay off the last core with O/S functions) of an Intel Xeon Phi 5110P coprocessor on which we have enabled the *icache_snoop_off* option in the kernel to gain additional memory bandwidth. We went "all in," asking for 4 threads per core, or 236 threads. To ensure that only the first 59 cores were used we set compact affinity using the `KMP_AFFINITY` environment variable. After verifying correctness, we achieved the output from the timing test shown in Figure 9.10 showing a performance of 34.8 GFLOPS in single precision, and around 25.2 GFLOPS in double precision.

This figure seems somewhat low. How does it compare to running on a Intel Xeon processor? As a comparison, we ran on a dual socket Intel Xeon E5-2560 (codenamed Sandy Bridge) processor, 2.0 GHz,

```
QDP uses OpenMP threading. We have 236 threads
Lattice initialized:
  problem size = 32 32 32 64
  layout size = 32 32 32 64
  logical machine size = 1 1 1 1
  subgrid size = 32 32 32 64
  total number of nodes = 1
  total volume = 2097152
  subgrid volume = 2097152
Finished init of RNG
Finished lattice layout
Running Test: timeDslash

        Timing with 50 counts
        50 iterations in 1.988364 seconds
        39767.28 u sec/iteration
        Performance is: 34805.5064364473 Mflops (sp) in Total
        Performance is: 34805.5064364473 per MPI Process

        Timing with 50 counts
        50 iterations in 2.748181 seconds
        54963.62 u sec/iteration
        Performance is: 25182.4810665673 Mflops (dp) in Total
        Performance is: 25182.4810665673 per MPI Process
  OK
Summary: 1 Tests Tried
         1 Tests Succeeded
         0 Tests Failed on some nodes
of which 0 Tests Failed in Unexpected Ways on some nodes
```

FIGURE 9.10

Timings of the naive Dslash on an Intel Xeon Phi coprocessor 5110P using 59 cores, or 236 threads. We see a single precision performance of 34.8 GFLOPS in single precision and 25.2 GFLOPS in double precision.

with 2×8 cores, and hyperthreading enabled, giving us 32 threads. Further, since we know that the memory allocation in this code is not NUMA aware we used the `numactl` utility to interleave memory allocation between the sockets using the `numactl --interleave=0,1` command to launch the code. Without enabling the SSE optimization code-branches, the result we obtained on the processor was 34.7 GFLOPS in single precision and 19.3 GFLOPS in double. So a single coprocessor performed roughly as fast (slightly faster) than a dual socket Xeon system using the same code.

While this is not an unreasonable first performance *ratio* between Intel Xeon processor and Intel Xeon Phi coprocessor, the result is nonetheless somewhat disappointing in terms of absolute performance. Our models tell us that the code should be memory bandwidth bound, so one immediate question is how much memory bandwidth are we utilizing? To answer this we profiled the code using VTune, using its bandwidth collection experiments which reported the code sustaining a memory bandwidth of 42.3 GB/s in the single precision Wilson-Dslash on the Intel Xeon Phi coprocessor.

EVALUATION OF THE NAIVE CODE

At this point we should pause and reflect. VTune reported that our single precision memory bandwidth on Intel Xeon Phi coprocessor was 42.3 GB/s. Taking the most naive arithmetic intensity of 0.86 FLOP/byte (no caching, no compression, no streaming stores), the model predicts a performance of 36.4 GFLOPS as our maximum. We are sustaining 34.8 GFLOPS of this, which is around 96% of the model prediction. However, the 42.3 GB/s is quite a low bandwidth for the Intel Xeon Phi coprocessor.

Second, right now we are not really using the vector units on the Intel Xeon Phi coprocessor, at least not deliberately. If the compiler were to generate code to carry out our scalar arithmetic using just one lane of the vector units, then the peak performance we can expect is two flops per cycle (a multiply and add), which at 1.053 GHz from 60 cores is 126.36 GFLOPS. If we could exhaust our bandwidth of 150 GB/s our most naive arithmetic intensity of 0.86 FLOP/byte predicts a performance of 129 GFLOPS. This is a little higher than, but still in the same ballpark as, the peak performance of unvectorized arithmetic. However, our most optimistic intensity of 2.29 FLOP/byte (cache reuse, compression, streaming stores) would predict 343.5 GFLOPS, which is substantially more than can be achieved with unvectorized arithmetic. Therefore, we need to ensure we make more effective use of the vector units than is done in the current version of the code.

Finally, our measured performance (34.8 GFLOPS) is commensurate with not getting any cache reuse at all ($R = 0$), stopping us from attaining our more optimistic model estimates. Therefore, it is necessary to improve our cache reuse.

OPTIMIZED CODE: QPhiX AND QPhiX-CODEGEN

In this section, we will illustrate how to solve the problems of the original code regarding cache reuse, vectorization, and better memory handling (prefetching). We will use the *QPhiX* code which is available on GitHub, and is also included in the code-package for this chapter. QPhiX is essentially an evolution of `cpp_wilson_dslash` and has two main parts: First, it deals with looping on the lattice to implement the technique of 3.5D blocking and it also implements a heuristic-based load balancing scheme to schedule the blocks to the cores. Second, it contains *kernels* to evaluate Dslash, on a *tile of sites* in parallel, in order to efficiently utilize the vector units of the Intel Xeon Phi coprocessor. These kernels are generated by a *code-generator* in a package called `qphix-codegen` and can then be copied into the `qphix` source package. The current `qphix` package on GitHub contains the best known performing kernels already pregenerated. In the Code package, we provide several variants of `qphix` with different selections of kernels to illustrate our points regarding optimization. Before launching into the optimizations, let us consider the important features of QPhiX and the code-generator.

DATA LAYOUT FOR VECTORIZATION

In our first attempt to optimize Dslash, we wanted to vectorize wholly over the X dimension; however, this proved rather restrictive. Since we split our lattice into even and odd subsets by dividing the global X dimension, for a lattice of dimensions $L_x \times L_y \times L_z \times L_t$ we have checkerboarded subsets of size $L_x/2 \times Ly \times L_z \times L_t$. For full vector utilization in single precision (16 floats), we would have had to have L_x be multiples of 32. While this is fine for our working example of $L_x = 32$, it places a strong constraint on our choice of problem sizes. To ameliorate this problem we have decided to vectorize over X-Y tiles. We could fill the length 16 vector registers using either 16 sites along X, a tile of size 8×2 in the X-Y plane, or a tile of size 4×4 in the X-Y plane. By using the gather engine on Intel Xeon Phi coprocessor, we could have been even more flexible, but we found that using *load-unpack* and *pack-store* instructions was more efficient, and it allowed us these combinations. As a result, instead of the *AoS* layout we had in our original code, we have opted to use a *Array of Structures of Arrays* (AoSoA) layout which we define in the file `geometry.h` in the `include/qphix` directory of the `qphix` package.

We have two key parameters which we supply as templates to almost every component of *QPhiX*. The length of the vector unit which we call VECLEN or V and the length of the inner arrays of the AoSoA structures, which we call the SOA length SOALEN or S in the code. We show the basic data types for Spinors and Gauge fields in QPhiX in Figure 9.11. We see that the FourSpinorBlock has an innermost array dimension of S, and we will have to *gather* ngy=V/S such blocks into a vector register. These blocks will come from ngy consecutive values of the y coordinate as shown in Figure 9.12.

The TwoSpinorBlock type is used only internally in our multinode implementation to store the results of projections on the faces of the lattice. By this time, the gathers have taken place prior to the projection so it is fine to leave the inner length as V for this type.

We have several comments about the type SU3MatrixBlock which represents the gauge fields. First, we have made the choice to double copy the gauge field, which means we store not just the four forward links from each site, but also the four backward links. This was done so that the fields could be accessed in unit stride access, hence the leftmost array dimension is eight, for the eight directions. Second, the gauge fields are read only, never written, and so, we could absorb the gather operation of the spinor blocks into a layout re-definition, essentially *pregathering* the gauge field. Hence, it has V as its innermost length. Finally, we implemented the two-row compression technique. It has turned out that, for Intel Xeon processors, the hardware prefetcher would still read the third row of the gauge fields, even when we did not reference its elements directly in the code, and thus we did not realize the benefits of compression on processors initially (although we did on Intel Xeon Phi coprocessors). One way to

```
template<typename T, int V, int S, const bool compressP>
class Geometry {
public:
    // Later change this to depend on compressP
    typedef T  FourSpinorBlock[3][4][2][S];
    typedef T  TwoSpinorBlock[3][2][2][V];
    typedef T  SU3MatrixBlock[8][ ( compressP ? 2 : 3 ) ][3][2][V];
    ...
```

FIGURE 9.11

The basic data types in QPhiX.

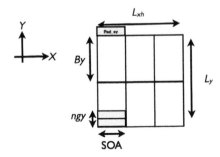

FIGURE 9.12

Schematic view of the data layout. We show blocking in the *Y*-direction with block length B_y, and vectorization in the *X*-*Y* plane, where blocks of length SOA in *X* are gathered from ngy consecutive values of the *Y*-coordinate. Additionally the padding can be introduced between *X*-*Y* slices of the lattice (Pad_xy in the figure) and also between *XY Z* volumes (Pad_xyz—not shown).

circumvent this was to reduce the number of rows in the data structure explicitly from 3 to 2, when compression is enabled. However, this is a compile time decision, hence we have an extra template parameter: compressP and the number of rows is decided based on this template at compile time. Finally, we added the option of padding our fields both following each X-Y plane of the lattice and after every X-Y-Z subvolume.

3.5D BLOCKING

The basic strategy in QPhiX was to implement a technique known as 3.5D blocking. In the form previously discussed for Intel Xeon (codenamed Westmere) processors in "High-performance lattice QCD for multicore-based parallel systems using a cache-friendly hybrid threaded-MPI approach" (see the "For more information" section), considered vectorizing over the X dimension of the lattice, and blocking over the Y and Z dimensions, while streaming up through the T dimension. With the tiled layout for vectorization, the idea still holds, except the Y-Z blocks now must contain an integer number of tiles. The idea here can be followed looking at Figure 9.3. As one scans along a Y-Z block, at T coordinate t, one needs in principle to bring in only the neighbor with coordinate $t + 1$. The co-planar X-Y-Z neighbors should have been brought into cache when working on the previous T-slice. The Y-Z plane of the lattice can then be divided into blocks, resulting in $Y ZT$ bricks, which can be assigned to the individual cores as shown in Figure 9.13. The width of these blocks can be denoted B_y and B_z, and need to be chosen so that at least three T-slices of spinors fit into cache. Data that is on the Y-Z boundaries of a

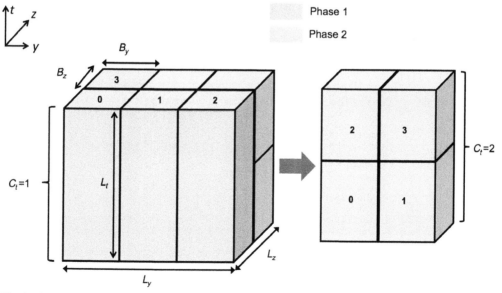

FIGURE 9.13

We show our load balancing scheme, with six blocks scheduled over four cores. In the first round, each core is assigned a full block. In the second round, the two remaining blocks are split in the time direction, to yield four blocks, each with shorter T-extent. These are then scheduled to the four cores, keeping all four cores occupied.

$B_y \times B_z$ block is needed both by the block, and its neighbor, however, if the computations are appropriately orchestrated and the cores working on the neighboring blocks are synchronized, this may result in both cores being able to use the data in each other's L2 cache rather than going to main memory.

LOAD BALANCING

It may be the case, depending on the lattice size and B_y and B_z, that there are comparatively few blocks given the number of cores. For example, in our test case of $32^3 \times 64$ sites, with $B_y = B_z = 4$ on Intel Xeon Phi coprocessor, one has only 64 blocks. This could result in two rounds of block processing, one in which up to 60 cores are fully engaged, and a second round where only 4 blocks are working and the remaining 56 are idle. To ameliorate this situation, we developed a heuristic load balancing scheme, which we describe below and show in Figure 9.13.

We perform the traversal of blocks in *phases*. In any given phase, if there are more blocks than cores, we simply assign one block per core, and all the cores are fully occupied. We keep repeating this until we have either finished processing all the blocks or we arrive at a phase that we have fewer blocks than cores. Once we have fewer blocks then cores, we consider splitting them in the time direction, which will increase the number of remaining blocks. If the number of blocks is now more than or equal to the number of cores, we carry on as before, and so on. Ultimately, the time-lengths of the blocks may be so short, that it will not be worth splitting them further. At this point, we take the load imbalance and finish the work in the final phase.

In terms of implementation, we keep a list of blocks and the number of splits in the time dimension; C_i for each phase. We can compute the block assignments for each phase up front on constructing the Dslash. In the QPhiX code, the basic phase info is set up in the geometry.h file in the include/qphix directory, as shown in Figure 9.14. In the code, rem stores the number of remaining blocks. This is initialized to ly*lz where ly and lz are the number of blocks in Y and Z, respectively. In each iteration, a value of p.Ct is computed. Depending on p.Ct the number of cores over which the Y-Z blocks can be allocated is found: p.Cyz. The first block for this phase is noted in p.startBlock after which p.Cyz

```
int ly = Ny_ / By;
int lz = Nz_ / Bz;
int rem = ly * lz;
int stblk = 0;
n_phases = 0;
int n_cores_per_minct = num_cores / MinCt;
while(rem > 0) {
   int ctd = n_cores_per_minct / rem;
   int ctu = (n_cores_per_minct + rem - 1) / rem;
   CorePhase& p = getCorePhase(n_phases);
   p.Ct = (ctu <= 4 ? ctu : ctd)*MinCt;
   p.Cyz = num_cores / p.Ct;
   if(p.Cyz > rem) p.Cyz = rem;
   p.startBlock = stblk;
   stblk += p.Cyz;
   rem -= p.Cyz;
   n_phases++;
}
```

FIGURE 9.14

Load balancing phase set-up in geometry.h.

blocks are removed from the block-list and the next phase is processed. In addition, one can set a minimum value of C_t (known as minCt), which can be useful for example, in a multisocket situation where minCt can be set to the number of sockets. When allocating memory, the phases are traversed and the right core can touch the appropriate area of memory in a cc-NUMA aware implementation. Our heuristic termination criterion for the splitting is to not split the T dimension into more than four MinCt blocks.

This concludes the setup of the assignment of cores to phases; however, it is also useful to be able to look up information about how the blocks are assigned to phases. This is done in the *constructor* for Dslash in the file dslash_body.h in include/qphix that we show in Figure 9.15. Here, for each thread, we set up which block it should process in each phase. For each phase, the thread ID is split into a core-ID and SMT-thread ID. The core-ID (cid) is split into a T-coordinate and YZ-coordinate (binfo.cid_t and binfo.cid_yz, respectively) and the coordinates of the block origin, binfo.by, binfo.bz, and binfo.bt are computed along with the temporal extent for the blocks binfo.nt.

SMT THREADING

With four SMT threads available on each core of Intel Xeon Phi coprocessor, we have a variety of ways we can imagine traversing a Y-Z block. We show three possible ways in Figure 9.16. In the end, we have opted to let the user specify the "shape" of the SMT threads, by specifying a S_y and S_z as the dimensions of a Y-Z grid. The lattice sites in a Y-Z block are then interleaved between the SMT threads. It is simplest to describe this in the case of the Y interleaved case ($S_y = 4, S_z = 1$). In this instance, thread 0 will work with a site that has Y-coordinate y, thread 1 will work with the site with Y-coordinate $y + 1$, thread 2 will

```
#pragma omp parallel shared(num_phases)
    {
        int tid = omp_get_thread_num();
        int cid = tid / n_threads_per_core;
        int smtid = tid - n_threads_per_core * cid;
        int ly = Ny/By;

        for(int ph =0; ph < num_phases; ph++){
            const CorePhase& phase = s->getCorePhase(ph);
            BlockPhase& binfo = block_info[num_phases*tid+ph];

            int nActiveCores = phase.Cyz * phase.Ct;
            if( cid > nActiveCores )  continue;
            binfo.cid_t = cid / phase.Cyz;
            binfo.cid_yz = cid - binfo.cid_t * phase.Cyz;
            int syz = phase.startBlock + binfo.cid_yz;
            binfo.bz = syz / ly;
            binfo.by = syz - binfo.bz * ly;
            binfo.bt = (Nt*binfo.cid_t) / phase.Ct;
            binfo.nt = (Nt*(binfo.cid_t+1)) / phase.Ct - binfo.bt;
            binfo.by *= By;
            binfo.bz *= Bz;
            int ngroup = phase.Cyz*Sy*Sz;
            binfo.group_tid = tid % ngroup;
        }
    } // OMP parallel
```

FIGURE 9.15

Load balancing block phase set-up in dslash_body.h.

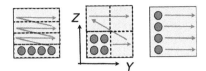

FIGURE 9.16

We show three possible ways for four SMT threads to traverse the sites in a block: lexicographic in *Y* interleaved (left), a 2 × 2 block in *Y-Z* interleaved (middle) or scanning along *Y* for four separate *Z*-coordinates interleaved (right).

work with *Y*-coordinate $y + 2$, and thread 3 will work with $y + 3$. Then thread 0 will work with $y + 4$, thread 1 will work with $y + 5$, and so forth traversing the block essentially lexicographically. Another alternative would be to assign *sub-blocks* to each SMT thread. So, for example, in a block with (B_y, B_z) = (4,4), we could have each thread work with a 2 × 2 sub-block. However, we restricted ourselves to the interleaved traversals in the hope that interleaving the SMT threads among the sites would improve sharing in the L1 cache.

LATTICE TRAVERSAL

Armed now with knowledge about the phases from load balancing, the SMT thread layout, and the specifics of the vectorization, we can look at a simplified form of the traversal of the lattice. We show some code from the file `dslash_body.h` from the function `DyzPlus` in Figure 9.18, where we have removed a lot of the minor details and computation of prefetch pointers for clarity. The full code is available in the source package. The crucial points to make are the following: each thread loops over the phases, first identifying its block in that phase or whether it is idle. Once the block is found, looping is over T, Z, and Y as we expect. The loop over Z is done in increments of Sz and the loop over Y is done in increments of $ngy*Sy$ (actually misspelled `nyg` in the code) where Sy and Sz are the SMT thread grid dimensions. The X loop is over SOAs (`nvecs` is the number of SOA lengths in the checkerboarded X dimensions).

Accessing the neighbors of the current X-Y tile in the Z and T dimensions is straightforward, and their tiles can be identified as soon as the Z and T coordinates are known. They are pointed to by pointers `tfBase` (*T* forward), `tbBase` (*T* backward), `zfBase`, and `zbBase`.

However, because of vectorization in X and Y, accessing the neighbors in these dimensions is tricky as it may need data from neighboring tiles. We show a simple case in Figure 9.17. Depending on the Y-coordinate, the first site of a given color (e.g., red) may be truly the first site for that Y-coordinate in the lattice (xodd=0 in the figure). In that case, its forward neighbors come from the first tile of the other checkerboard in a straightforward way. However, it can be that the first site of the given checkerboard is actually the second site in the lattice (xodd=1). In this case, the forward neighbor sites actually come from two different tiles of the other color and must be blended together. Further, due to periodic boundary conditions, one has to separate the cases for when the output tile under consideration is at the beginning or end of the X dimension (with wraparound to the tiles at the opposite end) or not. The necessary offsets are precomputed in the constructor into arrays `xbOffs_x0_xodd` (back neighbors at start of X dimension) and `xfOffs_xn_xodd` (forward neighbors at end of X dimension), and

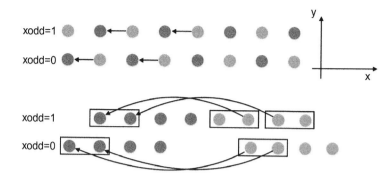

FIGURE 9.17

Locating neighbors in the forward X-direction, in a simple case with an X-Y tile size of 2 × 1. In the top diagram, we show the sites as they appear in the lattice. We show the forward neighbors needed by the first two red-sites in each row by connecting them to their partner sites with arrows. In the lower diagram, we have separated the differently colored sites into separate arrays, which are then tiled over. For the first red tile on line xodd=0, one needs only the same corresponding blue tile. However, for the first red tile on line xodd=1, the neighboring blue sites come from two blue tiles and need to be blended.

xbOffs_xodd (back X neighbor offsets) and xfOffs_xodd (forward X neighbor offsets) for the other cases. Likewise, similar offset arrays exist to identify neighbors in Y.

The last steps in the X-loop in Figure 9.18 are to identify whether one has the case of xodd=0, or xodd=1, and to select from the precomputed offsets appropriately depending on the x-coordinate into xfOffs, xbOffs (backward and forward X offsets, respectively) and similarly into ybOffs and yfOffs for the Y-direction. The pointer oBase is the pointer to the base of the Y-Z tile of the output spinor, gBase is the pointer to the appropriate portion of the gauge field. Other quantities computed (in the source but not printed here) are mostly prefetch pointers for the next iteration of work for this thread.

Once everything is worked out, the code finally calls the dslash_plus_vec function which carries out the work of the Dslash for the pointers identified in this loop. This is code that is generated by the *code-generator*, which we now turn to consider.

CODE GENERATION WITH QphiX-CODEGEN

We now consider how we write the kernels for the key functions dslash_plus_vec and its variants. To do this we decided to write a code generator, which can be found in the code distribution under the subdirectory qphix-codegen but can also be obtained from GitHub (see the "For more information" section).

Our initial motivations for writing the code-generator were the following: first, we wanted to eventually insert prefetches into the code to improve memory traffic. This was awkward to do when we had the code split into lots of little inline functions. It made sense to have a little code generator which could produce the fully inlined body of the Dslash kernel for an entire vector (and later X-Y tile). Using the code generator also allowed us to use compiler intrinsics and access streaming stores, gathers, load-pack, and other instructions directly. A second feature of the code-generator was once we had written

```
int num_phases = s->getNumPhases();
 for(int ph=0; ph < num_phases; ph++) {
   const CorePhase& phase = s->getCorePhase(ph);
   const BlockPhase& binfo = block_info[tid*num_phases + ph];
   ...
   // Loop over timeslices
   int Nct = binfo.nt;
   for(int ct = 0 ; ct < Nct; ct++) {
     int t = ct + binfo.bt;   // add origin to local loop variable
     ...
     // Loop over z. Start at smtid_z and work up to Ncz
     // in steps of Sz
     // (Ncz truncated for the last block so should be OK)
     for( int cz = smtid_z; cz < Bz; cz += Sz ) {
         int z = cz + binfo.bz; // Add on origin of block
         ...
         // Base address for XY tile for neighbors.
         const FourSpinorBlock *xyBase = &psi[t*Pxyz+z*Pxy];

         // Base address for neighbor tiles in Z & T
         const FourSpinorBlock *zbBase = &psi[t*Pxyz] + ... ;
         const FourSpinorBlock *zfBase = &psi[t*Pxyz] + ... ;
         const FourSpinorBlock *tbBase = &psi[z*Pxy] + ...;
         const FourSpinorBlock *tfBase = &psi[z*Pxy] + ...;

         // Base address for output
         FourSpinorBlock *oBase = &res[t*Pxyz+z*Pxy];
         ...
         // Loop over 'y' in nyg * Sy steps (should be ngy :( )
         for( int cy = nyg*smtid_y; cy < By; cy += nyg*Sy ) {
           int yi = cy + binfo.by;   // Offset local y-coordinate with
                 block origin
           // work out if first x-coordinate is on boundary...
           const int xodd = (yi + z + t + cb) & 1;

           // cx loops over the soalen partial vectors
           for(int cx = 0; cx < nvecs; cx++) {
             // Base address for gauge fields
             const SU3MatrixBlock *gBase = &u[...];
             int X=nvecs*yi+cx;
             ...
             // Offsets for gathering neighbors from back and forward x
             // may be in different tiles
             xbOffs = (cx == 0 ? xbOffs_x0_xodd[xodd] : xbOffs_xodd[xodd])
                 ;
             xfOffs = (cx == nvecs-1 ? xfOffs_xn_xodd[xodd] : xfOffs_xodd[
                 xodd]);

             ...
             // Offsets for gathering neighbors from back and forward Y
             // may be in different tiles
             ybOffs = (yi == 0 ? ybOffs_y0 : ybOffs_yn0);
             yfOffs = (yi == Ny - nyg ? yfOffs_yn : yfOffs_ynn);

             ...
             // Call kernel with appropriate pointers
             dslash_plus_vec<FT,veclen,soalen,compress12>(...)
           }
         } // End for over scanlines y
     } // End for over scalines z
     if( ct % BARRIER_TSLICES == 0 ) barriers[ph][binfo.cid_t]->wait(
         binfo.group_tid);
   } // end for over t
 } // phases
```

FIGURE 9.18

The basic loop structure in QPhiX, with a lot of auxiliary computations removed for clarity such as the indices of the next site, prefetch computations, etc. The full code is available in `include/dslash_body.h`, for example, in the function `DyzPlus`.

the code for Xeon-Phi intrinsics, it was straightforward also to replicate the features for AVX intrinsics to target Intel Xeon processors. Currently we feature a "scalar" target (no vectorization) and there are even targets for BlueGene/Q vectorization with QPX intrinsics, and Intel AVX2, although these latter targets are still experimental.

We should note that the use of small domain-specific code generators is not a new idea in itself. In QCD, there have been several frameworks including BAGEL and QA0. The QUDA library for GPUs has also at one point used an internal Python code generator. The BAGEL generator, for example, also performs some simulation of architectural pipelines and generates assembly code rather than intrinsics. In our case, the simple generator we wrote was more for convenience and saving typing when trying to re-space prefetches.

QphiX-CODEGEN CODE STRUCTURE

The code generator is called qphix-codegen and can be found as the subdirectory of the same name within the code-package. In qphix-codegen, we consider three primary objects: *instructions*, *addresses*, and *vector registers*. These are defined in the instructions.h and address_types.h files. In particular, the vector registers are referred to as FVec, and instructions and addresses are derivations of the base Instruction and Address classes. We also distinguish between regular Instructions and those that access memory (MemRefInstruction-s).

The FVec objects contain a "name" which will be the name of the identifier associated with the FVec in the generated code. All instructions and addresses have a method called serialize() which return the code for that instruction as a std::string. Since we are generating code, we need a couple of auxiliary higher level "instructions" to add conditional blocks, scope delimiters, or to generate declarations.

Ultimately, the code-generator generates lists of Instruction-s that are held in a standard vector from the C++ standard library. We alias the type of such a vector of instructions to type InstVector (for Instruction Vector). In turn, the instructions reference FVec and Address objects.

The remaining attributes for addresses and instructions were mostly added so we can perform analysis on the generated code. For example, one could look for MemRefInstructions, and extract their referenced Address-es for automatic prefetch generation, or to count the balance of arithmetic versus memory referencing instructions.

Finally, at the end of the file instructions.h we define some utility functions such as mulFVec that take an instruction vector, two FVec-s from which they generate a MulFVec object and insert is into the instruction vector. The majority of the code for the Dslash is written with these utility functions.

IMPLEMENTING THE INSTRUCTIONS

The actual implementations of the Instructions are in a variety of files with names like inst_sp_vec16.cc? that, in particular, refers to generating single precision code working with length 16 vectors, that is for Intel Xeon Phi coprocessor. First and foremost we declare the actual types of FVec-s as __m512. After this, we basically declare the serialize() methods of the various instructions which is where we generate the actual intrinsics. We show the example for LoadFVec and an FMA (fused multiply-add) in Figure 9.19 but, of course, the entire source is available in the Code package. We note that we have implemented the use of 16-bit precision in this work and the LoadFVec shows how

```
string LoadFVec::serialize() const
{
    std::ostringstream buf;
    string upConv = "_MM_UPCONV_PS_NONE";
    string lmask = mask;

    if(mask.empty()) {
        lmask = fullMask;
    }

    if(a->isHalfType()) {
        upConv = "_MM_UPCONV_PS_FLOAT16";
    }

    buf << v.getName() << " = _mm512_mask_extload_ps("
        << v.getName() << ", " << lmask << ", " << a->serialize()
        << ", " << upConv << ", _MM_BROADCAST32_NONE, _MM_HINT_NONE);" <<endl
        ;

    return buf.str();
}

string FMAdd::serialize() const
{
    if(mask.empty()) {
        return   ret.getName()+" = _mm512_fmadd_ps("+a.getName()+", "+b.
            getName()+", "+c.getName()+");" ;
    }
    else {
        return   ret.getName()+" = _mm512_mask_mov_ps(" + ret.getName() + ", "
            + mask + ", _mm512_fmadd_ps(" +a.getName()+", "+b.getName()+", 
            "+c.getName()+"));" ;
    }
}
```

FIGURE 9.19

The serialize methods for `LoadFVec` and `FMadd` instructions from `qphix-codegen`. They can be found in the file `inst_sp_vec16.cc`.

a vector of `unsigned short`-s can be loaded using *up-conversion* in the `_mm512_mask_extload_ps` intrinsic.

GENERATING DSLASH

Generating Dslash is coded in the `dslash.cc` and `dslash_common.cc` files. The basic Dslash body is reproduced in code Figure 9.20, although we have removed some of the branches relating to having to emulate masking for clarity. Modulo some code for dealing with additional scale factors to multiply into the results on accumulation (`beta_vec`), and adding conditionals and masks for accumulating (to do with boundary processing in a multinode implementation), the structure should be very similar to the pseudocode in Figure 9.2.

To round out this story, we show a brief snippet of the code to multiply $SU(3)$ matrices with three-vectors in Figure 9.21, from the file `dslash_common.cc`. First, we declare a global set of `FVec`-s, for each spin, color and complex component that we will use. In our case, b refers to the result of the projection and ub refers to the result of the multiplication. It is convenient to collect these `FVec`-s into arrays with indices mirroring our desired index structure, as shown in the code for the half-spinor

```
void dslash_body(InstVector& ivector, bool compress12, proj_ops *ops,
    recons_ops *rec_ops_bw, recons_ops *rec_ops_fw, FVec outspinor[4][3][2])
{
    for(int dim = 0; dim < 4; dim++) {
        for(int dir = 0; dir < 2; dir++) {
            int d = dim * 2 + dir;
            stringstream d_str;
            d_str << d;
            string mask;
            bool adjMul;
            recons_ops rec_op;

            if(dir == 0) {
                adjMul = true;
                rec_op = rec_ops_bw[dim];
            }
            else {
                adjMul = false;
                rec_op = rec_ops_fw[dim];
            }
            ifStatement(ivector,"accumulate[" + d_str.str() + "]");
            {
                declareFVecFromFVec(ivector, beta_vec);
                loadBroadcastScalar(ivector, beta_vec, beta_names[d],
                    SpinorType);
                if(requireAllOneCheck[dim]) {
                    mask = "accMask";
                    declareMask(ivector, mask);
                    intToMask(ivector, mask, "accumulate[" + d_str.str() + "]
                        ");
                }

                for(int s = 0; s < 2; s++) {
                    project(ivector, basenames[d], offsnames[d], ops[d],
                        false, mask, d, s);

                    if(s==0) {
                        loadGaugeDir(ivector, d, compress12);
                    }

                    matMultVec(ivector, adjMul, s);
                    recons_add(ivector, rec_op, outspinor, mask, s);
                }
            }
            endScope(ivector);
        }
    }
}
```

FIGURE 9.20

The basic code to generate the body of the Dslash (excluding additional code to deal with software emulated masking on non-Intel Xeon Phi coprocessor platforms.

b_spinor. Finally, we generate the matrix multiply in the function matMultVec using convenience functions defined earlier for complex arithmetic. Note that there is a loop in the function. When the function is executed that loop will essentially create all the operations in the matrix multiply into a single contiguous instruction stream.

```
FVec b_S0_C0_RE("b_S0_C0_RE");
FVec b_S0_C0_IM("b_S0_C0_IM");
...

FVec b_spinor[2][3][2] = {
    { {b_S0_C0_RE, b_S0_C0_IM}, {b_S0_C1_RE, b_S0_C1_IM}, {b_S0_C2_RE,
        b_S0_C2_IM} },
    { {b_S1_C0_RE, b_S1_C0_IM}, {b_S1_C1_RE, b_S1_C1_IM}, {b_S1_C2_RE,
        b_S1_C2_IM} }
};
...

// r is an array of length 2, as are s1 and s2 — for complex numbers
void mulCVec(InstVector& ivector, FVec *r, FVec *s1, FVec *s2, string &mask)
{
    mulFVec(ivector, r[RE], s1[RE], s2[RE], mask);
    fnmaddFVec(ivector, r[RE], s1[IM], s2[IM], r[RE], mask);
    mulFVec(ivector, r[IM], s1[RE], s2[IM], mask);
    fmaddFVec(ivector, r[IM], s1[IM], s2[RE], r[IM], mask);
}
...
// deal with spin component 's'
void matMultVec(InstVector& ivector, bool adjMul, int s)
{
    string mask;

    for(int c1 = 0; c1 < 3; c1++) {
        if(!adjMul) {
            mulCVec(ivector, ub_spinor[s][c1], u_gauge[0][c1], b_spinor[s
                ][0], mask);
            fmaddCVec(ivector, ub_spinor[s][c1], u_gauge[1][c1], b_spinor[s
                ][1], ub_spinor[s][c1], mask);
            fmaddCVec(ivector, ub_spinor[s][c1], u_gauge[2][c1], b_spinor[s
                ][2], ub_spinor[s][c1], mask);
        }
        else {
            mulConjCVec(ivector, ub_spinor[s][c1], u_gauge[c1][0], b_spinor[s
                ][0], mask);
            fmaddConjCVec(ivector, ub_spinor[s][c1], u_gauge[c1][1], b_spinor
                [s][1], ub_spinor[s][c1], mask);
            fmaddConjCVec(ivector, ub_spinor[s][c1], u_gauge[c1][2], b_spinor
                [s][2], ub_spinor[s][c1], mask);
        }
    }
}
```

FIGURE 9.21

Code to generate *SU*(3) matrix-vector multiply, from the `dslash_common.cc` file.

PREFETCHING

We implement prefetching in the code generator in two different ways, for L1 and L2 prefetching, respectively. We define custom L1 prefetch functions in the file `data_types.h` which we call explicitly just before starting to work with the data. We show the idea, for example, in the projection operation in Figure 9.22.

Our L2 prefetching is slightly different. We need to fetch further ahead than for L1, and our approach has been for every thread to prefetch the forward *T* neighbor of the next output block that it will work. While blocks that are co-planar in *Y* and *Z* should already be in L2, they may reside in

```
// File: dslash_common.cc
void project(InstVector& ivector, string base, string offset, proj_ops& ops,
    bool isFace, string mask, int dir)
{
    string tmask("");
    PrefetchL1FullSpinorDirIn(ivector, base, offset, dir);

    for(int s = 0; s < 2; s++) {
        for(int c = 0; c < 3; c++) {
            LoadSpinorElement(ivector, psi[0][RE], base, offset, ops.s[s][0],
                c, RE, isFace, mask, dir);
            LoadSpinorElement(ivector, psi[0][IM], base, offset, ops.s[s][0],
                c, IM, isFace, mask, dir);
            LoadSpinorElement(ivector, psi[1][RE], base, offset, ops.s[s][1],
                c, RE, isFace, mask, dir);
            LoadSpinorElement(ivector, psi[1][IM], base, offset, ops.s[s][1],
                c, IM, isFace, mask, dir);

            ops.CVecFunc[s](ivector, b_spinor[s][c], psi[0], psi[1], /*mask*/
                tmask); // Not using mask here
        }
    }
}
```

FIGURE 9.22

Generating L1 prefetches for the projection operation. We explicitly prefetch the whole spinor into L1, before element wise loading.

the caches of other cores than the one which needs them. Therefore, we allow the possibility of prefetching up to four neighboring spinors. For each of these we supply a pointer and an offset. The base pointers are xyBase (current tile), pfBase2, pfBase3, and pfBase4. The prefetch offsets to these pointers are siprefdist1, siprefdist2, and so on up to siprefdist4. We also prefetch gauge fields with offset gprefdist from the current gBase and can prefetch the next output spinor with base outBase. Some of these are commented out or not used in the implementation, but that is the basic idea.

The base pointers and siprefdist offsets are calculated during the lattice traversal loop in functions like DyzPlus in the QPhiX library. In Figure 9.18, we have hidden these computations for clarity, but they can certainly be found in the attached code bundle.

When the code generation is run, the L2 prefetches are generated into a *separate instruction vector* from the mainline code, and are merged with the main Dslash code just before serializing to try and space them evenly through the generated code. This merging is done by the function mergeIvector-WithL2Prefetches in the source file dslash.cc

GENERATING THE CODE

Now that we have covered the mechanics, let us generate the code. To do this we need to look at two makefiles. One is the main Makefile. Here our main work is to choose the architecture by editing the variable mode in the first line. Right now, it is set to mic which is fine for Intel Xeon Phi coprocessors. We can also set it to, for example, avx for AVX code, or scalar for nonvectorized code.

Second, for each supported mode there is a file called customMake.xxx, where xxx is the mode. We can look, for example, at customMake.mic. In this file, we can set a variety of options for code generation, for example, whether to use streaming stores, or whether we should use L1, L2 prefetching, etc. We show a snippet of customMake.mic in Figure 9.23 where we enabled all the prefetching options and

```
#Prefetching options
# FOR MIC SET THESE ALL TO 1
#
PREF_L1_SPINOR_IN = 1
PREF_L2_SPINOR_IN = 1
PREF_L1_SPINOR_OUT = 1
PREF_L2_SPINOR_OUT = 1
PREF_L1_GAUGE = 1
PREF_L2_GAUGE = 1
PREF_L1_CLOVER = 1
PREF_L2_CLOVER = 1

# Gather / Scatter options
USE_LDUNPK = 1           # Use loadunpack instead of gather
USE_PKST = 1             # Use packstore instead of scatter
USE_SHUFFLES = 0         # Use loads & Shuffles to transpose spinor when
        SOALEN>4
NO_GPREF_L1 = 1          # Generate bunch of normal prefetches instead of
        one gather prefetch for L1
NO_GPREF_L2 = 1          # Generate bunch of normal prefetches instead of
        one gather prefetch for L2

# Enable nontemporal streaming stores
ENABLE_STREAMING_STORES ?= 1
USE_PACKED_GAUGES ?= 1    # Use 2D xy packing for Gauges
```

FIGURE 9.23

Code generation options for Intel Xeon Phi coprocessor, from `customMake.mic`. We set every prefetching option, as well as asking for the use of *load-unpack*, *pack-store* and the use of streaming stores.

asked to use *load unpack* and *pack-store* operators for gather-scatter like operations. As a result, we do not want to generate *gather prefetches* and we have disabled those.

Once all these options are set, one can execute the makefile by running `make xxx` where, again, xxx is the value used for mode. The code generator should then build and run, with the resulting code being placed in the xxx subdirectory as a bunch of files. We note that these files are just the bodies of functions (not even containing function prototypes, etc.). In the QPhiX packages, these files get placed in the directory `include/qphix/xxx/generated` where as usual xxx is the value of the mode. There are files in `include/qphix/xxx` that define the function headers and include these files appropriately using a mixture of templates, and C-preprocessor macros. In the case of the mic target, these files are in `include/qphix/mic` and are called `dslash_mic_complete_specializations_form.h` which defines either the base templates for functions like `dslash_plus_vec`, or if certain preprocessor macros are defined, it defines a specialization, which includes the appropriate generated file.

This inclusion, is driven by the second file: `dslash_mic_complete_specialization.h` which cycles through the various possibilities of the macros, defines them, includes the `_form.h` file and then undefines the macros. This approach is rather messy and we wish a better one was available.

PERFORMANCE RESULTS FOR QPhiX

After chewing our way through the structure of QPhiX and the code-generator, it is finally time to see how well all this hard work has paid off. We will look at the following cases of generated code:

- *scalar*: this uses code generated for the `scalar` mode of the code-generator. It uses all of the 3.5D looping, but no prefetch or vectorization. A version of QPhiX with this set of generated files is available in the Code package in directory `Scalar`.
- *vector*: this uses code generated for the `mic` target but apart from generating vector code, all prefetching options have been turned off. The code for this in the package is in `Vector`. We use explicitly a vector length of 16, and an SOA length of 16.
- *vector + L2*: this is the vector code with L2 prefetches. Code is in `VectorPrefL2`.
- *vector + L1*: this is the vector code with L1 prefetches but not L2. Code is in `VectorPrefL1`.
- *vector + L1 + L2*: this is the vector code with both L1 and L2 prefetching, code is in `VectorPrefL1L2`.
- *vector + L1 + L2 + Barrier*: this is the previous code, but every now and again we resynchronize the cores using a lightweight barrier—similar in style to the Plesiochronous Phasing Barriers discussed in Chapter 5 of the first volume of High Performance Parallelism Pearls. The code for this is in `VectorPrefL1L2Barrier`.
- *vector + L1 + L2 + Barrier, SOALEN=8*: this is the previous code, but using an SOALEN=8, instead of 16. In other words, this test will work with an 8×2 tile. The code for this is in `VectorPrefL1L2BarreirS8`.

We ran all these tests on an Intel Xeon Phi coprocessor model 5110P, booted with the *icache_snoop_off* feature enabled to gain some extra memory bandwidth. We used 59 out of the 60 cores, and an affinity setting of `KMP_AFFINITY=compact,granularity=thread`. We added one unit of padding to our data structures in the *XY* plane, to be free of associativity misses. We present the results in the table shown in Figure 9.24. A couple of things to notice: just moving to the QPhiX lattice traversals, but keeping the code unvectorized, did have some benefit, but not very much. The performance only jumped from 35 GFLOPS (Original) to 51 GFLOPS. However, vectorization even without prefetching had a large impact. The performance reached 184 GFLOPS when using compression.

Looking at the difference between the vector + L1 case and the vector + L2 case, it is clear that L1 prefetching without L2 prefetching is not very beneficial, since probably most L1 prefetches will not hit

Mode	Performance No Compression (GFLOPS)	Performance 2-Row Compression (GFLOPS)
Original	35	N/A
Scalar	51	43
Vector	172	184
Vector+L1	144	169
Vector+L2	176	212
Vector+L1+L2	191	239
Vector +L1+L2+barrier	199	250
Vector +L1+L2+barrier, SOA=8	234	286

FIGURE 9.24

Performance tests run on a lattice with $32^3 \times 64$ sites, using 59 cores (236 threads) on an Intel Xeon Phi coprocessor model 5110P with *icache_snoop_off* feature enabled.

in L2. In contrast, L2 prefetching was very effective. Combining L1 and L2 prefetching we reached 239 GFLOPS with compression.

Finally we note that occasional synchronization with lightweight barriers is beneficial. Let us consider this for a moment, since it is often said that we should avoid synchronizations if we can, since typically they are quite costly. In this situation, we use lightweight barriers contributed by Intel corporation, and the barriers are not global. In any given *phase* of the lattice traversal barriers are called only among a group of cores that work on blocks of the same time-length chunk. This information is set up when we set up the block-phase information (see Figure 9.15)—a `group_tid` is computed for each thread in each block. At construction each `group_tid` is assigned its own barrier. As the threads step through the time-coordinates of a given block, when it comes time to synchronize, threads with the same `group_tid` call a wait on their barrier as can be seen at the end of Figure 9.18. Even within this chunk, we can tune the frequency of the barriers. In our case, we found that we got the highest performance when we execute them once every 16 t-slices. The barriers help, because slight drifts in synchronization may mean that cores which are supposed to be working on the same T-slice may end up working on different slices. In this situation, it could be that a core which could otherwise access a piece of data from the cache of another core, instead has to go to memory. The cost of this can outweigh the cost of the occasional lightweight barrier. This is similar in spirit to the use of plesiochronous phasing barriers described by Jim Dempsey in Chapter 5 of the first volume of High Performance Parallelism Pearls.

We finish off this discussion by noting that we got the best performance by switching to using a layout with *SOALEN=8*, rather than 16. This seems to hold up generally. We find it surprising, since loading two chunks of 8 instead of a single chunk of 16 seem like it ought to need higher bookkeeping overhead, and possibly more instructions.

We have come a long way from the performances seen in the original code. When we examine the memory bandwidth utilization of the best performing configuration with VTune, the memory bandwidth utilized is now reported as 130 GB/s. For this bandwidth, our model predicts a performance of 298 GFLOPS. Our 286 GFLOPS is 96% of this prediction.

OTHER BENEFITS

We may recall that our original code performed at the level of around 34.7 GFLOPS on a particular dual socket Intel Xeon processor. One of the benefits of all our hard work with blocking and the code generator is the improved performance of the new code on Intel Xeon processors. In the Code package, we have a setup to build QPhiX with AVX vectorization in the `FinalAVX` directory. This build does not perform barriers, and because of the excellent hardware prefetching on Intel Xeon processor, we have disabled software prefetching too. Finally, since this is a dual socket cc-NUMA system, we run the code setting the minimum number of time-splits C_t to be 2, which is the number of sockets. With the `KMP_AFFINITY` set to `compact` and because array initialization proceeds in lattice traversal order, the code has become NUMA-aware. Thanks to the large-shared L3 cache of the Intel Xeon processor we can choose slightly larger blocks. A choice of $(B_y, B_z) = (8,8)$ allows for 16 blocks in the Y-Z plane, which after the further split by the minimum value of C_t becomes 32, with 16 blocks assigned to each 8-core socket. This workload can then be processed in two phases without imbalance. We keep the

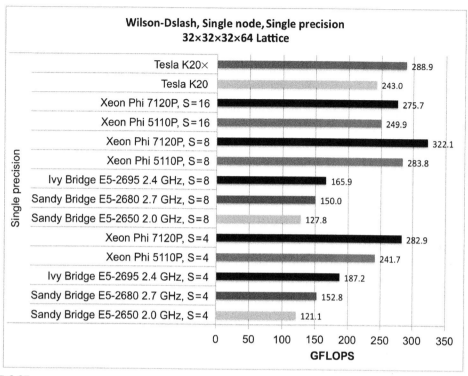

FIGURE 9.25

Performance of single node, singe precision Wilson-Dslash with two-row compression on a variety of systems. The GPU performance numbers were generated using the QUDA library.

same padding parameters, but set the SMT thread geometry to 1×2 in the Y-Z plane, since we have only two hyperthreads. On our system, the Wilson-Dslash timing test ran at **127 GFLOPS**, *a speed-up of about 3.6× over the original code without SSE optimizations*

To be completely fair to the original code, we have also built it with SSE optimizations enabled, and, as before ran it with the `numactl-interleave=0,1` command to ameliorate its non-NUMA nature. We find that the best performance on our test case in single precision is 48-49 GFLOPS. So QPhiX also gains over this configuration by a factor of 2.6×, which is a very significant gain. Further, we should note that it is possible that the processor may have entered its *turbo-boost* mode during our tests, we have not investigated this aspect in significant detail.

We shown in Figure 9.25 the performance of on a variety of systems including a comparison to a Wilson-Dslash code running on NVIDIA K20, and K20X GPUs. The GPU performances were measured using the QUDA library running with comparable options (single precision, two-row compression) and the same volume. We show also performance on the Intel Xeon Phi coprocessor model 7120P, and consider varying the SOA-length. In this plot, the final result for Intel Xeon Phi coprocessor model 5110P with SOA-length 8 is 283.8 GFLOPs, which is two to three GFLOPS less than the numbers we have measured earlier. This we take to be simply a fluctuation which at this rate is at about the 1% level. Finally we note that in the same way that Intel Xeon Phi coprocessor performed best with an SOA-length of 8 (half its vector length), in a similar way, the Xeon results are best with an SOA-length of 4 (half of its vector length).

We do make the disclaimer that to get this level of performance on the Intel Xeon Phi coprocessor requires the *icache_snoop_off* feature to be enabled at boot time. Without this feature performances on the Xeon Phi can be lowered compared to our numbers. As an example on a 61 core Xeon Phi in the Intel Endeavor cluster (*icache_snoop_off* enabled) we sustained 320 GFLOPS for a particular benchmark. The same problem size running on Stampede (similar 61 core Xeon Phi part) without the *icache_snoop_off* feature ran at 271 GFLOPS.

THE END OF THE ROAD?

Of course not! However, we are approaching the end of the chapter. We have gone through a lot of work to optimize the single node performance of Wilson-Dslash and the effort has been very fruitful. However, there are many avenues left, which we have not had the space to explore in this chapter.

One very important aspect is scaling Wilson-Dslash onto multiple nodes, either of Intel Xeon Phi coprocessors or Intel Xeon processors. The code to do this is present in *QPhiX* as well as the original code (although that uses a slightly different algorithm). In its current setting as a PCIe card, several challenges have been encountered with multinode scaling which could merit their own chapter. The interested reader should refer to the "For more information" section at the end of this chapter.

Another important consideration is that the Wilson-Dslash operator is typically the computationally most expensive piece of larger composite operators. Typically one needs to solve linear equations with the larger composite operator. Recently there have been advances in how to solve these systems, not just by the usual Krylov subspace methods such Conjugate Gradients or Stabilized Bi-Conjugate Gradients but also by newer algorithms such as Generalized Conjugate Residuals or Flexible GMRES, which allow the use of Domain Decomposed preconditioners and deflation, and also by Algebraic Multi-Grid approaches. In particular, the domain decomposed preconditioners have very nice properties: small domains can be blocked into L2 cache on the Intel Xeon Phi coprocessor, essentially moving the bandwidth bottleneck from main memory bandwidth to cache bandwidth. A thorough exposition of optimizing a solver with a domain decomposed preconditioned for Intel Xeon Phi coprocessor can be found in our Supercomputing 2014 paper (see the "For more information" section).

When one needs to solve for several systems, one can also consider vectorizing over the systems, which can lead to simpler vectorization than considered in QPhiX. This was done for the different way of formulating QCD than presented here in the "HISQ inverter" paper (see the "For more information" section), and work on Wilson-Dslash is in progress with promising preliminary results.

What would we like to emphasize as the take home messages from this chapter? Perhaps the following:

- To exploit the system for maximum efficiency, it helps to have some model of the performance. Is it memory bound? Is it compute bound? Can expected performance be related to system parameters?

In our case, we made several refinements to our model, for example, to take account of streaming stores, cache reuse, or compression.

- In our case, several optimization steps had to be employed. Just threading for parallelism was not sufficient to get the best performance. Vectorization, prefetching, blocking, and some synchronization were also needed.
- Be prepared for surprises. In our case, these came from the improvement from barriers, and from the finding that an SOA-length that is half of the vector length somehow was more performant than working with an SOA-length equal to the vector length.
- Domain-specific code generators can be helpful. They need not be super sophisticated, and can lower the pain of exploring certain optimizations (e.g., strategies to load, prefetch, etc.). In some cases, like ours, they can also help with performance on other architectures.

FOR MORE INFORMATION

- Babich, R., Brannick, J., Brower, R.C., Clark, M.A., Manteuffel, T.A., et al., 2010. Adaptive multigrid algorithm for the lattice Wilson-Dirac operator. Phys. Rev. Lett. 105, 201602.
- Babich, R., Clark, M.A., Joó, B., Shi, G., Brower, R.C., Gottlieb, S., 2011. Scaling lattice QCD beyond 100 GPUS. In: Proceedings of 2011 International Conference for High Performance Computing, Networking, Storage and Analysis, SC '11, New York, NY, USA. ACM, pp. 70:1-70:11.
- Boyle, P.A., 2009. The {BAGEL} assembler generation library. Comput. Phys. Commun. 180 (12), 2739-2748. 40 {YEARS} {OF} CPC: a celebratory issue focused on quality software for high performance, grid and novel computing architectures.
- Clark, M.A., Babich, R., Barros, K., Brower, R.C., Rebbi, C., 2010. Solving lattice QCD systems of equations using mixed precision solvers on GPUs. Comput. Phys. Commun. 181, 1517-1528.
- Edwards, R.G., Joó, B., 2005. The Chroma software system for lattice QCD. Nucl. Phys. Proc. Suppl. 140, 832.
- Frommer, A., Kahl, K., Krieg, S., Leder, B., Rottmann, M., 2014. Adaptive aggregation based domain decomposition multigrid for the lattice Wilson-Dirac operator. SIAM J. Sci. Comput. 36, A1581-A1608.
- Frommer, A., Nobile, A., Zingler, P., 2012. Deflation and flexible SAP-preconditioning of GMRES in lattice QCD simulation. ArXiv e-prints, April.
- Heybrock, S., Joó, B., Kalamkar, D.D., Smelyanskiy, M., Vaidyanathan, K., Wettig, T., Dubey, P., 2014. Lattice QCD with domain decomposition on Intel® Xeon Phi™ co-processors. In: Proceedings of the International Conference for High Performance Computing, Networking, Storage and Analysis, SC '14, Piscataway, NJ, USA. IEEE Press, pp. 69-80.
- Hestenes, M.R., Stiefel, E., 1952. Methods of conjugate gradients for solving linear systems. J. Res. Natl Bur. Stand. 49 (6), 409-436.
- Jeffers, J., Reinders, J., 2013. Intel® Xeon Phi™ Coprocessor High-Performance Programming, first ed. Morgan-Kauffman, Elsevier, Waltham, MA, USA.
- Jeffers, J., Reinders, J., 2014. High Performance Parallelism Pearls, first ed. Morgan-Kauffman, Elsevier, Waltham, MA, USA.

- Joó, B., Kalamkar, D.D., Vaidyanathan, K., Smelyanskiy, M., Pamnany, K., Lee, V.W., Dubey, P., Watson, W., 2013. Lattice QCD on Intel Xeon Phi coprocessors. In: Kunkel, J.M., Ludwig, T., Meuer, H.W. (Eds.), Supercomputing, volume 7905 of Lecture Notes in Computer Science. Springer, Berlin, Heidelberg, pp. 40-54.
- O. Kaczmarek, Schmidt, C., Steinbrecher, P., Mukherjee, S., Wagner, M., 2014. HISQ inverter on Intel Xeon Phi and NVIDIA GPUs, CoRR abs/1409.1510, http://arxiv.org/abs/1409.1510.
- Luscher, M., 2007. Local coherence and deflation of the low quark modes in lattice QCD. JHEP 0707, 081.
- McClendon, C., 2001. Optimized Lattice QCD Kernels for a Pentium 4 Cluster. Technical Report JLAB-THY-01-29, Jefferson Lab, September.
- Nguyen, A., Satish, N., Chhugani, J., Kim, C., Dubey, P., 2010. 3.5D blocking optimization for stencil computations on modern CPUS and GPUS. In: Proceedings of the 2010 ACM/IEEE International Conference for High Performance Computing, Networking, Storage and Analysis, SC '10, Washington, DC, USA. IEEE Computer Society, pp. 1-13.
- Pochinksy, A.V. QA0 Code Generator. http://www.mit.edu/~avp/qa0.
- Jefferson Lab GitHub Projects. CPP Wilson-Dslash. https://github.com/jeffersonlab/cpp_wilson_dslash.git.
- Jefferson Lab GitHub Projects. QPhiX-Codegen Code Generator. https://github.com/jeffersonlab/qphix-codegen.git.
- Jefferson Lab GitHub Projects. QPhiX Library. https://github.com/jeffersonlab/qphix.git.
- Smelyanskiy, M., Vaidyanathan, K., Choi, J., Joo, B., Chhugani, J., Clark, M.A., Dubey, P., 2011. High-performance lattice QCD for multicore based parallel systems using a cache-friendly hybrid threaded-MPI approach. In: 2011 International Conference for High Performance Computing, Networking, Storage and Analysis (SC), November, pp. 1-10.
- van der Vorst, H.A., 1992. Bi-CGSTAB: a fast and smoothly converging variant of bi-CG for the solution of nonsymmetric linear systems. SIAM J. Sci. Stat. Comput. 13 (2), 631-644.
- Vaidyanathan, K., Pamnany, K., Kalamkar, D.D., Heinecke, A., Smelyanskiy, M., Park, J., Kim, D., Shet, G.A., Kaul, B., Joo, B., Dubey, P., 2014. Improving communication performance and scalability of native applications on Intel Xeon Phi coprocessor clusters. In: 2014 IEEE 28th International Parallel and Distributed Processing Symposium, May, pp. 1083-1092.
- Download the code from this, and other chapters, http://lotsofcores.com.

COSMIC MICROWAVE BACKGROUND ANALYSIS: NESTED PARALLELISM IN PRACTICE

10

James P. Briggs*, Simon J. Pennycook[†], James R. Fergusson*, Juha Jäykkä*, Edward P. Shellard*

University of Cambridge, UK* Intel Corporation, UK[†]

The best current explanation of how our universe began is with a period of rapid exponential expansion, termed inflation. This created the large, mostly empty, universe that we observe today. The principle piece of evidence for this comes from the cosmic microwave background (CMB)—a microwave frequency background radiation, thought to have been left over from the big bang, that is observed to be approximately the same in every single direction we look in the sky. This has been measured by several experiments, the most recent being the European Space Agency's (ESA) Planck satellite, whose measurement is shown in Figure 10.1a. The CMB is from the time when the universe was approximately 300,000 years old. At this time the universe was so hot that it was opaque and so we cannot see back to any time before this. Today's theoretical physicists perform complex calculations with computers to test the plausibility of their theoretical models of the universe against what we see in the CMB.

In the remainder of this chapter, we show the steps taken to optimize and modernize Modal, a cosmological statistical analysis code developed by theoretical physicists at the University of Cambridge. We show the steps taken to port the code to many-core architectures and find that we require nested parallelism to achieve higher levels of performance and to reduce the memory footprint. Besides the optimization story, we compare the different nested parallelism approaches available in OpenMP, discussing the strengths and weaknesses of each and their increasing relevance to future microarchitectures.

ANALYZING THE CMB WITH MODAL

One of the key successes of the inflationary model is that it provides a natural mechanism for the generation of fluctuations in density from which all structure in the universe grew. These primordial seeds were created by the microscopic quantum fluctuations during inflation being stretched to galactic size. These fluctuations have been measured to very high precision in the CMB radiation, most recently by the Planck satellite experiment (see Figure 10.1a). Another key prediction of the simplest inflationary models is that these fluctuations should be Gaussian (i.e., follow a simple normal or "bell" curve). Deviations of these statistics from a Gaussian distribution would be direct evidence for interesting new physics.

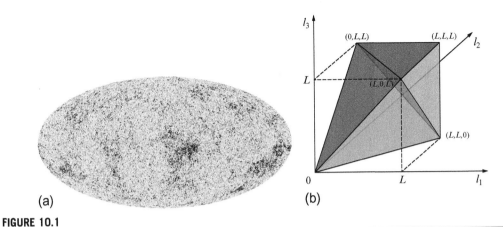

FIGURE 10.1

(a) The tiny density fluctuations in the CMB as measured by the Planck satellite experiment. (b) The nonrectangular integration domain within which the bispectrum is well defined by satisfying the triangle condition.

The Modal code we discuss here is currently the only completely general method for constraining deviations from this Gaussian prediction for the CMB. It does so via the *bispectrum*, or three-point correlator, of the CMB. This can be thought of as searching for any correlations between any three points defined by the corners of a given triangle (as such, we will see that the code frequently involves triple products). To do this, the inflationary bispectrum must be evolved forward in time and then projected onto a spherical shell defined by the CMB in a way that can be easily compared to data. For this work, we have extracted this part of the calculation from the rest of the code and turned it into a mini-app called *miniModal*.

The code employs two sets of three-dimensional basis templates: a theoretical one that has been evolved from the end of inflation until the time of observation (and hence involves an integration over r, which is the distance along a line of sight) and one defined on the 2D CMB itself—$\tilde{Q}_n$ and Q_n, respectively. These basis templates have been chosen as their form greatly simplifies the estimation part of the code (which would otherwise be seven-dimensional and hence intractable). The code in miniModal calculates the decomposition of the evolved primordial basis into the CMB basis. If we define the matrix Γ such that $\tilde{Q}_n = \sum_r \Gamma_{nr} Q_r$, then Γ can be calculated using the equation shown in Figure 10.2a. Thus for optimizing the calculation of Γ we only need to focus on optimizing the evaluation of the inner product. The majority of the calculation time is in evaluating the second inner product due to the radial integral inherent in $\tilde{Q}$, so we will restrict our attention to that alone.

Writing it out explicitly, the calculation performed in miniModal is shown in Figure 10.2b. There is a known mapping $n \rightarrow ijk$, and the values of ℓ_1, ℓ_2, and ℓ_3 are determined by the Wigner-3J symbol, shown in Figure 10.2c. The Wigner-3J symbol has two important properties: first, it is zero when the three ℓ_i treated as lengths are unable to form a triangle (the triangle condition); and second, it is zero whenever $\ell_1 + \ell_2 + \ell_3$ is odd (the parity condition), otherwise its value is unity. These constraints are a geometric effect which comes from conservation of momentum when projected onto the spherical shell. This integration domain is visualized in Figure 10.1b. The maximum value of any of the three ℓ values is fixed at 2000.

$$\Gamma_{nm} = \sum_r \langle Q_n, Q_r \rangle^{-1} \left\langle Q_r, \tilde{Q}_m \right\rangle$$

(a) Transfer function

$$\langle Q_n, \tilde{Q}_{n'} \rangle = \sum_{\ell_1=2}^{\ell_{max}} \sum_{\ell_2=2}^{\ell_{max}} \sum_{\ell_3=2}^{\ell_{max}} \frac{\theta_{\ell_1 \ell_2 \ell_3}}{72\pi^2} \frac{(2\ell_1 + 1)(2\ell_2 + 1)(2\ell_3 + 1)(L + 1/3)}{(L+1)(L_1 + 1/3)(L_2 + 1/3)(L_3 + 1/3)}$$

$$\times \sqrt{\frac{(L_1 + 1/6)(L_2 + 1/6)(L_3 + 1/6)}{(L + 1/6)C_{\ell_1} C_{\ell_2} C_{\ell_3} v_{\ell_1}^2 v_{\ell_2}^2 v_{\ell_3}^2}} \, (q_i(\ell_1) q_j(\ell_2) q_k(\ell_3) + 5 \, \text{perms})$$

$$\times \int r^2 dr \, (\tilde{q}_{i'}(r, \ell_1) \tilde{q}_{j'}(r, \ell_2) \tilde{q}_{k'}(r, \ell_3) + 5 \, \text{perms})$$

(b) Inner product

$$\begin{pmatrix} \ell_1 & \ell_2 & \ell_3 \\ 0 & 0 & 0 \end{pmatrix}$$

(c) Wigner-3J symbol

FIGURE 10.2

Key equations in the Modal pipeline.

Computing the solution to this inner product requires $\approx 2.4^{13}$ operations, and is therefore intractable on a single CPU. The original code utilizes multi-node parallelism via the message passing interface (MPI) to speed-up the calculation. The list of $n \rightarrow ijk$ triples is evenly divided among the MPI tasks, restricting the amount of parallelism available based on the length of the list. For a production run with the original code, the whole calculation takes approximately 6 hours on 512 Intel® Xeon® processor E5-4650L cores. Furthermore, it has to be run many times to cross-validate results, representing a significant bottleneck in the Modal pipeline. Any performance improvement for this calculation will have high impact on the Modal pipeline, and the cosmology research that depends on it.

The calculation performed by Modal is a prime candidate for Intel® Xeon Phi™ coprocessors—the inner product calculations are computationally very expensive, independent of one another, and require very little memory (with production runs using only $\mathcal{O}(100)$ MB of RAM and writing only $\mathcal{O}(1)$ MB to disk). However, the code as written does not express this calculation in a way that is conducive to the utilization of modern hardware. Our acceleration of Modal therefore has two components: tuning the code to ensure that it runs efficiently (i.e., optimization); and enabling the code to scale across vectors and many cores (i.e., modernization). Extracting performance from current and future generations of Intel Xeon processors and Intel Xeon Phi coprocessors is impossible without parallelism, and the process of optimization and modernization presented here is imperative for ensuring that COSMOS stay at the forefront of cosmological research.

OPTIMIZATION AND MODERNIZATION

The core of the theoretical bispectrum calculation lies in a routine called `calculate_gamma_3d`. The main loop nest of this routine, which is the codified version of the second equation from Figure 10.2, is shown in Figure 10.3. The n and m loops iterate over ijk and $i'j'k'$ triples, respectively (`terms`, or N_{terms}, represents the length of the sets of basis templates and hence the number of triples). The loop over m, which calls the function `plijk`, represents the second line of the equation and the call to function `calculate_xint` represents the third line of the same equation.

Originally, this loop nest was parallelized on the outermost loop using only MPI. This outermost loop iterates over the total number of eigenmodes used, which for production calculations typically ranges between 100 and 2000, providing sufficient parallelism for the code to run and scale well on a small cluster of processors. However, running a large number of MPI ranks per coprocessor is likely to incur significant performance overheads, and so the code as written should not be expected to perform well there. As shown by many other case studies, efficient use of a coprocessor requires the introduction of threads and a move to a hybrid MPI/OpenMP programming model, enabling parallelism at a finer granularity and reducing overheads associated with storing redundant data. The question is not whether to introduce threads, but how.

SPLITTING THE LOOP INTO PARALLEL TASKS

Examining the loops in Figure 10.3 more closely, it is apparent that there is a huge source of untapped parallel potential there. The output of the whole loop nest is the resultant array `mvec`—the whole loop nest is simply an array *reduction* pattern, and there is parallelism available in all of the $n\ell_1\ell_2\ell_3$ loop nests. The headache arising from this is that the constraints on the values of $\ell_1\ell_2\ell_3$ from the Wigner-3J symbol (the third equation in Figure 10.2) result in an irregular loop structure. Specifically, the loop between ℓ_1 and ℓ_2 is upper triangular, and the ℓ_3 loop is also upper triangular with respect to ℓ_2. Furthermore, the ℓ_3 loop strides by 2, and its start and end points depend on ℓ_1. A reduced version of the full iteration space, for $\ell_1 = \ell_2 = \ell_3 = 10$, is displayed visually in Figure 10.4.

```
for (n=0; n<terms; n++) {
    for (l1=0; l1<lsize; l1++) {
        for (m=0; m<terms; m++) mvec[m] = 0.0;
        for (l2=l1; l2<lsize; l2++) {
            for (l3=l2+l1%2; l3<min(l1+l2,lmax)+1; l3+=2) {
                x = calculate_xint(l1,l2,l3,n,xsize,xvec,yvec,task);
                ...
                z = permsix(l1,l2,l3)*calculate_geometric(l1,l2,l3)/sqrt(s1*
                    s2*s3);
                for (m=0;m<terms;m++) {
                    y = plijk(m,l1,l2,l3);
                    mvec[m] += x*y*z;
                }
            }
        }
    }
    // array reduction of mvec into gamma matrix
}
```

FIGURE 10.3

Code snippet for the hotspot in miniModal.

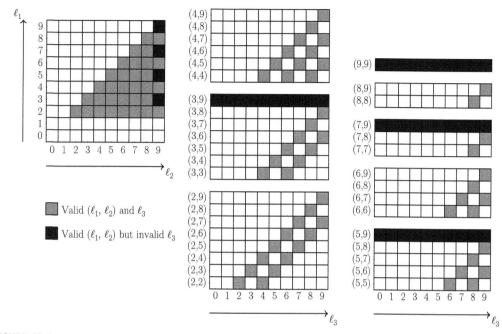

FIGURE 10.4

Structure of the $\ell_1\ell_2\ell_3$ iteration space with valid and invalid iterations shown.

Adding threads to the ℓ_1 loop would give an MPI/OpenMP hybrid code that could scale to use $\mathcal{O}(1000)$ coprocessors with 2000 parallel tasks per coprocessor. Although this sounds like a great idea, the problem with this setup is that the triangular structure of the nested loops would lead to load imbalance in the ℓ_1 loop, which is visualized in Figure 10.5 for four threads. Imbalanced loops in OpenMP are typically handled through the use of dynamic scheduling or task-based parallelism. In our experiments, we found that these approaches suffered from poor cache behavior and low levels of data reuse, due to an inability to bind particular groups of parallel tasks to the same core. Furthermore, this approach only puts a plaster over the problem and does not address the underlying algorithmic issue.

An ideal solution is to flatten the entire $\ell_1\ell_2\ell_3$ loop nest into a one-dimensional iteration space and divide the iterations between threads as evenly as possible. OpenMP provides the `collapse` pragma to do precisely this; however, it cannot be used in cases like ours where there are dependencies between loop bounds. We instead choose to manually restructure the loop such that it can be run from a specified start $\ell_1\ell_2\ell_3$ triple to a specified end triple, as shown in Figure 10.6. This way, the work assigned to a given parallel task on the coprocessor can be represented neatly by six bounds: (`lower_l1`,`lower_l2`, `lower_l3`,`upper_l1`,`upper_l2`,`upper_l3`).

To determine these bounds we first execute a "trial run" of the entire loop nest to count the total number of iterations N. Next, we evenly divide the iterations between our P parallel workers, spreading the remainder across the first $N \bmod P$ workers. Finally, another pass through the loop records the $\ell_1\ell_2\ell_3$ bounds for each of the workers, based on the number of iterations assigned to them. This gives an

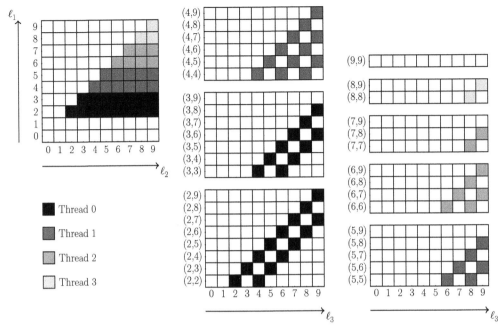

FIGURE 10.5

A naïve attempt to parallelize the loop nest. Each color corresponds to a different thread.

```
int start_l1 = lower_l1;
int end_l1 = upper_l1+1;
for (l1=start_l1; l1<end_l1; l1++)
{
        int start_l2 = l1 == lower_l1 ? lower_l2 : l1;
        int end_l2 = l1 == upper_l1 ? upper_l2+1 : lsize;
        for (l2=start_l2; l2<end_l2; l2++)
        {
                int start_l3 = l2+(l1%2);
                int end_l3 = min(l1+l2,lmax)+1;
                if ((l1==lower_l1) && (l2==lower_l2))
                {
                        start_l3 = lower_l3;
                }
                if ((l1==upper_l1) && (l2==upper_l2))
                {
                        end_l3 = upper_l3;
                }
                for (l3 = start_l3; l3 < end_l3; l3 += 2)
                {
                        // loop interior...
                }
        }
}
```

FIGURE 10.6

The flattened version of the loop shown in Figure 10.3 that can run between arbitrary *lower* and *upper* points in the triangular iteration space.

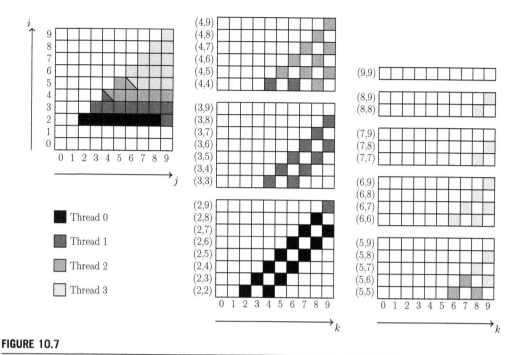

FIGURE 10.7

The optimal thread scheduling (with respect to iteration count) for the loop nest.

optimally load-balanced loop (assuming that all iterations take the same amount of time, which empirically we have seen to be the case) as shown in Figure 10.7.

Now that we have a working offload implementation, we can start the iterative process of optimization to close the gap between processor and coprocessor performance. Looking at a profile of the code running on the coprocessor, we see that over half of its execution time is spent in the function `plijk` seen in Figure 10.3. This is a simple inlined function that indexes some arrays and computes the second line of the second equation in Figure 10.2 for a given $\ell_1\ell_2\ell_3$. This function is already well-vectorized by the compiler, so there is not much that can be gained from just microoptimization—however, looking closely at the code in Figure 10.3, we can see that `plijk` is called N_{terms}^2 times for each $\ell_1\ell_2\ell_3$ triple. This can be reduced to N_{terms} calls by changing the loop order, bringing the n loop inside the ℓ loops and storing the result inside an array `x[n]`. The reordered version of the loop nest is shown in Figure 10.8.

Following this reordering of the loop nest, it becomes clear that the MPI parallelization of the original code was inefficient; parallelizing over n distributes the work of `calculate_xint`, but redundantly computes `plijk` on all processors. As was the case for threads, we must now find a way to distribute the triangular loop nest across MPI ranks. Luckily, the approach previously described for threads can easily be extended to divide work across multiple levels of a parallel hierarchy: we divide iterations first across MPI tasks, and then subdivide those iterations across OpenMP threads.

```
for (13 = start_13; 13 < end_13; 13 += 2)
{
        for (n = 0; n < terms; n++)
        {
                x[n] = calculate_xint(l1,l2,l3,n,xsize,xvec,yvec,thread_data[
                    tid].task_spl);
        }
        double s1 = svec[l1]; double s2 = svec[l2]; double s3 = svec[l3];
        double z = permsix(l1,l2,l3)*calculate_geometric(l1,l2,l3)/sqrt(s1*s2*
            s3);

        for (m = 0; m < terms; m++)
        {
                double y = plijk(m,l1,l2,l3);
                for (n = 0; n < terms; n++)
                {
                        mmat[m][n] += x[n] * y * z;
                }
        }
}
```

FIGURE 10.8

The rearranged version of the loop body shown in Figure 10.3.

INTRODUCING NESTED PARALLELISM

Although the new loop structure reduces algorithmic complexity and thus the total amount of work required, it is important to consider its use of memory—a naïve implementation requires every thread to store the outer product of x and plijk in a temporary matrix mmat, which has N_{terms}^2 elements. For typical sizes of N_{terms}, mmat requires $\mathcal{O}(10\text{MB})$ of memory per thread, far exceeding the capacity of the 512 kB L2 cache on Intel Xeon Phi coprocessors and potentially causing capacity issues for the larger L3 caches available on Intel Xeon processors. The fact that we would like to run two to four threads per core only makes this worse (see Figure 10.9), and competition between threads for capacity may even lead to thrashing.

Ideally, we should aim to keep only a single copy of mmat per core, avoid redundant calculations, and tightly control data placement to maximize cache re-use and avoid false sharing. It is only possible to achieve all of these goals simultaneously by rearranging the loop to accommodate *nested parallelism*, splitting the outer l loop over cores and the inner n and m loops over the threads on each core. This simple remapping of threads to work reduces memory requirements significantly, and also ensures that

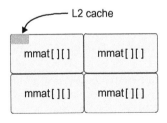

FIGURE 10.9

The temporary data of each thread, mmat, is larger than the L2 cache on a coprocessor core. With four threads per core this problem is four times worse.

threads *cooperate* rather than *compete* (i.e., cache lines accessed by one thread are expected to be re-used by others on the same core). We can improve memory behavior further through cache blocking, chunking together iterations of $\ell_1\ell_2\ell_3$ such that a single location in mmat is updated multiple times before being evicted from cache.

We explore three alternative ways to implement nested parallelism:

1. nested omp parallel constructs;
2. the new omp teams construct from OpenMP 4.0; and
3. manual thread decomposition, similar to the technique used by Dempsey in the "Plesiochronous phasing barriers" chapter of the previous High Performance Parallelism Pearls book.

Each of these options expresses nested parallelism differently, and uses different terminology. To simplify discussion here, we refer to the threads spawned at the outer level as "team leaders" and to the threads spawned at the inner level as "team members." We expect there to be performance differences between the approaches, but which performs best and under what circumstances is an open question.

All of the experiments that we have performed to compare different nested parallelism approaches use only Intel Xeon Phi coprocessors, primarily because the COSMOS supercomputer is not configured to support hyperthreading on its Intel Xeon processors. However, we are confident that the approaches outlined are applicable to any system with multiple threads sharing limited resources—including the next generation of Intel Xeon Phi coprocessors, where two cores (a maximum of eight threads) share a 1-MB L2 cache—and hope to demonstrate this in future work.

NESTED OpenMP PARALLEL REGIONS

The most obvious and intuitive method of implementing nested parallelism within an OpenMP code is to simply nest two (or more) OpenMP parallel regions. For an existing OpenMP code, employing this method is simple—the outer parallel region is set to spawn a fixed number of threads (e.g., 60), and an additional parallel region is set to spawn a smaller fixed number of threads (e.g., 4). An example of this for a simple loop nest is shown in Figure 10.10.

By default, an OpenMP thread encountering a nested OpenMP parallel region will serialize the section. In order to get the desired behavior (i.e., spawning additional threads), it is necessary to override the default behavior with an environment variable (OMP_NESTED=TRUE) or function call (omp_set_nested(true))—although this functionality is not necessarily supported by all OpenMP runtimes. Where it is supported, nesting OpenMP parallel regions in this manner are often not recommended, due to the repeated high overheads of creating and destroying the threads involved. These

```
#pragma omp parallel for num_threads(60)
for (l = 0; l < lsize; l++)
{
    #pragma omp parallel for num_threads(4) schedule(static,1)
    for (n = 0; n < terms; n++)
    { ... }
}
```

FIGURE 10.10

Example of nested OpenMP parallel regions.

costs are prohibitively expensive when the nested regions are encountered often, such as when the threads are spawned for an inner-most loop.

There is, however, support for an experimental feature in the Intel® OpenMP runtime (Version 15 Update 1 or later) known as "hot teams" that is able to reduce these overheads, by keeping a pool of threads alive (but idle) during the execution of the non-nested parallel code. The use of hot teams is controlled by two environment variables: KMP_HOT_TEAMS_MODE and KMP_HOT_TEAMS_MAX_LEVEL. To keep unused team members alive when team sizes change we set KMP_HOT_TEAMS_MODE=1, and because we have two levels of parallelism we set KMP_HOT_TEAMS_MAX_LEVEL=2.

Care must also be taken with thread affinity settings. OpenMP 4.0 provides new environment variables for handling the physical placement of threads, OMP_PROC_BIND and OMP_PLACES, and these are compatible with nested parallel regions. To place team leaders on separate cores, and team members on the same core, we set OMP_PROC_BIND=spread,close and OMP_PLACES=threads.

OpenMP 4.0 TEAMS

The teams and distribute constructs were added to OpenMP 4.0 as part of its support for accelerators, and are similar to the "gang" and "worker" model provided by OpenACC. An example of this for a simple loop nest is shown in Figure 10.11.

Employing teams requires more extensive code changes than simple nesting, as there are some restrictions on how it can be used. First, a teams construct must be contained within a target construct and therefore cannot easily be used for nested parallelism on the host—a teams region can only be executed on the host when the "if" clause of a target construct evaluates to false! Second, it must be the first statement to appear in that target construct, so switching between serial and parallel code requires separate target constructs (causing unnecessary host-device synchronization for offload codes). Third, although threads within a team can be synchronized with an OpenMP barrier, threads in different teams cannot be synchronized (except by the closing of the teams and target regions).

These restrictions make this approach less flexible than simple nesting, and also force developers to maintain separate versions of the same code for host and device. Retro-fitting OpenMP 4.0 teams into our preexisting code was difficult, as it was not designed with these restrictions in mind. For codes that are already divided into parallel kernels (e.g., CUDA, or OpenCL codes), this retro-fitting process would require less extensive changes.

```
#pragma omp target device(0)
partition_block(lsize, omp_get_num_teams(), &start_l, &end_l);

#pragma omp target device(0)
#pragma omp teams num_teams(60) thread_limit(4)
for (l = start_l; l < end_l; l++)
{
    #pragma omp parallel for num_threads(4) schedule(static,1)
    for (n = 0; n < terms; n++)
    { ... }
}
```

FIGURE 10.11

Example of OpenMP teams region. The teams construct must be called immediately after the target construct.

MANUAL NESTING

The final approach to nesting that we consider is a "manual" nesting approach, in which the threads created by OpenMP are partitioned and assigned work depending on their global thread ID (`tid=omp_get_thread_num()`), core ID (`tid / threads_per_core`), and local thread ID (`tid % threads_per_core`). We designate any thread with a local ID of 0 to be a team leader and all other threads to be team members. An example of this for a simple loop nest is shown in Figure 10.12.

Although implementing nested parallelism in this manner is fairly simple, there are some nonobvious pitfalls when it comes to thread synchronization with the OpenMP `barrier` construct. First, there is a performance issue. Although we have divided our threads into teams, there is no way to convey this manual partitioning to the OpenMP runtime and therefore any barrier will synchronize *all* of the threads. Such a global barrier is expensive compared to a team-local barrier (since barrier costs scale $\mathcal{O}(\log_2(N))$), and may also cause inefficiencies where slight load imbalance exists between teams. Second, there is a potential correctness issue. If our teams do not run exactly the same number of iterations (which may be the case, due to load imbalance) and do not hit exactly the same number of global barriers, then threads will get stuck and the code will deadlock. To work around these two issues we introduce a custom barrier implementation enabling synchronization between only the threads in a team. The code for this local barrier, provided by Larry Meadows of Intel Corporation, is shown in Figure 10.13.

At its core, the implementation is much simpler than one might expect. We use a 4 byte `int` as a barrier variable, and each of our (up to) four threads owns 1 byte. Each time a thread arrives at the barrier, it toggles its byte (i.e., from 0 to 1 or vice versa) and waits for the other threads to arrive. Since the barrier variable is a single `int`, we can check whether all threads have arrived simply by comparing its value to a precomputed wait value (`waitval`), which is either 0 or 0x01010101 depending on how many times the barrier has been used. Most of the complication in the code relates to ensuring correct operation of the barrier in corner cases and/or improving performance. If two barriers occur back-to-back, then it is possible that one thread will reach the second barrier before the other threads have left the first. If such a situation does occur, and the arriving thread signals its arrival by toggling its byte, the other threads will *never* leave the barrier—we have created a deadlock. To avoid this corner-case behavior, it is necessary to use two different barrier variables, and to switch between them after each synchronization point. To improve performance, the `corebarrier_t` struct containing our two barrier `int`s is aligned and padded to 64 bytes, thus ensuring it occupies exactly one cache line. This cache line

```
#pragma omp parallel num_threads(240)
{
    partition_block_grouped(lsize, omp_get_num_threads() / threads_per_core,
        &start_l, &end_l);
    for (l = start_l; l < end_l; l++)
    {
        int start_n = tid % threads_per_core;
        int end_n = terms;
        for (n = start_n; n < end_n; n += threads_per_core)
        { ... }
        userCoreBarrier();
    }
}
```

FIGURE 10.12

Example of manual nested OpenMP.

```
typedef __declspec(align(64)) struct corebarrier_t
{
    volatile int barrier[2]; // volatile ensures that the compiler won't
                             // optimize out reads in the while loop
    int padding[14];
} corebarrier_t;

typedef __declspec(align(64)) struct barrier_t
{
    int barrier_id;     // which barrier to use this time (0 or 1)
    int core_tid;       // local thread id on the core (tid % 4)
    int flag[2];        // value to write this time (0 or 1)
    int waitval;        // value to wait on if threads are writing 1s
    corebarrier_t* me;  // corebarrier_t shared by all threads on the core
} barrier_t;

void cpu_pause()
{
    // pause, sleep, or delay this thread
}

void corebarrier(barrier_t *bar)
{
    // determine which barrier and values to use
    int barrier_id = bar->barrier_id;
    int core_tid = bar->core_tid;
    int flag = bar->flag[barrier_id];
    int waitval = (flag) ? bar->waitval : 0;

    // loop until all threads have written to this barrier
    corebarrier_t *me = bar->me;
    ((char *)&me->barrier[barrier_id])[core_tid] = flag;
    while (me->barrier[barrier_id] != waitval)
        cpu_pause();

    // toggle the barrier/flag for next time
    bar->flag[barrier_id] = 1 - flag;
    bar->barrier_id = 1 - barrier_id;
}
```

FIGURE 10.13

Example implementation of a fast, on-core, barrier.

will only ever be accessed by threads in the same team, and this prevents false sharing of the barrier variables between threads on different cores. On the coprocessor, this barrier allows us to synchronize the threads on one core in only ≈ 50 cycles.

INNER LOOP OPTIMIZATION

Now that we have sufficiently prepared the ground for efficient usage of the coprocessor, we now begin the process of tuning the performance of the innermost loop. We once again profile the code running with $N_{terms} = 601$, and see that by far the biggest bottleneck is the routine that solves the integral over dr in the equation in Figure 10.2b. This integral is calculated by the routine calculate_xint which is shown in Figure 10.14.

The integral is evaluated using a (cubic) spline-based numerical integration method. Originally this was implemented using the routine gsl_spline_eval_integ from the GNU Scientific Library (GSL), but one of our first optimization steps replaced this with an equivalent and better optimized routine

```
double calculate_xint(int l1, int l2, int l3, int n, int rsize, double* r,
      double* y, DFTaskPtr task) {
   find_perm_prim(n,&a1,&a2,&a3);
   ...
   for (i=0; i < rsize; i++) {
       double p1 = beta[l1][a1][i];
       double p2 = beta[l1][a2][i];
       double p3 = beta[l1][a3][i];
       double p4 = beta[l2][a1][i];
       double p5 = beta[l2][a2][i];
       double p6 = beta[l2][a3][i];
       double p7 = beta[l3][a1][i];
       double p8 = beta[l3][a2][i];
       double p9 = beta[l3][a3][i];

       double t1 = p1*p5*p9;
       double t2 = p2*p6*p7;
       double t3 = p3*p4*p8;
       double t4 = p3*p5*p7;
       double t5 = p2*p4*p9;
       double t6 = p1*p6*p8;

       double _y = r[i] * r[i] * (t1+t2+t3+t4+t5+t6) * sixth;
       if (i < 10 && fabs(_y) > 1e-18) _y = 0;
       y[i] = _y;
   }
   ...
   // integrate : r^2 y(r) dr
   status = dfdConstruct1D(task, DF_PP_SPLINE, DF_METHOD_STD);
   status = dfdIntegrate1D(task, DF_METHOD_PP, 1, llim, DF_NO_HINT, rlim, \
                     DF_NO_HINT, 0, 0, &result, DF_NO_HINT);

   return result;
}
```

FIGURE 10.14

Code snippet for `calculate_xint` using a spline integration method.

from the Intel® Math Kernel Library (Intel® MKL) (shown in the last lines of code in the figure). There are two problems with this spline-based integration method: first, it requires a lot of extra memory in order to store the cubic polynomial coefficients for each data point; and second, it is bandwidth-inefficient, as it needs to solve a system of equations representing the global system. Ultimately, the Intel MKL routine is better suited to solving a single very large vector of data rather than the many short vectors of data we see in Modal.

Replacing the Intel MKL routine with a simpler numerical integration routine allows us to solve both of these problems. We find that using a simple trapezium rule integrator combined with hand-selected sampling points (to improve accuracy in areas of interest) provides sufficient numerical accuracy to obtain a physically meaningful result, and the reduced space and time requirements of this simplified method give a speed-up of $\mathcal{O}(10\times)$.

This leaves two fairly equal hotspots in the profile: the array reduction stage, where the blocks of x and plijk values are reduced into the mmat matrix; and the part of the computation inside the calculate_xint function that is not performing integration.

The initial implementation of the array reduction code is shown in Figure 10.15a. Here we attempted to perform the reduction using the nested threads, vectorizing the outer loop over *n*. The performance of this reduction suffered from poor L2 cache locality and, rather than tune it further

```
int start_m = workerid;              if (workerid == 0)
int end_m = terms;                   {
for (m=start_m; m<end_m; m+=4)           cblas_dgemm(CblasRowMajor,
{                                                    CblasTrans,
    #pragma omp simd private(n,l)                    CblasNoTrans,
    for (n=0; n<terms; n++)                          terms, terms,
    {                                                blocksize,
        double tmp = mvec[m][n];                     1.0, &plijkz[0][0],
        for (l=0; l<blocksize; l++)                  terms, &x[0][0],
        {                                            terms, 1.0,
            tmp += x[l][n] *                         &mmat[0][0], terms);
                   plijkz[l][m];             }
        }                                 userCoreBarrier(threadData[tid].bar);
        mmat[m][n] = tmp;
    }
}
```

(a) Our initial reduction routine, with multiple threads and outer loop vectorization.

(b) The current reduction routine, with one thread calling DGEMM while the others in the team wait.

FIGURE 10.15

The array reduction stage was one of the bottle necks in the inner loop. Our attempt at the reduction is shown in (a). This is equivalent to a matrix-matrix multiply and so we replaced it with DGEMM as shown in (b), with much performance improvement.

through manual cache-blocking, we realized that the whole operation could be expressed as a matrix-matrix multiply. The DGEMM provided by Intel MKL is already cache-blocked, solving all of the issues experienced by our implementation. Note that we currently use only the team leader to call this function—it should be possible to have all team members cooperate here, and we are in the process of investigating why our early attempts have resulted in a slow-down.

The remaining bottleneck in `calculate_xint` is the loop over i in Figure 10.14. The array beta is accessed with some indirection over the ℓ and a variables, but is read directly over i, and the compiler is thus able to auto-vectorize the code well out-of-the-box. However, we can improve memory behavior by aligning and padding the multidimensional beta array such that its rows start on 64-byte boundaries. We can also improve the quality of the prefetches generated by the compiler through use of the prefetch and loop count pragmas—prefetching beta, y and r with a prefetch distance of 1 gives the best performance for this loop. However, these changes do not completely banish the cache-misses, and this function remains the hotspot in our final version of the code. Although there is a large amount of data reuse inside a core, every thread has 11 memory streams, which is too many for the prefetchers to effectively hide the latency of the L2 accesses. We expect that the introduction of out-of-order execution and improved prefetching hardware in the next generation of Intel Xeon Phi coprocessors (previously codenamed "Knights Landing") will improve the performance of cases such as this.

RESULTS

Throughout this section we present results from a dual socket Intel Xeon processor E5-4650L and an Intel Xeon Phi coprocessor 5110P. The technical specifications of these are given in Figure 10.16. The host processors are based on the Intel microarchitecture previously code-named "Sandy Bridge," and the coprocessors on the microarchitecture previously code-named "Knights Corner." All experiments

Results

	Intel Xeon Processor E5-4650L	Intel Xeon Phi Coprocessor 5110P
Sockets × cores × threads	2 × 8 × 1	1 × 60 × 4
Clock (GHz)	2.6	1.053
Double Precision GFLOP/s	332.8	1010.88
L1/L2/L3 cache (kB)	32 / 256 / 20,480	32 / 512 / –
DRAM (per node)	128 GB	8 GB GDDR
STREAM bandwidth	52.8 GB/s	165 GB/s
PCIe bandwidth		6 GB/s
Compiler version		Intel® Composer XE 2015 (v15.0.0.090)
MPSS version		3.2.1

FIGURE 10.16

System configuration.

(unless otherwise stated) use all of the cores available within a node, with the maximum number of threads supported—four threads on the coprocessor and one thread on the processor (hyper-threading is disabled on the host system)—and the thread affinity is set using `KMP_AFFINITY=close,granularity=fine`. The coprocessor is used in offload mode, and no additional flags are passed to the compiler beyond those used for the processor: `-O3 -xHost -mcmodel=medium -restrict -align -fno-alias -qopenmp`. All experiments are repeated five times, and we present the average (mean), in order to account for system noise and any nondeterministic performance effects arising from threading.

The graph in Figure 10.17 shows the speed-up (higher is better) resulting from each of our optimizations, relative to the original code running on a dual-socket processor. A mapping from version number to a description of the optimizations is given for reference in the table shown in Figure 10.18, along

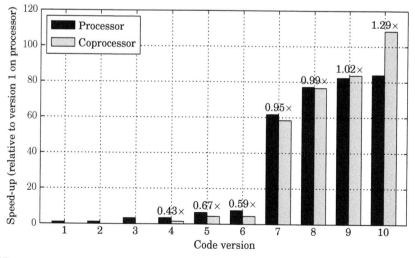

FIGURE 10.17

Speed-up for miniModal at each stage of optimization.

Version	Processor (s)	Coprocessor (s)	Comment
1	2887.0	–	Original code
2	2610.0	–	Loop simplification
3	882.0	–	Intel MKL integration routines and function inlining
4	865.9	1991.6	Flattened loops and introduced OpenMP threads
5	450.6	667.9	Loop reordering and manual nested threading
6	385.6	655.0	Blocked version of the loop (for cache)
7	46.9	49.5	Numerical integration routine (Trapezium Rule)
8	37.4	37.7	Reduction with DGEMM
9	35.1	34.5	Data alignment (for vectorization)
10	34.3	26.6	Tuning of software prefetching distances

FIGURE 10.18

Execution times of miniModal at each stage of optimization.

with execution times in seconds. Note that since we are utilizing the coprocessor in offload mode, we do not present results for it prior to the introduction of OpenMP threads—offloading to a single thread would have been very slow!

Code Versions 1-3 show that the speed-ups resulting from "low-hanging fruit" can be quite significant ($3.2\times$ on the processor), and that the impact of following best practices should not be underestimated. Versions 4-6 see the total speed-up grow further ($7.5\times$ on the processor, $3.0\times$ on the coprocessor), but the coprocessor remains slower due to the large memory footprint of Intel MKL's cubic spline routines. It is not until we make a dramatic change to the core algorithm in Version 7 (by switching to numerical integration) and subsequently tune it in Versions 8-10 that the coprocessor overtakes the processor, and we reach a performance ratio similar to what we should expect: specifically, a single coprocessor being $\approx 1.5\times$ faster than two processor sockets. In the final version, the number of vector instructions issued per cycle on the coprocessor was measured by Speedometer to be 39.8% of peak. This shows that our work in optimizing the inner loop in miniModal was quite successful in making effective use of the hardware, but still some inefficiencies remain due to the number of memory streams per thread being too high for the prefetchers to effectively hide the latency of cache accesses.

The total speed-up relative to the original baseline code is close to $100\times$ on both platforms. Further, the results shown here use only two processor sockets or one coprocessor—by dividing the complete problem space across nodes using MPI, and then subdividing across the processor and coprocessor present in each node, the calculation can be accelerated even further. These optimizations have thus enabled COSMOS to completely change the way in which the code is used; rather than running on the entire system for hours, after careful selection of cosmological parameters, Modal can now be incorporated as part of a larger Monte Carlo pipeline to quickly evaluate the likelihood of alternative parameters.

COMPARISON OF NESTED PARALLELISM APPROACHES

The graph in Figure 10.19 shows the execution time of the fully optimized miniModal, using each of the three nested parallelism approaches described earlier. For nested OpenMP parallel regions, we present two sets of results: one for the default behavior and another for the behavior with the experimental hot teams functionality enabled.

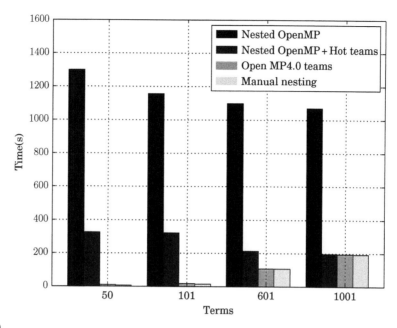

FIGURE 10.19

Runtime comparison of the different nested parallel approaches on an Intel Xeon Phi coprocessor for a range of problem sizes.

For small problem sizes, there is a clear difference in performance between nested OpenMP regions and the other approaches. Although use of hot teams provides a significant improvement to performance, it does not completely remove all thread creation/destruction overheads—the runtime must still obey OpenMP semantics (e.g., data movement for private variables) and the runtime must be able to handle any number of threads requested at any level of nesting. Interestingly, the gap between the different approaches is closed to almost zero for the largest problem size, as the overheads are able to be amortized over the increased amount of work assigned to each thread.

The Intel OpenMP runtime also supports an environment variable (KMP_BLOCKTIME) that controls the amount of time that threads spend spinning at the end of an OpenMP region prior to going to sleep. The graph in Figure 10.20 shows how the performance of hot teams is affected by three different values of this variable: 200 ms (the default); 0 (causing threads to sleep immediately and free up core resources); and infinite (causing threads to spin forever, ensuring they are awake when the next parallel region is encountered). Since we expect to encounter many parallel regions in quick succession, setting the blocking time to infinite should have the most effect, and this is reflected in our results. Setting KMP_BLOCKTIME correctly closes the performance gap between nested parallel regions and manual nesting for the 601 problem, a speed-up of 2×, but is still not enough to save the smaller problem sizes.

The table in Figure 10.21 compares the different nested parallelism approaches in terms of usability and friendliness to programmers. Since these metrics are not objective, they are opinions based on our experience with miniModal—readers should feel free to disagree! We feel that the best option today is the manual nesting approach introduced in this chapter, since it hits a "sweet spot," consistently

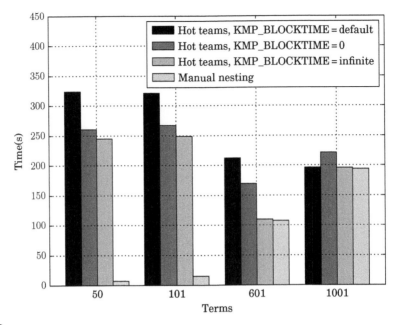

FIGURE 10.20

Runtime comparison for different values of KMP_BLOCKTIME on an Intel Xeon Phi coprocessor. For larger problem sizes, setting this variable to "infinite" gives comparable times to the manual nested approach.

	Nested OpenMP	Hot Teams	OpenMP Teams	Manual
Standard	Yes	No	Yes (4.0)	Yes
Overhead	High	Medium	Low	Low
Affinity	OMP_PROC_BIND OMP_PLACES	OMP_PROC_BIND OMP_PLACES	None	KMP_AFFINITY
Code Changes	Minimal	Minimal	Extensive	Localized
Restrictions	None	None	target only	Requires core barrier
Ranking	4	2	3	1

FIGURE 10.21

Comparison of the usability and programmer-friendliness of the different nesting approaches.

providing high levels of performance across problem sizes (due to its low overhead), enabling high levels of programmer control and requiring only local code changes (i.e., the addition of a few simple branches). However, manual thread decomposition is ugly, and we hope that the performance and usability of the two pragma-based approaches continues to improve over time. Nested OpenMP parallel regions (with hot teams) comes second, as it can be made to achieve high levels of performance with the right settings and is by far the simplest approach to use. The teams construct comes third because, although it gives very good levels of performance, we feel that it requires further refinement in future iterations of the OpenMP specification before it is ready for use in production codes. Specifically, the inability to set affinities for teams could negatively impact performance for other runtimes, while the inability to use `teams` outside of `target` regions reduces its utility significantly. Finally, based on our results, it would be very difficult to recommend the use of nested OpenMP parallel regions without hot teams!

SUMMARY

In this chapter, we have walked through a number of changes to miniModal, a proxy code for the Modal3D application employed at COSMOS to analyze CMB radiation. These changes improve performance by a factor close to 100 on both Intel Xeon processors and Intel Xeon Phi coprocessors, and the resulting code is suitable to be run on systems comprised of processors, coprocessors, or a combination of both.

Many of the techniques applied in this chapter to *optimize* the code (e.g., load balancing, cache blocking, tuning prefetch distances) should be familiar to any developer of high-performance applications, providing further evidence of the strengths of the "neo-heterogeneous" approach to parallel programming (i.e., using a single programming model across a heterogeneous system). However, the largest performance increase by far for miniModal results from switching the cubic spline integration routine in Intel MKL for a custom numerical integration routine, highlighting the need to analyze and ultimately replace unsuitable algorithms, *modernizing* code and enabling it to scale across wide SIMD vectors and many cores.

Although efficient numerical integration routines may not be directly applicable to other codes, it is a perfect example of the inherent danger in relying on "black box" routines to behave optimally in all circumstances. Through the use of nested parallelism, our integration routines are able to exploit both domain and hardware knowledge to reduce memory footprint and unnecessary cache traffic on microarchitectures capable of executing multiple hardware threads per core. Further, we show that, contrary to popular belief, a purely pragma-based implementation *can* match the performance of a manual one, given sufficient work to hide thread creation and destruction overheads. We are confident that future iterations of the OpenMP standard and/or improvements to the Intel OpenMP runtime will be able to improve the performance and usability of these pragma-based solutions even further.

FOR MORE INFORMATION

Here are some additional reading materials we recommend related to this chapter:

- Fergusson, J.R., et al., 2010. General CMB and primordial bispectrum estimation: mode expansion, map making, and measures of F NL. Phys. Rev. D 82 (2), 023502.
- Fergusson, J.R., et al., 2007. Primordial non-Gaussianity and the CMB bispectrum. Phys. Rev. D 76 (8), 083523.
- Cosmic Microwave Background image. www.esa.int.
- Bispectrum integration domain image. Planck 2015 results. XVII. Constraints on primordial non-Gaussianity. http://arxiv.org/abs/1502.01592.

- OpenMP 4.0 Application Program Interface Version 4.0. http://www.openmp.org/mp-documents/OpenMP4.0.0.pdf.
- Dempsey, J., 2014. Plesiochronous phasing barriers. In: High Performance Parallelism Pearls: Multicore and Many-Core Programming Approaches. Morgan Kaufmann, Waltham, MA, pp. 87-115.
- Speedometer. https://01.org/simple-performance-tools
- The Stephen Hawking Centre for Theoretical Cosmology. http://www.ctc.cam.ac.uk/

Download the code from this, and other chapters. http://lotsofcores.com.

VISUAL SEARCH OPTIMIZATION 11

Prashanth Thinakaran*, Diana Guttman*, Mahmut Taylan Kandemir*, Meenakshi Arunachalam[†],
Rahul Khanna[†], Praveen Yedlapalli*, Narayan Ranganathan[†]

Pennsylvania State University, USA[*] Intel Corporation, USA[†]

We are in the era of exponential growth of digital data in the form of text, images, and videos through multiple feeds, where real-time analytics of these data is becoming a bigger challenge. Owing to the inherent data-level parallelism in these analytics-based applications, compute accelerators like the Intel® Xeon Phi™ coprocessor, with multiple SIMD cores, come to the rescue by catering to these applications' real-time needs.

Image matching is an important application where a set of images is compared against a large database of images for feature similarity. There are numerous applications of image matching. Many multimedia systems such as Internet search engines, multimedia content analysis software, and image database classification tools use image matching as an intermediate step, making it a critical target for both performance and power optimizations.

Existing research on image matching focuses mostly on exploring algorithmic techniques and handling real-time processing constraints. With emerging architectural trends, such as many-core coprocessors, nonvolatile memories, and 3D stacking, it is becoming increasingly important to study the impact of image-matching applications on these computing platforms. Among the critical issues to be investigated are (1) different types of parallelism exhibited by image mapping applications; (2) how these applications scale when mapped to many-core coprocessors; (3) whether they require custom code parallelization techniques and/or data layout optimization to take advantage of many-core-specific features such as multiple memory channels, on-chip networks, and wide SIMD units; and (4) whether they can take advantage of 3D stacking and nonvolatile memories given the high memory bandwidth provided by GDDR memory on the Intel Xeon Phi coprocessor compute cores since the accelerated kernels are data parallel.

This chapter primarily focuses on the first two questions and represents a step toward understanding the behavior of one specific image-matching application (machine perception of facial detection and recognition) by investigating its performance when mapped to an Intel Xeon Phi coprocessor-based system.

In this chapter, we present a client-server application to perform image classification of a given dataset using the Fast Library for Approximate Nearest Neighbors (FLANN) as the underlying search algorithm. We discuss different parallelization techniques of this application on a coprocessor platform. In particular, the impacts of three important parameters (DBThreads, FLANNThreads, and K-dimensional (KD)-trees) on performance are studied. Presentation of experimental results using three different databases on the coprocessor system. Our results indicate that, while the tree creation part of the application scales well up to 120 threads, the search portion scales up to 32 threads. Furthermore, the best performance for the end-to-end application is achieved when using a combination of FLANN and DBThreads threads. We also explain the barriers preventing further scalability and quantify their individual roles.

To our knowledge, this work represents the first effort toward mapping such an image-matching application to a many-core Intel Xeon Phi coprocessor platform.

IMAGE-MATCHING APPLICATION

An image search methodology allows a system to browse, search, and retrieve images from a large database of digital images. It includes methods to acquire, process, and analyze images in order to synthesize and interpret information related to an active decision-making process. The process of automating decision processes through computer-aided image (or object) recognition tends to duplicate the abilities of human vision by perceiving and understanding the images. Recent advancements in mobile and integrated image retrieval systems (visual devices supported by smartphones) and use of highly parallel or specialized hardware have facilitated many use cases related to visual surveillance, object-modeling, information retrieval, computer-human interaction, robot-vision, smart-manufacturing, selective advertising, autonomous vehicles, smart classrooms, and social interactions. In many cases, it is not only crucial to retrieve and process the image in a speedy and power-efficient manner, but also required to transmit and match the attributes of the image over cloud infrastructures to retrieve necessary information related to that image in real time. For example, in visual surveillance, the image acts as an index into the personal information that can drive the social interaction based on the retrieved information. As illustrated in Figure 11.1, if we augment the visual information with gesture and audio keywords, we can become more selective in extracting the attributes of the information facilitated by the image-based index searches.

In this work, we focus on machine perception of facial detection and recognition used commonly in virtual reality applications, surveillance and social interactions. The time-critical nature of these applications drives us to develop image analysis algorithms that can sustain real-time constraints in the realm of video frame-rates (15-30 frames per second). Furthermore, since facial detection and recognition algorithms are compute-intensive operations, we need to identify methods that can parallelize the algorithmic operations for large-scale information exchange in real time. Emergence of low-cost graphic processing units (GPU), many-core architectures, and high-speed internet connectivity provides us with sufficient compute and communication resources to accelerate facial detection and recognition. We use the many-core Intel Xeon Phi SE10P coprocessor that offers up to one double precision teraFLOP/s peak of computing on a single coprocessor, which can be employed in solving larger and more complex scientific challenges.

IMAGE ACQUISITION AND PROCESSING

A digital image is produced using image sensors resulting in a 2D or 3D image data representation of one or a sequence of images. The data comprise spatial characteristics such as light intensity, depth, and absorption. In this work, we assume an input image needs to be compared with a large number of

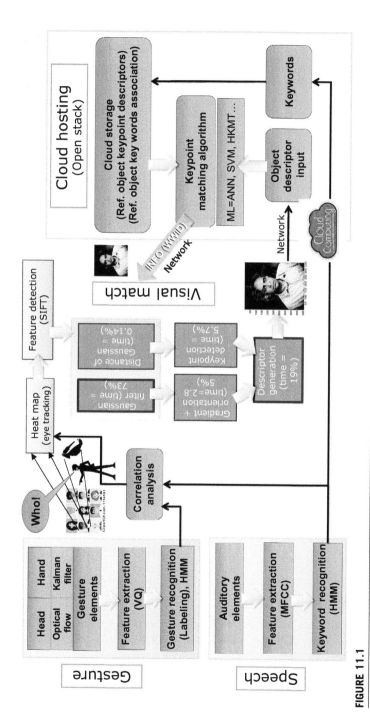

FIGURE 11.1

Information retrieval using visual facial recognition in conjunction with gesture and speech attributes.

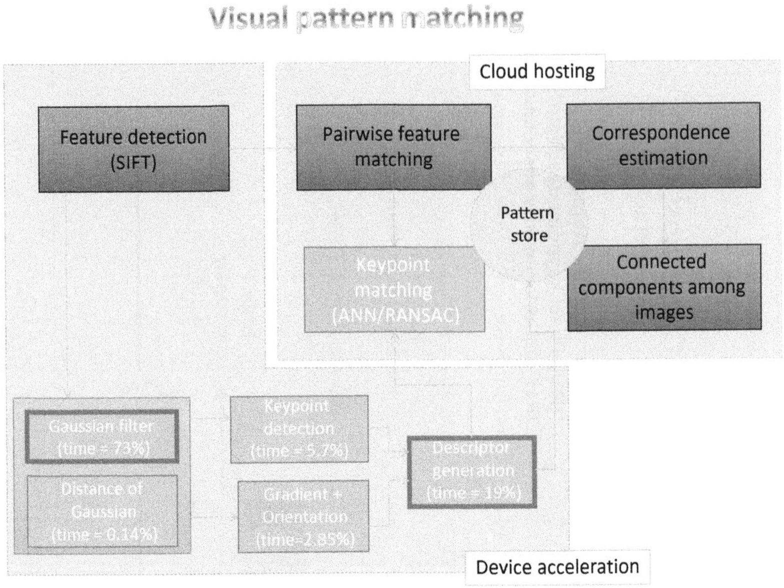

FIGURE 11.2

High-level view of Visual Pattern Matching using Scale Invariant Feature Transform (SIFT).

images archived in a database. The input image is preprocessed by reducing noise and enhancing contrast to enable extraction of relevant attributes and suppression of false information. To study the scalability and performance of the image-search (or matching), we use Scale-Invariant Feature Transform (SIFT) as an algorithm to detect and describe local features in images. The SIFT method is invariant to image scaling and rotation, and partially invariant to illumination changes and affine distortions even in the presence of occlusion, clutter, or noise. A large number of features can be extracted from a typical image that are highly distinctive and can be matched accurately to a large database of features for object, facial, or scene recognition. The runtime proportion of SIFT processing is illustrated in Figure 11.2. The SIFT library is an open-source library referenced in section "For more information," where one can extract invariant feature points out of any given database of images. Various stages of SIFT can be summarized as follows:

SCALE-SPACE EXTREMA DETECTION

This is the first stage of the SIFT framework that searches over all the scales and image locations called keypoints. The image undergoes Gaussian convolution at different scales to produce images separated by a constant factor. This convolution is followed by subtracting adjacent image scales to produce the difference-of-Gaussian (DoG) images. These images identify potential interest points invariant to scale and orientation. DoG images identify keypoints that are local minima/maxima of the DoG images across scales. Each pixel in the DoG image is compared to its eight neighbors at the same scale and nine corresponding neighboring pixels in each of the neighboring scales. A candidate keypoint is represented by a pixel whose value is the maximum or minimum among all compared pixels.

KEYPOINT LOCALIZATION

Once the keypoint candidates are selected, a detailed fit is performed to the nearby data for location, scale, and ratio of principal curvatures. This information allows some keypoints to be rejected that have low contrast (and are therefore sensitive to noise) or are poorly localized along an edge. Keypoints with strong edge response in a single direction are rejected.

ORIENTATION ASSIGNMENT

In this step of SIFT, each keypoint is assigned one or more orientations based on local image gradient directions. The keypoint can be referenced relative to this orientation and thereby achieves invariance with respect to image rotation.

KEYPOINT DESCRIPTOR

The local image gradients are measured at the selected scale in the region around each keypoint. These are transformed into a representation that allows for significant levels of local shape distortion and change in illumination. Figure 11.3 illustrates the keypoint selection on a facial image. Keypoints are displayed as vectors indicating scale, orientation, and location.

KEYPOINT MATCHING

Keypoint matching is the final step in the image (or object) recognition. Image recognition is performed by matching an individual keypoint to the archive of keypoints corresponding to the training images. The best match is found by identifying the nearest neighbor in the archive of keypoints of training images. The nearest neighbor is identified as the keypoint with minimum Euclidean distance for the invariant descriptor vector. One can use approximate nearest neighbor (ANN) matching features extracted from a real-time image to the database of features extracted from training images. Approximate nearest neighbor search includes locality-sensitive hashing, best bin first, and balanced box-decomposition tree-based search. FLANN is one such library for performing fast approximate nearest neighbor searches. FLANN is written in the C++ programming language. It performs fast approximate nearest neighbor searches in high-dimensional spaces. This computational efficiency of image recognition can be improved by using binary trees as proposed by the Approximated Nearest Neighbor (ANN) library. The two primary metrics that determine the performance of the application are (1) the time taken to create KD-trees and (2) the time taken to search the trees that are built to compare the images to find the best match. Creating KD-trees for the whole database of images is computationally costly. Therefore, we tried to save the computed parameters and reuse them the next time an index is created from similar data points (coming from the same distribution). In this chapter, we propose an Intel Xeon Phi coprocessor implementation of the FLANN-based image search algorithm and we compare its performance relative to various scaling parameters.

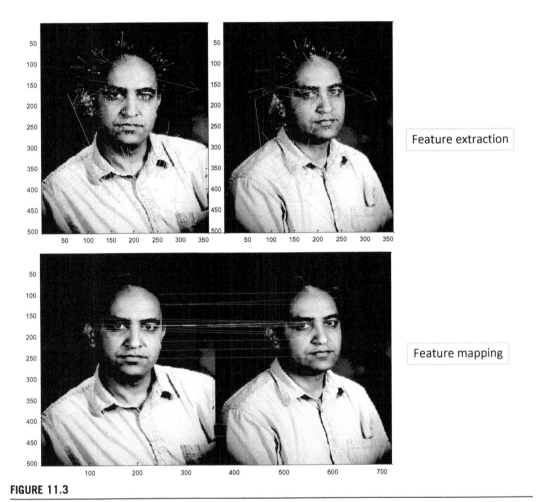

FIGURE 11.3

Keypoint selection and mapping between two images with different facial orientation.

APPLICATIONS

Mobile phones, sophisticated cameras, and ubiquitous wireless connectivity are revolutionizing our social behavior, which will change and adapt as we develop and improve image search technologies. We will be able to exploit the ability to perform automated image search using a hybrid mechanism composed of local processing on mobile phones and high-speed backend processing on remote servers. We will be able to overcome the limitations of real-time image search using tradeoffs involving energy, delay, accuracy, and cost. Visual queries are posed using the preconfigured programs (like video surveillance) or user-specific attributes (like gestures or speech). Specific applications that require real-time responses to visual queries can be exemplified in the following areas:

HOSPITALITY AND RETAIL INDUSTRY

Validating premier customers in restaurants, casinos, hotels, and shopping malls and identifying their unique needs would help to improve customer satisfaction and enhance the brick-and-mortar experience to be comparable to the online experience. Given a time-critical interaction between service-provider and customer, real-time response to a visual query is the key to develop that experience. The service-providers can remember customers' names and can greet them accordingly.

SOCIAL INTERACTIONS

Real-time information related to objects or people can enhance the social experience by identifying information that can be mutually beneficial. For example, a facial image can index into publically available information (such as a Facebook profile) related to that person's attributes, social standing, or interests. The time it takes to link the facial image to the person's profile determines the performance of the image recognition system.

SURVEILLANCE

High-security areas like ports, restricted buildings, and airports require constant monitoring of human traffic. Schools, public transportation, and border security are other use cases where visual surveillance can be of great interest. The power of the search capabilities will group similar faces from multiple cameras together. Algorithms can be developed to track and analyze suspicious movements by tracing spatiotemporal patterns of similar visual information. Given a large number of moving subjects, real-time response to visual queries is critical to avoid gaps in the information processing.

A STUDY OF PARALLELISM IN THE VISUAL SEARCH APPLICATION

The visual search application exhibits inherent parallelism in the way it looks for a nearest neighbor image with a specified precision by building KD-trees. The application can be parallelized in two dimensions—namely, *at the database level* or *within the FLANN library*—and it is crucial to choose the right amount of parallelism for each of these dimensions to maximize the performance that can be extracted from the underlying computing system. Since the application is designed as a client-server model as depicted in Figure 11.4, we run the server on the coprocessor and the client on the host. The host in our case is an Intel® Xeon® processor, but it could be anything able to connect to the same port number that the server is listening to. The server initializes the image database on the coprocessor and once the client is connected to the server, it sends the query image to the server. The server goes through the entire image database comparing with the query image and then returns the top four results to the client. In addition to this processor + coprocessor version of the code, we also have a processor-only version where both the server and client run on the processor.

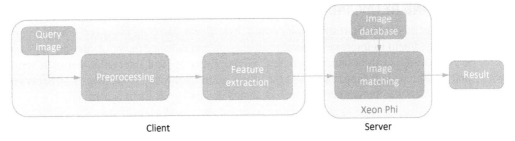

FIGURE 11.4

Client Server image-matching application.

DATABASE (DB) LEVEL PARALLELISM

One parallelization strategy for this application is to partition the number of images in the database across the number of threads available in the machine. Therefore,

$$\text{Compute load per thread} = \frac{\text{Total number of images in the database}}{\text{Total number of threads in the machine}}$$

Relative to the size of the database and number of threads in the machine, each thread works on a set of images from the database to look for the nearest neighbor match using the call image-matching module, which uses FLANN library calls. As can be seen from Figures 11.5 and 11.6, we use pthreads to create threads, and these threads are assigned their respective chunks of images from the database. Note also that the threads are affinitized to the individual cores dynamically. In the end, the top four nearest

```
for (int t = 0; t < thread_count; t++) {
   th_data[t].threadcount = t;
   int rc = pthread_create(&threads[t], NULL,
call_image_matching_module,(void *) &th_data[t]);

   if (rc){  printf("ERROR; return from pthread_create() is %d\n",
rc);
    exit(-1); }
   else {  cout << "Thread " << t << " Created Successfully\n"; }
   }
   for (int t = 0; t < thread_count; t++) {
      pthread_join(threads[t], NULL);}
```

FIGURE 11.5

DB thread creation code.

```
int BindToCpu(int cpu_num) {
        cpu_set_t cs;
        CPU_ZERO(&cs);
        CPU_SET(cpu_num, &cs);
        pthread_t current_thread = pthread_self();
        int status;

        status = pthread_setaffinity_np(current_thread,
    sizeof(cs), &cs);
        for (int i = 0; i < CPU_SETSIZE; i++) {
            if (CPU_ISSET(i, &cs)) {
            }
        }
}
```

FIGURE 11.6

DB threads affinity.

neighbor matches are sent to the client from the server. The total number of threads is a major parameter in determining the average search time for each thread. In this work, we name these threads DBthreads.

FLANN LIBRARY PARALLELISM

The other approach to exploit the inherent parallelism in this application is to make use of the internal parallelism in the FLANN library. This enables the FLANN compute kernel to partition each image into sub-images and search in parallel with the given input image. As shown in Figure 11.7, which has function calls to the FLANN library in server.cpp, the FLANN library has a parameter named cores that is a member of the FLANNParameters structure and can be set to the number of threads for the intra-image parallel search. This approach uses OMP threads and the OMP calls in the library dynamically load balance threads during runtime. We name these threads FLANNthreads.

The Flann_build_index() library call creates a search index from the initial dataset of points, which is used later for fast nearest-neighbor searches in the dataset. The parameters it takes specify the type of index to be built and the index. These parameters play a huge role in determining the performance of the new search index (nearest-neighbor search time) and the memory required to build the index values. The optimal parameter values depend on the dataset characteristics, e.g., the number of dimensions, and the distribution of points in the dataset. For the dataset that the application uses to compare key-value features extracted from the images, it is appropriate to use randomized KD-trees, and similarly, the number of randomized KD-trees generated can also be specified. The algorithm splits the data into half at each level of the tree on the dimension for which the data exhibit large variations. Therefore, this parameter should be chosen carefully by identifying the optimal split dimension.

```
struct FLANNParameters p;

p = DEFAULT_FLANN_PARAMETERS;

p.algorithm = FLANN_INDEX_KDTREE;

p.trees = KDT;

p.checks = 32;

p.target_precision = 0.6;

p.cores = FT; //Set the Desired FLANN threads


for (int i = from; i < to; i++)

{

  result = (int*) malloc(client_packet.num_keys * NN *
  sizeof(int));

  dists = (float*) malloc(client_packet.num_keys * NN *
  sizeof(float));


  index_id = flann_build_index(&hdf5_data_files[MAX_IMAGES * i],
  keys_data[i], DIM, &speedup, &p);


  flann_find_nearest_neighbors_index(index_id,
  &hdf5_query_files[MAX_IMAGES * client_packet.img_id],
  client_packet.num_keys, result, dists, NN, &p);


  images_searched++;

}
```

FIGURE 11.7

DB thread creation code.

Finally, the flann_build_index() function returns the newly created index, which is passed into the subsequent flann_find_nearest_neighbors_index() function.

Note that DBThreads and FLANNThreads represent inter- and intra-image parallelism respectively, and tuning each of them in a synergistic manner presents an interesting optimization problem. In particular, one can choose to employ both intra-image and inter-image parallelism in the same application. Thus, for example, in the case of 400 images in a database and 4 DBthreads, each thread gets 100 images to perform nearest neighbor search at the same time. When each DBthread is using the FLANN library calls, FLANN threads are created to partition the image into sub-images to parallelize the search within the image itself. Hence, if the FLANN thread parameter is set to 2, each image is further split into two, meaning that a total of 800 (400 × 2) FLANN threads are forked and joined by 4 DBthreads. In this way, maximum parallelization in the search step can be achieved.

Figure 11.8 gives the portion of the code in server.cpp that would be offloaded to the coprocessor, which copies the database and the respective working set structures into the coprocessor memory from the host. This `dispatch_to_worker_threads()` function calls the `flann_build_index()` and `find_flann_nearest_neighbors()` functions on the coprocessor and is given in Figure 11.7. Note that the Xeon code version would be Figure 11.8 without the offload pragmas and with both the server and the client running on the host. Since a two-dimensional array cannot be offloaded directly onto the coprocessor owing to the SIMD nature of vector registers, we had to serialize the array into one dimension and pass the image key features.

Figure 11.9 gives the command line to execute the client/server image search application. Both `DBthreads` and `FLANNthreads` can be set as the command line arguments while running the server. The number of randomized KD-trees that need to be built can also be specified as a command line argument. The server is run first, which initializes the image database, and then the client is run, which connects to the same port on which the server is listening. Following that, the client sends a query image to the server for which the nearest neighbor has to be searched. The server returns the top four image matches to the client.

```
#pragma offload target(mic) inout(imageInfo) in(client_packet)
in(hdf5_data_files:length(MAX_IMAGES*MAX_IMAGES) ALLOC)
in(keys_data) in(th_data:length(MAX_CORES) ALLOC)
in(query_file){}


#pragma offload target(mic) nocopy(imageInfo)
nocopy(client_packet)
nocopy(hdf5_data_files:length(MAX_IMAGES*MAX_IMAGES))
nocopy(keys_data) nocopy(th_data:length(MAX_CORES))
nocopy(query_file)


gettimeofday(&offloadstart, NULL);


dispatch_to_worker_threads(num_data_images, thread_count,
th_data, imageInfo);


gettimeofday(&offloadend, NULL);


#pragma offload target(mic) out(imageInfo)nocopy(client_packet)
nocopy(hdf5_data_files:length(MAX_IMAGES*MAX_IMAGES) FREE)
nocopy(keys_data) nocopy(th_data:length(MAX_CORES) FREE)
nocopy(query_file){}
```

FIGURE 11.8

Offloaded region of the FLANN library calls.

```
./server <Port #> ~/path/to/alldb.txt 0 <# of DBthreads>
~/path/to/data/ ~/path/to/input <# of FLANNthreads> <# of KD-
trees>


./client localhost <Port #> ~/path/to/input
```

FIGURE 11.9

Command line to execute our server and client image search applications.

EXPERIMENTAL EVALUATION

This section explains the infrastructure setup and the scalability study of our application. The image search application is compiled on the host with offload pragma calls for image search. We perform experiments with three different database sizes of 400, 800, and 1200 images. The goal behind the experiments presented below is to investigate the scalability of the application with respect to DBThreads and FLANNThreads, and identify the problems preventing scalability beyond a certain thread count.

SETUP

The scalability experiments are performed on the following configuration where the host architecture is an Intel Xeon E5-2680 processor running at 2.7 GHz with 32 GB (8 × 4 channels) memory, and the coprocessor on the host is an Intel Xeon Phi SE10P coprocessor running at 1.1 GHz with 8 GB GDDR5 memory. The motherboard chipset is Dell C8220, Intel PQI C610 Chipset with QPI interconnect at 8 GT/s. Intel compiler ICC version 13.1.0 is used to compile the application, and the Intel Composer XE version 2013.2.146 package is used for the rest of the tools. Figure 11.10 shows the environment variables used in our experiments.

DATABASE THREADS SCALING

In this section, scalability with respect to the different database sizes is investigated. The FLANN threads and KD-tree size are kept constant at 1, while increasing the DB thread count. Figure 11.11 plots the execution time (Y-axis) with three different database sizes, under varying DB thread counts (X-axis). One can observe from the results for our 400-image database that the application scales

```
export MIC_ENV_PREFIX=Phi
export Phi_KMP_AFFINITY=balanced
export Phi_KMP_PLACE_THREADS=60c,2t
export Phi_OMP_NUM_THREADS=120
```

FIGURE 11.10

The values of the environment variables in our experiments.

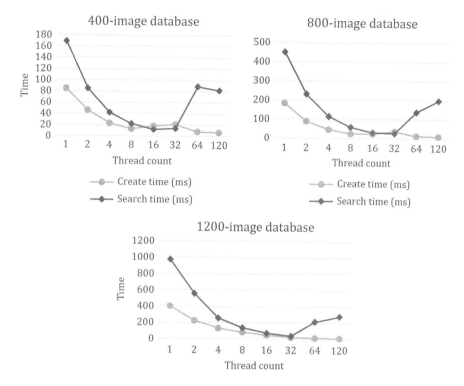

FIGURE 11.11

Scalability analysis of DBThreads across different database sizes.

reasonably well until 32 threads. Beyond that, we see degradation in the performance of the search component. Nevertheless, compared to the single-thread case, using 120 threads brings a speedup of around 18× in the KD-tree creation. When we compare the scaling results across larger database sizes, we observe similar scaling pattern, in both 800 and 1200 image databases, wherein the tree creation time hits a valley beyond 64 threads while the search time improvement shoots up to 6× when moving from 32 threads to 64 threads.

We used Intel VTune Amplifier profiler to investigate the scaling overhead through hotspot analysis. Figure 11.13a shows the hotspot analysis of the application when running with 120 threads in which libiomp5.so library dominates the CPU time. It is an internal OpenMP library that manages the OpenMP threads while they are executing. The kmp_fork_call in this library is the hottest function. Further investigating the issue resulted in learning that OpenMP threads created once live in a thread pool for the program's lifetime actively spinning, ready for dispatch at the next parallel region of the code. This effect due to idle spinning is further amplified when increasing the number of OpenMP threads to 64 or 120. We also analyzed the lock and wait times as seen in Figure 11.13c along with the call stacks, and found that a significant portion is spent in the clone module of libc, which is the internal library that does thread creation. This overhead is attributed to the large number of thread creations and associated idle spinning waiting for a critical section's lock.

FLANN THREADS SCALING

Since the DB thread scalability hits a valley beyond 64 threads with the different workloads, we next tried to vary the number of FLANN threads, keeping `DBThreads` and `KD-trees` constant. It can be observed from Figure 11.12 that increasing the number of `FLANNthreads` decreases the tree creation time, but increases the search time. This is due to the fact that the FLANN threads primarily exploit parallelism in the KD-tree creation part of the application. We observe 23-58% decrease in the tree creation time across varying database sizes. It is to be noted that each DB thread in parallel creates FLANN threads. For example, if the `FLANNThreads` parameter is set to 2, in case of an 800-image database, 1600 (800 × 2) FLANN threads are created in total. Therefore, from a practical angle, this parameter cannot go beyond 2 or 4, and it is necessary to decide upon the optimum KD-tree parameter considering the number of FLANN threads.

As seen in Figure 11.13b, which shows the VTune top four hotspots of the FLANN two-threaded version, the OpenMP overhead dominates the computation time as in the case of DB threads. Furthermore, it can be observed from Figure 11.13d that the CPU utilization of the FLANN kernel is taken over by system library overheads. From Figure 11.13e, the CPU utilization is dominated by `kmpc_global_-thread_num`, and consequently, the spin locking time has increased 14 times when compared to single-threaded version FLANN version.

KD-TREE SCALING WITH DBTHREADS

To overcome the law of diminishing returns, we tried to increase the number of randomized KD-trees that are to be searched with the best DBThread parameter (which is 16) and kept the number of FLANNthreads the same at 1. It is important to emphasize that when we increase KD-trees, we effectively increase the total workload processed by a thread, that is, as if we were working with larger inputs. As a result, one can see from Figure 11.14 that, with our 400-image database, the tree creation time and search time of 16 KD-tree increases by 72× and 31× with respect to the single KD-tree case. However, a KD-tree size of 16 or 32 is more realistic for a practical setting, as it gives a more reasonable workload to each thread, thereby increasing its compute density. It can be observed that the workload increases with the number of KD-trees with respect to both the create time and search time. The

Number of Images	DB,Flann,KD-trees	Create Time (ms)	Search Time (ms)
400	16,1,1	16	15
	16,2,2	13	92
800	16,1,1	28	29
	16,2,2	19	325
1200	16,1,1	57	47
	16,2,2	39	642

FIGURE 11.12

FLANNThread reads scaling across different database sizes. The values under the second column correspond to <DB threads, FLANN threads, and number of KD-trees>.

Module	CPU Time
libiomp5.so	5.52
vmlinux	0.45
FLANN::searchLevel	0.08
FLANN::meanSplit	0.06

(a)

Module	CPU Time
libiomp5.so	1.03
FLANN::meanSplit	0.66
FLANN::searchLevel	0.58
FLANN::selectDivision	0.93

(b)

```
flann::NNIndex<flann::L2<float>>::knnSearch          libiomp5.so
_flann_find_nearest_neighbors_index                  libflann.so.1.8.4
_flann_find_nearest_neighbors_index<float, float>    libflann.so.1.8.4
flann_find_nearest_neighbors_index                   libflann.so.1.8.4
call_flannC                                          server
call_image_matching_module                           server
clone                                                libc-2.12.so
```

(c)

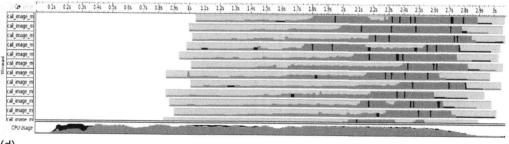

(d)

▷ __kmpc_global_thread_num	27.350s	24.537s	libiomp5.so
▷ __kmp_fork_call	9.109s	9.109s	libiomp5.so
▷ flann::KDTreeIndex<flann::L2<float>>::searcr	1.701s	0s	libflann.so.1.8.4
▷ flann::KDTreeIndex<flann::L2<float>>::mean:	0.300s	0s	libflann.so.1.8.4
▷ std::__adjust_heap<__gnu_cxx::__normal_itera	0.090s	0s	libflann.so.1.8.4
▷ flann::KDTreeIndex<flann::L2<float>>::select	0.040s	0s	libflann.so.1.8.4
▷ flann::KNNSimpleResultSet<float>::addPoint	0.030s	0s	libflann.so.1.8.4

(e)

FIGURE 11.13

VTune analysis when using 120 DBThreads and 2 FLANN Threads in a database of 800 images. (a) hotspots 120 DBThreads, (b) hotspots 2 FLANN Threads, (c) lock and wait times with DBThreads, (d) CPU utilization by thread with FLANN threads, (e) CPU utilization by modules with FLANN threads.

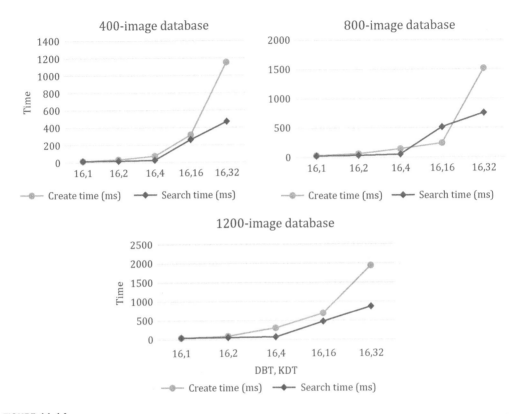

FIGURE 11.14

Scaling KD-trees with DBThread count configuration. The values on the X-axis are <DBThreads, KD-trees>.

memory overhead in using multiple KD-trees also increases linearly along with the number of KD-trees being built. Therefore, in the next set of experiments, we fix the number of KD-trees to be built at 32.

We also investigated the scalability with 32 KD-trees (Figure 11.15) and varying number of DBThreads. We find that increasing the computational density by building more randomized KD-trees aids in improving the image search precision. At the same time, we can overcome the scalability problem beyond 32 cores shown in Figure 11.11. It is seen that by picking the right KD-tree parameter, we observe over 6× improvement in scalability from 32 to 120, when compared to the scaling of Figure 11.11. We also compared the same parameter configuration against the processor alone. In Figure 11.16, we compare the processor performance with the combination of processor+coprocessor with varying number of KD-trees. The time taken to create the KD-trees increases in both the configurations, if we compare the single-threaded processor performance against the coprocessor, we observe 34% and 18% improvement in the tree creation and search times, respectively, with the latter mainly due to the fact that the KD-trees, which are created once for a database, are reused when it is run multiple times on the coprocessor.

We also analyzed the effects of vectorization in the coprocessor code (Figure 11.17). The highest level of vectorization O3 is doing a mere 4% better than the baseline without any optimizations, the

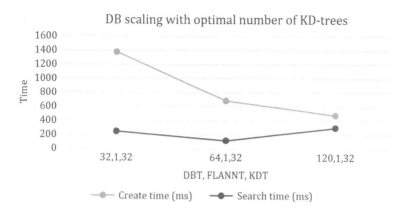

FIGURE 11.15

DBThread scaling with 32 KD-trees. Note that each point on the X-axis represents a different combination of <DBThreads, FLANNThread, KD-trees>.

DB,KD-trees	Xeon Create Time (ms)	XeonSearch Time (ms)	MIC Create Time (ms)	MIC Search Time (ms)
4,2	58	103	43	87
8,4	55	72	49	59
16,8	123	56	98	47
32,16	353	27	343	23

FIGURE 11.16

DBThread scaling with respect to KD-trees comparing Xeon versus Xeon Phi.

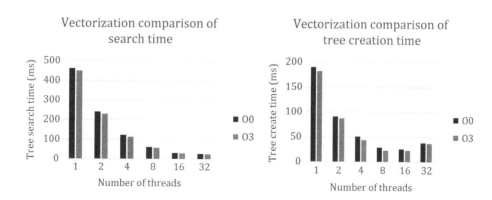

FIGURE 11.17

Impact of vectorization on tree creation and search time.

reason being that the main kernel FLANN library involves in building KD-trees and searching the trees in parallel with the threads created. The tree creation kernel does not take advantage of the wide vector register length to its fullest. Hence, we do not see a major performance improvement due to vectorization. In future, we would like to try to add vector intrinsics like SIMD and IVDEP to the hot loop nests that could potentially impact the performance.

SUMMARY

In this chapter, we presented an image-matching application that can take advantage of emerging many-core architectures. We detailed our application's functional modules and the associated libraries, as well as different parallelization strategies that can take advantage of inter- and intra-image parallelism. Two main metrics that determine the application performance—tree creation time and search time—were studied in the context of scalability. We articulated the challenges in obtaining application scalability on many-core architectures. Important insights obtained from our profiler-based analysis helped us to identify the challenges in scalability of DB threads. It made us further investigate the problem by increasing the number of KD-trees with respect to DB threads to find out the number of KD-trees with respect to DB threads that performs best. Then, the scalability with respect to increasing DBThreads with optimal KD-trees was shown to lead to 5.8× speedup in create time and 2.8× speedup in search time in the case of 120 threads when compared to single-threaded coprocessor performance.

Overall, although the image search application did not exhibit ideal scalability, it has potential to further exploit what many-cores have to offer. One main reason why the FLANN threads do not scale well is the limited number of features extracted from the image as key values; this restricts the ability of many-cores and multiple threads to exploit intra-image parallelism. The affinity parameter also played a crucial role in deciding the application scalability as the compact and scatter affinities do not exploit the inherent reuse in building KD-trees. Since we achieve very good scalability in KD-tree creation when compared to the image search step, it would also be interesting to see a selective offload of just the KD build tree module to the coprocessor, and to run the search on the host to get the best of both the worlds. One can also try to increase the size of the input database and see whether it helps in mitigating the libiomp.so overhead by increasing the parallel computational density of the code.

We also compared the processor performance with the coprocessor and found that the code performs 34% and 18% better on the coprocessor in tree creation time and search time, respectively. Overall, we can conclude from our analysis that individual parameters such as DBThreads, FLANNThreads, and KD-trees must be tuned carefully when scaling this application for performance on many-core architectures like the Intel Xeon Phi coprocessor.

FOR MORE INFORMATION

Here are some additional reading materials we recommend related to this chapter.

- FLANN Library, http://www.cs.ubc.ca/research/flann/.
- FLANN Library Usage Manual, http://www.cs.ubc.ca/research/flann/uploads/FLANN/flann_manual-1.8.4.pdf.

- Scale Invariant Feature Transform (SIFT) at http://robwhess.github.io/opensift/.
- Muja, M., David, G.L., 2009. Fast approximate nearest neighbors with automatic algorithm configuration. VISAPP (1) 2.
- Lowe, D.G., 2004. Distinctive image features from scale-invariant keypoints. Int. J. Comput. Vis. 60(2) 91-110.
- Muja, M., Lowe, D.G., 2009. Fast approximate nearest neighbors with automatic algorithm configuration. In: International Conference on Computer Vision Theory and Applications.
- Andoni, A., Piotr, I., 2006. Near-optimal hashing algorithms for approximate nearest neighbor in high dimensions. FOCS'06. 47th Annual IEEE Symposium on Foundations of Computer Science. IEEE.
- Arya, S., et al., 1994. An optimal algorithm for approximate nearest neighbor searching in fixed dimensions. In: Proceedings of the 5th ACM-SIAM Symposium on Discrete Algorithms.
- Mikolajczyk, K., Matas, J., Improving descriptors for fast tree matching by optimal linear projection.
- Huang, F.-C., Shi-Yu, H., Ji-Wei, K., Yung-Chang, C., 2012. High-performance SIFT hardware accelerator for real-time image feature extraction. IEEE Trans. Circ. Syst. Video Technol. 22(3) 340-351.
- Download the code from this, and other chapters, http://lotsofcores.com.

RADIO FREQUENCY RAY TRACING

12

Christiaan Gribble, Jefferson Amstutz

SURVICE Engineering, USA

Understanding the propagation of radio frequency (RF) energy in the presence of complex outdoor terrain features, such as in urban environments, is critical to planning, optimizing, and analyzing wireless communication and data networks. Unfortunately, simulating and visualizing RF energy propagation can be a difficult and time-consuming task because RF energy propagates throughout these environments via a combination of direct line-of-sight, reflection, and diffraction, all of which must be modeled accurately to obtain high fidelity results. Moreover, features within the environment—trees, buildings, and so forth— typically exhibit different permittivity and absorption properties with respect to the energy being measured and also impact simulation fidelity. Finally, energy produced from a single transmitter may arrive at a given point in space from a variety of paths, each with a different length and, thus, with different time-delay characteristics.

Many of these planning, optimization, and analysis tasks are difficult with existing RF simulation models. These models run slowly for moderate to large numbers of transmitter/receiver pairs in part because they are not designed to take advantage of modern multicore computer architectures. Moreover, these models do not account for noise caused by multipath scatter, but instead use unacceptably large estimates for its effects.

In this chapter, we discuss StingRay, an interactive environment for combined RF simulation and visualization based on ray tracing (Figure 12.1). StingRay is explicitly designed to support high performance, high fidelity simulation, and visualization of RF energy propagation in complex urban environments by exploiting modern multicore computer architectures, particularly Intel® Xeon® processors and Intel® Xeon Phi™ coprocessors. Our ray-based approach offers high performance: simulations involving 100 million or more rays complete in seconds or minutes using modern multicore platforms, thereby allowing analysts quickly identify the propagation phenomena of interest, ultimately reducing time-to-insight. Importantly, our ray-based simulation approach also offers high fidelity results that include important physical effects—including more accurate multipath scatter—for RF prediction. Finally, our modern, explicitly parallel simulation and visualization codes scale gracefully: for a machine with more cores, either similar quality results are computed in less time or higher fidelity results are computed in similar time.

StingRay comprises a high performance ray-based RF simulation engine and a collection of visualization components integrated via an extensible GUI. High performance RF simulation is achieved with the Intel open source Embree ray tracing kernels, and custom modules extending the Intel open source OSPRay rendering engine provide high fidelity visualization of the resulting data. You can find links to these libraries in the "For more information" section at the end of this chapter. In this chapter,

FIGURE 12.1

High performance radio frequency ray tracing with StingRay. A high performance ray-based RF simulation engine and a collection of visualization components are integrated via an extensible GUI to support visual analysis of RF energy propagation. Here, StingRay interactively simulates and visualizes RF energy propagation in an urban environment.

we present an overview of radio frequency ray tracing (RFRT) and the StingRay system architecture. We then explore two strategies for exploiting parallelism in StingRay and evaluate their performance on a modern workstation-class system. We utilize task-level parallelism expressed in OpenMP for scaling and ispc for vectorization in what prove to be our most optimized versions.

BACKGROUND

Ray-based methods have been used to approximate the solution of wave equations for electromagnetic fields in nondissipative media for at least four decades. Typically, these methods proceed in two steps. First, ray paths connecting source and receiver are found; in complex environments, this step is often the most time-consuming. Second, the wave equation is applied to compute field transport along identified ray paths. These classical ray-based approaches typically require hours of run time to simulate areas out to a kilometer or more.

In contrast, our approach to RF modeling uses ray tracing techniques from computer graphics, or *optical ray tracing*. Optical ray tracing simulates the propagation of visible light in complex 3D environments and elegantly handles dominant visual phenomena such as reflection, refraction, and shadows. We observe that RF energy is also a form of electromagnetic energy, albeit at a very different frequency than visible light; thus, methods in optical ray tracing offer a possible approach for simulating physical phenomena in the RF domain.

RFRT offers several advantages over traditional RF simulation methods. First, modifications necessary to capture important physical phenomena such as diffraction and interference are fairly straightforward. Second, RFRT generates the full signal trajectory, allowing computation and visualization of signal characteristics that are extremely costly, or even impossible, with other methods. Finally, RFRT scales effectively, both with geometric complexity and with processor count. These characteristics, combined with nearly 35 years of research in high performance techniques, make optical ray tracing an ideal method on which to base an interactive combined RF simulation and visualization tool for understanding RF propagation phenomena.

```
1: function TRACERAY(ray, depth)
2:     event ← OBJECTS.INTERACT(ray)
3:     if event then
4:         ray ← GENERATERAY(newDirection, newEField)
5:         TRACERAY(ray, depth + 1)
6:     end if
7: end function
```

FIGURE 12.2

RF simulation with Monte Carlo path tracing.

In particular, Monte Carlo path tracing formulates a solution to the wave equations for electromagnetic fields using a geometric optics approximation that models interesting visual phenomena. Path tracing probabilistically selects just one path of a (possibly) branching tree at each ray/object interaction. This approach drastically reduces the number of ray/object interactions that must be computed, thereby improving computational efficiency. We adapt the path tracing algorithm to compute energy propagation characteristics, including those arising from wave-based phenomena, in the RF domain (Figure 12.2).

Together with our collaborators at the University of Utah, we previously developed the Manta-RF RFRT system. As in classical ray-based techniques, Manta-RF utilizes the ray concept; however, transport properties are computed directly by launching many rays—on the order of 10^8 to 10^{11} or more—and using the statistical properties of ray distribution and density to represent received power. Whereas classical rays are defined by the order and location of their interactions with environmental features, rays in Manta-RF are more appropriately described as RF photons—discrete packets of electromagnetic energy in the RF portion of the spectrum. Validation against several measured datasets shows that a Monte Carlo approach to ray-based RF simulation offers high fidelity results comparable to those produced by classical ray-based methods (Figure 12.3). Moreover, simulations based on Monte Carlo ray tracing typically complete in seconds or minutes on modern multicore platforms, compared to the several hours or more required by those based on classical methods.

These characteristics—high fidelity and high performance—combine to provide a scalable RF simulation and visualization environment for modern multicore platforms. StingRay builds on the ray-based RF simulation techniques developed for Manta-RF, but leverages recent advances in high performance ray tracing and visualization APIs to provide a fully interactive combined RF simulation and visualization environment.

STINGRAY SYSTEM ARCHITECTURE

Combined simulation and visualization of RF energy propagation promotes deeper understanding of these phenomena, thereby reducing time-to-insight for critical analysis tasks. However, the complexity of typical RF analysis scenarios, including the underlying physical environment and the sheer number of ray/object interactions, can lead to issues with scale and visual clutter. Such issues necessitate a flexible, interactive environment in which analysts control both inputs and results at runtime.

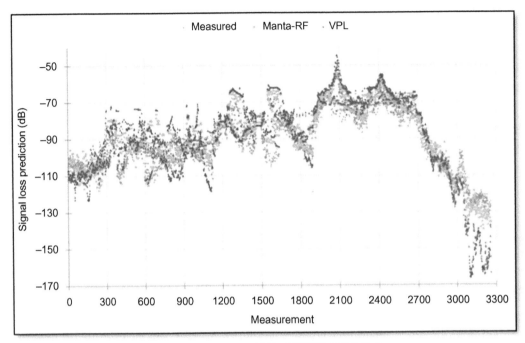

FIGURE 12.3

High fidelity RF simulation via Monte Carlo path tracing. Comparison of signal loss predictions using RFRT and VPL (top), a classical ray-based RF simulation approach, against measured data from Rosslyn, VA (bottom). These data show that a Monte Carlo path tracing approach to RF modeling provides high fidelity results comparable to those produced by classical ray-based methods.

Source: Data and image courtesy of Konstantin Shkurko, University of Utah.

StingRay satisfies these constraints via an extensible, loosely coupled plug-in architecture. The simulation and visualization components promote flexibility with user-controlled features, while an extensible GUI enhances a user's ability to perform debugging and analysis tasks by enabling easier navigation and exploration of the data in real-time.

The key components of the StingRay system architecture (Figure 12.4) combine to form an analysis process that is functional, flexible, and extensible. The design of StingRay leverages the following concepts:

- *Plug-in architecture.* StingRay is built around a set of configurable components that follow a specific design pattern to create a flexible infrastructure in which to implement RF simulation and visualization. We provide a set of core components to perform common tasks, but the plug-in architecture enables a programmer to create new components and extend the core facilities with arbitrary functionality.
- *Pipelined rendering.* StingRay uses a pipeline model for rendering, coupled with lazy evaluation for necessary values to avoid recomputation in later stages. The pipeline model leads to a layered visualization approach in which results of individual components are combined, under control of the user and at runtime, to achieve the desired result.

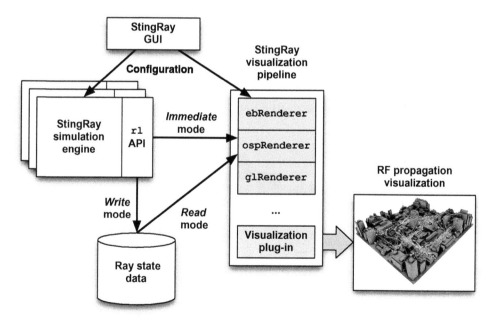

FIGURE 12.4

StingRay system architecture. Interactive simulation and visualization coupled with a ray state recording and processing API and a loosely coupled plug-in architecture creates a functional, flexible, and extensible system for visual analysis. A set of core components implements RF simulation and visualization, but the plug-in architecture enables a programmer to extend the core facilities with arbitrary functionality. These components are integrated via an interactive GUI that enables comprehensive control of the entire analysis process.

- *Extensible GUI.* The simulation and visualization components are integrated via an extensible GUI to enable comprehensive control of the entire analysis process. These components can tailor their user interface, exposing input parameters in a manner consistent with the functionality they provide. These features provide fine-grained control of the entire analysis process, making StingRay ideally suited to a wide variety of analysis tasks.

This design enables layered visualization within the spatial domain of computation (Figure 12.5) by compositing visual elements from several components to generate the final image.

The StingRay RF simulation engine implements the key RF propagation phenomena using a collection of C++ objects, including scene geometry, diffraction edge proxy geometry, and ray path loggers. Simulation functionality is exposed to client applications through a multithreaded controller object that provides a straightforward API. We explore parallelization in the RF simulation via OpenMP later in this chapter.

As noted, we adopt a layered visualization approach in which elements from separate visualization components are composited to generate the final image. StingRay currently supports several visual elements for RF visualization including underlying scene geometry, diffraction edge proxy geometry, and ray glyphs. StingRay also supports visualization of scalar volume data generated from simulation results: client applications can configure the engine to capture detailed information regarding the full path generated for each transmitter sample. These data allow computation and visualization of signal characteristics that are extremely costly, or even impossible, with other RF simulation methods. For example, RF energy characteristics at arbitrary locations in the environment can be visualized by collecting ray paths during simulation, converting the data to a scalar volumetric representation, and rendering the resulting data using traditional volume rendering techniques or as a participating medium (Figure 12.6). We explore parallelization when rendering scalar volume data as a participating medium via ispc later in this chapter.

Additional details regarding StingRay's RFRT approach can be found in the resources listed at the end of this chapter.

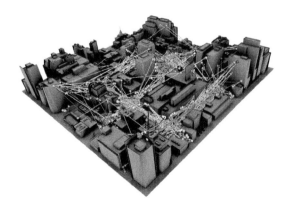

FIGURE 12.5

Layered visualization. The pipeline rendering model adopted by StingRay enables sophisticated visualization by layering results of several components to generate the final image. Here, glyphs depicting ray paths are composited over a rendering of the simulation domain, providing insight into the dominant energy transport paths in this scene.

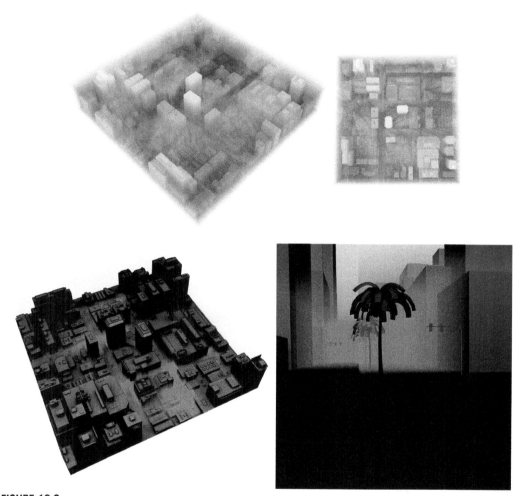

FIGURE 12.6

Scalar volume data generated from RF simulation results. By capturing detailed information about the full path generated for each transmitter sample, StingRay enables computation and visualization of signal characteristics that are extremely costly, or even impossible, with other RF simulation methods. Here, RF energy characteristics are visualized using traditional volume rendering (top) and as a participating medium (bottom).

OPTIMIZATION EXAMPLES

Ray tracing applications are often parallelized by exploiting task-level parallelism among rays. For example, in ray-based rendering, pixel color calculations are embarrassingly parallel: the computations along each ray are independent of those required by every other ray. In the same way, each path traced from a transmitter in RFRT is independent of every other path.

Similarly, certain ray tracing operations benefit from vectorization through implementations leveraging single instruction, multiple data (SIMD) instruction sets. Effective vectorization requires careful attention to *ray coherence*, or the tendency of spatially local rays traveling in similar directions to perform similar operations during rendering—to traverse the same nodes in an acceleration structure, for example, or to test the same primitives for intersection.

In this section, we examine three strategies to exploit task-level parallelism and we explore methods for effective vectorization in RF simulation and visualization. We evaluate the resulting performance of each strategy on Intel Xeon processors and Intel Xeon Phi coprocessors.

PARALLEL RF SIMULATION WITH OpenMP

Modern ray tracing engines, including Intel's Embree ray tracing kernels, exploit ray coherence to achieve high performance. In a typical ray-based renderer, primary rays, in particular, exhibit a high degree of coherence, and much of the recent work in high performance ray tracing examines techniques to identify and exploit coherence for other types of rays, including shadow rays, reflection rays, refraction rays, and so forth.

In this case, vector processing—for example, via implementation with modern SIMD instruction sets—can accelerate low-level traversal, intersection, and shading operations to improve ray tracing performance. However, paths traced by the RF simulation engine vary in both path depth and computational demand. As path length increases, even initially coherent paths tend to diverge, both spatially and in terms of path length itself. This behavior is often exaggerated in RF simulation due to the nature of path generation—in this case, even primary rays tend not to exhibit coherence.

Vectorization is particularly difficult in this context, and simply relying a high performance ray tracing engine to accelerate RFRT is not sufficient to achieve our performance goals. Other opportunities to exploit parallelism—for example, the task-level parallelism noted above—must be identified and expressed carefully to maximize simulation performance.

For example, one way to parallelize the basic RF path propagation loop (Figure 12.7) is to simply assign live path segments to each thread in a thread pool. This approach attempts to balance work across threads by assigning the same type of task to each one: threads simply trace the next segment of the assigned path in the core simulation loop.

This path-level parallelism is expressed in OpenMP by allocating a collection of live paths among threads using an `omp parallel for` construct over the core loop (Figure 12.8). If any path completes, a new path is created, and propagation begins in the next iteration of the `for` loop. The `omp parallel for` construct is embedded in a `while` loop that stops only after the simulator leaves the `running` state.

To understand the impact of parallelization using the OpenMP `parallel for` construct, we measure performance of the RF simulator on a modern multicore workstation using a varying number of threads. The test machine features two Intel Xeon E5-2699 processors with 36 cores running at 2.30 GHz and 64 GB of RAM. The machine is also equipped with a Intel Xeon Phi 7120X coprocessor with 61 cores running at 1.24 GHz and 16 GB of RAM. We first execute the naive RF path propagation loop (Figure 12.7) in a single thread for 5 s to establish baseline performance. The naive implementation achieves about 3.74 millions of rays per second on the test machine.

Next, we execute the simulator using the `omp parallel for` parallelization strategy and scale number of threads from 1 to 64. Each configuration runs for 5 s, and we again measure the resulting performance in terms of millions of rays per second (Figure 12.9).

```
while (running)
{

  // Generate path originating from current transceiver
  Transceiver *tr = transceivers[txrx\%ntxrx];
  Path path(tr->samplePrimaryRay(), tr->getPower());

  // Trace next segment in path to completion
  while (!path.traceNextRay(scene))
    ;

  // Record state, advance to next transceiver
  ...

} // End while
```

FIGURE 12.7

Single-threaded RF simulation loop. In each iteration of the outer `while` loop, this implementation simply traces to completion the next path from the current transceiver. Importantly, this version does not exploit opportunities for path-level parallelism inherent to RF path propagation; however, it serves as the starting point for expressing path-level parallelism and as the baseline for understanding the impact of the parallelization strategies described in this section. (Code snippet from `StingRay/Simulation.cpp:408-422`.)

```
while (running)
{
  #pragma omp parallel for num_threads(nthreads)
  for (auto i = 0; i < npaths; ++i)
  {
    Path& path = livePaths[i];

    // Trace next segment in path... if current path completes,
    //    create a new one
    if (path.traceNextRay(scene))
    {
      // Create a new path
      ...
    }

  } // End for

} // End while


// Simulation has been stopped, finish in-flight paths and
//    terminate
#pragma omp parallel for num_threads(nthreads)
for (auto i = 0; i < npaths; ++i)
{
  // Finish tracing path
}
```

FIGURE 12.8

Using OpenMP `parallel for` to express path-level parallelism. The first approach to parallel RF path propagation simply assigns live path segments to each thread in a thread pool, expressed in OpenMP using an `omp parallel for` construct. However, this approach induces unnecessary synchronization among threads and hinders parallel performance. (Code snippet from `StingRay/Simulation.cpp:451-476`.)

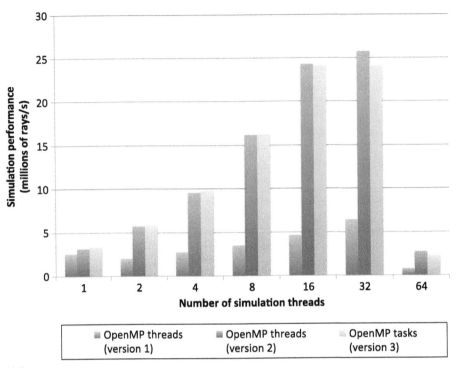

FIGURE 12.9

Parallel RF simulation with OpenMP. Tracing RF propagation paths is an embarrassingly parallel operation; however, careful attention to the expression of task-level parallelism in this context is required to maximize performance. These results depict scalar simulation performance, measured in terms of millions of rays per second, on two Intel Xeon E5-2699 processors using each of the three OpenMP parallelization strategies we explore.

As can be seen, when implemented in this way, simulator performance does not scale well with thread count. In fact, this version requires at least 16 threads before even a modest increase in performance is evident. This somewhat surprising behavior is a result of an implied barrier imposed at the end of the loop imposed by the `parallel for` construct. Each path segment will likely have a different computational cost due to variations in complexity of ray/object interactions or termination of the current path. Unfortunately, the barrier prevents other threads from making forward progress if any one segment is expensive to trace or if any one thread must create a new path. This parallelization strategy, though straightforward, induces unnecessary synchronization.

There are two approaches we examine to eliminate this unnecessary synchronization. One is to specify "nowait" which says that we do not want the implied barrier imposed at the end of the `for` loop. Another is to use the very flexible "task" capability of OpenMP.

First, we find that more careful use of OpenMP directives, by including the "nowait" clause, alleviates this issue (Figure 12.10). As before, this implementation spawns some number of threads using the `omp parallel` construct, but does so at the level of the `while` loop—not the nested `for` loop—so that

```
#pragma omp parallel num_threads(nthreads)
{
  while (running)
  {
    #pragma omp for nowait
    for (auto i = 0; i < npaths; ++i)
    {
      Path& path = livePaths[i];

      // Trace next segment in path... if current path completes,
      //    create a new one
      if (path.traceNextRay(scene))
      {
        // Create a new path
        ...
      }

    } // End for

  } // End while

} // End omp parallel


// Simulation has been stopped, finish in-flight paths and
//    terminate
for (auto i = 0; i < npaths; ++i)
{
  // Finish tracing path
}
```

FIGURE 12.10

Using OpenMP `parallel` and `for nowait` to express path-level parallelism. The first approach to parallel RF path propagation induces unnecessary synchronization among threads and hinders parallel performance. This version more carefully expresses the available parallelism using a combination of `omp parallel` and `omp for`, together with the `nowait` clause, to maximize performance. (Code snippet from `StingRay/Simulation.cpp:498-537`.)

each thread now executes the entire loop. Note that there is an implied barrier at the end of the `omp parallel` construct.

Within the `while` loop, the `omp for` construct indicates that the current team of threads works together to execute the iterations of the corresponding `for` loop. However, the `nowait` clause at the end of the `omp for` construct indicates that threads executing the `for` loop do not need to wait on other threads before moving on. This clause removes the unnecessary synchronization point that was implied by the `omp parallel for` construct in the first OpenMP parallelization strategy. As before, threads run until the simulator is stopped, at which point threads complete their current path and the simulator terminates.

This approach improves performance by as much as 6.9× relative to single-threaded RF path propagation and recovers a factor of 3.07× (on average) relative to the first OpenMP parallelization strategy (Figure 12.9). In this case, each thread actually executes independently of every other thread—without synchronization—and performance scales nicely with thread count, as expected.

An alternative expression of path-level parallelism—using OpenMP tasks—can also be used to avoid unnecessary synchronization (Figure 12.11). Here, the implementation spawns threads using the `omp parallel` construct, but creates `npaths` tasks, one for each live path, using a single thread from

```
#pragma omp parallel num_threads(nthreads)
{
  #pragma omp single
  {
    for (auto i = 0; i < npaths; ++i)
    {
      #pragma omp task
      {
        Path& path = livePaths[i];

        while (running)
        {
          // Trace next segment in path... if current path completes,
          //    create a new one
          if (path.traceNextRay(scene))
          {
            // Create a new path
            ...
          }

        } // end while


        // Simulation has been stopped, trace each path to
        //    completion
        while (!path.traceNextRay(scene))
          ;

      } // End omp task

    } // End for

  } // End omp single

} // End omp parallel
```

FIGURE 12.11

Using OpenMP tasks to express path-level parallelism. A third approach to parallel RF path propagation generates tasks using a single thread, expressed by the OpenMP omp single construct, and defers synchronization until the end of the surrounding omp parallel construct. As in the second OpenMP parallelization strategy, each path-trace task actually executes independently of every other task, and performance scales nicely. However, the task generation loop imposes unnecessary serialization in the RF path propagation loop, so absolute performance is generally not as high as with the second approach. (Code snippet from StingRay/Simulation.cpp:549-593.)

the pool. This arrangement is expressed by embedding the omp single construct immediately within the omp parallel construct. In this case, the first thread that arrives at the omp single construct executes the task creation loop. A task created in this manner can be executed immediately by any thread in the pool. Finally, once task creation is complete, the corresponding thread joins the other threads in executing the newly created tasks. As before, threads run until the simulator is stopped, at which point threads complete their current path and the simulator terminates.

This approach improves performance by as much as 6.5× relative to single-threaded RF path propagation and recovers a factor of 3.47× (on average) relative to the first OpenMP parallelization strategy (Figure 12.9). As in the second OpenMP parallelization strategy, each task actually executes

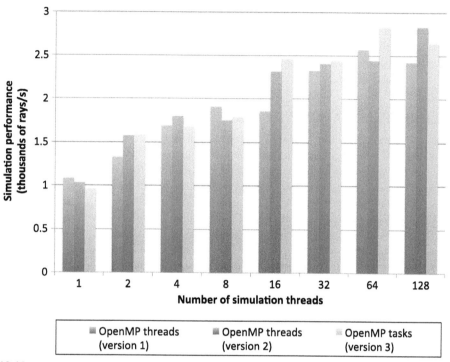

FIGURE 12.12

Parallel RF simulation on an Intel Xeon Phi 7120X coprocessor. These results depict scalar simulation performance, measured in terms of thousands of rays per second, on an Intel Xeon Phi 7120X coprocessor using task-level parallelism with 1-128 threads. Behavior of these codes is similar to that of the corresponding CPU versions; however, absolute performance suffers due to scalar code paths and memory bandwidth bottlenecks. Vectorized RF path propagation is an important area of future work, but is beyond the scope of this chapter.

independently of every other task—without synchronization—and performance scales nicely with thread count. However, the task generation loop imposes unnecessary serialization in the RF path propagation loop, so absolute performance is generally not as high as with the second approach.

Task-level parallelism also improves performance of RF path propagation on Intel Xeon Phi coprocessors (Figure 12.12). Behavior of these codes on Intel Xeon Phi coprocessors is similar to that of the corresponding codes on Intel Xeon processors: the second and third OpenMP parallelization strategies best express the available parallelism and generally achieve the best performance among the strategies we explore. However, absolute performance suffers due to scalar code paths and memory bandwidth bottlenecks. As noted above, vectorization of RF path propagation is particularly difficult, due to lack of coherence, even in primary rays. Vectorization in this context is an important area of future work, but is beyond the scope of this chapter.

Instead, we highlight the role of vector processing in StingRay's scalar volume visualization component, as described below. In particular, we explore the use of Intel's SPMD Program Compiler (ispc) to vectorize a visualization component that renders scalar volume data generated from RF simulation results as a participating medium.

PARALLEL RF VISUALIZATION WITH ispc

Visualization of RF simulation results in StingRay is a classic rendering problem: given a collection of 3D objects and a viewing specification, generate the 2D image of these objects as seen by the virtual camera. There are several ways to implement a parallel renderer for Intel Xeon processors and Intel Xeon Phi coprocessors, and a large body of work has explored methods that do just that; the interested reader can find additional details in the resources listed at the end of this chapter.

StingRay's plug-in architecture and layered visualization approach provide flexibility in the way analysts view RF simulation results by allowing individual visualization components to ingest and render data in whatever manner is most appropriate to its goals. In this example, we highlight the use of ispc to vectorize a visualization component that renders scalar volume data as a participating medium (Figure 12.6, middle-right and far-right).

We use a probabilistic approach to render volume data as a participating medium: at each sample point along a ray, the volume data are queried and the corresponding value is converted to a density. If a random value is less than accumulated density, a ray/volume interaction occurs; otherwise, the ray march continues to the next sample. In the case of ray/volume interaction, accumulated density is converted to color, lighting computations are applied, and the ray march is terminated.

In contrast to RF path propagation (where paths diverge almost immediately), rendering scalar volume data as a participating medium operates with rays that tend to be far more coherent: spatially local rays march through the volume in near lock-step and, therefore, access nearly the same cells. As a result, data-level parallelism, expressed in an SIMD implementation, can be exploited more effectively than in the RF simulation engine.

The ispc implementation of cleanly vectorized rendering code (Figure 12.13) is both easy to read and nearly identical to the corresponding multithreaded scalar code—porting this functionality from standard C++ to ispc is straightforward.[1] More importantly, ispc code is ISA-portable: the ispc compiler automatically maps code to different vector widths without source-level changes. These features keep the implementation footprint small and make the code portable across a wide range SIMD instruction sets.

Importantly, ispc enables high performance with low maintenance overhead: the ispc participating media implementation highlighted here improves performance by as much as $1.61\times$ relative to an AVX2 auto-vectorized scalar implementation (Figure 12.14). These improvements are achieved simply by retargeting the ispc compiler for different vector widths; no source-level changes to the ispc rendering code are required.

---

[1]The ispc language provides syntax to specify variables that correspond to vector types (varying) and single scalar types (uniform). (Note that variables not explicitly marked as uniform or varying are assumed by ispc to be varying.) In our experience, using these type qualifiers correctly is the trickiest part of porting SIMD-friendly routines, such as the participating media rendering code, to ispc.

```
/* March ray through volume and probabilistically shade sample point */
inline Vec3f marchRay(...)
{
  if (!intersect(volume->bounds, ray))
  {
    color[0] += 1.f;
    color[1] += 1.f;
    color[2] += 1.f;
  }
  else
  {
    const float texit  = min(ray.tfar, image->dbuffer[pid]);
    const float offset = frandom(&rngs)*tstep;
    const float random = frandom(&rngs);

    float t = ray.tnear + offset;
    float d = 0.f;
    while (t < texit)
    {
      const float<3> point = ray.org + t*ray.dir;
      const float      value = sampleVolume(volume, point)*volume->imax;

      d += value;

      if (random < d*iscale)
      {
        float<3> toLight = 1 - point;
        Normalize(toLight);

        const RGB scolor = { 0.f, d, d };

        RGB result = Ka*acolor*scolor;

        float<3> N =
        {
          camera->eye[0] - point[0],
          camera->eye[1] - point[1],
          camera->eye[2] - point[2],
        };

        Normalize(N);

        color += (Ka*acolor + Kd*max(0.f, Dot(N, toLight))*lcolor)*scolor;

        break;
      }

      t += tstep;
    }

    if (t > texit)
    {
      color[0] += image->fbuffer[pid][0];
      color[1] += image->fbuffer[pid][1];
      color[2] += image->fbuffer[pid][2];
    }
  }

  return color;
}
```

FIGURE 12.13

Rendering volume data as a participating medium with ispc. This cleanly vectorized ispc code implements a probabilistic approach to rendering volume data as a participating medium. Importantly, the code is easy to read, easy to maintain, ISA-portable, and highly performant. (Function interfaces omitted for brevity. Code snippet adapted from visbench/traceVolume.ispc:258-310.)

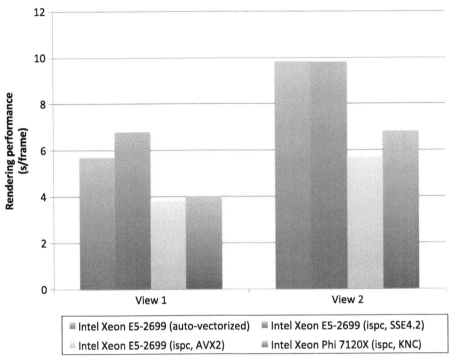

FIGURE 12.14

Parallel RF visualization with `ispc`. When visualizing scalar volume data as a participating medium, `ispc` enables a readable, ISA-portable, and high performance SIMD implementation with low maintenance overhead. These results depict rendering performance, measured in seconds per frame, on Intel Xeon E5-2699 processors and an Intel Xeon Phi 7210X coprocessor. Performance improves by as much as 1.61× relative to that of an AVX2 auto-vectorized scalar implementation for Intel Xeon processors.

SUMMARY

RF simulation and visualization is critical to planning, analyzing, and optimizing wireless communication networks. An interactive tool supporting visual analysis of RF propagation characteristics in complex environments will enable analysts to better understand RF propagation phenomena.

StingRay provides an interactive combined RF simulation and visualization environment that satisfies these constraints. Derived from first principles, StingRay's ray-based RF simulation engine provides a high fidelity approach for RF prediction in complex environments. StingRay is explicitly designed for Intel Xeon processors and Intel Xeon Phi coprocessors, which provide high performance compute capabilities for physics-based simulation. Moreover, the Embree ray tracing engine provides high performance ray tracing for problems in optical and nonoptical domains, and the OSPRay high fidelity visualization framework enables scalable visualization capabilities for understanding RF propagation phenomena.

In this way, StingRay combines best-known methods in high performance ray tracing and high fidelity visualization with low-level, architecture-specific optimizations for Intel Xeon processors and Intel Xeon Phi coprocessors to provide an interactive environment for predictive simulation and visualization of RF energy propagation in complex environments.

ACKNOWLEDGMENTS

We gratefully acknowledge the contributions of the Intel Parallel Visualization Engineering Team, including Jim Jeffers, Ingo Wald, Carsten Benthin, Greg P. Johnson, Greg S. Johnson, Brad Rathke, and Sven Woop. We also thank Erik Brunvand, Thiago Ize, and Konstantin Shkurko (University of Utah), Lee Butler (U.S. Army Research Laboratory), and Henry Bertoni (NYU Polytechnic) for their contributions to the early research, development, and reporting efforts that lead to the RF simulation methodology on which StingRay is based.

FOR MORE INFORMATION

The following resources provide additional details on many of the topics covered in this chapter:

- Embree—High Performance Ray Tracing Kernels: http://embree.github.io.
- Intel SPMD Program Compiler (ispc): http://ispc.github.io.
- OpenMP: http://www.openmp.org.
- OSPRay—A Ray Tracing Based Rendering Engine for High-Fidelity Visualization: http://ospray. github.io.
- StingRay–Combined RF Simulation/Visualization Environment: http://code.survice.com/survice/ stingray.
- Gribble, C., Amstutz, J., 2015. StingRay: high-performance RF energy propagation modeling in complex environments. DSIAC J. 2(2), 16-24 (Spring).

Download all codes from this, and other chapters, http://lotsofcores.com.

EXPLORING USE OF THE RESERVED CORE

13

John Holmen, Alan Humphrey, Martin Berzins

SCI Institute and School of Computing, University of Utah, USA

In this chapter, we illustrate benefits of thinking in terms of thread management techniques when using a centralized scheduler model along with interoperability of MPI and PThreads. This is facilitated through an exploration of thread placement strategies for an algorithm modeling radiative heat transfer with special attention to the 61st core. This algorithm plays a key role within the Uintah Computational Framework (UCF) and current efforts taking place at the University of Utah to model next generation, large-scale clean coal boilers. In such simulations, this algorithm models the dominant form of heat transfer and consumes a large portion of compute time. Exemplified by a real-world example, this chapter presents our early efforts in porting a key portion of a scalability-centric codebase to the Intel® Xeon Phi™ coprocessor. Specifically, this chapter presents results from our experiments profiling the native execution of a reverse Monte-Carlo ray tracing (RMCRT)-based radiation model on a single coprocessor. These results demonstrate that our fastest run configurations utilized the 61st core and that performance was not profoundly impacted when explicitly oversubscribing the coprocessor operating system thread. Additionally, this chapter presents a portion of radiation model source code, an many integrated core (MIC)-centric UCF cross-compilation example, and less conventional thread management techniques for developers utilizing the PThreads threading model.

THE UINTAH COMPUTATIONAL FRAMEWORK

Regularly maintained as open-source software (MIT License), the UCF consists of a set of simulation components and libraries facilitating the simulation and analysis of complex chemical and physical reactions. These reactions are modeled by solving partial differential equations on structured adaptive mesh refinement grids. This framework was originally developed as part of the University of Utah's Center for the Simulation of Accidental Fires and Explosions (C-SAFE) initiative in 1997. Since then, it has been widely ported and used to develop novel techniques for understanding large pool eddy fires and new methods for simulating fluid-structure interactions.

Released in January of 2015, UCF release 1.6.0 features four primary simulation components:

- *ARCHES*: This component targets the simulation of turbulent reacting flows with participating media radiation.
- *ICE*: This component targets the simulation of both low-speed and high-speed compressible flows.

- *MPM*: This component targets the simulation of multimaterial, particle-based structural mechanics.
- *MPM-ICE*: This component corresponds to the combination of the ICE and MPM components for the simulation of fluid-structure interactions.

Though small-scale simulations are supported, the UCF emphasizes large-scale simulations. This in mind, the UCF must be able to leverage the increasing adoption of the Intel® MIC architecture within current and emerging heterogeneous supercomputer architectures. Aligning with this need, our research efforts have targeted porting the UCF's RMCRT-based radiation model to this architecture. This radiation model has been chosen to support the University of Utah's Carbon Capture Multi-Disciplinary Simulation Center's (CCMSC) goal of simulating a 350-MWe clean coal boiler being developed by Alstom Power.

RADIATION MODELING WITH THE UCF

ARCHES was initially developed using the parallel discrete ordinates method and P1 approximation to aid in solving the radiative transport equation. Though scalable, this approach resulted in solution of the associated linear systems being the main computational cost of reacting flow simulations.

To reduce this cost, recent attention has been given to exploring more efficient RMCRT methods. These efforts have resulted in the development of a stand-alone RMCRT-based radiation model capable of being used with any of the UCF's simulation components.

RMCRT leverages reciprocity in radiative transfer and Monte-Carlo methods. The resulting approach samples a simulation mesh by tracing rays *toward* their origin. During traversal, the amount of incoming radiative intensity absorbed by the origin is computed to aid in solving the radiative transport equation.

This approach creates the potential for scalable parallelism as multiple rays can be traced simultaneously at any given cell and/or timestep. Additionally, it also eliminates the need to trace rays that may never reach a given origin. Note, however, this is achieved at the expense of an all-to-all communication between timesteps.

For these experiments, the primary hotspot was a function known as **updateSumI**(). Critical to RMCRT, this function traverses rays using a ray-marching algorithm while simultaneously computing each ray's contribution to the incoming radiative intensity. Putting this into perspective, upwards of 200 million rays were cast at each compute timestep during these experiments.

Figures 13.1 and 13.2 present portions of code corresponding to **updateSumI**(). Referring to the version of Uintah used for this chapter, **updateSumI**() can be found in **RMCRTCommon.cc**. Note that Figures 13.1 and 13.2 have been abbreviated so as not to include special scenarios that were not explored during these experiments.

To learn more about radiative heat transfer and the UCF's radiation models, please refer to the "For more information" section.

CROSS-COMPILING THE UCF

For this port, cross-compilation and resolution of third-party dependences have been the primary challenges.

```
RMCRTCommon::updateSumI ( Vector&              ray_direction,
                          Vector&              ray_location,
                          const IntVector&     origin,
                          const Vector&        Dx,
                          constCCVariable< T >& sigmaT4OverPi,
                          constCCVariable< T >& abskg,
                          constCCVariable<int>& celltype,
                          unsigned long int&   nRaySteps,
                          double&              sumI,
                          MTRand&              mTwister) {

    IntVector cur       = origin;
    IntVector prevCell = cur;

    // Step and sign used for ray marching
    int   step[3]; // Gives +1 or -1 based on sign
    bool sign[3];

    // Update step and sign to determine whether dimensions are incremented
    // or decremented as cell boundaries are crossed
    Vector inv_ray_direction = Vector( 1.0 ) / ray_direction;
    findStepSize( step, sign, inv_ray_direction );
    Vector D_DxRatio( 1, Dx.y() / Dx.x(), Dx.z() / Dx.x() );

    // Compute the distance from the ray origin to the nearest cell boundary
    // for a given dimension
    Vector tMax;
    tMax.x( (origin[0] + sign[0] - ray_location[0]) *
            inv_ray_direction[0] );
    tMax.y( (origin[1] + sign[1] * D_DxRatio[1] - ray_location[1]) *
            inv_ray_direction[1] );
    tMax.z( (origin[2] + sign[2] * D_DxRatio[2] - ray_location[2]) *
            inv_ray_direction[2] );

    // Compute the distance required to traverse a single cell
    Vector tDelta = Abs( inv_ray_direction ) * D_DxRatio;

    // Intialize per-ray variables
    bool   in_domain            = true;
    double tMax_prev            = 0;
    double intensity            = 1.0;
    double fs                   = 1.0;
    double optical_thickness    = 0;
    double expOpticalThick_prev = 1.0;

    // Traverse a given ray until the incoming intensity that would arrive
    // at the origin falls below a user-defined threshold
    while ( intensity > d_threshold ) {

      DIR face = NONE;

      // Traverse a given ray until it leaves the simulation mesh
      while ( in_domain ) {

        prevCell = cur;
        double disMin = -9; // Represents ray segment length

        T abskg_prev = abskg[prevCell];
        T sigmaT4OverPi_prev = sigmaT4OverPi[prevCell];
```

FIGURE 13.1

RMCRT-based radiation modeling hotspot.

```
// Determine which cell the ray will enter next
if ( tMax[0] < tMax[1] ) {     // X < Y
  if ( tMax[0] < tMax[2] ) { // X < Z
    face = X;
  } else {
    face = Z;
  }
} else {
  if ( tMax[1] < tMax[2] ) { // Y < Z
    face = Y;
  } else {
    face = Z;
  }
}

// Update ray marching variables
cur[face]  = cur[face] + step[face];
disMin     = ( tMax[face] - tMax_prev );
tMax_prev  = tMax[face];
tMax[face] = tMax[face] + tDelta[face];

// Update ray location
ray_location[0] = ray_location[0] + ( disMin * ray_direction[0] );
ray_location[1] = ray_location[1] + ( disMin * ray_direction[1] );
ray_location[2] = ray_location[2] + ( disMin * ray_direction[2] );

// Check if the cell is in the simulation mesh
in_domain = ( celltype[cur] == d_flowCell );

optical_thickness += Dx.x() * abskg_prev * disMin;

nRaySteps++;

double expOpticalThick = exp(-optical_thickness );

sumI += sigmaT4OverPi_prev *
        ( expOpticalThick_prev - expOpticalThick ) *
        fs;

expOpticalThick_prev = expOpticalThick;

} // End of in_domain while loop

T wallEmissivity = abskg[cur];

// Ensure that wall emissivity does not exceed one
if ( wallEmissivity > 1.0 ) {
  wallEmissivity = 1.0;
}

intensity = exp( -optical_thickness );

sumI += wallEmissivity * sigmaT4OverPi[cur] * intensity;

intensity = intensity * fs;

// Terminate a ray upon reaching mesh boundaries
if(!d_allowReflect) intensity = 0;

  } // End of intensity while loop
} // End of updateSumI function
```

FIGURE 13.2

RMCRT-based radiation modeling hotspot (continued).

When preparing to build the UCF, a developer must first cross-compile any required libraries that are unavailable on the coprocessor or feature conflicting versions between architectures. For this work, the UCF required cross-compilation of *libxml2* and *zlib* as demonstrated in Figures 13.3 and 13.4.

After resolving dependences, a developer then constructs a configure line denoting how to build the UCF executable. Figure 13.5 demonstrates how to cross-compile the UCF with utilities only.

With cross-compilation complete, a developer must then transfer coprocessor executables, UCF problem specifications, and dynamically linked libraries to the coprocessor.

```
wget http://xmlsoft.org/sources/libxml2-2.7.8.tar.gz
tar xvf libxml2-2.7.8.tar.gz
cd libxml2-2.7.8
./configure \
    --prefix=$HOME/installs/mic/libxml2-2.7.8 \
    --host=x86_64-k1om-linux \
    --enable-static \
    --without-python \
    CC=icc \
    CXX=icpc \
    CFLAGS="-mmic" \
    CXXFLAGS="-mmic" \
    LDFLAGS="-mmic"
make -j32 all
make install
```

FIGURE 13.3

Cross-compiling *libxml2-2.7.8* for the coprocessor.

```
wget http://zlib.net/zlib-1.2.8.tar.gz
tar xvf zlib-1.2.8.tar.gz
cd zlib-1.2.8
CC=icc CXX=icpc CFLAGS="-mmic" CXXFLAGS="-mmic" LDFLAGS="-mmic" \
    ./configure \
    --prefix=$HOME/installs/mic/zlib-1.2.8 \
    --static
make -j32 all
make install
```

FIGURE 13.4

Cross-compiling *zlib-1.2.8* for the coprocessor.

```
../src/configure \
    --host=x86_64-k1om-linux \
    --enable-64bit \
    --enable-optimize="-O2 -mkl=parallel -mmic -mt_mpi" \
    --enable-assertion-level=0 \
    --enable-static \
    --with-libxml2=$HOME/installs/mic/libxml2-2.7.8 \
    --with-mpi=/opt/intel/impi/5.0.1.035/mic \
    --with-zlib=$HOME/installs/mic/zlib-1.2.8 \
    CC=mpiicc \
    CXX=mpiicpc \
    F77=mpiifort
```

FIGURE 13.5

Configure line for an MIC-specific UCF build.

To learn more about obtaining, installing, and using the UCF, please refer to the "For more information" section.

TOWARD DEMYSTIFYING THE RESERVED CORE

On the 61-core coprocessor, the last-most physical core contains logical cores 241, 242, 243, and 0. Though /proc/cpuinfo core id: 60 in practice, this physical core is commonly referred to as the 61st core. The 61st core is unique in that logical core 0 is reserved for the Xeon Phi operating system. Additionally, the 61st core is also reserved for the offload daemon. While it is reportedly safe to use all 244 threads for native execution, this begs the question—How does one effectively manage the 61st core when executing natively?

To explore this question, we have experimented with a number of thread placement strategies featuring varying affinity patterns and thread counts. Detailed information regarding the parameters explored can be found in the subsequent sections and the "Simulation configuration" section. These parameters have been chosen to examine a multitude of strategies for handling the 61st core. On coprocessors with less than 61 cores, we believe that the results would be similar when using the last core.

EXPLORING THREAD AFFINITY PATTERNS

Structured around a task-based, MPI + PThreads parallelism model, the UCF features a task scheduler component. This component is responsible for computing task dependences, determining task execution order, and ensuring correctness of inter-process communication.

As of UCF release 1.6.0, the default multithreaded scheduler is the Threaded MPI Scheduler. This dynamic scheduler features nondeterministic, out-of-order task execution at runtime. This is facilitated using a control thread and *nThreads*-1 task execution threads, where *nThreads* equals the number of threads launched at runtime.

Given this centralized model, we have experimented with the affinity patterns described below. Referring to the version of Uintah used for this chapter, implementations of these affinity patterns can be found in **ThreadedMPIScheduler.cc**. Note that *nt* corresponds to the number of threads per physical core (TPPC).

- *Compact*: This pattern binds task execution threads incrementally across logical cores 1 through *nt* in a given physical core first and then across physical cores 1 through 61. This pattern is modeled after OpenMP's **KMP_AFFINITY = compact** with values of **61c,2t**, **61c,3t**, and **61c,4t** for the **KMP_PLACE_THREADS** environment variable.
- *None*: This pattern allows both the control and task execution threads to run anywhere among all 244 logical cores.
- *Scatter*: This pattern binds task execution threads incrementally across physical cores 1 through 60 first and then across logical cores 1 through *nt* in a given physical core. This pattern is modeled after OpenMP's **KMP_AFFINITY = scatter** with values of **60c,2t**, **60c,3t**, and **60c,4t** for the **KMP_PLACE_THREADS** environment variable. Note that threads are spread across physical cores 1 through 60 only to support our exploration of the 61st core.

- *Selective*: This affinity pattern binds the control thread to either logical core 240, 241, 242, 243, or 0 depending upon the values of *nt* and *nThreads*. Task execution threads are allowed run anywhere among the logical cores preceding the control thread.

To facilitate exploration of the 61st core with the *Compact, Scatter*, and *Selective* affinity patterns, multiple values of *nThreads* are used to increment the number of logical cores used on the 61st core from 0 to *nt*. For example, a run configuration featuring *nThreads* = 180 and *nt* = 3 uses 0 logical cores on the 61st core. This in mind, the control thread is bound to the last logical core used by a given pattern. For example, a run configuration featuring *nThreads* = 180 and *nt* = 3 binds the control thread to logical core 240.

THREAD PLACEMENT WITH PTHREADS

Alluded to in the prior section, OpenMP users are provided with environment variables to specify thread placement. Such environment variables include **KMP_PLACE_THREADS** and **KMP_AFFINITY**. To learn more about these environment variables, please refer to the **OpenMP Support** section in Intel's *User and Reference Guide* for the corresponding compiler.

In contrast to OpenMP, PThreads requires that developers manually implement affinity patterns. This is attainable using the **CPU_ZERO()**, **CPU_SET()**, and **sched_setaffinity()** functions found within the **sched.h** header file. Given these functions, the **mask** parameter in **sched_setaffinity()** is of key interest. This bit mask determines which logical core(s) a thread is eligible to run on. Figure 13.6 demonstrates how to bind a thread (identified by *pid*) to a single logical core (identified by *logCore*). Referring to the version of Uintah used for this chapter, our use of code in Figure 13.6 can be found in **set_affinity()** in **Thread_pthreads.cc**.

Note, however, Figure 13.6 is insufficient for allowing a thread to run among a subset of logical cores. To accomplish this, **CPU_SET()** may be used repeatedly to add additional logical cores to the bit mask. Figure 13.7 demonstrates how to allow a thread to run among a subset of logical cores

```
cpu_set_t mask;
unsigned int len = sizeof( mask );
CPU_ZERO( &mask );
CPU_SET( logCore, &mask );
sched_setaffinity( pid, len, &mask );
```

FIGURE 13.6

Specifying one-to-one thread binding.

```
cpu_set_t mask;
unsigned int len = sizeof( mask );
CPU_ZERO( &mask );
for ( int logCore = 1; logCore < nThreads; logCore++ ) {
  CPU_SET( logCore, &mask );
}
sched_setaffinity( pid, len, &mask );
```

FIGURE 13.7

Specifying one-to-many thread binding.

(specifically, anywhere among logical cores 1 through *nThreads*-1). Referring to the version of Uintah used for this chapter, our use of code in Figure 13.7 can be found in **set_affinityMICMainOnly()** in **Thread_pthreads.cc**.

Note

If not explicitly changed, a user-defined **mask** persists for subsequently launched threads. Attention to this detail is critical when implementing affinity patterns with selective thread binding. Such cases require a combination of the methods described in Figures 13.6 and 13.7.

IMPLEMENTING SCATTER AFFINITY WITH PTHREADS

The scatter affinity pattern requires more effort to implement than other patterns we have discussed. For this reason, Figure 13.8 demonstrates how to implement the scatter affinity pattern with PThreads. This example assumes that each thread is uniquely identified by a *threadID* and calls **scatterAffinity()** to denote which logical core it is eligible to run on. Note that Figure 13.8 supports values of 0 through 243 for *threadID*, where *threadID*=0 is mapped to logical core 0.

Referring to the version of Uintah used for this chapter, our use of code in Figure 13.8 can be found in **run()** in **ThreadedMPIScheduler.cc**. Note that our implementation differs slightly from Figure 13.8. Specifically, our implementation handles the 61st core as a special case and spreads threads across physical cores 1 through 60 only. This has been done to support our exploration of the 61st core.

```
void scatterAffinity( int threadID ) {

    int scatterPhysCores    = 61;
    int logCoresPerPhysCore = 4;
    int logCoreIndex        = 0;
    int physCoreIndex       = 0;
    int overallIndex        = 0;

    // Determine whether the thread will be bound to the 1st, 2nd,
    // 3rd, or 4th logical core in a given physical core
    logCoreIndex = floor(( threadID-1 ) / scatterPhysCores ) + 1;

    // Determine which physical core the thread will be bound to
    physCoreIndex = ( threadID - (( logCoreIndex-1 ) * scatterPhysCores ));

    // Determine the specific logical core the thread will be bound to
    overallIndex = logCoreIndex + ( physCoreIndex-1 ) * logCoresPerPhysCore;

    // Bind the thread to its corresponding logical core
    cpu_set_t mask;
    unsigned int len = sizeof( mask );
    CPU_ZERO( &mask );
    CPU_SET( overallIndex, &mask );
    sched_setaffinity( 0, len, &mask );
}
```

FIGURE 13.8

PThreads-based implementation of the scatter affinity pattern.

EXPERIMENTAL DISCUSSION

This section describes our experimental setup and concludes with discussion of our experimental results.

MACHINE CONFIGURATION

These experiments were performed on a single-node machine using one MPI process and double-precision floating point numbers.

Host-side simulations were launched with 32 threads distributed among 16 physical cores. This was accomplished using two Intel Xeon E5-2680 processors in a dual-socket configuration.

Coprocessor-side simulations were launched with as many as 244 threads distributed among 61 physical cores. This was accomplished using one 16 GB Intel Xeon Phi 7110P coprocessor.

SIMULATION CONFIGURATION

Below are key parameters explored on the coprocessor-side:

- Three physical core usage levels (2, 3, and 4 hardware TPPC):
  - For 2 hardware TPPC, 3 thread counts were used to allot 0-2 threads for the 61st core (120-122 threads).
  - For 3 hardware TPPC, 4 thread counts were used to allot 0-3 threads for the 61st core (180-183 threads).
  - For 4 hardware TPPC, 5 thread counts were used to allot 0-4 threads for the 61st core (240-244 threads).
- Four affinity patterns (*Compact*, *None*, *Scatter*, and *Selective* affinity).
- Four mesh patch counts (facilitating ratios of 1, 2, 4, and 8 patches per thread [PPT]).

Below are notes regarding simulation configuration:

- Simulation meshes are decomposed into mesh patches consisting of individual cells.
- Tasks are executed by threads, which are bound to logical cores.
- Tasks reside on mesh patches, which are computed serially using a single thread.
- Different threads may be used to compute tasks resident to a particular mesh patch.
- Tasks are assigned to idle threads without regard to spatial locality of the mesh patch data that they access.
- Simulations were performed using a single-level 128^3 simulation mesh as this was the largest supported by the coprocessor.
- Radiation modeling calculations were performed over 10 consecutive timesteps.
- At each compute timestep, the simulation mesh was sampled using 100 rays per cell.
- Host-side simulations explored the use of 32 threads with the aforementioned affinity patterns and mesh patch counts.

COPROCESSOR-SIDE RESULTS

Figures 13.9 through 13.12 visualize results from the 192 simulations performed on the coprocessor-side. Below are notes regarding coprocessor-side results:

- Marks correspond to the average elapsed execution time per compute timestep (in seconds).
- TPPC corresponds to the number of hardware threads utilized per physical core.
- Reserved core usage (RCU) corresponds to number of hardware threads utilized on the reserved core. For clarity, each value of RCU has been enumerated below:
  - RCU=0 corresponds to use of 120, 180, and 240 threads facilitating 2, 3, and 4 hardware TPPC, respectively.
  - RCU=1 corresponds to use of 121, 181, and 241 threads facilitating 2, 3, and 4 hardware TPPC, respectively.
  - RCU=2 corresponds to use of 122, 182, and 242 threads facilitating 2, 3, and 4 hardware TPPC, respectively.
  - RCU=3 corresponds to use of 183 and 243 threads facilitating 3 and 4 hardware TPPC, respectively.
  - RCU=4 corresponds to use of 244 threads facilitating 4 hardware TPPC.
- PPT corresponds to the ratio of mesh patches to threads. Note that each thread is not guaranteed to compute this number of mesh patches.
- Over 10 identical coprocessor-side simulations, there existed not more than a 4.29% difference in performance between two identical runs.
- At 2, 3, and 4 hardware TPPC, there existed 30.14%, 42.60%, and 149.33% differences in performance, respectively, between the fastest and slowest run configurations.

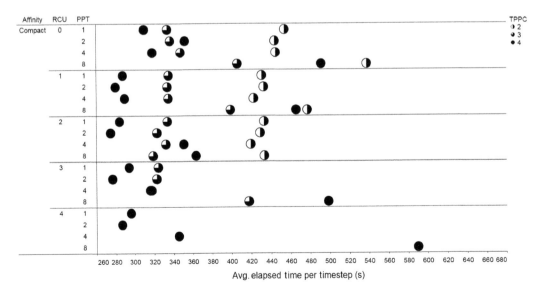

FIGURE 13.9

Coprocessor-side results for the *Compact* affinity pattern.

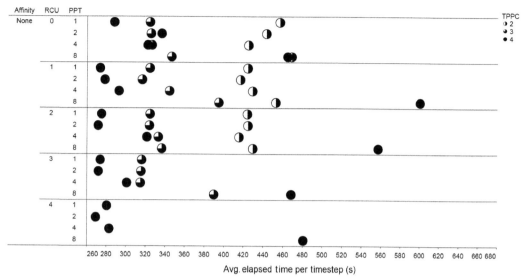

FIGURE 13.10

Coprocessor-side results for the *None* affinity pattern.

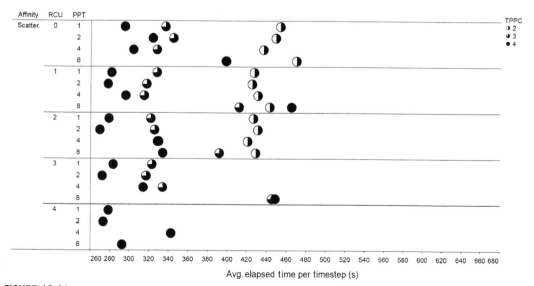

FIGURE 13.11

Coprocessor-side results for the *Scatter* affinity pattern.

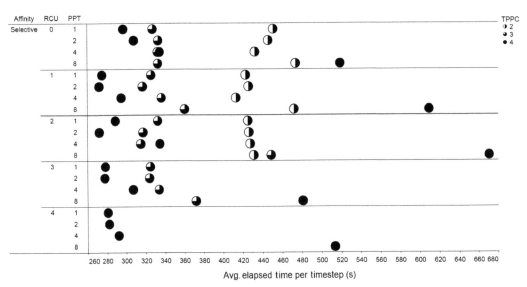

FIGURE 13.12

Coprocessor-side results for the *Selective* affinity pattern.

HOST-SIDE RESULTS

Figure 13.13 visualizes results from the 16 simulations performed on the host-side. Below are notes regarding host-side results:

- Marks correspond to the average elapsed execution time per compute timestep (in seconds).
- PPT corresponds to the ratio of mesh patches to threads. Note that each thread is not guaranteed to compute this number of mesh patches.
- Over 10 identical host-side simulations, there existed not more than a 3.35% difference in performance between two identical runs.
- There existed a 10.14% difference in performance between the fastest and slowest run configurations.

FURTHER ANALYSIS

Addressing comparisons between architectures first, the two Xeon processors outperformed the single Xeon Phi coprocessor. Specifically, there existed a 39.43% difference in performance between the fastest run configurations for each architecture. Regarding accuracy, simulation results computed by each architecture were identical to one another up to a relative tolerance of 1E-15 digits.

Given this has been a naive port of our CPU-based algorithm, these results are encouraging as they leave ample opportunity to shift performance in favor of the coprocessor. Having not yet adequately pursued such optimizations, effective memory management and vectorization are believed to be the factors attributing to these differences. Supporting this conclusion, version 15.0 compiler optimization reports and experimentation with simpler vectorization approaches (e.g., SIMD directives) suggest that

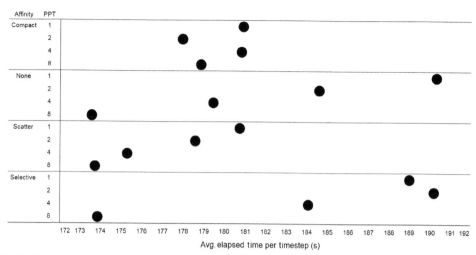

FIGURE 13.13

Host-side results.

little, if any, vectorization is being achieved. Further, predominantly 100% core usage during compute timesteps suggests that thread-level parallelism is sufficient.

Turning to observations, performance disparities among coprocessor-based results deserve attention. As more hardware TPPC were utilized, the difference in performance between fastest and slowest run configurations increased. This is likely attributed to the sharing of the 512 kB per core L2 cache among four hardware threads. Though it offered better run times, use of more hardware TPPC further divided the amount of L2 cache available to a given thread. This resulted in increased sensitivity to simulation mesh decomposition.

Moving forward, the overarching takeaway from these native execution-based experiments is that no one thread placement strategy dominated performance. For similar algorithms, this suggests that time may be best spent by first pursuing more favorable areas of optimization.

Returning to the question motivating this work, our fastest run configurations utilized the 61st core. Further, performance was not profoundly impacted when explicitly oversubscribing the coprocessor operating system thread. For similar algorithms, this suggests that use of the 61st core may be both forgiving and capable of offering modest performance improvements.

SUMMARY

These experiments have helped establish valuable baselines for our future efforts addressing both single-node performance and scalability. Perhaps more important, they have also provided valuable insight regarding potential challenges and areas to address as we strive to achieve performance with the Intel Xeon Phi products. When considering these results, it is important to remember that we have examined native execution exclusively. When operating in offload mode, Intel guidance is to refrain from using the reserved core as it actively supports offloading.

ACKNOWLEDGMENTS

These research efforts have been supported by the National Nuclear Security Administration's PSAAP II project. This work utilized equipment donations to the University of Utah's Intel Parallel Computing Center (IPCC) at the SCI Institute. We would also like to thank Aaron Knoll, IPCC Principal Investigator, for his assistance along the way.

FOR MORE INFORMATION

To learn more about the UCF, please refer to the link below:

- http://www.uintah.utah.edu/

To explore Uintah and C-SAFE-related publications, please refer to the link below:

- http://www.uintah.utah.edu/pubs/pubs.html

To learn more about radiative heat transfer and the discrete ordinates method-based radiation model, please refer to the publication referenced below:

- Spinti, J.P., Thornock, J.N., Eddings, E.G., Smith, P.J., Sarofim, A.F., 2008. Heat transfer to objects in pool fires. In: Transport Phenomena in Fires. WIT Press, Southampton, UK.

To learn more about the RMCRT-based radiation model, please refer to the publication referenced below:

- Humphrey, A., Meng, Q., Berzins, M., Harman, T., 2012. Radiation modeling using the Uintah heterogeneous CPU/GPU runtime system. In: Proceedings of the 1st Conference of the Extreme Science and Engineering Discovery Environment (XSEDE12). ACM.

To download the version of Uintah used for this chapter, please refer to the link below:

- http://lotsofcores.com/downloads

To learn more about installing and using the UCF, please refer to the link below:

- http://uintah-build.sci.utah.edu/trac/wiki

HIGH PERFORMANCE PYTHON OFFLOADING

14

Jussi Enkovaara*, Michael Klemm[†], Freddie Witherden[‡]

CSC, Finland* Intel Corporation, Germany[†] Imperial College of London, United Kingdom[‡]

Python applications, running on a host processor, can use the *pyMIC* module to load and execute code on the Intel® Xeon Phi[TM] coprocessor. This chapter demonstrates the usage of pyMIC within two high performance computing (HPC) applications, GPAW and PyFR. This chapter also reviews the design, implementation, and performance of pyMIC.

It is worth noting that Python code can be run directly on a coprocessor using PyPhi. That is not covered in this chapter but there are references at the end of this chapter for PyPhi.

The pyMIC offload model supports management of data transfers and offloading at various levels of control. Programmers can start from a naïve, simplistic solution and incrementally increase the level of control to gain additional performance or extend the offloaded code regions. The current version of pyMIC requires the programmer to write the offload kernels in C, C++, or Fortran, and compile them for native coprocessor execution. In contrast to the native version of Python that ships with the Intel® Manycore Platform Software Stack (MPSS), Python code runs on the host while the offloaded code relies on native execution and multithreading for maximum performance. At the end of this chapter, the "For more information" section contains links for pyMIC (offload from Python to a coprocessor) and PyPhi (run Python on a coprocessor).

BACKGROUND

Python is one of the most commonly used programming languages within the computing industry. Throughout its existence, Python has proven to be an easy-to-use, elegant scripting language that allows for rapid prototyping and development of highly flexible software. Python has gained substantial popularity in the HPC community. Add-on packages such as Numpy and SciPy provide efficient implementations of containers for bulk floating-point data and typical number-crunching algorithms. Extensions like these usually use compiled languages such as C or Fortran for performance. Therefore, Python can provide the performance needed for widespread HPC usage.

GPAW is one prominent example of a Python HPC application. It is a versatile open-source software package for various electronic structure simulations of nanostructures and materials science research problems. GPAW is based on the density-functional theory (DFT) and time-dependent DFT, and it offers several options for discretizing the underlying equations, such as uniform real-space grids, plane waves, and localized atomic orbital basis. GPAW can be run on wide variety of HPC systems, and depending on the input data, simulations can scale up to tens of thousands of traditional CPU cores. GPGPUs have already been shown to be beneficial for speeding up GPAW, and the Intel Xeon Phi coprocessor appears as an appealing alternative for GPU-based accelerators. GPAW is implemented as a combination of Python and C, thus the ability to operate on coprocessors from the high-level Python code is considered highly beneficial.

PyFR is another example of using Python in the context of HPC. It is an open-source Python framework for solving the unsteady compressible Navier-Stokes equations in the vicinity of complex geometrical configurations. This is accomplished by employing the flux reconstruction approach of Huynh. These schemes have a variety of desirable computational properties including: high-order accuracy in space, support for mixed unstructured grids, and good locality. As such, they are a prime candidate for acceleration. Being a relatively new code, PyFR has been designed from the ground-up to support a variety of hardware platforms. This is accomplished through the use of pluggable "backends." Kernels are written once in a C-like domain-specific language which is then translated, at run-time, into the native language of the backend. These are then compiled, linked, and loaded at start-up. PyFR offloads all computation onto the backend. Scalability up to hundreds of GPUs has been shown and PyFR is capable of obtaining ~50% of peak FLOPS on both CPU and GPU architectures for real-world simulations.

THE pyMIC OFFLOAD MODULE

The pyMIC module follows Python's philosophy of being easy-to-use and being widely applicable. It supports several levels of abstraction that range from high-level kernel invocation to fine-grained control over each aspect of memory allocation and data copying. We explicitly designed our module to blend in with the widely used Numpy package for storing bulk floating-point data. The module uses the *LIBXSTREAM* library to provide a stream interface with asynchronous offloads.

LIBXSTREAM is a library to program with streams, events, and to enqueue user-defined functions for asynchronous execution while preserving the predecessor/successor relationship of a stream. The library is available as open-source for Intel Architecture (x86) and supports offloading work to an Intel Xeon Phi coprocessor. One of the strengths of the library is its terse and ease-of-use API and high-performance offloading capabilities. The stream programming model offered is augmented with I/O functions (copy-in, copy-out) used to (asynchronously) transfer data to/from a coprocessor.

DESIGN OF pyMIC

As stated before, the pyMIC module was designed to be an easy-to-use, slim interface to enable offloading to the Intel Xeon Phi coprocessor from the Python level. The main focus is to start with a rather simple offloading solution that can later be refined by adding more and more fine-grained control over buffer management, data transfers, and the offloading itself. The guiding principle is to allow for a first, quickly working implementation in an application, and then offer the mechanisms to incrementally increase complexity to improve the first offload solution. Because Numpy is a well-known package for dealing with (multi-dimensional) array data, pyMIC is crafted to blend well with Numpy's ndarray class and its corresponding array operations. As we will see later, instances of Numpy's ndarray data structure are used for buffer management and data transfer between host and coprocessors at a high-level.

Finally, we require pyMIC to integrate well with other offload programming models for the Intel Xeon Phi coprocessor, most notably the Intel Language Extensions for Offloading (LEO) and the `target` extensions of OpenMP 4.0. Several HPC applications not only use Python code but also implement parts of their application logic in C/C++ and/or Fortran. The pyMIC module is flexible, so that advanced programmers can freely mix Python offloading with C/C++ or Fortran offloading in Python extension modules. For instance, one could allocate data in an `ndarray`, transfer it to the coprocessor through the pyMIC interface, and then use the data from an offloaded C/C++ code region in a Python C/C++ extension module.

THE HIGH-LEVEL INTERFACE

The pyMIC interface consists of several key classes that provide different levels of abstractions for offloading: `OffloadDevice`, `OffloadStream`, `OffloadArray`, and `OffloadLibrary`. The `OffloadDevice` class provides the interface to interact with offload devices in a stream-oriented manner through the methods of the `OffloadStream` class. Most operations are implemented as asynchronous operations, such that the host thread can continue executing Python code, while a particular request is being processed for a coprocessor. The `OffloadArray` class provides an easy, high-level access to array buffer management, array data transfers, and coprocessor resident array data primitive operations.

Figures 14.1 and 14.2 form a first simplistic example of how to invoke a kernel that takes no arguments and that sleeps a few seconds before returning. The code first imports the pyMIC module and retrieves the stream object associated with coprocessor device 0. All available coprocessors are enumerated through the module variable `devices` and can be selected through their numerical ID. The pyMIC module offers a module-scope function (`number_of_devices`) to query the number of devices available to the application. If the requested device ID does not match an available offload target, an exception is raised.

```
 1  import pymic
 2
 3  # acquire an offload target and a stream
 4  device = pymic.devices[0]
 5  stream = device.get_default_stream()
 6
 7  # load library w/ kernel
 8  library = device.load_library("libsimple.so")
 9
10  # invoke kernel and wait for completion
11  stream.invoke(library.sleepy)
12  stream.sync()
```

FIGURE 14.1

simple.py: Simplistic offload example to acquire an offload device and invoke a kernel.

```
1   /* compile with:
2    icc −mmic −fPIC −shared −o libsimple.so simple.c
3   */
4
5   #include <pymic_kernel.h>
6   #include <unistd.h>
7
8   PYMIC_KERNEL
9   void sleepy(void) {
10      /* sleep 5 seconds */
11      sleep(5);
12  }
```

FIGURE 14.2

simple.c: Empty kernel implementing the sleepy kernel of Figure 14.1.

The next step for the code in Figure 14.1 is to load the library that contains the kernel code to be invoked. The application can load an (almost) arbitrary number of different libraries that may contain multiple kernels and that may also link to other external libraries such as the Intel Math Kernel Library. After a library has been loaded successfully, all its kernel symbols (identified by the function attribute PYMIC_KERNEL) become available as methods of the library and can be used as a function argument for the invoke function.

A kernel function may receive any number of formal parameters but its signature needs to match the actual arguments of invoke at the Python level. The type of the formal parameters of kernel functions are pointers to the C equivalent of a Python scalar type (int64_t, long int, double, or double complex); the offload engine always passes the actual arguments for the kernel invocation as pointers. The pyMIC infrastructure automatically marshals and unmarshals the scalar and bulk-data arguments, so that the kernel function can simply access the arguments without calling runtime functions. It is the kernel's responsibility to access the passed pointers appropriately to avoid data corruption when accessing scalar or array data.

Figures 14.3 and 14.4 show a more sophisticated example of a dgemm kernel that uses three Numpy arrays plus scalar data (the matrices' dimensions as well as α and β) to invoke the kernel. The code first creates and initializes three Numpy arrays to store the matrices a, b, and c. The input matrices a and b are initialized with random values, the result matrix c is initialized with zeros.

The code invokes the mydgemm kernel of the loaded library, passing in the three matrices plus the additional scalar arguments needed for perform the dgemm operation. The underlying pyMIC offload infrastructure detects the type of the arguments and automatically issues data transfers for all the arguments; this provides programmers with very convenient invocation semantics similar to the well-known concept of remote procedure calls. For each Numpy ndarray and each scalar argument, pyMIC automatically enqueues a data transfer before the kernel invocation is enqueued into the stream (copy-in). It also inserts a request for a data transfer back to the host for array arguments (copy-out). Scalars are ignored for copy-out because they are immutable objects in Python.

```
1   import pyMIC
2   import numpy
3
4   # size of the matrices
5   m, n, k = 4096, 4096, 4096
6
7   # create some input data
8   alpha = 1.0
9   beta = 0.0
10  a = numpy.random.random(m*k).reshape((m, k))
11  b = numpy.random.random(k*n).reshape((k, n))
12  c = numpy.zeros((m, n))
13
14  # load kernel library
15  device = pymic.devices[0]
16  stream = device.get_default_stream()
17  library = device.load_library("libdgemm.so")
18
19  # perform the offload and wait for completion
20  stream.invoke_kernel(library.mydgemm,
21                       a, b, c, m, n, k, alpha, beta)
22  stream.sync()
```

FIGURE 14.3

dgemm.py: Using pyMIC to perform a dgemm operation on the coprocessor.

```
1   #include <pymic_kernel.h>
2   #include <mkl.h>
3
4   PYMIC_KERNEL
5   void mydgemm(const double *A, const double *B, double *C,
6                const int64_t *m, const int64_t *n,
7                const int64_t *k,
8                const double *alpha, const double *beta) {
9       /* invoke dgemm of the cblas wrapper of MKL */
10      cblas_dgemm(CblasRowMajor, CblasNoTrans, CblasNoTrans,
11                  *m, *n, *k, *alpha, A, *k, B, *n, *beta, C, *n);
12  }
```

FIGURE 14.4

dgemm.c: Kernel in C implementing the offload part of Figure 14.3.

The table shown in Figure 14.5 summarizes the operations that are offered by the `OffloadArray` class. In addition, the `OffloadArray` implements the full set of array operations for element-wise addition, multiplication, etc. The operations are all performed on the target device and only require a data transfer if the input data of the second operand is not yet present on the target.

THE LOW-LEVEL INTERFACE

In addition to the high-level interface of the `OffloadArray` class, pyMIC exposes the internal low-level interface for buffer management for additional flexibility and optimization opportunities (see Figure 14.6). The low-level interface consists of a `memcpy`-like interface that supports allocation and deallocation of device memory, data transfers to and from host and coprocessor as well between buffers on the coprocessor. These operations are also part of the streaming API of `OffloadStream` and thus interact with the high-level API in a natural way. By using this low-level API, programmers gain full control of the memory management and can control every aspect of it. It even becomes possible to perform pointer arithmetic on both host and device data. While this low-level programming may lead to improved performance, it is generally advised to stay with the high-level interfaces to avoid hard-to-find errors that arise from using Python in a nonstandard way.

Operation	Semantics
update_host()	Transfer the buffer from the device
update_device()	Transfer the buffer to the device
fill(value)	Fill the buffer with the parameter
fillfrom(array)	Copy the content array to into the offload buffer
zero()	Fill the buffer with 0 (equivalent to fill(0.0))
reverse()	Reverse the contents of the buffer
reshape()	Modify the dimensions of the buffer; creates a new view

FIGURE 14.5

Operations of the `OffloadArray` class.

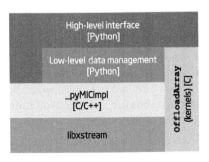

FIGURE 14.6

Architecture of the pyMIC module.

Underneath the low-level API module, a Python extension module (_pyMICimpl) bridges the gap between the Python level and the low-level offload interfaces and libraries. This layer is written in C/C++ and performs the mapping between the Python data types and APIs into the world of C/C++ data types and low-level functions. The lowest level, the offload library, is based on LIBXSTREAM that implements asynchronous data transfers and offloads. In addition, pyMIC ships with a library that contains kernels for offloading the operations of the OffloadArray class to implement the typical array operations on the coprocessor.

EXAMPLE: SINGULAR VALUE DECOMPOSITION

The following, more extensive, example of an image compression/decompression program that uses the singular-value decomposition (SVD) shows how pyMIC allows programmers to choose offload abstractions at different levels.

Figure 14.7 shows six images that have been processed with SVD for different quality and thus different rates of compression. The upper left image shows the original image in JPEG format (original resolution 1920×2560). The compression starts with the image as a gray-scale image of $n \times m$ pixels;

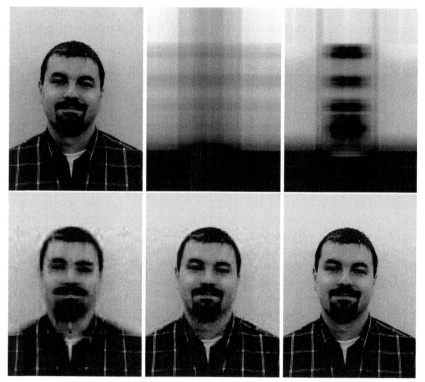

FIGURE 14.7

SVD algorithm applied to a gray-scale picture.

each pixel of the image is stored as a matrix M of floating-point values that correspond to the gray-scale value of each pixel. The compression then performs the SVD to calculate three matrices U, Σ, and V such that $M = U\Sigma V^T$. If M is a matrix with real numbers, then U is a unitary $m \times m$ matrix, Σ is $n \times m$ diagonal matrix, and V^T is a transposed $n \times n$ unitary matrix. To compress the image, the algorithm creates a new diagonal matrix Σ' that only contains some values of the Σ matrix, for example, by restricting it to a submatrix or by dropping values that are close to zero or below a threshold value. Correspondingly, rows and columns of U and V may be removed to match the dimensionality of Σ', leading to U' and V'

To reconstruct the image, the decompression algorithm computes $M' = U'\Sigma'V'^T$ and uses the resulting matrix M' as the output image. One particularly interesting property of this algorithm is that even with very low dimensionality of Σ', the most important features of the compressed image become visible as shown by Figure 14.7. The images in the upper row of Figure 14.7 are the result of retaining only one and two values in the Σ matrix, whereas the lower row contains the outcome of keeping 10, 25, and 100 values in Σ'. This corresponds to a data reduction of 99.9% and 99.8% for the images in the top row, and 99.0%, 97.7%, and 90.7% for the lower row.

The corresponding compression code for the construction of the SVD is shown in Figure 14.8. The read_image function takes a file name as the argument, reads the image from disk, and converts it to gray-scale data. Another function, compute_svd, converts the image data into Numpy's matrix data type and then applies the SVD algorithm to compute and pass back the three matrices. For the sake of brevity, we rely on Numpy's implementation of the SVD algorithm.

The functions read_image and compute_svd are called from the compress_image function, which then restricts each of the matrices according to the compression factor. The factor determines how many rows and columns of the matrices will be preserved; the lower the factor, the higher the compression. The function decompress_image implements the inverse operation by calculating M' by applying two matrix-matrix multiplications.

Using the offloaded mydgemm kernel of Figure 14.4 and pyMIC's high-level offloading, one can easily replace the matrix multiplications with invocations of mydgemm (see Figure 14.9). The Numpy array tmp is supposed to store the result of multiplying U and Σ, M_prime will store the result of the second dgemm operation. After preparing all needed arguments, the code performs two offloads to compute the two matrix multiplications. In this example, it is easy to see that pyMIC's copy-in/copy-out semantics leads to superfluous data transfers; tmp and M_prime are copied to the coprocessor, although they will be overwritten there. In addition, the matrix tmp is transferred from the coprocessor to the host and is then immediately copied back.

For applications that have more complex algorithms, it will be more difficult to see when and in which part of the code data transfers are happening. To help optimize data transfers and/or offloads, pyMIC comes with some basic debugging and performance analysis features. Setting the environment variable PYMIC_TRACE to a value greater than 1 enables the tracing feature of pyMIC. After the application finishes, pyMIC outputs a postmortem list of all call sites of its API and the respective stack traces of these call sites. The pyMIC module also supports on the fly debugging output of key API calls. The environment variable PYMIC_DEBUG enables the additional output to visualize all requests for both implicit and explicit data transfers as well as invocations of offloaded kernels. Please see the documentation of pyMIC for further information.

Figure 14.10 shows how to avoid the aforementioned unnecessary data transfers for the SVD reconstruction. Instead of working on the Numpy data structures, the optimized version of

```
1   import numpy
2   from PIL import Image
3
4   def read_image(file):
5       # open the image and convert it to gray scale
6       img = Image.open(file)
7       img = img.convert("LA")
8       return img
9
10  def compute_svd(image):
11      # convert the gray-scale image into a numpy.matrix
12      mtx = numpy.asarray(image.getdata(band=0), float)
13      mtx.shape = (image.size[1], image.size[0])
14      mtx = numpy.matrix(mtx)
15      U, sigma, V = numpy.linalg.svd(mtx)
16      return U, sigma, V
17
18  def compress_image(file, factor):
19      # read image and decompose it
20      image = read_image(file)
21      U, sigma, V = compute_svd(image)
22
23      # compress
24      c = numpy.matrix(U[:, :factor])
25      Sc = numpy.diag(sigma[:factor])
26      Vc = numpy.matrix(V[:factor, :])
27
28  def decompress_image(U, sigma, V):
29      # reconstruct the image data
30      M_prime = U * sigma * V
31      image = Image.fromarray(M_prime)
32      return image
```

FIGURE 14.8

svd.py: Constructing the SVD for an image stored as JPEG data.

reconstruct_image creates OffloadArrays to store the matrices and the temporary data. For the matrices U, Σ, and V it uses the bind operations to create an offload buffer that is associated with the existing Numpy arrays. For tmp and M_prime, it allocates empty buffers on the coprocessor to store the data. Passing False as the update_host argument instructs pyMIC to only allocate the buffer, but to not transfer the data to the host memory. The code then invokes the kernels as before, but now passes the offload arrays instead of the Numpy arrays. The pyMIC module recognizes this and does not issue the copy-in/copy-out requests for the arrays. Finally, the update_host method of OffloadArray is used to update and retrieve a host copy of the M_prime array.

```
1  def reconstruct_image (U, sigma, V):
2      alpha, beta = 1.0, 0.0
3      tmp = numpy.empty ((U.shape [0], U.shape [1]), dtype=float)
4      m_prime = numpy.empty ((U.shape [0], V.shape [1]), dtype=float)
5
6      # tmp = U * sigma
7      m, k, n = U.shape [0], U.shape [1], sigma.shape [1]
8      stream.invoke (library.mydgemm,
9                          U, sigma, tmp, m, n, k, alpha, beta)
10
11     # m_prime = tmp * V
12     m, k, n = tmp.shape [0], tmp.shape [1], V.shape [1]
13     stream.invoke (library.mydgemm,
14                          tmp, V, m_prime, m, n, k, alpha, beta)
15     stream.sync ()
16
17     # reconstruct the image from the matrix
18     image = Image.fromarray (m_prime)
19     return image
```

FIGURE 14.9

svd_decompress_simple.py: Decompression routine with offloading to the coprocessor.

GPAW

The GPAW code is the first full application that we will examine that uses the pyMIC module to offload computation from the host to the Intel Xeon Phi coprocessor.

OVERVIEW

GPAW is an open-source software package for electronic structure calculation for various research problems related to materials and nanoscience. GPAW is based on the DFT, and it implements also various post-DFT approaches, such as time-dependent DFT, GW approximation, and Bethe-Salpeter equation. GPAW utilizes the projector-augmented wave (PAW) method for treating the region near atomic nuclei, and different basis sets, that is, uniform real-space grids, plane waves, numerical atomic orbitals can be used for discretizing the equations. In this work, we focus on the basic DFT calculation with uniform real-space grids.

Traditionally, compiled languages like Fortran and C are used in HPC applications. On the contrary, GPAW uses a combination of Python and C. High-level algorithms are implemented in Python, allowing the application developer to benefit from the high-level features of Python, while key numerical kernels are implemented in C or utilize libraries such the Intel Math Kernel Library. This approach provides high programmer productivity while still retaining high performance.

Even though on standard CPUs the Python overhead is typically small (5-10%), the Python parts are serial and it is not feasible to execute them natively on the Intel Xeon Phi coprocessor. However, the

```
 1  def reconstruct_image (U, sigma, V):
 2      alpha, beta = 1.0, 0.0
 3
 4      # create offload buffers
 5      offl_U = stream.bind(U)
 6      offl_sigma = stream.bind(sigma)
 7      offl_V = stream.bind(V)
 8      offl_tmp = stream.empty((U.shape[0], U.shape[1]),
 9                              dtype=float, update_host=False)
10      offl_M_prime = stream.empty((U.shape[0], V.shape[1]),
11                              dtype=float, update_host=False)
12
13      # tmp = U * sigma
14      m, k, n = U.shape[0], U.shape[1], sigma.shape[1]
15      stream.invoke(library.mydgemm, offl_U, offl_sigma, offl_tmp,
16                      m, n, k, alpha, beta)
17
18      # M_prime = tmp * V
19      m, k, n = offl_tmp.shape[0], offl_tmp.shape[1], V.shape[1]
20      stream.invoke(library.mydgemm,
21                          offl_tmp, offl_V, offl_M_prime,
22                          m, n, k, alpha, beta)
23      M_prime = offl_M_prime.update_host().array
24      stream.sync()
25
26      image = Image.fromarray(M_prime)
27      return image
```

FIGURE 14.10

svd_decompress_opt.py: Decompression routine with offloading to the coprocessor.

pyMIC interface allows one to launch kernels and control data transfers from GPAW's high-level Python code, making the offload approach a viable option.

DFT ALGORITHM

In the following, we use the atomic units ($\hbar = m = e = \frac{4\pi}{\epsilon_0} = 1$). The so-called Kohn-Sham equations of the ground state DFT can be written as

$$H\psi_n(r) = e_n\psi_n(r), \tag{14.1}$$

$$H = -\frac{1}{2}\nabla^2 + v_{eff}(r) = -\frac{1}{2}\nabla^2 + v_H(r) + v_{ext}(r) + v_{xc}(r), \tag{14.2}$$

$$\nabla^2 v_H(r) = -4\pi\rho(r), \tag{14.3}$$

$$\rho(r) = \sum_i |\psi_i(r)|^2, \tag{14.4}$$

where e_n and $\psi_n(r)$ are the Kohn-Sham energy and Kohn-Sham wave function of electron n, respectively, v_{eff} is the effective potential consisting of the classical electrostatic Hartree potential v_H, the external potential due to atomic nuclei v_{ext}, and the so-called exchange-correlation part v_{xc} (the main physical approximation in DFT).

The system of equations is nonlinear, as the charge density $\rho(r)$ depends on the wave functions. The equations are typically solved by self-consistent iteration, where one starts from initial guess for charge density, then determines the Hamiltonian and solves the eigenvalue problem of Eq. (14.1), and finally calculates the new charge density. The iteration is stopped when the density no longer changes. From the wave functions, eigenenergies, and charge density, one can determine other physical quantities such as total energies and forces acting on the atoms.

When the equations are discretized on a real-space grid, the wave functions, potentials, and charge density are represented by their values at the grid points, ψ_{nG}, ρ_G, $v_{H,G}$, etc., with the three real-space grid indices condensed into single G index. The Laplacian in the Hamiltonian, Eq. (14.2), is approximated by finite differences. The PAW method adds some nonlocal contributions to the Hamiltonian in terms of atomic Hamiltonian matrix elements $H^a_{i_1 i_2}$ and projector functions $p^a_i(r)$, which are defined within augmentation sphere centered on atom a. In discretized form the Hamiltonian operator H in PAW approximation is

$$H_{GG'} = -\frac{1}{2}L_{GG'} + v_{\text{eff},G}\delta_{GG'} + \sum_{i_1 i_2}p^a_{i_1 G}H^a_{i_1 i_2}p^a_{i_2 G'}, \tag{14.5}$$

where the $L_{GG'}$ is the finite-difference stencil for the Laplacian. The sparse Hamiltonian matrix is never stored explicitly, one only needs to be able to apply the Hamiltonian to a function, that is, evaluate a matrix-free matrix-vector product.

The most numerically intensive parts in the DFT algorithm are:

1. The Poisson equation

$$\nabla^2 v_H = -4\pi\rho \tag{14.6}$$

is solved using a multigrid algorithm. The basic operations in this algorithm are finite-difference derivatives, and restriction and interpolation of functions between a fine grid and a coarse grid.

2. Subspace diagonalization involves application of Hamiltonian operator to wave functions and diagonalizing a Hamiltonian matrix

$$H_{nn'} = \sum_G \psi_{nG} \sum_{G'} H_{GG'}\psi_{n'G'} = \sum_G \psi_{nG}(H\psi)_{n'G}. \tag{14.7}$$

When applying the Hamiltonian operator, one needs finite-difference derivatives of wave functions, integrals of projector functions times wave function

$$P^a_{ni} = \sum_{G^a} p^a_{iG^a}\psi_{nG^a} \tag{14.8}$$

and addition of projector function times matrix to the wave function

$$\psi'_{nG^a} = \psi_{nG^a} + \sum_i O^a_{ni}p^a_{iG^a}. \tag{14.9}$$

The grid points G^a are defined inside the augmentation sphere of atom a. Finally, the wave functions are multiplied by the diagonalized matrix $H^D_{nn'}$,

$$\psi'_{nG} = \sum_{n'} H^D_{nn'} \psi_{n'G}.$$ (14.10)

3. Iterative refinement of wave functions requires applications of Hamiltonian to wave functions as well as multigrid preconditioning which uses restriction and interpolation operations similar to the Poisson problem.

4. Orthonormalization of wave functions requires construction of an overlap matrix

$$S_{nn'} = \sum_G \psi_{nG} \sum_{G'} S_{GG'} \psi_{n'G'},$$ (14.11)

where the overlap operator involves the same operations with the projector functions as the subspace diagonalization. The overlap matrix is Cholesky decomposed and inverted to get a matrix $S^D_{nn'}$, after which orthonormal wave functions are obtained as

$$\psi'_{nG} = \sum_{n'} S^D_{nn'} \psi_{n'G}.$$ (14.12)

The two main parameters characterizing the amount of computations are the number of grid points, N_G, and the number of electronic bands, N_b, both of which are directly proportional to the number of atoms in the system, N_a. The computational complexities of the key operations are summarized in the table shown in Figure 14.11.

OFFLOADING

The description of the DFT algorithm in the previous section indicates that in large-scale calculations the $\mathcal{O}(N^3)$ operations in the subspace diagonalization and orthonormalization will dominate the computing time (see Figure 14.11). In order to quantify the computational bottlenecks further, Figure 14.12 presents the execution profile of a relatively large production-like benchmark case. The benchmark consists of two fullerene molecules on a Pb surface with a total of 232 atoms in the system. The benchmark system is shown in Figure 14.13.

Operation	Complexity
Poisson equation	$\mathcal{O}(N_a)$
Subspace diagonalization	$\mathcal{O}(N_a^3)$
Refinement of wave functions	$\mathcal{O}(N_a^2)$
Orthonormalization	$\mathcal{O}(N_a^3)$

FIGURE 14.11

Computational complexity of various parts of the DFT algorithm with N_a as the number of atoms in the calculation.

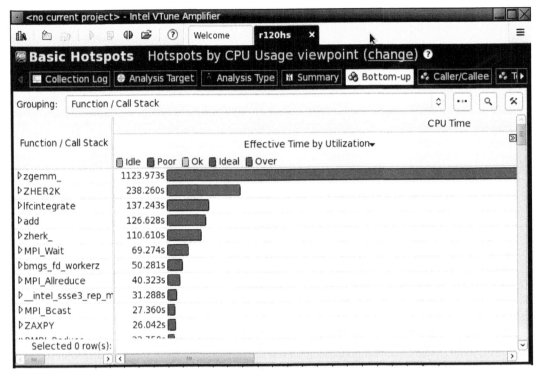

FIGURE 14.12

Hotspot profile of a GPAW benchmark (no offloading) in Intel VTune Amplifier XE.

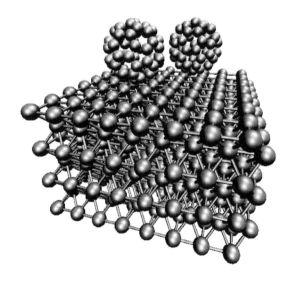

FIGURE 14.13

Benchmark system consisting of two fullerene molecules on a Pb surface.

The profile in Figure 14.12 shows that the major part of the computing time is spent in complex matrix-matrix multiplications (zgemm), which corresponds to the operations in Eqs. (14.7), (14.10), (14.11), and (14.12). The second prominent hotspot in the profile is the symmetric rank 2 update zherk2k, which also takes place during the subspace diagonalization and orthonormalization. Thus, these BLAS functions are the natural targets for offloading.

Automatic offloading provided by Intel Math Kernel Library would be one option to offload the most time-consuming matrix operations to the Intel Xeon Phi coprocessor. However, as the algorithm allows some large arrays to remain on the coprocessor during host execution, more explicit control of the offload execution and data transfers can provide substantial savings in data transfer times. In addition, some of the data transfers can be performed asynchronously with host execution to further overlap computation and communication.

Since the high-level algorithms in GPAW are implemented in Python, the pyMIC interface provides a very convenient way of controlling of data transfers and offload execution. Figure 14.14 shows a routine snippet that initializes arrays on the real grid, and only minimal modifications allow the array to be allocated also on the coprocessor. Later on, if input arrays are of type OffloadArray the matrix multiplication is offloaded as shown in Figure 14.15. Figure 14.16 shows how to transfer data asynchronously and overlap with host execution.

Even though there is a hybrid MPI/OpenMP version of GPAW, in most practical situations the pure MPI implementation is currently faster. Therefore, an execution model with one MPI task per core in the host processor is the most appropriate. As typical hardware configurations contain one or two coprocessors per node, there would be more MPI tasks than there are coprocessors. Thus, the coprocessor is partitioned in smaller pieces, so that each MPI task utilizes only part of the coprocessor. Because MKL uses the Intel OpenMP runtime on the coprocessor, this can be accomplished in a straightforward manner with the KMP_PLACE_THREADS environment variable. Based on the number of coprocessors and the number of host cores per node, a wrapper script can generate a proper KMP_PLACE_THREADS value for each MPI task as shown in Figure 14.17. The wrapper script is inspired by the coprocessor partitioning that has been shown in Chapter 17 of High Performance Parallelism Pearls, volume 1.

```
1   from gpaw.mic import stream
2   # ...
3
4   def zeros(self, n=(), dtype=float, global_array=False,
5             pad=False, usemic=False):
6       array = self._new_array(n, dtype, True, global_array, pad)
7       if usemic:
8           oa = stream.bind(array)
9           stream.sync()
10          return oa
11      else:
12          return array
```

FIGURE 14.14

gd_zeros.py: Using OffloadArrays in the array initialization method of GPAW.

```
 1  def integrate(self, a_xg, b_yg=None,
 2                  global_integral=True, hermitian=False,
 3                  _transposed_result=None):
 4      # ...
 5      if isinstance(a_xg, mic.OffloadArray):
 6          result_yx_mic = stream.bind(result_yx)
 7          stream.sync()
 8
 9      # ...
10      if isinstance(a_xg, mic.OffloadArray):
11          mic_gemm(self.dv, a_xg, a_yg, 0.0, result_yx_mic, 'c')
12      else:
13          gemm(self.dv, a_xg, a_yg, 0.0, result_yx, 'c')
14
15      if isinstance(a_xg, mic.OffloadArray):
16          result_yx_mic.update_host()
17          stream.sync()
18
19      # ...
20      return result_yx
```

FIGURE 14.15

gd_integrate.py: Matrix multiplication with offload arrays in GPAW.

```
 1  if use_mic:
 2      psit_xG.update_device()
 3      wfs.apply_pseudo_hamiltonian(kpt, hamiltonian,
 4                                    psit_xG.array,
 5                                    result_xG.array)
 6      result_xG.update_device()
 7      stream.sync()
 8  else:
 9      wfs.apply_pseudo_hamiltonian(kpt, hamiltonian, psit_xG,
10                                    result_xG)
```

FIGURE 14.16

gpaw_async.py: Asynchronous data transfers in GPAW.

```bash
1  #!/bin/bash
2
3  # cores per node is given as input variable
4  ppn=$1
5  shift
6  rank=$PMI_RANK
7
8  # number of devices in the system
9  ndev=2
10
11 # number of cores per device
12 nphcores=61
13 nphcores=$((nphcores - 1))
14
15 # number of threads per physical core
16 tpc=4
17
18 # ranks per device
19 rpd=$((ppn / ndev))
20 if [ "$rpd" == "0" ]; then
21     rpd=1
22 fi
23
24 # physical cores per device
25 ncores=$((nphcores / rpd))
26
27 # partition number of the current rank on its device
28 partition=$((rank % rpd))
29
30 # offset for the current rank
31 offset=$((ncores * partition))
32
33 # build core selection string
34 places="${ncores}c,${tpc}t,${offset}o"
35
36 # fire up the actual run
37 MIC_KMP_AFFINITY=compact,verbose MIC_KMP_PLACE_THREADS=$places $@
```

FIGURE 14.17

affinity_wrapper.sh: Script for partitioning coprocessor for multiple MPI tasks.

PyFR

The PyFR framework is the other full application we are going to explore in this chapter. It uses pyMIC in a different way to integrate the coprocessor into applications using the PyFR framework.

OVERVIEW

PyFR is an open-source Python framework for solving advection-diffusion problems of the form

$$\frac{\partial u}{\partial t} + \nabla \cdot \mathbf{f}(u, \nabla u) = S(\mathbf{x}, t), \tag{14.13}$$

where $u(\mathbf{x}, t)$ is a state vector representing the solution, $\mathbf{f}$ a flux function, and S a source term. A prominent example of an advection-diffusion type problem are the compressible Navier-Stokes equations of fluid dynamics. PyFR is based around the flux reconstruction (FR) approach of Huynh. In FR, the computational domain of interest is first discretized into a mesh of conforming elements. Inside of each element, two sets of points are defined: one in the interior of the element, commonly termed the *solution points*, and another on the boundary of the element, termed the *flux points*.

   The objective of FR is to obtain an approximation of $\nabla \cdot \mathbf{f}$ that sits in the same polynomial space as the solution which can be used to march forwards in time. Accomplishing this requires two kinds of distinct operations (i) moving quantities between flux/solution points, and (ii) evaluating quantities (such as $\mathbf{f}$) at either individual solution points or pairs of flux points. When moving quantities, say from the solution points to the flux points, the value at each flux point is given as a weighted sum of the quantity at each solution point

$$q_{e,i}^{(f)} = \sum_j \alpha_{e,ij} q_{e,j}^{(u)}, \tag{14.14}$$

where q represents the quantity, e the element number, i the flux point number, and $\alpha_{e,ij}$ is a matrix of coefficients that encodes the numerics. This can be identified as a matrix-vector product; or in the case of an N-element simulation, N matrix-vector products. If the quantities are first mapped from physical space to a reference space then the $\alpha_{e,ij}$ coefficients become identical for each element of a given type. Hence, the above operation can be reduced to a single matrix-matrix product. Depending on the order of accuracy, PyFR spends between ~50% and ~85% of the wall clock time performing such multiplications. The remaining time is spent in the point-wise operations. These kernels are a generalization on the form `f(in1[i], in2[i], ..., &out1[i])`. As there are no data dependences between iterations, the point-wise kernels are both trivial to parallelize and highly bound by available memory bandwidth.

RUNTIME CODE GENERATION

PyFR aims to support a variety of modern hardware platforms. While the matrix multiplications can be offloaded to a vendor supplied BLAS library, the point-wise operations must be coded up once for each key platform. This presents both a barrier to entry with respect to adding new physics into the code and further represents a significant maintenance burden. To avoid this, the point-wise kernels in PyFR are specified in a C-like domain-specific language built on top of the Mako template engine. The language exploits the fact that—at least for point-wise operations—the major parallel programming languages

C/OpenMP, CUDA, and OpenCL differ only in how kernels are prototyped and how elements are iterated over. PyFR is therefore able to use Mako to substitute a common function body into a variety of platform-specific templates in order to yield a suitable kernel. All kernel generation is performed at run-time.

Along with portability across multiple platforms the above arrangement confers several other advantages.

- The Mako templating language enables Python to be used to help generate source code for a kernel. This is significantly more flexible than the C preprocessor and much simpler than C++ templates.
- Since the source ends up as a Python string it is possible to post-process it before compilation. A good use-case for this capability is to ensure that when running in single precision all floating point constants are prefixed by ".f". Doing so helps to eliminate cumbersome casts inside of the body of the kernel and prevents unwanted auto-promotion of expressions.
- By compiling the code at run-time it is possible to avoid the need for an explicit build/install phase. Packaging and distribution are also simplified.
- Further, it is also trivial to allow for user-defined functions and expressions to be inserted into a kernel. PyFR, for example, permits the form of source term, $S(\mathbf{x},t)$, to be specified on the command line. Without runtime code generation this would require an expression evaluation library and is unlikely to be competitive with the code generated by an optimizing C compiler.

To illustrate the utility of templating consider the task of writing a generic form of the BLAS function AXPBY

$$\mathbf{y} \leftarrow \alpha\mathbf{x} + \beta\mathbf{y}, \tag{14.15}$$

which instead computes

$$\mathbf{x}_0 \leftarrow \sum_{i}^{N} \alpha_i \mathbf{x}_i, \tag{14.16}$$

where the number of arrays, N, is known at code generation time. A Mako template for generating a pyMIC kernel for this function, termed AXNPBY, can be seen in Figure 14.18. In the listing, both the number of parameters and the data type are templated. Within the template itself Python expressions can be used. A good example of which is the dot-product on line 12. Figure 14.19 shows how to use Mako to render the template. Although it is possible to write this rendering out to disk and compile it statically it is more elegant to do so dynamically at run-time. A simple Python class for compiling, linking, and loading generated code is shown in Figure 14.20.

OFFLOADING

Each backend in PyFR provides methods for: allocating/deallocating memory, copying slices of these blocks to/from the device, compiling kernels for the templates, and invoking these kernels. The first two requirements are satisfied by the low-level interface provided by `OffloadStream`. Kernel compilation can be handled by a class similar to the one sketched above and, finally, `OffloadStream.invoke()` can be used to call these kernels.

Domain decomposition in PyFR is slightly different to that of GPAW. To run PyFR on multiple nodes, a mesh is first decomposed using a graph partitioning library—such as METIS or

```
1   void
2   axnpby(const int64_t *n,
3           ${', '.join('{0} *x{1}'.format(dtype, i)
4                       for i in range(nv))},
5           ${', '.join('const double *a{0}'.format(i)
6                       for i in range(nv))}
7   )
8   {
9   #pragma omp parallel for
10      for (int64_t i = 0; i < *n; i++)
11          x0[i] = ${' + '.join('*a{j}*x{j}[i]'.format(j=j)
12                      for j in range(nv))};
13  }
```

FIGURE 14.18

axnpby.mako: Sample Mako template for a generic kernel for performing $x_0 = \sum_{i=0}^{N_v} a_i x_i$. Here nv and dtype are template parameters used to generate the kernel.

```
1   from mako.template import Template
2
3   # Load the Mako source into a string
4   tpl = ...
5
6   # Render the kernel
7   print Template(tpl).render(dtype='double', nv=4)
```

FIGURE 14.19

render_tpl.py: Python snippet for rendering the AXNPBY template.

SCOTCH—into as many segments as there are packages. A package can be either a CPU, coprocessor, or GPU. Each MPI rank is then allocated as segment of the mesh to operate on. On account of this, there is no need to partition the cores of the MIC itself; a single MPI rank will have exclusive use of the device. Nevertheless, thread placement and count is vital for good sgemm and dgemm performance. For best performance, we again leave one core of the coprocessor free for communication and choose compact thread placement using four threads per physical core.

PERFORMANCE

For the performance evaluation we use the Taito cluster of CSC, Finland. The nodes are equipped with two Intel Xeon E5-2620v2 processors with 2.1 GHz (turbo mode disabled and Intel Hyper-Threading enabled) and a total of 32 GB of DDR3 memory at 1600 MHz. The node is equipped with two Intel

```
1   import itertools as it
2   import os
3   import shutil
4   import subprocess
5   import tempfile
6
7   class MICSourceModule(object):
8       _dir_seq = it.count()
9
10      def __init__(self, src, dev):
11          # Create a scratch directory
12          tmpidx = next(self._dir_seq)
13          tmpdir =
14              tempfile.mkdtemp(prefix='pymic-{0}-'.format(tmpidx))
15
16          try:
17              # Write the source code out
18              with open(os.path.join(tmpdir, 'tmp.c'), 'w') as f:
19                  f.write(src)
20
21              # Compile and link
22              cmd = (
23                  'icc -shared -std=c99 -O3 -mmic -fopenmp '
24                  '-fPIC -o libtmp.so tmp.c'
25              )
26              subprocess.check_call(cmd.split(), cwd=tmpdir)
27
28              # Load
29              self._mod =
30                  dev.load_library(os.path.join(tmpdir,
31                                                'libtmp.so'))
32          finally:
33              shutil.rmtree(tmpdir)
34
35      def function(self, name):
36          return getattr(self._mod, name)
```

FIGURE 14.20

runtime.py: Python class for compiling and linking pyMIC kernels at run-time.

Xeon Phi 7120P coprocessors with 61 cores at 1238 MHz (maximum turbo upside 1333 MHz) and 16 GB of GDDR5 memory each. The host runs Red Hat Enterprise Linux (RHEL) 6.5 (kernel version 2.6.32-358.6.2) and MPSS 3.3.30726 (coprocessor kernel 2.6.38.8+mpss3.3). We use Intel Composer XE 2013 for C/C++ version 14.0.3.174 to compile the Python extension modules and the coprocessor kernels. The Python interpreter is the standard CPython interpreter (version 2.6.6) shipped with RHEL. Numpy is version 1.8.2 and has been setup to use the multithreaded Intel Math Kernel Library shipped with Intel Composer XE.

PERFORMANCE OF pyMIC

We test the performance of the pyMIC module by a series of micro-benchmarks that evaluate the primitive operations of the module at the lowest levels. Because we are interested in how the module performs when communicating to a coprocessor, these benchmarks are run on a single processor package and we compare them against one coprocessor. A 1:1 ratio of processors to coprocessors improves locality and yields optimal offload performance, because each processor package is assigned one coprocessor and only communicates to the assigned coprocessor. In all measurements, we leave one core of the coprocessor empty to handle the operating system load and offload data transfers.

The table shown in Figure 14.21 shows the average latency of the data transfer and kernel invocation methods of pyMIC. Each of the benchmarks runs for 1,000,000 repetitions to avoid jitter. Associating a Numpy array with one element (8 bytes) on the host with a buffer on the coprocessor takes about 0.16 ms. This includes the time required on the coprocessor to allocate physical pages on the device and to transfer 8 bytes (which is negligible). The time of course also includes all overhead of the pyMIC module's Python code and the glue code of the extension module. Similar figures can be observed for the transfer of data to and from the coprocessor. Because no allocation/deallocation is performed in these cases, they expose a much lower latency.

Figure 14.22 shows the achievable bandwidth for data transfers for different data sizes ranging from 8 bytes to 2.1 GiB. For small data, the latency of the operation dominates and thus the achieved bandwidth stays low. At about 32 MiB of data, bandwidth increases and the latency effects have less impact on performance. With large data sizes, transfer bandwidth reaches the peak bandwidth that can be achieved with the PCIe bus (gen 2). Again, the update_device and update_host operations perform slightly better, because in contrast to bind they do not require the allocation of physical pages on the coprocessor.

Operation	Latency
bind (8 bytes)	0.16
update_device (8 bytes)	0.03
update_host (8 bytes)	0.03
invoke (empty kernel)	0.07

FIGURE 14.21

Latency (in milliseconds) of offload operations.

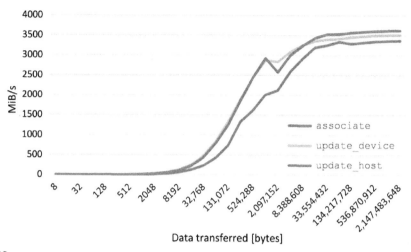

FIGURE 14.22

Bandwidth achieved with the pyMIC `OffloadArray` classes transfer functions.

GPAW

The possible benefits of offloading depend on the overhead due to data transfers and the performance differences between the host and the coprocessor. One can make a simple performance model for the speed up obtainable from coprocessor as follows: assuming that the performance of host and coprocessor, P_h and P_c (GFLOPS), as well as the bandwidth between host and coprocessor, B (MB/s), do not depend on the size of the matrices, the times required for matrix-matrix operations in host T_h and in the coprocessor T_c are

$$T_h = \frac{aN_GN_b^2}{P_h} \tag{14.17}$$

$$T_c = \frac{aN_GN_b^2}{P_c} + \frac{bN_GN_b}{B}, \tag{14.18}$$

where a and b are constant prefactors. Thus, the cross over at which offloading becomes beneficial, that is, $T_c < T_h$, is directly proportional to the number of electronic bands N_b:

$$N_b > \frac{bP_hP_c}{aB(P_c - P_h)}. \tag{14.19}$$

In reality, all the performance parameters P_c, P_h, and B depend also on the size of the matrices, as seen in Figure 14.22, and the performance of the dgemm and zgemm operations. However, Eq. (14.19) shows that offloading is necessarily not beneficial in small systems (small number of atoms, small number electronic bands), but with increasing number of atoms/bands one should reach the maximum available speedup. As an example, Figure 14.23 shows the performance of subspace diagonalization Eq. (14.10) as a function of N_b with fixed N_g. It can be seen that offloading on the Taito cluster can speed up this part of the DFT algorithm up to factor of 4-5.

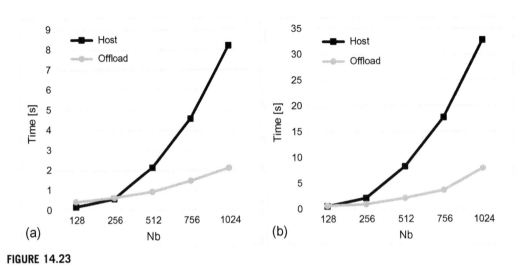

FIGURE 14.23

Performance of the subspace diagonalization on the host and in the offload mode. Number of grid points is fixed to $N_G = 64^3$. (a) Real valued data. (b) Complex valued data.

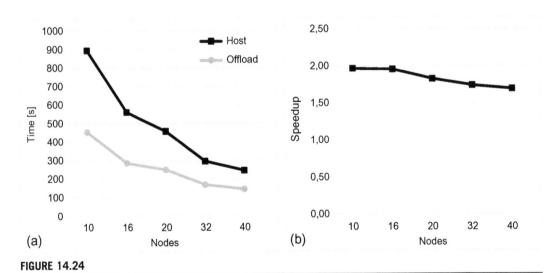

FIGURE 14.24

Performance of full GPAW calculation. (a) Wall clock time. (b) Speedup from offloading.

The speed-up for the full calculation naturally depends on the proportion of the offloaded operations to the total computing time. In Figure 14.24, we present the performance of the benchmark case of Figure 14.13 with different number of nodes in the cluster. The parallel scaling of the host-only version is slightly better (which is natural as computation to communication ratio is higher). However, the offload calculation shows still good parallel scaling, as an example the speedup from 20 to 40 nodes is $1.7\times$. Overall, the speedup obtainable from offloading in the current benchmark varies from $1.9\times$ to $1.7\times$.

PyFR

As a benchmark problem, we consider the case of flow over a circular cylinder at Mach 0.2 and Reynolds number 3900. The domain was meshed with 46610 hexahedra and run with fourth-order solution polynomials. A visual depiction of the simulation can be seen in Figure 14.25. When running at double precision this gives a working set of ~3.1 GiB. One complete time step using a fourth-order Runge-Kutta scheme requires on the order of ~4.6×10^{11} floating point operations with large simulations requiring on the order of half of million steps. The performance of PyFR in sustained GFLOPS for this problem on an Intel Xeon Phi 3120A coprocessor (57 cores at 1.1 GHz) can be seen in Figure 14.26. Results for a 12-core Intel Xeon E5-2697v2 CPU using the OpenMP backend are also included. Using pyMIC a speedup of approximately 1.85×can be observed. Further, 11 of the CPU cores are freed up in the process to run either alternative workloads or a heterogenous PyFR simulation using two MPI ranks to exploit both the CPU cores and the coprocessor.

FIGURE 14.25

Isosurfaces of density colored by velocity magnitude for the cylinder benchmark problem.

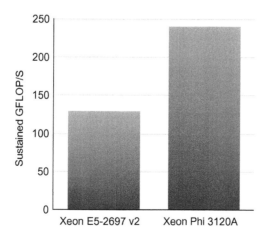

FIGURE 14.26

Sustained performance of PyFR for the cylinder flow problem using the C/OpenMP backend on a 12-core Xeon E5-2697 CPU and the pyMIC backend on an actively cooled Xeon Phi.

SUMMARY

This chapter has shown how to utilize the compute power of the Intel Xeon Phi coprocessor from Python HPC applications. The pyMIC module provides an easy-to-use, flexible way to offload applications kernels to the coprocessor. It supports a streaming interface for asynchronous data transfers and kernel execution. Through the various layers of abstractions and invocation semantics, pyMIC allows for an incremental enabling of offload execution in the Python code.

The two example applications, GPAW and PyFR, show how pyMIC can be employed in different application scenarios with different requirements. Where as GPAW offloads manually selected compute kernels that constitute the hotspots of the application, PyFR uses runtime code generation to dynamically create and compile kernels for offloading. Both applications show that the Intel Xeon Phi coprocessor provides a way to reduce time-to-solution without sacrificing too much productivity of the Python language.

As of today, pyMIC requires programmers to use compiled kernels written in C/C++ or Fortran for offloading. The roadmap of pyMIC contains plans to support offloading of Python code to the coprocessor so that programmers gain additional flexibility for offloading kernels. It is also planned that pyMIC will support host fallback, that is, compile and invoke kernels in a way that they can execute on the host if a coprocessor device is not installed in the system.

The pyMIC module can be downloaded from https://github.com/01org/pyMIC. The download also contains the codes snippets of the Figures 14.1–14.10 as in the `examples` directory. Please find GPAW's website at https://wiki.fysik.dtu.dk/gpaw/. PyFR is located at http://www.pyfr.org/. You can find the remainder of the code examples of this chapter at these locations.

ACKNOWLEDGMENTS

The work on GPAW is supported by an Intel® Parallel Computing Center Grant.

FOR MORE INFORMATION

- The PyMIC project. http://github.com/01org/pyMIC.
- Python for Scientific Computing on Intel's Xeon Phi MIC Platform. https://github.com/bpartridge/pyphi.
- LIBXSTREAM. http://github.com/hfp/libxstream.
- GPAW. https://wiki.fysik.dtu.dk/gpaw/.
- Enkovaara, J., Rostgaard, C., Mortensen, J.J., Chen, J., Dułak, M., Ferrighi, L., Gavnholt, J., Glinsvad, C., Haikola, V., Hansen, H.A., Kristoffersen, H.H., Kuisma, M., Larsen, A.H., Lehtovaara, L., Ljungberg, M., Lopez-Acevedo, O., Moses, P.G., Ojanen, J., Olsen, T., Petzold, V., Romero, N.A., Stausholm-Møller, J., Strange, M., Tritsaris, G.A., Vanin, M., Walter, M., Hammer, B., Häkkinen, H., Madsen, G.K.H., Nieminen, R.M., Nørskov, J.K., Puska, M., Rantala, T.T., Schiøtz, J., Thygesen, K.S., Jacobsen, K.W., 2010. Electronic structure calculations with GPAW: a real-space implementation of the projector augmented-wave method. J. Phys. Cond. Matter. 22 (25), 253202.

- Hakala, S., Havu, V., Enkovaara, J., Nieminen, R., 2013. Parallel electronic structure calculations using multiple graphics processing units (GPUs). In: Manninen, P., Öster, P. (Eds.), Applied Parallel and Scientific Computing, volume 7782 of Lecture Notes in Computer Science. Springer, Berlin, Heidelberg, p. 63.
- Romero, N.A., Glinsvad, C., Larsen, A.H., Enkovaara, J., Shende, S., Morozov, V.A., Mortensen, J.J., 2013. Design and performance characterization of electronic structure calculations on massively parallel supercomputers: a case study of GPAW on the Blue Gene/P architecture. Concurr. Comput. Pract. Exper. 27, 69–93, http://dx.doi.org/10.1002/cpe.3199.
- Mako Templates for Python. http://www.makotemplates.org/.
- NumPy. http://www.numpy.org/.
- pyFR. http://www.pyfr.org/.
- Witherden, F.D., Farrington, A.M., Vincent, P.E., 2014. PyFR: an open source framework for solving advection-diffusion type problems on streaming architectures using the flux reconstruction approach. Comput. Phys. Commun. 185 (11), 3028-3040.
- SciPy. http://www.scipy.org/.
- Download the code from this, and other chapters. http://lotsofcores.com.

FAST MATRIX COMPUTATIONS ON HETEROGENEOUS STREAMS

15

Gaurav Bansal, Chris J. Newburn, Paul Besl

Intel Corporation, USA

A heterogeneous system offers differing compute capabilities which need to be given work to do, fed data, and synchronized. The Intel® hStreams library offers an abstraction that controls these capabilities of a system with "streams of actions" made up of computations, data transfers, and synchronizations. This simple first-in first-out (FIFO) stream abstraction is very powerful, flexible, and can yield both performance and performance portability. This chapter illustrates the library's usage and performance on Intel® Xeon® processors and Intel® Xeon Phi™ coprocessors. Performance results highlight four key benefits of using hStreams: (1) concurrency of computes across nodes and within a node, (2) pipelined concurrency among data transfers, and between data transfers and computes, (3) ease of use in exploring the ptimization space, and (4) separation of concerns between scientists and tuners, between those who may wish to be minimalists, and those who wish to have visibility and exert full control over performance.

THE CHALLENGE OF HETEROGENEOUS COMPUTING

You have a challenge on your hands. You have a heterogeneous platform. You have a scientific problem to be solved. The platforms you will run your application on supports lots of parallelism. Thankfully, you can decompose the problem to create concurrency among tasks. But, some of the tasks have dependences among them, and some do not. You can vary the degree of problem decomposition and how the resources of the platform should be partitioned, but you have not come up with a clear heuristic for determining what those parameters should be. After all, you are a scientist, not a computer scientist. You may have a friend who is good at tuning, but he does not know much about science. He is very busy, and does not have a lot of time. He wants a system that makes it easy to explore the performance optimization space. And as someone who likes to take initiative, you may want to explore the performance optimization space yourself, but you do not have time to learn complicated techniques and new languages. It has to be quick and easy so that you get back to real science. Oh, and your code will need to be portable, long after you and your domain expertise are gone. It will be ported to a variety of heterogeneous platforms, some of which have not been invented yet. How can you do all of this?

After reading this chapter,

- You may realize that your view of where and how your code could run, for example, native or offload, may have been overly limited, given the increasing commonality of heterogeneous system platforms with *computing domains* such as an Intel Xeon processor acting as root node, a set of Intel Xeon Phi coprocessors, remote Intel Xeon processors and (with the introduction of the many-core processor codenamed Knights Landing) self-booting many-core processors. The world is your platform.

- You may become dissatisfied with any system that does not provide a clear separation of concerns between the view of the scientist, who wants to express algorithms and expose parallelism, and the view of the tuner, who will map and optimize that parallelism for a variety of platforms. You may experience a yearning for frameworks that lead to portable code, to flexible expressions of parallelism that enable a quick and easy exploration of a tuning space.
- You may become excited about being able to harvest concurrency on many fronts: among computing domains, among tasks running on subsets of computing resources within a computing domain, among computation and communication.
- You may find that outstanding performance is possible with tractable effort.
- You will know how to achieve all of the above with a new library for heterogeneous streaming, called **hStreams**.

In this chapter, we walk the path to parallelism by example, by considering problems from the field of linear algebra. The most basic case in linear algebra, matrix multiply, will serve our purposes. We describe the algorithm, show how the problem can be decomposed by tiling the matrices to increase concurrency, and express it with hStreams. We will then highlight four key benefits of hStreams with some performance results: (1) concurrency of computes across nodes and within a node, (2) pipelined concurrency among data transfers, and between data transfers and computes, (3) ease of use in exploring the optimization space, and (4) separation of concerns between scientists and tuners, between those who may wish to be minimalists, and those who wish to have visibility and exert full control over performance.

Once that is established, we will reveal more details of what hStreams is, what its features are, how it works, and how it compares with other approaches. We then expand on matrix multiply with a presentation of how hStreams is used to parallelize Cholesky factorizations. Finally, we wrap up with a recap of the chapter's contributions and highlights of future work.

In short, hStreams is a library that enables ease of use with a simple FIFO streaming abstraction. It can be used to map task parallelism across a heterogeneous platform. Task compute, data transfer, and synchronization actions are enqueued in **streams** that enforce a FIFO semantic, and whose endpoints are bound to subsets of computing resources. Concurrency is available across streams that are bound to different computing domains, such as a multicore Intel Xeon processor and a many-core Intel Xeon Phi coprocessor, and among subsets of cores in a many-core computing domain. Concurrency is also available within or across streams, by pipelining and overlapping computation and communication.

MATRIX MULTIPLY

Matrix multiplication is arguably the most basic building block of linear algebra. Concurrency scales nonlinearly with problem size, and matrix multiplies are amenable to parallelization among decomposed tasks, thread parallelism within tasks, and vectorization within threads. We focus on task parallelism, executing tasks on nonoverlapping subsets of computing resources that vary in the number of threads and computing capability. We do not focus on optimization of the work with each task, since for matrix multiplication and other applications discussed later in this chapter, the kernels executed by those tasks are implemented by the Intel® Math Kernel Library (MKL) functions, which are already highly parallelized.

```
1: for i = 1, m do
2:     for j = 1, n do
3:         C_{i,j} = 0
4:         for s = 1, k do
5:             C_{i,j} = C_{i,j} + A_{i,s} * B_{s,j}
6:         end for
7:     end for
8: end for
```

FIGURE 15.1

Elemental matrix multiplication algorithm.

BASIC MATRIX MULTIPLY

The basic form of a multiplication of two input matrices, **A**, with m rows and k columns, by **B**, with k rows and n columns, to get the matrix product **C** with m rows by n columns, is shown in Figure 15.1. Subscripts i and j represent the row i and column j. The computational cost of multiplying matrices that are N elements on a side is on the order of N^3: there are k multiplications and k additions, or $2k$ floating point operations (flops) for each element, yielding a total of $2mnk$ flops. Good: plenty of concurrency. Now we need to get concurrency at the granularity of tasks, via tiling.

TILING FOR TASK CONCURRENCY

Matrices can be decomposed into tiles. The top row in Figure 15.2 shows matrices divided into 3×3 tiles. Figure 15.3 shows a tiled algorithm that makes use of the MKL function for double-precision (DP) matrix multiplication (cblas_dgemm), although not all input parameters to cblas_dgemm are shown. Defining each call to a cblas_dgemm as the compute task, there is a high task concurrency because there is no dependence between cblas_dgemm calls which compute different tiles of the **C** matrix. The results of cblas_dgemm calls which compute the same **C** tile (i.e., the inner most loop) must be accumulated, which is obtained by setting the *beta* parameter in the cblas_dgemm call to one.

For simplicity of illustration, we assumed that matrices **A** and **B** are square and the number of tiles in each direction is equal for both matrices (=T). Note that the total compute for the tiled matrix multiplication is the same as that for the elemental matrix multiplication. In this case, the average

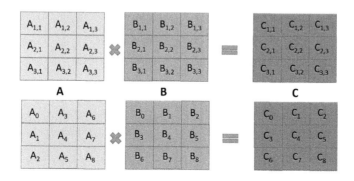

FIGURE 15.2

Decomposition and tile numbering of input matrices **A** and **B** and output matrix **C** into tiles. Top row: for the tiled matrix multiplication algorithm. Bottom row: for the tiled hStreams matrix multiplication algorithm.

```
1: for i = 1, T do
2:     for j = 1, T do
3:         Set C_{i,j} to 0.
4:         for s = 1, T do
5:             cblas_dgemm(A_{i,s}, B_{s,j}, C_{i,j});
6:         end for
7:     end for
8: end for
```

FIGURE 15.3

Tiled matrix multiplication algorithm.

concurrency is given by T^2. This is because each of the tiles of the $\mathbf{C}$ matrix can be computed independent of each other. The total tasks is given by T^3 since to compute each tile of $\mathbf{C}$ matrix, T calls to cblas_dgemm is required.

While decomposition of a matrix multiplication into smaller tasks can be done with few and simple dependences among tasks, the task graph can be more complicated for other algorithms. The more dependences that there are the less average concurrency there tends to be in the task graph. Concurrency tends to increase with the degree of tiling. Figure 15.4 shows the increase in average concurrency and total tasks with increasing degree of tiling, and the increase in concurrency from Cholesky to LU to matrix multiply, which have progressively fewer dependences. There is a corresponding increase in performance, which is due in part to this increase in concurrency. The algorithms and task graphs for Cholesky are described later in the chapter (reference Figure 15.20 for the task graph of Cholesky). For this plot of concurrency, we consider only *compute* concurrency, that is, how many compute tasks can be executed in parallel. A broader notion of concurrency considers data transfers in addition to

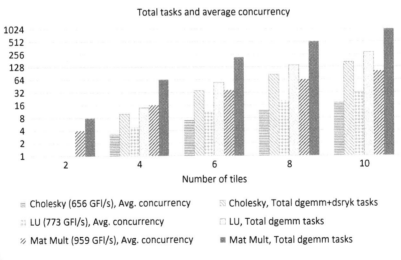

FIGURE 15.4

Concurrency of computes. Cholesky, LU, and matrix multiply have an increasing amount of total tasks and average concurrency, which correlates to performance, shown in parentheses. GFlops/sec (GFl/s) numbers are given for input matrix size of 16,000.

computes. This type of concurrency also increases with the number of tiles, because we can perform data transfers for some input tiles of matrix **A** and **B** overlapped with computes for some output tiles of **C**. Below, we introduce the concept of streams that enable harnessing many kinds of concurrency to boost performance.

We next describe some of the key features of hStreams through which one can exploit the various forms of concurrencies available in the scientific problem, again working through our matrix multiplication example. We will introduce facets of hStreams as we go, and the hStreams section later describes the hStreams features in detail.

HETEROGENEOUS STREAMING: CONCURRENCY AMONG COMPUTING DOMAINS

Once tiling is applied to a matrix multiply, we have task concurrency. What if a different computing domain, such as a many-core processor or newer Intel Xeon processor reached over the fabric, or a many-core coprocessor reached over PCIe, is more capable, but there is a cost in moving the data there and back? We have seen that the computational load is $O(N^3)$ for square matrices with N elements on a side. But since the number of elements is only $O(N^2)$, transferring the computation to be executed in another computing domain is worthwhile once the advantage in computational power outweighs the cost of allocating remote space and moving data back and forth, which happens for a large enough N. A detailed analysis of the value of N for which this becomes true, as a function of data transfer rates, and relative computational efficiency, can be found in the hStreams resources on the book's website (http://lotsofcores.com/hStreams). We call the mechanism for managing *data transfer*, *compute*, and *synchronization actions*, for work that happens on a particular subset of computing resources a **stream**. Both hStreams and the Intel compiler's Offload Streams feature support this kind of streaming. Differences between the two are described in the related work section.

Transferring work from one computing domain to another may boost efficiency. Concurrency is achieved by executing tasks both at the originating computing domain and at the offload endpoints. hStreams allows the use of a *single*, *unified streams abstraction* to transfer, complete, and synchronize work on any set of resources, rather than having to make the abstraction used depend on where the work happens. Figure 15.7 shows how performance is better when offloaded over PCIe to a coprocessor for more than 1200 or so elements on a side. Figure 15.20 shows similar results for Cholesky. These results are discussed in detail later. The machine configuration on which we have done all the performance tests presented in this chapter is given in Figure 15.5.

PIPELINING WITHIN A STREAM

If we treat tasks that are executed in another computing domain in isolation, we must transfer the data, do the work, and transfer the data back before processing the next task. That is a serial, synchronous sequence. If we have multiple such tasks, and do not treat them in isolation, we can use *pipelining within a stream* to overlap and perhaps even hide most of the communication behind the computation. That creates *concurrency between computation and communication* (data transfers). We show the impact of pipelining and stream concurrency below.

Specification	Intel Xeon Processor E5-2697v2	Intel Xeon Phi Co-processor 7120A
Sockets × cores × SMT	2 × 12 × 2	1 × 61 × 4
Clock (GHz)	2.7	1.33 (turbo-on)
RAM	64 GB DDR3-1600 MHz	16 GB GDDR5
L1 data cache (kB)	32	32
L1 instruction cache (kB)	32	32
L2 cache (kB)	256	512
L3 cache (kB)	30,000 (shared, per socket)	
	—	
OS	RHEL 6.4	Linux
Compiler	Intel 15.0.1	Intel 15.0.1
MPSS	MPSS 3.5	MPSS 3.5

FIGURE 15.5

Machine configuration.

STREAM CONCURRENCY WITHIN A COMPUTING DOMAIN

With hStreams, the heterogeneous streams are not limited to one per computing domain. Any given computing domain can be subdivided, where *streams are associated with subsets of resources*. As shown in Figure 15.6, using multiple streams, with a smaller number of cores each, boosts overall native (not offload) throughput of independent dgemm tasks on a coprocessor. For this plot, the number of independent concurrent dgemms executed is given as 60/number of cores. For example, if only 2 cores per dgemm is used, then 30 concurrent dgemm tasks are executed. While that data pertain to native

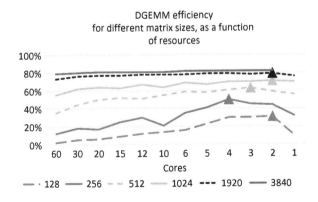

FIGURE 15.6

Native compute efficiency versus concurrency. As the number of cores per dgemm task decreases, the number of concurrent dgemms increases, bringing increasing throughput performance for independent native dgemms up to a small number of cores per task. The benefits are greater for smaller matrices, though the overall performance is lower for smaller sizes. Performance is measured relative to peak efficiency. Performance can fall off at the right, where the number of independent dgemms is very large.

execution, the same principle applies to offload using. If you stream transfer, compute, and synchronization actions, concurrently to several subsets of resources spread across the many different computing domains in your heterogeneous platform, you may be able to increase your overall performance.

TRADE-OFFS IN PIPELINING, TILING, AND OFFLOAD

A key value of hStreams is that it makes it easier to explore the optimization space where there are many trade-offs to make. First, we highlight trade-offs in pipelining, tiling, and offload; next, we will look at trade-offs in degree of tiling and number of streams. Let us take a look at matrix multiplication performance, as measured in GFlops/s, as a function of matrix size, using the MKL `cblas_dgemm` function, in Figure 15.7a. In this figure, we show the impact of host versus coprocessor, coprocessor-compute-only versus offload, 2×2 tiling versus untiled, pipelined versus nonpipelined, and one stream versus four streams. Figure 15.7b shows the zoomed-in plots for matrix sizes less than 2000. Coprocessor-compute-only refers to using the compiler to offload dgemm but measuring only the time for the compute on the coprocessor and ignoring the data transfer times to/from the coprocessor. Compiler offload refers to using the compiler to offload dgemm and measuring time for both data transfers to/from and compute on the coprocessor. Both of these are untiled, not pipelined, and have no concurrency. Tiled hStreams offload refers to the program which we describe in Figure 15.11, which is tiled, pipelined by default, and has concurrency across streams. Two cases, with one and four streams are evaluated for the tiled hStreams offload for the 2×2 matrix tiling. For one stream, results for a pipelined as well as nonpipelined (sequential) case are reported. Finally, an untiled hStreams offload case with one stream is also reported.

The performance of all offload cases are lower than coprocessor-compute-only because they include the additional data transfer overheads. The only exception is the untiled hStreams offload case with one stream which performs better than the coprocessor-compute-only case for the smallest matrix sizes of 400 and 600. Untiled hStreams offload with one stream matches the untiled compiler offload for matrix sizes greater than about 3000, and has performance similar to the compiler Offload Streams, with which it shares common infrastructure. For smaller matrix sizes, the untiled hStreams offload with one stream performs the best among the offload programs. The impact of pipelining is shown as the difference between the nonpipelined and pipelined hStreams lines, for one stream and 2×2 tiling. The 2×2 tiling has lower performance in the nonconcurrent one stream case, compared to the untiled compiler offload case, up until matrices that are nearly 12,000 elements on a side. Finally, tiled hStreams with four pipelined streams and 2×2 tiling beats the compiler-offloaded untiled matrix for all but some very small sizes. Offloading beats host performance for all but very small sizes, since the coprocessor offers higher performance. For the untiled case with a single stream, pipelining does not make any difference as there is dependence among transfer and compute tasks, so it was not shown.

Small matrix performance

To see where and why tiled hStreams has performance advantages and disadvantages, we take a closer look at what happens at small sizes in Figure 15.8. The key performance factors at small sizes are (1) fixed overheads for asynchronous transfers, (2) efficiency of tiling at the sink, and (3) opportunity to cover transfer time. The solid line shows *relative* performance for 2×2 tiled hStreams with four pipelined streams compared to untiled compiler offload. That line almost always remains above 0, only exception being matrix size of 800, and is often 25% or more in this range. It tracks the dip in the

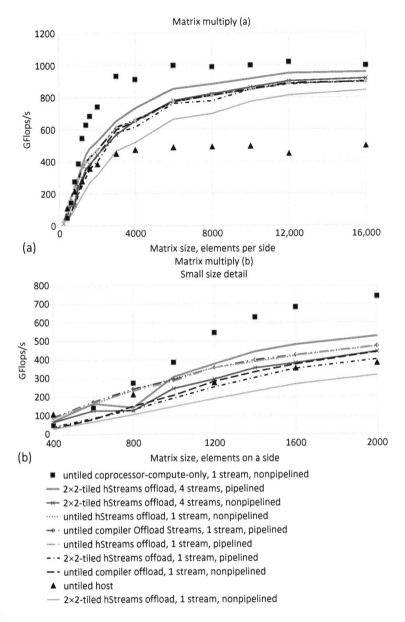

FIGURE 15.7

(a) Performance of matrix multiplication programs with MKL `cblas_dgemm`. (b) Zoomed-in plots of (a) for matrix sizes less than 2000. The legend applies to both. The computation is either on the host, coprocessor-compute-only (no transfers), offloaded with the compiler, offloaded with compiler Offload Streams, or offloaded with hStreams. The matrices are either full-sized or 2 × 2 tiled. The streams for hStreams cases are either pipelined or nonpipelined. Tiled hStreams offload with four pipelined streams and 2 × 2 tiling is up to 2.1× host, 2.2× (for now, until a known issue is fixed) untiled compiler offload, and 0.96× of untiled coprocessor-compute-only. With one stream, 2 × 2 tiling hurts up until matrices with 12,000 elements on a side, as seen from comparing one pipelined stream 2 × 2 tiled with untiled compiler offload. Forcing streams to be sequentialized has the impact seen in the difference between the pipelined and nonpipelined lines for one stream case with 2 × 2 tiling. The performance of compiler Offload Streams is similar to hStreams.

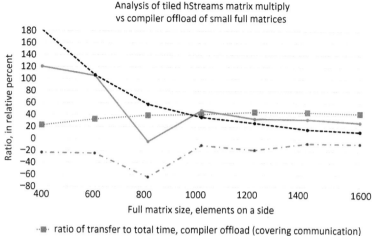

Analysis of tiled hStreams matrix multiply
vs compiler offload of small full matrices

- ·■· ratio of transfer to total time, compiler offload (covering communication)
- —■— ± % of 2×2 tiled hStreams/untiled compiler offload
- –•– ± % of untiled hStreams/untiled compiler offload
- –•· ± ratio of tiled/untiled native (size impact)

FIGURE 15.8

Analysis of relative performance improvement for small matrix sizes. All lines are relative ratios, with units of percentages. The solid line shows % gain of 2 × 2-tiled hStreams offload with four streams over offloading a full-size (untiled) matrix with the compiler offload. That line's general downward trend tracks the simple-dashed line, which shows a decreasing benefit as a fixed cost is amortized over an increasing amount of work. The fixed cost in this case is due to an early version of the offload compiler's temporary lack of an optimization to avoid unnecessary host-side synchronization. The 1.8× (for 2 × 2 tiling) or 2.2× (for untiled) performance impact shows how important it is to optimize asynchronous offload performance at small sizes. The solid line differs from the dashed line in two key ways. The divot at a full matrix size of 800 is due to the fact that native MKL has negative performance anomaly at 400 elements on a side, such that 2 × 2 tiling is much worse there; this pulls the solid line down accordingly. The dotted line, which shows the ratio of transfer time to total time rises in the range shown, and buoys up the solid line at the right.

dot-dashed line on the bottom, which shows the relative performance of running 4 concurrent dgemms for matrices of size $N/2$ elements on a side, compared to running 1 dgemm for matrix of size N, both in a native setting (not offload). So the solid line dips lowest for 2 × 2 tiles of 400 elements, for a total matrix size of 800, where MKL has a negative performance anomaly, which is also shown in Figure 15.10. The shape is dominated by the effect of a fixed synchronization overhead for asynchronous actions, which an old version of the offload compiler had not eliminated: the dashed line comparing hStreams with that older offload compiler on an untiled offload drops parabolically with increasing matrix size. Note that the Offload Streams implementation has fixed this: in Figure 15.7, the lines for untiled hStreams offload and compiler Offload Streams for one stream are nearly identical. Finally, the greater the fraction of total time that is spent on transfers, shown in the dotted line, the greater the impact that tiling can have. The ratio of data transfer times to/from the coprocessor to total time can climb as high as 45%, and that overhead falls gradually after 1200. For large enough sizes (not shown) the plot follows a $1/N$ dependence, where N is the matrix size. This is because the compute is $O(N^3)$ whereas data transfers are $O(N^2)$. In the tiled hStreams case, the communication overhead can be partially covered by reducing the latency before which computation begins, by starting after just small tiles of data are sent, versus having to wait for the full **A** and **B** matrices to arrive at the coprocessor. This plot gives an idea of the upper bound of how much one can hope to recover by concurrent invocation of data transfers and computes by using the hStreams framework.

In this section, we looked at binary questions: to tile or not to tile, to pipeline or not to pipeline, to offload or not to offload. We saw above that **tiling generally helps**, the **pipelining is beneficial** in all but anomalous cases, and once matrix sizes are big enough, **using more efficient computing domains tends to be better than keeping all computation local**.

TRADE-OFFS IN DEGREE OF TILING AND NUMBER OF STREAMS

Trade-offs in the degree of tiling and the number of streams are more subtle. There are no robust heuristics that we know of for determining the optimal degree of tile decomposition, or the optimal number of streams per computing domain. We first illustrate that there are trade-offs, then explain some of the underlying effects that have performance impact, and then we will show how we can formulate the matrix multiply algorithm to enable easy exploration of the optimization space.

Figure 15.9 shows the performance of the tiled hStreams matrix multiply program for a variety of choices of number of tiles per side (T) and number of streams (nstreams). Note the large variation in performance. The performance significantly drops when number of tiles on a side is 4 and number of streams is either 8 or 16. Neither four streams nor four tiles on a side are always best. In the case of

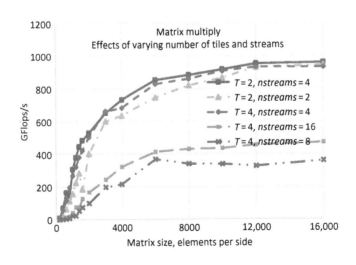

FIGURE 15.9

Performance of tiled hStreams matmult program for different choices of number of tiles per side (T) and number of streams (*nstreams*). Performance is highly sensitive to the choice of these parameters. It is difficult to predict *a priori* what is an optimal choice, but hStreams makes it very easy to explore the optimization space.

Cholesky, presented later in the chapter (see Figure 15.20), there is even less of a clear winner over the range of matrix sizes. So experimentation may be necessary to identify the optimal choice of the parameters.

Increasing the number of tasks via tiled decomposition can help, because of greater concurrency and better load balancing, or it can hurt, because of lower computational efficiency, because of higher overheads, and because of more intense bursts of demands on limited resources. Cache effects can go either way. We now explain these in more detail, and use the data in Figure 15.10 to illustrate some of these trade-offs. The configurations are shown across the x-axis, for example, 4 × 15 means 4 streams of 15 cores each on the coprocessor. With each consecutive configuration, the degree of tiling is increased so that there are four times as many total tiles (or two times as many tiles per side). The compute efficiency is on the y-axis; more is better. There is a line each for several matrix sizes, as measured by elements per side. Independent dgemms are executed in each stream.

First, let us consider the relationship between tiling and utilization. Look at the line in Figure 15.10 for matrices that are 512 elements on a side. In the 4 × 15c case, tiles are 512/2 = 256 elements on a side, and each tile is executed on 15 cores; 256 does not divide evenly by 15, so there is some load imbalance within each task. In the 15 × 4c case, tiles are 512/4 = 128 elements on a side, and 128 divides evenly by 4, leaving each task with a balanced load. This is why the line for 512 bends up from 4 × 15c to 15 × 4c. Load balance across tasks is relevant when there are more tasks than streams. If there are not as many

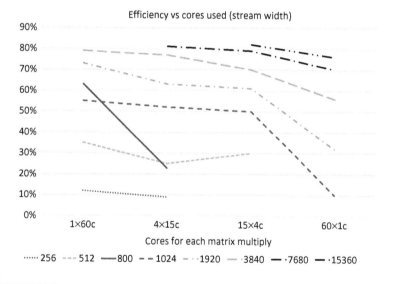

FIGURE 15.10

Compute efficiency versus degree of tiled decomposition. Configurations are (number of streams) × (cores per stream). The trade-offs for breaking a larger matrix up into tiles are complex. For matrix multiply, the trend is that more concurrent tasks reduces the compute efficiency. But that trend is superseded when load balance is better, for example, 512 (elementers per side) is divisible by 4 but not by 15, so performance is better for 15 × 4 compared to 4 × 15; 1920 is divisible by 60 so performance falls smoothly from 60 to 15 cores. Note that the line for 800 is an anomaly: it has a higher value for 1 × 60c than 1024, but drops below 512 for 4 × 15c. This corresponds to the drop in tiled performance for the 800 case discussed before.

tasks as streams, decomposition from tiling helps to use the whole machine. For example, if 40 independent untiled dgemm tasks were put onto 60 streams, the utilization, 40/60 would be less than 1. But if 6×6 tiling is applied, both underutilization and load balancing would be addressed. The average concurrency (not total tasks) from tiling matrix multiply by T goes up by T^2, as seen in Figure 15.4. So we have $40 \times 6 \times 6/60 = 4 \times 6 \times 60/60$ tasks per stream, which is a whole number, 24. So both changing the degree of tiling and changing the number of streams may help with load balance.

But there can be downsides to over-decomposition. The general trend shown in Figure 15.10 is that the efficiency drops as more tasks execute concurrently. As the task size decreases but fixed overheads (thread and vector parallelism, data movement, invocation, etc.) stay the same, efficiency drops. Burst effects can also come into play. The MKL matrix multiply does internal copies to re-layout data for optimal processing. For large matrices, the re-formatted data does not fit in the caches, and each matrix multiply instance incurs DRAM bandwidth demand. If there are more instances, it is possible to get bursts of DRAM bandwidth demand that approach or exceed the machine's bandwidth capacity, and we found that bottleneck to negatively impact performance in some cases. Specifically, for 1920 elements on a side, the peak DRAM bandwidth demand indicated by Intel® VTune™ jumped from 78 GB/s for $15 \times 4c$ to 128 GB/s for $60 \times 1c$. We found the execution overhead for invocation to be negligible, but for very large numbers of streams, the current implementation of COI (Coprocessor Offload Infrastructure on which hStreams depends) may run into some scaling issues with significant performance impact that have yet to be addressed as of this writing.

Because of the complex effects of number of tiles and number of streams, increase in concurrency, and decrease in compute efficiency, it is difficult to predict *a priori* what the optimal degree of tiled decomposition is.

TILED hStreams ALGORITHM

hStreams provides a mechanism to explore this many-dimensional optimization space with relative ease. One can vary these parameters with little or no change to the corresponding application program. Of course, care must be taken while designing algorithms for these programs so that they can be flexible. Let us describe, in detail, the algorithm for our matrix multiplication example. This will help us understand how to design algorithms using the hStreams framework while keeping in mind the flexibility as well performance considerations.

For this purpose, let us divide the matrices **A** and **B** into tiles, such that **A** contains *mtiles* × *ktiles* and **B** contains *ktiles* × *ntiles*. Thus, each block of **A** contains *m/mtiles* × *k/ktiles* elements and each tile of **B** contains *k/ktiles* × *n/ntiles* elements.

An example for square matrices divided into 3×3 tiles is shown in the bottom row of Figure 15.2. Note that here we have ordered the tiles for **A** in a column-major order and the tiles for **B** and **C** in a row-major order. By this ordering, we obtain some useful generalizations which are a key to make the algorithm flexible in exploring the optimization space. Expanding the entries for C_i's:

$$
\begin{aligned}
C_0 &= A_0 \times B_0 + A_3 \times B_3 + A_6 \times B_6 \\
C_1 &= A_0 \times B_1 + A_3 \times B_4 + A_6 \times B_7 \\
C_2 &= A_0 \times B_2 + A_3 \times B_5 + A_6 \times B_8 \\
C_3 &= A_1 \times B_0 + A_4 \times B_3 + A_7 \times B_6 \\
&\vdots \\
C_8 &= A_2 \times B_2 + A_5 \times B_5 + A_8 \times B_8
\end{aligned}
$$

The first generalization that we obtain pertains to the validity of the multiplication of the tiles of **A** and **B**. The multiplication between a tile $\mathbf{A_i}$ and $\mathbf{B_j}$ is valid if and only if it satisfies Eq. (15.1). Otherwise the multiplication does not contribute to any of the tiles of the result matrix **C**.

$$\left\lfloor \frac{i}{mtiles} \right\rfloor = = \left\lfloor \frac{j}{ntiles} \right\rfloor, \tag{15.1}$$

where $\lfloor x \rfloor$ denotes the greatest integer less than or equal to x.

The other useful generalization is for the index k of the tile of **C**, $\mathbf{C_k}$, obtained as a result of multiplying a valid $\mathbf{A_i}$ and $\mathbf{B_j}$ pair. Equation (15.2) gives the result.

$$k = (i \% mtiles) * ntiles + j \% ntiles. \tag{15.2}$$

Using these two generalizations, we can write an algorithm which does the matrix multiplication for a generic tile size. The key steps of the algorithm are shown in Figure 15.11. The various functions used in the algorithm related to partitioning the device, creation of streams, data transfer between host and device, compute on the device, etc. are all available using the hStreams APIs. These are marked by green(*hS) in the algorithm. These steps can be described as follows. First partition the device into a small number of physical partitions and create and associate a stream per partition. Let us say total number of streams created is equal to *nstreams*. Start transferring the matrix tiles from matrix **A** and matrix **B** to the device in streams. The stream used to transfer tiles is given by the tile subscript modulo *nstreams*. This maps the transfers on to the streams in a round-robin manner. Next, queue up multiplications on the coprocessor. For this, when the device receives a new tile for **A** then, loop over all **B** tiles residing on the device and if the multiplication of the new **A** tile with the existing **B** tile is valid, then queue up the multiplication. Similarly, queue up multiplications when a new **B** tile is received. The computes are queued in a stream given by the tile subscript for the **C** tile modulo *nstreams*. Finally, transfer over all the computed **C** tiles from device to host. Note that using this algorithm, we are able to queue up compute on the device in a "greedy" manner, that is as soon as the two input matrices for compute are available on the device, the computation is queued. This maximizes the interleaving of compute and data transfer. Moreover, to minimize the need for stream synchronization, each individual tile of output matrix **C** is computed in a fixed stream. This way, we can rely on the FIFO characteristics of the stream to give correct answers without the need for extra synchronizations. This *pipelining* of data transfers to the device and compute on the device, and running computes for various tiles concurrently on the device, provides performance advantages for the *tiled hStreams* code over a code which does direct offload of the compute for the full matrix. Note that we can also interleave the data transfers from the device to the host for tiles of the results matrix **C** with the rest of the computes and transfers (though not implemented in the present code). This may offer further performance advantages. Since all the data transfers as well as computes are queued in stream given by the tile subscript modulo *nstreams*, we can easily vary the *nstreams* as an input parameter to explore the optimization space without any change to the program.

As mentioned earlier, there is often a choice to target a particular computing domain for a given kernel within the application. This will be shown later for the Cholesky application, where one particular kernel gives better performance if run on the host CPU. Once again, the ability of hStreams to easily switch where to run the kernels makes this happen, together with a flexible algorithm behind the program.

The matrix multiplication example and the associated discussion so far gives the reader a high-level idea about what hStreams is all about and what one can achieve by using it. Before we discuss the

```
 1: Partition the card into nstreams places, and create 1 logical stream per place   (*hS)
 2: // Let the total streams created be nstreams
 3: define totalTilesA = mtiles * ktiles, totalTilesB = ktiles * ntiles.
 4: set countA = -1, countB = -1
 5: //
 6: // Send the tiles from host to card =========
 7: while ((countA < totalTilesA − 1) OR (countB < totalTilesB − 1)) do
 8:     if (countA <= countB) then
 9:         increment countA
10:         transfer A_countA to card in stream id: countA % nstreams   (*hS)
11:     elseif (countB < countA)
12:         increment countB
13:         transfer B_countB to card in stream id: countB % nstreams   (*hS)
14:     end if
15:     //
16:     // new A tile received ===========
17:     if (countA > countB) then // A new A_countA is received
18:         for (j = 0; j <= countB; j++) do // loop over all B_j's on card
19:             if (⌊countA/mtiles⌋ == ⌊j/ntiles⌋) then // Check validity per Eq. 1
20:                 define countC = (countA % mtiles) * ntiles + j % ntiles
21:                 Call cblas_dgemm in streamd id: countC % nstreams   (*hS)
22:                     ⟹ C_countC = C_countC + A_countA × B_j
23:             end if
24:         end for
25:     else
26:         // new B tile received========= // A new B_countB is received
27:         for (i = 0; i <= countA; i++) do // loop over all A_i's on card
28:             if (⌊i/mtiles⌋ == ⌊countB/ntiles⌋) then // Check validity per Eq. 1
29:                 define countC = (i % mtiles) * ntiles + countB % ntiles
30:                 Call cblas_dgemm in stream id: countC % nstreams   (*hS)
31:                     ⟹ C_countC = C_countC + A_i × B_countB
32:             end if
33:         end for
34:     end if
35: end while
36: // retrieve C tiles (output data) from the card =========
37: Transfer computed tiles of C from card to host   (*hS)
```

FIGURE 15.11

Tiled hStreams matrix multiplication. A full version of compilable C++ source code is included as the last section of the paper following the "For more information" section. The two-and-a-half-page listing includes a host call to MKL `cblas_dgemm` to check the results of the tiled hStreams matrix multiplier.

details of the Cholesky program, lets first describe the hStreams library and the associated framework in greater detail in the next section.

THE hStreams LIBRARY AND FRAMEWORK

The Intel® hStreams library provides a portable abstraction of memory, data transfers, invocation, and synchronization on heterogeneous platforms. This abstraction facilitates a separation of concerns: scientists are free to focus on specifying the "what" in the form of algorithms, while performance tuners and runtimes have the freedom to improve the "how," to map the parallelism that is available in the algorithm onto parallel hardware, and to portably change that mapping over time. Both the scientist and the tuner are free to operate in areas of their own expertise. Every effort is made to avoid putting unnecessary burdens on users, by allowing them to be *descriptive* rather than *prescriptive*. hStreams also seeks to give those who want it, full control and transparency over actual execution. This "best of both worlds" approach is necessary to satisfy the divergent audience of developers.

hStreams enables users to expose the following forms of task-related parallelism:

- Concurrent execution of tasks on different devices.
- Concurrent execution of tasks within a many-core device.
- Concurrent execution of task computation and communication of data consumed by and produced by tasks.
- Minimal and efficient synchronization among tasks.

A key part of making the management of task parallelism easy is making dependences implicit rather than explicit. Some users prefer to expose task parallelism in task graphs, but that is not hStreams' approach. Some programming models and plumbing systems require users to link producer and consumer tasks with explicit dependences. While hStreams enables the explicit linkage of dependent tasks where necessary, it uses a simple stream abstraction, which is an FIFO pipeline, to avoid the need for that where possible. Actions placed in a given stream, such as computes and data transfers, are implicitly ordered via that FIFO semantic. But, wherever the implementation can determine that actions are free to execute concurrently or out of order, it is free to optimize, since such concurrency and reordering is not visible at the semantic level. That separation of concerns between the semantic layer and physical implementation layer is one of hStreams' key values.

In heterogeneous systems, there are many parameters that may vary. These include the number of physical memory coherence domains; the number, capabilities, and ISA of the computing resources; the capacity and types of storage, and the fabric that connects them. hStreams enables the specification of work at a *logical level* that allows these differences to be abstracted away, making such systems easier for the high-level user to target. It also provides facilities to enumerate the physical platform properties, and to bind the logical resources to the physical resources in ways that are controlled by the tuner of a runtime in order to optimize performance. hStreams makes it relatively easy to compile the same task across different processing capabilities, and to have hStreams invoke the code that is appropriate to where the task executes. Nodes in a heterogeneous cluster with a sizable collection of computing resources, such as a many-core processor or coprocessor, can have those resources subdivided and used for concurrent execution of smaller tasks. Tasks may expose functional parallelism, by doing different work, or may expose data parallelism by performing the same work on different data through data domain decomposition. Either way, tasks can execute concurrently with one another on different resources, and the communication of data between storage in those different domains can be seamlessly overlapped with the computation.

There are several streams-based implementations of software projects owned by independent software vendors (ISVs). For many such ISVs, changing the compiler or updating the version incurs a large cost, so they do not wish to make the frequent changes to keep up with the latest compilers, as may be necessary for compiler-based language interfaces that manage parallelism. They prefer a library-based approach, which is exactly what hStreams offers. And since ISVs tend to not want to be tied to specific languages, for example, C++, hStreams provides a C-only interface, on top of which interfaces can be built for Fortran, Python, etc.

hStreams is intended to be an interoperable plumbing layer, rather than just a top-level language interface. For example, it has been used as a plumbing layer in OmpSs to enable efficient offload to Intel Xeon Phi coprocessors. It has been intermixed with the Intel® Language Extensions for Offload (LEO) in large manufacturing applications. Some manufacturing ISVs create a proprietary interface for internal developers that provides a platform-agnostic streaming interface. hStreams is one of several implementation choices for that target-agnostic streaming interface, alongside NVidia's CUDA® Streams and OpenCL. This has enabled code that has already been written for a streams interface to be easily ported to Intel Xeon Phi products with competitive performance. hStreams tasks are free to use any kind of programming models that the developer wishes, including MKL, OpenMP threading and vectorization, Threading Building Blocks, and SIMD vectorization.

FEATURES

The essential component building blocks of hStreams are *domains*, *streams*, and memory *buffers*. Each of these provide abstractions that both enhance programmer productivity and enable transparency and control. Each of these is treated in turn in this section.

A **physical domain** is a set of computing and storage resources which share coherent memory. Examples of physical domains include a node in a cluster, a coprocessor, or a GPU. Physical domains are discoverable and enumerable to users. Each physical domain has a set of properties that include the number, kind and speed of hardware threads, and the amount of each kind of memory type. A **logical domain** is an abstraction of a physical domain. Logical domains may have a many-to-one mapping to physical domains, but they may not span physical domains. Logical domains have a CPU mask property that specifies the subset of the physical domain's computing resources that are associated with the logical domain. A user might write code for two logical domains, one bound to an Intel Xeon processor with a very large memory, and one bound to an Intel Xeon Phi coprocessor for accelerating highly parallel code. When that code is retargeted for a later-generation self-booting many-core processor (e.g., codenamed Knights Landing processor) that includes a more limited sized high-bandwidth memory with a large DRAM backing store, the code may be easily ported by changing the two lines of code related to binding: map the two logical domains to disjoint resources on the single physical domain of the new target, and change the memory type of the buffers residing in high-bandwidth memory.

The **stream** abstraction implements an FIFO pipeline semantic. Streams have a **source** endpoint, from which actions are issued, and a **sink** endpoint, at which actions occur. **Actions** such as *compute*, *data transfer*, and *synchronize* are queued into the stream in order. They are free to execute and complete out of order, as long as the effect of such optimizations is not visible at the semantic level, that is, they do not violate the sequential *FIFO semantic* of the stream. Computation is conducted at the sink, on a set of resources indicated by the stream's logical domain and CPU mask. All actions are associated with a particular stream via a user-supplied identifier. There can be a many-to-one mapping between stream identifiers and a set of computing resources, enabling users to have a different stream identifier for each tile that they operate on, if they wish. Users specify the work to be done in a stream, but this does not require that users explicitly bind the work to a particular set of resources. Suppose a task uses OpenMP thread parallelism within it. The OpenMP parallel directive within the task implicitly makes use of whatever number and affinity of threads the stream has assigned to it. Thus the same task could seamlessly execute on a whole 240-thread coprocessor, or on just a subset, or on a single thread.

Compute, data transfer, and synchronization actions can specify **memory operands**. These memory operands are the basis for data dependence analysis. If a given sequence of actions within a stream has nonoverlapping memory operands, then the runtime is free to execute and complete those actions out of order. Actual dependences among actions within a stream are implicitly specified by their FIFO order and their memory operands, and they are faithfully enforced. There are no implicit dependences implied among actions in different streams, or between actions in streams and what is done at the source; those must be explicitly specified using synchronization actions. The use of hStreams is shown in Figure 15.12.

Memory buffers may be instantiated on one or more logical domains. This allows them to be materialized only where needed. Memory locations are referred to by their **source proxy address**. Data that is transferred among physical domains are commonly materialized at the source, for example, on a host CPU. But some memory needs to be instantiated only in other domains. So memory is always virtually allocated at the source, providing the source proxy address, but it is physically allocated only where and when it is needed. The physical address may be different in each domain, so address

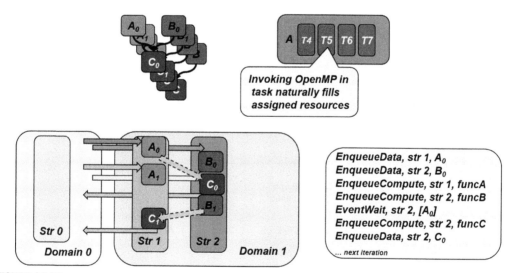

FIGURE 15.12

Dependences between tasks A, B, and C in each of several iterations are illustrated at the upper left. Tasks are implicitly bound to, and expand to fill the resources of the stream on which they execute, for example, an OpenMP team of hardware threads T4-T7. No explicit task graph is needed; APIs to move data, invoke the tasks, and synchronize actions are issued sequentially into streams Str1 and Str2, as shown in pseudocode. Domains 0 and 1 may be different nodes in a cluster, where Domain 1 has two streams. Dependences within each stream are implicit, but the dependence between the completion of task A in Str1 and the start of task C in Str2 must be explicitly called out by the programmer. The programmer is responsible for explicitly moving data among domains.

translation may be necessary. Compute actions (tasks), data transfers, and synchronization specify their memory operands as arguments. As actions in a stream are processed, a simple and efficient translation is applied to transform the source proxy address into the address needed at the sink.

HOW IT WORKS

hStreams uses a layered design, as shown in Figure 15.13. hStreams currently supports offloading from an Intel Xeon host processor to a coprocessor. The lowest-level interface that abstracts the PCIe connection to the coprocessor is the Symmetric Communication Interface, SCIF. The next level up is the Coprocessor Offload Interface, COI. Forthcoming versions of COI will support offload over fabric (i.e., the high-speed cluster interconnect) to self-booting computing resources, not just to captive cards over PCIe. There are currently two application programming interfaces (APIs) in hStreams: a *core* **API** layer and an *app* **API** layer. The core API layer encapsulates COI, so that it is free to be re-targeted to other plumbing infrastructures. The core API provides a rich and capable set of functions. The app API is a simplified, higher-level abstraction of selected core APIs that are easier to use, and that cover the common case. The app APIs provide for initialization and finalization, buffer creation, data transfers, invocation, and many flavors of synchronization. They also include some convenience functions for remote execution, for example, selected Intel MKL APIs, `memset`, and `memcpy`.

Users often wish to write their own functions for remote invocation. hStreams enables this. Users create their own source-side and sink-side interfaces for their functions. The user-defined functions that are called from source side must marshall operands and call the hStreams API for remote invocation. The marshalling is required because hStreams is a library, not a compiler that is capable of parsing the number, type, and order of arguments. The user-supplied sink-side interface is responsible for

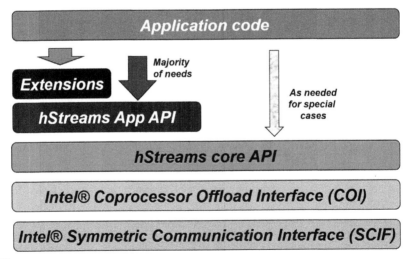

FIGURE 15.13

Layering of hStreams APIs on top of lower plumbing interfaces.

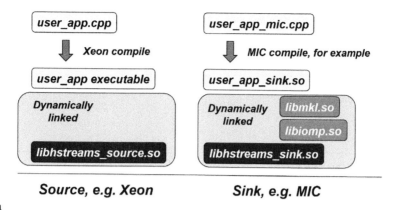

FIGURE 15.14

Users provide their own source and sink-side application code and can freely link to dynamic libraries.

de-marshalling operands from the hStreams remote invocation interface, and implementing the user-defined functionality. Helper functions that make marshalling easier are envisioned for future product releases. The hStreams runtime manages the dependences, the remote signaling, the passing of parameters, and the memory operand address translation.

hStreams executables have multiple parts: an executable for the source, for example, a Xeon host, and a dynamic library for the sink, for example, a coprocessor, as shown in Figure 15.14. Each side is separately compiled and has its own references to dynamically loaded libraries, as usual. If users follow the convention that the sink-side dynamic library has the same name as the source-side executable, but with a _mic extension, then the sink-side dynamic library name need not be specified.

RELATED WORK

hStreams is most similar to CUDA Streams from NVidia. While CUDA Streams uses FIFO semantics within each stream, hStreams' ability for actions to execute and complete out of order creates greater performance opportunities. hStreams' event interfaces are designed to be easier to use, and to allow greater concurrency. First, each action has an associated event; events do not need to be created separately after actions are enqueued. Events do not need to be explicitly created, registered, and destroyed. It is possible to wait for a set of events, for example, within a stream.

The hStreams interface does not need the boilerplate code that OpenCL does. Unlike tasks in SyCL, MPI, OmpSs, Qualcomm MARE, CnC, and others, task dependences need not be explicitly specified. Unlike SyCL, Phalanx, CnC, UPC++, CHARM++, and Chapel, there is no current dependence on C++ or other language mechanisms. As a library, hStreams does not depend on users to stay current with the latest versions of compilers, as is the case for the Offload Streams feature of the Intel compiler (under development as of this writing). The current hStreams interfaces are at a lower level than related systems such as Trilinos and Legion. Other frameworks that deal with distributed environments, like Global Arrays and TIDA or simple offloading, like OpenMP TR3 do not offer the FIFO stream abstraction of hStreams. hStreams offers a distinction between logical and physical abstractions that are not available in LIBXSTREAM or Offload Streams, and it provides a mechanism to specify a number of streams per domain that resources should be divided among, which lets it flexibly adapt to different SKUs or kinds of platforms which vary in their number of resources, without changing the user code.

In the next section, we switch gears and describe the Cholesky factorization application as enabled by the use of the hStreams library.

CHOLESKY FACTORIZATION

Cholesky factorization (or Cholesky decomposition) is a decomposition of Hermitian, positive-definite matrix into the product of a lower triangular matrix and its conjugate transpose, useful for efficient numerical solutions and Monte Carlo simulations. When it is applicable, the Cholesky factorization is roughly twice as efficient as LU factorization for solving systems of linear equations.

If we define a square matrix $\mathbf{A}$ having m rows by m columns, then the Cholesky factorization is of the form:

$$\mathbf{A} = \mathbf{LL}^T, \tag{15.3}$$

where $\mathbf{L}$ is a $m \times m$ lower triangular matrix, and $\mathbf{L}^T$ is its transpose.

Every Hermitian positive-definite matrix (and thus also every real-valued symmetric positive-definite matrix) has a unique Cholesky factorization. The standard algorithm for Cholesky factorization, is a variant of Gaussian elimination that operates on both the left and the right of the matrix at once, preserving and exploiting symmetry. When Cholesky factorization is implemented, only half of the matrix (upper or lower triangular part) and the diagonal elements are operated on and need to be represented or stored explicitly. One variant of the algorithms for Cholesky factorization is called the "right-looking" Cholesky factorization, this is described in Figure 15.15.

The computational complexity of this algorithm is dominated by the innermost loop. A single execution of this line: $A_{i,j} = A_{i,j} - A_{i,k} * A_{j,k}$ requires one multiplication and one subtraction, or

```
1: for k = 1, m do
2:     A_{k,k} = √(A_{k,k})
3:     for i = k + 1, m do
4:         A_{i,k} = A_{i,k}/A_{k,k}
5:     end for
6:     for i = k + 1, m do
7:         for j = k + 1, i do
8:             A_{i,j} = A_{i,j} - A_{i,k} * A_{j,k}
9:         end for
10:    end for
11: end for
```

FIGURE 15.15

Right-looking Cholesky factorization algorithm.

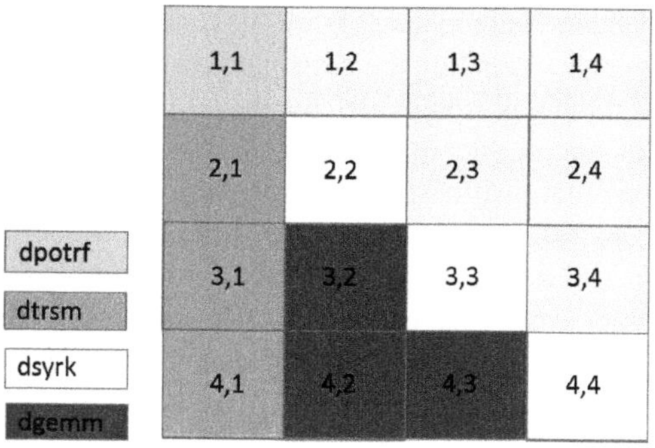

FIGURE 15.16

4 × 4 tiling of matrix for tiled Cholesky factorization. The tiles are colored according to the BLAS operations that are applied to them in the first pass of the outer-loop for the algorithm in Figure 15.17.

two operations. For the inner most loop, this requires: $2 * (i - (k + 1) + 1)$ or $2 * (i - k)$ operations. Thus total complexity is written as:

$$\Sigma_{k=1}^{m} \Sigma_{i=k+1}^{m} 2(i-k) = 2\Sigma_{k=1}^{m} \frac{(m-k+1)(m-k)}{2} \approx \Sigma_{k=1}^{m} k^2 \approx \frac{m^3}{3}. \tag{15.4}$$

To make use of the high-performance BLAS level-3 functions of the MKL library, we next show a tiled version of the Cholesky factorization algorithm. For this, the matrix is divided into square tiles as shown in Figure 15.16. The algorithm is given in Figure 15.17. The matrix is divided into T tiles for each side.

In Figure 15.16, each tile color corresponds to an MKL BLAS operation, namely, dpotrf, dtrsm, dsyrk, and dgemm. The actual MKL function names for the C-interface for these functions are `LAPACKE_dpotrf`, `cblas_dtrsm`, `cblas_dsyrk`, and `cblas_dgemm`, respectively. For details on these MKL functions, the reader is referred to the MKL reference manual. The colored tiles in the figure are the ones which are processed in the first iteration of the outer k-loop of the algorithm. In a right-looking algorithm, these colors (and corresponding BLAS operations) move to the right for each outer-loop iteration. The tiles in

```
 1: for k = 1, T do
 2:     A_{k,k} ← LAPACKE_dpotrf(A_{k,k})
 3:     for m = k + 1, T do
 4:         A_{m,k} ← cblas_dtrsm(A_{k,k}, A_{m,k})
 5:     end for
 6:     for n = k + 1, T do
 7:         A_{n,n} ← cblas_dsyrk(A_{n,k}, A_{n,n})
 8:         for m = n + 1, T do
 9:             A_{m,n} ← cblas_dgemm(A_{m,k}, A_{n,k}, A_{m,n})
10:         end for
11:     end for
12: end for
```

FIGURE 15.17

Tiled Cholesky factorization algorithm.

each column get finalized (contain factored data) as we move through the outer loop. Note that only the lower triangular half of the matrix (including the diagonal tiles) are operated on. The white tiles are not operated on. The overall compute is dominated by the cblas_dgemm operation at the inner most loop which executes on the matrix tile of size *tile_size*. The cost of this dgemm on the tile is $2 * (tile\_size)^3$. The total computational cost for the tiled algorithm is also $m^3/3$ (not derived), which is the same as the elemental algorithm, where m is the matrix size, with $m = T * tile\_size$.

Using this tiled algorithm as baseline, we next describe an offload algorithm for tiled Cholesky factorization. The offload algorithm uses both the host CPU and coprocessor using the hStreams framework. Before describing the algorithm, it is important to understand the data and compute dependences in a tiled Cholesky program as described above. For this, we construct a task-graph for the tiled Cholesky program. Figure 15.18 shows this task-graph for a 4 × 4 tiling. For each outer-loop iteration, the compute

FIGURE 15.18

Task dependence graph for 4 × 4-tiled Cholesky factorization. Solid connections indicate dependences within the same outer-loop iteration of algorithm in Figure 15.17, and dashed connections indicate dependences between the current and subsequent outer-loop iteration. The rectangles indicate compute operations and parallelograms indicate input matrix data.

dependences are as follows: dpotrf is computed first on the "hot" diagonal tile (hot tiles are tiles that contain the final factored data after the current iteration of the outer-loop), dtrsm operations are conducted next on the tiles in the hot column, dgemm and dsyrk operations are finally conducted on all the remaining tiles on the right of hot column, but only for the lower-triangular part of the matrix. Note that dpotrf requires only the data for its own tile, dtrsm requires two input tiles—its own tile and the diagonal tile directly above its own tile on which dpotrf was executed. dsyrk also requires two input tiles—its own tile and the hot tile on which dtrsm was executed in the same block row as itself. Lastly, dgemm requires three input parameters—its own tile, and two hot tiles on which dtrsm was executed, one corresponding to the row-index and other corresponding to the column-index of its own tile. Also note, that dgemm and dsyrk operations do not depend on each other and can be concurrently executed. Thus, the concurrency (i.e., how many BLAS operations can be executed in parallel) for a 4×4 tiled matrix, changes dynamically *within* the same outer loop iteration: first 1 dpotrf operation, then 3 dtrsm operations, and finally 3 dgemm and 3 dsyrk operations together for $k = 1$. So the maximum concurrency of 6 comes from the concurrent execution of dsyrk and dgemm operations. One can follow the dependence graph as we move to the next iteration of outer-loop. In general, the concurrency can be written as $(T - k) + \frac{1}{2}(T - k - 1) * (T - k)$ for T tiles at kth outer-loop iteration. Understanding of concurrency is very important for optimal scheduling of compute and data transfers to the streams. It is important that the number of streams be smaller than the maximum concurrency so that we do not under-subscribe the coprocessor, at least for the first few outer-loop iterations. The load balancing will be better if the concurrency is an integer multiple of number of streams for as many outer-loop iterations as possible.

For the offload tiled Cholesky algorithm using the hStreams library (hereafter called "tiled hStreams Cholesky"), we first define an important concept called "function-specific targeting," which means executing functions on architectures for which they are best suited. For example, executing a function which does not have much parallelism on the host processor (which has good serial performance) and a function which as a great deal of intrinsic parallelism on the coprocessor. For this algorithm, we execute the dpotrf on the diagonal hot tile on the processor as dpotrf does not have a lot of parallelism because of task dependences. All the other functions (i.e., dtrsm, dsyrk, and dgemm) are executed on the coprocessor. At the time of writing this chapter, running streams with the host processor as sink is not implemented in the hStreams library so we execute the dpotrf using the host thread and MKL library takes care of spawning multiple host threads to parallelize the dpotrf. There is ongoing work to extend the hStreams capability so that one can concurrently run streams on *both* host processor and the coprocessor. With that capability, seamless function-specific targeting of kernels of the application will be possible.

NOTE

Use *function-specific targeting* to execute kernels of an application on either the host or the coprocessor depending on the kernel characteristics such as inherent parallelism.

The algorithm for tiled hStreams Cholesky is given in Figure 15.19. The entries of the input matrix **A** are overwritten with those of the Cholesky factored matrix as the algorithm proceeds. The algorithm details steps for the first iteration of the outer-loop ($k = 1$) for brevity. For the other outer-loop iterations, one also needs to add extra synchronization steps between each outer-loop iteration by following the task-graph in Figure 15.18. Note also that all the data transfers for the input matrix required for the coprocessor are completed by the end of the first iteration of outer-loop. The algorithm starts by

1: **Partition** card into *nstreams* partitions and **create** one stream per partition (*hS)
2: **Define** integers *q_potrf*, *q_trsm*, and *q_syrk_gemm* and **set** them all to zero.
3: **Call** LAPACKE_dpotrf on the host CPU for the diagonal hot tile ($\mathbf{A}[1][1]$).
4: **Transfer** the diagonal hot tile ($\mathbf{A}[1][1]$) to the card in stream id: *q_potrf%nstreams*
    (*hS) . Associate an hStreams event, *eventCpyTo*[1][1] with this transfer (*hS) . Incre-
    ment *q_potrf* by 1.
5: **for** $m = 2, T$ **do**
6:     **Transfer** tile $\mathbf{A}[m][1]$ to card in stream id: *q_trsm%nstreams* (*hS)
7:     **Wait** for event *eventCpyTo*[1][1] to finish (*hS)
8:     **Call** cblas_dtrsm on card in stream id: *q_trsm%nstreams* (*hS) . Associate an
    event, *eventTrsm*[m][1] with this compute (*hS) .
9:     **Transfer** tile $\mathbf{A}[m][1]$ to host in stream id: *q_trsm%nstreams*. Increment *q_trsm*
    by 1 (*hS)
10: **end for**
11: **for** $n = 2, T$ **do**
12:     **Transfer** tile $\mathbf{A}[n][n]$ to card in stream id: *q_syrk_gemm%nstreams* (*hS) .
13:     **Wait** for event *eventTrsm*[n][1] to finish (*hS) .
14:     **Call** cblas_dsyrk for tile $\mathbf{A}[n][n]$ on card in stream id: *q_syrk_gemm%nstreams*
    (*hS) . Increment *q_syrk_gemm* by 1.
15:     **for** $m = n + 1, T$ **do**
16:         **Transfer** tile $\mathbf{A}[m][n]$ to card in stream id: *q_syrk_gemm%nstreams* (*hS) .
17:         **Wait** for event *eventTrsm*[m][1] to finish (*hS) .
18:         **Wait** for event *eventTrsm*[n][1] to finish (*hS) .
19:         **Call** cblas_dgemm for tile $\mathbf{A}[m][n]$ on card in stream id: *q_syrk_gemm%nstreams*
    (*hS) . Increment *q_syrk_gemm* by 1.
20:     **end for**
21: **end for**

FIGURE 15.19

Tiled hStreams Cholesky factorization.

partitioning the coprocessor into a number of physical partitions and associating one stream per partition. Once again, in the figure, all the operations which are a part of the hStreams API are specified
with (*hS) in the algorithm. We define three queues, one for dpotrf, one for dtrsm, and one for both
dsyrk and dgemm. These queues are incremented after every compute queued on the coprocessor,
and wrap around the maximum number of streams available, thus providing good load balancing.
As mentioned earlier, dpotrf is executed on the host for the diagonal hot tile. After dpotrf execution
finishes, the diagonal hot tile is transferred to the coprocessor for subsequent use. The rest of the
algorithm, follows the host native tiled Cholesky algorithm as given in Figure 15.17, with data transfers
and synchronization events inserted.

PERFORMANCE

We now look at the performance for Cholesky factorization. For this, we will look at two versions of
tiled hStreams offload program.

The first program follows the algorithm in Figure 15.19, where we use the host CPU to compute the
dpotrf on the diagonal tile and the rest of the computes (i.e., dtrsm, dsyrk, and dgemm) are done on the
coprocessor. For comparison to this, we look at the performance of the auto-offload (AO) feature of
MKL for dpotrf function. Figure 15.20 shows these performance results. For the tiled hStreams version,

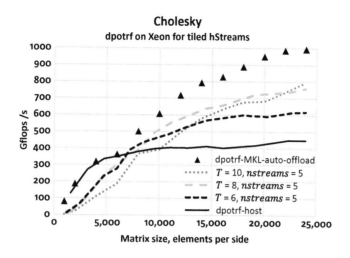

FIGURE 15.20

Performance of the Cholesky factorization programs. The tiled hStreams offload program (following the algorithm in Figure 15.19) is shown in various dashed lines corresponding to different numbers of tiles on a side (T) and number of streams (*nstreams*). The triangle symbols are for MKL AO performance for dpotrf, while the solid line is for dpotrf on the host.

three different plots are shown corresponding to different values of number of tiles, T, and number of streams (=number of coprocessor partitions), *nstreams*. First, we note that the performance of tiled hStreams program is sensitive to the choice of T and *nstreams*. It is observed that for small matrices the $T = 6$, *nstreams* $= 5$ case performs best and for large matrices $T = 10$, *nstreams* $= 3$ case performs best. $T = 8$, *nstreams* $= 5$ case shows good performance over the entire range of matrix sizes. It is difficult to predict *a priori* what combination of these parameters is best for a given matrix size. This is because of the complexities associated with (a) a change in compute efficiency on the coprocessor as a function of matrix size and different sensitivities of different functions namely dtrsm, dsyrk, and dgemm; (b) concurrency of transfers and computes; and (c) dynamic level of total compute concurrency which affects the load balancing of computes on the streams or partitions. In general, a larger number of tiles should offer benefits for hiding data transfer latencies, and if the concurrency of compute tasks is an integer multiple of number of streams, we should get good load balancing. It should, however, be kept in mind that the total compute concurrency is a function of the outer-loop iteration index as discussed earlier. Thus, it is best to experiment with a range of values for these parameters to obtain the best possible values for a given matrix size. Another thing we note in Figure 15.20 is that the performance of tiled hStreams program is lower than the MKL AO performance. This is expected because the tiled hStreams program does not make much use of the host processor apart from computing dpotrf on the diagonal tile which makes a small percentage of the total compute, whereas MKL AO makes good use of both the host processor and coprocessor card. Even then it is interesting to see that the tiled hStreams performance is quite close to the MKL AO performance for matrix sizes between 5000 and 10,000. In the near future, when the ability to run streams on host processor is added to the hStreams API, we should be able to fully utilize the processor concurrently with the coprocessor giving a boost to the performance of tiled hStreams programs.

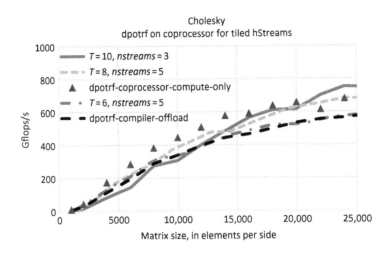

FIGURE 15.21

Pure offload performance for tiled hStreams program for various values of number of tiles on a side (*T*) and number of streams (*nstreams*), and for compiler-offload program. Also shown is dpotrf coprocessor-compute-only performance.

To have better insight into the benefits of tiling and concurrently invoking transfers and computes, we next show another set of performance results. For these runs, the tiled hStreams program is modified such that all compute happens on the coprocessor, even the dpotrf on the diagonal tile. For this purpose, the algorithm is modified slightly and some different synchronization events are added following the task graph shown in Figure 15.18. We refer to this approach as "pure offload" since the host is not involved in the computation at all. Figure 15.21 shows the performance of tiled hStreams and dpotrf-compiler-offload programs in the pure offload mode. It also shows the coprocessor-compute-only performance for dpotrf (on the full untiled matrix) which does not include the transfer times and only includes the time on the coprocessor. The overall performance for the pure offload tiled hStreams program and dpotrf-compiler-offload program are smaller than the corresponding numbers for tiled hStreams program and dpotrf-MKL-auto-offload shown in Figure 15.20 since the host is not contributing to the compute in the pure offload case. We again note a sensitivity to the parameters *T* and *nstreams* for the tiled hStreams program. With a good choice of these parameters, the tiled hStreams program can further hide the latency of data transfers performing better than the dpotrf-compiler-offload version. It is interesting to note that the case $T = 10$, $nstreams = 3$ performs even better than the dpotrf-coprocessor-compute-only case at the largest matrix sizes. This shows the advantages of the tiled algorithm over the dpotrf function called on an untiled matrix.

LU FACTORIZATION

We hope that our examples so far have adequately illustrated the use of hStreams to have you interested in this method of programming for a heterogeneous machine. We left an important related example of hStreams usage, LU factorization, out of the book for space considerations. For LU factorization, tiled hStreams achieved 1.95× performance compared to host-native runs for LAPACKE_mkl_dgetrfnpi at large matrix sizes. It is available freely online along with some examples from mechanical engineering problems where LU factorization is a key step in obtaining numerical solutions. These can be found in the hStreams resources on the book's website (http://lotsofcores.com/hStreams). The online treatment of LU factorization using hStreams builds on the discussion in the prior section on Cholesky factorization, so please read that first.

CONTINUING WORK ON hStreams

We are working on several enhancements to the hStreams library to extend the functionality as well as improve the performance. Some of the key areas of focus are the following.

- Full heterogeneity: Enable running hStreams on multiple kinds of processors, including the host processor, which is especially relevant for the upcoming Intel Xeon Phi processor, codenamed Knights Landing. This enables seamless and concurrent data transfers and computation for heterogeneous platforms consisting of any kind of processor and interconnect that our underlying plumbing supports, whether that is over fabric or PCIe.
- Support for concurrent sets of partially overlapping streams: Creating overlapping sets of streams that partition of resources that we can dynamically switch back and forth among, for example, five streams each using one-fifth of the compute resources, and a partition with a single stream using the entire compute resources. This will enable dynamic load balancing for cases where the compute concurrency is variable, such as in Cholesky and LU factorizations.
- Indicators for load balancing: The ability to obtain details on stream load which would enable the scheduling of tasks on the most-available resources, thus facilitating dynamic load balancing.
- We may explore opportunities and performance for matrix factorizations with pivoting, but such formulations tend to have less concurrency, and tuning for these may involve multidimensional data movement, which is not yet fully supported in hStreams.

ACKNOWLEDGMENTS

We would like to thank those who reviewed this document, and especially Efe Guney and Konstantin Arturov, for their contributions to MKL data collection and analysis, and Dmitry Prohorov, for his help in extending and applying Intel® VTune™ Amplifier.

RECAP

The hStreams library offers the ability to:

- Flexibly bind computation to target **heterogeneous architectures** that excel at either serial or highly parallel computation, and remotely invoke it there. For example, dpotrf runs better on Xeon, while other MKL functions are run on the Xeon Phi coprocessor, as shown in differences between Figures 15.20 and 15.21.
- Concurrently execute tasks that individually **lack adequate data parallelism** within a multicore target: Figures 15.6 and 15.10 show the trade-offs between task concurrency and compute resources allocated per task.

- **Move data** among domains only when necessary: Even though several streams are mapped to a given domain, they share the same address space and need not move data between them; they only need to synchronize across streams when necessary, as shown in Figure 15.12.
- Enable remote invocation, data movement, and synchronization to be **asynchronous**, to maximize concurrency, for example, via pipelining: the benefits of pipelining are exhibited in Figure 15.7, and the impact of steps taken to minimize latency are revealed in Figure 15.8.
- Manage dependences between tasks, while minimizing the effort involved in specifying those dependences and necessary synchronization, using a simple streaming abstraction that allows users to **think sequentially** about what happens within each stream, and where dependence enforcement is only an issue across streams: compute and data movement actions are invoked in order, but may proceed out of order, as shown in Figure 15.12. As an example, in the tiled hStreams matrix multiply program (shown in Figure 15.11), we do not need to synchronize computes (dgemm calls) which contribute to the same result matrix tile since they are all enqueued in a fixed stream for a given result matrix tile.
- Users can either use convenience functions from hStreams, or write their own remotely invoked functions.

We expose and manage **concurrency** is several ways. Tiling is a key optimization technique, but it is not unique to hStreams. Several features of hStreams make it easier to gain performance from tiling. Tiling decomposes tasks to create the opportunity to start one subtask while transferring data to the next. Simply queuing a sequence of data transfers and remote invocations into a stream makes harvesting pipeline parallelism between computation and communication possible; these benefits are highlighted in Figure 15.7. The concurrency within a multicore target supported by hStreams can either enable more efficient execution or degrade it; both cases are shown in Figure 15.10. Users can expose parallelism in tasks at a logical level, and can explore the optimal binding of tasks, which can each have their own logical stream if desired, to different numbers of physical streams in a separate tuning step that specifies the number of physical streams. This helps manage complexity, and lets resource decisions be managed by a savvy performance tuner versus needing to be hardcoded by the scientifically minded user. Figures 15.9, 15.20, and 15.21 show that there are trade-offs between the number of tiles and streams used, as a function of matrix size. We have further insights that can prune the search space for the best trade-offs, but space limitations do not allow inclusion of that detail in this chapter.

We presented **algorithms** for some of the most common matrix operations in mechanical engineering as well as other physical simulation fields: matrix multiplication and Cholesky factorization. The discussions for each of these operations builds up from an elemental version of the algorithm, to a tiled algorithm for running natively on a given platform, and then finally to a tiled algorithm that employs the hStreams library to run on heterogeneous platforms such as a host processor and a connected Intel Xeon Phi coprocessor.

SUMMARY

The hStreams library makes it relatively easy to expose task parallelism, to pipeline computation and communication, and to achieve task concurrency within and across heterogeneous targets such as an Intel Xeon processor and one or more Intel Xeon Phi coprocessors. This chapter contains examples of how coding in hStreams allows programming by simply specifying a number of streams, and tasks can be modulo-mapped to those streams, without rewriting code, configuring OpenMP, fiddling with affinitization, etc. Thus, use of hStreams facilitates design exploration of systems where there are complex trade-offs to be made that are not statically predicted with ease.

Overall, hStreams **performance** fared well. We demonstrated a performance gain over using just the Intel Xeon processors and over simple compiler offloading to the Intel Xeon Phi coprocessor, in Figures 15.7, 15.20, and 15.21. hStreams achieved these gains by exploiting concurrency of data transfers and computes to hide the communication latency using multiple asynchronous streams, using pipelining benefits within a stream to overlap data transfers with computes when possible, and enabling *function-specific targeting*. For matrix multiplication, we explored the trade-offs for small matrices, and correlated performance differences between tiled hStreams offload and untiled compiler-offload with fraction of time spent on communication and the impact of smaller tiles on compute efficiency (see Figure 15.8).

For matrix multiply, tiled hStreams offload achieved up to $2.1\times$ host, $2.2\times$ (for now, until a known issue is fixed) untiled compiler offload, and $0.96\times$ of untiled coprocessor-compute-only performance. For Cholesky factorization, tiled hStreams offload (with dpotrf conducted on host) achieved $0.80\times$ of MKL automatic offload performance for large matrix sizes, even though the hStreams implementation used the host only for dpotrf computation on the diagonal tile, and tiled hStreams for pure offload case achieved $1.11\times$ of coprocessor-compute-only performance for large matrix sizes.

For both matrix multiply and Cholesky, we noted that the performance of tiled hStreams programs is sensitive to the choice of parameters namely number of tiles and number of streams (or number of many-core coprocessor partitions). With a careful choice of these parameters, very good overall performance can be obtained for the entire range of matrix sizes. The same observation holds for LU factorization (an analysis of LU is available online along with other material which did not fit in this chapter, see http://lotsofcores.com/hStreams).

The **reference codes** for each of matrix multiply, Cholesky and LU are installed automatically with the Intel MPSS 3.5 release, and we also have them on the book's website. Please just build and run them to give them a try!

FOR MORE INFORMATION

- COI: Coprocesor offload interface. Available from: https://software.intel.com/en-us/articles/intel-manycore-platform-software-stack-mpss.
- hStreams resources (details) as companion to this book. Available from: http://lotsofcores.com/hStreams.
- Intel compilers. Available from: https://software.intel.com/en-us/compiler_15.0_ug_c.
- Intel Math Kernel Library, MKL. Available from: https://software.intel.com/en-us/mkl_11.1_ref.
- libxstream: library to program with streams, events, and queue functions into a stream. Available from: https://github.com/hfp/libxstream.
- MPI (Message Passing Interface). Available from: http://www.mpi-forum.org/docs/.
- NVidia CUDA. Available from: http://docs.nvidia.com/cuda/pdf/CUDA_C_Programming_Guide.pdf.
- OpenCL. Available from: https://www.khronos.org/registry/cl.
- OpenCL BLAS. Available from: https://github.com/clMathLibraries/clBLAS.

- OpenCL SYCL, cross-platform abstraction layer. Available from: https://www.khronos.org/opencl/sycl.
- Parallel computing (MARE). Available from: https://developer.qualcomm.com/mobile-development/maximize-hardware/parallel-computing-mare.
- PCIe. Available from: https://www.pcisig.com/specifications/pciexpress.
- Duran, A., 2011. OmpSs: a proposal for programming heterogeneous multicore architectures. Parallel Process. Lett. 21 (2), 173-193.
- Unat, D., Chan, C., Zhang, W., Bell, J., Shalf, J., 2013. Tiling as a durable abstraction for parallelism and data locality. In: Workshop on Domain-Specific Languages and High-Level Frameworks for High Performance Computing.
- Bauer, M., Treichler, S., Slaughter, E., Aiken, A., 2012. Legion: expressing locality and independence with logical regions. In: Proceedings of the International Conference on High Performance Computing, Networking, Storage and Analysis, SC '12, Los Alamitos, CA, USA. IEEE Computer Society Press, pp. 66:1-66:11.
- Bianchi, L., Dorigo, M., Gambardella, L.M., Gutjahr, W.J., 2009. A survey on metaheuristics for stochastic combinatorial optimization. Nat. Comput. 8 (2), 239-287. Available from: http://dx.doi.org/10.1007/s11047-008-9098-4.
- Borges, L., 2012. Experiences in developing seismic imaging code for Intel Xeon Phi Coprocessor. http://software.intel.com/en-us/blogs/2012/10/26/experiences-in-developing-seismic-imaging-code-for-intel-xeon-phi-coprocessor.
- Chamberlain, B.L., Callahan, D., Zima, H.P., 2007. Parallel programmability and the chapel language. Int. J. High Performance Comput. Appl. 21 (3), 291-312.
- Garland, M., Kudlur, M., Zheng. Y., 2012. Designing a unified programming model for heterogeneous machines. In: Proceedings of the International Conference on High Performance Computing, Networking, Storage and Analysis, SC '12, Los Alamitos, CA, USA. IEEE Computer Society Press, pp. 11.
- Heroux, M.A., Bartlett, R.A., Howle, V.E., Hoekstra, R.J., Hu, J.J., Kolda, T.G., Lehoucq, R.B., Long, K.R., Pawlowski, R.P., Phipps, E.T., Salinger, A.G., Thornquist, H.K., Tuminaro, R.S., Willenbring, J.M., Williams, A., Stanley, K.S., 2005. An overview of the Trilinos Project. ACM Trans. Math. Softw. 31 (3), 397-423.
- Jeannot, E., 2012. Performance analysis and optimization of the tiled Cholesky factorization on NUMA machines. In: PAAP 2012-IEEE International Symposium on Parallel Architectures, Algorithms and Programming.
- Kale, L.V., Krishnan, S., 1993. Charm++: a portable concurrent object oriented system based on C++. In: Proceedings of the Eighth Annual Conference on Object-Oriented Programming Systems, Languages, and Applications, OOPSLA '93, New York, NY, USA, ACM. pp. 91-108.
- Kim, W., Voss, M., 2011. Multicore desktop programming with Intel threading building blocks. IEEE Softw. 28 (1), 23-31.
- Nieplocha, J., Palmer, B., Tipparaju, V., Krishnan, M., Trease, H., Apr, E., 2006. Advances, applications and performance of the global arrays shared memory programming toolkit. Int. J. High Performance Comput. Appl. 20 (2), 203-231.
- OpenMP Language Working Group. OpenMP Technical Report 3 on OpenMP 4.0 enhancements, 2014. Available from: http://openmp.org/TR3.pdf.
- Trefethen, L.N., Bau III, D., 1997. Numerical Linear Algebra. SIAM.

- Zheng, Y., Kamil, A., Driscoll, M.B., Shan, H., Yelick, K., 2014. UPC++: a PGAS extension for C++. In: 2014 IEEE 28th International Parallel and Distributed Processing Symposium, May, pp. 1105-1114.

Download the code from this, and other chapters, http://lotsofcores.com.

TILED hStreams MATRIX MULTIPLIER EXAMPLE SOURCE

```
#include <stdio.h>
#include <math.h>
#include <mkl.h>
#include <hStreams_source.h>  // <-----hStreams Core API
#include <hStreams_app_api.h>// <-----hStreams App API
typedef double MATRIX_TYPE;
void randomInit(MATRIX_TYPE *data, int size) { for (int i = 0; i < size; ++i) {
   data[i] = rand() / (MATRIX_TYPE)RAND_MAX;
} }
int main() { // compile and link with $ icpc apicalls.cpp -lhstreams_source -mkl
   HSTR_OPTIONS hstreams_options; // <-----hStreams
   int partitions = 4;  // computing partitions per card
   int max_log_str = 4; // number of logical streams: can be bigger
   int nIter=3, blocksize = 128; // run 3 times, 1st run is slow owing to MKL init
   int numRowsA=512, numColsA=1024, numColsC=5120;
   int numRowsB = numColsA, numColsB = numColsC, numRowsC = numRowsA;
   int Aindex, Bindex, Cindex;
   const MATRIX_TYPE alpha = 1.0; const MATRIX_TYPE beta = 1.0;
   hStreams_GetCurrentOptions(&hstreams_options, sizeof(hstreams_options));
   hstreams_options.verbose = 0;
   hstreams_options.domains_limit = 256; // Limit to 256 domains
   hStreams_SetOptions (&hstreams_options); // <-----hStreams
   int mblocks = (int)numRowsA/blocksize;
   int kblocks = (int)numColsA/blocksize;
   int nblocks = (int)numColsC/blocksize;
   int totalblocks_A = mblocks * kblocks;
   int totalblocks_B = kblocks * nblocks;
   int totalblocks_C = mblocks * nblocks;
   unsigned int size_A = numColsA * numRowsA;
   unsigned int size_B = numColsB * numRowsB;
   unsigned int size_C = numColsC * numRowsC;
   // allocate host memory for matrices A and B and C
   MATRIX_TYPE *h_A = new MATRIX_TYPE[size_A];
   MATRIX_TYPE *h_B = new MATRIX_TYPE[size_B];
   MATRIX_TYPE *h_C = new MATRIX_TYPE[size_C];
   MATRIX_TYPE *reference = new MATRIX_TYPE[size_C];
   MATRIX_TYPE** h_Ablock = new MATRIX_TYPE*[totalblocks_A];
   MATRIX_TYPE** h_Bblock = new MATRIX_TYPE*[totalblocks_B];
   MATRIX_TYPE** h_Cblock = new MATRIX_TYPE*[totalblocks_C];
```

```
unsigned int mem_size_Ablock = sizeof (MATRIX_TYPE) * size_A/totalblocks_A;
unsigned int mem_size_Bblock = sizeof (MATRIX_TYPE) * size_B/totalblocks_B;
unsigned int mem_size_Cblock = sizeof (MATRIX_TYPE) * size_C/totalblocks_C;
//the second arg is logStrPerParition! not perCard
int iret = hStreams_app_init(partitions, 1); // <-----hStreams
if( iret != 0 ) { printf("hstreams_app_init failed!\r\n"); exit(-1); }
// malloc & initialize blocks of A/B/C on host and device
for (int i = 0; i < totalblocks_A; ++i) {
  h_Ablock[i] = new MATRIX_TYPE[size_A/totalblocks_A];
  hStreams_app_create_buf((void *)h_Ablock[i], mem_size_Ablock); //<-----hStreams
  randomInit(h_Ablock[i], size_A/totalblocks_A);
}
for (int i = 0; i < totalblocks_B; ++i) {
  h_Bblock[i] = new MATRIX_TYPE[size_B/totalblocks_B];
  hStreams_app_create_buf((void *) h_Bblock[i], mem_size_Bblock); //<-----hStreams
  randomInit(h_Bblock[i], size_B/totalblocks_B);
}
// Create buffers on the card
for (int i = 0; i < totalblocks_C; ++i) {
  h_Cblock[i] = new MATRIX_TYPE[size_C/totalblocks_C];
  hStreams_app_create_buf((void *) h_Cblock[i], mem_size_Cblock); //<-----hStreams
}
// Assemble full size matrices A & B for host compute check for comparison purposes
for (int i = 0; i < kblocks; i++) {
  for (int k = 0; k < numRowsB/kblocks; k++) {
    for (int j = i*nblocks; j < (i+1)*nblocks; j++) {
      for (int l = 0; l < numColsB/nblocks; l++) {
        Bindex = numColsB*(i*numRowsB/kblocks+k) + ((j-i*nblocks)*numColsB/nblocks+l);
        h_B[Bindex] = h_Bblock[j][l + k*numColsB/nblocks];
} } } }
for (int i = 0; i < mblocks; i++) {
  for (int k = 0; k < numRowsA/mblocks; k++) {
    for (int j = i; j <= i + (mblocks)*(kblocks-1); j = j + mblocks) {
      for (int l = 0; l < numColsA/kblocks; l++) {
        Aindex = numColsA*(i*numRowsA/mblocks+k) + (((j-i)/mblocks)*numColsA/kblocks+l);
        h_A[Aindex] = h_Ablock[j][l + k*numColsA/kblocks];
} } } }
HSTR_EVENT *eventAcpy = new HSTR_EVENT[totalblocks_A]; // <-----hStreams
HSTR_EVENT *eventBcpy = new HSTR_EVENT[totalblocks_B]; // <-----hStreams
HSTR_EVENT *eventCcpy = new HSTR_EVENT[totalblocks_C]; // <-----hStreams
HSTR_EVENT *eventCset = new HSTR_EVENT[totalblocks_C]; // <-----hStreams
for (int iter = 0; iter < nIter; iter++) { // do multiple runs on device & 1st use MKL slow
  int qindex; int cblock_index = 0; int countA = -1, countB = -1;
  div_t divresult1, divresult2;
  // Memset h_Cblock to zero initially
  for (int i = 0; i < totalblocks_C; ++i) {
    hStreams_app_memset(h_Cblock[i], 0, mem_size_Cblock, (i%max_log_str),
                                           &eventCset[i]); //<-----hStreams
  }
  while (countA < totalblocks_A-1 || countB < totalblocks_B-1) {
    if ((countA <= countB || countB == totalblocks_B-1) && (countA < totalblocks_A-1)) {
      countA++;
```

```
     hStreams_app_xfer_memory( h_Ablock[countA], h_Ablock[countA], //<-----hStreams
      mem_size_Ablock,(int)countA%max_log_str, HSTR_SRC_TO_SINK, &eventAcpy[countA]);
     }
    else if ((countB < countA || countA == totalblocks_A-1) && (countB < totalblocks_B-1)) {
     countB++;
     hStreams_app_xfer_memory( h_Bblock[countB], h_Bblock[countB], //<-----hStreams
      mem_size_Bblock,(int)countB%max_log_str, HSTR_SRC_TO_SINK, &eventBcpy[countB]);
     }
    // start multiplications
    if ((countA + countB) >= 0) {
     if (countA > countB) { //received a new A block: issue a DGEMM call on the card
      for (int j = 0; j <= countB; j++) {
        divresult1 = div(countA, mblocks);
        divresult2 = div(j, nblocks);
        if (divresult1.quot == divresult2.quot) { //validity checking
          cblock_index = divresult1.rem*nblocks + divresult2.rem;
          hStreams_app_event_wait(1, &eventBcpy[j]); // <---------hStreams
          hStreams_app_event_wait(1, &eventAcpy[countA]); // <---------hStreams
          hStreams_app_event_wait(1, &eventCset[cblock_index]); //<----hStreams
          //Async compute using MKL DGEMM on the device
          qindex = (int)cblock_index % max_log_str;
          hStreams_app_dgemm(CblasColMajor, CblasNoTrans, CblasNoTrans, //<---hStreams
            numColsB/nblocks, numRowsA/mblocks, numRowsB/kblocks,
            alpha, h_Bblock[j], numColsB/nblocks, h_Ablock[countA], numColsA/kblocks,
            beta, h_Cblock[cblock_index], numColsC/nblocks,
            qindex, &eventCcpy[cblock_index]);
      } } }
     else { //received a new B block: issue a DGEMM call
      for (int i = 0; i <= countA; i++) {
        divresult1 = div(i, mblocks);
        divresult2 = div(countB, nblocks);
        if (divresult1.quot == divresult2.quot) { //validity check
          cblock_index = divresult1.rem*nblocks + divresult2.rem;
          hStreams_app_event_wait(1, &eventBcpy[countB]);    // <---------hStreams
          hStreams_app_event_wait(1, &eventAcpy[i]);         // <-------hStreams
          hStreams_app_event_wait(1, &eventCset[cblock_index]); //<----hStreams
          //Async compute using MKL DGEMM on the device
          qindex = (int)cblock_index % max_log_str;
          hStreams_app_dgemm(CblasColMajor, CblasNoTrans, CblasNoTrans, //<---hStreams
            numColsB/nblocks, numRowsA/mblocks, numRowsB/kblocks,
            alpha, h_Bblock[countB], numColsB/nblocks, h_Ablock[i], numColsA/kblocks,
            beta, h_Cblock[cblock_index], numColsC/nblocks,
            qindex, &eventCcpy[cblock_index]);
    } } } }
// copy result from device back to host
for (int i = 0; i < totalblocks_C; ++i) {
  //Synchronize before transferring the result back
  hStreams_app_stream_sync(i%max_log_str); // <-----hStreams
  hStreams_app_xfer_memory(h_Cblock[i], h_Cblock[i], mem_size_Cblock, //<-----hStreams
          (int)i%max_log_str, HSTR_SINK_TO_SRC, &eventCcpy[i]);
}
// assemble fullsize C matrix from the blocks for comparison purposes
```

```
for (int i = 0; i < mblocks; i++) {
  for (int k = 0; k < numRowsC/mblocks; k++) {
    for (int j = i*nblocks; j < (i+1)*nblocks; j++) {
      for (int l = 0; l < numColsC/nblocks; l++) {
        Cindex = numColsC*(i*numRowsC/mblocks+k) + ((j-i*nblocks)*numColsC/
        nblocks+l);
        h_C[Cindex] = h_Cblock[j][l + k*numColsC/nblocks];
} } } }
// check h_A*h_B = Creference on host against h_C computed on device
memset(reference,0,size_C*sizeof(MATRIX_TYPE));
cblas_dgemm(CblasRowMajor, CblasNoTrans, CblasNoTrans, numRowsA, numColsB, numColsA,
    1.0, h_A, numColsA, h_B, numColsB, 0.0, reference, numColsC);
bool resACBLAS = true; uint32_t num_mismatch = 0;
for (int i = 0; i < size_C; ++i) {
  MATRIX_TYPE diff = fabs(reference[i] - h_C[i]);
  if ( reference[i] != 0 ) diff /= reference[i];
  if ( diff > 1.0e-14 ) { num_mismatch++;
    if ( resACBLAS ) { printf("MKL Dgemm: 1st Problem at i=%d: ref=%g actual=%g\n",
          i, reference[i], h_C[i]);
        }
    resACBLAS = false; break;
} }
if( resACBLAS ) {
  printf("If no MKL Dgemm problems, then Block Multiplication was successful.\r\n");
}
}
// Free Memory... and exit
delete [] reference; delete [] h_A; delete [] h_B; delete [] h_C;
delete [] eventAcpy; delete [] eventBcpy; delete [] eventCcpy; delete [] eventCset;
for (int i = 0; i < totalblocks_A; ++i)  { delete [] h_Ablock[i]; }
for (int i = 0; i < totalblocks_B; ++i)  { delete [] h_Bblock[i]; }
for (int i = 0; i < totalblocks_C; ++i)  { delete [] h_Cblock[i]; }
//Synchronize after transferring the result back
hStreams_app_thread_sync(); // <-----hStreams
hStreams_app_fini(); // <-----hStreams
return(0); }
```

MPI-3 SHARED MEMORY PROGRAMMING INTRODUCTION

16

Mikhail Brinskiy*, Mark Lubin[†], James Dinan[†]

Intel Corporation, Russia* Intel Corporation, USA[†]

MOTIVATION

The message passing interface (MPI) is one of the most popular parallel programming models for distributed memory systems. As the number of cores per node has increased, programmers have increasingly combined MPI with shared memory parallel programming interfaces, such as the OpenMP programming model. This hybrid of distributed-memory and shared-memory parallel programming idioms has aided programmers in addressing the concerns of performing efficient internode communication while effectively utilizing advancements in node-level architectures, including multicore and many-core processor architectures, such as Intel® Xeon® processors and Intel® Xeon Phi™ coprocessors.

Version 3.0 of the MPI standard, adds a new MPI interprocess shared memory extension (MPI SHM). This new extension is now supported by many MPI distributions, including versions 5.0.2 and beyond the Intel® MPI Library. The MPI SHM extension enables programmers to create regions of shared memory that are directly accessible by MPI processes within the same shared memory domain. In contrast with hybrid approaches, MPI SHM offers an incremental approach to managing memory resources within a node, where data structures can be individually moved into shared segments to reduce the memory footprint and improve the communication efficiency of MPI programs.

We present application developers with an introduction to MPI SHM and a tutorial on how to start using MPI SHM on systems with Intel Xeon processors with Intel Xeon Phi coprocessors. We discuss the two central optimization challenges that are addressed by MPI SHM: communication efficiency and memory capacity pressure. We further demonstrate the potential for performance improvement from these new capabilities through a halo exchange example taken from the MPPTEST test suite, which we have extended to include MPI SHM. Halo exchange is a prototypical neighborhood exchange communication pattern. In such patterns, the adjacency of communication partners often results in communication with processes in the same node, making them good candidates for acceleration through MPI SHM. By applying MPI SHM to this common communication pattern, we demonstrate that direct data sharing can be used instead of communication, resulting in significant performance gains.

MPI'S INTERPROCESS SHARED MEMORY EXTENSION

MPI SHM was added in version 3.0 of the MPI specification as an extension to the remote memory access (RMA) interface. The MPI RMA interface was added in version 2.0 of the MPI specification. The MPI RMA API provides a set of operations that can be used to remotely access data located in the memory of different MPI processes, using one-sided communication between MPI processes. In contrast with conventional two-sided communication, where both processes participate through matched send and receive operations, one-sided communications are performed by the initiator without a corresponding operation at the target. For this reason, MPI refers to the process that initiates a one-sided communication operation as the *origin process* and the process that contains the memory being accessed as the *target process*.

In the MPI RMA model, processes open *windows* into their address space through a setup operation that results in a *window object*. Window object creation is performed collectively—i.e., by all processes—on an existing parent MPI communicator, such as MPI_COMM_WORLD. A handle to the resulting window object is returned in all participating processes; this handle can then be used in subsequent communication operations to access the windows of all other processes that are participants in the window object.

While memory in a process is private by default, opening a window allows other processes to access data contained within the window memory directly using one-sided *put* and *get* copy operations, as well as atomic update operations, including *compare-and-swap*, *accumulate*, and *get-accumulate*. MPI also defines several synchronization methods that are used to coordinate remote accesses, ensure data consistency, and provide ordering among remote access operations.

MPI SHM extends the MPI RMA interface with a set of new operations that can be used to:

- identify which processes are located within the same shared memory domain,
- allocate interprocess shared memory, and
- coordinate accesses to the shared memory allocation.

In contrast to conventional MPI windows, shared memory windows can be queried for a direct pointer to the window memory, and window memory can be directly accessed using the pointer. In the coming sections, we discuss the MPI SHM interface in detail and demonstrate its usage. While our discussion focuses on MPI's interprocess shared memory extension, the same concepts and techniques can be applied in the context of interprocess shared memory mechanisms provided by other communication libraries, such as OpenSHMEM.

WHEN TO USE MPI INTERPROCESS SHARED MEMORY

MPI's interprocess shared memory extension addresses two key challenges faced by programmers of modern HPC systems: communication efficiency and memory capacity pressure. As the number of cores per node continues to grow, there is potential for more data exchange to occur within the node, which can be performed more efficiently through direct, shared memory accesses, rather than conventional message passing. At the same time, memory is a resource that is shared by the cores in a node. In conventional MPI programs, the memory of each process is private and when every MPI process needs the same data, it is replicated. As a result, the same data may be stored multiple times in a node's memory.

To address these challenges, many programmers utilize hybrid MPI and OpenMP programming, where MPI processes are multithreaded and assigned multiple cores using OpenMP facilities. The OpenMP model provides a variety of appealing primitives for expressing shared memory computations, including parallel loops and task parallelism, which are not provided by MPI SHM. However, in contrast with MPI SHM, utilizing hybrid MPI+OpenMP programming model requires the management of two parallel programming systems as well as two levels of parallel decomposition. OpenMP simd constructs also support the vectorization. MPI SHM also can serve as an alternative to the OpenMP approach for the applications where MPI-style domain decomposition of OpenMP is employed, leaving OpenMP to be used where it is most efficient, e.g., at the loop level. In addition, MPI SHM supports a structured approach, where data is private until it is explicitly shared and augments the existing MPI model with an interface that can be used to incrementally move data into shared segments as needed.

Usage Model	Memory Footprint Per Node
Single-threaded MPI	M_P*C_N
Multithreaded MPI	M_P*C_N/C_P
Single-threaded MPI SHM	$(M_P-M_S)*C_N+M_S$
Multithreaded MPI SHM	$(M_P-M_S)*C_N/C_P+M_S$

The table above shows the total memory footprint per node for several usage models. In a single-threaded MPI program, where M_P memory is required per process and there are C_N cores per node, the total memory requirement is M_P*C_N. In contrast, when C_P cores are used per process, C_N/C_P processes are used per node, effectively shrinking the per-node memory footprint by a factor of C_P. When the MPI SHM extension is used and an MPI process is run on every core, a similar memory reduction is achieved by moving shared data of size M_S into a shared memory window, resulting in a memory requirement of $(M_P-M_S)*C_N+M_S$.

While both hybrid MPI+OpenMP and MPI SHM extend conventional MPI programming with shared memory, in certain situations their usage can be complementary. Depending on the behavior of the application, OpenMP parallel regions within an MPI process may not scale efficiently to large numbers cores or serial sections may contribute a significant fraction of execution time. In such scenarios, multiple hybrid MPI+OpenMP processes are run within the same node. In this usage model, optimizing the communication and memory consumption across the hybrid MPI processes is still possible through the use of MPI SHM, yielding a per-node memory footprint of $(M_P-M_S)*C_N/C_P+M_S$.

1-D RING: FROM MPI MESSAGING TO SHARED MEMORY

We illustrate the semantics of the MPI SHM API through a simple one-dimensional communication ring example. In this example, each MPI process uses nonblocking send and recv operations to exchange data with its left and right neighbors. For illustrative purposes, we replace send and receive operations with

```
MPI_Irecv (&buf[0],…, prev,…, MPI_COMM_WORLD, &reqs[0]);
MPI_Irecv (&buf[1],…, next,…, MPI_COMM_WORLD, &reqs[1]);
MPI_Isend (&rank,…, prev,…, MPI_COMM_WORLD, &reqs[2]);
MPI_Isend (&rank,…, next,…, MPI_COMM_WORLD, &reqs[3]);
         {do some work}
MPI_Waitall (4, reqs, stats);
```

FIGURE 16.1

Nearest neighbor exchange in a 1-D ring topology and corresponding MPI code.

direct memory copies and later we demonstrate that even this simple change can lead to performance improvements. Additional benefits can be obtained by further code transformations to replace memory copies with direct accesses to shared data. Starting from this code, we will show how MPI SHM can be used to replace these communication operations with interprocess shared memory (Figure 16.1).

On systems with multicore nodes, the above code can be made more efficient by eliminating communication between MPI processes in the same node. The function MPI_Comm_split_type enables programmers to determine the *maximum* groups of MPI ranks that allow such memory sharing. Note that an MPI communicator contains an ordered set of processes. Each process in a group is associated with a unique integer *rank*. Rank values start at zero and go to $N-1$. Hence, *rank* is just a unique number, i.e., "name" of process in context of specific communicator. An MPI process versus rank comparison would be somewhat similar to the thread vs. thread ID. The function MPI_Comm_split_type has a powerful capability to decompose a communicator into shared memory "islands" in the output communicator shmcomm:

```
MPI_Comm shmcomm;
MPI_Comm_split_type(MPI_COMM_WORLD,MPI_COMM_TYPE_SHARED,0,MPI_INFO_NULL,&shmcomm);
```

Using the shared memory communicator at a given process, a shared memory window can now be created. This function is performed collectively on shmcomm and directs the MPI library to allocate interprocess shared memory and expose it in an RMA window. Each process contributes alloc_length to the total amount of space allocated and is returned a handle to the window object as well as a local pointer to the start of the memory belonging to that process. By default, this function allocates the shared window buffers contiguously in memory, making it possible to treat the resulting shared memory as a single contiguous buffer, even though individual chunks are logically associated with different processes. An alternative noncontiguous model can be used to optimize for nonuniform memory access (NUMA) latencies, which we will cover later.

```
MPI_Win_allocate_shared (alloc_length, 1, info, shmcomm, &mem, &win);
```

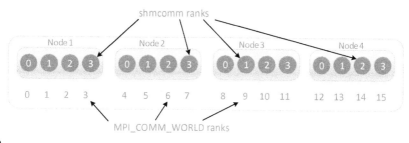

FIGURE 16.2

Mapping of global ranks to `shmcomm` ranks. If some of the neighbors' ranks are residing on a different node, their mapping in the resulting array `partners_map` will be a predefined constant `MPI_UNDEFINED`.

In order to execute point-to-point MPI send and receive operations between the nodes (as in the original example) and to execute MPI SHM functions within each node, we need a mechanism to distinguish between ranks that fit into the same node versus ranks belonging to different nodes. To accomplish this, we first query the MPI groups from the global communicator and shared memory communicator `shmcomm`.

```
MPI_Comm_group (MPI_COMM_WORLD, &world_group);
MPI_Comm_group (shmcomm, &shared_group);
```

Next, we map global rank numbers onto the `shmcomm` ranks numbers and store this mapping into the array `partners_map`, shown in Figure 16.2.

```
MPI_Group_translate_ranks (world_group, n_partners, partners, shared_group, partners_map);
```

The routine `MPI_Win_shared_query` routine can be used to query the address of shared memory belonging to a peer process. Whenever a peer process j is accessible via shared memory, i.e., `partners_map[j]!=MPI_UNDEFINED`, the `partners_map[j]` entry contains the peer's rank in `shmcomm`. To avoid repeatedly calling `MPI_Win_shared_query`, we cache the pointers in the `partners_ptrs` array. These pointers can be used to perform simple loads and stores, rather than copying data between processes using send and receive operations. A caveat is, because of how most operating systems provide interprocess shared memory; these pointers may be different at each process and should not be directly exchanged between processes (Figure 16.3).

```
for (j=0; j<n_partners; j++) {
  if (partners_map[j] != MPI_UNDEFINED)
      MPI_Win_shared_query (win, partners_map[j],…,
&partners_ptrs[j]);
  }
```

FIGURE 16.3

MPI_Win_shared_query can return different process-local addresses for the same physical memory on different processes.

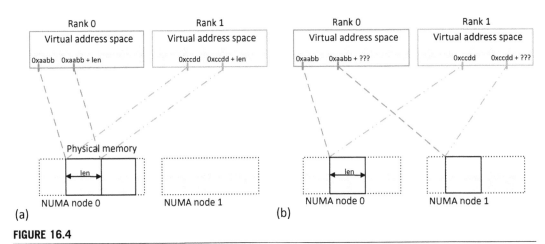

FIGURE 16.4

Different allocation strategies implied by MPI_Win_allocate_shared: (a) Contiguous memory allocation: peers address can be calculated based on the basic segment address and size of peer blocks and (b) Noncontiguous memory allocation: peers address can't be calculated, MPI_Win_shared_query API should be used.

The default behavior of MPI_Win_allocate_shared is to allocate memory where contributions from each process form a contiguous segment. In this model, the full segment can be treated as a contiguous array. The MPI standard also provides an info hint, alloc_shared_noncontig that can be used by advanced users to optimize for memory access latencies. Once it is provided to MPI_Win_allocate_shared call, it allows the MPI implementation to allocate the memory for each process separately, allowing it to be placed in a location that optimizes accesses from the owning process. In this case, the segment can be noncontiguous and the MPI_Win_shared_query function is required to obtain the remote process memory address. In our example, we do not use the alloc_shared_noncontig info hint, but MPI_Win_shared_query may still provide a convenient way in retrieving pointers to the peer memory addresses.

Figure 16.4 shows that process local addresses may be different even though they point to the same physical memory location. It also shows examples on contiguous and noncontiguous memory allocation strategies.

Unlike the point-to-point message passing model, the MPI SHM interface requires explicit use of synchronizations to ensure memory consistency and that the changes in memory are visible to the other processes. In some cases, it enables higher performance at the cost of more complex code that each developer needs to understand and maintain. Therefore in this chapter, we focus on the semantics of these new synchronizations and their effect on performance.

We choose to use the MPI_Win_lock_all and MPI_Win_lock_all functions to demarcate the time interval, called an RMA access epoch, when remote memory operations are allowed to occur. The name *lock* here does not have the same connotation familiar to shared memory programmers, such as mutexes. During this epoch, the MPI_Win_sync function is used to ensure completion of memory updates without closing the RMA epoch, and MPI_Barrier is used to synchronize processes on the node (Figure 16.5):

```
//Start passive RMA epoch
MPI_Win_lock_all (MPI_MODE_NOCHECK, win);


// write into mem array hello_world info
mem[0] = rank;
mem[1] = numtasks;
memcpy(mem+2, name, namelen);


MPI_Win_sync (win); // memory fence - sync node exchanges
MPI_Barrier (shmcomm); //time barrier
```

FIGURE 16.5

Passive RMA synchronizations are needed for MPI SHM updates. The performance assertion
`MPI_MODE_NOCHECK` hints that the epoch can begin immediately at the target.

Note: On some platforms an additional `MPI_Win_sync` is required after the call to `MPI_Barrier` to
ensure that updates to shared memory are visible to the reader. Thus, it is highly recommended to use a
second `MPI_Win_sync` to maintain code portability across various platforms.

MPI RMA provides several synchronization methods in addition to the lock-all method. The
`MPI_Win_lock` method can be used, which involves performing lock and unlock operations around
accesses to shared memory for a specified rank. These operations can further be used in an exclusive
mode, which provides mutually exclusive access to window data at the target process. Because the lock
and unlock calls ensure data consistency, `MPI_Win_sync` is typically not needed in this model. In our
source code examples, to get better performance, we have not used mutual exclusion in `MPI_Win_lock`.
We will describe specifics of our implementation using `MPI_Win_lock` in the next section.

A second alternative is the collective active target MPI RMA synchronization model that relies on a
pair of `MPI_Win_fence` operations surrounding memory updates. The `MPI_Win_fence` method is less
verbose compared to lock/unlock epochs since it already includes barrier synchronizations but the collective nature of this synchronization model can have higher overheads.

With correct synchronizations in place, all processes can retrieve their neighbors' data either via
shared memory or using standard point-to-point communications when neighbor processes are located
on the different nodes (Figure 16.6).

After completion of MPI SHM communications we can close the access epoch using `MPI_Win_`
`unlock_all`, and at the same place synchronize the internode communications by using `MPI_Waitall` as usual.
The resulting code is available for download (see "For more information" at the end of this chapter).

MODIFYING MPPTEST HALO EXCHANGE TO INCLUDE MPI SHM

We next evaluate the performance of the MPI SHM implementation provided by the Intel MPI library
5.0.2 using clusters based on Intel Xeon processors and Intel Xeon Phi coprocessors. We modified the
halo exchange algorithm from the MPPTEST benchmark using the same approach as the 1-D ring

```
for (j=0; j<n_partners; j++){
  if (partners_map[j] != MPI_UNDEFINED) {
    i0 = partners_ptrs[j][0]; //load ops from MPI SHM!
    i1 = partners_ptrs[j][1];
    i2 = partners_ptrs[j]+2;

    ...
  } else { // inter-node non-blocking MPI
    MPI_Irecv (&rbuf[j],…, partners[j], 1 ,
               MPI_COMM_WORLD, rq++);
    MPI_Isend (&rank,…, partners[j], 1 , MPI_COMM_WORLD,
               rq++);

  }
}
```

FIGURE 16.6

Halo exchanges using MPI SHM on the node and standard nonblocking MPI send/recv for internode communications.

example described in the previous section. Although the MPPTEST halo test does not have the computational kernels present in many real applications, it provides us with an unhindered view of how different order halo exchanges, message sizes, and MPI synchronization operations may affect performance.

As described already, MPI SHM improves performance by eliminating send and receive operations to copy data between processes in the same node. It also eliminates other overheads associated with MPI point-to-point communication operations, including those incurred by the MPI software stack, interprocess synchronization, and protocols used to copy data between address spaces within the same node. However, some synchronization is still required in order to ensure that updates are stored correctly and can be read reliably by peer processes, and the synchronization method can have a significant performance impact.

We implemented three new halo patterns for the MPPTEST suite, *mpi3shm_lockall, mpi3shm_lock,* and *mpi3shm_fence* that can be used as new MPPTEST configuration parameters. All of them use the same MPI SHM communication scheme, but they employ different MPI RMA synchronization primitives:

- *mpi3shm_lockall*. It relies on MPI_Win_lock_all and MPI_Win_unlock_all to open and close an access epochs, and on MPI_Barrier and MPI_Win_sync for processes synchronization (memory and time).
- *mpi3shm_lock*. The same as above but using separate MPI_Win_lock and MPI_Win_unlock calls for each neighbor in the halo exchange.
- *mpi3shm_fence*. A pair of successive MPI_Win_Fence calls ensures that any local stores to the shared memory executed between them are consistent, and thus there is no need for any other synchronization primitives.

In MPPTEST, every process has a separate memory block for each partner, simulating that different message is intended for each neighbor. We followed the same approach in our code and allocated memory chunk which fits data for all neighbors:

```
MPI_Win_allocate_shared(n_partners * msg_size, 1, MPI_INFO_NULL, shmcomm, &exch_buf,
&win);
```

This approach allows us to directly replace send and receive operations with memory copies and to measure the baseline performance benefits associated with eliminating MPI calls. Additional improvements to performance and reductions in per-node memory footprint are possible by further replacing memory copies with direct accesses to shared data.

The resulting code is similar to the 1-D ring example, except the communication phase is repeated a predefined number of iteration times. MPI_Win_lock_all, MPI_Win_lock, MPI_Win_unlock_all, and MPI_Win_unlock calls open and close RMA access epoch just once per test rather than on each iteration step. Therefore, their costs are reduced with the growing number of iterations. The number of synchronizations also plays a significant role in realizing performance benefits; we reduce this overhead by performing a single synchronization, based on MPI_Barrier and MPI_Win_sync, following all these exchanges, as it is shown in code listing on Figure 16.7. The MPI_Win_sync is needed for memory synchronization. Its cost, which depends on the target platform, is typically low, as it is a local operation. The most time-consuming synchronization is MPI_Barrier which is collective operation over all processes in the node rather than point-to-point. As a result, MPI_Barrier call may incur excess overhead when the number of processes per node is much larger that the set of processes being communicated with.

We also used MPI_Win_lock and MPI_Win_unlock calls in similar to MPI_Win_lock_all way by opening an access epoch to every partner prior to any data exchange (−*mpi3shm_lock* option). Using personal locks for each partner may save us some time, especially when number of neighbors is significantly less than number of processes on the node, because the MPI_Win_lock_all function assumes opening an access epoch to all processes in the given window, which means all processes on the node in our case.

To investigate different process topologies in halo exchanges, we introduced a new configuration parameter into the MPPTEST halo benchmarks: *-dimension*. This parameter instructs MPPTEST to use one of two available processes decompositions, 1-D or 2-D, with the latter used by default. An example based on nine processes and four partners is shown on Figure 16.8. In the case of 1-D decomposition the partners of the rank 4 process are ranks 2, 3, 5, and 6, while in the 2-D case, its neighbors would be ranks 1, 3, 5, and 7.

Finally, we modified the reported time by adjusting it to the time for a process with the biggest execution time. The current MPPTEST approach reports overall time as the time of a rank 0, which might not be representative, especially in nonperiodic cases where rank 0 typically has fewer neighbors than other processes.

EVALUATION ENVIRONMENT AND RESULTS

In our performance studies, we used Intel's Endeavour cluster, where each node is equipped with a dual Intel Xeon E5-2697 processors, one Intel Xeon Phi 7120P coprocessor, and one Mellanox Connectx-3 InfiniBand adapter connected to the same socket. The cluster was running Red Hat Enterprise Linux 6.5 OS, Intel MPSS 3.3.30726, and OFED 1.5.4.1. We used Intel MPI Library v5.0.2, Intel® C++ Compiler v15.0.1, and the MPPTEST benchmark with the modifications described above.

```
MPI_Win_lock_all(MPI_MODE_NOCHECK, win);
for (i=0;i<reps;i++) {
  for (j=0; j<n_partners; j++) {
      if (partners_map[j] == MPI_UNDEFINED) {
        MPI_Irecv (my_buf +offset, len, MPI_BYTE,
                    partner, i, MPI_COMM_WORLD, rq++);
        MPI_Isend (exch_buf + offset, len, MPI_BYTE,
                    partner, i, MPI_COMM_WORLD, rq++);
      } else {
        memcpy (my_buf + offset, partners_ptrs[j]+offset,
                len);

      }
    offset += len;
  }
  if (n_node_partners > 0) {
    MPI_Win_sync(win);
    MPI_Barrier( shmcomm );
    MPI_Win_sync(win);
  }
  if (n_inter_partners > 0) {
    MPI_Waitall(2*n_inter_partners, reqs,
              MPI_STATUS_IGNORE);
  }
}
MPI_Win_unlock_all(win);
```

FIGURE 16.7

Communication scheme based on `MPI_Win_lock_all` and `MPI_Win_unlock_all`, which are called just once per test.

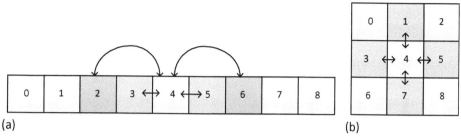

(a) (b)

FIGURE 16.8

Processes decomposition: (a) 1-D with four neighbors and (b) 2-D with four neighbors.

The following command line was used to obtain the performance data:

```
mpirun -n 64 -machinefile hostfile ./mpptest -halo -waitall -logscale -n_avg 1000
-npartner 8 -dimension 2
```

where the argument after *–halo* specifies the particular communication pattern for ghost cell exchanges, e.g., -*waitall* is used in case of point-to-point messages; -*logscale* indicates that we want to run the powers of two message sizes tests, starting from 4 bytes up to 128 kB; -*n_avg* specifies the number of iterations to be used and finally -*npartner* determines the number of neighbors per process. As described above, we introduced three new parameters corresponding to our new benchmarks: -*mpi3shm_lock*, -*mpi3shm_lockall*, and -*mpi3shm_fence* that can be used in place of -*waitall*. The -*dimension* parameter is optional (the default dimension is 2) and this was also previously described.

Figure 16.9 shows the results obtained on one coprocessor with 32 processes and 8 partners. In this case, the MPI SHM feature noticeably outperforms the regular point-to-point pattern regardless of synchronization type (please note the logarithmic scale of the both axes). However, we should note that with a relatively small number of updates (i.e., iterations in MPPTEST) the synchronization

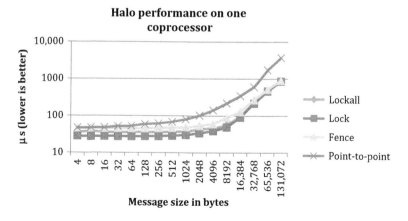

FIGURE 16.9

Different halo patterns on one coprocessor with 32 processes and 8 partners.

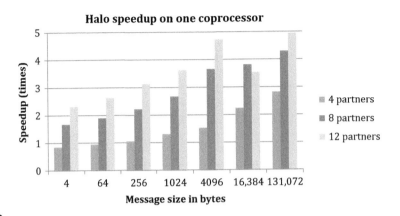

FIGURE 16.10

Speedup of MPI SHM approach compared to the point-to-point based (measured on 1 coprocessor with 32 processes).

overhead based on locks might become crucial. This is because we do locking once per test, thus its contribution to the overall time is an inverse to the number of iterations. Another observation is that using separate locks provides better performance than locking all the processes. This may become especially significant when the number of node neighbors to exchange the data with is significantly fewer than the number of processes bound to the interested window (thus calling `MPI_Win_lock_all` and `MPI_Win_unlock_all` may lead to unnecessary communication with all the processes rather than to the neighbors only). Also we see that using `MPI_Win_fence` gives the worst result of the sync primitives selected for this comparison.

We analyzed how the number of neighbors in halo exchanges impacts overall performance. Figure 16.10 shows the speedup of MPI SHM with lock synchronization in comparison with the common `MPI_Isend`/`MPI_Irecv` approach. We see that the performance advantage of our approach grows with the number of processes partners. This is to be expected because the relative cost of MPI SHM synchronizations stays the same regardless of number of partners, while the performance advantage of simple memory copies compared to point-to-point operations grows with every other exchange. With 12 partners per process, we get up to 2.6× improvement with small message sizes and as much as 4.9× with relatively large message sizes.

We repeated the measurements on two Intel Xeon Phi coprocessors connected to different nodes. We used 64 processes, 32 per coprocessor. The results depicted on Figure 16.11 shows lower speedup than we observed on a single node. This is because some exchanges are done via the network and the cost of intranode communication is just a part of the overall cost. We see that a personal lock-based shared memory approach is the best for almost all message sizes except very small messages, where the standard point-to-point scheme performs better. The experiments described so far have been done with the default 2-D neighbor's topology. Using the 1-D process topology, the personal locks based MPI SHM approach outperforms all other approaches at small message sizes too. Also starting from 4 kB messages all shared memory-bound patterns outperform the point-to-point-based ones.

The speedup of the lock-based approach as compared to the reference point-to-point one with different numbers of neighbors is shown in Figure 16.12. We see that with four partners, our approach is

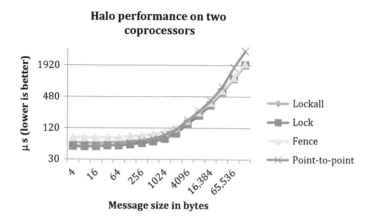

FIGURE 16.11

Different halo patterns on two coprocessors with 64 processes (32 per card) and 8 partners.

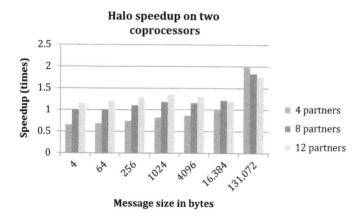

FIGURE 16.12

Speedup of MPI SHM approach compared to the point-to-point based (measured on 2 coprocessors with 64 processes).

beneficial only above medium-sized messages. However, as it was with the one-node case, the performance benefit becomes more significant with a growing number of neighbors. With 8 and 12 partner processes, we get up to $1.2\times$ improvement on small message sizes and $1.8\times$ on big ones.

The preliminary studies with larger number of nodes using both processors and coprocessors show similar results when 1-D process topology is used. With 2-D topology, MPI SHM pattern did not reveal performance benefits and typically showed worse results than point-to-point-based pattern. This behavior is explained by the different number of local node neighbors in 1-D and 2-D process decomposition cases as a result of how the processes are laid out on the cluster (we have not used any MPI topology aware algorithms in modifications of MPPTEST). The default processes placement used in Intel MPI Library currently is compact placement. This means that for a multicore node, sequential MPI ranks

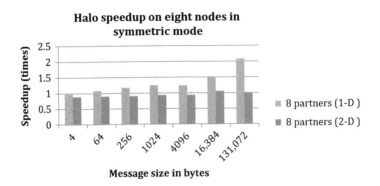

FIGURE 16.13

Speedup of MPI SHM approach compared to the point-to-point based, measured with eight neighbors and different processes decompositions (1-D and 2-D) measured on 8 nodes with 480 processes in symmetric mode. Each node contains one processor and one coprocessor.

are placed on the same node creating in case of 1-D very compact neighbors assignments while for 2-D decomposition and relatively big number of processes, most of the partners are non-local processes. As we stated in the previous chapter, number of local node partners has direct impact on the overall performance. Figure 16.13 shows speedup obtained on eight Intel Xeon processors and eight Intel Xeon Phi coprocessors in symmetric mode. The program execution is called symmetric when the complete program runs on both the host and the coprocessor as peers (not using explicit offload programming). This mode is only logically symmetric although, the host and coprocessor may have different computational and communication performances. In case of pure MPI applications, developer may choose a different number of processes per node. We ran the test with 480 processes, 28 per processor, and 32 per coprocessor and different process topologies corresponding to Figure 16.8.

These experiments confirm that the overall performance of MPI SHM pattern depends on the number of local neighbors rather than on the total processes count. Therefore, the proposed approach has good scaling potential with the proper partner assignments.

SUMMARY

An interprocess shared memory extension was added in MPI 3.0. We have described this extension, and how it can be used to perform communication efficiency and memory footprint optimization. We demonstrated how to apply this new feature in a simple 1-D ring "hello world" example and extended it for several node runs. Using a modified MPPTEST benchmark, we achieved up to 4.9× improvement over a standard point-to-point communication approach on one Intel Xeon Phi coprocessor. Moreover, we showed that the proposed approach may benefit halo exchanges even for multi-node cases, and we obtained up to 1.8× improvement with two Intel Xeon Phi coprocessors. Finally, we showed that the benefits of MPI SHM grow as we increase the number of intranode neighbors for halo exchanges.

FOR MORE INFORMATION

- Hoefler, T., et al., 2012. Leveraging MPI's one-sided communication interface for shared-memory programming. Recent Advances in the Message Passing Interface—19th European MPI Users' Group Meeting, EuroMPI 2012, Vienna, Austria, vol. 7490, September 23-26, 2012.
- Brinskiy, M., et al. Mastering Performance Challenges with the new MPI-3 Standard, PUM issue 18: http://goparallel.sourceforge.net/wp-content/uploads/2014/07/PUM18_Mastering_Performance_with_MPI3.pdf.
- Hoefler, T. et al., 2013. MPI+MPI: a new hybrid approach to parallel programming with MPI plus shared memory, Computing 95 (12) 1121.
- Gropp, W.D., Thakur, R., Revealing the performance of MPI RMA implementations, PVM/MPI'07 Proceedings of the 14th European Conference on Recent Advances in Parallel Virtual Machine and Message Passing Interface, pp. 272-280.
- Message Passing Interface (MPI) Tutorial, https://computing.llnl.gov/tutorials/mpi/#Non-Blocking_Message_Passing_Routines.
- Gropp, W.D., et al., 2014. Using Advanced MPI. Modern features of the Message-Passing Interface. MIT Press, November 2014.
- A Message-Passing Interface Standard 3.0, http://www.mpi-forum.org/docs/mpi-3.0/mpi30-report.pdf.
- Download the code from this, and other chapters, http://lotsofcores.com.

COARSE-GRAINED OpenMP FOR SCALABLE HYBRID PARALLELISM

17

Enda O'Brien

Irish Centre for High-End Computing (ICHEC), Ireland

This chapter illustrates the benefit of using OpenMP parallelism in a more "coarse-grained" way. This requires inserting directives at the highest possible level in source code, and using domain decomposition concepts that are closely analogous to those of Message-Passing Interface (MPI), so that multiple copies of thread-local arrays do not lead to excessive memory consumption. On massively parallel, heterogeneous hardware systems, an efficient nesting of such coarse-grained OpenMP within distributed-memory MPI parallelism may be the best approach for obtaining optimal performance from a large class of applications.

COARSE-GRAINED VERSUS FINE-GRAINED PARALLELISM

It has been abundantly clear since at least 2004 (when Herb Sutter famously declared "The Free Lunch Is Over") that individual processor cores are not getting any more powerful and the primary way to obtain better performance from numerical applications is through increased parallelism.

The two main parallel programming "standards" that have been available to developers since the last years of the twentieth century are OpenMP and the MPI. These two standards take quite different approaches to parallelism.

OpenMP is intrinsically "fine-grained," by which is meant that parallel regions are created and destroyed multiple times during the running of each executable job, and interspersed with sequential regions, however short. The amount of work done during the lifetime of any individual parallel processing element (or "thread" in the case of OpenMP) is relatively small. OpenMP is also often (though not always) implemented at a relatively low "loop-level" in source, since that is usually the easiest and least disruptive way to exploit parallelism. In this way, it is possible to introduce OpenMP directives into source code without knowing much at all about the larger problem that the code is trying to solve: developers can just look for compute-intensive loops, check that the loop iterations can be done in any order (that they do not contain dependencies), and add in simple OpenMP directives which parallelize each loop by distributing the loop iterations among the available number of threads. One major limitation of OpenMP is that is restricted to shared-memory systems only and cannot exploit parallelism across multi-node clusters.

MPI, in contrast, is intrinsically "coarse-grained," since the parallelism is built-in at the highest possible level—the entire executable. The entire job may be thought of as one big parallel region that exists from start to finish. The amount of work done by each individual processing element (i.e., each MPI process) is large—ideally 1/Nth the work done by the corresponding sequential job, where N is the number of MPI processes, but usually somewhat larger than this, given the overheads of cooperating with the other MPI processes in the parallel job. MPI parallelism is invariably built-in at the highest possible "domain-level." Parallelizing a program with MPI requires developers to think "physically" and have a good idea of the overall problem the code is trying to solve. Part of the appeal of MPI, in contrast with OpenMP, is that it can orchestrate parallel processes across multiple nodes of distributed-memory systems.

So which is "better"—"coarse-grained" or "fine-grained" parallelism; OpenMP or MPI? Of course the answer, as you might expect, is "it depends." Each of those two paradigms is naturally suited to somewhat different situations, and each has its advantages and disadvantages. Nevertheless, one purpose of this chapter is to address the question: given the option of using either OpenMP threads or MPI processes to utilize the computing resources of a host node or coprocessor device, which works better, or what is the best "mix" between them, and why? To some extent, the answer also depends on the "quality" of the OpenMP multi-threading. As we will see, the more coarse-grained the multi-threading can be, or the higher up the call-tree the OpenMP directives can be placed, the better the performance seems to be.

Of course there is nothing new or surprising in this: coarse-grained parallelism has fewer overheads than the fine-grained variety, and so should perform better. The only reason why many applications do not use OpenMP in a more coarse-grained way is that making OpenMP programs optimally coarse-grained is hard—just about as hard as writing code to use MPI. Until recently, anyone going to all that trouble was better off investing in an MPI version (for its distributed-memory capabilities) than in OpenMP.

However, from now and most likely far into the future, the standard way to run really large numerical applications (such as weather-forecasting models or turbulent flow simulations) will be on massively parallel systems using heterogeneous architectures. Obtaining good and scalable performance from such systems will almost certainly require use of nested parallelism, with MPI for internode parallelism, and OpenMP (or something very like it) for intranode parallelism. The MPI component will need to avoid "all-to-all" type global communications, since these will not scale to the thousands of MPI processes that will be required (if N is the number of MPI processes, then the number of all-to-all messages grows as N^2). Similarly, the multi-threaded component will need to be maximally coarse-grained; both to avoid thread creation overheads and to avoid other negative side effects such as memory blow-up as the thread count increases.

It should be noted that "vectorization" provides a third layer of "parallelism," at the instruction level, below both OpenMP and MPI and largely independent of both of them. Efficient vectorization of application code is becoming ever more important as vector lengths increase (e.g., via the AVX or "advanced vector extensions" on Intel® Xeon® processors), and offer proportionately increased performance.

Nevertheless, the focus of this chapter is really on coarse-grained multi-threading and the value it has over its fine-grained counterpart. More and more, the effort required to convert a fine-grained OpenMP program into a coarse-grained one is becoming worthwhile, and some time in the future it may even be necessary.

In this chapter, we use a very simple FORTRAN program to put some numerical flesh on the conceptual bones we have just introduced. The program performs repeated smoothing or "filtering" of an arbitrarily large three-dimensional array and is representative of the kind of "stencil" operations that are used widely in many different applications. The "stencil-test" program is parallelized with both MPI and OpenMP, and in different versions, the OpenMP directives are inserted in either a fine-grained or a coarse-grained way. The key characteristics are illustrated with specific code examples, and results are shown from both standard Intel® Xeon® processor nodes and Intel® Xeon Phi™ coprocessors.

FLESH ON THE BONES: A FORTRAN "STENCIL-TEST" EXAMPLE

Many of the ideas mentioned above can be illustrated using a simple FORTRAN application that starts with a three-dimensional gridded field on an arbitrarily-sized domain and repeatedly "smooths" or "filters" it by replacing the field value at each point with a weighted average of the surrounding points in the three-dimensional space. The code is therefore quite representative of a large class of "stencil" operations. The application itself is contrived principally as a way to test (and indeed to learn!) different parallel methods. Otherwise, there is very little value in the answers it produces—other than to check that the answers remain the same regardless of how the code is parallelized.

Consider an "input array," `arr_in`, dimensioned with NX, NY, and NZ points in the x, y, and z directions, respectively. It may help to think of this as a physical field such as temperature, or tracer concentration. The basic calculation is then to replace the value at each grid-point with a weighted average of the point itself along with the six points to the north, south, east, west, above, and below. The result is stored in a separate "output array," `arr_out`. Alternatively, if memory is truly scarce, it is possible to simply over-write `arr_in` with its own smoothed values. However, I prefer to save to the separate `arr_out`, since first it is more representative of real-world code, and second, any over-writing would require the introduction of extra temporary variables and extra lines of code to handle the data dependencies that would be introduced. Moreover, those dependencies would seriously complicate the introduction of OpenMP directives, so using `arr_out` instead really simplifies the multi-threading.

If the (NX,NY,NZ) domain represents a physical space with rigid boundaries, then the stencil operations at the walls, edges, and corners all need special treatment, since, e.g., the eastern boundary points cannot be smoothed using neighboring points to the east. Normally, such "special treatment" simply means an extra set of smaller loops to handle the smoothing at those locations. Computationally, however, it is convenient to define an "extended" domain, of size (NX+2,NY+2,NZ+2), with an extra layer of "shadow" points (sometimes known as a "halo") beyond the physical boundaries, which can be filled with the values desired (e.g., the same values as on the boundaries). This means that the central set of nested loops can span the entire physical domain. It also eliminates the need for a messy set of extra small loops to handle conditions at the boundaries, simplifies the parallelization, and makes the entire code more efficient, and (arguably) more elegant.

FINE-GRAINED OpenMP CODE

Figure 17.1 shows the central part of the code, which is a set of nested loops to perform the smoothing over the entire physical domain (i.e., the interior of the extended domain). The array names `ext_in` and `ext_out` are used instead of `arr_in` and `arr_out`, respectively, to signify that they span the extended domain, not just the physical one.

```
!        do k=2,nz+1
!$OMP PARALLEL DO PRIVATE(i,j,k)
         do k=2,nz_loc+1
!          do j=2,ny+1
           do j=2,ny_loc+1
!            do i=2,nx+1
             do i=2,nx_loc+1
               ext_out(i,j,k) = w1*ext_in(i,j,k) + w2*(
     &              ext_in(i-1,j,k) + ext_in(i+1,j,k) +
     &              ext_in(i,j-1,k) + ext_in(i,j+1,k) +
     &              ext_in(i,j,k-1) + ext_in(i,j,k+1) )
             end do
           end do
         end do
!$OMP END PARALLEL DO
```

FIGURE 17.1

Fine-grained: the central loops of the hybrid parallel stencil code using MPI and fine-grained OpenMP.

The code shown in Figure 17.1 is part of a "hybrid" parallel implementation, i.e., one that uses both MPI and OpenMP. The OpenMP directives span only this set of loops, so is clearly a "fine-grained" version. The main effect of using MPI is simply to replace the "global" domain limits (NX, NY, NZ) with the MPI-local subdomain limits (NX_LOC, NY_LOC, NZ_LOC). The vestige of the sequential version that spans (NX, NY, NZ) may be seen in the commented-out lines in Figure 17.1.

Of course, another consequence of using MPI is that the arrays ext_in and ext_out are now defined over the MPI subdomains (NX_LOC+2, NY_LOC+2, NZ_LOC+2) instead of the global extended domain (NX+2, NY+2, NZ+2). Note that the MPI subdomains are themselves "extended," with the values around the edges coming from MPI messages exchanged with other "nearest-neighbor" subdomains. The MPI messages are not shown here, but they are a very standard "halo-exchange" process, and may be seen in the complete code that is available from the repository provided with this book.

So far, this is very simple and very conventional. However, simplicity also makes for efficiency. Much of the simplicity here is a consequence of separating ext_out from ext_in and of using the "extended" computational domain instead of just the physical one.

PARTIAL COARSE-GRAINED OpenMP CODE

While the loops shown in Figure 17.1 are one of the computational "hot-spots" in the overall application, as is usually the case, they are not the only one. After a "halo-exchange" to update the "edges" of ext_out, a second smoothing pass is made through the field now contained in ext_out, this time saving the output in ext_in. So the initial values in ext_in are ultimately overwritten with updated (smoothed) values—just not within the same loop, where dependencies would complicate matters. This pair of smoothing passes, with intermediate MPI message passing, is repeated an arbitrary number of times (let's call this NCOUNT).

During the course of a complete program run, therefore, the OpenMP parallel region of Figure 17.1 is encountered NCOUNT times, as is the "sister" parallel region where ext_out is smoothed into ext_in, and as are the OpenMP parallel regions in the "halo-exchange" routines in each of the three directions (north-south, east-west, up-down). In a typical "fine-grained" fashion, the set of parallel threads is created and destroyed multiple times, with the number of threads in each set determined by the value of OMP_NUM_THREADS.

A key question of interest now is: how easy and how worthwhile is it to merge all those distinct OpenMP-parallel loops into a single large (i.e., coarse-grained) OpenMP parallel region?

In the case of this simple stencil-test, the answer to the first part of that question is that it is quite easy to do. The strategy (which is quite generic and applicable to other applications too) is to let any large arrays (i.e., ext_in and ext_out in the stencil case) remain "shared" (in the OpenMP sense). That means that for each MPI process, only a single copy of each array exists and is accessible by all OpenMP threads. In practice, of course, each thread should access only its own well-defined section of each "shared" array and take care not to step on the toes of any other thread accessing the same array! If possible, only scalars and small work-arrays should be declared "private" (in the OpenMP sense), so each thread has its own separate copy (usually with different values in each). The approach is shown schematically in Figure 17.2 for the stencil case.

Although Figure 17.2 is just schematic, here are some points to note:

- There is only one OpenMP parallel section, which encloses pretty much the entire rest of the code, including any I/O, any subroutine calls, and any MPI message-passing.
- Loops parallelized with "!$OMP PARALLEL DO" in Figure 17.1 just need the directive "!$OMP DO" in Figure 17.2.
- It usually makes sense to use only a single thread to do any I/O, hence the I/O section in Figure 17.2 is enclosed in an "OMP SINGLE" section.
- Usually (but not always) it also makes sense to use only a single thread for any message-passing, so the MPI calls in the "halo_exchange" subroutine are also enclosed in an "OMP SINGLE" section (not shown in Figure 17.2).

In a sense, the "fine-grained" OpenMP implementation (as in Figure 17.1) is a single-threaded program interspersed with multi-threaded parallel regions, in each of which a set of multiple threads are created and later destroyed. The more "coarse-grained" implementation shown schematically in Figure 17.2 is more of a multi-threaded program interspersed with single-threaded regions for operations such as I/O or message-passing. The set of multiple threads is only created once near the beginning and destroyed near the end.

The differences in the "halo_exchange" between the "fine-grained" and "coarse-grained" versions are essentially the same as listed above. Any "!$OMP PARALLEL DO" directives are replaced with the simpler "!$OMP DO," and all the calls to MPI functions are done within a new "!$OMP SINGLE" region in the "coarse-grained" version.

FULLY COARSE-GRAINED OpenMP CODE

The code shown schematically in Figure 17.2 is coarse-grained in the sense that it contains only one large OpenMP parallel section that starts at the top of the call-tree and encloses the entire working code. However, it may need further modification to make it as fully coarse-grained as it really should be. A hint as to the extra changes needed is provided by the bold-font of the variables nx_loc passed in the

```
! This section is as close as possible to top of program.
! May need a long list of "private" variables here:
!$OMP PARALLEL PRIVATE(i,j,k,i_loc,j_loc,k_loc, &
!$OMP& icount,xdist,ydist,zdist,...)
...
!$OMP SINGLE
        ! Only 1 thread does any I/O needed...
        ...
!$OMP END SINGLE
...
! Main loop over smoothing iterations:
        do icount=1,ncount
            call halo_exchange(ext_in,myrank,nx_loc,...)
            ...
!$OMP DO
!   Central smoothing nested loops as in Figure 1.1:
            do k=2,nz_loc+1
            ...
            end do
!$OMP END DO

            call halo_exchange(ext_out,myrank,nx_loc,...)

!$OMP DO
!   2nd smoothing pass, but from ext_out to ext_in:
            do k=2,nz_loc+1
            ...
            end do
!$OMP END DO
        end do    ! End of main outer loop over icount
!$OMP END PARALLEL
```

FIGURE 17.2

Partial coarse-grained: schematic code for coarse-grained OpenMP implementation of the stencil application. Note that the parallel section now encloses the main outer loop, I/O, and message-passing in the halo_exchanges.

argument list of halo_exchange in Figure 17.2. (Similar variables ny_loc and nz_loc are not shown for brevity, but the points made here about nx_loc apply equally to them too).

If NX is the number of (x-dimension) points in the "global" domain, nx_loc is the number of such points in each MPI subdomain. Any arrays of size nx_loc then span the entire subdomain. If any such arrays are declared inside an OpenMP parallel region (e.g., in the "halo_exchange" subroutine of the coarse-grained code in Figure 17.2), then *a separate copy of those arrays will be created for each thread.* This may not be a problem if OMP_NUM_THREADS is set to just 2 or 4 (e.g., to soak up hyper-threads on a Intel Xeon processor host node), but can be a major problem on a Intel Xeon Phi coprocessor, where OMP_NUM_THREADS could plausibly have a value as large as 244, but where memory is typically only a fraction of that available on a host node. If each OpenMP thread is allowed to allocate arrays that span the full MPI subdomain, then total memory consumption could increase almost in proportion to the number of threads used, and quickly exceed the memory available—especially on coprocessors, where the number of threads used is typically large, while memory is typically smaller than on a host node.

In order to avoid this problem, a second level of domain decomposition may need to be done. In that case, each thread then works with arrays of "thread-local" size, say nx_tloc instead of nx_loc. In other words, just as NX is decomposed into subdomains of size nx_loc for each MPI process, so nx_loc is decomposed into subdomains of size nx_tloc for each thread. The grand total of memory allocated does not then increase dramatically as more MPI processes or more threads are added to speed up the overall solution. Each MPI process and each OpenMP thread works on progressively smaller parts of the problem as more processes and more threads are added.

In principle, introducing a second level of domain decomposition for multiple threads presents many of the same coding difficulties and subtleties that occur when implementing a top-level decomposition for MPI. Just as each MPI process needs to know where to start and stop working in the global domain, so now each thread needs to know where to start and stop within each MPI subdomain. The bookkeeping calculations required in each case can be tricky, and in practice, any extra decomposition performed for multi-threading is likely to be much harder than simply merging and expanding OpenMP parallel regions!

Once nx_loc is decomposed into a separate nx_tloc for each thread, with thread-local arrays now of size nx_tloc instead of nx_loc, one important consequence is that each individual thread may now need to send and receive its own MPI messages. In that case, many smaller messages are exchanged between MPI processes (one for each thread), instead of a single large message. This raises several issues:

- First, this is regressive, since it is generally more efficient to exchange a few large messages between MPI processes rather than many small ones.
- Second, it requires that the MPI library be thread-safe and able to support multiple threads exchanging messages like this. Recent versions of Intel MPI are certainly thread-safe in this way, although other MPI implementations may not be.
- Finally, such thread-wise message passing requires that each thread have a counterpart thread on other MPI processes. This may not always be the case, especially when running a job in "symmetric mode" over both standard host nodes (where OMP_NUM_THREADS is typically small) and coprocessors (where OMP_NUM_THREADS is typically large).

Alternatively, each thread could "pack" its part of a larger work-array spanning a full MPI subdomain before a single thread sends a single large message. Similarly, each thread could "unpack" its part of a larger work-array from a single received message. Packing and unpacking like this is not ideal either, since it amounts to extra communication overhead. Nevertheless, such a trade-off may be necessary for the sake of avoiding memory blow-up as the thread count increases.

In our stencil code, the large working arrays are "shared" among all threads, so memory blow-up due to excessively large thread-local arrays is not a practical issue in this case. However, some thread-local arrays are still unnecessarily large, so the procedure for reducing their size and making the code fully coarse-grained is outlined here for illustrative purposes and should still apply quite generally.

Almost all the stencil code modifications required to implement the fully coarse-grained OpenMP (i.e., for each thread to have its own unique subdomain) were made in the "halo_exchange" subroutine as called in Figure 17.2. The representative key changes required are shown in Figure 17.3. As with

```
!!!real shado_E(ny_loc,nz_loc)   ! data moving eastwards
   real shado_E(ny_loc,nz_tloc)  ! data moving eastwards
   integer  itag_E                ! tag for messages east
   integer  idestE                ! MPI proc. to East.
!

   itag_E = 100 + mythread
   kmin = mythread*nz_tloc ! For thread-local point range
...
! Extract the "shadow-zone" part of main array:
!!!!$OMP DO
!!!    do k=2,nz_loc +1    ! Send east, receive from east
       do k=2,nz_tloc+1    ! Send east, receive from east
          do j=2,ny_loc+1
!!!          shado_E(j-1,k-1) = ext_in(nx_loc+1,j,       k)
             shado_E(j-1,k-1) = ext_in(nx_loc+1,j,kmin+k)
          enddo
       enddo
!!!!$OMP END DO


!=======================================================
!  Now to exchange some MPI messages...
!  Note: only messages from "even" to "odd" processes
!  shown here; data from "odd" processes sent already.
!=======================================================
!!!!$OMP SINGLE
!Use if MPI not thread-safe: !$OMP ORDERED
!!! call MPI_Recv(shado_W(1,1),ny_loc*nz_loc ,MPI_REAL, &
    call MPI_Recv(shado_W(1,1),ny_loc*nz_tloc,MPI_REAL, &
    &      idest_e,itag_w,MPI_COMM_WORLD,istatus,ierror)
!
!!! call MPI_Send(shado_E(1,1),ny_loc*nz_loc, MPI_REAL, &
    call MPI_Send(shado_E(1,1),ny_loc*nz_tloc,MPI_REAL, &
    &      idest_e,itag_e,MPI_COMM_WORLD,ierror)
!Use this if MPI not thread-safe:   !$OMP END ORDERED
!!!!$OMP END SINGLE
```

FIGURE 17.3

Full coarse-grained: part of the "halo_exchange" subroutine, showing some key changes made for the fully coarse-grained version. Lines from the partially coarse-grained version commented out with "!!!"

Figure 17.2, this is intended to be schematic rather than literal—e.g., only one half of the full set of MPI messages is shown. Lines commented out with "!!!" correspond to code from the "partially" coarse-grained version. Some key points to note from Figure 17.3 are:

- Thread-wise decomposition is done along one dimension only (i.e., in Figure 17.3, nz_loc is replaced with the thread-local nz_tloc, but ny_loc is retained). A two-dimensional decomposition is probably possible, but introduces further complications and was not necessary here.

- Thread-specific "tags" are defined for each message.
- A new variable (kmin) is introduced to identify the start of each nz_tloc range of points within nz_loc.
- The "!$OMP DO" directives are commented out because each thread now knows which part of the main ext_in array to work on, based on the (thread-local) index kmin.
- The "!$OMP SINGLE" directives are commented out because each thread now sends and receives its own messages.
- The "!$OMP ORDERED" directive was not needed with later versions of Intel MPI.

PERFORMANCE RESULTS WITH THE STENCIL CODE

A benchmark version of the stencil code was configured in order to evaluate the different kinds of multi-threading discussed in this chapter (i.e., fine-grained, partially coarse-grained, and fully coarse-grained). The grid-point dimensions of the global domain were chosen to be (NX,NY,NZ) = (800, 800, 1000), which correspond closely to the dimensions of the main arrays ext_in and ext_out, and which require a total memory allocation of approximately 10 GB. The number of pairs of smoothing passes, NCOUNT (i.e., number of iterations through the outer loop), was chosen to be 40, which was enough to get reasonable and representative run-times (10-40 s).

The code was built using the FORTRAN compiler and MPI from the Intel cluster studio V15.0 (2015). Compiler options were simply "-O3 –openmp" or "-O3 -openmp -xAVX" for the host-node executables, and "-O3 -openmp -mmic" for the coprocessor executable. According to the compiler "vector reports," all the key inner loops of the application vectorize without any reported problem. Nevertheless, vectorization is inhibited at run-time by the three-dimensional nature of the stencil, which accesses array elements that are scattered throughout memory and so prevents a uniform vector stride (even though all points on the stencil are "local" in the physical space representation). One consequence is that performance of this code is relatively insensitive to whether the –xAVX option is used or not.

Tests were run on a system consisting of a host node with dual 10-core 2.2 GHz Intel E5-v2 (code-name IvyBridge) processors and 64 GB memory, along with one Intel Xeon Phi 7000-series coprocessor, with 61 cores (244 threads) and 16 GB memory. Jobs were run either on the host node only, or in "native mode" entirely on the Intel Xeon Phi coprocessor.

Apart from that separation, all runs were configured to correspond as much as possible to the "real-life" situation where the parallelism expands to utilize all available resources. While this benchmark case does show good "strong scalability" (especially on the coprocessor), we are more interested here in the relative performance of MPI and OpenMP parallelism. Given 20 physical cores (or 40 logical cores) on the host node, is it better to run with 20 (or 40) single-threaded MPI processes, or just one MPI process with 20 (or 40) OpenMP threads—or some combination of the two?

Furthermore, does either of the "coarse-grained" OpenMP versions of the code ("partial" or "full") perform well enough relative to the "fine-grained" version to justify the extra work involved in developing them?

Some answers to these questions are given in the performance results shown in Figures 17.4–17.6.

Figure 17.4 shows run-times on the host node using the 20 physical cores (i.e., without hyper-threading), such that the product of MPI process count and OpenMP thread count is equal to 20 in

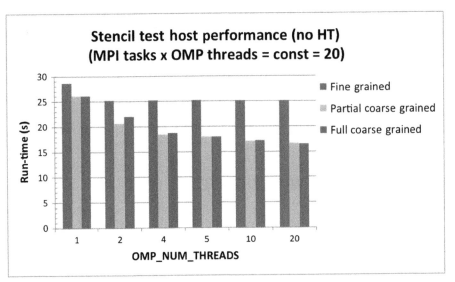

FIGURE 17.4

Stencil-test run-times on the standard host node as a function of OpenMP thread count (OMP_NUM_THREADS), and of MPI processor count, such that all 20 physical cores were used in all cases. Results are shown for each of the fine-grained, partial coarse-grained, and fully coarse-grained OpenMP code versions.

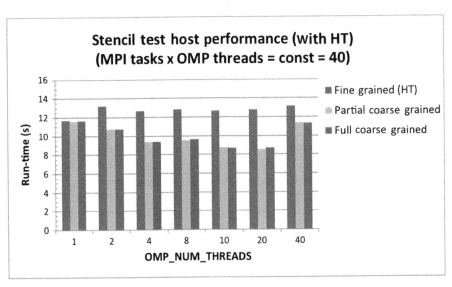

FIGURE 17.5

Stencil-test run-times on the standard host node as in Figure 17.4, but this time using all 40 logical cores (using hyper-threading).

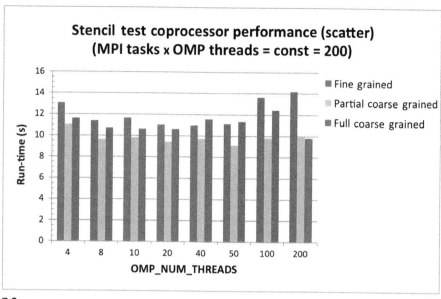

FIGURE 17.6

Stencil-test run-times as in Figures 17.4 and 17.5, but on the Intel Xeon Phi coprocessor, and using a total of 200 threads in all cases.

all cases. When using the fine-grained OpenMP version, performance improves from 1 thread to 2, but remains insensitive to the MPI/OpenMP "mix" after that. Both of the coarse-grained versions, on the other hand, perform better with more OpenMP and less MPI, and they perform significantly better than the fine-grained OpenMP version. That is really no surprise, at least for the larger thread counts, though it is perhaps more surprising for the single-threaded case. In principle a single thread has no "grain-iness" at all, neither coarse or fine, but Figure 17.4 suggests that the extra directives invoked in the fine-grained case do incur some overhead, even in the single-threaded case.

Figure 17.5 is similar to Figure 17.4, but for the case where hyper-threading was used, so for all results shown in Figure 17.5 the product of MPI processes and OpenMP threads is 40. Perhaps, the first point to make is that hyper-threading is very effective here: using it reduces run-times by almost a factor of 2. The fastest run-time in Figure 17.4 is 16.6 s (for the partial coarse-grained run with 20 threads), and in Figure 17.5 is 8.6 s (also for the partial coarse-grained run with 20 threads—but of course this time with the benefit of a second MPI process).

Otherwise, the main result of Figure 17.5 is the same as Figure 17.4, namely, that coarse-grained multi-threading performs better than fine-grained—significantly better for most thread counts, but also even for 1 thread, however marginally. For all runs in both Figures 17.4 and 17.5, the performance costs of the extra MPI messages in the full coarse-grained case are negligible—but they may become more noticeable if run over a network between multiple nodes.

Figure 17.6 is similar to Figures 17.4 and 17.5, but shows results from 200 threads of the Intel Xeon Phi coprocessor. Even though 240 threads were available, it was easier to divide the $800 \times 800 \times 1000$ domain in different ways among 200 threads rather than 240. In any case, runs using all 240 threads on the Intel Xeon Phi coprocessor produced only marginal improvements over the 200-thread results. Overall, run-times on the coprocessor (Figure 17.6) are closely comparable to run-times on the host-node with hyper-threading (Figure 17.5). Coprocessor performance is at its best (relative to the host) when the problem size is as large as possible to still fit on coprocessor memory. For smaller problem sizes, it is more difficult to efficiently exploit the massive parallelism of the coprocessor and in that case, performance on the host tends to be better.

Once again, Figure 17.6 shows that the partial coarse-grained OpenMP version is always faster than the fine-grained one. On the coprocessor, however, the extra small MPI messages in the fully coarse-grained version can impose a more significant performance penalty, since the latencies of all those messages can accumulate. MPI latency is much larger within a coprocessor than within the host node (approx. 2.5 vs. 0.5 μs).

Results on the coprocessor suggest that a balanced "mix" of OpenMP threads and MPI processes is usually better than putting most or all the parallelism into either OpenMP or MPI. Results on the host node (Figures 17.4 and 17.5) suggest that an efficient coarse-grained OpenMP favors using mostly OpenMP parallelism over MPI (at least within each node). However, insofar as the results in Figures 17.4 through 17.6 favor OpenMP relative to MPI, this is likely to be highly application-dependent, and simply reflects the fact that the simple dominant loops in the stencil code make it particularly well suited for multi-threaded parallelism.

PARALLELISM IN NUMERICAL WEATHER PREDICTION MODELS

Of the principal numerical weather prediction (NWP) and climate models in use today, all of them use MPI parallelism very efficiently. However, the design of many such models requires them to use MPI "all-to-all" type communications, which grow in proportion to N^2 as the MPI process count N increases. These "all-to-all" messages start to dominate the run-time profiles as the MPI process count increases, and eventually limit performance scalability. One way to postpone this scalability limit is to restrict the number of MPI processes to the number of nodes used, and use OpenMP multi-threading for all intra-node parallelism.

For this strategy to work well, the OpenMP implementation must be very efficient. This is certainly true for some models, but not for some others where the multi-threading is still very fine-grained. In yet other models, the OpenMP directives are inserted at a very high (truly coarse-grained) level in the call-tree, but suffer grievously from memory blow-up as the thread count increases, since the thread count (OMP_NUM_THREADS) is used explicitly as an extra dimension of working arrays, as in:

```
REAL*8 :: ARRAY(NPROMA,NLEV,OMP_NUM_THREADS)
```

Here, NPROMA is a horizontal "block-size," typically chosen for optimal cache usage, while NLEV is the number of vertical levels. In the MPI-only case, the OMP_NUM_THREADS variable in the third dimension reverts to 1. Meanwhile, the total number of physical grid-points in the subdomain grid (NGPTOT) is not used at all in any array declarations, but is used as the loop-limit over as many NPROMA blocks as required to complete the work over the full domain, as shown schematically in Figure 17.7.

Arrays in the subroutine CPG_GP (and in the many other subroutines below that) are then just two-dimensional of size (NPROMA,NLEV). Instead of the loop-index J working sequentially through each NPROMA-sized block, the OpenMP parallelism means that each thread can work on its own separate

```
!$OMP PARALLEL DO PRIVATE(J,K,…)
    DO J = 1, NGPTOT, NPROMA
        !(calculate offsets, start & end pts. etc.)
        . . .
        K = OML_MY_THREAD    ! Includes 1 for MPI-only
        CALL CPG_GP(J, K, ARRAY(1,1,K),...)
        . . .
    ENDDO
```

FIGURE 17.7

Schematic of a very high-level OpenMP loop in a weather model, which is highly parallel (in the partial coarse-grained sense) but profligate with memory (i.e., not fully coarse-grained) since working array sizes are proportional to thread count.

block simultaneously. This is highly efficient in the parallel sense, but extremely demanding of memory, since memory allocation increases almost in proportion to thread count.

Any "industrial-strength" application that is coded like this invariably runs out of memory before running out of threads on highly parallel, limited-memory platforms such as the Intel Xeon Phi coprocessor. Ideally, such codes should be rewritten to be fully coarse-grained (in the sense used throughout this chapter), in order to fully exploit multi-threaded parallelism within a fixed amount of memory.

One option to restructure the working arrays above would be to drop the third dimension completely (i.e., the OMP_NUM_THREADS dimension, which makes memory consumption directly proportional to thread count), and reorder the first two dimensions so that the declaration looks like:

    REAL*8 :: ARRAY(NLEV,NPROMA2)

Here, NPROMA2 could be optionally much larger than NPROMA, since the OpenMP parallelism will be applied to this dimension. The key point is that once chosen, NPROMA2 is fixed, and does not change with thread count. The OpenMP multi-threading could then "decompose" along this dimension, much as MPI can decompose all the grid-points along a meridian into N subdomains of size NGPTOT.

The main reason to switch the order of the NLEV and NPROMA dimensions is because it is (usually) easier to parallelize over the horizontal NPROMA (or larger NPROMA2) points than over the vertical NLEV points. Physical processes such as radiation and convection, at any given level in the vertical, typically involve interactions with variables at levels immediately above and below. Those interactions introduce dependencies that inhibit parallelization along the vertical dimension.

By the way, the final contents of the working arrays as declared above are ultimately saved to a large pointer-based state structure, which spans all NGPTOT points—but that is not a problem from the multi-threading point of view.

SUMMARY

This chapter illustrates, with the help of a simple program that performs repeated stencil-type operations, how the performance of simple loop-level or "fine-grained" OpenMP directives can be significantly improved by merging and expanding the OpenMP parallel regions into a single large "coarse-grained" parallel region that spans as much of the code as possible. The technique is not particularly novel, or particularly difficult, but the need for efficient multi-threaded parallelism nested in high-level distributed-memory parallelism (e.g., MPI) is becoming ever more urgent, as high-performance computing platforms evolve more and more into heterogeneous systems with massively parallel hardware components.

As OpenMP directives are moved higher up the call-tree to become more coarse-grained, an important consideration that arises (especially on devices like the Intel Xeon Phi coprocessor where memory is limited) is to avoid excessive memory blow-up due to each thread having its own copy of large private arrays. Such memory blow-up can be prevented by introducing a second-level domain decomposition, whereby each MPI subdomain is further decomposed into a set of "thread-local" sections. While this effectively saves memory, it comes at the price of extra coding complexity and can give rise to inefficiencies such as each thread (within an MPI process) sending its own MPI messages.

Performance tests with the stencil code on both a standard host-node and a coprocessor demonstrate the value of coarse-grained over fine-grained OpenMP and also show the penalty paid (often negligible, but it can be significant) by making the multi-threading fully coarse-grained and introducing the second-level domain decomposition. This effect will vary from application to application, but developers (especially for limited-memory devices such as the coprocessor) should be aware of the propensity of OpenMP to be profligate with memory, and also be aware of the trade-offs involved in managing this.

We can be reasonably confident that the practice of using memory in proportion to thread count must soon come to an end, even though future generations of coprocessors will undoubtedly have a lot more memory (indeed, as much memory as can fit on a host node). The more natural, and more sensible, approach is to select a problem size that fits in available memory, and then independently decompose that among an arbitrary number of threads. In other words, it will be worthwhile for future weather models to use truly coarse-grained OpenMP.

FOR MORE INFORMATION

Here are some additional reading materials we recommend related to this chapter.
- Herb Sutter's 2004 article "The Free Lunch Is Over: A Fundamental Turn Towards Concurrency in Software," http://www.gotw.ca/publications/concurrency-ddj.htm.
- For a nice example of a small coarse-grained OpenMP program, only without MPI, see: http://faculty.washington.edu/rjl/classes/am583s2014/notes/jacobi1d_omp2.html. There is a link to an MPI version on that page too, but no "hybrid" (mixed MPI/OpenMP) version.
- Stencil Code, http://wikipedia.org/wiki/Stencil_code.
- Stencil computation optimization and auto-tuning on state-of-the-art multicore architectures, http://dl.acm.org/citation.cfm?id=1413375
- Download the code from this, and other chapters, http://lotsofcores.com

EXPLOITING MULTILEVEL PARALLELISM IN QUANTUM SIMULATIONS

18

Jeongnim Kim, Lawrence Meadows

Intel Corporation, USA

Proper considerations of how to express and use nested parallelism can have a profound impact on performance. This chapter segments this challenge into two parts: nesting of OpenMP within an message passing interface (MPI) program, and then use of nesting within OpenMP itself. This logical decomposition of a program is quite approachable once the concepts are explained in the course of discussing real-world examples.

Using OpenMP within an MPI program has become common. It is especially important when the amount of parallelism at a node level becomes very high. The presence of Intel® Xeon Phi™ coprocessor(s) on a node definitely qualifies as a very high level of parallelism. The coprocessor can be exploited with a handful of MPI ranks, each rank made up of a number of cores from the coprocessor, and each using OpenMP within the rank.

Within an MPI rank, we can utilize OpenMP including its nesting capabilities. OpenMP nesting is turned off by default by most implementations, and is generally consider unsafe by typical users due to concerns of oversubscription and the resulting poor application performance. This chapter shows how properly using nested parallelism can boost performance.

One difference between nested parallelism as defined by OpenMP, and other similar solutions such as Intel Threading Building Blocks (TBB), is that OpenMP truly creates nested teams of threads. TBB (and OpenMP tasking) can have nested tasks, but the tasks themselves are executed by a single team of threads. The use of nested OpenMP thread teams is particularly valuable for modern SMP machines that have hierarchical (e.g., multilevel caches) memory systems. Outer teams can be created at higher levels of the hierarchy (e.g., cores) and inner teams can be created at lower levels of the hierarchy (e.g., hardware thread contexts). This chapter shows how exploiting nested parallelism can also take better advantage of hierarchical machine organization.

SCIENCE: BETTER APPROXIMATE SOLUTIONS

"The underlying physical laws necessary for a large part of physics and the whole of chemistry are thus completely known, and the difficulty is only that the exact applications of these laws lead to equations much too complicated to be soluble."—Dirac, P., 1929. Proc. R. Soc. Lond. 123 (792).

Much of theoretical physics and chemistry has been devoted to finding ever more accurate approximate solutions to the equations governing the behavior of matter at the quantum level. Through the decades, the coupling of more advanced methods with the exponential increase in computing power has led to progress from qualitatively correct models based on empirically determined parameters to truly first-principled calculations, that is, *ab initio* methods.

For a system with N electrons, the computational complexity in obtaining the exact solution grows as $O(e^N)$. The computation of the density functional theory (DFT) method, one of the most widely used electronic structure (ES) methods and the least expensive, grows as $O(N^3)$. The memory use increases with similar powers of N. Increasing computing power either by adding more computing processing units or by using more powerful computing units is the only way to enable more accurate simulations of larger quantum systems without increasing the time to solution, and thus sustaining the productivity of scientists (as measured by the number of discoveries in a given time).

Since distributed computers have become the mainstream platform for parallel computing, ES code developers have adopted the MPI as their primary parallel programming model. Numerous parallel ES codes are available to the community and have become invaluable tools in probing the ES properties of molecules and crystalline systems starting from the Si surface reconstruction in 1992. Quantum simulations are the enabling tools for the Materials Genome Initiatives, providing quantitative insights into critical materials (e.g., dielectric materials in microprocessors and batteries) that complement our understanding of the materials through experiments and theories. The demand for ever faster solutions for bigger and higher fidelity quantum simulations is greater than ever.

One of the main trends of HPC systems is the increasing parallelism available in a single SMP node. The average number of nodes of big clusters has not increased in recent years but the compute capacity of a node has been steadily increasing through multiple cores, multiple hardware threads per core, and wider single instruction multiple data (SIMD) units. Many-core architecture expands the parallelism on a node dramatically. For example, the current generation of Intel Xeon Phi coprocessors have up to 61 cores, 244 threads and a double-precision SIMD width of 8. While partitioning a node with MPI tasks (e.g., 61 or even 244 MPI tasks on a single coprocessor) is possible, one quickly realizes the limitations of such approaches: the memory available for each MPI task is limited; MPI communication overhead is higher due to more MPI data exchanges; collectives, such as `MPI_Allreduce` and `MPI_Alltoall`, scale $O(N_{MPI}\log N_{MPI})$ at best; and a fine-grained data partition at the MPI level results in latency-limited communication patterns.

The limitation of the pure MPI implementations is even more acute for the ES applications. The performance-limiting communication patterns of these methods are "collective" and require global communications either by reduction operations or by all-to-all data exchange. Employing fewer MPI tasks can benefit these applications by increasing per task computational density, while decreasing the communication-to-compute ratio. The amount of memory used in a run can be significantly reduced by eliminating data replications that are frequently used to lessen the impact of communication. The data exchange can take advantage of highly optimized asynchronous bulk DMA engines, facilitating complete overlaps of computations with the communications.

So, how can these applications effectively exploit the parallelism of SMP nodes based on many-core processors? In this chapter, we use a model application and computational kernels that capture the characteristics of this class of applications. We will expose the parallel opportunities of these applications and explore multiple ways to express the parallel algorithms with OpenMP. We analyze representative computational kernels to design a performance-portable parallel application that can adapt to the problem and the hardware.

ABOUT THE REFERENCE APPLICATION

The DFT methods map the $3N$-dimensional problems onto a coupled set of N three-dimensional problems using one-particle orbitals (bands) $\{\Psi\}$. The essence of the DFT methods are expressed as

$$E = \min_{\{\Psi\}} \sum_{\mathbf{k}}^{n_{\mathbf{k}}} w_{\mathbf{k}} \sum_{i}^{N} \sum_{j}^{N} \left(\hat{S}^{\mathbf{k}}\right)^{-1}_{i,j} \left(\Psi_j^{\mathbf{k}}\right)^{\dagger} \hat{H}_{\mathbf{k}} \Psi_i^{\mathbf{k}}, \tag{18.1}$$

where $\hat{S}^{\mathbf{k}}_{i,j} = \left(\Psi_i^{\mathbf{k}}\right)^{\dagger} \cdot \Psi_j^{\mathbf{k}}$. The theory is all captured by the Hamiltonian operator $\hat{H}^{\mathbf{k}}$ and a wide range of approximate forms to the exact Hamiltonian are used in real simulations. The only important information of this operator for our readers is that (i) it depends on $\{\Psi\}$ under the constraint that the inverse of the overlap matrix $\hat{S}$ exists and (ii) we can compute $\hat{H}_{\mathbf{k}}\Psi$. The self-consistent nature of the solution results in iterative methods which update $\{\Psi\}$ until the solution, the minimum energy, has been reached. The subscript $\mathbf{k}$ denotes the $\mathbf{k}$-points introduced to handle the periodic boundary conditions of a crystalline system. To reduce computational cost, the selection of the $\mathbf{k}$-points exploits the symmetry of the computational unit cell, where the weight $w_{\mathbf{k}}$ includes all the contributions from the equivalent $\mathbf{k}$-points in the Brillouin zone of the simulation cell (see Figure 18.1 for an example).

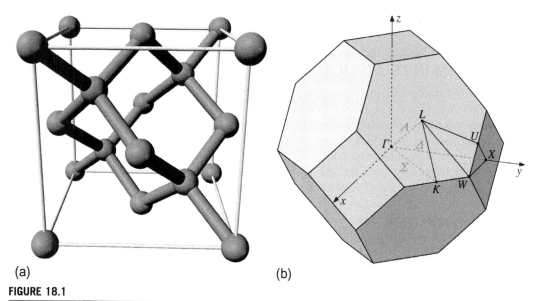

(a)   (b)

FIGURE 18.1

(a) Ball-and-stick rendering of crystalline silicon in a diamond structure. The box shows the boundary of a 8-atom unit cell. (b) The Brillouin zone of a 2-atom diamond structure.

The computation at each $\mathbf{k}$ is independent at each self-consistent field method (SCF) step and the number of SCF cycles vary from a few to hundreds depending upon the chosen algorithm and materials properties. To accelerate the convergence to the solution, extra bands are employed and N_{band}^{tot} denotes the total number of bands used in the figure computations.

The representation of Ψ is arbitrary and any nonsingular basis set can be used, for example, δ-functions on a regular spatial 3D grid or Gaussian orbitals centered at the ions. The computational details of $\hat{H}_{\mathbf{k}}\Psi$ depend on Ψ. For the concreteness of our discussions, we will use plane-wave basis sets to represent each Ψ as

$$\Psi_i^{\mathbf{k}}(\mathbf{r}) = \sum_{\mathbf{G}} C_{i,\mathbf{k}}^{\mathbf{G}} \exp^{(i\mathbf{r}\cdot\mathbf{G})}, \tag{18.2}$$

where $\mathbf{G}$ denote the plane-wave basis set. For an orthorhombic cell of $L_x \times L_y \times L_z$, $\mathbf{G} = (n_x 2\pi/L_x, n_y 2\pi/L_y, n_z 2\pi/L_z)$ where n_x, n_y, and n_z are integers. The coefficients $C_{i,\mathbf{k}}^{\mathbf{G}}$ are the variables to be updated during the SCF cycles. In the plane-wave basis set, a part of $\hat{H}_{\mathbf{k}}\Psi$ is performed in the spectral space, while some terms are computed in $\mathbf{r}$ on the spatial grid, thus requiring a 3D Fast Fourier transform (FFT) of the bands during an SCF cycle.

There are important characteristics of the ES simulations that will impact how we parallelize these applications with OpenMP as well as with MPI.

- The number of electrons N varies from few to 10^4.
- The number of $N_{\mathbf{k}}$ ranges from 1 to 10^6 depending upon the desired accuracy and the intended use of these bands.
- Fewer $N_{\mathbf{k}}$ are used for bigger N. For large-scale simulations or molecular systems, $N_{\mathbf{k}} = 1$.
- The size of the plane-wave basis set, $N_{\mathbf{G}}$, increases as N (the volume of the unit cell) and the target accuracy of the solution. Typically, $N_{\mathbf{G}} > 10^3$.

PARALLELISM IN ES APPLICATIONS

Equation (18.1) manifests the inherent parallel opportunities that exist in the DFT methods. The loosely coupled computations at each $\mathbf{k}$-point are carried out independently and the reduction over the $\mathbf{k}$-points is performed after the completion of the computations. MPI supports process grouping capability to form a virtual communicator (MPI Group) consisting of a subset of MPI tasks. Using these MPI Group routines, an application can map each $\mathbf{k}$-point or a set of $\mathbf{k}$-points onto an MPI group of N_{MPI} tasks and distribute N_{band}^{tot} bands over the tasks. The tasks within an MPI group are tightly coupled as the double loop $\sum_i \sum_j$ implies. The shaded block in Figure 18.2 represents the data owned by an MPI task. This data partition is commonly used by ES applications and will be the baseline of our experiments.

Each band can be further broken into multiple tasks, necessitating a distributed memory (cluster) FFT with all-to-all transpose. The optimal data distribution will depend on many factors. For large problems $N_{\mathbf{G}} \gg 1$, it may not be feasible for a task to own a complete band. Also, there are algorithms that can benefit from distributing the bands over the tasks. These are the implementation details of a real application that need to be addressed by the developers at the design stage to optimize the use of MPI and will not be discussed further here. However, the principal findings of this chapter that show the advantage of OpenMP within an SMP node are applicable to any data-partition scheme at the MPI level.

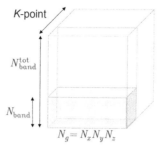

FIGURE 18.2

The simulation parameters and a prototype data distribution in a ES code.

Assuming the data partition scheme of Figure 18.2, the computation for each MPI task can be simplified as shown in Figure 18.3. We make a further simplification by choosing N_{band} to be identical for each MPI task. This is not a requirement but is a common practice adopted by applications to load balance among the tasks. The details of what is involved in do_mpi are critical for the performance and the scalability. We assume that the applications have adopted the best solutions within their implementation.

```
1   void main()
2   {
3     int nband_tot=480;
4     int nband=nband_tot/mpi_tasks;
5     PWBands  psi(nband);
6     PWBands*  psi_remote=&psi;
7
8     for(int ip=0; ip<mpi_tasks; ++ip)
9     {
10      for(int i=0; i<nband; ++i)
11      {
12        fft(psi[i]);
13        compute_g(psi[i],psi_remote);
14        ifft(psi[i]);
15        compute_r(psi[i],psi_remote);
16      }
17      do_mpi(...); //visit all the remote bands
18    }
19  }
20
21  void compute_g(PWBand& me, PWBand* others)
22  {
23    const int i= me.id;
24    const int mband=others->size();
25    Matrix overlap(nband,mband);
26    for(int j=0; j<mband; ++j)
27      overlap(i,j)=dot(me,others[j]);
28    for(int x=0; x<nions; ++x)
29      do_more(me,x,others);//gemm,gemv,
30  }
```

FIGURE 18.3

A pseudo plane-wave ES code.

The typical computation within the loop over N_{band} (lines 12-15 in Figure 18.3) includes forward and backward FFT transformations and computations in the real and spectral spaces. compute_g shows the kind of computations that are performed to complete the innermost loop over j in Figure 18.3. Similar computational patterns appear in compute_r.

Astute readers will quickly observe that the parallelization of the loop over the bands is straightforward. This is, in fact, how the MPI parallelization is done and the communication is coordinated to allow independent tasks with local bands and remote bands. The key computation kernels can be further parallelized. Intel's MKL library provides highly optimized threaded implementations for FFT. The inner loops (lines 26 and 28 in Figure 18.3) have sufficient parallel work to do as long as do_more is implemented in a thread-safe way. Trusting our ability to remove any write conflicts and to avoid well-known pitfalls of OpenMP, we arrive at an OpenMP parallelized application in Figure 18.4.

We have discovered that multiple-level of parallelisms exist in the DFT method and learned that standard features provided by MPI to group processes, and by OpenMP to nest parallel regions, allow composable codes that can express the parallelism in a flexible way. Now, let us examine how this approach can improve the performance of these applications on Intel Xeon Phi architectures and perform numerical experiments to make projections of realistic problems on a given computational node.

```
1   void main()
2   {
3     int nband_tot=480;
4     int nband=nband_tot/mpi_tasks;
5     PWBands  psi(nband);
6     PWBands*  psi_remote=&psi;
7
8     for(int ip=0; ip<mpi_tasks; ++ip)
9     {
10  #pragma omp parallel for
11      for(int i=0; i<nband; ++i)
12      {
13        fft(psi[i]);
14        compute_g(psi[i],psi_remote);
15        ifft(psi[i]);
16        compute_r(psi[i],psi_remote);
17      }
18      do_mpi(...); //visit all the remote bands
19    }
20  }
21
22  void compute_g(PWBand& me, PWBand* others)
23  {
24    const int i= me.id;
25    const int mband=others->size();
26    Matrix overlap(nband,mband);
27  #pragma omp parallel
28    {
29  #pragma omp for nowait
30      for(int j=0; j<mband; ++j)
31        overlap(i,j)=dot(me,others[j]);
32  #pragma omp for
33      for(int x=0; x<nions; ++x)
34        do_more(me,x,others);//gemm,gemv,
35    }
36  }
```

FIGURE 18.4

A pseudo plane-wave code with nested OpenMP parallelization.

MULTICORE AND MANY-CORE ARCHITECTURES FOR QUANTUM SIMULATIONS

Multicore and many-core processors are all similar. They consist of a number of cores. Each core typically has its own L1 caches, and may have its own L2 cache or may share that cache with another core. Multicore processors usually have an additional shared L3 cache, while many-core processors do not.

The cores are connected by some form of network. Memory is also connected to that network. This often leads to a nonuniform memory architecture (NUMA) in which some memory is closer to a given core than other memory. Multi-socket systems always have NUMA characteristics.

Since access to cache is many times faster than access to main memory, it is important to optimize algorithms so that they reuse data from cache as much as possible. Many ES applications have already done this sort of optimization. This also helps to mitigate any issues caused by the NUMA architecture.

Each core has two or more hardware threads, which share the core's resources but have their own register states and other internal state. Using hardware threads is a good way to hide memory latency; one thread can compute while another thread is waiting for a memory operation to complete. When the memory result is available the hardware will execute the waiting thread.

Cores also have SIMD (aka vector) units, enabling them to operate on several integer or floating-point numbers at the same time. Compilers will usually automatically vectorize innermost loops (e.g., over N_G). The user can assist with directives and by assuring that data are properly aligned and padded to fit the SIMD width.

Intel provides optimized FFT and BLAS libraries that are tuned for multicore and many-core architectures, so, in many cases, the application writer will find that much of the work has already been done.

OpenMP 4.0 AFFINITY AND HOT TEAMS OF INTEL OpenMP RUNTIME

A node contains multiple parallel units—multiple cores, multiple sockets, multiple hardware threads, and optionally coprocessors. The ability to bind OpenMP threads to physical processing units has become increasingly important to achieve high performance on these modern CPUs. OpenMP 4.0 affinity features provide standard ways to control thread affinity that can have a dramatic performance effect. This impact is especially true on current generation Intel Xeon Phi coprocessors: four hardware threads share the L1/L2 cache of an in-order core. We use OpenMP runtime environments to optimally bind MPI tasks and OpenMP threads. For instance, when using 5 MPI and 12 OpenMP threads for the band loop and 4 OpenMP threads for compute, they are set as

```
export OMP_NESTED=true
export OMP_NUM_THREADS=12,4
export OMP_PLACES=threads
export OMP_PROC_BIND=spread,close
mpirun -np 5 ./myapp
```

By default, Intel MPI runtime will partition the 5 MPI ranks over 60 cores so that each MPI task is allocated 12 cores. The OpenMP 4.0 affinity environment variables, OMP_PLACES and OMP_PROC_BIND, are set to bind one top-level thread per core and to bind four second-level threads (including the single top-level thread) to the hardware threads on the core.

Nested OpenMP is an optional feature of the OpenMP standard. Its support is subject to the compilers and runtime libraries. The default is to ignore OpenMP parallel regions within a running parallel region; in OpenMP parlance, the nested regions are serialized. This can be overridden by setting OMP_NESTED=true. The Intel OpenMP runtime has greatly improved performance for nested OpenMP since releasing Intel Composer XE 15.1 with so-called HOT_TEAMS. They are enabled in our experiments by setting these environment variables:

```
export KMP_HOT_TEAMS_MODE=1
export KMP_HOT_TEAMS_MAX_LEVEL=2
export MKL_DYNAMIC=false
```

Note that we set MKL_DYNAMIC=false so that MKL library does not override the number of threads for DGEMM or FFT when they are used within an OpenMP parallel region.

HOT TEAMS MOTIVATION

"Hot teams" is an extension to OpenMP supported by the Intel runtimes that can substantially reduce the overhead of OpenMP parallelism. It works with standard OpenMP code but enhances performance. It is a logical extension that may inspire similar capabilities in other implementations.

To understand "hot teams," it is important to know that any modern implementation of OpenMP, in order to avoid the cost of creating and destroying pthreads, has the OpenMP runtime maintain a pool of OS threads (pthreads on Linux) that it has already created. This is standard practice in OpenMP runtimes because OS thread creation is normally quite expensive.

However, OpenMP also has a concept of a thread team, which is the set of pthreads that will execute a given parallel region. The thread team is a set of internal data-structures that determine which pthreads will be used, what the enumeration is (value of omp_get_thread_num()), values for OpenMP "internal control variables," and how the runtime will communicate when performing barriers or fork/join using the team. Since its almost always the case that an OpenMP program will execute many parallel regions with the same set of parameters (number of threads), as well as keeping the threads themselves alive, we keep the team structure alive. Teams whose teams structure already exists are "hot," because we expect them to be reused, and we already have the data structure created, so avoid the cost of tearing it down at the end of a parallel region only to recreate it at the next.

Traditionally, a runtime had only one hot team, for the top-level parallel region. Any teams used for nested parallel regions were created each time they were needed and destroyed again at the end of the parallel region.

Since nested parallelism has become more important (for instance with people using 60 threads at the outer level, for a coprocessor, and then 60 four-thread teams inside that), Intel implemented support for "nested hot teams."

These hot teams are controlled by the KMP_HOT_TEAMS environment variable. The value set will be the maximum depth for which hot teams will be maintained. The default is 1, which replicates the previous behavior so that only the outermost parallel region is treated as a hot team.

By setting KMP_HOT_TEAMS=2, the team structures will be maintained for two levels of parallelism. For this to make sense you also must have OMP_NESTED=true.

The effect of this is that code such as

```
1  #pragma omp parallel num_threads(60)
2  {
3    for (int i=0; i<1000000; i++)
4    {
5  #pragma omp parallel num_threads(4)
6    . . .
7    }
8  }
```

should run faster, because with `KMP_HOT_TEAMS=2` the runtime creates the 60 inner teams once and does not destroy them. Without this, the runtime would create and destroy them a million times.

The extension is Intel specific, the `KMP_` prefix tells us that. Things defined in the OpenMP standard all have an `OMP_` prefix.

This capability applies to both processors and coprocessors. `KMP_HOT_TEAMS_MAX_LEVEL` and `KMP_HOT_TEAMS_MODE` are documented starting in the Intel OpenMP documentation for the 15.1 compilers (January 2015).

SETTING UP EXPERIMENTS

The primary motivations of using parallel computers and developing parallel applications are to solve problems faster, to solve bigger and longer problems, and to solve more complex problems. Some users will pay for more resources to solve a problem faster, while some users will choose to use less resources per simulation to maximize the total number of simulations. In all cases, the goal is to maximize productivity by optimally utilizing the available resources. Any attempt to parallelize applications should deliver sustained throughput, while reducing the time-to-solution. In the following sections, we will show that multilevel parallel applications using hybrid MPI and OpenMP programming can deliver high performance on modern CPU architectures, especially on Intel Xeon Phi coprocessors. We will show how the developers design their applications to exploit the microarchitectures and future-proof them and how the users use these high performance applications and resources to maximize their science outcome.

Inspection of the profile of real DFT simulations reveals that the top hotspots of these applications are mostly MKL routines, FFT, xGEMM (DGEMM or ZGEMM), xGEMV, and other BLAS functions. One possible solution to enable OpenMP in existing MPI applications is to use threaded numerical libraries and, in fact, that has been common practice by the developers. The effectiveness of this solution varies widely depending upon the problem size and how these library routines are used in the user code. In general, the matrix sizes for BLAS operations are small (10-1000). It is well known that the performance of BLAS on small matrices is low compared to that of large matrices on any architecture. By parallelizing the local band with OpenMP, these computations are executed concurrently and the lack of performance or scalability of these routines becomes immaterial. This so-called "batched" method turns out to be a simple but very effective solution to obtain high performance of these applications, independent of the problem size and the resources.

Our starting point for the model application employs MPI to parallelize over the entire set of bands. Taking advantage of the concurrent nature of the computations between MPI communications, we parallelize the loop over the local bands using OpenMP as shown in Figure 18.4. The computation per band can be abstracted as a series of computational kernels, such as FFT. There may be dependences between computational kernels. For instance, compute_g needs the result of the forward FFT of each band. Regardless of the complexity of the operations for a band, they can be executed in parallel using any number of OpenMP threads N_{OMP}. We use $N_{band} = nN_{OMP}$ where n is an integer. This choice puts a constraint on N_{band}^{tot} but does not affect the fidelity of the result or overall performance.

Figure 18.5 shows how the test code measures the performance of one compute kernel. The test is set up to use any number of MPI tasks and OpenMP threads and to vary problem sizes to mimic the real applications. The initialization and finalization steps are omitted for brevity. The timers are placed to exclude any MPI overhead and the maximum of the compute time is used to measure the throughputs and the wall-clock time per operation for each kernel. Note that the total number of computations (nband_tot*niters) is fixed for any combination of MPI and OpenMP.

The download file includes mini apps (dgemm.cpp, fft3d.cpp, and diffusion.c) that are used to generate the data in the following sections. Makefile and run scripts on Intel Xeon Phi coprocessor 7120P (61 cores) and Intel® Xeon® processor E5-2697 (dual socket, 14 cores per socket) are also included in the file. We use MPI, OMP, MKL to denote the number of MPI tasks, the number of OpenMP threads at the band level and the number of OpenMP threads in the nested parallel regions, respectively. Note that the code examples in the text do not match to the real codes literally but are used to highlight the key concepts.

MPI VERSUS OpenMP

First, we address an important question: "Is the additional use of OpenMP profitable?" Although we have assumed that the parallelization over the local bands using OpenMP is as simple as putting a pragma omp parallel for, the reality is much more complicated. Real applications have much more complex data and logic dependences and correctly parallelizing this loop is not as simple as we have

```
1   void dft_kernel(int nband_tot, int niters)
2   {
3     int nband=nband_tot/mpi_task;
4     PWBand  psi[nband];
5     double start=time();
6   #pragma omp parallel
7     {
8        for(int t=0; t<niters; ++t)
9   #pragma omp for
10          for(int i=0; i<nband; ++i)
11            compute(psi[i]);
12     }
13     double dt=time()-start;
14     mpi_allreduce(dt,MPI_MAX);
15   }
```

FIGURE 18.5

A pseudo code to test a compute kernel. PWBand includes all the abstraction to manage nband bands for each task. Two main applications fft3d.cpp and dgemm.cpp in the download files replace compute by 3D FFT and dgemm calls, respectively.

pretended in our model application and the mini apps. Achieving high performance may require fundamental changes in the applications.

The main difference between MPI and OpenMP in parallelizing the primary loop over the band is how the data are allocated and initialized. The data locality is enforced in MPI: each task owns its data and there is no conflict in terms of read or write and of cache interference.

In an OpenMP program, many threads are all sharing the same address space and may thus suffer from factors such as false sharing (where two different threads are accessing different parts of the same cache line). NUMAs can also interfere with performance, because data may be allocated in "far" memory. Policies such as first-touch in modern operating systems alleviate this; in particular, it is helpful to initialize data structures in parallel, so that the thread that initializes a piece of data is also the thread that will work on that data. The mini apps, `dgemm.cpp` and `fft3d.cpp`, employ this allocation-and-initialization per thread method to maximize the data locality.

Because of these intricate memory policies and because of other overhead (such as starting the OpenMP threads the first time), the experiments ignore the timings for initialization and for the first call to any MKL routine.

Figure 18.6a shows the performance of a batch of 240 DGEMMs on an Intel Xeon Phi coprocessor 7120P for the problem sizes for which using 240 MPI tasks is feasible. These results, which can be also reproduced on any Intel Xeon processors as shown in Figure 18.6b, should assure developers that OpenMP itself does not compromise performance compared to MPI. The performance gain coming from the expanded memory available for the applications is obvious: there is no more need to waste cores by using fewer MPI tasks per node because the memory demand is high. In real simulations, this flexibility of mixing MPI and OpenMP at the same efficiency allows the users to partition a node to meet the memory requirement, to minimize any NUMA impact, and to optimize the on-node and off-node communications.

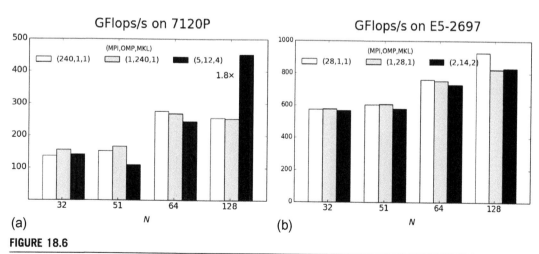

FIGURE 18.6

Total GFlop/s of concurrent DGEMMs C=A(N,N)*B(N,N) (a) on Intel® Xeon Phi™ coprocessor 7120P @1.24 GHz and (b) on Intel® Xeon® processor E5-2697 @2.60 GHz, each size N tested with all MPI, all OpenMP, and hybrid of OpenMP/MKL within MPI.

Now, we will exercise several kinds of parallelism: MPI and OpenMP parallelization over the bands and nested OpenMP parallelization within a `compute` kernel.

DGEMM EXPERIMENTS

The total throughputs (GFlop/s) of 60 DGEMMS of various square matrices are presented in Figures 18.7a and 18.8a. The overall performance is not sensitive to the choice of MPI and OpenMP at the primary parallelization level over the bands. Using five MPI tasks and 12 OpenMP threads will optimize the throughput for this range of N on Intel Xeon Phi coprocessors. The overhead of nested OpenMP grows as more OpenMP threads are used to parallelize the bands and it becomes more noticeable when the problem size is small, because the compute time becomes small compared to the synchronization time. The same trends are observed on Intel Xeon processor E5-2697 as shown in Figure 18.7b.

The additional parallelization provided by the MKL library boosts the performance by as much as $1.8\times$ for $N = 128$: 455 GFlop/s compared to 250 GFlop/s with 240 MPI tasks (or OpenMP threads) in Figure 18.6. We attribute the improved performance with `MKL_NUM_THREADS=4` to higher cache hits and reduced TLB pressure. This is directly translated into reduced time-to-solution by the same factor through the use of nested OpenMP without any extra investment by the developers.

Traditionally, HPC applications (with at most two hyperthreads per core) have not made much use of hyperthreading on Xeon. In fact, many Xeon machines are booted with hyperthreading disabled. One reason for this is that the out-of-order nature of Xeon cores provides many of the benefits, such as latency tolerance, that are provided by the extra threads on Intel Xeon Phi coprocessor. Another reason is that naive thread scheduling will often unexpectedly place two threads on the same core, resulting in performance degradation (since there is only one set of caches and computational units). However, using the techniques described here allow hyperthreads to improve performance over using a single

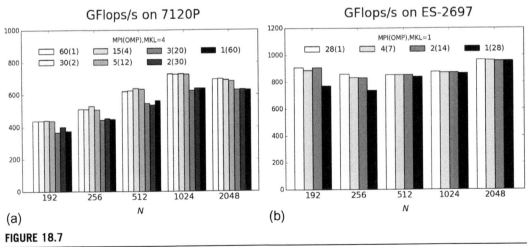

FIGURE 18.7

Total throughputs in GFlops/s of DGEMMs (a) on a 7120P and (b) on a E5-2697 node. The number of concurrent DGEMMs is the number of cores per node: (a) 60 and (b) 28. Each size N tested with different number of MPI ranks using OpenMP when rank count is less than core count.

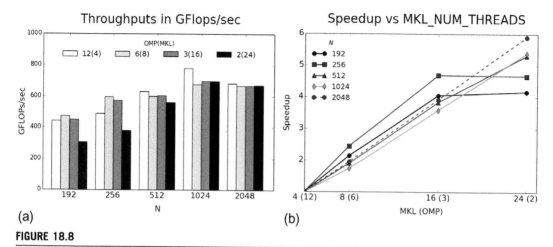

FIGURE 18.8

DGEMMs on 7120P: (a) total throughputs in GFlops/s of DGEMMs and (b) speedup ($T_{MKL=4}/T_{MKL}$) with respect to `MPI_NUM_THREADS=4`. The number of MPI tasks is fixed at 5.

thread per core, by adding an additional level of latency tolerance and also by keeping the core busy with instructions issued by two threads at once. Using both threads does come at the cost of a reduction in the resources used for out-of-order execution. This is evident in the case of DGEMM. In contrast to Intel Xeon Phi coprocessors, using two hardware threads per core to perform a DGEMM does not boost the performance on Intel Xeon processors as shown in Figure 18.6b.

Our goal is not only to obtain sustained performance with the multilevel parallel schemes. We also seek to reduce the time-to-solution using more resources. This can be achieved by using more threads to perform each DGEMM while using more compute nodes. Figure 18.8 shows the throughputs (GFlops/s/node) and the speedup, $T_{MKL=4}/T_{MKL}$, where T denotes the time per DGEMM. We choose 5 MPI tasks per node, which gives the optimal performance on Intel Xeon Phi coprocessor. The speedup of $N = 2048$ is close to ideal, linear to `MKL_NUM_THREADS`. Figure 18.9 presents the speedup on Intel[®] Xeon[®] processor E5-2697.

FFT EXPERIMENTS

The performance characteristics of FFT kernels are similar to DGEMM as shown in Figures 18.10 and 18.11. The scalability of FFT for typical problem sizes of $N \sim 100$-1000 is excellent over a wide range of `MKL_NUM_THREADS`. The only factor for production runs is the amount of memory needed to represent a complete band and the resources (core hours and human time) they can afford for each simulation.

USER CODE EXPERIMENTS

Our experiments with a batch of DGEMMs and FFTs show that applications can reap the benefits of the parallel capacity of a node by exploiting MPI and OpenMP standards and optimized numerical libraries. The parallel opportunities that exist in the applications are mapped to MPI tasks and OpenMP threads to decrease the memory use and maximize throughputs in the weak-scaling and strong-scaling

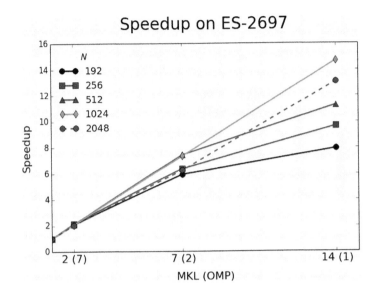

FIGURE 18.9

Speedup of DGEMM ($T_{MKL=1}/T_{MKL}$) on Intel® Xeon® processor E5-2697. The number of MPI tasks is fixed at 2, that is, one per socket.

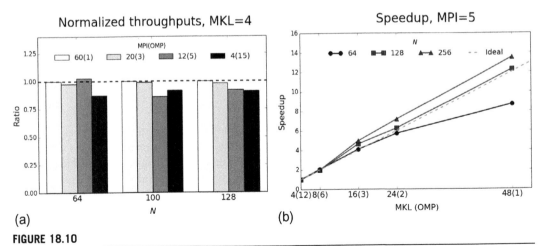

(a)   (b)

FIGURE 18.10

On 7120P: (a) the throughputs (number of FFT transforms per second) normalized by those at 60 MPI tasks and 1 OpenMP, while using `MKL_NUM_THREADS = 4`. (b) Strong scaling of FFT of $N_{FFT} = N^3$ with respect to `MKL_NUM_THREADS`. The number of MPI tasks is fixed at 5.

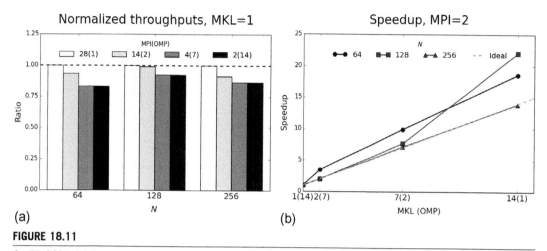

FIGURE 18.11

On E5-2697, (a) the throughputs (number of FFT transforms per second) normalized by those at 2 MPI tasks and 14 OpenMP, while using `MKL_NUM_THREADS=1`. (b) Strong scaling of FFT of $N_{FFT} = N^3$ with respect to `MKL_NUM_THREADS`. The number of MPI tasks is fixed at 2.

use modes. Now, we turn our attention to user codes and discuss how we can apply similar techniques to boost their performance.

We use the 3D diffusion code (referenced below) as a prototype. The stencil operations on a regular 3D grid of the diffusion code are representative of the class of computations performed by `compute_r` in the ES codes. We will skip the discussion of the performance of hybrid MPI/OpenMP of a user kernel at the band level, since there are no special properties of these kernels that will prevent the same parallel performance with any distribution of the bands over MPI and OpenMP. The performance of the nested OpenMP is predictable when this kernel is called within the band loop.

A more interesting scenario we will consider is when this user code is used at the same level of the band loop as shown in Figure 18.12. This is the realistic use case. For instance, the computations of Coulomb interactions between the electrons and ions in the ES codes use the charge density, $\rho(\mathbf{r}) = \sum_{\mathbf{k}} w_{\mathbf{k}} \sum_i |\Psi_i^{\mathbf{k}}(\mathbf{r})|^2$, that is computed in the preceding loop over the bands.

Amdahl's scaling law states that the speedup of parallel computing is limited by the sequential fraction of the program and we need to make sure the user codes (e.g., `diffusion`) do not limit the performance of the applications.

The diffusion code used in our experiments has been already parallelized by OpenMP and several optimizations were made to achieve high performance on Intel Xeon Phi coprocessors as discussed in Chapter 5 in High Performance Parallelism Pearls (HPPP), ©2015, James Reinders and Jim Jeffers, Morgan Kaufmann Publications. We use the tiled version of the diffusion code in Figure 5.3 (p. 91) in HPPP as the reference. We recommend the readers to review the step-by-step improvement in the diffusion code through padding, cache blocking, and peeling as detailed by Dempsey. Finally, `collapse(2)` is used to extract enough parallelisms after the blocking and `pragma vector nontemporal` to increase streaming storage bandwidth. All these resulted in 10× speedup over the basic OpenMP code which is included in `diffusion.c`.

```
1   void main()
2   {
3     int nband_tot=480;
4     int nband=nband_tot/mpi_tasks;
5     PWBands  psi(nband);
6     PWBands*  psi_remote=&psi;
7
8     for(int ip=0; ip<mpi_tasks; ++ip)
9     {
10  #pragma omp parallel for
11      for(int i=0; i<nband; ++i)
12      {
13        //do_band
14      }
15      do_mpi(...); //visit all the remote bands
16    }
17
18    diffusion();
19  }
```

FIGURE 18.12

A pseudo code showing diffusion following the computation over the bands. The mini application diffusion.c in the download files only measures the performance of diffusion kernel.

When nested OpenMP is disabled at runtime, the reference implementation will utilize the same pool of OpenMP threads as the rest of the application. With nested OpenMP enabled, only a fraction of the active threads will be used for the computation. This loss of resource utilization can be ignored, if the gain in other parts is great. But, let us assume that diffusion is an important hotspot that can potentially become the bottleneck once everything else is fully parallelized and optimized.

A solution is to restructure the loops to expose the two-level parallelism. The use of collapse(2) provides a hint that the diffusion code can be expressed as a double loop: the outer loop over z and the inner loop over y. Recall that this optimizes the hyper-thread phalanx effect (HPPP) and therefore we express the nested parallelism to preserve this data access pattern. Figure 18.13 shows the main part of the reference implementation diffusion_tiled and the modified version with nested OpenMP diffusion_nested. We introduce a precomputed range array majorIndex using a simple blocking method. The load difference between the primary threads is 1 at worst and is perfect if nz%OMP=0. It is straightforward to explicitly partition the y-loop at the initialization stage using the same method and use the precomputed ranges for the computation instead of parallel for in line 11 in Figure 18.13b. Also shown is diffusion_twoyz. This explicit "2D" method does not use nested OpenMP. Instead, it partitions the data and the threads to accomplish the same data access pattern of the tiled and nested OpenMP methods using minorIndex. np_minor is equivalent to the number threads of the nested OMP region in diffusion_nested.

Figure 18.14 presents the speed up of various diffusion implementations over Tiled(60) using 60 threads (cores) by setting

```
export OMP_PLACES=cores
export OMP_PROC_BIND=close
```

Alternatively KMP_AFFINITY can be set for the same thread placement. In addition to Tiled(240) and nested OpenMP, Figure 18.14 shows the speedup of alternative implementations: (i) PC and PCO using

(a)

```
1   void diffusion_tiled(REAL *f1, REAL *f2, ...) {
2   #pragma omp parallel
3     for (int i = 0; i < count; ++i)
4     {
5       REAL *f1_t = (i&1)?f2:f1;
6       REAL *f2_t = (i&1)?f1:f2;
7   #define YBF 14
8   #pragma omp for collapse(2)
9       for (int yy = 0; yy < ny; yy += YBF) {
10        for (int z = 0; z < nz; z++) {
11          int ymax = yy + YBF;
12          if (ymax >= ny) ymax = ny;
13          for (int y = yy; y < ymax; y++) {
14            //computation on x-axis at[z][y][x]
15          }
16        }
17      }
18  #pragma omp barrier
19    }}
```

(b)

```
1   void diffusion_nested(REAL *f1, REAL *f2, ... {
2   #pragma omp parallel
3     for (int i = 0; i < count; ++i)
4     {
5       REAL *f1_t = (i&1)?f2:f1;
6       REAL *f2_t = (i&1)?f1:f2;
7       const int ip=omp_get_thread_num();
8       const int z0=majorIndex[ip];
9       const int z1=majorIndex[ip+1];
10
11  #pragma omp parallel for firstprivate(z0,z1)
12      for(int y=0; y<ny; y++){
13        for (int z = z0; z < z1; z++) {
14          //computation on x-axis at[z][y][x]
15        }
16      }
17  #pragma omp barrier
18    }}
```

(c)

```
1   void diffusion_twoyz(REAL *f1, REAL *f2, ...) {
2   #pragma omp parallel
3     for (int i = 0; i < count; ++i)
4     {
5       REAL *f1_t = (i&1)?f2:f1;
6       REAL *f2_t = (i&1)?f1:f2;
7       const int ipz=omp_get_thread_num()/np_minor;
8       const int ipy=omp_get_thread_num()%np_minor;
9       const int z0=majorIndex[ipz];
10      const int z1=majorIndex[ipz+1];
11      const int y0=minorIndex[ipy];
12      const int y1=minorIndex[ipy+1];
13
14      for (int z = z0; z < z1; z++) {
15        for(int y=y0; y<y1; y++){
16          //computation on x-axis at[z][y][x]
17        }
18      }
19  #pragma omp barrier
20    }}
```

FIGURE 18.13

Code snippets of (a) diffusion_tiled, the reference diffusion, (b) diffusion_nested, and
(c) diffusion_twoyz. The full implementations are in diffusion.c.

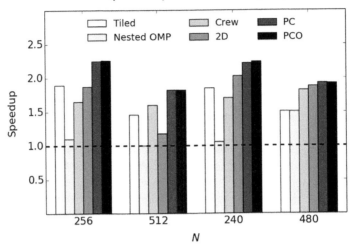

FIGURE 18.14

Speedup of alternative OpenMP parallel implementations of `diffusion` over `diffusion_tiled` using 60 threads; 240 threads are used for Tiled(240), nested OpenMP, Crew, and 2D, while 244 threads are used for PC (PlesioChronous) and PCO (PC over the outer loop).

plesiochronous phasing barriers by J. Dempsey (Chapter 5 in HPPP), (ii) Crew using experimental Intel compiler directives developed by A. Robison, J. Cownie, and X. Tian for the nested parallel region on Intel Xeon Phi coprocessors, and (iii) 2D, an explicit data partition scheme.

Using more hardware threads per core on Intel Xeon Phi coprocessors is beneficial, as indicated by 1.5-2× speedup of `diffusion_tile` using 240 threads. The benefit of using nested OpenMP is not big, but it does not negatively affect the performance for the same number of primary threads. This simply reflects the overhead of implicit barriers and synchronizations of the nested parallel regions as dictated by OpenMP standards. On the other hand, the speedup of nested OpenMP at N=480 is as good as other methods. The performance of Crew which has less overhead than OpenMP indicates that further improvement of OpenMP runtime is possible. Figure 18.15 shows the relative performance of two methods shown in Figure 18.13 on Intel Xeon processor E5-2697. Note that nested OpenMP boosts the performance significantly on Intel Xeon processors. All these suggest that we have several knobs to maximize the performance. It is only a matter of determining what is the optimal granularity for the data partition over the distributed memory space (MPI tasks) and for the computation in a shared memory space (OpenMP threads).

SUMMARY: TRY MULTILEVEL PARALLELISM IN YOUR APPLICATIONS

We have demonstrated that the multilevel parallel methods based on MPI and OpenMP standards provide developers with flexible parallel programming tools. Many resources like MKL and community libraries are available to further enhance the productivity of the developers and the users. How can we exploit these tools in your applications?

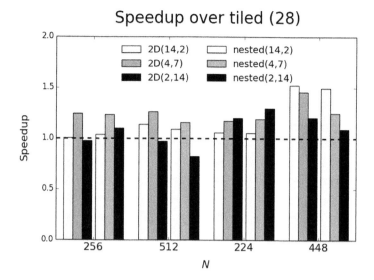

FIGURE 18.15

Speedup of alternative OpenMP parallel implementations of `diffusion_twoyz` (2D) and `diffusion_nested` (nested) over `diffusion_tiled` using 28 threads on Intel® Xeon® processor E5-2697.

The starting point is to determine the data distribution to minimize the memory use and data movement between MPI tasks and to maximize concurrent computations between data exchange. The data partition must meet the requirements of good high performance parallel programming.

- *Load balance*: In parallel computing, the slowest parallel unit sets the time scale of a simulation and ensuring the load balance at all parallel levels is critical for high performance.
- *Computational granularity*: `compute` units are structured to extend the computation time between implicit/explicit synchronizations and hide data movement.
- *Data locality*: Increasing both temporal and spatial locality is essential on cache-based architectures such as Intel Xeon processors and Intel Xeon Phi coprocessors.

Once the best design decision is made, applying OpenMP to parallelize the task can become as simple as placing `pragma omp parallel` as in our model application.

FOR MORE INFORMATION

We thank Jim Dempsey for useful discussion and for sharing his diffusion codes.

- Brommer, K.D., Needels, M., Larson, B., Joannopoulos, J.D., 1992. *Ab initio* theory of the Si(111)-(7×7) surface reconstruction: a challenge for massively parallel computation. Phys. Rev. Lett. 68, 1355-1358.
- Dempsey, J., 2014. Plesiochronous phasing barriers. In: High Performance Parallelism Pearls: Multicore and Many-Core Programming Approaches. Morgan Kaufmann, Waltham, MA, pp. 87-115.

- Hohenberg, P., Kohn, W., 1964. Inhomogeneous electron gas. Phys. Rev. 136, B864-B871.
- Mills, B., 2007. Ball-and-Stick Model of the Unit Cell of Silicon. http://commons.wikimedia.org/wiki/File:Silicon-unit-cell-3D-balls.png
- Wikipedia, 2008. A diagram of the first Brillouin zone of a face-centred cubic (FCC) lattice. http://commons.wikimedia.org/wiki/File:Brillouin_Zone_(1st,_FCC).svg

Download all codes from this, and other chapters: http://lotsofcores.com.

OpenCL: THERE AND BACK AGAIN

19

Matthias Noack*, Florian Wende*, Klaus-Dieter Oertel[†]

Zuse Institute Berlin, Germany* Intel Corporation, Germany[†]

This chapter presents a case study on optimizing the Hexciton kernel of the GPU-HEOM code for multicore and many-core processors. We start with a naive reference implementation and develop a fully optimized OpenCL kernel by analyzing different optimization techniques. For instance, we compare automatic and manual vectorization, optimize the memory layout for contiguous vector loads and locality, and exploit the runtime kernel-compilation in OpenCL. We shed some light on the question of portable performance by comparing the tuned kernels with a GPGPU optimized implementation. In the second part, we port the OpenCL kernel back to native C++ by using a generalizable approach to replace the OpenCL-runtime with OpenMP 4.0 constructs. For manual vectorization, we replace OpenCL's vector types with C++ equivalents that encapsulate SIMD intrinsics. These are provided by different third-party libraries, which we compare against each other and compiler-assisted vectorization. Overall, we achieve an overall performance gain of $5.9\times$ for OpenCL and $6.4\times$ for C++ with OpenMP on the Intel® Xeon Phi™ coprocessor.

THE GPU-HEOM APPLICATION

GPU-HEOM is an implementation of the Hierarchical Equations Of Motion (HEOM) method. It bridges biology, material sciences, and quantum physics by simulating molecular light-harvesting complexes. Natural light-harvesting complexes are crucial for photosynthesis of biological organisms. Artificial complexes are relevant for future organic-materials solar cells. The goal of these simulations is to understand the energy transport from an initial excitation, due to photon absorption, to the reaction center or electrode of the system. The HEOM method is a general approach to compute the time evolution of the density operator of open quantum systems. Thus, the results for this code are relevant for other domains, too.

From the computational perspective, the HEOM method deals with a hierarchical network of relatively small, dense complex matrices. For each of these matrices, there is a time-dependent differential equation to solve. These equations are coupled according to the edges of the hierarchy. The size of the matrices depends on the number of sites of the simulated molecular complex. The depth of the hierarchy is crucial for the accuracy of the simulation, and is limited by its exponential growth per added layer and the available compute and memory resources. Currently, only small systems, for example, green sulfur bacteria with seven sites, are feasible. One goal is to scale the capabilities toward larger complexes, like the photosystem II with 42 sites, found in higher plants such as spinach. Improving the capabilities of this code by leveraging modern multicore and many-core architectures is crucial for enabling new results in the natural sciences.

The GPU-HEOM code is a relatively young and compact OpenCL code without any legacy parts. This makes it an ideal candidate for experimenting with different programming models and target architectures. It consists of four kernels. Three of them deal with individual terms of the density operator equation, while the fourth is a classical Runge-Kutta integrator. There are reference implementations and a Nvidia GPGPU optimized variant of each kernel. In this case study, we summarize the experiences we made with the Hexciton kernel. The main focus is on the code efficiency with respect to vectorization and memory access, since these are most crucial for leveraging the potential of current and future multicore and many-core processors.

Our work with this code started within the Intel Parallel Compute Center (IPCC) at the Zuse Institute Berlin (ZIB) and focuses on optimizing the code for Intel® Xeon® processors and Intel Xeon Phi coprocessors.

By now, we have funding from the German Research Foundation (DFG) to scale the application to large many-core HPC systems. This will allow the simulation of more complex systems, deeper equation hierarchies, and will yield new insights for both, computer and natural sciences.

THE HEXCITON KERNEL

The Hexciton kernel computes a commutator term for a large set of small, complex matrices σ and a complex Hamiltonian H of the same dimension. This kind of computation is relevant in many quantum dynamics' computations. The relevant part of the differential equation for the time evolution for the auxiliary density operator is:

$$\frac{d}{dt}\sigma(t) = -\frac{i}{\hbar}[H, \sigma(t)] + \cdots = -\frac{i}{\hbar}(H\sigma(t) - \sigma(t)H) + \cdots$$

For the benchmark code used throughout this chapter, we reimplemented the corresponding part of the GPU-HEOM algorithm, where Δt is the constant time step of the integrator.

$$\sigma_k, \sigma_{k+1}, H \in \mathbb{C}^{n \times n}$$

for all the σ_k **in Hierarchy do**

$$| \quad \sigma_{k+1} = -\frac{i}{\hbar}(H\sigma_k - \sigma_k H)\Delta t + \cdots$$

end

The computation is fairly simple, but in contrast to a conventional matrix multiplication kernel that operates on one large matrix, this kernel processes hundreds of thousands of rather small matrices which are used as left-hand and right-hand operands.

BUILDING EXPECTATIONS

As an estimate for the computational effort, we count the two matrix multiplications with $2n^2(n \cdot \text{mult} + n \cdot \text{add})$ FLOP, where "mult" and "add" are complex operations. A complex multiplication counts six FLOP (four multiplications and two additions) and a complex addition two FLOP. If everything is accumulated in-place, and the Hamiltonian is prescaled with $-\Delta t \frac{i}{\hbar}$, all other operations can be performed implicitly in the implementation and thus are not counted. All in all, we get $2n^2(6n + 2n) = 16n^3$ FLOP per commutator. In our benchmarks, we use $n = 7$ (the light-harvesting complex of green sulfur bacteria has seven Chlorophylls), a hierarchy of 2^{19} σ-matrices and double precision. For this setup, we get a lower bound of 2.9 GFLOP per iteration. The actual value can be higher depending on the specific kernel.

The Intel Xeon Phi 7120P coprocessor has a peak performance of 1.208 TFLOPS and a peak memory bandwidth of 352 GiB/s. In practice, about half of the memory bandwidth can be achieved, for example, 174 GiB/s for the stream triad benchmark. This means an ideal application, that utilizes the whole coprocessor, would have a computational intensity of 6.5 FLOP/byte being at the exact sweet-spot between compute- and memory-bound.

The Hexciton kernel reads from one buffer and accumulates the output into another, touching $2n^2$ complex matrix elements for each σ. The Hamiltonian is the same for all σ and can be neglected due to the high number of σ-matrices. For the benchmark setup, this amounts to 784 MiB of accessed memory. Together with the FLOP estimate from above, we get a computational intensity of only 3.5 FLOP/byte. The kernel clearly is memory-bound.

The ratio of the optimal and actual computational intensity provides us with an upper bound for the achievable performance. In case we manage to fully utilize the memory bandwidth, we could at most get 54% of the coprocessor's peak computational performance, that is, 654 GFLOPS. This gives us a lower bound for the runtime per iteration of 4.4 ms for the benchmark setup. For a single Intel Xeon E5-2697v3 processor, which we use for benchmarking, we get a lower bound of 11.3 ms using the same method. In practice, these runtimes will be hard to achieve, because there are lots of performance-relevant constraints we did not take into consideration, for instance, caching efficiency, memory access patterns, vectorization, integer/address arithmetic, or the instruction mix.

However, it is important to have at least some idea of the theoretical bounds of the application and hardware to define an approximate goal for the optimization efforts. For more complex applications, performance counters are an alternative to theoretical analysis. In the remainder of this chapter, we investigate how close to the theoretical bounds we can actually get using different programming models and optimization strategies.

OPTIMIZING THE OpenCL HEXCITON KERNEL

In this section, we describe our different approaches for optimizing the initial OpenCL Hexciton kernel for multicore and many-core processors using the Intel OpenCL SDK.

OpenCL IN A NUTSHELL

OpenCL has some advantages over other parallel programming models. First of all, it is the only one of the "open" standards for which there actually are implementations by all major vendors—unlike for OpenMP or OpenACC. The level of vendor support, however, is a different story. OpenCL is a library that can be used with any C/C++ compiler, which makes it independent of additional tools. The kernels are written separately in a C-like language and compiled at runtime for the present hardware. The kernel compiler comes with the OpenCL implementation provided by the hardware vendor. A kernel written in OpenCL will run everywhere, including conventional CPUs, Intel Xeon Phi coprocessors, GPGPUs, some FPGAs, and even mobile devices.

OpenCL programs are divided into host and kernel code. Only the latter is executed on the compute device. In the host program, kernels and memory movements are queued into command queues associated with a device. The kernel language provides features like vector types and additional memory qualifiers. A computation must be mapped to work-groups of work-items that can be executed in parallel on the compute units (CUs) and processing elements (PEs) of a compute device. A work-item is a single instance of a kernel function. For each kernel-call, an NDRange (n-dimensional range) specifies the dimension, number, and shape of the work-groups. Global synchronization during the execution of a kernel is unavailable. Work-items inside a work-group can be synchronized. OpenCL provides a complex memory model with a relaxed consistency. For more information on OpenCL, please refer to the "For more information" section at the end of this chapter.

THE HEXCITON KERNEL OpenCL IMPLEMENTATION

The GPU-HEOM code comes with two OpenCL implementations, a straight-forward implementation of the algorithm and a GPGPU-optimized variant. GPGPU-optimized OpenCL code usually makes heavy use of the architecture's complex memory hierarchy with its fast local memory in each CU. These are also part of the OpenCL memory model, but have no physical equivalent on multicore and many-core processors. Hence, using them will result in some software emulation that will at best not degrade the runtime performance. Accordingly, the straight-forward implementation of the Hexciton kernel yielded the best initial performance of the existing GPU-HEOM kernel variants on the Intel Xeon processor and Intel Xeon Phi coprocessor. We will come back to performance portability later in this section.

Our Hexciton benchmark code resembles the structure of the original Hexciton kernel of GPU-HEOM. We refactored this kernel into multiple variants to explore the space of possible optimizations. In these kernels, each work-item evaluates the commutator term for one σ-matrix. This might sound like a lot to those who have experience in GPGPU programming, where the natural thing to do would be to map the computation of a single element of the result matrix to one work-item. This is the first thing to keep in mind: The Intel Xeon processor and Intel Xeon Phi coprocessor have far fewer and more complex cores processing the work-items. Hence, having too fine-grained work-items results in very small work-loads per work-group causing lots of runtime overhead.

The original kernel uses `double2` as substitute for complex numbers. This is discouraged, since it can interfere with vectorization, causes avoidable load operations, and implies a memory layout where real and imaginary parts are stored together. We modified the code to access real and imaginary parts by means of indices and distinct scalar variables.

We also prescaled the Hamiltonian with $-\Delta t \frac{i}{\hbar}$ during initialization, since otherwise this computation would have been performed identically by each work-item. Interestingly, this is hardly measurable in the runtime, because either way, the kernel is memory bound and the avoided computations would work on already loaded data. Still, as a general rule, moving identical computations out of the kernel and passing the results as arguments or compile time constants is a good idea.

In preparation of evaluating different memory layouts, we separated index computations from the commutator arithmetic by using function-like macros. Using actual functions can prevent compiler optimizations or introduce runtime overhead. Splitting up complex index computations into terms depending on different loop variables and moving them to outer loops also has a negative impact on performance. Even if in theory it would prevent unnecessarily repeating index computations in the inner-most loop, it prevents the compiler from recognizing memory access patterns.

Figure 19.1 shows a refactored variant of the kernel that uses the prescaled Hamiltonian and directly stores into sigma_out. Other variants accumulate the result in temporaries, or permute the j and k loops to cache the [k,j] accesses in temporary variables.

```
__kernel
void commutator_ocl_refactored_direct(__global real_t const* restrict sigma_in,
                                      __global real_t* restrict sigma_out,
                                      __global real_t const* restrict hamiltonian,
                                      const uint num, const uint dim,
                                      const real_t hbar, const real_t dt)
{
  // number of package to process == get_global_id(0)
  #define sig_real(i, j) (sigma_id + 2 * ((i) * dim + (j)))
  #define sig_imag(i, j) (sigma_id + 2 * ((i) * dim + (j)) + 1)

  #define ham_real(i, j) (2 * ((i) * dim + (j)))
  #define ham_imag(i, j) (2 * ((i) * dim + (k)) + 1)

  uint sigma_id = get_global_id(0) * dim * dim * 2;

  // compute commutator: (hamiltonian * sigma_in[sigma_id] - sigma_in[sigma_id] *
      hamiltonian)
  uint i, j, k;
  for (i = 0; i < dim; ++i)
  {
    for (j = 0; j < dim; ++j)
    {
      for (k = 0; k < dim; ++k)
      {
        sigma_out[sigma_imag(i, j)] -= hamiltonian[ham_real(i, k)] * sigma_in[
            sigma_real(k, j)];
        sigma_out[sigma_imag(i, j)] += sigma_in[sigma_real(i, k)] * hamiltonian[
            ham_real(k, j)];
        sigma_out[sigma_imag(i, j)] += hamiltonian[ham_imag(i, k)] * sigma_in[
            sigma_imag(k, j)];
        sigma_out[sigma_imag(i, j)] -= sigma_in[sigma_imag(i, k)] * hamiltonian[
            ham_imag(k, j)];
        sigma_out[sigma_real(i, j)] += hamiltonian[ham_real(i, k)] * sigma_in[
            sigma_imag(k, j)];
        sigma_out[sigma_real(i, j)] -= sigma_in[sigma_real(i, k)] * hamiltonian[
            ham_imag(k, j)];
        sigma_out[sigma_real(i, j)] += hamiltonian[ham_imag(i, k)] * sigma_in[
            sigma_real(k, j)];
        sigma_out[sigma_real(i, j)] -= sigma_in[sigma_imag(i, k)] * hamiltonian[
            ham_real(k, j)];
      }
    }
  }
}
```

FIGURE 19.1

Refactored initial Hexciton OpenCL kernel. The arithmetic inside the loop maps to eight fused multiply-add instructions (FMA). The kernel prior to refactoring, and all others, are included in the downloadable examples. See the Readme for a mapping of figures and source files.

VECTORIZATION IN OpenCL

In order to achieve performance on multicore and many-core processors, the code generated by the OpenCL compiler must make efficient use of the SIMD hardware. There are two approaches to achieve this goal: (a) leave it to the compiler, and (b) manually vectorize the code using the appropriate vector types provided by OpenCL. In both cases, understanding the vectorization strategy is crucial for optimizing the memory layout for contiguous vector loads and stores.

The automatic vectorizer of the Intel OpenCL SDK maps work-items to SIMD lanes. This means there is no vectorization applied to the loops inside the kernel. This basically is outer loop vectorization if you think of the OpenCL runtime as loop over work-items. The kernel can be seen as an SIMD function that processes n work-items in parallel across the SIMD lanes, with n being the SIMD width of the target hardware.

Manual vectorization allows for the same, and also for different, vectorization schemes. We applied the same outer loop vectorization scheme for the manually vectorized kernel, because it allows a trivial transition between automatic and manual vectorization by substituting scalar types with vector types and creating n times less work-items in the host code. Each kernel then processes n times the work. In case of HEOM that is n commutator terms for n σ-matrices.

For manual vectorization, the automatic vectorizer must be deactivated by declaring the kernel with:

```
__kernel __attribute__((vec_type_hint(double8))) commutator(...)
```

Any vector type passed to the `vec_type_hint` attribute will disable automatic vectorization. This is a documented, implementation-specific behavior of the Intel OpenCL SDK.

For the Hexciton kernel, outer loop vectorization over the work-items and thus over the number of σ-matrices also resolves most of the remainder problems that occur when some problem-specific size is not divisible by the SIMD width. With inner loop vectorization, we would have to pad each matrix to a dimension that fits the SIMD width, or risk running scalar code. Instead we only need to add a few sigma matrices at the end of our buffer, or have one suboptimal work-group in the NDRange.

MEMORY LAYOUT OPTIMIZATION

Now that we know how OpenCL makes use of the SIMD hardware, we can use that knowledge to optimize the memory layout. In the original layout, all σ-matrices are stored one after another in a row-major format. Each element is a complex number; that is, two contiguous floating point numbers encoding the real and the imaginary part. This layout resembles what is often referred to as Array of Structures (AoS), with the matrix of elements being the structure, and the set of all σ-matrices being the array. With n work-items processing n of the σ-matrices in parallel across n SIMD lanes, each access to a matrix element happens to n corresponding matrix elements in parallel. These elements must be loaded into or stored from a vector register, but are a matrix-size stride away from each other. This means each access will generate an expensive gather or scatter instruction.

The other extreme would be a Structure of Arrays (SoA) layout, where all corresponding elements of all σ-matrices would be stored in contiguous arrays. This would allow for contiguous vector loads and stores, but there would be a huge stride between the ith and the $(i + 1)$th matrix elements needed for subsequent arithmetic operation.

The solution is a hybrid SoA or AoSoA layout. Figure 19.2 shows all three layouts by ways of declaring them. The size of the inner array is set to the SIMD width or a small multiple of it. The hybrid SoA layout is long known to combine locality when accessing different structure elements with contiguous iteration over the corresponding elements of multiple structures. In fact, it is already mentioned in the *IA-32 Intel® Architecture Optimization Reference Manual* from 1999, but rarely found in the wild. It is a generalization which collapses to SoA if the outer array size is one, and to AoS if the inner size is one. With the major fraction of today's and tomorrow's processor's FLOPS coming from SIMD hardware of growing width, hybrid SoA becomes more relevant than ever to achieve contiguous vector loads/stores.

The Hexciton benchmark code uses no explicit data structures. Instead the layout is applied with a set of index computations that work on a large buffer of floating point elements. The original and the optimized memory layout are shown in Figure 19.3. This allows a memory layout exchange by swapping the index computations without modifying the application's arithmetic code. Figures 19.4 and 19.5 show the relevant parts of the host and kernel code for both automatic and manual vectorization.

```
// AoS                // SoA                // AoSoA or hybrid SoA
struct data_t {       struct data_t {       struct data_t {
  type_t elem;          type_t elem[N];       type_t elem[VEC_LEN];
  // ...                // ...                // ...
};                    };                    };
data_t data[N];       data_t data;          data_t data[N/VEC_LEN];
```

FIGURE 19.2

The different memory layouts declared as their name implies for a buffer `data`.

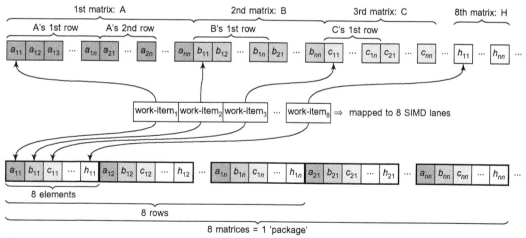

FIGURE 19.3

Memory accesses to matrix elements that result from the outer loop vectorization scheme of OpenCL for the Hexciton kernel (for an SIMD width of eight). The original SoA memory layout leads to noncontiguous gather/scatter operations. The improved interleaved AoSoA layout results in fully contiguous memory accesses. Not shown: real and imaginary parts of complex numbers are separated into two adjacent blocks of eight elements.

The code for the automatically vectorized kernel is more complex since a number of constraints must be met to make the compiler generate the intended code. First, the VEC_LENGTH must be set to 16 in any case, and second, a part of the index computation must be moved outside the kernel into a special NDRange shape. Otherwise, the compiler does not recognize the contiguous access pattern.

In a native C or C++ Kernel, we could verify whether the compiler did as expected, or still emitted gather and scatter instructions, by means of the optimization report of the compilers included as part of Intel® Composer. Since the Intel OpenCL compiler does not provide a detailed optimization report, the only way to find out what the compiler actually did is to look at the assembly. During this process, we also identified an alignment issue that impacts the performance of the automatically vectorized kernel.

```
/* in the host program */
#define VEC_LENGTH 16 // for the MIC: regardless of float or double!
size_t work_dim = 2;
size_t global_work_size[] = {VEC_LENGTH, num_sigma / VEC_LENGTH};
size_t local_work_size[] = {VEC_LENGTH, 1};
clEnqueueNDRangeKernel(queue, kernel, work_dim, 0, global_work_size,
    local_work_size, 0, 0, 0);

/* in the kernel code */
#define package_id ((get_group_id(1)) * (VEC_LENGTH * 2 * DIM * DIM)) // the
    package of matrices processed by this work-group
#define sigma_id get_local_id(0) // the sigma matrix processed by this work-item

#define sigma_real(i, j) (package_id + 2 * VEC_LENGTH * (DIM * (i) + (j)) +
    sigma_id)
#define sigma_imag(i, j) (package_id + 2 * VEC_LENGTH * (DIM * (i) + (j)) +
    VEC_LENGTH + sigma_id)

#define ham_real(i, j) ((i) * DIM + (j))
#define ham_imag(i, j) (DIM * DIM + (i) * DIM + (j))
```

FIGURE 19.4

Kernel call and indexing scheme for the hybrid SoA memory layout for the automatically vectorized kernel. The compiler needs a VEC_LENGTH of 16. The two-dimensional NDRange is necessary to directly map sigma_id to the local id of work-group dimension 0. Otherwise, the contiguous access pattern is not recognized.

```
/* in the host program */
size_t work_dim = 1;
size_t global_work_size[] = {num_sigma / VEC_LENGTH};
clEnqueueNDRangeKernel(queue, kernel, work_dim, 0, global_work_size, 0, 0, 0, 0);

/* in the kernel code */
// number of package to process == get_global_id(0)
#define package_id (get_global_id(0) * DIM * DIM * 2)

#define sigma_real(i, j) (package_id + 2 * (DIM * (i) + (j)))
#define sigma_imag(i, j) (package_id + 2 * (DIM * (i) + (j)) + 1)

#define ham_real(i, j) ((i) * DIM + (j))
#define ham_imag(i, j) (DIM * DIM + (i) * DIM + (j))
```

FIGURE 19.5

Kernel call and indexing scheme for the hybrid SoA memory layout for the manually vectorized kernel. We leave the work-group shape to the OpenCL implementation, and create one work-item for every package of VEC_LENGTH matrices.

As far as the OpenCL standard is concerned, the alignment matches the buffer type—which is scalar. There is no way to convey another alignment to the compiler, nor does the Intel OpenCL implementation enforce the proper alignment by itself. As a result, vector loads are contiguous but unaligned. This is a known issue and will hopefully be fixed in future releases. Until then, the manual vectorization yields considerably better performance, as will be shown later in this section.

COMPILE-TIME CONSTANTS

An optimization strategy unique to OpenCL is to exploit its runtime kernel compilation. The kernel code of an OpenCL application is compiled via a set of OpenCL library calls in the host code. This allows it to take input values known only at runtime, for instance, the matrix dimension of the σ-matrices, and pass them as "compile-time" constant to the kernel.

In case of the Hexciton benchmark code, this enables loop-unrolling and allows the compiler to resolve larger parts of the index computations. By counting the FMA instructions (4 vfmadd and 4 vfnmadd per inner loop iteration) in the assembly code, the applied loop unrolling can be easily verified. However, for the variants of the kernel that have gathers and scatters, the loop unrolling is not beneficial. This means some metric of the compiler that decides whether loop unrolling is applied or not seems to fail in these cases.

We also use compile time constants to pass the SIMD width as VEC_LENGTH to the kernel. This is used in the index computations and to map real_vec_t to the correct OpenCL vector type, for example, double4 on the Intel Xeon processor and double8 on the Intel Xeon Phi coprocessor.

PREFETCHING

Prefetching refers to activity that brings data into caches before it is actually used. It is designed to mask the long latencies required to fetch data from memory. Many processors will automatically, or implicitly, perform prefetching based on heuristics. There are also programming methods for explicit prefetching to benefit from the expertise of the programmer and her knowledge of the specific algorithms.

OpenCL provides a built-in function for explicit prefetching. For the manually vectorized kernel variant without any temporaries, adding a manual prefetch as shown in Figure 19.6 measurably improve the kernel runtime. For all other variants, it does not.

Another possibility to influence software prefetching is the Intel-specific OpenCL compiler option -auto-prefetch-level=n, where *n* is a value between 0 and 3. A value of 0 disables automatic prefetching, all other values subsequently increase the amount of automatic prefetching. According

```
for (i = 0; i < DIM; ++i) {
  // prefetch result memory for the inner loops
  j = 0;
  prefetch(&sigma_out[sigma_real(i, j)], 2 * DIM);
  for (j = 0; j < DIM; ++j) {
    for (k = 0; k < DIM; ++k) {
      /* commutator arithmetic */
    }
  }
}
```

FIGURE 19.6

An example of explicit prefetching that actually is beneficial for the manually vectorized kernel.

to the documentation, the default value of 2 performs best in most cases. Lower levels are recommended for compute-bound kernels. On the Intel Xeon processor, we could hardly measure any effect from this setting for the Hexciton kernel. On the Intel Xeon Phi coprocessor, levels 1-3 perform equally for all kernel variants.

As expected, disabling automatic prefetching decreases the performance of some kernel variants. For others, it has no effect. However, for some variants, a significant improvement of more than 2× can be observed from disabled prefetching, although the kernel is clearly memory bound. Hence, we suggest to at least compare a value of 0 and the default of 2 on the Intel Xeon Phi coprocessor. Further information on automatic software prefetching can be found in the Intel OpenCL Optimization Guide referenced in the "For more information" section at the end of this chapter.

OpenCL PERFORMANCE RESULTS

We evaluated a large set of kernel variants on an Intel Xeon processor (Sandy Bridge and Haswell) and on an Intel Xeon Phi coprocessor using the Intel OpenCL 1.2 SDK (4.6.0.92). The metric used is the average kernel runtime per iteration, measured over 50 runs of 100 iterations plus 5 warm-up iteration each. The error bars in the plots depict minimum and maximum values. The runtime reflects the execution time of one iteration of the Hexciton kernel computing the commutator for 2^{19} complex 7×7 matrices, excluding OpenCL buffer transfers and host code execution. Measuring the surroundings of the kernel would make it harder to quantify the efficiency of the generated code. Figure 19.7

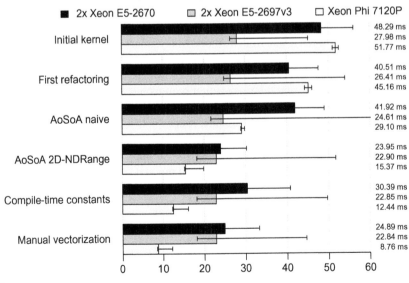

FIGURE 19.7

Effects of the different optimization strategies applied to the Hexciton benchmark kernel. We achieve a speed-up of 2.0× and 1.2× on the Sandy Bridge and Haswell Intel Xeon processor, respectively, and 5.9× on the Intel Xeon Phi coprocessor over the initial version.

shows the impact of the different optimization strategies, subsequently applied to the initial kernel. We choose this order, because it shows an improvement with every step—at least for the Intel Xeon Phi coprocessor. When we experimented with the code, we had to explore a large combinatorial space, even for such a small kernel, to finally end up with these educational variants. The downloadable Hexciton benchmark code contains more incarnations of the kernel than can be shown here.

During our work on the code, there were always situations where one optimization would actually have a negative effect in one kernel, but would improve the performance in another one. For instance, the compile-time constants became beneficial only after the memory accesses were contiguous. If applied earlier, the resulting loop-unrolling decreases the performance significantly. The unfortunate consequence is that optimization approaches, that is, dimensions in the search space for the optimal solution, cannot be discarded just because they were unsuccessful in one context. However, the most important optimization, that will most likely never lead to performance degradation, is the transition to a memory layout that allows for contiguous vector loads and stores. This requires exact knowledge about the applied vectorization strategy, regardless of it being implemented manually or generated by the compiler. While the strategy of the Intel OpenCL vectorizer is well-documented, the automatic vectorization of native C/C++ kernels is much less obvious. But also for OpenCL code, that is not intended for a specific device, no general assumption can be made about the vectorization strategies of the device-specific compilers that might be used at host program runtime to compile the kernel. In fact, we cannot even assume that the target hardware has some kind of SIMD hardware. In GPU-HEOM, OpenCL is used as means to create efficient kernels for different platforms within the same programming model, language, and toolset—not to write a single kernel and hope for the miracle of portable performance to happen (even though the idea is appealing).

Figure 19.8 compares the differences between manual and automatic vectorization for otherwise identical kernels on the Intel Xeon processor and Intel Xeon Phi coprocessor. The gap between the fastest manually and automatically vectorized code is 40% for the Intel Xeon Phi coprocessor. The reason is the alignment issue, we described earlier. It causes unaligned vector loads and stores in the automatically vectorized code. Currently, manual vectorization in OpenCL is mandatory for efficient code generation on the Intel Xeon Phi coprocessor. For the Intel Xeon processor, both approaches perform similar with only small differences on Sandy Bridge. On Haswell, there are basically no ($<1\%$) differences at all—not between manual and automatic vectorization, and not even across the different kernels. In fact, every kernel optimization in addition to the new memory layout in combination with the correct NDRange had no effect on the measured performance on the Haswell architecture.

PERFORMANCE PORTABILITY IN OpenCL

Although OpenCL offers code portability across a wide variety of homogeneous and heterogeneous platforms, performance portability is a quite different matter. While the general thoughts to optimizing a kernel may be similar across the different OpenCL platforms, getting the highest achievable performance requires the use of platform-specific optimization strategies. This often leads to situations where optimizations increase the performance on one platform, but considerably decrease it on another.

There are two choices, (a) completely refrain from device-specific optimizations and aim for a single implementation with portable but suboptimal performance, or (b) maintain multiple optimized but device-specific implementations. Whether (b) is worth the effort obviously depends on how suboptimal

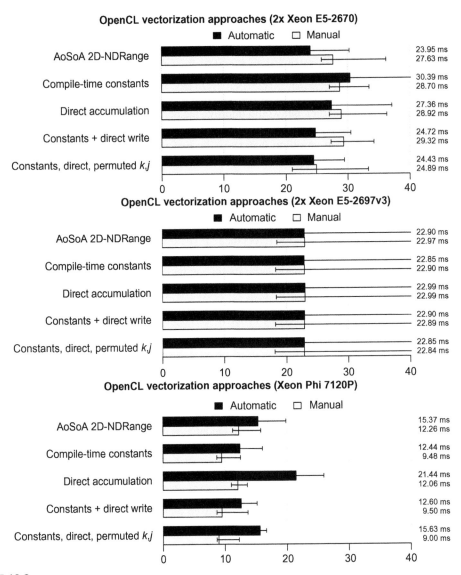

FIGURE 19.8

Runtimes per iteration for manually and automatically vectorized variants of the OpenCL Hexciton kernel on the Sandy Bridge and Haswell Intel Xeon processor, and Intel Xeon Phi coprocessor.

the performance of (a) is. For the Hexciton kernel, we choose (b), since it is memory bound and thus must exploit the highly device-specific memory hierarchies of multicore and many-core processors, and GPGPUs in order to perform well. In the first *High Performance Programming Pearls* book, the chapter "Portable performance with OpenCL" focuses on (a) for a compute-intensive application.

In this section, we analyze the performance of the different Hexciton kernel implementations across platforms. First, we compare the optimization techniques we used on a GPGPU with those shown for multicore and many-core processors. Then, we analyze the benchmark results of the different implementations across platforms. We recommend reading the best practices and optimization guides for the different OpenCL implementations, referenced at the end of this chapter, to get an impression of what is important on each architecture.

NVIDIA GPGPU-SPECIFIC OPTIMIZATIONS

We optimized the Hexiton kernel for the Nvidia Tesla K40m (Kepler) GPGPU (hereafter, just GPGPU). Although there already was a GPGPU-optimized version, we put some more effort into the implementation for a better comparability of the results.

Mapping of work-items to hardware threads

Our fastest coprocessor version of the Hexiton kernel uses OpenCL's built-in vector data type `double8` to manually address SIMD in the kernel code. On GPGPU, SIMD execution is implicit, that is, work-items are directly mapped to hardware threads which then execute on the GPGPU's PEs in "same instruction, multiple-thread" (SIMT) mode—32 successive work-items, starting from 0, form an "SIMT group." As there are no SIMD units on the PEs, using vector data types of length n gives n-fold the amount of work to each work-item compared to using scalars instead.

The usual way of implementing the matrix-matrix multiplication $C = A \cdot B$ on the GPGPU is to assign to each work-item just one of the matrix elements c_{ij} for computation, and to instantiate N^2 work-items in case of A, B, and C being of dimension N^2. Compared to our kernel for the Intel Xeon Phi coprocessor, the number of work-items on the GPGPU then would be larger by a factor $8 \cdot N^2$, where the factor 8 results from processing bunches of eight matrices at once using the `double8` data type on the coprocessor. Depending on the particular workload, increasing the amount of work per work-item can be beneficial on the GPGPU, too, to gain instruction-level parallelism. In our Hexciton kernel implementation, each work-item processes $n = 2$ matrix elements c_{ij} at once. Thereby, the real and the imaginary parts are stored and processed separately using local memory and the `double2` built-in data type.

The differences of processing the σ-matrices, between the Intel Xeon Phi coprocessor version of the Hexiton kernel and its GPGPU equivalent, are shown in Figure 19.9.

Work-groups

On GPGPUs at most 1024 work-items can form a work-group, and at least 128 work-items per work-group are required to achieve 100% device occupancy—at most 16 concurrent work-groups are scheduled on each CU. Our implementation uses two-dimensional work-groups $\{d_x, d_y\}$, where the first dimension d_x corresponds to the number of matrix elements, and the second dimension is chosen appropriately so as to have at least 128 work-items per work-group. In the case of $d_y > 1$, multiple matrices are processed within a single work-group. Additionally, we pad the first dimension so that d_x becomes a multiple of the native execution width—which on the Tesla K40m is 32. That is,

$$d_x = \text{ceil}\,(N^2, 32), \quad \text{ceil}\,(a,b) = \lfloor \frac{a+b-1}{b} \rfloor b,$$

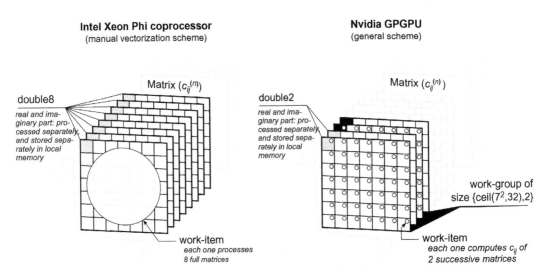

FIGURE 19.9

Assignment of matrix elements $c_{ij} \in \mathbb{C}$ to work-items for computation: (left) Intel Xeon Phi coprocessor and (right) Nvidia GPGPU. On the coprocessor, each work-item (denoted by open circles) processes eight full matrices using the built-in `double8` vector data type. On GPGPU, each work-item is assigned matrix elements c_{ij} of two successive matrices—we use the `double2` data type, where real and imaginary parts are stored and processed separately in local memory. In the schematic, work-groups on the GPGPU have size {ceil(7^2,32),2} = {64,2} according to the padding scheme described in the text.

for matrix dimension N^2. The padding requires in the kernel to mask out work-items for which `get_local_id(0)<(N*N)` does not hold. The assignment of the remaining work-items to matrix elements $c_{ij}^{(n)}$ within the kernel is as follows:

```
int i = get_local_id(0) / N;
int j = get_local_id(0) % N;
int n = get_group_id(0) * DY + get_local_id(1);
```

For a total of NUM matrices to be processed, NUM/d_y work-groups need to be instantiated. The NDRange then is {(NUM/d_y) d_x,d_y} together with the work-group size {d_x = ceil(N^2, 32), d_y = DY}. *Note:* Due to the 1024 work-items per work-group restriction on GPGPUs, the matrix dimension N can be at most 32 with this implementation. For larger matrices, blocking would be needed.

Local memory

Unlike the Intel Xeon Phi coprocessor, GPGPUs provide direct access to fast on-chip local memory within OpenCL kernels using the address space qualifier `_local`. Work-items within the same work-group can use it to share data and to coordinate their acting. The size of the local memory per CU is 48 KiB for the Tesla K40m GPGPU. It is organized in 32-bit memory banks; 64-bit words are accessed by reading/writing from/to two successive local memory banks. Work-items i and $i + 16$ within the same SIMT group hence access the same local memory banks when reading/writing the

64-bit words ...[i], respectively, ...[i+16]. The latter results in two-way bank conflicts, and lowers the effective local memory bandwidth.

For the Hexiton kernel, we load both the Hamiltonian and the input σ-matrices into the local memory. All matrix elements $c_{ij} \in \mathbb{C}$ thereby are split into 64-bit real and imaginary part, and are stored in separate fields ...real[N*N] and ...imag[N*N] in local memory. Placing both real and imaginary part of c_{ij} to local memory one after another would result in four-way bank conflicts. With the 64-bit splitting, we hence take the lesser evil—two-way bank conflicts.

Our final local memory layout, e.g., for $d_y = 2$, incorporating the point that each work-item processes two matrices at once using the double2 built-in vector data type, is shown in Figure 19.10.

The amount of local memory consumed by that kernel is $M = (2 + 4 \cdot d_y) \cdot 8 \cdot N^2$ bytes per work-group. In case of $N = 7$ and work-group size {64,2}, it takes $M = 3920$ bytes of the local memory. The maximum number of concurrent work-groups on each of the GPGPU's CUs then is $\lfloor (48 \cdot 1024 \text{ bytes})/(3920 \text{ bytes}) \rfloor = 12$, which corresponds to 1536 work-items per CU, and hence 75% maximum device occupancy. Our final GPGPU kernel consumes 40 registers (32-bit) per work-item, or at most 61,440 registers overall per CU. The total register count of 65,536 per CU thus is not exceeded, and the stated maximum device occupancy hence remains the same. By not using the double2 built-in vector data type for internal computation, we can achieve 100% device occupancy instead. However, the increased per-work-item instruction-level parallelism when using double2 processing overcompensates the reduced occupancy.

```
__local double h_real[N*N];
__local double h_imag[N*N];
__local double sin_real[2][DY][N*N]; // input sigma
__local double sin_imag[2][DY][N*N]; // matrices

// load Hamiltonian -> h_real, h_imag
// load input sigma matrices -> sin_real, sin_imag
int dy=get_local_id(1);

double2 sout1_ij=0.0; // Output sigma
double2 sout2_ij=0.0; // matrices: element (i,j)
for (int k=0; k<N; ++k)
{
  // compute commutator sout<x>=[h,sin<x>] (x=1,2)
  // *** h_ik*sin_kj ***
  double2 s_kj_real=(double2)(sin_real[0][dy][k*N+j],
                              sin_real[1][dy][k*N+j]);
  double2 s_kj_imag=(double2)(sin_imag[0][dy][k*N+j],
                              sin_imag[1][dy][k*N+j]);
  sout1_ij+=h_real[i*N+k]*s_kj_real;
  sout2_ij+=h_imag[i*N+k]*s_kj_imag;
  sout1_ij+=..
  // *** sin_ik*h_kj ***
  double2 s_ik_real=(double2)(sin_real[0][dy][i*N+k],
                              sin_real[1][dy][i*N+k]);
  // ...
```

FIGURE 19.10

Part of the Nvidia K40m optimized OpenCL Hexciton Kernel. The entire kernel can be found in the downloadable examples. See the Readme for a mapping of figures and source files.

Memory layout

As our GPGPU version of the Hexiton kernel uses the local memory to speed up access to both the Hamiltonian and the input sigma matrices within the work-groups, transformations of the memory layout are applied when loading data from global to local memory. For each matrix element c_{ij} both its real and imaginary parts are loaded and stored using the double2 data type. Within the kernel, the two 64-bit components are separated and grouped together into one matrix containing all real parts, and another containing all imaginary parts (see Figure 19.10).

The short message of this section is: even though the OpenCL kernel code will run everywhere, the considerations regarding code optimization are profoundly different when comparing GPGPUs with multicore and many-core processors.

OpenCL PERFORMANCE PORTABILITY RESULTS

To quantify the performance portability, we benchmarked the GPGPU-optimized kernel, and the fastest Intel Xeon processor and Intel Xeon Phi coprocessor variants across all three platforms. The results are shown in Figure 19.11. Obviously, there is no such thing as portable performance for the Hexciton kernel. Due to their architectural similarity, the same kernel can perform well on Intel Xeon processor and Intel Xeon Phi coprocessor. The GPGPU does not do well with the heavy work-loads of the Intel Xeon processor and Intel Xeon Phi coprocessor-optimized code, while the GPGPU-optimized kernel achieves a surprisingly good device-utilization on the Intel Xeon processor. We ran this benchmark for a total of 20 different Hexciton kernel variants, none of which where able to achieve a high degree of device utilization on all three devices. However, the Haswell Intel Xeon processor shows something like an inverse performance portability, that is a good performance across a wide variety of implementation variants of the same kernel.

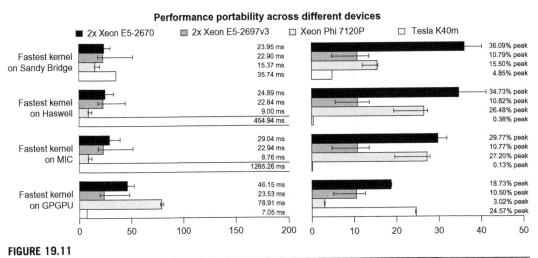

FIGURE 19.11

The left plot depicts the runtimes per iteration of the fastest kernel variants across all platforms. The right plot shows the achieved percentage of the device's theoretical peak performance. The low peak percentage of the Haswell originates from its high theoretical peak, but relatively low memory bandwidth.

PORTING THE OpenCL KERNEL TO OpenMP 4.0

As stated earlier, the goal of this case study is to compare programming models and methodologies with respect to the efficiency of the generated code for multicore and many-core processors. We started with OpenCL, since the original GPU-HEOM application is written in it. Our next step was to evaluate a native C++ implementation with OpenMP 4.0 to see how the results compare. The basic idea is to take the optimized OpenCL kernels and apply the same vectorization strategy for which we already optimized the memory layout. Therefore, we have to find substitutes for certain OpenCL constructs, that is, the runtime and the vector types.

Some advice on vectorization terminology: strictly speaking, *automatic* vectorization refers to everything the compiler can do by its own and possibly with some hints like `ivdep`. When you read *explicit* vectorization, probably in an Intel document, this refers to adding directives that force the compiler into vectorizing code, like `simd`. We use the term automatic vectorization for both, since the distinction is not relevant here. By *manual* vectorization, we refer to writing code where the programmer deals with actual vector types and operations that address the SIMD hardware.

OpenMP 4.0 VS. OpenCL

Directive-based approaches like OpenMP modify semantics of the underlying language and allow passing additional information to the compiler, which is needed for parallelization and optimization. This accommodates evolutionary change with minimal effort. In contrast, the OpenCL runtime model and kernel language are more of a revolution, designed for parallelism from the beginning. OpenCL originates from offloading to accelerator devices like GPGPUs in heterogeneous systems, while OpenMP's roots lie in thread-parallelism on homogeneous multicore processors. Practically, there is a large overlap. OpenCL can be used to run kernels on multicore and many-core processors of homogeneous systems as well, while OpenMP 4.0 started to provide directives for offloading in heterogeneous systems. Unlike GPGPUs, the Intel Xeon Phi coprocessor allows both offloading and native execution. Native means, running an application solely on the coprocessor, completely independent of the host. We chose the native execution for this study, since its scope is the efficiency of the generated code, not the offload performance of the OpenMP or OpenCL runtime. At the time this is being written, the future support of OpenCL on the Intel Xeon Phi coprocessor is unknown, while the continued support for OpenMP is beyond debate.

SUBSTITUTING THE OpenCL RUNTIME

As shown in Figure 19.12, OpenCL work-groups are executed using thread-parallelism, while the work-items within a work-group are mapped to SIMD-lanes. This allows us to replace the OpenCL runtime with an OpenMP parallel region containing two nested loops. An outer `parallel for` loop iterating over the work-groups, and an inner `simd` loop for the work-items. Inside these loops, we can then basically copy and paste the OpenCL kernel code. The necessary global and local work-group and work-item IDs can be derived from the loop indices. In case of manual vectorization, where a single work-item puts work on all SIMD-lanes by using OpenCL's vector types (e.g., `double8`), only the outer loop is needed. Additionally, we need a substitute for the vector types which is addressed in the next section. Figure 19.13 shows the respective code.

OpenCL runtime	OpenCL platform	Multicore and many-core	OpenMP
NDRange	Device	Processo r	Parallel section
work-groups	Compute unit	Core	Parallel for
work-items	Processing element	SIM D lane	simd

FIGURE 19.12

Mapping of OpenCL entities to the actual hardware and the corresponding OpenMP construct.

```
/* OpenMP replacement for the OpenCL runtime, auto. vectorization */
#pragma omp parallel for
for(int group_id = 0; group_id < N / VEC_LEN; ++group_id)
  #pragma omp simd
  for(int local_id= 0; local_id < VEC_LEN; ++local_id)
    /* kernel code */

/* OpenMP replacement for the OpenCL runtime, manual vectorization */
#pragma omp parallel for
for(int group_id = 0; group_id < N / VEC_LEN; ++group_id)
  /* kernel code with library vector types */
```

FIGURE 19.13

OpenMP replacements for the OpenCL runtime.

C++ SIMD LIBRARIES

The direct approach to manual vectorization in C/C++ are intrinsics. They allow programming at a very low abstraction level that is only a small step away from writing assembler code. Intrinsics are specific to a certain SIMD instruction set (SSE, AVX, AVX2, etc.) and so is the resulting code. A better approach is to encapsulate intrinsics into C++ vector type classes that overload arithmetic operators. There already is a number of libraries implementing that pattern. In this section, we introduce three of them and use them to replace the OpenCL vector types in the ported OpenCL kernel code.

In general, manual vectorization using vector types has some advantages over automatic and directive-based vectorization. If you already know which vectorization strategy and memory layout you want to implement, vector types enable you to write the corresponding code in a straight-forward fashion and get exactly what you want. With automatic and directive-based approaches, it can be much harder to achieve the same. They are more suited for cases where minimal code changes in legacy codes have the highest priority. Another problem with automatic vectorization is debugging incorrect application results, because the vectorized code cannot not be easily instrumented. Also, with manually vectorized code, there are no surprises with changed vectorization behavior that comes with the next compiler update. In fact, using SIMD library types makes the code both compiler and hardware independent. The performance is on the same level as manually written intrinsics code, but the programming happens on a higher abstraction level. However, using intrinsics, directly or indirectly can impair compiler optimizations in some cases. For the Hexciton benchmark, we compare the following SIMD implementations for the manually vectorized OpenMP kernels:

- *Intel header:* Intel provides two header-only libraries that contain very basic C++ SIMD types for the Intel Xeon Phi coprocessor (micvec.h) and the Intel Xeon processor (dvec.h). They are supplied as part of Intel Composer.
- *VCL / VCLKNC:* A similar implementation is the Vector Class Library (VCL) by Agner Fog. Intel Xeon Phi coprocessor support is provided via VCLKNC, an extension developed by Przemysaw Karpiski at CERN.
- *Vc:* The Vc project provides a more advanced C++ library. In contrast to the other implementations, its API provides a generic vector type of an abstract SIMD width. Vc also offers a scalar fall-back implementation for architectures without actual SIMD hardware, utility functions for memory management, and vector math functions. Vc is developed at the Goethe University Frankfurt.

Figure 19.14 shows the mapping of the corresponding types of OpenCL and the SIMD libraries. In our OpenCL and OpenMP code, we use an abstract `real_t` and `real_vec_t`. This, in combination with a compile time constant for the actual SIMD width, and another one for switching between single and double precision, makes sure the code remains portable. The Hexciton benchmark code can be built using any of the three SIMD libraries using a compile time switch.

FURTHER OPTIMIZING THE OpenMP 4.0 KERNEL

After porting the fully optimized OpenCL kernels with the described pattern, we applied further optimizations that were not possible or beneficial in OpenCL. For the automatically vectorized kernel, we manually permuted the `simd` loop. Moving it from the second to the third level had the highest impact on performance. We also noticed that declaring the buffer pointers with the `restrict` keyword is very important for the efficiency of the generated memory accesses, while it made no difference in the OpenCL kernel. In this context, we also learned that using explicit vectorization, like the `simd` directive, can lead to a completely different compilation result, i.e., performance, compared with just hinting the vectorization potential via `ivdep` to the compiler. It often is a particular combination of directives,

OpenCL	micvec.h	VCLKNC	Vc	HEOM
double4	F64vec4	Vec4d	Vc::double_v	real_vec_t
double8	F64vec8	Vec8d	Vc::double_v	real_vec_t
float8	F32vec16	Vec16f	Vc::float_v	real_vec_t
float16	F32vec8	Vec8f	Vc::float_v	real_vec_t
···	···	···	···	···

FIGURE 19.14

Vector types of OpenCL and the different C++ SIMD libraries. Only Vc offers types with an abstract size which directly allows for writing portable code that works on different SIMD extensions. In the HEOM code, we defined a single vector type that is mapped to one of the other types at compile time.

attributes, and keywords that can make a surprising difference. For the manually vectorized code, the last bit of performance gain could be mobilized by adding `unroll` and `nounroll` directives to the inner loops.

On the Intel Xeon Phi coprocessor, the Intel compiler provides the command line option `-opt-prefetch-distance=n1,n2` which allows to define the prefetch distance as a number of loop iterations. The first value n1 affects the prefetches from the memory to the L2 cache, while the n2 value does the same for prefetches from the L2 to the L1 cache. Prefetching can be disabled by setting the values to 0. We experimentally determined a value of 6,1 to be most beneficial for the otherwise optimized Hexciton kernel variants.

Another noteworthy observation is that we encountered many code changes that made a significant difference when benchmarked on a small scale like just two threads on a single core, were not even measurable in runs on the whole system. Permuting the j and k loops to move loading the elements indexed with (i,k) one loop up is such an example. Hence, it is a good idea to regularly benchmark on a realistic scale.

Figure 19.15 shows the complete source of the fastest OpenMP kernel.

OpenMP BENCHMARK RESULTS

For benchmarking the OpenMP kernel, we used the same hardware as for the OpenCL benchmarks. We used the Intel C/C++ compiler, version 15.0.1. Since the subject of this study is the efficiency of the generated code, we executed the kernels natively on the Intel Xeon Phi coprocessor, not via offloading. The runtimes reflect the mere execution time per iteration for the identical input as used for the OpenCL kernels. Figure 19.16 shows the runtime per iteration for a selection of kernels, each of them vectorized either automatically or manually. The surprising result here is that there actually is a single kernel, the one shown in Figure 19.15, that provides the best result on all three architectures. Both, automatic and manual vectorization techniques, were able to achieve the same final performance on the Intel Xeon Phi coprocessor of around 8.1 ms. Another interesting result, which we have already seen with OpenCL, is that the Haswell system is not sensitive to any of the optimizations beyond the improved memory lay-out. The average values deviate by no more than 6%. For Sandy Bridge, it is 23%, and for the Intel Xeon Phi coprocessor 84%.

By comparing the best results we achieved with OpenCL against those of OpenMP, we can quantify the performance gap between them as 42% and 82% on the Sandy Bridge and Haswell Intel Xeon processor, respectively, and 8% on the Intel Xeon Phi coprocessor, all in favor of OpenMP.

We also measured runtimes for all kernels with all three SIMD libraries. VCLKNC had a performance bug which we fixed in the downloadable benchmark code. On the Sandy Bridge system Vc is 2-44% slower for all kernels that directly accumulate their result in the output buffer. Other than that there is no difference between the libraries. On the Haswell system, there are no significant differences at all. For the Intel Xeon Phi coprocessor, we observed differences of up to 23% when compiling the same kernel with the different SIMD libraries. However, there is no obvious pattern, that is, for each library there is a kernel where it is the fastest and another one where it is the slowest. The Intel Xeon Phi coprocessor in general seems to be the architecture with the largest variances. It will be interesting to see, if this remains valid for its future generations.

```
void commutator_omp_perm2to3 (real_t const* restrict sigma_in,
                              real_t* restrict sigma_out,
                              real_t const* restrict hamiltonian,
                              const int num, const int dim,
                              const real_t hbar, const real_t dt)
{
#pragma omp parallel for
  for (int group_id = 0; group_id < (num / VEC_LENGTH); ++group_id)
  {
    #define package_id (group_id * VEC_LENGTH * 2 * DIM * DIM)
    #define sigma_id local_id

    #define sigma_real(i, j) (package_id + 2 * VEC_LENGTH * (DIM * (i) + (j)) + (
        sigma_id))
    #define sigma_imag(i, j) (package_id + 2 * VEC_LENGTH * (DIM * (i) + (j)) +
        VEC_LENGTH + (sigma_id))

    #define ham_real(i, j) ((i) * DIM + (j))
    #define ham_imag(i, j) (DIM * DIM + (i) * DIM + (j))

    for (int i = 0; i < DIM; ++i)
    {
      // manual loop permutation
      #pragma vector aligned
      #pragma simd
      for (int local_id = 0; local_id < VEC_LENGTH; ++local_id)
      {
        for (int k = 0; k < DIM; ++k)
        {
          for (int j = 0; j < DIM; ++j)
          {
            sigma_out[sigma_imag(i,j)] -= hamiltonian[ham_real(i,k)] * sigma_in[
                sigma_real(k,j)];
            sigma_out[sigma_imag(i,j)] += sigma_in[sigma_real(i,k)] * hamiltonian[
                ham_real(k,j)];
            sigma_out[sigma_imag(i,j)] += hamiltonian[ham_imag(i,k)] * sigma_in[
                sigma_imag(k,j)];
            sigma_out[sigma_imag(i,j)] -= sigma_in[sigma_imag(i,k)] * hamiltonian[
                ham_imag(k,j)];
            sigma_out[sigma_real(i,j)] += hamiltonian[ham_real(i,k)] * sigma_in[
                sigma_imag(k,j)];
            sigma_out[sigma_real(i,j)] -= sigma_in[sigma_real(i,k)] * hamiltonian[
                ham_imag(k,j)];
            sigma_out[sigma_real(i,j)] += hamiltonian[ham_imag(i,k)] * sigma_in[
                sigma_real(k,j)];
            sigma_out[sigma_real(i,j)] -= sigma_in[sigma_imag(i,k)] * hamiltonian[
                ham_real(k,j)];
          }
        }
      }
    }
  }
}
```

FIGURE 19.15

Complete source code of the fastest OpenMP kernel. The kernel can also be found in the downloadable examples. See the Readme for a mapping of figures and source files.

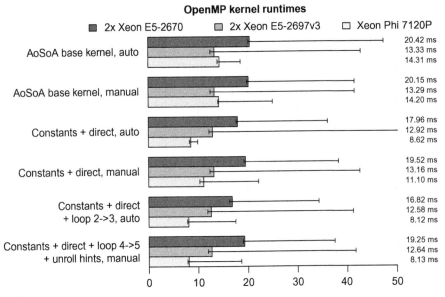

FIGURE 19.16

Runtime results for two kernels directly ported from their OpenCL equivalents, and the best performing automatic and manually vectorized OpenMP kernel that have been subject of further optimization. *Constants* means the matrix size known at compile time, while *direct* means no temporaries were used for accumulation.

Note

The downloadable example code for this chapter contains all kernel variants and the benchmarks we used. See the Readme for further instructions on how to build and run the code, and for a complete mapping of figures and source files.

SUMMARY

Both OpenCL and OpenMP are suitable for generating efficiently vectorized code for Intel Xeon processors and Intel Xeon Phi coprocessors. OpenCL kernels run everywhere but performance portability is, if at all, hard to achieve. Even so, maintaining multiple kernel variants within the same programming model, language and toolset is still better than having a completely different application branch for each target architecture. Intel has nearly two decades of experience supporting and optimizing OpenMP, which is reflected by up to 8% better performance on the Intel Xeon Phi coprocessor and up to 42% and 84% on the Sandy Bridge and Haswell Intel Xeon processor, respectively. We presented a simple recipe for porting OpenCL kernels to OpenMP. Our goal for the future is to automate this approach to maintain a single code base that can be used with both models.

With an optimized implementation, the Hexciton kernel can be efficiently computed on multicore and many-core processors and GPGPUs. It is memory-bound on all three platforms and achieves a percentage of the peak performances of up to 36%. The over-all speedups are $2.9\times$ on the Intel Xeon processor and $6.4\times$ on the Intel Xeon Phi coprocessor. The performance gain for the Intel Xeon Phi coprocessor over a dual Sandy Bridge and a dual Haswell Intel Xeon processor is $2.1\times$ and $1.5\times$, respectively.

Many optimization techniques have interacting effects, which means after successfully applying one optimization, previously failed approaches could become beneficial again and have to be retried. This process, especially with directive-based vectorization can be very unsatisfying. Manual vectorization using vector types offers a straight-forward and abstract way of implementing efficient code for SIMD architectures and offers multiple advantages such as compiler independence and a higher level of control. It is important to write such codes for an abstract SIMD width in order to keep the code portable. Using manual vectorization should at least be taken into consideration whenever writing new code or rewriting major portions of legacy code.

The most important lesson learned here is that not vectorization alone, but only the combination of vectorization and an optimized memory layout for the resulting access pattern are the foundation for performance on today's and tomorrow's multicore and many-core processors. Additionally, the use of compile time constants to specialize kernels for specific input instances can significantly improve performance by enabling better compiler optimization.

We will continue our work on the GPU-HEOM code with the remaining kernels. Currently, we are working on a generalization and automatization of the OpenCL to OpenMP transition, and hope to find an elegant equivalent to OpenCL's runtime kernel compilation. Either by including multiple precompiled kernels into the binary or by actually building and linking in kernels at runtime.

ACKNOWLEDGMENTS

This work was supported by the German Research Foundation (DFG projects RE 1389/8, KR 2889/7) and the Intel Parallel Computing Center at ZIB. We would like to thank Tobias Kramer and Christoph Kreisbeck, the authors of the GPU-HEOM code, and our colleagues at Intel for the productive cooperation, especially Chris J. Newburn, Georg Zitzlsberger, and Serguei Preis.

FOR MORE INFORMATION

The C++ SIMD libraries can be downloaded at:

VCL: http://www.agner.org/optimize/#vectorclass
VCLKNC: https://bitbucket.org/veclibknc/vclknc
Vc: http://code.compeng.uni-frankfurt.de/projects/vc

The following papers and technical documents provide more detailed insights in the topics discussed in this chapter.
- Advanced Micro Devices, Inc., AMD Accelerated Parallel Processing OpenCL Programming Guide: Revision: 2.7.
- Intel Corporation., Intel^{TM} SDK for OpenCL Applications XE 2013 R2, Optimization Guide.

- Kreisbeck, C., Kramer, T., Aspuru-Guzik, A., 2014. Scalable high-performance algorithm for the simulation of exciton dynamics. Application to the light-harvesting complex II in the presence of resonant vibrational modes. J. Chem. Theory Comput. 10 (9), 4045-4054.
- McIntosh-Smith, S., Mattson, T., Portable performance with OpenCL. Chapter 22 of High Performance Parallelism Pearls: Multicore and Many-Core Programming Approaches, pp. 359-376, Morgan Kaufmann, Waltham, MA, 2015.
- NVIDIA Corporation., NVIDIA OpenCL Best Practises Guide.
- Opencl, K., Munshi, A., The OpenCL Specification Version: 1.2 Document Revision: 15.
- OpenMP Architecture Review Board., OpenMP application program interface version 4.0.

Download all codes from this, and other chapters, http://lotsofcores.com.

OpenMP VERSUS OpenCL: DIFFERENCE IN PERFORMANCE?

20

Julia Fedorova, Sergei Vinogradov, Dmitry Prohorov

Intel Corporation, Russia

The comparison of OpenMP and OpenCL is interesting as they offer different constructs for describing data parallelism, so it is logical to wonder if one has an advantage over the other in performance. In this chapter, we explore this question by studying a set of benchmarks that initially seem to show an advantage for OpenCL when using the OpenMP and OpenCL programming models to offload calculations to an Intel® Xeon Phi™ coprocessor. We show that the performance advantages came from optimization work present only in the OpenCL versions of the code. Applying these optimizations in both versions of the code resulted in OpenMP implementations that matched or exceeded the performance of OpenCL implementations for these benchmarks.

FIVE BENCHMARKS

This chapter presents case studies with five benchmarks from the Rodinia suite comparing the performance of their OpenMP implementations with their OpenCL counterparts. We have chosen the Rodinia suite because it is being developed to benchmark heterogeneous systems, is freely available, and most of its benchmarks have both OpenCL and OpenMP implementations. We were also intrigued by the lower performance data reported for the OpenMP implementations of some benchmarks when compared with their OpenCL counterparts. As you will see, we found that the OpenMP implementations were not equivalently optimized and we show in this chapter how we were able to quickly improve them.

Figure 20.1 presents the timing for the OpenCL implementations and initial (baseline) OpenMP implementations. All implementations mentioned in this chapter refer to benchmarks offloading their computations onto an Intel Xeon Phi coprocessor.

Over the course of this case study, we investigated the OpenMP and OpenCL implementations of the benchmark, made sure that the OpenMP version implemented the same algorithm as done in OpenCL, and then applied several refinements to the OpenMP code. We discovered that the OpenMP version of the *LUD* benchmark implemented a different, "naive," algorithm versus the one implemented using OpenCL. Other OpenCL benchmarks expose some optimizations using algorithmic differences and specific language features of OpenCL. In our quest to find a fair comparison, we needed to apply similar transformations to the OpenMP implementations as well.

Benchmark	Benchmark Parameters	Optimized OpenCL time, sec	Original OpenMP time, sec	Optimized OpenMP time, sec
HotSpot	Grid size: 2048 X 2048 # of iterations: 4800	22.2	65.9	8.11
LUD	predefined well-conditioned matrix, size: 8000 X 8000	3.32	368	3.24
NW	sequence length: 16384 penalty value: 10	5.52	11.3	3.63
CFD	pre-generated file with 193K elements	9.36	28.3	9.03
BFS	pre-generated file with 16M nodes and 100M edges	1.59	1.03	0.71

FIGURE 20.1

Benchmarks used in the case study, the benchmark parameters, and timing of the OpenCL and baseline OpenMP implementation. All benchmarks are run in offload mode from an Intel® Xeon® processor host to an Intel Xeon Phi coprocessor.

First, we extended the OpenMP code with target pragmas to enable the code to utilize the Intel Xeon Phi coprocessor. The OpenCL code ran on the Intel Xeon Phi coprocessor out of the box. Then, we successively modified the OpenMP code and used the Intel® VTune™ Amplifier XE which helped us to explore inefficiencies and identify where to apply our optimization effort.

In this chapter, we look at the optimization of the *HotSpot* benchmark in depth; explaining the optimization techniques used and presenting the results. We review other benchmarks where similar optimization techniques have been applied and present their results. We conclude with a summary of results and a discussion of the particularly performance-sensitive differences between the OpenMP and OpenCL standards.

EXPERIMENTAL SETUP AND TIME MEASUREMENTS

We use the following system in our case study:

- Intel® Xeon® E5 processor @ 3.10 GHz: two sockets with eight cores per socket and two hardware threads per core, 32 Gb RAM as a host connected via PCI-E.
- Intel Xeon Phi 7120P coprocessor (formerly code named Knights Corner) with 61 cores where each one runs 4 hardware threads, for total of (61 × 4=) 244 threads. OpenMP and OpenCL

run-times leave one core for offload runtime services (aka "the COI demon"), providing up to 240 threads available for a user application.

- Red Hat Enterprise Linux Server release 6.5 as a host OS.
- Intel® Manycore Platform Software Stack (Intel® MPSS) version 3.4.2.

We built the benchmarks with Intel® C++ Compiler version 15.0 and used Intel® OpenCL™ Runtime 14.2 for Intel® CPU and Intel® Xeon Phi™ Coprocessor for Linux.

We used the same approach and implementation as Rodinia for time measurement. The times reported out and compared with for the benchmarks and their versions include the data transfers time, to and from, the coprocessor, the execution time on the coprocessor and, host time required to offload code fragments to the coprocessor when used by the runtime. Data initialization read from files and OpenCL kernel compilation are not included into the measured time. Timestamps are captured using the `gettimeofday()` function.

HotSpot BENCHMARK OPTIMIZATION

HotSpot is a 2D-transient thermal modeling kernel that computes the final state of a grid of cells from a given set of initial conditions (temperature and power dissipation per cell). The application iteratively updates the temperature values in all cells in parallel and stops simulation after a fixed number of iterations. The OpenMP version of the workload is located in the `openmp/hotspot/hotspot_openmp.cpp` source file. The compilation command is:

```
icc -g -fopenmp -O2 hotspot_openmp.cpp -o hotspot_offload
```

The OpenCL program is located in the `opencl/hotspot/` directory. There you can find `hotspot.c` that is the source for the program submitting work to the device and `hotspot_kernel.cl` that is the OpenCL device kernel. The OpenCL kernel is compiled with compiler default options and only the work group size is given via the definition in the OpenCL compilation command: `-DBLOCK_SIZE=16`.

The benchmark takes seven input parameters:

1. the size of the grid (two parameters),
2. the number of iterations,
3. the number of OpenMP threads to use,
4. the files containing initial temperature and power values, and
5. the output file into which to store the result temperature values.

In our case study, we use a 2048 × 2048 grid, 4800 iterations, and 240 threads.

In the OpenMP code, the computations are made within the `compute_tran_temp()` function that calls the `single_iteration()` function in the iteration loop.

As a first step, we extended the code of the benchmark with OpenMP target pragmas to run a computation on the Intel Xeon Phi coprocessor. We modified the `compute_tran_temp()` function as shown in Figure 20.2 and placed an OpenMP target pragma before the iteration loop. This version takes 65.9 s to run (shown in Figure 20.1).

To understand the performance characteristics of **HotSpot,** we ran the VTune Amplifier's *General Exploration Analysis* on the OpenCL and baseline OpenMP versions of the code and compared their results as shown in Figure 20.3. The key differences are marked in Figure 20.3 with numbers 1, 2, and 3:

```
void compute_tran_temp(FLOAT *result, int num_iterations,
    FLOAT *temp, FLOAT *power, int row, int col)
{
  FLOAT grid_height = chip_height / row;
  FLOAT grid_width = chip_width / col;

  FLOAT Cap = FACTOR_CHIP * SPEC_HEAT_SI*
     t_chip * grid_width * grid_height;
FLOAT Rx = grid_width /
     (2.0 * K_SI * t_chip * grid_height);
FLOAT Ry = grid_height /
     (2.0 * K_SI * t_chip * grid_width);
FLOAT Rz = t_chip /
     (K_SI * grid_height * grid_width);

FLOAT max_slope = MAX_PD /
      (FACTOR_CHIP * t_chip * SPEC_HEAT_SI);
FLOAT step = PRECISION / max_slope / 1000.0;

int array_size = row*col;
#pragma omp target \
   map(temp[0:array_size]) \
   map(to: power[0:array_size]) \
   map(to: row, col, Cap, Rx, Ry, Rz) \
   map(to: step, num_iterations) \
   map(result[0:array_size])
  {
   for (int i = 0; i < num_iterations ; i++)
   {
     single_iteration(result, temp, power, row,
  col, cap, Rx, Ry, Rz, step);
   }
  }
}
```

FIGURE 20.2

HotSpot `compute_tran_temp()` is a main computational function of the OpenMP code.

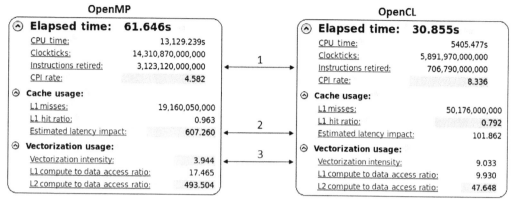

FIGURE 20.3

Intel VTune Amplifier XE General Exploration Analysis Summary for the baseline OpenMP and the OpenCL implementations of HotSpot benchmark.

- The number of retired instructions is significantly higher, at more than four times, for the OpenMP code versus the OpenCL version.
- The **Estimated Latency Impact** metric, which approximates an average number of cycles taken to service L1 cache misses, is about six times higher for the OpenMP code versus the OpenCL code.
- The **vectorization intensity** metric, which approximates the ratio of the total number of data elements processed by vector instructions to the total number of vector instructions, is about 2.25 times lower for the OpenMP code versus the OpenCL code. As HotSpot uses single-precision floats in the calculations, the ideal value for this metric is 16.

These differences suggested that there could be opportunities for the OpenMP version to be optimized. Therefore, we decided to modify the OpenMP code to make it more amenable to auto-vectorization, to run fewer instructions, and also to improve its data access pattern.

AVOIDING AN ARRAY COPY

The `single_iteration()` function contains two OpenMP parallel regions (see Figure 20.4):

- The first one calculates new values of the temperature based on `temp` and `power` values and stores these new values in the `result` array.
- The second one copies the `result` array to the `temp` array to use new values on the next iteration.

However, we can avoid copying the array and thereby remove the second parallel region by just swapping pointers to the `result` and the `temp` arrays on each iteration step. This is what the version written in OpenCL code did. We therefore removed the second parallel region from the `single_iteration()` function and correspondingly changed the offloaded region in the `compute_tran_temp()` as shown in Figure 20.5.

This change removed unnecessary work and makes the simulation time a little faster: 62.6 s versus 65.9 s.

```
void single_iteration (FLOAT *result, FLOAT *temp,
                       FLOAT *power, int row, int col,
                       FLOAT Cap, FLOAT Rx, FLOAT Ry,
                       FLOAT Rz, FLOAT step)
{
    FLOAT delta;
    #pragma omp parallel for schedule(static) \
            shared(power, temp, result) \
            private(r, c, delta) firstprivate(row, col)
    for (int r = 0; r < row; r++) {
        for (int c = 0; c < col; c++) {
            /* Boundaries */
            if ( (r == 0) || (c == 0) ||
                 (r == row-1) || (c == col-1) ) {...}
            /* Internal Area */
            else {
                delta = (step / Cap) * (power[r*col+c] +
                    (temp[(r+1)*col+c] + temp[(r-1)*col+c]-
                    2.0*temp[r*col+c]) / Ry +
                    (temp[r*col+c+1] + temp[r*col+c-1] -
                    2.0*temp[r*col+c]) / Rx +
                    (amb_temp - temp[r*col+c]) / Rz);
            }
            result[r*col+c] =temp[r*col+c]+ delta;
        }
    }
    #pragma omp parallel for shared(result, temp) \
            private(r, c) schedule(static)
    for (r = 0; r < row; r++) {
        for (c = 0; c < col; c++) {
            temp[r*col+c]=result[r*col+c];
        }
    }
}
```

FIGURE 20.4

The baseline code of the single_iteration() function with two OpenMP regions. The second region is doing an array copy.

APPLYING BLOCKING AND REDUCING THE NUMBER OF INSTRUCTIONS

As the single_iteration() function code review suggests (see Figure 20.4), one OpenMP thread processes grid elements from several grid rows (Figure 20.6b). However, if we consider an element access stencil (illustrated in Figure 20.6a) that uses the elements of the temp array temp[i][j], temp[i-1][j], temp[i+1][j], temp[i][j-1], temp[i][j+1] to calculate result[i][j], we discover that in the best case a grid element is reused only three times as a thread moves over the row.

```
int array_size = row*col;
#pragma omp target \
        map(temp[0:array_size]) \
        map(to: power[0:array_size]) \
        map(to: row, col, Cap, Rx, Ry, Rz) \
        map(to: step, num_iterations) \
        map( result[0:array_size])
{
    FLOAT* r = result;
    FLOAT* t = temp;
    for (int i = 0; i < num_iterations ; i++)
    {

        single_iteration( r, t, power, row, col, Cap,
                    Rx, Ry, Rz, step );
        FLOAT* tmp = t;
        t = r;
        r = tmp;
    }
}
```

FIGURE 20.5

Modified code of the `compute_tran_temp()` function used to eliminate the second OpenMP region in the single_iteration() function.

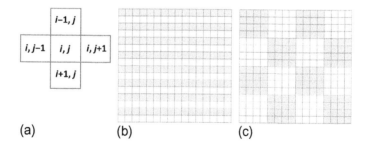

(a)   (b)   (c)

FIGURE 20.6

(a) HotSpot kernel data access stencil. (b) Baseline row-major work distribution pattern. (c) Blocked work distribution pattern.

A better work distribution would have a thread process elements in a grid block as suggested in Figure 20.6c. Within such a block, a `temp` array element is reused up to five times for calculating adjacent `result` elements.

The OpenCL code was already using a similar approach by breaking down the grid into square blocks and passing a square block as a work group to the computational kernel. This is how the OpenCL programming model specifies data decomposition, and so we applied this optimization to the OpenMP version.

Further experiments with different block sizes suggested that the optimal block size is 16×16 elements, which is the same in both the OpenCL and the OpenMP codes. Possible reasons for this size are:

1. 16 elements is a sweet spot for vectorization as a thread can process 16 (single precision) elements in one instruction.
2. Data required by four threads per core for a 16×16 block fits into L1 cache: data size ~ 12 kB ($16 \times 16 \times 4$ (size of float) $*3$ (number of arrays) $\times 4$ (threads)), while the L1 cache size is 32 kB.

To implement blocking in the OpenMP code, we transformed a two-dimensional loop into a one-dimensional loop by traversing blocks over the grid as shown in Figure 20.7.

Another transformation applied with the blocked code is related to separation of code processing blocks adjacent to the grid boundary from the "pure" inner bocks (this was done for individual elements in the code in Figure 20.4). Such a transformation enables decreasing the number of dynamic instructions by preventing excessive "if-else" constructs for inner blocks at runtime. The code with this change implemented is shown in Figure 20.7.

The OpenCL code enforces uniform processing of individual elements by introducing halo elements on the grid boundaries.

As a result, the number of retired instructions is significantly decreased for this version of the OpenMP code: from 3123 billion instructions at the baseline to 2634 billion instructions. Correspondingly, the simulation duration decreased from 65.9 to 45.4 s.

CHANGING DIVISIONS TO RECIPROCALS

The OpenCL computational kernel that implements the code for the `single_iteration()` function exchanges the division operations with multiplication through pre-calculated reciprocals that are passed to the kernel as parameters. This is much more efficient than having the division operation applied to each element during code execution.

We applied the same approach to the OpenMP version of the code.

VECTORIZATION OF THE INNER BLOCK CODE

Profiling using VTune Amplifier (Figure 20.8) showed that the code processing the inner blocks is a major hotspot. VTune Amplifier also reported the **vectorization intensity** metric of the `single_iteration()` function as one. A value of one can happen when scalar instructions are used, or when vector instructions are used in a scalar mode. Actual examination of the assembly code can be confusing, in the latter case, because vector instructions are present but underutilized which is inefficient use of the vector processing unit. This is why it is important to use the vectorization intensity metric that accounts for a number of active elements in vector instructions in dynamics. Based on the initially low vectorization intensity reported, for optimization, we focused our efforts on making the code run in vector mode.

To understand the reasons for the poor vectorization, we generated a vectorization report from the compiler by adding `-offload-option,mic,compiler,"-qopt-report-phase=vec -qopt-report=5"` to the compiler compilation command. Therefore, the compiler outputs a vectorization report for the code generated for the Intel Xeon Phi coprocessor. The vectorization report fragment presented in

```
#define BLOCK_SIZE_R    16
#define BLOCK_SIZE_C    16

void single_iteration(FLOAT *result, FLOAT *temp,
                      FLOAT *power,
                      int row, int col, FLOAT Cap,
                        FLOAT Rx, FLOAT Ry, FLOAT Rz,
                        FLOAT step)
{
    FLOAT delta;
    int num_chunk = row*col/(BLOCK_SIZE_R*BLOCK_SIZE_C);
    int chunks_in_row = col/BLOCK_SIZE_C;
    int chunks_in_col = row/BLOCK_SIZE_R;

    #pragma omp parallel for schedule(static) \
            shared(power, temp, result) \
            private(chunk, r, c, delta) \
            firstprivate(row, col, num_chunk, \
                         chunks_in_row)
    for ( int chunk = 0; chunk < num_chunk; ++chunk ) {
        int r_start = BLOCK_SIZE_R*(chunk/chunks_in_col);
        int c_start = BLOCK_SIZE_C*(chunk%chunks_in_row);
        int r_end = (r_start + BLOCK_SIZE_R) > row ?
                        row : (r_start + BLOCK_SIZE_R);
        int c_end = (c_start + BLOCK_SIZE_C) > col ?
                        col : c_start + BLOCK_SIZE_C;
        /* Boundaries */
        if ( r_start == 0 || c_start == 0 ||
             r_end == row || c_end == col ) {
            for ( r = r_start; r < r_end; ++r ) {
                for ( c = c_start; c < c_end; ++c ) {
                    ...
                    /* Update Temperatures */
                    result[r*col+c] = temp[r*col+c] +
                                        delta;
                }
            }
            continue;
        }
        /* Internal area */
        for ( int r = r_start; r < r_end; ++r ) {
            for ( int c = c_start; c < c_end; ++c ) {
                /* Update Temperatures */
                result[r*col+c] = temp[r*col+c]+
                        (step / Cap * (power[r*col+c] +
                        (temp[(r+1)*col+c] +
                         temp[(r-1)*col+c] -
                         2.f*temp[r*col+c]) / Ry +
                        (temp[r*col+c+1] + temp[r*col+c-1] -
                         2.f*temp[r*col+c]) / Rx +
                        (amb_temp - temp[r*col+c]) / Rz));
            }
        }
    }
}
```

FIGURE 20.7

Code listing of the single_iteration() function with blocking applied.

```
271     for ( chunk = 0; chunk < num_chunk; ++chunk )                                    5.523s|
272     {                                                                                 1.028s|
273         int r_start = BLOCK_SIZE_R*(chunk/chunks_in_col);                             9.890s|
274         int c_start = BLOCK_SIZE_C*(chunk%chunks_in_row);                             1.028s|
275         int r_end = r_start + BLOCK_SIZE_R > row ? row : r_start + BLOCK_SIZE_R;      0.257s|
276         int c_end = c_start + BLOCK_SIZE_C > col ? col : c_start + BLOCK_SIZE_C;      0.835s|
277         /* Boundaries */
278         if ( r_start == 0 || c_start == 0 || r_end == row || c_end == col )           1.734s|
279         {
280             for ( r = r_start; r < r_start + BLOCK_SIZE_R; ++r ) {                    0.385s|
281                 for ( c = c_start; c < c_start + BLOCK_SIZE_C; ++c ) {                5.394s|
282                     /* Corner 1 */
283                     if ( (r == 0) && (c == 0) ) {                                     1.670s|
284                         delta = (Cap_1) * (power[0] +
285                             (temp[1] - temp[0]) * Rx_1 +
286                             (temp[col] - temp[0]) * Ry_1 +                            0.193s|
287                             (amb_temp - temp[0]) * Rz_1);
288                     }   /* Corner 2 */
289                     else if ((r == 0) && (c == col-1)) {                              0.064s|
290                         delta = (Cap_1) * (power[c] +                                 0.064s|
291                             (temp[c-1] - temp[c]) * Rx_1 +                            0.321s|
292                             (temp[c+col] - temp[c]) * Ry_1 +
293                             ( amb_temp - temp[c]) * Rz_1);
294                     }    /* Corner 3 */
295                     else if ((r == row-1) && (c == col-1)) {                          1.477s|
296                         delta = (Cap_1) * (power[r*col+c] +                           0.064s|
297                             (temp[r*col+c-1] - temp[r*col+c]) * Rx_1 +
298                             (temp[(r-1)*col+c] - temp[r*col+c]) * Ry_1 +              0.450s|
299                             ( amb_temp - temp[r*col+c]) * Rz_1);
300                     }   /* Corner 4    */
301                     else if ((r == row-1) && (c == 0)) {                              0.064s|
302                         delta = (Cap_1) * (power[r*col] +                             0.064s|
303                             (temp[r*col+1] - temp[r*col]) * Rx_1 +
304                             (temp[(r-1)*col] - temp[r*col]) * Ry_1 +
305                             (amb_temp - temp[r*col]) * Rz_1);                         0.257s|
306                     }   /* Edge 1 */
307                     else if (r == 0) {
308                         delta = (Cap_1) * (power[c] +                                 0.193s|
309                             (temp[c+1] + temp[c-1] - 2.0*temp[c]) * Rx_1 +            0.450s|
310                             (temp[col+c] - temp[c]) * Ry_1 +                          0.128s|
311                             (amb_temp - temp[c]) * Rz_1);                             0.193s|
312                     }   /* Edge 2 */
313                     else if (c == col-1) {                                            1.541s|
314                         delta = (Cap_1) * (power[r*col+c] +                           3.147s|
315                             (temp[(r+1)*col+c] + temp[(r-1)*col+c] - 2.0*temp[r*col+c]) * Ry_1 +   2.761s|
316                             (temp[r*col+c-1] - temp[r*col+c]) * Rx_1 +                0.193s|
317                             (amb_temp - temp[r*col+c]) * Rz_1);                       9.119s|
318                     }   /* Edge 3 */
319                     else if (r == row-1) {                                            1.092s|
320                         delta = (Cap_1) * (power[r*col+c] +                           0.321s|
321                             (temp[r*col+c+1] + temp[r*col+c-1] - 2.0*temp[r*col+c]) * Rx_1 +   0.450s|
322                             (temp[(r-1)*col+c] - temp[r*col+c]) * Ry_1 +              0.064s|
323                             (amb_temp - temp[r*col+c]) * Rz_1);                       0.257s|
324                     }   /* Edge 4 */
325                     else if (c == 0) {                                               0.963s|
326                         delta = (Cap_1) * (power[r*col] +                            3.596s|
327                             (temp[(r+1)*col] + temp[(r-1)*col] - 2.0*temp[r*col]) * Ry_1 +   2.761s|
328                             (temp[r*col+1] - temp[r*col]) * Rx_1 +                   0.064s|
329                             (amb_temp - temp[r*col]) * Rz_1);                        0.257s|
330                     }
331                     result[r*col+c] =temp[r*col+c]+ delta;                           17.982s|
332                 }
333             }
334             continue;
335         }
336         /* Internal Area */
337         for ( r = r_start; r < r_end; ++r ) {                                        29.606s|
338             for ( c = c_start; c < c_end; ++c ) {                                     99.862s|
339                 /* Update Temperatures */
340                 result[r*col+c] =temp[r*col+c]+                                       1258.523s|
341                     ( Cap_1 * (power[r*col+c] +
342                     (temp[(r+1)*col+c] + temp[(r-1)*col+c] - 2.f*temp[r*col+c]) * Ry_1 +   607.780s|
343                     (temp[r*col+c+1] + temp[r*col+c-1] - 2.f*temp[r*col+c]) * Rx_1 +   233.505s|
344                     (amb_temp - temp[r*col+c]) * Rz_1));                              62.422s|
```

FIGURE 20.8

VTune Amplifier Source View for the single_iteration() function of the OpenMP implementation with blocking applied. Time annotations on the right indicate that the inner block processing code is a hotspot.

```
*MIC* Begin optimization report for:
single_iteration(FLOAT *, FLOAT *, FLOAT *, int,
int, FLOAT, FLOAT, F

LOAT, FLOAT, FLOAT)


     Report from: Vector optimizations [vec]


LOOP BEGIN at hotspot_openmp.cpp(337,9)
     remark #15541: outer loop was not auto-
vectorized: consider using SIMD directive
     LOOP BEGIN at hotspot_openmp.cpp(338,13)
          remark #15344: loop was not vectorized:
vector dependence prevents vectorization
          remark #15346: vector dependence: assumed
FLOW dependence between result line 340 and temp
line 340
       remark #15346: vector dependence: assumed ANTI
dependence between temp line 340 and result line
340
       LOOP END
LOOP END
```

FIGURE 20.9

Vectorization report for the single_iteration() function.

Figure 20.9 identifies that the loop in line 338 (also identified as a hotspot) is not vectorized due to assumed dependencies between the `temp` and the `result` arrays.

However, based on the code access patterns, we know that there are no dependencies between the `temp` and `result` arrays across iterations of the loop. Therefore, the loop can be safely vectorized with no side effects. So, we add a `#pragma omp simd` to the inner loop out of the two loops over block elements to inform the compiler to ignore the dependency and use vector instructions.

The result rewards us with the **vectorization intensity** metric value jumping to 10, as reported in VTune, and the computation time reduced to 13 s! This result provides a very favorable comparison to 45.4 s after blocking and 65.9 s for the baseline code.

It is possible to improve the performance even further by explicitly setting the number of loop iterations enabling the compiler to successfully unroll the inner loop. Therefore, we rewrote the inner block processing loop as shown in Figure 20.10 specifying that it has a constant number of iterations equal to the block size.

```
void single_iteration(FLOAT *result, FLOAT
*temp,
                      FLOAT *power,
                      int row, int col, FLOAT
Cap_1,
                      FLOAT Rx_1, FLOAT Ry_1,
FLOAT Rz_1,
                      FLOAT step)
{
FLOAT delta;
int num_chunk = row*col /
              (BLOCK_SIZE_R *
BLOCK_SIZE_C);
   int chunks_in_row = col/BLOCK_SIZE_C;
   int chunks_in_col = row/BLOCK_SIZE_R;

   #pragma omp parallel for schedule(static) \
          shared(power, temp, result) \
          private(chunk, r, c, delta) \
          firstprivate(row, col, num_chunk,
chunks_in_row)
      for( int chunk = 0; chunk < num_chunk;
++chunk ) {
         int r_start =
BLOCK_SIZE_R*(chunk/chunks_in_col);
         int c_start =
BLOCK_SIZE_C*(chunk%chunks_in_row);
         int r_end = (r_start + BLOCK_SIZE_R) >
row ?
                     row : (r_start +
BLOCK_SIZE_R);
         int c_end = (c_start + BLOCK_SIZE_C) >
col ?
                     col : (c_start +
BLOCK_SIZE_C);
         /* Boundaries */
         if ( r_start == 0 || c_start == 0 ||
            r_end == row || c_end == col ) {
            for ( r = r_start; r < r_end; ++r )
{
               for ( c = c_start; c < c_end;
++c ) {
                  ...
                  result[r*col+c]
=temp[r*col+c] +
                                    delta;
               }
            }
            continue;
         }
         /* Internal area */
         for(int r = r_start; r < r_start +
BLOCK_SIZE_R;
```

FIGURE 20.10

Final version of the single_iteration() function. The loop for the inner blocks has a constant number of iterations.

```
                        ++r)
              {
    #pragma omp simd
                for(int c = c_start;
                    c < c_start + BLOCK_SIZE_C; ++c)
                {
                /* Update Temperatures */
                    result[r*col+c] =temp[r*col+c]+
                        (Cap_1 * (power[r*col+c] +
                        (temp[(r+1)*col+c] +
                        temp[(r-1)*col+c] -
                        2.f*temp[r*col+c]) * Ry_1
    +
                        (temp[r*col+c+1] +
    temp[r*col+c-1] -
        2.f*temp[r*col+c]) * Rx_1
    +
                        (amb_temp - temp[r*col+c])
    * Rz_1));
                }
            }
        }
    }
```

FIGURE 20.10,   Cont'd.

Inspection of assembly instructions shows that the loop is now unrolled. This provides another boost in the performance reducing the simulation time to 10.8 s.

With this last transformation, the number of retired instructions reported by the VTune Amplifier drops to 171 billion. The **vectorization intensity** metric jumps up to 17 (Figure 20.11a). The value 17 is not definitive since the VTune Amplifier cannot measure it precisely and approximates it from the hardware events. However, it indicates that a significant number of vector instructions process all 16 SIMD lanes at a time.

The VTune Amplifier reports 706 billion retired instructions and the **vectorization intensity** equal to 9 for the OpenCL code. Inspection of the OpenCL binary code in the VTune Amplifier Source View shows

1. The number of the instructions of the OpenCL kernel is bigger than the number of the OpenMP single_iteration() function instructions.
2. The hottest basic block of the OpenCL computational kernel has the vectorization intensity equal to ~17. However, the **vectorization intensity** values for the other basic blocks are lower. So when this metric is calculated for the whole kernel, it averages to the lower value.

This analysis suggests that the OpenCL implementation based on halo elements is less efficient than the optimized OpenMP code, and probably could be optimized to run less instructions in the computational kernel and thereby reduce simulation time.

FINAL TOUCH: LARGE PAGES AND AFFINITY

To improve temporal and spatial cache reuse, we set up the MIC_KMP_AFFINITY=compact environment variable to make the OpenMP runtime place OpenMP thread <n+1> on a free thread context as close as possible to the thread context where OpenMP thread <n> was placed. While running with the default OpenMP scheduler, the same placement is made for every iteration, so array data loaded into L1 and L2 is reused between iterations.

The profiling data in Figure 20.11a show that the **Estimated Latency Impact** metric is still too high. A key contributor appears to be L1 TLB misses (whose ratio is also high). The Translation Lookaside Buffer (TLB) is a hardware unit responsible for the translation of virtual addresses into physical ones. The optimization technique for fighting TLB misses is to use large 2 MB pages versus standard 4 kB pages. The offload runtime allocates buffers on a large 2 MB page if the MIC_USE_2MB_BUFFERS=<...> environment variable is set. For example, MIC_USE_2MB_BUFFERS=64K instructs the runtime to allocate buffers of greater than 64 kB into large pages.

Note that the OpenCL runtime uses large pages on the Intel Xeon Phi coprocessor by default. One can check it by dumping /proc/meminfo while an OpenCL program is running on the Intel Xeon Phi coprocessor.

These modifications improve performance further: the simulation time is reduced to 8.1 s.

HotSpot OPTIMIZATION CONCLUSIONS

The table in Figure 20.12 summarizes the optimization steps, the performance metrics, and the simulation time achieved in each step. During optimization, the performance is improved by a factor of eight.

⊙ **Elapsed time: 16.921s**		⊙ **Elapsed time: 14.769s**	
CPU time:	2380.450s	CPU time:	1941.248s
Clockticks:	2,594,690,000,000	Clockticks:	2,115,960,000,000
Instructions retired:	171,220,000,000	Instructions retired:	114,520,000,000
CPI rate:	15.154	CPI rate:	18.477
⊙ **Cache usage:**		⊙ **Cache usage:**	
L1 misses:	7,189,000,000	L1 misses:	7,014,000,000
L1 hit ratio:	0.899	L1 hit ratio:	0.856
Estimated latency impact:	330.525	Estimated latency impact:	280.491
⊙ **Vectorization usage:**		⊙ **Vectorization usage:**	
Vectorization intensity:	17.421	Vectorization intensity:	17.375
L1 compute to data access ratio:	4.329	L1 compute to data access ratio:	6.318
L2 compute to data access ratio:	42.746	L2 compute to data access ratio:	43.872
⊙ **TLB usage:**		⊙ **TLB usage:**	
L1 TLB miss ratio:	0.047	L1 TLB miss ratio:	0.000
L2 TLB miss ratio:	0.000	L2 TLB miss ratio:	0.000

(a)   (b)

FIGURE 20.11

Intel VTune Amplifier XE General Exploration Summary illustrating how affinity and large pages reduce the Estimated Latency Impact metric and number of L1 TLB misses. (a) Profiling data prior to applying large pages and affinity. (b) Profiling data for the optimized version with large pages and MIC_KMP_AFFINITY=compact enabled.

Optimization Step	time, s	Instruction Retired, billions	Cycles per Instruction (CPI)	Vectorization Intensity	Estimated Latency Impact
Baseline	65.9	3,123	4.6	3.9	607
Avoiding array copy	62.6	3,431	5.2	4.0	658
Blocking	62.2	3,241	5.6	4.0	745
Separate boundaries processing	45.4	2,634	5.5	2.7	681
Hoisting common expressions and using reciprocals	14.8	512	7.0	1.0	357
Vectorization - simd	13	356	8.9	10.0	332
Inner loop unrolled	10.8	171	15.2	17.4	330
KMP_AFFINITY = compact	10.4	182	14.3	17.4	332
Big pages	8.1	114	18.5	17.4	280

FIGURE 20.12

The sequence of optimization steps for the HotSpot benchmark and profiling characteristics reported by the VTune Amplifier. The variations in performance metrics between steps where no transformation that might impact the corresponding metric is done should be attributed to the statistical noise or variations in the OpenMP runtime (e.g., scheduler, wait functions, etc.).

To a great extent, the speedup is achieved due to the decreased number of retired instructions where eliminating redundant computations and enabling vectorization is a key.

The work distribution and, therefore, data access pattern also help in performance improvement by enabling vectorization and decreasing data access latency through better data reuse and locality.

Optimal data access can result in an even bigger speedup for the code where a working set is significantly bigger than the cumulative size of L2 cache. For the HotSpot case, the impact is not that big because the working set is 48 MB ($=2048 \times 2048$ (grid size) $\times$ 4 (size of float) $\times$ 3 (number of arrays)) that is just 1.5 times bigger than 30 MB of the combined L2 cache size ($=512K$ (per core) $\times$ 60 (number of cores)).

It is interesting to note that focusing only on the CPI metric (Cycles per Instruction) can be highly misleading for the case where algorithm and instruction mix changes are done over the steps of optimization. Our goal should be to get better performance through dynamic work shrinking and vectorization usage, both targeting a smaller number of retired instructions, the number of retired instructions better correlates with performance. Therefore, when we optimize code, vectorization intensity and Instruction Retired are much better metrics to watch and compare between runs. Figure 20.12 shows us that CPI does not correlate with the simulation elapsed time. This also illustrates why the OpenCL code takes longer time to run than the optimized OpenMP code, given how OpenCL is implemented required far more instructions to run (706 billion).

OPTIMIZATION STEPS FOR THE OTHER FOUR BENCHMARKS

In the other four benchmarks, the optimization work and results echoed with those we examined in detail for the first benchmark. We focused on applying the same techniques that we learned while working on the HotSpot benchmark. However, there are a few other interesting techniques used. They are highlighted in the following sections.

LUD BENCHMARK

The *LUD* benchmark runs LU factorization for a predefined well-conditioned matrix. There is a big difference in performance between the OpenCL version (blocked LU): 3.3 s, and the baseline OpenMP version (naïve LU): 368 s (see Figure 20.1). This difference is the result of the naïve algorithm being used, especially in regard to how the code traverses the data. The blocked algorithm used in the OpenCL code is much better in terms of data locality.

Implementing blocked LU factorization in the OpenMP code provided a huge performance boost: decreasing the computation time from 368 to 48.5 s.

The blocked algorithm is composed of three functions that compute "in-place" different submatrices (blocks) of the input matrix. This is done through executing a loop transforming the input matrix into a resultant one that holds final L and U matrices at its low diagonal and upper diagonal parts.

In the blocked code, the hotspot is an update of an inner submatrix marked as "I" in Figure 20.13, therefore most of optimizations were done on this code region.

The following transformations/steps were applied to the LUD OpenMP code:

- Implemented blocked LU factorization algorithm significantly improving data locality. Experiments determined that the best block size is 16.
- `#pragma omp simd` applied to the internal loops in the hotspot region.
- Local arrays added in the hotspot. They store block data (copied from the input matrix) in a compact manner, which enables efficient non-strided memory accesses and full vectorization of the inner loop.
- `MIC_USE_2MB_BUFFERS=64K` environment set to make the offload runtime allocate 2 MB pages for better use of TLB.

With these changes, the *LUD* OpenMP benchmark achieves 3.1 s computation time, which is on-par with the OpenCL code time.

Sub-matrices in the blocked LU factorization algorithm
and two iterations of the algorithm

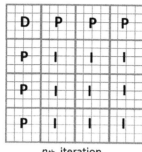 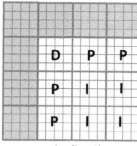

*n*th iteration   *n*+1 th iteration

FIGURE 20.13

Blocked LU factorization data breakdown. The input matrix is viewed as a set of submatrices (blocks), which are updated one by one. There are three types of submatrices depending on their position in the input matrix: diagonal (D), perimeter (P), and inner (I) blocks. At each iteration, the input matrix shrinks down as elements at the diagonal and perimeter submatrices get their result values and these submatrices do not "participate" in the next iteration (in gray).

CFD BENCHMARK

The **CFD** benchmark is an unstructured-grid finite-volume solver for the three-dimensional Euler equations with compressible flow. The CFD solver iteratively calculates fluxes and updates an array of structures (AoS) that contain density, density power, and momenta. The benchmark has three compute kernels; each of them contains a single OpenMP parallel loop.

After we put target pragmas to the OpenMP code, it ran about three times slower than the OpenCL code. In this case, the compiler does not vectorize the loop annotated with the OpenMP `parallel for` directive.

To enable compiler vectorization, we added one more loop over blocks as shown in Figure 20.14. With this, the OpenMP scheduler works at a coarser block level and at the same time each block gets vectorized within a thread. Such a transformation gave some performance boost but not enough to reach the OpenCL code performance.

Setting the `MIC_USE_2MB_BUFFERS=64K` environment variable to make the offload runtime allocate large pages for the OpenMP version does not improve the performance. At the same time, VTune Amplifier shows that the OpenMP code still has some potential vectorization improvements (see Figure 20.15a).

Here, we noticed that there is one big difference between the OpenCL and OpenMP implementation. The OpenCL version stored density, density power, and momentums data as a structure of arrays (SoA), while the OpenMP version stored the same data as an AoS.

While AoS allows writing code that is easy to understand and maintain, it does not lend itself well to data locality and SIMD execution. In contrast, SoA in the OpenCL implementation enables better locality and vectorization and, consequently, performance. Switching the OpenMP code to use SoA helps to reach better **vectorization intensity**, cache utilization (see Figure 20.15b), and to achieve the same performance as the OpenCL code.

```
// nelr - number of elements
#pragma omp parallel for   default(shared)
schedule(static)
for(int blk = 0; blk < nelr/block_length; ++blk)
{
    int b_start = blk*block_length;
    int b_end = (blk+1)*block_length > nelr ?
                nelr : (blk+1)*block_length;
#pragma omp simd
    for(int i = b_start; i < b_end; ++i)
    {
        ...
    }
}
```

FIGURE 20.14

Code fragment illustrating manual blocking and enabling vectorization of an inner loop.

Array of structures		Structure of arrays	
⊘ Elapsed time: 16.423s		**⊘ Elapsed time: 15.180s**	
CPU time:	2578.312s	CPU time:	2431.055s
Clockticks:	2,810,360,000,000	Clockticks:	2,649,850,000,000
Instructions retired:	426,300,000,000	Instructions retired:	286,160,000,000
CPI rate:	6.592	CPI rate:	9.260
⊘ Cache usage:		**⊘ Cache usage:**	
L1 misses:	15,622,950,000	L1 misses:	13,923,000,000
L1 hit ratio:	0.912	L1 hit ratio:	0.881
Estimated latency impact:	147.764	Estimated latency impact:	164.592
⊘ Vectorization usage:		**⊘ Vectorization usage:**	
Vectorization intensity:	8.486	Vectorization intensity:	12.276
L1 compute to data access ratio:	10.898	L1 compute to data access ratio:	8.310
L2 compute to data access ratio:	124.587	L2 compute to data access ratio:	70.050
⊘ TLB usage:		**⊘ TLB usage:**	
L1 TLB miss ratio:	0.002	L1 TLB miss ratio:	0.019
L2 TLB miss ratio:	0.000	L2 TLB miss ratio:	0.000
(a)		(b)	

FIGURE 20.15

Intel VTune Amplifier XE General Exploration Summary for OpenMP version of CFD, original code using AoS (a) and modified to use SoA (b).

The following modifications were done in the OpenMP version of CFD solver:

- Blocking algorithm implemented to enable compiler vectorization
- `MIC_USE_2MB_BUFFERS=64K` environment set to make the offload runtime allocate 2 MB pages for better use of TLB
- Memory layout changed from AoS to SoA.

NW BENCHMARK

The *NW* (Needleman-Wunsch) is a dynamic programming algorithm used in bioinformatics to align protein or nucleotide sequences. It consists of three steps: initialization of the score matrix, calculation of scores, and deducing the alignment from the score matrix. The second step is parallelized using OpenMP and OpenCL correspondingly.

Initially, the OpenMP version ran about two times slower than the OpenCL version. Again, the OpenCL code uses a blocked algorithm to traverse the data and copies blocks of data to local memory before processing. The following modifications in the OpenMP version help to achieve better performance than the OpenCL implementation:

- The same blocking algorithm implemented in the OpenMP code and blocks of data placed to local arrays before doing calculations
- `#pragma omp simd` applied to the inner loops of the parallel region
- `MIC_USE_2MB_BUFFERS=64K` environment set to make the offload runtime allocate 2 MB pages for better use of TLB
- `MIC_KMP_AFFINITY=compact` environment set for better data locality.

After these optimizations, the OpenMP version performs ~1.5 times better than the OpenCL version (3.63 s vs. 5.52 s). Comparing the profiles suggests that the OpenCL runtime scheduler introduces more overhead than the OpenMP default static scheduler. The OpenCL scheduler overhead becomes significant for this benchmark because the size of a single computation task varies along the iteration space. We think that the combination of the compact affinity and the static OpenMP scheduler helps the OpenMP code run faster. This case highlights some room for improvement in the OpenCL runtime.

BFS BENCHMARK

The BFS is the Breadth-First Search algorithm implemented in parallel. The algorithm contains two kernels:

- The first kernel visits all nodes on the current layer to find their non-visited children and updates the corresponding costs.
- The second kernel marks visited nodes and sets a mask for the nodes that should be visited on the next layer.

The second kernel was not run in parallel in original OpenMP version. We merely had to add the `#pragma omp parallel for` declaration for the second kernel and make the offload runtime allocate memory with 2 MB pages.

The optimized OpenMP version beats the OpenCL version with a two times performance increase (0.71 vs. 1.59 s). We associate this difference with the OpenCL scheduler issue similar to the one described for the NW benchmark.

SUMMARY

In this chapter, we have described optimization techniques applied to the five benchmarks in the Rodinia suite. Most optimizations were already present in the OpenCL versions and were easily duplicated in the OpenMP versions of the code. These techniques enabled the OpenMP code to offload

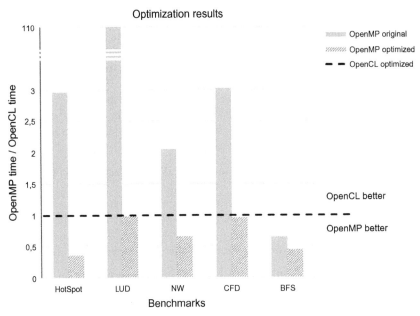

FIGURE 20.16

Performance results.

computations to the Intel Xeon Phi coprocessor and achieve the same or better performance versus its OpenCL counterpart. Figures 5.16 and 5.17 show the relative and absolute performance numbers.

The baseline performance gaps were caused, to a great extent, by the differences in the algorithms or data access patterns implemented in the OpenCL and OpenMP codes. After extending the OpenMP versions with the optimizations that were implemented in the OpenCL code, similar or better performance was reached. OpenMP versions with better performance may suggest opportunities to further optimize the OpenCL versions.

We also observed that the OpenCL programming model constrain users to write kernel code that vectorized out of the box. Data decomposition into work groups, implied by the OpenCL model, inspires implementation of algorithms directed toward exploiting data locality.

While the OpenMP programming model does not impose such constrains, implementing an OpenMP code exhibiting vectorization and locality properties (with right algorithm in hands) is not difficult. Applying the OpenMP `pragma omp simd` to the inner loops known to have no dependencies helps vectorize OpenMP code. Exploiting data locality is governed by the algorithm (which is independent on programming model) and data access patterns.

The parallel work scheduling is another factor that should be taken into account when comparing programming models. We saw differences in the performance due to the OpenCL and OpenMP schedulers. However, to make definitive conclusions, the examined benchmarks do not suffice—more benchmarks with imbalanced tasks are required.

Through this case study, we have learned that similar performance can be achieved with either programming model: OpenMP or OpenCL, with similar efforts. The most important factors that repeatedly impacted performance were (1) algorithm choice, (2) memory layout, and (3) data access patterns.

Benchmark	Optimized OpenCL time, sec	Original OpenMP time, sec	Optimized OpenMP time, sec
HotSpot	22.2	65.9	8.11
LUD	3.32	368	3.24
NW	5.52	11.3	3.63
CFD	9.36	28.3	9.03
BFS	1.59	1.03	0.71

FIGURE 20.17

Performance results.

FOR MORE INFORMATION

Here are some additional reading materials that we recommend related to this chapter:

- OpenCL:
  - https://www.khronos.org/opencl/
  - Intel® OpenCL™ SDK and run-times: https://software.intel.com/en-us/articles/intel-code-builder-for-opencl-api
- OpenMP: http://openmp.org/wp/openmp-specifications/
- Rodinia benchmark suite:
  - http://www.cs.virginia.edu/~skadron/wiki/rodinia/index.php/Rodinia:Accelerating_Compute-Intensive_Applications_with_Accelerators
  - Che, S., Sheaffer, J.W., Boyer, M., Szafaryn, L.G., Wang, L., Skadron, K., 2010. A characterization of the Rodinia benchmark suite with comparison to contemporary CMP workloads. In: Proceedings of the IEEE International Symposium on Workload Characterization, December 2010
  - http://www.mcs.anl.gov/events/workshops/p2s2/2012/slides/JieShen_P2S22012_presentation.pdf
- Performance analysis and optimization for Intel® Xeon Phi™ Coprocessor: https://software.intel.com/en-us/articles/optimization-and-performance-tuning-for-intel-xeon-phi-coprocessors-part-2-understanding
- Download the code from this, and other chapters, http://lotsofcores.com

PREFETCH TUNING OPTIMIZATIONS

21

Diana Guttman*, Meenakshi Arunachalam[†], Vlad Calina[‡], Mahmut Taylan Kandemir*

Pennsylvania State University, USA[*] Intel Corporation, USA[†] Intel Corporation, Romania[‡]

In this chapter, we explore various techniques for tuning prefetching in throughput applications and show up to $3\times$ speed-up from such optimizing of prefetching on a coprocessor. Although we show specific applications as examples, these applications are diverse enough to require different optimization strategies. We show that tuning prefetching can optimize performance on both processors and coprocessors; the effects of tuning prefetching prove more significant for the cores using in-order execution on the Intel® Xeon Phi™ coprocessor than for the out-of-order cores on an Intel® Xeon® processor. We hope that readers tuning the performance of other applications can try some or all of these strategies to get the best performance possible from their own code.

THE IMPORTANCE OF PREFETCHING FOR PERFORMANCE

Modern processor architectures generally include some level of prefetching support in their memory hierarchies via combinations of hardware, software (compiler-guided), and intrinsics for application developers. Prefetching aims to issue data accesses before an application actually needs that data thereby reducing the observed memory latencies and lowering the number of cache misses. This may significantly improve the application performance by effectively hiding memory access latencies while other useful work is done on the processor. Figure 21.1 illustrates how prefetching overlaps memory latency with computation. Sophisticated prefetchers detect patterns in workload access streams, tune their aggressiveness, and throttle each other dynamically. The goal of the prefetcher is to increase coverage in order to mitigate as many demand cache misses as possible while improving efficiency by targeting only prefetching candidates that will actually improve performance. Careful targeting is needed because prefetching speculatively utilizes processing resources such as memory bandwidth. There are multitudes of factors that the designer takes into account to make optimal implementations including throttling so that aggressive pursuits do not result in kicking useful data out of the caches, bringing in data too far ahead of time, or even in plain wasted useless prefetches. It is a balancing act to maximize benefits while using microarchitectural resources efficiently in tune with the access patterns and workload needs.

Much of this decision making is done in hardware or by the compiler. However, sufficient control is also given to the application writer, who knows their workload best. The challenge is in tuning prefetchers to your application by thoroughly understanding what they can do and tuning them to get maximum performance efficiency. In this chapter, we discuss the prefetcher support available on Intel Xeon

Without prefetching:

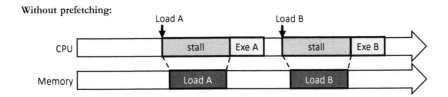

With prefetching:

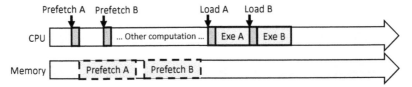

FIGURE 21.1

The first request to a data item (cold cache miss) can cause the CPU to stall for hundreds of cycles waiting for memory to provide the data. Prefetching allows the processor to request data ahead of time, overlapping the memory access latency with other computation. After the data has been prefetched into the on-chip cache, the first access to it will be a hit.

processors and Intel Xeon Phi coprocessors and give examples showing how it can be used effectively. More specifically, we demonstrate through three different workloads—Stream Triad, Smith-Waterman, and SHOC MD (Scalable Heterogeneous Computing Molecular Dynamics)—how to tune processor and coprocessor prefetchers for each of their differing access patterns and needs. Hardware and software prefetcher tuning together yield a whopping 6× bandwidth improvement for Stream Triad as its streaming access pattern is amenable to optimal prefetching behavior. The out-of-order execution found in Intel Xeon processor cores also shows benefits from tuning prefetching but with slightly less magnitude, as expected. Even with SHOC MD, which does indirect accesses that cannot be easily determined at compile time, we see benefits using _mm_prefetch runtime intrinsics. On both processors and coprocessors, it is imperative that all applications evaluate the benefits that prefetching can bring and tune them to their advantage.

PREFETCHING ON INTEL XEON PHI COPROCESSORS

Prefetching is especially important for the coprocessor compared to out-of-order, more complex processors. Because the cores are in-order, they cannot hide memory latency as easily. An out-of-order processor can work on later instructions while earlier instructions are stalled waiting for memory requests; in an in-order processor, a stalled instruction prevents any later instructions from executing until the data return from memory. Also, the lack of an L3 cache on the coprocessor means that L2 misses have to access the slower memory subsystem. Another way to hide latency in parallel applications is to spawn large numbers of threads. Compared to GPUs with thousands of threads, an Intel Xeon Phi coprocessor can run up to 244 threads, so this latency hiding technique is less viable, and other techniques become more important. There are two types of prefetching for the coprocessor: software prefetching and hardware prefetching.

SOFTWARE PREFETCHING

The compiler may issue prefetch instructions that target future iterations of a loop. This optimization helps in improving performance for applications with regular memory accesses. For each memory access inside a loop, the compiler may issue two prefetch instructions:

- VPREFETCH1—prefetches data from memory to L2
- VPREFETCH0—prefetches data from L2 to L1. The prefetch distance of these instructions is generally shorter than for VPREFETCH1

Ideally, software prefetching should bring data from main memory into the L2 cache first, before prefetching from the L2 cache to the L1 cache, as shown in Figure 21.2. The prefetch instructions are described in more detail in the Intel Xeon Phi Coprocessor Instruction Set Architecture Reference Manual.

COMPILER INTRINSICS FOR VPREFETCH INSTRUCTIONS

The `_mm_prefetch(char const* p, int i)` intrinsic function and other intrinsics for the coprocessor are described in the Intel Intrinsics Guide. This function is used when a programmer wishes to force the compiler to insert a VPREFETCH0 or VPREFETCH1 instruction for a specific memory address. The first argument is the memory address to be fetched (1 byte) and the second argument is a hint to the compiler about which level of cache to bring the data to (L2 or L1). When using manually inserted intrinsic prefetches, automatic compiler prefetching can be turned off at the command line (with `-no-opt-prefetch`) or using `#pragma noprefetch` for a single loop nest.

HARDWARE PREFETCHING

The last-level (L2) caches contain hardware stream prefetchers that are trained on streams of misses and software prefetches. If a hardware prefetcher detects a pattern in the misses it sees, it will begin prefetching future addresses in that pattern. Hardware prefetching is turned on by default and for the

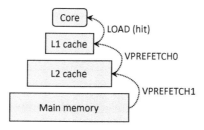

FIGURE 21.2

The ideal flow of prefetching for a memory access. Prefetching brings data into the L2 cache first, then from the L2 to the L1 cache. When the processor requests data, it finds it in the L1 cache.

most part it helps performance. The hardware prefetchers can throttle themselves in response to software prefetching, so even if hardware prefetching is not effective for a certain application, it does not need to be disabled because it will remain mostly inactive.

THROUGHPUT APPLICATIONS

The coprocessor is designed and well suited for running throughput applications, and we will focus on three multithreaded applications that each benefit from different prefetching strategies. All three applications use a large amount of data and measure their performance in throughput or bandwidth, such as gigabytes per second (GB/s).

The code we have provided for these three applications is written for Intel Xeon Phi coprocessors, although it may also run on other architectures.

STREAM TRIAD

Stream is a synthetic benchmark developed by John McCalpin that measures the sustainable memory bandwidth for four vector kernels: Copy, Scale, Add, and Triad. The source code for these four kernels is shown in Figure 21.3 and can be found in stream.c in the source code. In the following study, we

```
void tuned_STREAM_Copy()
{
        ssize_t j;
#pragma omp parallel for
        for (j=0; j<STREAM_ARRAY_SIZE; j++)
            c[j] = a[j];
}

void tuned_STREAM_Scale(STREAM_TYPE scalar)
{
        ssize_t j;
#pragma omp parallel for
        for (j=0; j<STREAM_ARRAY_SIZE; j++)
            b[j] = scalar*c[j];
}

void tuned_STREAM_Add()
{
        ssize_t j;
#pragma omp parallel for
        for (j=0; j<STREAM_ARRAY_SIZE; j++)
            c[j] = a[j]+b[j];
}

void tuned_STREAM_Triad(STREAM_TYPE scalar)
{
        ssize_t j;
#pragma omp parallel for
        for (j=0; j<STREAM_ARRAY_SIZE; j++)
            a[j] = b[j]+scalar*c[j];
}
```

FIGURE 21.3

Code listing of the Stream benchmark kernels found in stream.c of the STREAM source code. The main performance metric is based on the last kernel, Stream Triad.

analyze the performance of the Triad kernel from this benchmark, which does a combination of the operations from the Copy, Scale, and Add kernels.

SMITH-WATERMAN

The Smith-Waterman algorithm performs local sequence alignment for determining similar regions between two strings and is used in genomic applications to find out structural or functional similarities between nucleotides on amino acid sequences.

For this study, we used a highly tuned code that uses intrinsics to fully exploit the vector units of the coprocessor. These intrinsics are specific to 512-bit wide vectors found first on the Intel Xeon Phi coprocessor; our intrinsics should be easily adapted to Intel Xeon Phi processors with AVX-512 support (Knights Landing) and Intel Xeon processors with AVX-512 support (Skylake). The two hot loops for this application are found at approximately lines 134 and 148 in `SmithWatermanMIC()` in SmithWaterman.cpp in the Smith-Waterman source code.

SHOC MD

The MD benchmark from the SHOC benchmark suite is a molecular dynamics kernel based on the Lennard-Jones potential. It models the interactions between nearby atoms or molecules by iteratively updating all forces in the system.

The kernel for this application is `compute_lj_force()`, found in MD.cpp. An abridged version of this function is shown in Figure 21.4.

Note the three nested loops in this function. The outermost loop (k) runs for the number of iterations required by the simulation parameters. The next inner loop (i) loops over the atoms, and the innermost loop (j) traverses the neighbors of each atom. In the body of this loop, the forces on each atom are computed based on the distance between an atom and its neighbor.

Notice that the values of the neighbors' positions (`jposx`, `jposy`, `jposz`) come from an *indirect array access*, that is, using the values of a second "index array" (`neighList[]`) as the indices into the `position[]` array. This means that the elements of `position[]` are not necessarily accessed in sequential order; the order that they are accessed depends on the values in the `neighList[]` array. Therefore, it is very difficult for the compiler to predict a pattern of memory accesses to prefetch.

At each iteration, the item at `position[neighList[j + i * maxNeighbors]]` is accessed. This requires two memory accesses, first to get the value of `neighList[]` for the iteration, then a second memory access to the array `position[]` using that value as an index. If the accesses to this array followed a sequential or strided pattern, they would be easy to predict. However, because this code uses an index array, the access pattern is determined by the values in `neighList[]`. A diagram of the index array problem is shown in Figure 21.5. Prefetching these locations manually can help overlap the latency of memory accesses with the computation of previous iterations.

TUNING PREFETCHING

In the following sections, we demonstrate strategies for tuning prefetching using our three example applications. The first step in tuning an application should be to determine the hot functions or loops that take up the majority of the runtime. This analysis is available for the processor and coprocessor using a tool such as Intel® VTune™ Amplifier.

```
#pragma omp parallel
{
    for (int k = 0; k < nIters; k++)
    {
        #pragma omp for
        for (int i = 0; i < inum; i++)
        {
            T iposx = position[i].x;
            T iposy = position[i].y;
            T iposz = position[i].z;

            T fx = 0.0f;
            T fy = 0.0f;
            T fz = 0.0f;

            #pragma simd reduction(+:fx,fy,fz)
                      vectorlengthfor(float)
            for (int j = 0; j < maxNeighbors; j++)
            {

                T jposx = position[neighList[j+i*
                                 maxNeighbors]].x;
                T jposy = position[neighList[j + i *
                                 maxNeighbors]].y;
                T jposz = position[neighList[j + i *
                                 maxNeighbors]].z;

                T delx  = iposx - jposx;
                T dely  = iposy - jposy;
                T delz  = iposz - jposz;
                T r2inv = delx*delx + dely*dely + delz*delz;

                if (r2inv < cutsq)
                {

                    r2inv   = 1.0f  / r2inv;
                    T r6inv = r2inv * r2inv * r2inv;
                    T force = r2inv * r6inv * (lj1*r6inv-lj2);

                    fx += delx * force;
                    fy += dely * force;
                    fz += delz * force;

                }

            } // End current atom

            force3[i].x = fx;
            force3[i].y = fy;
            force3[i].z = fz;

        } // End iteration

    }
}
```

FIGURE 21.4

Code listing of the SHOC MD kernel showing indirect array accesses and the force calculations. This kernel can be found in the compute_lj_force() function of md/MD.cpp in the SHOC source code.

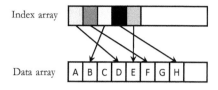

FIGURE 21.5

Indirect accesses to an array of data using an index array can lead to unpredictable access patterns.

PREFETCH DISTANCE TUNING ON THE COPROCESSOR

A critical parameter for success is the prefetching "distance," which is how many iterations ahead we issue a prefetch instruction prior to using the data. To inspect the prefetch distance used automatically by the compiler, we can use compiler optimization reports. The loop optimizations are generated using the *-qopt-report-phase = loop* compiler options (Intel C Compiler 2015). To generate the highest level of detail, we use the option *-qopt-report = 5*.

Sometimes it is useful to tune the prefetch distance manually instead of relying on the compiler to determine it. This is done by using the *-qopt-prefetch-distance = n1,n2* compiler option. *n1* represents the distance for prefetching from memory L2, while *n2* represents the distance for prefetching from L2 to L1. To tune the distance for individual loops, the compiler directive `#pragma prefetch var:` `hint:distance` can be used.

RESULTS—PREFETCH TUNING EXAMPLES ON A COPROCESSOR

Using Stream Triad, Smith-Waterman, and MD as examples, we will show how software prefetching can be tuned to improve performance on the coprocessor.

PREFETCHING METRICS FOR STREAM TRIAD

To show why prefetching affects performance, we can look at the hardware performance counters, which can be collected using Intel VTune Amplifier. We use the values of these counters to develop two low-level metrics of prefetching effectiveness: coverage and efficiency. A useful prefetch is one that takes a miss off the critical path of the program by bringing data into the cache before it is used.

Coverage is a measure of how well prefetches replace demand misses in the execution, which should lead to higher performance. In other words, perfect coverage means that all the data used were prefetched into the cache and the program experienced no misses (other than prefetches). Coverage is calculated as follows:

$$\text{Coverage} = \frac{\text{Misses}_{\text{NoPrefetching}} - \text{Misses}_{\text{WithPrefetching}}}{\text{Misses}_{\text{NoPrefetching}}} = \frac{\text{Saved Misses}}{\text{Total Misses}}$$

Efficiency measures how expensive prefetching was. If many useless prefetches are issued, the cost of prefetching might outweigh the benefits. Efficiency also affects the performance because a large number of useless prefetches may pollute the cache and waste memory bandwidth. We calculate the percent of prefetches that were actually beneficial as follows:

$$\text{Efficiency} = \frac{\text{Misses}_{\text{NoPrefetching}} - \text{Misses}_{\text{WithPrefetching}}}{\text{Total Prefetches}} = \frac{\text{Good Prefetches}}{\text{Total Prefetches}}$$

See the section on Useful Coprocessor Hardware Event Counters for more details about how to calculate these metrics using hardware event counters.

We measured the performance of Stream on an Intel Xeon Phi coprocessor and also collected hardware event counters using VTune. To compare the performance of prefetching, we ran the application multiple times with different prefetchers enabled or disabled. Note that software prefetching can only be disabled by recompiling the source code. The total misses and resulting performance with three combinations of prefetching settings are shown in Figure 21.6. Note that "no prefetching" is not a realistic setting because it is difficult to disable hardware prefetching, and disabling all prefetching leads to poor performance for most workloads. Here, we use it for comparison to show the benefits of prefetching. In most systems, hardware prefetching should be left on.

Compared to no prefetching, hardware prefetching improves performance by 6.8×, and the combination of hardware and software prefetching improves performance by nearly 9×. In a more realistic setting where hardware prefetching is always enabled, the combination of hardware and software prefetching improves performance by 1.3× over software alone.

The number of prefetches of each type for the two prefetching-enabled configurations is shown in Figure 21.7. The small number of software prefetches in the hardware-only case comes from prefetches already existing in related code such as libraries, not from the compiler. Notice that in the combined case, even though the hardware prefetcher is enabled, there are much fewer hardware prefetches issued. This is because the hardware prefetcher does not train itself on streams of misses that have been filtered out by the software prefetches.

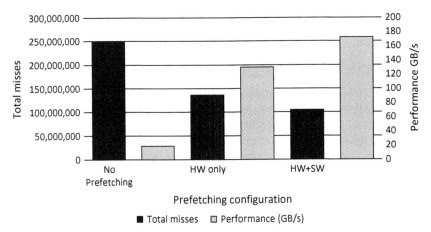

FIGURE 21.6

Total number of misses and performance achieved on the coprocessor with three prefetching configurations. The results for each configuration were obtained by running the application multiple times with each type of prefetching enabled or disabled.

Configuration	Hardware Prefetches	Software Prefetches
Hardware only	276,920,142	1232
Hardware and software combined	401,853	323,021,840

FIGURE 21.7

Number of prefetches of each type for Stream Triad when software prefetching is disabled and enabled.

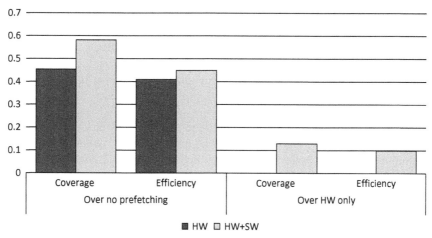

FIGURE 21.8

Coverage and efficiency values for Stream Triad with prefetching-off and hardware-prefetching-only as baselines.

To explain these observations, we consider our prefetching metrics: coverage and efficiency. For both metrics, the best value is 1.0 (or 100%) and the worst is 0. Figure 21.8 shows the coverage and efficiency when both no prefetching and hardware-only are considered as baselines. In both cases, we can see that adding software prefetching increases coverage, leading to higher performance. However, we do not have perfect coverage, indicating that some demand misses were not covered by prefetches.

Both configurations have similar efficiency values, but software prefetching was slightly more accurate. This is to be expected because software prefetching benefits from sophisticated compile-time analysis of the loops in the program, whereas the hardware prefetchers have to predict streams of misses at runtime.

USEFUL COPROCESSOR HARDWARE EVENT COUNTERS FOR MORE IN-DEPTH ANALYSIS

Readers who would like to evaluate these metrics for themselves, or develop other low-level metrics of prefetching can use the hardware event counters accessible through VTune. On the Intel Xeon Phi coprocessor, counter data can be collected using the command `amplxe-cl -collect-with runsa-knc -knob event-config=<EVENT>`. Note that usually only one or two event counters can be collected in the same run. Counter collection using VTune is described in more detail in the VTune Amplifier XE manual.

Some event counters relevant to prefetching are listed in Figure 21.9. In Figure 21.10, we show the formulas we used to calculate our prefetching metrics. Calculating these metrics requires running the program multiple times with and without prefetching.

COMPILER PREFETCH DISTANCE TUNING FOR STREAM TRIAD

Stream Triad is an application that does not get the best performance from the default compiler settings for prefetch distance. In order to tune this application, we start by compiling it with the default compiler options for prefetching and obtain a baseline performance of 129.3 GB/s.

We present in Figure 21.11 an interpretation of the loop optimization report for the Triad kernel main loop. The compiler issued four prefetch instructions for the loop at line 344 in the code. The L2 prefetch distance is 8 (dist = 8 in remark #25019), while the L1 distance was set to 4 (second-level distance in remarks #25139 and #25139).

In order to find out the best prefetch distance configuration, we fixed the L1 distance to 4 and scaled the L2 prefetch distance from 4 to 128. Note that for L2 distance = 8, we obtained similar performance to the default options. The best performance is achieved when using L2 distance = 64 (175.4 GB/2).

Counter	Description
L2_READ_HIT_E	L2 ReadHit E State
L2_READ_HIT_M	L2Read Hit M State
L2_READ_HIT_S	L2 Read Hit S State
L2_READ_MISS	L2 Read Misses
L1_DATA_PF2	VPREFETCH1 requests seen by L1
L2_DATA_PF2	VPREFETCH1 requests seen by L2
L2_DATA_PF1_MISS	VPREFETCH0 requeststhat missed in L2
L2_DATA_PF2_MISS	VPREFETCH1 requeststhat missed in L2
HWP_L2HIT	Hardware prefetches that hit in L2
HWP_L2MISS	Hardware prefetches that missed in L2

FIGURE 21.9

Intel Xeon Phi coprocessor hardware event counters related to prefetching.

Metric	Formula
Total demand misses (L2M)	L2_READ_MISS - L2_DATA_PF2_MISS
Total prefetches (L2P)	L1_DATA_PF2 + HWP_L2HIT + HWP_L2MISS
Total data requests (L2D)	L2_READ_HIT_M + L2_READ_HIT_E + L2_READ_HIT_S + L2_READ_MISS
Coverage	(L2M[Pf off] – L2M[Pf on]) / L2M[Pf off]
Efficiency	(L2M[Pf off] – L2M[Pf on]) / (L2P[Pf on] - L2P[Pf off])

FIGURE 21.10

Formulation of prefetching metrics.

```
LOOP BEGIN at stream.c(344,2)
    remark #25018: Total number of lines prefetched=4
    remark #25019: Number of spatial prefetches=4, dist=8
    remark #25021: Number of initial-value prefetches=6
    remark #25139: Using second-level distance 4 for prefetching
spatial memory reference  [ stream.c(345,13) ]
    remark #25139: Using second-level distance 4 for prefetching
spatial memory reference  [ stream.c(345,25) ]
    remark #25015: Estimate of max trip count of loop=8000000
LOOP END
```

FIGURE 21.11

Loop optimization report for Stream Triad showing the prefetch distances determined automatically by the compiler.

L1 Prefetch Distance = 4	
L2 Prefetch Distance	Performance GB/s
4	102.4
8	129.6
16	147.3
32	168.1
64	175.2
128	174.8

L1 Prefetch Distance = 8	
L2 Prefetch Distance	Performance GB/s
8	114.0
16	142.6
32	165.6
64	175.4
128	175.3
256	174.3

FIGURE 21.12

Stream Triad performance when L1 prefetch distance is fixed and L2 prefetch distance is varied.

We repeated the experiment by fixing the L1 distance to 8 and the best performance was obtained for the same 64 L2 distance (**175.4 GB/s**). The results of these experiments are shown in Figure 21.12. This leads us to the conclusion that 64 is the optimal value for the L2 prefetch distance for this benchmark.

Next, we scaled the L1 distance while fixing L2 distance to 64 and obtained the best performance for L1 distance of 8. The results of this experiment are shown in Figure 21.13. By simply fixing L2 distance of 64 and L1 distance of 8, we increased performance from 129.3 GB/s with the default settings to 175.4 GB/s with optimal settings. This represents a **35% increase** in performance obtained by only recompiling the code with the appropriate compiler options.

COMPILER PREFETCH DISTANCE TUNING FOR SMITH-WATERMAN

Smith-Waterman is our second example of an application that benefits from prefetch distance tuning. After compiling the application with default prefetch options, the application reports a performance of **46.17 GCUPS** (billion cell updates per second). When inspecting the loop optimization report generated by the compiler for the hot loops of the program (lines 134 and 148 from SmithWaterman.cpp), we discover that no L1 prefetch instructions are issued (no second-level distance reported). This report is shown in Figure 21.14. The prefetch distance for the L2 prefetches is set to 2 (dist=2 in remarks #25035 and #25019).

L2 Prefetch Distance = 64	
L1 Prefetch Distance	Performance GB/s
4	175.2
8	175.4
16	168.2
32	172.8
64	115.4

FIGURE 21.13

Stream Triad performance with optimal L2 prefetch distance

```
LOOP BEGIN at SmithWaterman.cpp(134,5)
    remark #25018: Total number of lines prefetched=1
    remark #25021: Number of initial-value prefetches=1
    remark #25035: Number of pointer data prefetches=1, dist=2

    LOOP BEGIN at SmithWaterman.cpp(148,9)
        remark #25018: Total number of lines prefetched=4
        remark #25019: Number of spatial prefetches=4, dist=2
        remark #25021: Number of initial-value prefetches=4
    LOOP END

    LOOP BEGIN at SmithWaterman.cpp(203,9)
        remark #25460: No loop optimizations reported
    LOOP END
LOOP END
```

FIGURE 21.14

Loop optimization report for Smith-Waterman showing the prefetch distances determined by the compiler.

In order to tune the prefetch distance, we analyzed various L1 prefetch distances from 0 (indicating L1 prefetching is off completely) to 32. For each L1 distance, we tested all valid L2 distances from 1 to 256. For an L2 distance to be valid, it needs to be greater than or equal to the L1 distance. These results are shown in Figure 21.15. We observe that the best score is obtained for L2 distance = 16 with no L1 prefetching (**74.22 GCUPS**). Considering the performance of the application when compiled with default prefetch options, this results in **60% performance gain** from tuning prefetching distance.

USING INTRINSIC PREFETCHES FOR HARD-TO-PREDICT ACCESS PATTERNS IN SHOC MD

When an application cannot fully exploit automatic prefetching because of an irregular access pattern, application developers can consider using prefetching intrinsics. As discussed earlier, the access pattern of MD is hard to determine at compile time because it relies on the values of an index array. We can still prefetch for these accesses by precalculating them at runtime and using intrinsics to instruct the compiler to insert prefetches for those addresses. The code with intrinsics added by the SHOC MD authors is shown in Figure 21.16. These calls calculate the value of neighList[] needed for the position 16 iterations ahead (hence the +16 term in the first argument). Depending on the size of data used, more bytes will be prefetched. In this code, the second argument (1) indicates the compiler hint _MM_HINT_T0 to prefetch into the L1 cache, and the value 2 indicates _MM_HINT_T1, which tells the compiler to prefetch into the L2 cache.

For SHOC MD, the effects of intrinsic prefetches are dramatic. As shown in Figure 21.17, the performance improves by approximately 300% when intrinsic prefetches are included in the code.

L1 dist.	L2 Distance								
	1	2	4	8	16	32	64	128	256
0	46.09	46.14	71.40	74.16	**74.22**	74.17	74.13	73.97	65.67
1	61.58	62.28	69.30	74.00	74.00	74.00	73.83	73.70	65.32
2		66.02	71.32	74.16	74.17	74.15	74.09	74.05	65.68
4			66.23	74.02	74.11	74.12	74.05	74.00	65.89
8				66.14	74.09	74.09	74.06	74.01	65.90
16					65.89	72.67	72.69	72.59	65.04
32						59.93	59.51	59.50	55.35

FIGURE 21.15

Smith-Waterman performance with every tested combination of L1 and L2 prefetch distance. The optimal configuration is with L1 prefetching off (L1 distance=0) and an L2 distance of 16.

```
#pragma noprefetch
#pragma simd reduction(+:fx,fy,fz) vectorlengthfor(float)
for (int j = 0; j < maxNeighbors; j++)
{
    _mm_prefetch((char*)&position[neighList[i * maxNeighbors +
j + 0 + 16]], 1);
    _mm_prefetch((char*)&position[neighList[i * maxNeighbors +
j + 1 + 16]], 1);
    _mm_prefetch((char*)&position[neighList[i * maxNeighbors +
j + 2 + 16]], 1);
    _mm_prefetch((char*)&position[neighList[i * maxNeighbors +
j + 3 + 16]], 1);
    _mm_prefetch((char*)&position[neighList[i * maxNeighbors +
j + 4 + 16]], 1);
    _mm_prefetch((char*)&position[neighList[i * maxNeighbors +
j + 5 + 16]], 1);
```

FIGURE 21.16

Code listing for the SHOC MD kernel with intrinsic prefetch methods. This kernel is found in compute_lj_force() in md/MD.cpp in the SHOC source code.

(continued)

```
        _mm_prefetch((char*)&position[neighList[i *
maxNeighbors + j + 6  + 16]], 1);
        _mm_prefetch((char*)&position[neighList[i *
maxNeighbors + j + 7  + 16]], 1);

    if(sizeof(T) == sizeof(float))
    {
        _mm_prefetch((char*)&position[neighList[i *
maxNeighbors + j + 8  + 16]], 1);
        _mm_prefetch((char*)&position[neighList[i *
maxNeighbors + j + 9  + 16]], 1);
        _mm_prefetch((char*)&position[neighList[i *
maxNeighbors + j + 10 + 16]], 1);
        _mm_prefetch((char*)&position[neighList[i *
maxNeighbors + j + 11 + 16]], 1);
        _mm_prefetch((char*)&position[neighList[i *
maxNeighbors + j + 12 + 16]], 1);
        _mm_prefetch((char*)&position[neighList[i *
maxNeighbors + j + 13 + 16]], 1);
        _mm_prefetch((char*)&position[neighList[i *
maxNeighbors + j + 14 + 16]], 1);
        _mm_prefetch((char*)&position[neighList[i *
maxNeighbors + j + 15 + 16]], 1);
    }
    // This conditional improves GFLOPS for S1, S2, S3 but
    // lowers GFLOPS for S4 with ~5%
    if ((inum > PF2_THRESHOLD) || (sizeof(T) ==
sizeof(double)))
    {
        _mm_prefetch((char*)&position[neighList[i *
maxNeighbors + j + 0  + 32]], 2);
        _mm_prefetch((char*)&position[neighList[i *
maxNeighbors + j + 1  + 32]], 2);
        _mm_prefetch((char*)&position[neighList[i *
maxNeighbors + j + 2  + 32]], 2);
        _mm_prefetch((char*)&position[neighList[i *
maxNeighbors + j + 3  + 32]], 2);
        _mm_prefetch((char*)&position[neighList[i *
maxNeighbors + j + 4  + 32]], 2);
```

FIGURE 21.16—Cont'd

(continued)

```
        _mm_prefetch((char*)&position[neighList[i *
maxNeighbors + j + 5  + 32]], 2);

        _mm_prefetch((char*)&position[neighList[i *
maxNeighbors + j + 6  + 32]], 2);

        _mm_prefetch((char*)&position[neighList[i *
maxNeighbors + j + 7  + 32]], 2);

        _mm_prefetch((char*)&position[neighList[i *
maxNeighbors + j + 8  + 32]], 2);

        _mm_prefetch((char*)&position[neighList[i *
maxNeighbors + j + 9  + 32]], 2);

        _mm_prefetch((char*)&position[neighList[i *
maxNeighbors + j + 10 + 32]], 2);

        _mm_prefetch((char*)&position[neighList[i *
maxNeighbors + j + 11 + 32]], 2);

        _mm_prefetch((char*)&position[neighList[i *
maxNeighbors + j + 12 + 32]], 2);

        _mm_prefetch((char*)&position[neighList[i *
maxNeighbors + j + 13 + 32]], 2);

        _mm_prefetch((char*)&position[neighList[i *
maxNeighbors + j + 14 + 32]], 2);

        _mm_prefetch((char*)&position[neighList[i *
maxNeighbors + j + 15 + 32]], 2);

    }


    //[...]
    // calculation using position[neighList[j + i *
    // maxNeighbors]]

}
```

FIGURE 21.16—Cont'd

Code Version	Prefetching Configuration	Performance (GB/s)	Improvement due to Compiler Prefetching	Improvement due to Intrinsic Prefetches
SP, no intrinsics	HW only	29.2928	–	–
	HW+SW	32.1697	9.8%	–
DP, no intrinsics	HW only	21.8806	–	–
	HW+SW	23.3263	6.6%	–
SP, with intrinsics	HW only	95.97505	–	3.3×
	HW+SW	96.42325	0.47%	3.0×
DP, with intrinsics	HW only	67.8325	–	3.1×
	HW+SW	67.8827	0.074%	2.9×

FIGURE 21.17

Comparison of different SHOC MD code versions under different prefetching configurations. The improvement due to intrinsics compares two versions with the same precision and automatic prefetching configuration.

The improvements of software prefetching over hardware-only prefetching are more modest (and disappear when intrinsics are used) because the access pattern is hard for the compiler to predict.

RESULTS—TUNING HARDWARE PREFETCHING ON A PROCESSOR

While prefetching is essential on the coprocessor, it brings comparatively modest performance gains on the processor. Intel Xeon processors use out-of-order processing cores, so executing other instructions during memory stalls already hides much of the memory latency. An Intel Xeon Phi coprocessor has in-order processing cores, which means that any instruction that stalls for memory will delay the instructions following it.

In this section, we show results for different hardware-prefetching configurations on the processor. However, the compiler optimizes code differently for these architectures. While the user has the ability to tune software prefetching on the coprocessor, on the processor, one can only turn on or off the hardware prefetchers. The processor also has several different hardware prefetchers available.

TUNING HARDWARE PREFETCHING FOR STREAM ON A PROCESSOR

In Figure 21.18, we present the impact of the processor hardware prefetchers on Steam Triad. By analyzing the results, we observe a gain of only 6.6% on the processor due to prefetching compared to the coprocessor where we had a gain of 35%. Of the four hardware prefetchers available on the Intel Xeon processor, the MLC Streamer Prefetcher helps the most with a performance improvement of 6.5%. This lower impact of prefetching on the processor is expected considering the out-of-order nature of the Xeon core, which can better hide latency caused by cache misses.

TUNING HARDWARE PREFETCHING FOR SMITH-WATERMAN ON A PROCESSOR

Using a processor version of Smith-Waterman, we compared the performance on a processor with different hardware-prefetching settings. The results are shown in Figure 21.19. Prefetching on the processor improves performance 30% improvement with all prefetchers enabled, which compares to the gain of 60% on the coprocessor.

Prefetch Configuration	Performance (GB/s)	Gain %
NO prefetcher—baseline	97.42	0.0
MLC streamer prefetcher	103.73	6.5
MLC spatial prefetcher	97.83	0.4
DCU streamer prefetcher	97.84	0.4
DCU IP prefetcher	97.59	0.2
ALL prefetchers—default setting	103.86	6.6

FIGURE 21.18

Stream Triad performance with various hardware-prefetching settings on an Intel Xeon processor.

Prefetch Configuration	Performance (GCUPS)	Gain %
NO prefetcher—baseline	145	0.0
MLC streamer prefetcher	175	20.9
MLC spatial prefetcher	154	6.7
DCU streamer prefetcher	159	9.7
DCU IP prefetcher	181	25.3
ALL prefetchers—default setting	188	30.0

FIGURE 21.19

Smith-Waterman performance with different hardware prefetchers on an Intel Xeon processor.

TUNING HARDWARE PREFETCHING FOR SHOC MD ON A PROCESSOR

Although the main benefit to SHOC MD comes from intrinsic prefetches, we can also look at the performance benefits of hardware prefetching on the processor. The results for the processor version of SHOC MD with intrinsics are shown in Figure 21.20. The performance improvement is minimal, with a maximum of 6.4% improvement for DP with all prefetchers enabled.

We also performed the same analysis after deactivating intrinsics, shown in Figure 21.21. The DCU IP Prefetcher is the best configuration for both SP and DP, but the gains are still small.

Even on the coprocessor, where prefetching is more important, automatic methods could not prefetch effectively, so it is not surprising to see such comparatively small gains on the processor. Notice that the performance improvement due to intrinsics on Xeon is only about 13-20%, compared to approximately 3× improvement due to intrinsics on Intel Xeon Phi coprocessors. While inserting prefetching intrinsics is necessary to hide latency on the coprocessor, the processor already has other latency-hiding techniques and it may not be worth the effort to use prefetching intrinsics for relatively modest gains.

Configuration	Performance SP (GFLOPS)	Performance DP (GFLOPS)	Gain SP %	Gain DP %
NO prefetcher—baseline	110.4	92.1	0.0	0.0
MLC streamer prefetcher	112.1	95.1	1.6	3.2
MLC spatial prefetcher	110.5	92.3	0.1	0.1
DCU streamer prefetcher	111.4	93.6	0.9	1.6
DCU IP prefetcher	112.5	96.2	2.0	4.4
ALL prefetchers—default setting	112.4	98.0	1.8	6.4

FIGURE 21.20

Performance of SHOC MD with intrinsics with different hardware prefetchers on an Intel Xeon processor.

Configuration	Performance SP (GFLOPS)	Performance DP (GFLOPS)	Gain SP %	Gain DP %
NO prefetcher — baseline	92.3	71.5	0.0	0.0
MLC streamer prefetcher	93.7	72.6	1.6	1.6
MLC spatial prefetcher	92.1	71.6	-0.2	0.1
DCU streamer prefetcher	89.4	69.6	-3.1	-2.6
DCU IP prefetcher	102.8	78.7	11.4	10.2
ALL prefetchers — default setting	99.2	76.4	7.6	6.9

FIGURE 21.21

Performance of SHOC MD without intrinsics with different hardware prefetchers on an Intel Xeon processor.

SUMMARY

Throughput applications running on high-performance systems with Intel Xeon Phi coprocessors require large amounts of data to keep the cores busy. Prefetching is an especially critical optimization for applications running on in-order processors such as the current Intel Xeon Phi coprocessors to obtain optimal performance. Prefetching is less important on out-of-order processors such as Intel Xeon processors, because the complex out-of-order pipeline already effectively hides memory latency.

In this chapter, we explored several ways to tune the prefetching settings of an application to extract more performance. The first strategy is to compare the application performance with difference compiler prefetching distances. The distances calculated automatically by the compiler may not be the best for every application or every loop within an application. For example, tuning the compiler prefetching distances led to improvements of 35% for STREAM and 60% for Smith-Waterman over versions using the distances set automatically by the compiler when run on the coprocessor. The out-of-order cores on Intel Xeon processors limited our best speed-up from tuning prefetching to a more modest 6.5% and 30%, respectively.

When automatic hardware and compiler prefetching struggle to predict an application's access pattern, we can use the second strategy: intrinsic prefetches. This method requires careful analysis of the memory accesses in a program to manually insert prefetches to specific memory locations. In the end, however, this hard work can pay off dramatically. In our example application, SHOC MD, we saw performance improvements of $3\times$ due to intrinsics that were not attainable with automatic prefetching alone.

ACKNOWLEDGMENTS

This work is supported in part by NSF grants 1213052, 1439021, 1409095, 0963839, and 1017882 and a grant from Intel.

FOR MORE INFORMATION

- Krishnaiyer, R. Compiler Prefetching for the Intel Xeon Phi coprocessor. https://software.intel.com/sites/default/files/managed/54/77/5.3-prefetching-on-mic-update.pdf.

- Jeffers, J., Reinders, J., 2013. Intel Xeon Phi coprocessor high-performance programming. In: Streaming Through Caches: Data Layout, Alignment, Prefetching, and so on. Morgan Kaufmann.
- Guttman, D., Kandemir, M., Arunachalam, M., Calina, V., 2015. Performance and Energy Evaluation of Data Prefetching on Intel Xeon Phi. ISPASS 2015.
- Krishnaiyer, R., Kultursay, E., Chawla, P., Preis, S., Zvezdin, A., Saito, H., 2013. Compiler-Based Data Prefetching and Streaming Non-temporal Store Generation for the Intel® Xeon Phi™ Coprocessor. IPDPSW 2013.
- Lee, J., Kim, J., Vuduc, R., 2012. When prefetching works, when it doesn't, and why. ACM Trans. Archit. Code Optim. 9(March).
- Baer, J.-L., Chen, T.-F., 1991. An effective on-chip preloading scheme to reduce data access penalty. In: ACM/IEEE Conference on Supercomputing, November 1991.
- Intel® Xeon Phi™ Coprocessor (codename: Knights Corner) Performance Monitoring Units. Intel Corporation, 2012.
- Intel® C++ Compiler XE 13.1 User and Reference Guides.
- Intel® VTune™ Amplifier User's Guide.
- Intel® Xeon Phi™ Coprocessor Instruction Set Reference Manual. Intel Corporation, 2012, https://software.intel.com/en-us/mic-developer/programming.
- Danalis, A., Marin, G., McCurdy, C., Meredith, J., Roth, P., Spafford, K., Tipparaju, V., Vetter, J., 2010. The scalable heterogeneous computing (SHOC) benchmark suite. Proceedings of the Third Workshop on General-Purpose Computation on Graphics Processors (GPGPU 2010), March 2010.
- McCalpin, J.D., 1995. Memory bandwidth and machine balance in current high performance computers. IEEE Computer Society Technical Committee on Computer Architecture (TCCA) Newsletter, December 1995. [STREAM Benchmark]
- Farrar, M.S., 2007. Striped Smith–Waterman speeds database searches six times over other SIMD implementations. Bioinformatics 23(2): 156-161.
- Source code from this and other chapters can be found at http://www.lotsofcores.com.

SIMD FUNCTIONS VIA OpenMP

22

George M. Raskulinec, Evgeny Fiksman

Intel Corporation, USA

In this chapter, we look at a *pearl* that can greatly enhance application performance on both Intel® Xeon Phi™ coprocessors and Intel® Xeon® processors through the use of OpenMP pragmas that facilitate the generation of SIMD (Single Instruction Multiple Data) vector loops for multiple processor architectures. This pearl focuses on (1) the use of the OpenMP pragma SIMD directive that explicitly tells the compiler to turn a loop into a SIMD vector loop and (2) the use of the OpenMP SIMD `processor(...)` clause that tells the compiler to generate a vector loop for one or more CPU architecture types. In combination, the SIMD directive and associated clauses give programmers the ability to create portable libraries and executables containing efficient vector loops for multiple CPU architectures. The appropriate vector loops are selected automatically at runtime—no recompilation is required—which is a significant advantage for developers who wish to support multiple processor architectures.

High floating-point performance on Intel Xeon processors and Intel Xeon Phi coprocessors can only be achieved when appropriate processor-specific vector instructions are utilized to access the vector units. The extensive history of $\times 86$ processors means that libraries and applications can potentially be required to support many different vector instruction sets, be they SSE2, SSE3, SSSE3, SSE4, AVX, AVX-2, or AVX-512. Incorrectly pairing the vector instruction set to the processor architecture means that a library or application may exhibit sub-optimal performance or even fail with an error message.

To ensure consistent vectorization, the OpenMP SIMD directive explicitly tells the compiler to vectorize a loop rather than relying on the compiler to infer the SIMD nature of a loop. Compilers are carefully designed to avoid generating incorrect code, no matter how bizarre the human-generated source code. Thus, they must—by necessity—be very conservative and consider a number of sometimes nonobvious corner cases when making vectorization decisions. As a result, we might see the compiler claiming that there are unresolved dependencies or other issues with a loop that can clearly be vectorized. The SIMD directive gives us the ability to tell the compiler to just go ahead and vectorize the loop. Of course, telling the compiler to vectorize a loop that does contain dependencies will likely result in program errors.

Even after a loop is vectorized, the compiler might need additional information such as which vector instruction set(s) to target. Through the use of the processor() clause, it is possible to target a particular processor architecture, and more importantly, multiple processor architectures. This gives programmers the ability to create portable libraries and applications that can transparently deliver high vector floating-point performance across many different CPU architectures. No user or programmer intervention is required as the choice of which vector loop to utilize is automatically made at runtime.

This chapter starts with an overview of vectorization and the performance benefits of SIMD-enabled applications. Next we focus on the use of SIMD-enabled functions using code examples taken from real-world applications that highlight typical pitfalls users may encounter. We present the original code, discuss issues that impact optimal vectorization present modified code, and show performance results. For those who are interested, we provide additional references in the "For more information" section to resources that provide a more comprehensive discussion of the OpenMP SIMD syntax and pragma capabilities.

SIMD VECTORIZATION OVERVIEW

Vectorization is the process of transforming a scalar operation acting on individual data elements (Single Instruction Single Data—SISD) to an operation where a single instruction operates concurrently on multiple data elements (SIMD). Modern Intel processor cores have dedicated vector units supporting SIMD parallel data processing. An example of an SIMD-enabled operation is shown in Figure 22.1.

Intel processors that support Intel® Advanced Vector Extensions (Intel® AVX) have one 256-bit vector unit per core. Thus, each core can process eight single-precision (e.g., 32-bit) floating point operations or four double-precision" (e.g., 64-bit) floating point operations using a single instruction. Intel® Advanced Vector Extensions 512 (Intel® AVX-512) double the number of registers and size of the vector unit to 512-bits so that each per-core vector unit can perform 16 single-precision or 8 double-precision operations per instruction. Some newer Xeon processors also support AVX-512 vector instructions, just like Intel Xeon Phi processors and practically the same as in 512-bit SIMD in the original coprocessors.

The larger vector units and increased functionality translate to significant speedups for many real-world applications. Figure 22.2 shows the performance results of a financial application that prices options using a trinomial tree. The first (shorter, lower performance bars) in each pair use only threads while the second (taller, higher performance bars) combine both parallel threads and vector units. The added speedup of vector units, especially in recent years, is dramatic.

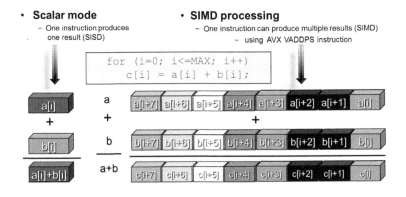

FIGURE 22.1

Intel® AVX vector operation (SIMD) example.

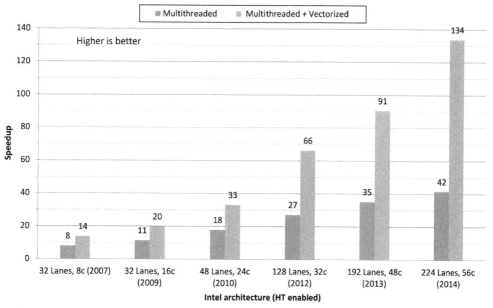

FIGURE 22.2

Speedup comparison between threaded and threaded + vectorized code.

DIRECTIVE GUIDED VECTORIZATION

There are various methods available to programmers who wish to utilize SIMD-enabled instructions to increase performance. Compiler intrinsic operations are one option, but they are architecture specific and tend to be difficult to use. A much simpler approach is to use compiler directives, or pragmas, to annotate the C, C++, or Fortran code and have the compiler generate the SIMD instructions.

The SIMD directives that are available in the OpenMP 4.0 standard give the programmer the ability to guide the compiler about when and which SIMD instructions to use. In this section, we demonstrate the basic usage of the OpenMP 4.0 extensions with examples and explain the usage of SIMD enabled functions.

LOOP VECTORIZATION

Figure 22.3 shows the implementation of a linear spline interpolation method in the Interpolate() function in C.

Most modern compilers are able to apply auto-vectorization algorithms that can decide if a loop can be vectorized, and when appropriate, perform the vectorization.

The following vector report shows that the critical loop in Figure 22.3 was not vectorized because the compiler could not determine if the call to the Interpolate() function was safe. The compiler switch

```c
static const int steps = 512;
static const int ARRAY_SIZE = 4096;

int main(int argc, const char* argv[]) {
    point vals[steps+1];
    double src[ARRAY_SIZE];
    double dst[ARRAY_SIZE];

    /* Set interpolation array */
    double delta = 1.0 / steps;
    double delta_inv = 1./delta;

    vals[0].c0 = 0.;
    vals[0].c1 = erfc(0.);

    double prev_val = vals[0].c1;
    // Fill interpolation array
    for(int ind=1; ind <= steps; ++ind) {
        double x = ind * delta;
        double val = erfc(x);
        double c0 = (val - prev_val)*delta_inv;
        double c1 = val - c0*x;
        vals[ind].c0 = c0;
        vals[ind].c1 = c1;
        prev_val = val;
    }

    /* Initialize input array */
    ...
```

FIGURE 22.3

Unoptimized C source code for a linear spline.

```
/*Critical loop requires vectorization */
for(int i=0; i<ARRAY_SIZE;++i) {
    dst[i] = Interpolate(src[i],vals);
}


/* Print results */
/* . . . full code on lotsofcores.com . . . */
return 0;
}


//Implementation of Interpolate() and FindPosition()
double Interpolate(double x, point* vals){
    int ind = FindPosition(x);
    const point* pnt = &vals[ind];
    double res = pnt->c0*x+pnt->c1;
    return res;
}


/* . . . full code on lotsofcores.com . . . */int
FindPosition(double x) {
    return (int)(x*steps);
}
```

FIGURE 22.3, Cont'd

---

to get these reports on Linux is –qopt-report=5 –qopt-report-phase=vec and on Windows /Qopt-report=5 /Qopt-report-phase=vec.

```
remark #15382: vectorization support: call to function
Interpolate(double, const point *) cannot be vectorized
[ main.c(56,18) ]
remark #15344: loop was not vectorized: vector dependence prevents
vectorization
```

While the message highlighted in boldface in the report is somewhat obscure to non-compiler savvy developers, it does tell us that the compiler cannot resolve all the dependencies associated with the Interpolate() function. In this particular situation, the compiler's auto-vectorization algorithm needs to rely on code inlining to resolve trip counts along with potential data, pointer, and loop dependencies. Since the Interpolate() function is not an inline function, the compiler takes a conservative approach and decides to not vectorize the loop.

Vectorization can be forced, as shown in Figure 22.4, through the use of the OpenMP 4.0 C/C++ *#pragma omp simd* directive which tells the compiler to ignore the built in vectorizer heuristics and vectorize the loop.

After applying the simd directive and recompiling, the vector report contains the messages shown in Figure 22.5.

The compiler now reports that the loop was vectorized, but it cannot find a suitable vector version of the Interpolate() function. Instead, the compiler is using a serial version. To be helpful, the compiler suggests that the programmer add a "*declare simd*" directive to identify Interpolate() as a vector-enabled function.

```
//Critical loop
#pragma omp simd
for(int i=0; i<ARRAY_SIZE;++i) {
    dst[i] = Interpolate(src[i],vals);
}
```

FIGURE 22.4

Apply #pragma omp simd to force vectorization.

```
LOOP BEGIN at main.c(55,9)
   ...
  remark #15525: call to function 'Interpolate' is serialized
                   [ main.c(56,18) ]
  remark #15301: OpenMP SIMD LOOP WAS VECTORIZED
   ...
  remark #15489: --- begin vector function matching report ---
  remark #15490: Function call: Interpolate(double, const point *)
                   with simdlen=2, actual parameter types:
                   (vector,uniform)[ main.c(56,18) ]
  remark #15545: SIMD annotation was not seen, consider adding
                   'declare simd' directives at function declaration
  remark #15493: --- end vector function matching report ---
   LOOP END
```

FIGURE 22.5

Report after applying *#pragma omp simd* to critical loop.

SIMD-ENABLED FUNCTIONS

Calling an SIMD-enabled function from within a vector loop means that multiple consecutive instances of the function execute in parallel. In OpenMP parlance, these vector functions operate on simdlen() chunks of data as if they were compiled as a part of the body of the vector loop.

The ability to create independent vector functions that can be linked, rather than compiled as an inline function, means that programmers now have the ability to create independent vector libraries that can be distributed as binary files rather than header files containing the full source code. The advantages to commercial software development should be obvious, as is the ability to utilize modular programming techniques.

The OpenMP 4.0 syntax for an SIMD-enabled function is `omp declare simd [clauses]`, preceded by `#pragma for` C/C++ and `!$omp` for Fortran. This pragma accepts a number of clauses as will be discussed in the following sections. Each clause provides additional information and detail such that the compiler can use to generate efficient, targeted vector code for the appropriate processor architecture.

By default, the width of the SIMD operation is determined by the function return type. In addition, the compiler will also default to generating code for an SSE2 CPU architecture, which utilizes 128-bit vector registers.

The following vectorization report was generated using default values. It shows that the compiler could not find a suitable vector version of the function "FindPosition."

```
remark #15397: Suitable vector variant of function 'FindPosition' was not found [ inter-
polate.c(16,15) ]
```

The reason for the incompatibility is that the return type of Interpolate() is a *double*, which means that the SIMD element count (also called simdlen) is set to 2 by default (since the compiler default is currently SSE). The return type of FindPosition() is *int*, which means it has a simdlen of 4 (again, due to the compiler default of SSE). Thus, relying on default values causes a calling convention incompatibility between the two vector functions (e.g., simdlen of 2 vs. 4) and hence the compiler tells us it cannot find a "suitable variant" of the function FindPosition().

The OpenMP 4 standard provides a *simdlen()* clause that modifies the default number of SIMD elements during a function call. We use the simdlen() clause, as shown in Figure 22.6, to modify the number of SIMD elements for the FindPosition() function.

After recompiling, we find that the vectorization warning (Figure 22.7) has disappeared from the vectorization report. We also see that the report confirms that the critical loop has been vectorized.

```
        #pragma omp declare simd
       double Interpolate(double x, point* vals);
/* . . . full code on lotsofcores.com . . . */
         #pragma omp declare simd simdlen(2)
        int FindPosition(double x);
/* . . . full code on lotsofcores.com . . . */
```

FIGURE 22.6

Identify Interpolate() and FindPosition() as a SIMD enabled functions in the function declaration.

```
LOOP BEGIN at main.c(55,9)
    remark #15388: vectorization support: reference src has aligned
                   access    [ main.c(56,18) ]
    remark #15388: vectorization support: reference dst has aligned
                   access    [ main.c(56,9) ]
    remark #15399: vectorization support: unroll factor set to 4
    remark #15301: OpenMP SIMD LOOP WAS VECTORIZED
    remark #15448: unmasked aligned unit stride loads: 1
    remark #15449: unmasked aligned unit stride stores: 1
  remark #15475: --- begin vector loop cost summary ---
  remark #15476: scalar loop cost: 107
  remark #15477: vector loop cost: 216.000
  remark #15478: estimated potential speedup: 1.980
  remark #15479: lightweight vector operations: 7
  remark #15480: medium-overhead vector operations: 1
  remark #15484: vector function calls: 1
  remark #15488: --- end vector loop cost summary ---
  remark #15489: --- begin vector function matching report ---
  remark #15490: Function call: Interpolate(double, const point *)
                 with simdlen=2, actual parameter types:
                 (vector,uniform)   [ main.c(56,18) ]
    remark #15492: A suitable vector variant was found (out of 2) with
                   xmm, simdlen=2, unmasked, formal parameter types:
                   (vector,vector)
    remark #15493: --- end vector function matching report ---
  LOOP END
```

FIGURE 22.7

Report after applying *#pragma omp declare simd* to Interpolate().

Unfortunately, closer inspection of the vector report shows that the parameter lists are not consistent. We see that the Interpolate() function call passes parameter types of *(vector, uniform)*, but the only vector variant match is *(vector, vector)*.

This report tell us that the second parameter, *point* vals*, is not a vector parameter type and treating it as such would generate inefficient code. The OpenMP *uniform()* clause is used to tell the compiler that the pointer address, *point* vals*, should be treated as invariant, which means it can safely be broadcast to all loop iterations (and in effect all SIMD lanes). The compiler can then generate more efficient

```
#pragma omp declare simd uniform(vals)
double Interpolate(double x, point* vals);
```

FIGURE 22.8

Applying *uniform* clause.

```
remark #15301: OpenMP SIMD LOOP WAS VECTORIZED

...

...

remark #15489: --- begin vector function matching report ---
remark #15490: Function call: Interpolate(double, const point *) with
               simdlen=2, actual parameter types: (vector,uniform)
remark #15492: A suitable vector variant was found (out of 2) with
               xmm, simdlen=2, unmasked, formal parameter types:
               (vector,uniform)
remark #15493: --- end vector function matching report ---

...
```

FIGURE 22.9

Vector report after adding uniform clause.

vector memory load/store instructions, which will result in better performance. The uniform() clause is highlighted in boldface in Figure 22.8.

Recompiling with the uniform() clause results in the vector report shown in Figure 22.9 that contains only positive messages.

TARGETING SPECIFIC ARCHITECTURES

In the previous sections, we discussed the OpenMP directives that help developers ensure both loop vectorization and the efficient use of vector instructions. Now we examine how to generate efficient code for multiple architectures including Intel's latest architectures like the Intel® Xeon® E5 v3 family and Intel® Xeon Phi™ product family.

OPTIMIZING FOR AN ARCHITECTURE WITH COMPILER OPTIONS AND THE PROCESSOR(...) CLAUSE

Compilers options (−x on Linux, and /Qx on Microsoft Windows) control which instructions the compiler uses within a function, while the processor(...) clause controls creation of non-standard functions using wider registers (YMM or ZMM) for passing SIMD data for parameters and results.

The processor(...) clause gives us direct control of what is produced. The use of processor(...) is not important when a function is inlined by the compiler since processor(...) only affects the interfacing of a function to the callers of the function. Wherever a function is inlined, the vectorization is controlled by the way the caller is compiled.

In order to support legacy architectures and maintain binary portability, the default Intel compiler options are set very conservatively to build binaries for SSE2-enabled architectures. This default behavior provides complete compatibility with the standard $\times 64$ ABI (Application Binary Interface) that is required to support custom binary libraries, but limits potential performance benefits.

Figure 22.10 illustrates an example where the "main" application is compiled with the Intel SSE4.2 instruction set and dynamically linked to a library which supports two architectures: Intel AVX and Intel AVX2. When the program is launched, the library runtime can choose the appropriate binary based on the underlying hardware.

Developers can change the default target architecture through command-line switches passed to the Intel compiler ($-x$ on Linux, and /Qx on Microsoft Windows). These command-line switches are also the mechanism that provides support for new instruction architectures such as Intel AVX-512 vector instruction set.

The vectorization report for our example when compiling under Linux for the Intel AVX2 instruction set using the –xCORE-AVX2 command-line flag is shown in Figure 22.11.

The boldface region of the vector report in Figure 22.15 shows the default use of XMM registers in the $\times 64$ ABI. This means the default SIMD length is still set to simdlen$=2$ even when compiled for Intel AVX2.

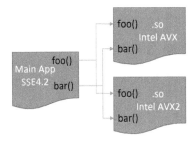

FIGURE 22.10

An application dynamically linked with a hardware dependent library.

```
...
remark #15489:  --- begin vector function matching report ---
remark #15490:  Function call: Interpolate(double, const point *)
                with simdlen=8, actual parameter types:
                (vector,uniform)    [ main.c(56,18) ]
remark #15492:  A suitable vector variant was found (out of 2)
                with xmm, simdlen=2, unmasked, formal parameter
                types: (vector,uniform)
remark #15493:  --- end vector function matching report ---
...
```

FIGURE 22.11

Vectorization report when compiled with –xCORE-AVX2.

On Intel AVX-enabled architectures, the YMM registers (256-bits wide) can be used for parameter passing and results as they have twice the bit width of the XMM registers (which are 128-bits wide). As this uses a nonstandard calling convention, it needs to be carefully specified for the function to affect the function compilation and calls to the function so that parameters and results are placed in YMM registers. To enable usage of YMM registers, the processor(…) clause needs to be added to the declaration directive as shown in Figure 22.12. In this case, the parameter-passing interface is changed to that of a core_4th_gen_avx architecture for this function. *Note*: this clause needs to be added separately to each function.

As can be seen in Figure 22.14, targeting the core_4th_gen_avx architecture increases the vector length to simdlen=4 due to the use of the YMM registers to pass parameters. Setting simdlen to anything other than a multiple of what fits in a YMM register does not make sense for efficiency. This means the programmer also needs to update the *simdlen(…)* clause of the FindPosition() function. The vector report after recompiling the modified sources is shown in Figure 22.13. Note that the correct simdlen=4 is highlighted in boldface.

```
#pragma omp declare simd uniform (vals)\
                       processor(core_4th_gen_avx)
double Interpolate(double x, const point* vals);


#pragma omp declare simd simdlen(4) \
                       processor(core_4th_gen_avx)
int FindPosition(double x);
...
```

FIGURE 22.12

Declaration of specific processor in a vector function.

```
...
remark #15489: --- begin vector function matching report ---
remark #15490: Function call: Interpolate(double, const point *)
               with simdlen=8, actual parameter types:
               (vector,uniform)    [ main.c(56,18) ]
remark #15492: A suitable vector variant was found (out of 2)
               with ymm2, simdlen=4, unmasked, formal parameter
               types: (vector,uniform)
remark #15493: --- end vector function matching report ---
...
```

FIGURE 22.13

Extending method declarations for uniform calls.

Target Processor	ISA Extension	ISA Class
pentium_4	SSE2	xmm
pentium_4_sse3	SSE3	xmm
core_2_duo_ssse3	SSSE3	xmm
core_2_duo_sse4_1	SSE4_1	xmm
core_i7_sse4_2	SSE4_2	xmm
core_2nd_gen_avx	AVX	ymm1
core_3rd_gen_avx	AVX	ymm1
core_4th_gen_avx	AVX2	ymm2
mic	Intel® Xeon Phi™ coprocessor (Knights Corner)	mic

FIGURE 22.14

processor() clause supported target processor types.

Figure 22.14 shows the processor architectures currently supported by the Intel 15.0 compiler. Newer versions of the compiler will support AVX-512 for future Intel Xeon processors and Intel Xeon Phi processors. Use of AVX-512 will enable the use of ZMM registers (512-bits wide) for parameters and results.

In addition to select the vector ABI, the *processor()* clause also specifies the vector instruction set used to generate the binary code for the relevant function thereby overriding the compiler architecture settings. For example, if we compile the file with the default architecture (SSE2), but use processor (core_4th_gen_avx) clause in the function declaration, then the compiler will only generate an Intel AVX2 version of the vector function.

If the architecture specified by the compiler command-line switch is a more recent generation than one specified by the processor() clause, then the command line switch will be used to generate the instructions for the binary code but not the vector ABI. In this case, a compiler warning will be generated. Example:

```
warning #13395: Command line flag overrides the target processor to 'core_4th_gen_avx'
for the vector function '...' where processor clause is 'core_2nd_gen_avx'
```

SUPPORTING MULTIPLE PROCESSOR TYPES

The Intel compiler is designed to support multiple processor architecture types in the same binary file. No user input is required as the runtime transparently decides which architecture version to use based on the current hardware platform. Care must be taken as the Intel documentation points out that the default behavior is to run a sequential loop if no matching hardware version has been defined for the software.

The additional architecture is specified by –ax (on Linux) or /Qax (on Windows) compiler flags. For example, in addition to the default SSE2 instruction set, the /QaxCORE-AVX2 will generate Intel AVX2 binary path. It is possible to combine –x(/Qx) flags with multiple –ax(/Qax) combinations,

```
#pragma omp declare simd simdlen(2) \
                    processor(core_i7_sse4_2)
#pragma omp declare simd simdlen(4) \
                    processor(core_4th_gen_avx)
int FindPosition(double x);


#pragma omp declare simd uniform(vals) \
                    processor(core_i7_sse4_2)
#pragma omp declare simd uniform(vals) \
                    processor(core_4th_gen_avx)
double Interpolate(double x, const point* vals);
```

FIGURE 22.15

Declaring support for multiple architectures.

wherein the architecture specified with –x(/Qx) is the eldest one. For example, −xSSE4.2 -axAVX -axCORE-AVX2.

When multiple architectures are specified, the compiler will generate a vector function for each architecture, specifically for SSE4.2, Intel AVX and Intel AVX2 in our example. Figure 22.15 lists the modified source code.

The following example vector report from the Intel compiler tells us that it included autodispatch code for some functions, like main, when compiling for two architectures with the -xSSE4.2 and -axCORE-AVX2 flags.

```
main.c(17): (col. 1) remark: main has been targeted for automatic
cpu dispatch
```

The autodispatcher is the software component that manages multiple architecture-specific binaries within a single executable file. It has the ability to identify the architecture of the processor that is running the executable and appropriately initialize internal variables such as the dispatch table to route execution through the most performant execution path.

The vectorization report in Figure 22.16 shows that detailed information is include by the Intel compiler all target architectures.

VECTOR FUNCTIONS IN C++

In this section, we discuss the usage of directive guided vectorization in C++. The mechanism for vectorization of a C++ class method is similar. However, there are few points that require special attention. In this section, we extend the C code example by declaring an Interpolator class, as shown in Figure 22.17.

Unfortunately, C++ virtual methods cannot be vectorized because they are implemented as function pointers, which reside in a virtual table. No guarantee is made that all the pointers in the virtual table point to objects from the same class type, which make virtual function impossible to vectorize.

```
...
remark #15489: --- begin vector function matching report ---
remark #15490: Function call: Interpolate(double, const point *)
               with simdlen=8, actual parameter types:
               (vector,uniform)    [ main.c(56,18) ]
remark #15492: A suitable vector variant was found (out of 4)
               with ymm2, simdlen=4, unmasked, formal parameter
               types: (uniform,vector)
remark #15493: --- end vector function matching report ---
...
remark #15489: --- begin vector function matching report ---
remark #15490: Function call: Interpolate(double, const point *)
               with simdlen=8, actual parameter types:
               (vector,uniform)    [ main.c(56,18) ]
remark#15492: A suitable vector variant was found (out of 4)
               with xmm, simdlen=2, unmasked, formal parameter
               types: (uniform,vector)
remark #15493: --- end vector function matching report ---
...
```

FIGURE 22.16

Vectorization report for multiple architectures.

Figure 22.18 shows the vector report for the C++ implementation.

Note that the critical loop was vectorized, but that there are some vector function matching issues, which are highlighted in boldface in Figure 22.18.

The call to the Interpolator::interpolate method has two parameters. The first parameter is a pointer to the instance of *Interpolator* class (*this*) and the second parameter is an input value. As the *interpolator* object is uniform and the data parameter is linear within the vectorized loop, the compiler is looking for *(uniform,vector)* version of the Interpolate::interpolate() method. However, the compiler can only locate a (vector,vector) version of this method. As discussed previously, this results in inefficient machine code being generated.

UNIFORM(THIS) CLAUSE

Similar to the C code example shown in Figure 22.8, this function parameter passing ambiguity is resolved by applying a *uniform(this)* clause to the declaration of the vector function as listed in Figure 22.19. In case of a multiple target architecture, this clause must be applied to all the "declare simd" pragmas.

These changes are reflected in the compiler vectorization report listed in Figure 22.20 showing that appropriate function version was called.

```cpp
class Interpolator {
public:
    /* . . . full code on lotsofcores.com . . . */
    #pragma omp declare simd simdlen(2) \
                            processor(core_i7_sse4_2)
    #pragma omp declare simd simdlen(4) \
                            processor(core_4th_gen_avx)
    int FindPosition(double x) const {
return (int)(x*delta_inv);
    }


    #pragma omp declare simd processor(core_i7_sse4_2)
    #pragma omp declare simd processor(core_4th_gen_avx)
    double Interpolate(double x) const {
        int ind = FindPosition(x);
  const point& pnt = val_ptr[ind];
  double res = pnt.c0*x+pnt.c1;
  return res;
    }
private:
    double delta;
    double delta_inv;
}
/* . . . full code on lotsofcores.com . . . */
int main(int argc, char* argv[])
{
    Interpolator interpolator(512);
/* . . . full code on lotsofcores.com . . . */
    #pragma omp simd
    for(int i=0; i<ARRAY_SIZE; ++i) {
        dst_ptr[i] = interpolator.Interpolate(src_ptr[i]);
    }
    /* . . . full code on lotsofcores.com . . . */
    return 0;
}
```

FIGURE 22.17

C++ class declaration with SIMD enabled methods.

```
...
LOOP BEGIN at main.cpp(111,14)
    remark #15388: vectorization support: reference src_ptr
                   has aligned access    [ main.cpp(106,35) ]
    remark #15388: vectorization support: reference dst_ptr
                   has aligned access    [ main.cpp(106,9) ]
    remark #15399: vectorization support: unroll factor set to 4
    remark #15301: OpenMP SIMD LOOP WAS VECTORIZED
    remark #15442: entire loop may be executed in remainder
    remark #15448: unmasked aligned unit stride loads: 1
    remark #15449: unmasked aligned unit stride stores: 1
    remark #15475: --- begin vector loop cost summary ---
    remark #15476: scalar loop cost: 112
    remark #15477: vector loop cost: 29.000
    remark #15478: estimated potential speedup: 7.720
    remark #15479: lightweight vector operations: 8
    remark #15480: medium-overhead vector operations: 1
    remark #15484: vector function calls: 1
    remark #15488: --- end vector loop cost summary ---
    remark #15489: --- begin vector function matching report ---
  remark #15490: Function call: Interpolator::Interpolate(const
                 Interpolator *, double) const with simdlen=8,
                 actual parameter types: (uniform,vector)
                 [ main.cpp(106,35) ]
  remark #15492: A suitable vector variant was found (out of 4)
                 with ymm2, simdlen=4, unmasked, formal parameter
                 types: (vector,vector)
  remark #15493: --- end vector function matching report ---
        LOOP END
  . . .
```

FIGURE 22.18

C++ code vectorization report.

```
class Interpolator {
/* . . . full code on lotsofcores.com . . . */
  #pragma omp declare simd\
                        processor(core_i7_sse4_2)
  #pragma omp declare simd uniform(this)\
                        processor(core_i7_sse4_2)
  #pragma omp declare simd\
                        processor(core_4th_gen_avx)
  #pragma omp declare simd uniform(this)\
                        processor(core_4th_gen_avx)
  double Interpolate(double x) const {
      int ind = FindPosition(x);
      const point& pnt = val_ptr[ind];
      double res = pnt.c0*x+pnt.c1;
      return res;
  }
  /* . . . full code on lotsofcores.com . . . */
}
```

FIGURE 22.19

Extending method declaration for uniform calls.

```
...
remark #15489: --- begin vector function matching report ---
remark #15490: Function call: Interpolator::Interpolate(const
               Interpolator *, double) const with simdlen=2,
               actual parameter types: (uniform,vector)
               [ main.cpp(106,35) ]
remark #15492: A suitable vector variant was found (out of 8)
               with ymm2, simdlen=4, unmasked, formal parameter
               types: (uniform,vector)
remark #15493: --- end vector function matching report ---
. . .
```

FIGURE 22.20

Extending method declaration for uniform calls.

The *uniform(this)* clause must be used appropriately. There are scenarios that may call different object instances; such as processing an array of interpolators. In such cases, a nonuniform variant of the function is used.

VECTOR FUNCTIONS IN FORTRAN

Figure 22.21 shows the implementation of a linear spline interpolation method in the Interpolate() function in Fortran

PERFORMANCE RESULTS

A summary of vector speedup is shown in Figure 22.22 with the following test configuration:

- OS = Linux RedHat Enterprise 6.5
- Intel Composer XE 2015, version 15.0.2, ×64
- Dual socket system-based Intel Xeon E5-2697 v3 family processor
- Intel Xeon Phi 7120A coprocessor
- All tests run using a single thread.

Performance testing shows that individual test speedup gains range from 2.03× using SSE2 to 4.54× using AVX2 compared to scalar code. The greater than 2× speedup of the AVX2 version over the SSE2 version is due partially to the 256 bit width of the AVX2 SIMD instructions (vs. the 128 bit width of SSE2) and the inclusion of an FMA (Fused Multiply Add) instruction. There is no observable overhead in multiarchitecture (SSE4.2 and Intel AVX2) binary support compared to a single architecture binary (Intel AVX2) despite expecting to see some because of architectural limitations in switching between SSE and AVX.

SUMMARY

Larger vector units and ever more capable vector instruction sets have both contributed to increasing hardware performance and efficiency. We expect this hardware trend will continue for the foreseeable future. Similarly, compilers have become increasing smarter in their ability to recognize vectorizable loops. Even so, the addition of the OpenMP SIMD declaration and associated clauses gives programmers the ability to ensure vectorization and create multiarchitecture libraries and applications that can run efficiently on both legacy and state-of-the-art processors including Intel Xeon Phi processors and coprocessors.

You are encouraged to download the code from lotsofcores.com, and experiment with compiling it and looking at the performance and optimization reports. While the optimization support for vectorization is probably best with the Intel compilers, the code will work with the GCC compiler as well. Making this code we provide useful for exploration of this SIMD vector capability on multiple compilers in addition to Intel's compilers.

```fortran
! . . . full code available on lotsofcores.com . . .
! . . . the interface declarations for SIMD function . . .
interface
double precision function Interpolate(a,vals)
!$omp declare simd(Interpolate) uniform(vals)
use points
double precision, intent(in) :: a
type(point), intent(in), dimension(:) :: vals
end function Interpolate
end interface

! . . . full code available on lotsofcores.com . . .
! . . . the call call site within the main program . . .
start_time = get_current_time()
do iter=1, ITER_COUNT, 1
   !$omp simd
   do i=1, ARRAY_SIZE, 1
      dst(i) = Interpolate(src(i),vals)
   end do
end do
end_time = get_current_time()

! . . . full code available on lotsofcores.com . . .
! . . . the SIMD functions themselves . . .
double precision function Interpolate(x, vals)
!$omp declare simd(Interpolate) uniform(vals) simdlen(8)
use points
double precision, intent(in) :: x
type(point), intent(in) :: vals(:)
integer FindPosition
integer :: ind
ind = FindPosition(x)
Interpolate = dlog(dexp( vals(ind)%c0 * x + vals(ind)%c1 ) )
end function Interpolate
```

FIGURE 22.21

Optimized with "simd" directives: Fortran source code for a linear spline.

Test #	Language	SIMD Width	Platform	Scalar Time (ms)	Vector Time (ms)	Vector Speedup
1	C	128	Intel Xeon v3	148.0	71.7	2.1X
2	C	512	Intel Xeon Phi coprocessor (Knights Corner)	565.1	142.6	4.0X
3	C	256	Intel Xeon v3	148.0	33.1	4.5X
4	C	128 & 256	Intel Xeon v3	149.2	33.2	4.5X
5	C++	128 & 256	Intel Xeon v3	147.9	32.6	4.5X
6	Fortran	128 & 256	Intel Xeon v3	151.4	36.0	4.2X
7	Fortran	512	Intel Xeon Phi coprocessor (Knights Corner)	583.7	145.1	4.0X

FIGURE 22.22

Vectorization speedup summary.

FOR MORE INFORMATION

Here are some recommended reading materials.
- Intel Compiler User Guide version 15, https://software.intel.com/en-us/compiler_15.0_ug_c.
- Explicit Vector Programming with OpenMP 4.0 SIMD Extensions, http://primeurmagazine.com/repository/PrimeurMagazine-AE-PR-12-14-32.pdf.
- Vector Function Application Binary Interface, https://www.cilkplus.org/sites/default/files/open_specifications/Intel-ABI-Vector-Function-2012-v0.9.5.pdf.
- A Guide to Vectorization with Intel® C++ Compilers, https://software.intel.com/en-us/articles/a-guide-to-auto-vectorization-with-intel-c-compilers.
- Download the code from this, and other chapters, http://lotsofcores.com.

VECTORIZATION ADVICE

23

Michael Seaton*, Luke Mason*, Zakhar A. Matveev[†], Stephen Blair-Chappell[‡]

STFC Daresbury Laboratory, UK[*] Intel, Russia[†] Intel, UK[‡]

Many chapters in this book show how to achieve performance using vectorization as a key optimization. This chapter highlights a tool to help analyze the opportunity for vectorization and give advice on how to solve it.

Using the new Intel® Vectorization Advisor to optimize your code is like having an expert sitting with you to help you get your code to vectorize. This chapter discusses considerations for vectorization in the context of using the Vectorization Advisor to analyze your program and guide you to greater performance.

This chapter shows how the Vectorization Advisor supports a three-step approach to helping us vectorize code: (1) profile and diagnose; (2) analyze and advise (trip counts, dependencies, memory access patterns, snapshot comparisons); and (3) make code changes, recompile, and repeat.

In this chapter, we look at how to analyze some code, identify a problem, and then fix it. In some cases, we analyze the code and discuss suggestions for the type of changes that need to be made. In our examples, we use the DL_MESO Lattice Boltzmann equation (LBE) code from Daresbury Labs.

This chapter focuses only on vectorization and does not attempt to cover threading or parallelism across cores. For simplicity, in all our examples, we turn off the threading and just run on one thread. Despite this, please do not misunderstand us, threading *is* very important, the Intel® Advisor tool provides support and dedicated analysis for threaded applications, but that is not the focus of this chapter.

THE IMPORTANCE OF VECTORIZATION

It is not hard to understand that *threading* offers more parallelism than *vectorization*; consider that hardware thread counts could be 244 on an Intel® Xeon Phi™ coprocessor, while SIMD could be "just" 16-way for single precision float-point computations. However, it is very important to understand the multiplicative effects when you add vectorization to a threaded program! The newest processor designs can favor programs dramatically when *both* threading and vectorization are used. Figure 23.1 shows an example of how dramatic this can be; Figure 23.1 shows parallel performance that is relatively limited with either threading or vectorization alone, but has much more dramatic advantage when used together. The graph also shows that this increased capability is growing rapidly with new processor generations.

When writing code for multicore Intel® Xeon® processors or many-core Intel Xeon Phi platforms, your code will only reach good performance if it is both parallel and efficiently vectorized. There are many different ways you can add vectorization to your code including:

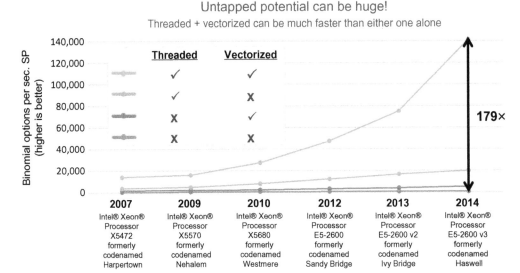

FIGURE 23.1

Vectorization and threading can be dramatically more powerful when used in combination.

- Letting the compiler automatically vectorize your code
- Adding pragmas or directives (such as the OpenMP simd pragmas/directives)
- Using libraries that are already vectorized, such as the Intel Math Kernel Library (MKL)
- Hand-coding using assembler instructions, vector intrinsic functions, or C++ vector classes (this approach is known to be less "portable" than others).

Whichever way you choose to produce vectorized code, it's important that the resultant code is efficient in exercising the vector units of the processor.

ABOUT DL_MESO LBE

DL_MESO_LBE can simulate lattice-gas systems using the LBE, modeling fluids at the mesoscale. The following properties and features are currently available:

- Multiple fluid components, solutes, and coupled heat transfers.
- Collisions: Bhatnagar-Gross-Krook (BGK) single-relaxation-time or Multiple-Relaxation-Time (MRT).
- Boundary conditions: Periodic, bounce-back (including stationary objects), constant pressure/velocity at planar surfaces.
- Mesoscale interactions: Shan-Chen pseudopotential method, Lishchuk continuum-based method.
- Initial conditions can either be determined by DL_MESO_LBE or specified by the user.

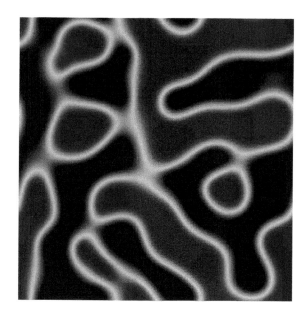

FIGURE 23.2

Visualization of the 3D_PhaseSeparation benchmark.

DL_MESO_LBE utilizes a right-handed Cartesian coordinate system with the x-axis from left to right in the horizontal direction, the y-axis from low to high in the vertical direction and z-axis from back to front. D2Q9, D3Q15, D3Q19, and D3Q27 lattice models have been included. The speed vectors and weight factors are arranged to allow the use of swap algorithms for propagation. MRT schemes exist for each lattice (except D3Q27) and can improve numerical stability compared with simpler BGK collisions. Interacting forces between fluid species can be calculated using either of the above mesoscale interaction schemes to provide immiscibility and interfacial tension, while diffusive and heat transfer processes can be modeled concurrently with fluid flow.

Figure 23.2 shows the cross-sectional plot of two initially mixed fluids from the 3D_PhaseSeparation benchmark at one particular point in time.

INTEL VECTORIZATION ADVISOR AND THE UNDERLYING TECHNOLOGY

The Vectorization Advisor is one of the two major features of the **Intel® Advisor XE 2016** product. Intel Advisor XE includes the **Vectorization Advisor** and **a Threading Advisor.**

The Vectorization Advisor is an analysis tool that lets you identify:

- If loops in your code use modern SIMD instructions.
- What prevents your code being vectorized.
- The performance efficiency of your code and how to increase it.

The advisor displays optimization information from the compiler in a user-friendly view and extends the information with other metrics, including loop **trip counts**, CPU time, **memory access patterns**, and **recommendations** for optimization. The Vectorization Advisor is most efficient when applied to user applications compiled with Intel Compiler. However, a solid subset of metrics is available for binaries built with other compilers as well.

The Intel C++ and Fortran Compilers use sophisticated code transformation techniques and static architecture analysis to generate optimized code. The decisions made by the optimization engine normally do not take into account the runtime behavior of the application you are developing. One of the consequences of this lack of runtime knowledge is that the resulting binary may run poorly, unless you are utilizing the profile-guided feedback mechanisms. With the Vectorization Advisor, we do not need to use the profile-guided feedback and we have the benefits of interactive advice and a rich set of dynamic binary profiles (which could even be obtained in multi-node cluster environment).

The Intel Vectorization Advisor Survey feature bridges the gap between compile time decisions and runtime behavior by using a combination of static and dynamic analysis, along with the optimization information embedded in the compiler-generated binaries.

In order to understand SIMD and Threading parallelism potential, it is often crucial to get knowledge about loop "call counts" and "trip counts" (the number of times loop is invoked and number of times loop bodies execute). Advisor technology makes it possible to obtain given information using the "Trip Counts" feature. This feature relies on dynamically instrumenting the running application; one side effect of this analysis is that the application will run between $2\times$ to $3\times$ slower.

The last (but not least) constituent of Advisor technology platform—is a set of *memory profiling* tools, implemented using conditional memory access load and store instruction tracking, providing a unique capability of (a) identifying the memory access pattern being used in Vectorized and Scalar codes (MAP feature) and (b) dynamically characterizing real loop-carried dependencies in scalar loops (Loop Dependencies feature).

A LIFE CYCLE FOR EXPERIMENTATION

As you try to improve the performance of your code, you'll almost certainly want to try different "experiments." Perhaps you'll first add a pragma or two to your code, and then maybe edit your code to build on some success you have already achieved. After a series of edits and experimentation, you may even decide to go back to the original code and start all over again!

When doing these sorts of experiments, we suggest you adopt the life cycle shown in Figure 23.3. In the figure, the steps shown parenthetically are optional.

- Profile & Diagnose
  - Firstly, build an **optimized version** (i.e., Release Mode) of your application, remembering to generate debug information using the -g (Linux) or /Zi (Windows) flags. Once you have built your application, the same binary should typically be used in the following steps.
  - Run a **Survey** analysis to look for the hotspots. The results will include how long each loop takes to run, any compiler optimization messages, the type of vectorization used, and, where appropriate, one or more recommendations in the advice panel.
- Analyze and Advise

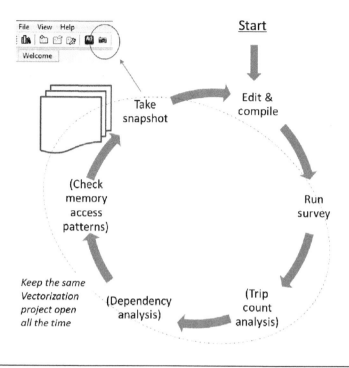

FIGURE 23.3

A life cycle for experimentation.

- Optionally run a **Trip Count** analysis to get see how many times particular loops run.
- Optionally run a **Dependencies** analysis to see if there are any loop-carried dependencies.
- Optionally run a **Memory Access Patterns (MAP)** analysis to see how your code is iterating through memory.
- Take a **Snapshot** of the results

The Dependencies analysis and MAP analysis are for performing a "deeper dive" into the workings of particular loops. Before you run an analysis, you must first select the loops you are interested in—which can be easily done from within the Survey results window. You should also try to reduce the amount of work your application does, as these steps add significant overhead to the runtime and the amount of memory used. Finally, the snapshot stores:

- Survey Report (including Trip Count)
- Refinement Reports (including Dependencies and MAP)
- Selective snapshots of user source code
- Various logging information

One of the benefits of this life-cycle is not only that your analysis results are saved in the snapshot but, as importantly, so are the code changes you make.

ANALYZING THE LATTICE BOLTZMANN CODE

Figure 23.4 shows the initial analysis of the DL_MESO code using the *vectorization advisor survey* feature of Intel Advisor XE. Depending on the input data set characteristics, such as the number of fluids or collision scheme type, the hotspots' distribution varies significantly.

The hotspots distribution has a "flat profile" pattern, which is fairly common for physics simulation codes, and contains a large number of hotspots, each taking only 3-5% of the time. Optimizing programs with this kind of "flat profile" can be time consuming, as you have to individually profile and develop each of the many hotspots.

Normally, when you start any optimization work, you should work on parts of the code that contribute most to the runtime. That is the biggest hotspot, but in our case, we chose to go in the reverse order, because we incrementally want to introduce different features of the Vectorization Advisor in the chapter. In fact, we even skip the third hotspot in fGetSpeedSite, because the fourth hotspot will serve our purposes better.

In this chapter, we look at three of the four hottest loops:

- **lbpSUB:744** in **fGetEquilibriumF** calculates the equilibrium for compressible fluids
- **lbpGET:42** in **fGetOneMassSite** calculates mass density
- **lbpSUB:1247** in **fPropogationSwap** moves particles to neighboring grid points

OPTIMIZING THE COMPUTE EQUILIBRIUM LOOP (lbpSUB:744)

In this section, we use the Advisor Survey Analysis to look at the constituent parts of the loop in fGetEquilibriumF, and then fix vectorization inefficiency by padding some of the data structures.

Function Call Sites and Loops	Self Time ▾	Total Time
[loop at lbpSUB.cpp:1247 in fPropagationSwapompparallel@1225]	12.118s	12.118s
[loop at lbpGET.cpp:42 in fGetOneMassSite]	9.751s	9.751s
[loop at lbpGET.cpp:281 in fGetSpeedSite]	6.710s	12.031s
[loop at lbpSUB.cpp:744 in fGetEquilibriumF]	6.570s	6.570s
[loop at lbpFORCE.cpp:98 in fCalcInteraction_ShanChen]	3.647s	6.644s
[loop at lbpSUB.cpp:1238 in fPropagationSwapompparallel@1225]	3.054s	3.054s
[loop at lbpFORCE.cpp:102 in fCalcInteraction_ShanChen]	**2.997s**	**2.997s**
[loop at lbpFORCE.cpp:37 in fCalcPotential_ShanChenompparallel@30]	1.260s	14.962s
[loop at lbpFORCE.cpp:116 in fCalcInteraction_ShanChen]	1.229s	1.229s
[loop at lbpBGK.cpp:30 in fSiteFluidCollisionBGK]	1.070s	1.070s

FIGURE 23.4

The results of an initial analysis.

```
int fGetEquilibriumF(double *feq, double *v, double rho)
{
  double modv = v[0]*v[0] + v[1]*v[1] + v[2]*v[2];
  double uv;

  for(int i=0; i<lbsy.nq; i++)
  {
    uv = lbv[i*3]   * v[0]
       + lbv[i*3+1] * v[1]
       + lbv[i*3+2] * v[2];

    feq[i] = rho * lbw[i]
           * (1 + 3.0 * uv + 4.5 * uv * uv - 1.5 * modv);
  }
  return 0;
}
```

FIGURE 23.5

Code listing—loop for calculating equilibrium distribution.

The fGetEquilibriumF function

This loop, shown in Figure 23.5, calculates the equilibrium distribution of compressible fluids. Depending on the number of fluids being modeled, this can be the hotspot with the most "self-time" and be responsible for up to 20% of program elapsed time; in other cases, it still tends to provide more than 2% impact even when modeling a single fluid.

The array lbv stores the velocities for of the lattice in each dimension, the loop count variable lbsy.nq being the number of velocities. In this chapter, we are using the D3Q19 lattice Boltzmann model that represents the three-dimensional 19-velocity lattice, so the value of lbsy.nq is 19.

The resulting equilibrium is stored in the array feq[i].

Advisor survey

Looking at Figure 23.6, which shows the advisor analysis for this loop, the upper part of the screenshot shows loop hotspots, and is sometimes referred to as the "bottom up" view. The lower part shows the Top Down view, which displays the call stack of the loops that are selected in the bottom up view.

Looking at the results you will notice that the compiler has generated several versions and blocks for the original loop:

- A vectorized loop body, accounting for almost 5 s of the total loop time of 6.57 s. The Vector Length is 4—that is four doubles held in the 256 bit-wide AVX registers.
- A scalar remainder that consumes almost 2 s.
- Two scalar versions of the loop to cater for potentially overlapping data (assuming loop dependencies). These are invoked from some initialization code and consume insignificant time.

Function Call Sites and Loops	●	Vector Issues	Self Time ▾	Total Time	Loop Type	Why No Vectorization?	Vectorized L... Vector I... E:
[loop at lbpSUB.cpp:744 in fGetEquilibriumF]		⌄ 5 Assumed depend...	6.570s▮	6.570s	Collapse	Collapse	AVX
[loop at lbpSUB.cpp:744 in fGetEquilibriumF]	■	⌄ Data type conversi...	4.820s▯	4.820s	Vectorized (body)		AVX
[loop at lbpSUB.cpp:744 in fGetEquilibriumF]			1.730s▮	1.730s	Remainder		
[loop at lbpSUB.cpp:744 in fGetEquilibriumF]		⌄ 1 Assumed depende...	0.010s▮	0.010s	Scalar	▣ vector dependence prevents vectorization	
[loop at lbpSUB.cpp:744 in fGetEquilibriumF]		⌄ 1 Assumed depende...	0.010s▮	0.010s	Scalar	▣ vector dependence prevents vectorization	

Function Call Sites and Loops	Total Time %	Total Time	Self Time	Loop Type	Why No Vectorization?	Vectorized Loops Vector I... Vector Length	Instruction Set Ana... Traits Data Types	Ad\
fCollisionBGKompparallel@827	33.0%▮	22.231s▮	2.720s					
fSiteFluidCollisionBGK	17.2%▮	11.620s▮	2.419s					
fGetEquilibriumF	12.1%▮	8.130s▮	1.580s					
[loop at lbpSUB.cpp:744 in fGet	9.7%▮	6.550s▮						
[loop at lbpSUB.cpp:744 in fG	7.2%▮	4.820s▮	4.820s	Vectorized (...		AVX 4	Type ... Float64; Int...	
[loop at lbpSUB.cpp:744 in fG	2.6%▮	1.730s▮	1.729s	Remainder				
[loop at lbpBGK.cpp:30 in fSiteFlui	1.6%▮	1.070s▮						

FIGURE 23.6

Analysis results of the loop at line 744 of lbpSUB.cpp: body – peel – remainder break-down.

Trip count analysis

One additional piece of information useful in analyzing loops is exactly how many times a loop body has been iterated and how many times a loop was invoked. You can use the Trip Count analysis in the Vectorization Advisor to find out these values. When you run a Trip Count analysis, you should expect the program to run between two and three times slower than the Advisor Survey.

In our given case, because of our knowledge of the code, we already know that the Trip Count will be 19 for this loop, but it is better to check Trip Counts and Call Counts data by running an analysis.

Fixing the problem

The Scalar Remainder is an unnecessary overhead introduced by vectorization, and our case takes about 25% of the total time for the loop. The existence of this remainder loop has a detrimental effect on the parallel efficiency—that is, the maximum speedup that could be achieved.

Note

You should always investigate any code where you see a significant proportion of a loops runtime being spent in either a scalar, remainder, or peeled loops—it indicates that vector parallel efficiency is sub-optimal and that there might be optimization opportunities.

The big remainder "overhead" in the function fGetEquilibriumF is actually caused by the loop (trip) count not being a multiple of the Vector Length (*VL*). When the compiler vectorizes the loop, it generates the vectorized body, which in our case executes loop iterations number 0–15. The remaining three iterations, 16–18, are executed by the scalar remainder code.

As the total loop count is quite small, then the three iterations remaining become a significant part of elapsed loop time. In an ideally optimized loop, and especially those with a low trip count, there should be no remainder code.

One technique we can apply to this code is to increase the loop iterations count to become a multiple of VL, i.e., 20 in our case—see Figure 23.7. This technique is called "data padding" and this is exactly what Advisor explicitly suggests in the "Recommendations" window for this loop (as seen in Figure 23.9). In order to "pad" the data we need to increase the size of the arrays feq[], lbv[] and lbw[] so that accessing the (unused) 20th location will not cause a segmentation violation or similar problem.

Figure 23.8 gives an example of the change that is needed. The value nq_full_width hard codes the padding value to be lbsy.nq + 1, but a more elegant and portable way could be to replace 1 with VL - (lbsy.nq mod VL).

You will also see that we have added the #pragma loop count (20) directive. By telling the compiler what the loop count will be, the compiler sees that the count is a multiple of the vector length and optimizes code generation for particular trip count value so that scalar remainder invocation code is omitted in runtime.

In the DL_MESO code, there are a number of similar equilibrium distribution code constructs that can be modified in the same way. In our example, we modified three other loops in the same source file and achieved a speedup of 15% on each loop.

```
int nq_full_width = lbsy.nq;
  if(lbsy.nq != 0)
    nq_full_width = lbsy.nq + 1;


if(lbsy.nq != 0) {
  lbw = new double[nq_full_width];  // was [lbsy.nq]
}
```

FIGURE 23.7

Code listing—example of code changes to memory allocation, with modifications shown in **bold**.

```
#pragma loop count (20)
for(int i=0; i<lbsy.nq + 1; i++)
{
  uv = lbv[i*3]   * v[0]
         + lbv[i*3+1] * v[1]
         + lbv[i*3+2] * v[2];

  feq[i] = rho * lbw[i]
             * (1 + 3.0 * uv + 4.5 * uv * uv - 1.5 * modv);
}
```

FIGURE 23.8

Code listing—the optimized loop, with modifications shown in **bold**.

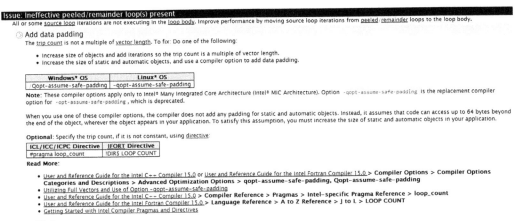

Issue: Ineffective peeled/remainder loop(s) present
All or some source loop iterations are not executing in the loop body. Improve performance by moving source loop iterations from peeled/remainder loops to the loop body.

○ Add data padding
The trip count is not a multiple of vector length. To fix: Do one of the following:

- Increase size of objects and add iterations so the trip count is a multiple of vector length.
- Increase the size of static and automatic objects, and use a compiler option to add data padding.

Windows* OS	Linux* OS
/Qopt-assume-safe-padding	-qopt-assume-safe-padding

Note: These compiler options apply only to Intel® Many Integrated Core Architecture (Intel® MIC Architecture). Option -qopt-assume-safe-padding is the replacement compiler option for -opt-assume-safe-padding, which is deprecated.

When you use one of these compiler options, the compiler does not add any padding for static and automatic objects. Instead, it assumes that code can access up to 64 bytes beyond the end of the object, wherever the object appears in your application. To satisfy this assumption, you must increase the size of static and automatic objects in your application.

Optional: Specify the trip count, if it is not constant, using directive:

ICL/ICC/ICPC Directive	IFORT Directive
#pragma loop_count	!DIR$ LOOP COUNT

Read More:

- User and Reference Guide for the Intel C++ Compiler 15.0 or User and Reference Guide for the Intel Fortran Compiler 15.0 > **Compiler Options > Compiler Options Categories and Descriptions > Advanced Optimization Options > qopt-assume-safe-padding, Qopt-assume-safe-padding**
- Utilizing Full Vectors and Use of Option -qopt-assume-safe-padding
- User and Reference Guide for the Intel C++ Compiler 15.0 > **Compiler Reference > Pragmas > Intel-specific Pragma Reference > loop_count**
- User and Reference Guide for the Intel Fortran Compiler 15.0 > **Language Reference > A to Z Reference > J to L > LOOP COUNT**
- Getting Started with Intel Compiler Pragmas and Directives

FIGURE 23.9

The Vectorization Advisor Recommendations for padding the data.

ANALYSIS OF THE CALCULATE MASS DENSITY LOOP (lbpGET:42)

In this section, we use Advisor to help spot an alignment issue of the loop in fGetOneMassSite, and then fix the problem by adding pragmas to the source code.

The fGetOneMassSite function

Figure 23.10 shows the code for the mass density calculations. The starting position in the grid is passed into the function fGetOneMassSite via the parameter startpos. The calculated mass is returned to the calling function.

```
double fGetOneMassSite(double* startpos)
{
  double mass=0.0;
  double *pt1;
  pt1= startpos;
  for(int i=0; i<lbsy.nq; i++) {
    mass += *pt1;
    pt1 ++;
  }
  pt1 = NULL;
  return mass;
}
```

FIGURE 23.10

Code listing—calculating the mass density.

Advisor survey

Despite the simplicity of the code, in our tests this function was the number two hotspot, and even in other test cases it often fell within the top five hotspots of the Survey Analysis—as in Figure 23.11. In the Analysis results you can see that there are four instances of the loop, those four versions being created by code in-lining that the compiler has carried out. Each version contains:

- A Vectorized Body—using packed AVX instructions.
- A Remainder Loop—added to compensate for the Trip Count not being a multiple of the Vector Length.
- A Peel Loop—this is a consequence of the array being referenced by `startpos` not being aligned correctly for AVX.

Twelve loops in total. In our case, the Peeled Loops are responsible for almost 60% of the total loops runtime, with the Vectorized Body taking just over 30%, leaving the Remainder Loops to consume 10%. Thus over 40% of the time is spent outside the Vectorized Body—this is something that needs investigation by analogy with the investigation we've undertaken in the previous section.

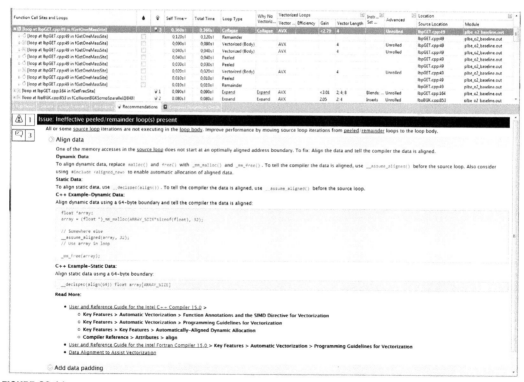

FIGURE 23.11

Analysis results of the loop in fGetOneMassSite. Alignment and padding advice given by Advisor Recommendations.

In the Recommendation section (the lower part of Figure 23.11), there are two problems in the fGetOneMassSite function that need fixing:

- The alignment of the array pointed to by startpos.
- The Trip Count and data padding.

Fixing the problem

In our code, the real problem is that the compiler was not certain if the array pointed to by startpos is aligned, and therefore assumes it is unaligned. To fix this, we simply use a pragma to tell the compiler the data are aligned:

```
#pragma vector aligned
```

In any codes that you work on, you must be certain that the array *is actually* aligned before using this pragma, otherwise your program may fail. If you need more help on getting your data aligned, you can go to one of the urls in section For more information. You can also confirm the alignment of your data at runtime using Advisor's Memory Access Pattern (MAP) tool, but this topic is out of scope for this chapter.

After dealing with alignment, we still need to fix the loop count (and remainder-driven overhead) issue. To do that, we repeat the padding steps done in the last loop, and also tell the compiler that the trip count is 20 via #pragma loop count. The code in Figure 23.12 shows the modified loop.

```
double fGetOneMassSite(double* startpos)
{
  double mass=0.0;
  double *pt1;
  pt1= startpos;

  #pragma loop count (20)
  #pragma vector aligned
  for(int i=0; i< lbsy.nq + 1; i++) {
    mass += *pt1;
    pt1 ++;
  }
  pt1--;
  mass -= *pt1;
  pt1 = NULL;
  return mass;
}
```

FIGURE 23.12

Code listing—calculating the mass density.

BALANCING OVERHEADS AND OPTIMIZATION TRADE-OFFS

The padding technique that we used for the first two loops has both performance and code maintenance costs.

- From a **performance** perspective, by padding we avoid overhead in the scalar part, but we introduce extra computations in the vector part.
- From a **code maintenance** perspective, we have to rework data structure allocations and potentially introduce workload-dependent pragma definitions.

Fortunately, in our case, the performance benefit outweighs any performance loss, and the code maintenance burden is light.

In our example, the loop trip count values are defined by number of velocities, which in our available data sets are limited to the values 15, 19, and 27 (according to lattices DnQm taxonomy). This means that the number of extra "padding" iterations needed in the loop remainder is always +1 for AVX/AVX2 platforms.

For future AVX-512 and current IMCI platforms, the D3Q15 data set should benefit from the doubling of the Vector Length on Intel Xeon Phi coprocessors, but D3Q19 and D3Q27 (due to wider VL) will be less optimal.

From a code maintenance perspective, the earlier suggestion of replacing nq_full_width with *trip count + VL – (trip count mod VL)* can be used to avoid hardcoding the number of padding iterations and loop counts. The pragma hardcoding (Figures 23.8 and 23.12) could either be addressed by using a more flexible pragma loop count *min, max, avg* clause or by using code parameterization techniques like C pre-processor conditionalization, C++ template specialization or by using C++11 functors.

OPTIMIZING THE MOVE PARTICLES TO NEIGHBORING GRID LOOP (lbpSUB:1247)

In this section, we deal with the loop in function fPropagationSwap, which is the loop that is also our number one hotspot. After doing a Dependency Analysis to confirm there are no dependencies, we vectorize the original scalar loop and then run a Memory Access Pattern analysis to find out why the loop is performing so badly. We then improve the performance by applying OpenMP4.0 standard #pragma simd directives at a different loopnest level.

The loop in function fPropagationSwap

This loop moves particles to neighboring grid points using a swap algorithm. This is the last of the loops we shall look at in this chapter. The code consists of a five-level nested loop within the function fPropagationSwap. At the deepest level, particles are swapped to their neighbors using the function fSwapPair—see Figure 23.13.

We already know from Section "Analyzing the Lattice Boltzmann code" that the loop at lbpSUB. cpp:1247 often takes more time than any other loop. Additionally (Figure 23.14), we can see that the loop:

```
#pragma omp for collapse(3)
for(int i=0; i<Xmax; i++)
  for(int j=0; j<Ymax; j++)
    for(int k=0; k<Zmax; k++) {
      il = (i * Ymax + j) * Zmax + k;
      for (int l=0; l<qdim; l++) {
        for (int m=1; m<=half; m++) {
          nextx = fCppMod(i + lbv[3*m],   Xmax);
          nexty = fCppMod(j + lbv[3*m+1], Ymax);
          nextz = fCppMod(k + lbv[3*m+2], Zmax);
          ilnext = (nextx * Ymax + nexty) * Zmax + nextz;
          fSwapPair(
              lbf[il*lbsitelength + l*lbsy.nq + m + half],
              lbf[ilnext*lbsitelength + l*lbsy.nq + m]);
        }
      }
    }
```

FIGURE 23.13

Code listing—The five-level nested loop in fPropagationSwap.

FIGURE 23.14

Why No Vectorization?" in advisor survey.

- Runs for over 12 s.
- Has scalar code.
- Cannot be vectorized due to loop dependencies.

When coming across vector dependencies, your role as a programmer is to confirm whether or not there are really dependencies in the code. It can be quite hard to do this, but fortunately with the help of the "Check Dependencies" feature of Advisor XE the task is much easier.

Dependency analysis

To run a dependency check, simply:

- Select the loops of interest in the Survey window in column 2 of the Survey window.
- Press the "Check Dependencies" button
- Wait for the results. Only select one loop at a time, as there is a large overhead when running this analysis.

Check for loop-carried dependencies in your application

Summary   Survey Report   Refinement Reports

Site Location	Loop-Carried Dependencies
[loop in fPropagationSwap at lbpSUB.cpp:1242]	No dependencies found
[loop in fPropagationSwap at lbpSUB.cpp:1247]	No dependencies found

FIGURE 23.15

Dependency analysis shows there are no loop-carried dependencies.

Running the analysis shows that there are no dependencies—see Figure 23.15.

Now, we are certain that there are no dependencies, so it safe to force vectorization for the given loop.

Introducing a dependency

A genuine dependency can be seen by artificially modifying `fSwapPair` function call so that the swapped address ranges become overlapping—see Figure 23.16.

Re-running the Dependency analysis on the modified code will produce a "Write After Read" diagnostic as shown in Figure 23.17.

EXPLORING POSSIBLE VECTORIZATION STRATEGIES

The "particles move" computational kernel has a slightly more complex structure than the previously considered kernels. Particularly, it has five possible levels where we could consider applying SIMD or threading-type parallelism.

For this kind of nested loop structure, the Advisor Source Views with diagnostics and dynamic data embedded into the code are very useful (Figure 23.18).

Notice that there are only three snippets of information embedded for the five loops. Loop-j and loop-k don't have any information associated with them. This actually correlates with what the programmer requested when specifying `#pragma omp for collapse(3)`—which means: "please merge iteration space to a depth of 3 nested loops." As a result, the three loops have been "collapsed" into a single physical loop (from a control flow graph perspective) and that's exactly what the tool reports out.

The embedded snippets for two inner loops tell us that they have not been vectorized:

```
fSwapPair(
            lbf[il*lbsitelength + l*lbsy.nq + m],
            lbf[il*lbsitelength + l*lbsy.nq + m + 1]);
```

FIGURE 23.16

Code listing—the changes in **bold** will produce a loop dependency.

Site Location		Loop-Carried Dependencies	Strides Distribution	Access Pattern
⟳ [loop in fPropagationSwap at lbpSUB.cpp:1247]	⦿ RAW:1		No information available	No information avail

Memory Access Patterns Report	Dependencies Report

Problems and Messages

ID	✇	Type	Site Name	Sources	Modules	State
P1	▣	Parallel site information	loop_site_72	lbpSUB.cpp	slbe_swap_overlap.exe	✔ Not a problem
P3	◎	Read after write dependency	loop_site_72	lbpSUB.cpp; malloc.c	slbe_swap_overlap.exe	⚑ New

Read after write dependency: Code Locations

ID	Description	Source	Function	Variable references	Module	State
⟊X3	Parallel site	⊟ lbpSUB.cpp:1255	fPropagationSwap		slbe_swap_overlap.exe	⚑ New
⊟X4	Read	⊟ lbpSUB.cpp:1255	fPropagationSwap		slbe_swap_overlap.exe	⚑ New

```
1253    fSwapPair (lbf[il*lbsitelength + l*lbsy.nq + m + half], lbf[ilnext*lbsitelength + l*lbs
1254 #else
1255    fSwapPair (lbf[il*lbsitelength + l*lbsy.nq + m + 1], lbf[il*lbsitelength + l*lbsy.nq +
1256 #endif
1257        }
```

⊟X5	Write	⊟ lbpSUB.cpp:1255	fPropagationSwap		slbe_swap_overlap.exe	⚑ New

```
1253    fSwapPair (lbf[il*lbsitelength + l*lbsy.nq + m + half], lbf[ilnext*lbsitelength + l*lbs
1254 #else
1255    fSwapPair (lbf[il*lbsitelength + l*lbsy.nq + m + 1], lbf[il*lbsitelength + l*lbsy.nq +
1256 #endif
1257        }
```

FIGURE 23.17

A dependency is reported in the Correctness Report.

- The m-loop is not vectorized due to conservative compiler assumptions about dependence (already proven by Advisor Correctness to be not the case for given workload).
- The l-loop is not vectorized by default, simply because it's an outer loop (against the m-loop). The message suggests that we can use simd pragma to force the compiler to vectorize the "outer loop."

Thus the first natural step here is to enable innermost m-loop SIMD-ization by "forcing" the compiler to vectorize the code either using the OpenMP4.0 standard SIMD pragma or the compiler-specific #pragma ivdep (abbreviated from "Ignore Vector DEPendence"). Surprisingly, after vectorizing the loop in that way and rerunning Advisor Survey analysis, we don't see any performance speedup at all, even though loop at the lbpSUB:1242 is now reported by Advisor as vectorized.

Projected gain and efficiency

In order to understand the root cause of our performance issue, we should first of all check "Gain" and "Efficiency" data provided by Advisor.

You can see how efficient the advisor thinks the vector code is by comparing the Estimated Gain against the Vector Length. For perfect efficiency, the two values will be the same. The Estimated gain is not measured, but is calculated by a heuristic in Advisor. In our case, we see:

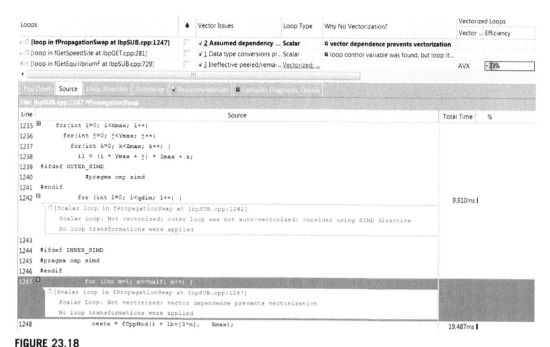

FIGURE 23.18

Diagnostics embedded in the code.

- A potential speedup of 1.22X.
- The Vector Length is 4, calculated from the fact that an AVX vector register can hold 4 doubles (for Intel Compiler 16.X and higher Advisor can also directly obtain this data from compiler vectorization engine).
- A speedup of 4X would be the optimum.

It may be that a speedup of 1.22 is good enough to justify not putting in any more effort, but we'll do a deeper exploration anyway.

There is one more clue that should alert you to a potential problem. In the "Performance Traits" column is written the word "Shuffles." The existence of such memory reorganization instructions indicates that there may be inefficient memory access.

Memory access patterns analysis

We can use the MAP analysis to see whether there are any inefficient memory access patterns. To do this we:

- Select the loop at line 1242 in the Survey (using the same selection approach as for Dependence Analysis, see Figure 23.19).

Function Call Sites and Loops	🔥	💡	Se
▷ 🔘 [loop at lbpSUB.cpp:805 in fGetEquilibriumC]		💡 3	
▷ 🔘 [loop at lbpGET.cpp:50 in fGetOneMassSite]		💡 3	
🔘 **[loop at lbpSUB.cpp:1284 in fPropagationSwap]**	☑	💡 1	

FIGURE 23.19

Selecting the loop at 1284.

- Run Memory Access Pattern collection.
- Wait for the results. This analysis is relatively expensive. An analysis that normally takes 30 s to run could run for up to 10 min.

Note

It's possible to get MAP results much faster by tracking the Memory Access Pattern log in the Advisor GUI. Once you notice the "site end" diagnostic for your loop of interest—consider manually pressing "Stop" on the Advisor Workflow panel; after "stopping" the analysis there will be an access pattern profile for at least one "instance" of the given loop. You can apply a Memory Access Pattern analysis to scalar or vector loops, but working with an original scalar loop might be slightly easier to investigate.

Figure 23.20 shows the result of the MAP analysis. You can see that:

- The Strides Distribution column shows there is a bad access pattern.
- Colors are used on-screen as indicated in the figure with annotations and arrows, the right two-thirds of the bar is colored red—indicating a poor access pattern.

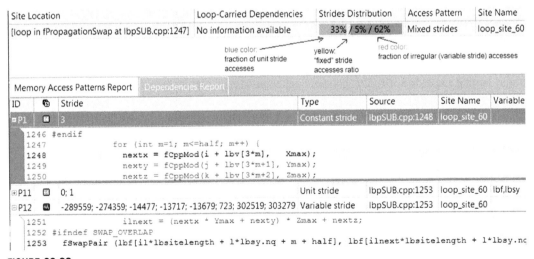

FIGURE 23.20

Memory Access Patterns Analysis for the innermost loop in `fPropagationSwap`.

Line	Source	Stride	Operand Type	Operand Size (bits)
1248	nextx = fCppMod(i + lbv[3*m], Xmax);	3	int	32:64
1249	nexty = fCppMod(j + lbv[3*m+1], Ymax);	3	int	32

FIGURE 23.21

Memory Access Pattern source view.

Looking at the patterns report in bottom of Figures 23.20 and 23.21 you can see that bad memory access comes from:

- Problems P1, P2, & P3 (colored yellow). Three simultaneous packed loads of three mutually related references at 3*m, 3*m+1, 3*m+2 positions—with additional shift of 3 every next scalar iteration (that's why it's classified as stride-3).
- Problem P12 has an "unpredictable" or random stride access coming from the swapping routine. It's not surprising to find random access here, as the address to be swapped is defined by the value in ilnext (being a complex function of lbv array values and m)—leading to a pure form of indirect referencing.

With such a terrible dynamic memory access pattern, at runtime we don't achieve the static estimated gain of 1.22; in fact, we don't experience any performance boost at all.

A final MAP analysis

Let's try to investigate vectorization for the "outer loop" now—hoping it proves to be better from memory usage perspective. First, we rerun MAP analysis for the outer loop (1-loop). Surprisingly MAP results are much more promising (see Figure 23.22); the random indirect referencing seems to have

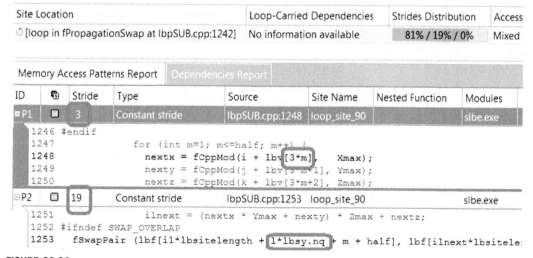

FIGURE 23.22

Memory Access Patterns Analysis for the outer loop in fPropagationSwap.

gone away! It was not obvious that the l-access pattern is so different from the m-access pattern without running the MAP analysis. But now, since the data claims an advantage for the l-loop—we can take a look at the code again and notice that, in fact, ilnext indices are not a function of the value of l so, as a result lbf[ilnext*lbsitelength+l*lbsy.nq+m] is not accessed randomly anymore, but instead exposes an induction of l*lbsy.nq, which should lead to a constant stride of lbsy.nq. A constant stride is again confirmed by tool output, where we see a stride of 19 which corresponds to the value of .nq for D3Q19 lattice model.

Fixing the problem

Figure 23.23 shows four different experiments we carried out. The pragma simd simdlen gives hints to the compiler on what the Vector Length is. (In versions of the Intel compiler *before* v16.0, use #pragma simd vectorlength(n))

Please note that we didn't use more elegant ways of parameterizing simdlen pragma, just for experimental simplicity. Production code will have to use more elegant and portable vector length parameterization.

Figure 23.24 shows the effect of adding the pragma to the inner and then the outer loop. As you can see, the best performance improvement happens when the outer loop is vectorized.

```
// different experiments - uncomment just one of these
// #pragma omp simd
for (int l=0; l<qdim; l++) {
// #pragma omp simd
// #pragma omp simd simdlen(2) //for default dataset with trip count
// of 2 and "avoid scalar remainder" advice from Advisor Recommendations
// #pragma omp simd simdlen(4) //for 7-fluids and other bigger
                            //input datasets
   for (int m=1; m<=half; m++) {
     nextx = fCppMod(i + lbv[3*m],   Xmax);
     nexty = fCppMod(j + lbv[3*m+1], Ymax);
     nextz = fCppMod(k + lbv[3*m+2], Zmax);
     ilnext = (nextx * Ymax + nexty) * Zmax + nextz;
     fSwapPair(
                 lbf[il*lbsitelength + l*lbsy.nq + m + half],
                 lbf[ilnext*lbsitelength + l*lbsy.nq + m]);
   }
 }
```

FIGURE 23.23

Code listing—experiments on the inner loops in fPropagationSwap.

Pragma Statement Inner Loop	Time Takes (s)			Speedup Estimate (Upper Bound)	Ratio of Nonunit-Stride Memory Access Instructions
	Body	**Remainder**	**Total**		
None	11.929	N/A	11.929	N/A	N/A
#pragma simd simlen(2)	11.747	1.270	13.017	1.15	Tbd
#pragma simd simlen(4)	8.149	1.400	9.549	1.28	**76%**
Outer Loop					
#pragma simd	6.879	N/A	6.879	1.99	**19%**

FIGURE 23.24

Table—The results of using pragma on loop lbpSUB:1242.

THE RESULTS

The table in Figure 23.25 shows the speedups we obtained. These values are comparing the code running on a 2-socket Intel Xeon E5-v2 processor, running the whole application single threaded.

SUMMARY

We showed that Vectorization Advisor supports a three-step approach to helping us vectorize code: (1) profile and diagnose; (2) analyze and advise (trip counts, dependencies, memory access patterns, snapshot comparisons); and (3) make code changes, recompile, and repeat.

To demonstrate this we used the Vectorization Advisor to analyze DL_MESO and, by adding some pragmas to the code, we were able to shave off between 10% and 19% of the time of three hotspots. We then applied similar techniques to several other less significant hotspots and gained additional speedups. As a total result the speedup of the application, using our data set, was about 18%.

The optimizations we did can be best described as "low-hanging fruit" in that we made no changes to the algorithm or data structures. It is clear from a Vector Advisor code analysis that further speedups should be possible by applying:

Code	Auto vectorized	Optimized	Speedup	Data Set (D3Q19)
Whole application	60.28s	51.27s	1.18	Number_of_solute = 7
fPropagationSwap	**17.3s**	**14.5s**	1.19	Number_of_solute = 7
GetEquilibriumC	**7.8s**	7.1s	1.10	fluids-4 only
GetEquilibriumF	**1.47s**	**1.29s**	1.14	Number_of_solute = 7

FIGURE 23.25

Sample speedup from the vectorization work.

- Simple SoA (or AoSoA) transformation for some data structures, especially for "lbv" arrays.
- Providing "natural" padding.
- Using Intel Xeon E5-v3 processors with support for AVX2.
- Further migration to many-core Intel Xeon Phi products with support for IMCI/AVX-512.

By using the Vectorization Advisor, the time taken to discover and apply these optimizations was much shorter than would have been otherwise. What a pearl!

FOR MORE INFORMATION

Here are some additional reading materials we recommend related to this chapter.

- Motivational webinar and overview Vectorize or Die—unlock performance secrets with data driven software design, Kevin O'Leary, Intel, http://tinyurl.com/vectorize-or-die.
- A Case for Improved C++ Compiler Support to Enable Performance Portability in Large Physics Simulation Codes. LLNL. Hornung, R.D., Keasler, J.A..
- Seaton, M.A., Anderson, R.L., Metz, S., Smith, W., 2013. DL_MESO: highly scalable mesoscale simulations. Mol. Sim. 39(10), 796-821. doi:10.1080/08927022.2013.772297.
- Seaton, M.A., 2012. The DL_MESO Mesoscale Simulation Package, STFC Scientific Computing Department, www.ccp5.ac.uk/DL_MESO.
- A Guide to Vectorization with Intel® C++ Compilers, https://software.intel.com/en-us/articles/a-guide-to-auto-vectorization-with-intel-c-compilers.
- Download the code from this, and other chapters, http://lotsofcores.com.

PORTABLE EXPLICIT VECTORIZATION INTRINSICS

24

Paulo Souza*, Leonardo Borges[‡], Cedric Andreolli[†], Philippe Thierry[†]

Petrobras, Brazil* Intel, France[†] Intel, USA[‡]

For more than a decade now, processor designs have shifted away from relying on higher frequencies to improve performance because of the so-called *power wall*. Increasing processor frequency would have led to prohibitive power consumption levels. Design innovations have found more power efficient solutions by relying on the growing number of transistors available at each new semiconductor fabrication technology for ways other than frequency increases to increase performance. From a programmer's perspective, this translates into two clear trends: more cores per processor and more operations per core. The first trend (more cores) implies that applications must be developed to exploit thread and/or process parallelism available on current processors with high core count. The second trend (more operations per core) is exemplified by vector units implementing SIMD (single instruction multiple data).

Popular ways to leverage the growing number of cores include open standards approaches such as MPI, OpenMP, TBB, and OpenCL. However, portable open standards to explicitly exploit processor vector units are not as prevalent or mature. For instance, the relatively recent OpenMP 4.0 finally introduced some vector processing focused features. Although some compilers do a remarkable job with auto-vectorization, array notation present in languages such as Fortran 90 (F90) or in language extensions like Cilk™ Plus can help users to express vectorization opportunities to the compilers; the reality is that these language extensions are either not portable or often they do not map directly into the typical hardware vector instructions present in current processors. F90 array notation is portable and standard but only gives a hint for vectorization opportunities. SIMD vector support in OpenMP 4.0 provides a standard-based method of writing vector code explicitly. We expect OpenMP standard-based vector programming to have wide acceptance among the programming community as a high-level approach to improve vectorization; in the same way, OpenMP has become a programmer's favorite way to write threaded code. In the following, we present a tool for critical sections of code that require explicit vectorization coding that matches intrinsic/assembly code performance, while maintaining the look and feel of high-level coding.

Today, the widest vector units found on a mass production processor are in the Intel® Xeon Phi™ coprocessor with its 512-bit vector registers. Each register has the capacity to store 16 single-precision floats per vector unit. Similarly, AVX-512 registers have the same capacity. These vector units have a single-precision peak performance gain of $16\times$ for single flop operations (like ADD, e.g.), and a theoretical gain of $32\times$ for compounded flop operations (like FMA, or fused-multiply-add). In practice, due to limiting factors like memory access latency, I/O demand, serial code sections, and global synchronization, the real performance improvement number is typically below the theoretical peak. Efficient use of SIMD units is mandatory to maximize performance on the Intel Xeon Phi products.

In this work, we present a portable way to take advantage of vector units across various processor SIMD architectures with a single, portable source code. This is accomplished by adding a vector type and hardware intrinsics support to C/C++ language through a header file that is compatible with gcc and commercially available compilers in general. We hide different hardware/compiler feature set under a common portable programming syntax. In addition, the implementation supports a scalar backend alternative to target unknown architectures. This implementation has been successfully demonstrated on multiple SIMD architectures including Intel SSE/AVX/AVX-512/IMCI, ARM NEON, and IBM Power VSX using only a common header file to enable the compiler to generate proper SIMD instructions for the given underlying architecture.

By providing a single set of intrinsics, this method offers an alternative for software developers to program explicit vectorization in their codes that is portable across different architectures. Code should prove to be future proof since new SIMD architectures could easily be added. Finally, we present performance results on three production codes using our portable method on source code with architecture-dependent hand-tuned implementations showing we achieve similar performance. Unlike intrinsics that are tightly tied to a particular instruction set, these intrinsics stress portable concepts that can be readily mapped by the header files to many SIMD instruction sets.

RELATED WORK

Explicit manual vectorization is not a new thing. Processor vendors provide a vendor-specific way to create SIMD codes for their architectures. Some examples of widely used intrinsics provided by vendors are ARM Neon, IBM VSX, IBM SPU (cell processor), and Intel SSE/SSE2/AVX/AVX2/AVX512/IMCI. Although manual vectorization can provide great performance, the code becomes specific to vendor and architecture, even when the same vendor adds new vector architecture features, for instance, from Intel SSE instructions to the wider vector Intel AVX instruction set. Other portable approaches like Apple Accelerate are locked on the vector size, that is, the datatype width is fixed and your code requires changes when SIMD width changes.

Proposed C++ libraries for SIMD vectorization like Boost SIMD, libsimdpp, and Vc, can lead to templatization overhead and also leave C and FORTRAN out of the picture. Intel's C++ SIMD Vector Class is a C++ Class abstraction to SIMD vector intrinsics. You can learn more about these implementations by checking "For more information" at the end of this chapter. Overloaded operators, class member functions, and friend functions make the program easier to write and maintain (i.e., has the look and feel of normal C/C++ code). However, the class definition itself is tied to the underlying hardware, so the programmer still has to recode when migrating between architectures.

Aside from portability, our two main goals are (1) to add as few preprocessing macros as possible in directly mapping our implementation to vendor proprietary intrinsics and (2) focus the implementation on the C standard (and not C++) to also accommodate C/FORTRAN developers.

WHY VECTORIZATION?

SIMD parallelism enhances the performance of computationally intensive applications that execute the same operation on distinct elements in a dataset. SIMD parallelism is typically accomplished by *vectorization* where successive instances of a scalar operation, which operates on a single pair of operands,

```
//scalar: 40 iterations
for (int i=0; i<40; i++)
    z[i] = x[i] + y[i];
```

```
//vector: 10 iterations
for (int i=0; i<40; i+=4)
    z[i:i+3]= x[i:i+3]+ y[i:i+3];
```

FIGURE 24.1

Scalar loop with 40 iterations vectorized to 10 iterations, assuming a processor with vector register that can hold 4 scalar elements.

are transformed into a vector instruction that operates on multiple pairs of operands at once, as exemplified in Figure 24.1.

Today, most commodity processors are based on hardware architectures that feature SIMD vector instructions. Intel MMX/SSE/VX/AVX-512, IBM Power AltiVec and Cell SPU, and ARM NEON are examples of instruction sets enabling loop vectorization.

This wide range of hardware implementations makes maintenance of explicit manual vectorization almost impossible across multiple architectures and vendors. The differences can be attributed to multiple factors like:

SIMD width: Intel's Streaming SIMD Extensions (SSE) supports vectorization of four single-precision floating-point or two double-precision floating-point values. More recently, the Advanced Vector Extensions (AVX) introduced 256-bit registers doubling from the SSE vectorization length to either eight packed single-precision floating-point values or four-packed double-precision floating-point values. Intel's Initial Many-Core Instructions (IMCI) vector instructions on the Intel® Xeon Phi™ coprocessor have 512-bit vector registers (16-packed single-precision, or 8-packed double-precision values) that are present in the AVX-512 instruction set. AltiVec is also a SIMD instruction set for integer and floating-point vector computations. It features 128-bit registers that allow computations with four-packed 32-bit integers or single-precision floating-point values (IBM Power6 or later) and two-packed 64-bit double-precision floating-point values (IBM Power7 or later). It is important to note that although the register width and the HPC functionality of interest (ADD, MUL, etc.) are basically similar between SSE and AltiVec, the translation between the associated intrinsics can be troublesome. NEON (or Advanced SIMD) is the counterpart of SIMD instruction set devised for ARM-based architectures. Depending on the version, it can support from 8-bit to 64-bit integers and 32-bit single-precision floating point. Its latest versions can process 128-bit (four single-precision floating-point values) in the same execution cycle (for each architecture, see "For more information" at the end of this chapter).

Extended instructions: AVX2 added fused-multiply-add support and nondestructive three-operand instructions that preserve source operands values. Together with IMCI, it also introduced comprehensive support for scatter/gather vector operations.

Register masking: AVX also greatly extended register masking functionality. This can be used to vectorize divergent code paths and implement conditional reduction primitives.

A good programming mode for explicit vectorization must allow developers to write single source code using all the above features, regardless of the underlined hardware architecture.

Some compilers have an auto-vectorizer that can be good at recognizing common patterns found in loops and issuing the proper vector instructions. But auto-vectorization often produces non-optimal vector code due to factors like complex loop structure, lack of information about data-dependency, improper data alignment, pipeline synchronization, etc. Hence, compilers typically provide many more ways for developers to drive the way compilers vectorize. The supported ways to improve code generation of vector instructions can range from high-level language extensions for array notation, SIMD-enabled functions, SIMD pragmas/directives, and standards like OpenMP 4.0; more lower-level coding approaches are SIMD vector intrinsics and inline assembly code.

In some cases, applications may contain very specific and delimited region(s) of code where the majority of the compute time is spent and squeezing every bit of performance is a critical matter. Under this circumstance, vector SIMD intrinsics may provide performance gains closer to the theoretical attainable performance of the architecture. Vector intrinsics have been greatly improved by hardware vendors providing APIs allowing intrinsic "functions" to be inserted in the source code. However, most of the current API implementations available are far from being cross-platform compatible.

PORTABLE VECTORIZATION WITH OpenVec

We developed a tool called OpenVec that enables portable explicit vectorization on different architectures. To get portability, the provided SIMD types are not tied to a fixed size; i.e., a float vector will contain a number of floats that is dependent on the target architecture SIMD width. There is a single vector type for float for all architectures. Figure 24.2 shows scalar saxpy and OpenVec saxpy.

On a four-way SIMD (four elements per instruction) CPU like ARM and Power, the first loop iteration (i==0) will make the following operations:

$y_0 = a*x_0 + y_0; y1 = a*x1 + y1; y2 = a*x2 + y2; y3 = a*x3 + y3;$

And first iteration (i==0) on eight-way CPU like AVX will make following operations:

$y_0 = a*x_0 + y_0; y1 = a*x1 + y1; y2 = a*x2 + y2; y3 = a*x3 + y3;$
$y4 = a*x4 + y4; y5 = a*x5 + y5; y6 = a*x6 + y6; y7 = a*x7 + y7;$

All these operations are done simultaneously on the CPU illustrating the performance gain potential of SIMD. Note that in AVX, there are eight elements per vector and on ARM only four, so that when using the ARM architecture the loop trip count will be two times greater than AVX.

Most of OpenVec is implemented using C/C++ macros. It maps a common set of portable intrinsics to proprietary intrinsics of the given underlying hardware architecture. Some OpenVec intrinsics are composed of more than one proprietary intrinsic. One of the goals is to map a common set of proprietary intrinsics to portable intrinsics. Another goal is to define a syntax that is also accessible to C and Fortran developers. By using macros, the added performance overhead is zero in C and can be zero with some C++ compilers, that's because in C++ we need to override proprietary vector type in order to define all operators.

The current OpenVec implementation supports 32-bit single-precision floats and 64-bit double-precision floats. The `ov_double` is used for double precision and all functions get the suffix

```
/* SCALAR SAXPY */

void saxpy(int n, float a, float* x, float* y)

{

  // n is the number of float elements

  for (int i=0; i<n; i++)    y[i] = a*x[i] + y[i];

}



/* OpenVec SIMD SAXPY */

void vsaxpy(int n, float a, ov_float* x, ov_float* y)

{

  //nv is the number of SIMD elements

  int const nv = (n-1)/OV_FLOAT_WIDTH + 1;

  for (int i=0; i<nv; i++) y[i] = a*x[i] + y[i];

}
```

FIGURE 24.2

Scalar SAXPY and OpenVec SIMD SAXPY.

"d," e.g., `ov_alld`. On Intel SSE, ARM Neon and IBM Altivec double precision is implemented with the scalar backend since there's no vector instructions for double precision. On these platforms, the OV_DOUBLE_WIDTH will be one. Never assume OV_DOUBLE_WIDTH to have the same value of OV_FLOAT_WIDTH.

THE VECTOR TYPE

To avoid overhead, all the implementation is contained in OpenVec header files. To enable OpenVec, the developer must include "openvec.h." This header file maps OpenVec portable intrinsics to vendor proprietary vector intrinsics. Also it creates proper arithmetic operator definitions if the language is C++.

The OpenVec vector type `ov_float` creates an instance of OV_FLOAT_WIDTH floats, you declare it like a regular `float`. For example in ARM Neon, IBM Altivec, and Intel SSE, OV_FLOAT_WIDTH=4 giving four floats per `ov_float` variable; on Intel IMCI and AVX-512 OV_FLOAT_WIDTH=16; therefore, the `ov_float` variable contains multiple float elements and all operations are performed on all elements.

The compile time constant OV_FLOAT_WIDTH represents the SIMD width for floats and is defined for each architecture as the number of floats per `ov_float` type. On the scalar backend, OV_FLOAT_WIDTH=1 and `ov_float` is defined as type `float`.

```
#include"openvec.h"      // Enable OpenVec

void vsaxpy(int n, float a, ov_float* x, ov_float* y)
{
    // nv is the number of SIMD elements
    int const nv = (n-1)/OV_FLOAT_WIDTH + 1;
    // make all elements = a
    ov_float const va = ov_setf(a);
    for (int i=0; i<nv; i++)
        y[i] = ov_maddf(va, x[i], y[i]);
}
```

FIGURE 24.3

OpenVec SAXPY with multiply and add intrinsic.

Figure 24.3 shows BLAS saxpy implemented with portable vector multiply and add (MADD) intrinsic:

If the target processor does not have a *multiply and add*, it will be replaced by a vector add instruction plus a vector multiply instruction.

The basic arithmetic operators like +, *, /, and - are defined for C++. The operations between vector/vector and vector/scalar are defined. By scalar, we mean a float variable like "a" in the first saxpy code example from Figure 24.3. We can see the scalar multiply by a vector operation " cx[i]." In C++, all scalars are promoted to vectors before operations; float "a" is promoted to ov_float with all elements equal to the scalar float "a".

The ov_setf intrinsic makes a SIMD vector from a single value, e.g., ov_setf(a) makes a SIMD float type containing {a, a, a, a} on a four-way SIMD CPU.

MEMORY ALLOCATION AND ALIGNMENT

More performance is achieved if vector types are memory aligned for the architecture. The alignment boundary is the size of one vector type, e.g., on an AVX platform the alignment boundary for floats is OV_FLOAT_WIDTH × size of (float) = $8 \times 4 = 32$ bytes. OpenVec provides memory allocation calls that allocate memory aligned to the size of one vector type. Here are the memory allocation functions:

```
void *ov_malloc(size_t size);
void ov_free(void *ptr);
void *ov_calloc(size_t count, size_t size);
```

The ov_malloc/ov_calloc function allocates aligned memory and it can be used as a direct replacement for the standard malloc/calloc. For convenience, the OpenVec header file replaces the standard malloc/calloc/free so you don't have to change your code to get the benefit. The ov_free frees memory allocated by ov_malloc/ov_calloc. Memory allocated by ov_malloc/ov_calloc must be free by ov_free.

Our current implementation uses posix_memalign inside ov_malloc function. The compile time constant OV_ALIGN is provided and it contains the alignment size in bytes, also ov_malloc allocates size+OV_ALIGN to make it unnecessary to handle vector tails, which will be discussed later.

When aligned memory is allocated, the address of the first element is aligned (i.e., to the address of array[0]), all indexes that are a multiple of OV_FLOAT_WIDTH will be at aligned addresses (i.e., array[index] is aligned if index modulo OV_FLOAT_WIDTH=0). There are different intrinsics to access aligned and unaligned addresses; usually, a performance penalty is incurred accessing unaligned addresses. Next, we will present these intrinsics.

BUILT-IN FUNCTIONS

OpenVec provides some basic built-in functions; most of them are direct mappings to SIMD hardware instructions. All built-in functions were tested on all supported architectures. These functions work applying its behavior on all elements of the vector type. E.g.: ov_sqrtf(x) will calculate the square root of all float elements of x. Figure 24.4 shows the provided portable intrinsics.

The ov_stream_stf and ov_nt_storef streaming store intrinsics will add performance benefit in some architectures that support it. In those that do not, it will map to regular aligned store ov_stf.

For example, the ov_maddf intrinsic maps to _mm512_fmadd_ps on AVX-512, vmlaq_f32 on ARM NEON and on SSE to a composition of _mm_mul_ps and _mm_add_ps.

The understanding of the intrinsics is very straightforward except for the LOAD/STORE (LD/ST) intrinsics. In C/C++ code, these operations tend to be implicit in the code. With OpenVec, we have implicit or explicit LD/ST. Figure 24.5 uses BLAS saxpy to demonstrate both implicit and explicit LD/ST.

The example assumes aligned data since the loop starts with index 0 and jumps OV_FLOAT_WIDTH every step, so all indexing will be aligned because for all steps:

```
i MOD OV_FLOAT_WIDTH =0
```

But if there is no safe assumption about alignment, the unaligned versions of load and store should be used, adding the prefix "u" as in ov_uldf and ov_ustf. Do not use implicit notation if data is not aligned.

The math operators symbols like + are defined in C++ but in plain C, developers must use intrinsics to do basic math operations, e.g., c=a+b should be written as c=ov_addf(a,b) with C.

```
ov_float a,b,c;
// C++ code with implicit call to ov_addf intrinsic
c =a + b;
/* equivalent C code with explicit call */
c =ov_addf(a,b);
```

With that limitation on C codes, C++ codes have the advantage to be more readable and maintainable than plain C code. It is notable that we observed some performance gain using plain C, the performance numbers will be presented later in this chapter. The OpenVec C implementation has **true zero overhead** since it is only mapping intrinsics with pre-processor macros.

New architectures can be easily added by mapping OpenVec intrinsics to the new architecture and creating a new header file based on a previous architecture. For example, the ARM NEON ov_float

Intrinsic	Operation / Description
ov_addf(x, y)	x + y
ov_subf(x ,y)	x - y
ov_mulf(x, y)	x * y
ov_divf(x, y)	x / y
ov_ldf(address)	Loads a vector from aligned address
ov_uldf(address)	Loads a vector from unaligned address
ov_stf(address, x)	Stores x vector to aligned address
ov_storeuf(address, x)	Stores x vector to unaligned address
ov_stream_stf(address, x)	Stream stores x vector to aligned address
ov_nt_storef(address, x)	Non temporal stores x vector to aligned address
ov_setzerof(x)	Make all values of x zero
ov_getzerof()	Return a zero valued vector
ov_setf(scalar)	Make a vector with all elements equal to scalar
ov_maxf(x,y)	Return per element maximum
ov_minf(x,y)	Return per element minimum
ov_rsqrtf(x)	Reciprocal square root 1/sqrt(x)
ov_sqrtf(x)	Square root
ov_sqrf(x)	x * x
ov_rcpf(x)	Reciprocal 1/x
ov_floorf(x)	Round to floor
ov_ceilf(x)	Round to ceil
ov_maddf(x,y,z)	(x*y) + z
ov_msubf(x,y,z)	(x*y) - z
ov_absf(x)	Absolute value

FIGURE 24.4

OpenVec portable intrinsic functions. There's an equivalent double-precision version with suffix d, e.g., ov_maddd.

```
void vsaxpy(int n, float a, ov_float* x, ov_float* y)
{
  int const nv = (n-1)/OV_FLOAT_WIDTH + 1;
  for (int i=0; i<nv; i++)
    y[i] = a*x[i] + y[i]; // Implicit LD/ST
}


void vsaxpy(int n, float a, float* x, float* y)
{
  // Where n is the number of floats
  // Jump to next vector address: +OV_FLOAT_WIDTH
  for (int i=0; i<n; i+=OV_FLOAT_WIDTH)
  {
    ov_float vy = ov_ldf(&y[i]); // Explicit LOAD
    ov_float vx = ov_ldf(&x[i]); // Explicit LOAD
    vy = a*vx + vy;
    ov_stf(&y[i], vy); // Explicit store
  }
}
```

FIGURE 24.5

Implicit and explicit load/stores.

vector type will be defined as float32x4_t and on the Intel AVX type it will be __m256. To give an idea on the implementation simplicity, the AVX header file has less than a hundred lines of codes to define the single-precision implementation. One of the goals of this project is to easily add new architectures and customization.

Power users can modify or create new platforms to match their applications and precision needs keeping the code portable. For example, ARM NEON does not have native SIMD division, so one can define division as:

```
#define ov_div(x,y) ov_mulf(x, ov_rcpf(y)) // x * (1/y)
```

which can be faster but less precise than the provided version for ARM NEON. Note that as illustrated by this example, users can customize OpenVec for variable precision.

IF ELSE VECTORIZATION

The main concept of SIMD architecture is to execute the same single instruction on all elements of a vector, but what happens in the case of divergent paths caused by if/else statements? Unfortunately, the same instruction must be applied on all elements of the vector type, the way divergent code can be vectorized is executing both if and else blocks and then merge both executions according to the code path of each element. Here's the common technique to vectorize an if/else:

- Get a bit mask set with one on the elements that evaluate for TRUE, these elements should enter the if block;
- Apply the mask on the result of the if code block, usually a bitwise AND;
- Apply an inverted mask on the result of the else code block;
- Merge both masked results, usually a bitwise OR;

Here's a simple if/else code:

```
for (int i = 0; i < n; i++){
    if (x[i] >y[i]) scalar_result[i] =x[i]-y[i];
    else scalar_result[i] =y[i] + x[i];
```

Figure 24.6 shows the OpenVec masked SIMD version:

As we can see in the code from Figure 24.6, the function ov_confitionalf hides the complexity of a few steps of mask merging; Figure 24.7 shows Intel SSE equivalent code.

The example from Figure 24.6, uses the C++ operator ">" for greater than comparison, in C the function ov_gtf(x,y) must be used and it means greater than float. It returns the mask with bits set to one where x>y. Here's all variations of this functionality:

```
for (int i=0; i<n; i+=OV_FLOAT_WIDTH)

{

      ov_float const vx=ov_ldf(&x[i]); // Load x and y

      ov_float const vy=ov_ldf(&y[i]);

            /* Merge two vectors depending on

                a comparison expression */

      ov_float result;

      result = ov_conditionalf(vx > vy, vx-vy, vy+vx);

      ov_stf(&simd_result[i], result); // Store the results

}
```

FIGURE 24.6

IF/ELSE vectorization.

```
/* OpenVec conditional merge */

ov_float result =

ov_conditionalf(mask, if_result, else_result);


        /* Intel SSE equivalent conditional merge

            with SSE intrinsics */

    __m128 result = _mm_or_ps(_mm_and_ps(mask,
    if_result),_mm_andnot_ps(mask, else_result));


    # SSE generated assembly code for ov_conditionalf

    andps       %xmm1, %xmm2   # Bitwise AND, applying the mask

    # Bitwise AND NOT, applying the inverted mask

    andnps      %xmm0, %xmm1

    orps        %xmm1, %xmm2   # Bitwise OR, merge results
```

FIGURE 24.7

Intel SSE IF/ELSE vectorization.

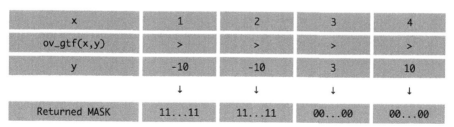

FIGURE 24.8

Behavior of ov_gtf function on an IBM Altivec four-way SIMD.

ov_eqf(x,y) mask bits = 1 on elements where $x == y$
ov_gtf(x,y) mask bits = 1 on elements where $x > y$
ov_gef(x,y) mask bits = 1 on elements where $x >= y$
ov_ltf(x,y) mask bits = 1 on elements where $x < y$
ov_lef(x,y) mask bits = 1 on elements where $x <= y$

Figure 24.8 shows an example of the greater than comparison function for floats: ov_gtf.

These functions return an `ov_maskf` type, which is architecture dependent; do not assume the size of `ov_maskf` to be equal to the size of `ov_floatf`. The next section will present an optimization to avoid execution of a masked code in certain conditions.

TO MASK OR NOT TO MASK?

What if only a few elements go to the else path? Imagine a loop that must handle the points in the edges of the data, this is very common on numeric simulations with special conditions on the borders of the simulation models. In these cases, the exception code is usually the else block, and it will be executed only at a few points at the border. If we do a simple masked vectorization, as done in previous section, many compute cycles will be wasted computing the else block and applying and merging masks, especially if the else code block has more calculations than the if.

OpenVec provides a simple but powerful way to optimize for a divergent path inside a SIMD vector: comparison reduction functions. For example, we can use the comparison reduction function `ov_allf` to detect if all comparisons are TRUE, the f suffix means float, this function will accept a float mask from a comparison expression like `vector_a < vector_b` or from a comparison function like `ov_ltf`. If all elements inside the SIMD vector evaluate to TRUE, they follow the same code path and there's no need to apply an expensive MASK merge of two code paths. We use the slower masked code only on the corner cases. Figure 24.9 shows an optimized version of the code from Figure 24.7 using a comparison reduction function:

Different than the functions to obtain a mask, the comparison reduction functions will return a single answer to all elements of the SIMD vector, a single TRUE or FALSE that can be used in conjunction

```
for (int i=0; i<n; i+=OV_FLOAT_WIDTH)
{
  ov_float const vx=ov_ldf(&x[i]); // load x and y
  ov_float const vy=ov_ldf(&y[i]);
  ov_float result;


  /* no apply MASK involved, no compute of else block */
  if (ov_allf(vx>vy)) result = vx-vy;
  /* If not all elements, then use slow masked version*/
  else result = ov_conditionalf(vx>vy, vx-vy, vy+vx);
  ov_stf(&simd_result[i], result); // Store the results
}
```

FIGURE 24.9

IF/ELSE vectorization optimization.

with an if statement, as shown in the example by the comparison reduction function ov_allf. Do not make the assumption that TRUE is integer 1 and FALSE is integer 0, for optimization reasons we keep architecture-dependent types the only valid assumption that will work in conjunction with if/else statements. Here are the reduction comparison functions:

```
ov_allf(mask) TRUE if all mask elements are true
ov_anyf(mask) TRUE if at least one mask element is true
```

We have variations for comparison to zero value because in some architectures this comparison is faster and is accomplished testing only the sign bits using dedicated instructions such as the SSE _mm_movemask_ps. These functions receive an ov_float vector and return a single answer. Here is a list of reduction comparison to zero functions:

```
ov_any_lt_0f(x) TRUE if at least one element <0.0f
ov_any_ge_0f(x) TRUE if at least one element > = 0.0f
ov_all_lt_0f(x) TRUE if all elements are <0.0f
ov_all_ge_0f(x) TRUE if all elements are > = 0.0f
```

HANDLING VECTOR TAILS

Up to now, all loop examples go from 0 to n-1, jumping OV_FLOAT_WIDTH elements every step, but what happens if n is not multiple of OV_FLOAT_WIDTH ? More elements will be done exceeding the upper limit n-1, to be more precise, n modulo OV_FLOAT_WIDTH more elements.

If you allocate memory with ov_malloc, it will allocate an extra tail of OV_FLOAT_WIDTH elements and if n is the total size of your array, then you code the loops like previous examples and it will work fine, the extra elements will be written to the extra allocated memory.

But if you are not updating the whole array in your loop or you need to exit your loop at exactly element length, than you have to code your loop twice, the first loop will handle the upper limit that's multiple of the SIMD size, and the second loop will be a scalar code loop to handle the remaining tail, the tail trip count will be always smaller than OV_FLOAT_WIDTH.

You can try to avoid making your grid first dimension (the dimension that runs faster in memory) multiple of OV_FLOAT_WIDTH, also if done that will keep the proper alignment constrains to get optimized code.

If you cannot avoid handling the vector tail, Figure 24.10 shows an array copy example handling a vector tail.

The first loop subtracts OV_FLOAT_TAIL from the upper limit, which will cause the next element to be done be multiple of OV_FLOAT_WIDTH and under the upper limit. The second loop will take the remaining elements (vector tail).

The provided constant OV_FLOAT_TAIL is equal OV_FLOAT_WIDTH minus one.

The compile time optimization with macro #if, creating the first loop only on SIMD sizes greater than one is not mandatory.

MATH REDUCTIONS

Sometimes you need to do operations with elements inside the vector type, like adding up all elements. OpenVec provides reductions functions like ov_all_sumf that takes one ov_float vector and returns a single float with the sum. Figure 24.11 shows a code to add all elements of one array:

```
void memcpy_f(float *dst, float*src, int upperLimit)
{
  // upperLimit is not always multiple of OV_FLOAT_WIDTH
  int i=0; /* first element */


  /* First loop: multiple of OV_FLOAT_WIDTH elements */
#if OV_FLOAT_WIDTH > 1
/* Loop below won't be compiled in the scalar backend */
  for (; i<upperLimit -OV_FLOAT_TAIL ; i+=OV_FLOAT_WIDTH)
  {
    ov_float vx = ov_ldf(&src[i]);
    ov_stf(&dst[i], vx);

  }
#endif


  /* Second loop goes up to upper limit
     it's regular scalar code */
  for (; i<upperLimit; i++) dst[i]=src[i];

}
```

FIGURE 24.10

Handling vector tails.

The results may get different compared to scalar sum because the order your sum floats will interfere in the final result, e.g., adding a huge value to a tiny value, the tiny value won't contribute to the sum.

In the current implementation, math reduction functions are not optimized for each architecture, we provide only scalar code for all architectures. However, since these functions are usually called only once for the trailing elements that are less than vector width, the performance impact should be small for large arrays. Here are math reduction functions:

```
/* n is not always multiple of OV_FLOAT_WIDTH */
float vsum=0.0f; /* Total sum = 0 scalar */
i=0;  /* first loop element */
#if OV_FLOAT_WIDTH > 1
/* In the scalar backend this LOOP won't be compiled */
ov_float tmp=ov_zerof; // Vector temp sum = {0,0,…,0,0}
for (; i<n-OV_FLOAT_TAIL; i+=OV_FLOAT_WIDTH)
{
  ov_float vx = ov_ldf(&x[i]);
  tmp = ov_addf(tmp, vx); // Add SIMD elements per step
}
vsum = ov_all_sumf(tmp); /* Reduction function */
#endif


/* Second loop handles the tail going up to n
   it's regular scalar code */
for (; i<n; i++) vsum += x[i];
```

FIGURE 24.11

Math reduction.

```
ov_all_sumf(x)   Sum all SIMD elements
ov_all_prodf(x)  Multiplies all SIMD elements
ov_all_maxf(x)   Returns maximum element
ov_all_minf(x)   Returns minimum element
```

COMPILING OpenVec CODE

To use OpenVec, the developer must include "openvec.h" header file; no library is needed. It auto detects the target architecture based on compiler flags, if you want to override auto-detection, use -D_OV_NOAUTO plus the desired architecture macro. Figure 24.12 shows compiler flags and correspondent override macro flags.

Override macro flags	Architecture	Compiler	Target flag
-D_OV_NOAUTO -D_OV_MIC	Intel KNC KNF	Intel C++	-mmic
-D_OV_NOAUTO -D_OV_AVX	Intel AVX	Intel C++	-xAVX
-D_OV_NOAUTO -D_OV_AVX2	Intel AVX 2	Intel C++	-xCORE-AVX2
-D_OV_NOAUTO -D_OV_AVX512	Intel AVX 512	Intel C++	-xCORE-AVX512
-D_OV_NOAUTO -D_OV_AVX	Intel AVX	g++/llvm	-mavx
-D_OV_NOAUTO -D_OV_AVX2	Intel AVX 2	g++/llvm	-mavx2
-D_OV_NOAUTO -D_OV_SSE	Intel SSE	g++/llvm	-msse
-D_OV_NOAUTO -D_OV_SSE4	Intel SSE4	g++/llvm	-msse4
-D_OV_NOAUTO -D_OV_SSE	Intel SSE	Intel C++	-xSSE
-D_OV_NOAUTO -D_OV_SSE4	Intel SSE4	Intel C++	-xSSE4.1
-D_OV_NOAUTO -D_OV_NEON	ARM Neon	g++/llvm	-mfpu=neon
-D_OV_NOAUTO -D_OV_NEON	ARM Neon 64 bit	g++/llvm	
-D_OV_NOAUTO -D_OV_ALTIVEC	IBM Altivec	g++	-mvsx -maltivec
-D_OV_NOAUTO	Any (scalar)	Any	Any

FIGURE 24.12

Compiler flags.

In all of our tests auto-detection worked fine so we found no need to use override macro flags. With the Intel Parallel Studio Compiler suite, you can use -xHOST to get the highest architecture set optimization for the machine that's compiling the code.

OpenVec is C89 compliant but some provided C examples use loop initial declarations which require the -std=c99 flag. The macro ov_restrict is defined and works as a C99 restrict modifier, so it can be used both in C and C++ codes.

REAL-WORLD EXAMPLE

Modern seismic acoustic imaging techniques like reverse time migration (RTM) and full waveform inversion are based on computing finite difference (FD) to model and generate the image of geological volumes, which in turn are used to find new reserves of oil and gas. Hence, optimizing this type of computations leads to performance improvements in seismic imaging processing.

```
for (int t=0; t<Time_Steps;  t++) // time steps
{
   for (int iz=0; iz<nz; iz++) // third (slow) dimension
     for(int iy=0; iy<ny; iy++) // second dimension
       for(int ix=0; ix<nx; ix++)// first (fast) dimension
       {
         u_0 = W[0]* U0(ix,iy,iz);
         for(int  k=1; k<=HL; k++)//Stencil Half-Length HL
           u_0 += W[k]*(
             U0(ix+k,iy  ,iz  ) + U0(ix-k,iy  ,iz  ) +
             U0(ix  ,iy+k,iz  ) + U0(ix  ,iy-k,iz  ) +
             U0(ix  ,iy  ,iz+k) + U0(ix  ,iy  ,iz-k));
           U1(ix,iy,iz)  = P(ix,iy,iz)*u_0  +
                             2*U0(ix,iy,iz)  - U1(ix,iy,iz);
       }
     swap U0 <--> U1
}
```

FIGURE 24.13

Pseudo-code for finite differences stencil computational kernel.

FD stencils typically arise in iterative finite-difference techniques employed to solve partial differential equations. For a given point in a regular grid, the stencil computation is a well-defined weighted contribution from a subset of neighbor points in both time and space. Computationally, the FD method can be schematically described as an outer-loop representing time steps of the iterative method where the values U0(ix, iy, iz) of the previous time step are used to compute the new values U1(ix, iy, iz). In the most simplest case of isotropic acoustic constant density wave equation, at each time step, triply nested loops in ix, iy, and iz update array U1 based on the values in array U0 and coefficients in array W, followed by its corresponding integration in time, as shown by the pseudocode in Figure 24.13. The order of the three-dimensional stencil is defined by its half-length (HL) value: as stencil of 8th-oder has half-length $HL = 8/2 = 4$, for example.

Graphically, a three-dimensional stencil of 8th order (25 points) can be represented as shown in Figure 24.14a. Recalling that elements in dimension X are contiguous in memory, suggests that they can be stored in SIMD registers. For example, in Figure 24.14b we have a graphical representation of 19

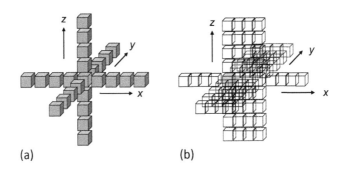

FIGURE 24.14

(a) Twenty-five-point stencil—a new value for the center cell (lighter cell) is obtained by weighted sum of the values in all the neighbor cells (dark cells). (b) Four stencils can be computed simultaneously with register blocking in SSE.

hypothetical SSE registers being used to compute four stencils simultaneously by storing four single-precision floating-point elements on each SIMD register. This informal observation suggests that the algorithm in Figure 24.13 is a good candidate for vectorization.

Following we have a weight k derivative pseudocode:

```
u_0 + = W[k]*(U0(ix + k,iy ,iz ) +U0(ix-k,iy ,iz ) +
              U0(ix ,iy + k,iz ) +U0(ix ,iy-k,iz ) +
              U0(ix ,iy ,iz + k) +U0(ix ,iy ,iz-k));
```

Figure 24.15 shows the same code but with AVX2 intrinsics:
And with C++ OpenVec:

```
u_0 + = W[k] * (
        ov_uldf(&U0[i + k ]) +ov_uldf(&U0[i-k ]) +
        ov_ldf(&U0[i + k*nx ]) + ov_ldf(&U0[i-k*nx ]) +
        ov_ldf(&U0[i + k*nxny]) + ov_ldf(&U0[i-k*nxny]));
```

In this work, we will not address boundary reflection, which is an important problem for RTM processing in bounded domains. Briefly, the idea to deal with the reflections is to construct an artificial boundary that absorbs incoming waves. Applying absorbing boundary conditions is a commonly used technique but it requires constant checking that the domain point being processed belongs to the absorbing area. Such conditional processing can potentially inhibit vectorization. Although this case is outside the scope of our example, one potential way to address this conditional processing is to take advantage of the if/else construct for masked vectorization with conditional reduction functions like `ov_allf` as proposed on this work.

PERFORMANCE RESULTS

We measure the OpenVec performance with saxpy kernel and finite-difference kernel. We benchmarked the same code on following platforms scalar, SSE, AVX, AVX2, Intel Xeon Phi coprocessor (IMCI), AVX512, Power7, ARM NEON and with following compilers, Intel C/C++, gcc, IBM XL, and

```
// u_0 += W[k]*(<summations>)
u_0 = _mm256_fmadd_ps(
            _mm256_set1_ps(W[k]),
            _mm256_add_ps(
                _mm256_add_ps(
                    // U0(ix+k,…) + U0(ix-k,…)
                    _mm256_add_ps(
                        _mm256_loadu_ps(&U0[i+k ]),
                        _mm256_loadu_ps(&U0[i-k ])),
                    // U0(…,iy+k,…) + U0(…,iy-k,…)
                    _mm256_add_ps(
                        _mm256_load_ps(&U0[i+k*nx ]),
                        _mm256_load_ps(&U0[i-k*nx ]))),
                // U0(…,iz+k) + U0(…,iz-k)
                _mm256_add_ps(
                    _mm256_load_ps(&U0[i+k*nxny]),
                    _mm256_load_ps(&U0[i-k*nxny]))),
            u_0);
```

FIGURE 24.15

AVX2 intrinsics version of the pseudocode for finite differences stencil computational kernel.

Float Elements	icc	icpc	Apple LLVM C	Apple LLVM C++
512	27,38	27,42	16,15	16,24
16384	15,05	14,92	7,49	7,54
524288	7,44	7,36	3,75	3,76

FIGURE 24.16

OpenVec with multiple compilers C and C++. Numbers in Gflops/s.

Apple LLVM. For AVX-512, we show it was validated through Software Development Emulator (SDE) (software) emulation.

We compare saxpy performance on multiple compilers. Figure 24.16 shows saxpy results in Gflops/s. The test was run on a Mac Mini (late 2012) with core i5 @ 2.5 GHz with AVX, compiled with Intel compiler, Apple LLVM with C and C++ languages.

The sizes (number of float elements) in Figure 24.16 were chosen to be equal the sizes from Boost SIMD paper (see "For more information" at the end of this chapter). The best BOOST result was 794

OpenVec Aligned	OpenVec Unaligned	Intel Vector Class
249,7	280,7	280,9

FIGURE 24.17

Performance in MSamples per second.

Gflops with Intel AVX processor, the comparison against BOOST SIMD is valid only to give an idea on performance since processors are different and probably the compilers.

In another test, we compare the finite-difference kernel using OpenVec and Intel C++ Vector class for AVX. Intel Vector Class for AVX (dvec.h) comes with Intel C++ compiler (icpc) and it provides only unaligned load and stores with loadu and storeu intrinsics. We note that this version of Intel Mac OS compiler was doing a better job if there's no use of aligned version of load/store intrinsics for aligned data. Figure 24.17 shows the comparison on a Mac Mini using both cores with OpenMP.

In this test, we got zero performance overhead in C++ compared to Intel Vector Class for AVX, using only unaligned LD/ST versions of OpenVec.

Now we compare OpenVec finite-difference kernel with hand-coded AVX2 using nonportable intrinsics and based on the code presented in Chapter 23 of the first edition of this book series (see "For more information"). Both codes use OpenMP for multicore parallelism. The iterative method is a finite-difference scheme for propagation in 16th order in space and 2nd order in time. Coefficients are symmetric and constant. The domain size is defined by nx = 704, ny = 670, and nz = 714.

Figure 24.18 shows results in Msamples per second per socket, comparing OpenVec C/C++ with hand-coded C with AVX2 intrinsics and auto-tuning from Pearls first edition's Chapter 23.

Tests were run on a single Intel Xeon CPU E5-2697 v3 @ 2.60 GHz with 14 cores using Intel Compiler Version 15.0.1.133 and gcc 4.4.7. All code samples are cache blocked and we also tested manual 4X unrolling of the finite-difference computation. All runs were NUMA locked to use cores and memory from one single socket (`numactl --cpunodebind=0 --membind=0 <executable>`, for example). Note that this version of gcc does not support AVX2.

DEVELOPING TOWARD THE FUTURE

Portable intrinsics can also provide a fast and effective way to develop and experiment with new or proposed hardware architectures. Instead of waiting for hardware availability and fully matured auto-vectorizers for an architecture, developers can use portable intrinsics to generate efficient vector code and take advantage of hardware emulators.

Here, we experiment with Intel's SDE to vary the quality of the assembler code generated for the codenamed Knights Landing (KNL) version of the Intel® Many Integrated Core (MIC) architecture. The SDE is available so that developers can experiment with new instruction sets or extensions to present sets before having the new hardware. The tool can help software to be ready for new instructions.

The C/C++ compiler supports code generation for the AVX-512 instruction set for KNL (`-xMIC-AVX512`), and the OpenVec header files implement AVX-512 using the compiler intrinsics; we can build the unrolled stencil sample code targeting the AVX-512 instruction set for KNL. To simplify our discussion here, we rebuild our stencil_unroll.c example to run single threaded (`-openmp-stubs`) and to perform a reasonable number of iterations of time steps (niter = 10, for example). The first is to not take

OpenVec

Compiler	Msamples/s
gcc	2217.1
gcc unroll	2413.3
g++ unroll	2147.7
g++	2081.9
icpc	2389.8
icpc unroll	2321.0
icc	2506.1
icc unroll	2483.7

Pearls C AVX-2 Intrinsics

Compiler	Msamples/s
icc	2681,6

FIGURE 24.18

OpenVec C and C++ versus Pearls 1st edition chapter 23 C AVX-2 Intrinsics. Numbers in millions of samples per second.

into account analysis of the OMP parallel runtime, and the latter is to amortize the influence of initialization steps and termination steps in the statistics for the actual finite-difference loop that we are interested. We build:

```
icc -std = c99 -ftz -O3 -xMIC-AVX512 -D_OV_AUTO -openmp stencil_unroll.c -o stencil-AVX512.exe
```

Clearly, the stencil-AVX512.exe is an AVX-512 executable and will not run older machines without support for AVX-512; the SDE can be used to validate output results and inspect the quality of the code generated on older machines. Here, we will exemplify the second case: the quality of vectorization. First, we run the executable under SDE to collect the instruction mix for KNL architecture:

```
<SDE install path>/sde -knl -mix -omix knl-mix.txt -- ./stencil-AVX512.exe
```

The above command line runs the SDE, emulating instruction set for KNL architecture (− knl), collecting instruction mix (−mix) in text output file knl-mix.txt (−omix) for the executable stencil-AVX512.exe. Detailed information about installing SDE and all available options can be found in the tool Web page (see "For more information" at the end of this chapter). Figure 24.19 shows the extract from the report with the total number of floating-point scalar and vector instructions of the total emulation run (end of knl-mix.txt) and the total number of instructions issued during the entire simulation:

```
*isa-set-AVX                                  99
*isa-set-AVX512ER_SCALAR                       1
*isa-set-AVX512F_512                 36618257964
*isa-set-AVX512F_SCALAR                       13
*isa-set-FMA                                   2
*isa-set-FXSAVE                                1
*isa-set-SSE                                   8
*isa-set-SSE2                                772
*isa-set-SSEMXCSR                              4
*isa-set-X87                                   1


*isa-ext-BASE                        12558923982
*total                               49177183652
```

FIGURE 24.19

OpenVec C and C++ versus C AVX-2 Intrinsics. Numbers in millions of samples per second.

That is, basically all FP instructions are AVX-512 vector instructions (isa-set-AVX512F_512 = 36618257964) as we would like. Additionally, from the total number of instructions issued during the execution (total = 49,177,183,652), the AVX-512 vector instructions correspond to 36,618,257,964/49,177,183,652 = 75% of the instructions issued. These are indications of good vectorization and not significant overhead of the integer computations mainly required to control the loops execution (isa-ext-BASE = 12558923982).

A more detailed analysis would take into consideration the SDE statistics for the execution block(s) taking most of the computing cycles, as reported by the SDE output. However, this would go beyond the scope of this example. It is worth noting that MPI-based programs can also be emulated. One way to achieve this is by running SDE on each MPI process together with the flag -i that adds process id to each output file name, producing an independent output file for each MPI process:

```
mpirun -n < # processes> <SDE install path>/sde -knl
  -mix -omix mix-knl.out -i-- < exec name>
```

SUMMARY

The gap between scalar performance and vector performance is getting bigger over time; today the maximum gap is 16X with 512-bit wide vectors. Future architectures may increase vector width making the potential gap even larger. With such large gaps, proper vectorization is becoming mandatory for HPC codes.

With this work, we provide a powerful and simple way to express vectorization closer to assembly level but in a portable way, supporting SIMD architectures from more than 15 years ago up through the latest architectures including AVX-512. The effort to add new architectures is low, typically 100 lines of code for a single-precision implementation.

The user code is expressed in architecture independent way; our datatypes are not tied to a fixed vector size, giving freedom to increase SIMD width for future architectures.

Vectorization is one aspect of performance optimization; there are more things to consider in high-performance codes, such as NUMA locality, cache blocking/associativity, threading, and more. If developers combine all these aspects with auto-tuning plus OpenVec, portable high-performance coding should be achievable.

The C++ implementation gives strong coding productivity; for the finite-difference kernel, it took less than one hour to convert C++ scalar to OpenVec, while keeping good readability.

FOR MORE INFORMATION

You can download OpenVec from:

```
https://github.com/OpenVec/OpenVec.git
```

Here are some additional reading materials that we recommend related to this chapter.

- Program Optimization through Loop Vectorization. [Online] http://software.intel.com/en-us/articles/program-optimization-through-loop-vectorization.
- Intel Intrinsics Guide. [Online] http://software.intel.com/sites/landingpage/IntrinsicsGuide/
- Intel SSE to PowerPC AltiVec migration. [Online] https://www.ibm.com/developerworks/community/wikis/home?lang=en#!/wiki/W51a7ffcf4dfd_4b40_9d82_446ebc23c550/page/Intel%20SSE%20to%20PowerPC%20AltiVec%20migration
- ARM NEON Intrinsics Reference. [Online] http://infocenter.arm.com/help/topic/com.arm.doc.ihi0073a/IHI0073A_arm_neon_intrinsics_ref.pdf
- BOOST.SIMD https://www.lri.fr/~falcou/pub/pact-2012.pdf
- Vc. [Online] http://code.compeng.uni-frankfurt.de/projects/v
- libsimdpp. [Online] https://github.com/p12tic/libsimdpp
- Intel® Software Development Emulator. [Online] https://software.intel.com/en-us/articles/intel-software-development-emulator
- Andreolli, C., Thierry, P., Borges, L., Skinner, G., Yount, C. High Performance Parallelism Pearls. Edited by Reinders, J., Jeffers, J. (Eds.) (Chapter 23).

POWER ANALYSIS FOR APPLICATIONS AND DATA CENTERS

25

Taylor Kidd*, Rob Farber[†], Belinda Liviero*, Evan Felix[‡]

Intel Corporation, USA[*] TechEnablement Corporation, USA[†]
Pacific Northwest National Laboratory, USA[‡]

INTRODUCTION TO MEASURING AND SAVING POWER

In this chapter, we look at two *pearls* that can potentially save megawatts of power on leadership class systems and provide significant reductions in power consumption on small clusters over the long term. These pearls are: (1) how to measure the performance per watt associated with running an application, analyze such measurements, and make changes to an application to improve its energy efficiency; and (2) how to acquire and understand power usage across a cluster environment through the use of waterfall plots.

With this in mind, we wrote this chapter in three sections: Sections "Introduction to measuring and saving power," "Application: Power measurement and analysis," and "Data center: Interpretation via waterfall power data charts." This section includes some power management and threading background, and provides an overall context for the subsequent sections. Section "Application: Power measurement and analysis" discusses the basics of how to measure and analyze performance per watt for a specific application. Section "Data center: Interpretation via waterfall power data charts" looks at techniques you can use to analyze data center power-performance.

MOTIVATION TO ACT: IMPORTANCE OF POWER OPTIMIZATION

Large data center installations have been experiencing a focus shift in operating metrics from maximum *performance* alone to *performance per watt*. Most of today's (and future) procurements specify system requirements that include the operational maximum and average power consumption envelope while the system is running the target applications it has been designed for. Therefore, performance per watt is a key driver of system design, and, more recently, of application development. "Performance at any cost" is no longer viable as supercomputer cluster operational costs are now on par with the hardware and software acquisition cost. It has been estimated that an exascale machine, built with technology available in 2014, would consume several gigawatts of power (versus contemporary petascale systems that consume 5-20 mW). New technology needs to be developed to make exascale computing practical. Furthermore, the environmental impact of large systems is substantial, causing data center location considerations to include less expensive and/or more environmentally friendly sources such as hydroelectric generation. As Jeff Goodell quipped, "coal was supposed to be the engine of the industrial revolution, not the Internet revolution." Regardless of motive—practicality, altruism or profit—procurement teams, system designers and application developers will want to learn how to measure and reduce power consumption.

PROCESSOR FEATURES: MODERN POWER MANAGEMENT FEATURES

Intel® processors, and the Intel® Xeon Phi™ coprocessor, have many advanced power management features that notably include idle states (C-states) and performance states (P-states). C-states are used to minimize consumption when a processor can be idle; P-states prevent the processor from consuming too much when work is being done. For reducing energy usage, the primary mechanism is through the use of C-states. Processors enter idle states when they are not actively executing instructions. The C-states consume dramatically less energy than any executing state while negligibly affecting performance, and is the best way to save energy and reduce average power. C-states do not affect instantaneous power usage, another important consideration in a cluster environment. For reducing instantaneous power draw, the primary mechanism is through the use of P-states. P-states are an automatic reduction in instruction execution (or clock) rate. A P-state is both a frequency and voltage operating point since both are scaled as higher numbered P-states are reached. P-state management keeps the total energy usage capped while doing a given amount of computation but may spreads it over a longer period of time when the current power draw needs to be reduced (e.g., instantaneous power draw exceeds a monitored threshold).

THREAD MAPPING MATTERS: OpenMP AFFINITY

The OpenMP environment variable KMP_AFFINITY specifies how software threads are distributed across available hardware threads and cores. This applies to both processors and the Intel Xeon Phi coprocessor. The most important affinity types are "type = none," "type = compact," and "type = scatter." The default is "none" which specifies no explicit affinity between software and hardware threads. In this case, the operating system's policy, independent of OpenMP, may enforce some type of implicit affinity. Use of "compact" causes OpenMP to place threads as close as possible to one another so that they can potentially share common resources. Use of "scatter" distributes threads, as much as possible across separate cores, maximizing the resources available to each individual thread.

One reason to use "compact" affinity is to exploit data locality between threads launched at the same time. This affinity type allows potential common data sharing, e.g., data in a shared cache as in the case when four threads are executed on the same core on an Intel® Xeon Phi™ coprocessor. In this case, if there are eight threads, numbered 0 through 7, "type = compact" would keep threads as close to each other as possible, e.g., core0 holds threads 1, 2, 3, and 4, and core1, threads 5, 6, 7, and 8.

Use of "type = scatter" causes the thread distribution to be on separate cores as much as possible. An example scenario is when each different thread has very little shared data in common, and are best served by each thread utilizing all a core's resources, such as cache lines. Use of "type = scatter" will distribute application threads across different cores. For example, thread0 on core0, thread 1 on core1, thread 2 on core 2, and so on. Only after OpenMP utilizes all cores does it allocate more than one thread per core.

As we will see, thread mapping not only affects performance of an application but also affects its power utilization.

APPLICATION: POWER MEASUREMENT AND ANALYSIS

In this section, we explore power measurement options that can improve application performance per watt. Some seemingly benign and simple application changes can have a significant performance per watt impact. We offer a basic methodology for measuring power-performance, and show how to do some first-order analysis.

The inspiration for this section is from a paper, by Lawson, Sosonkina, and Shen, which explored how affinity affects workload power performance on the Intel Xeon Phi coprocessor across several NAS parallel benchmark (NPB) applications.

BASIC TECHNIQUE

Download and compile the NPB EP workload. Follow the directions in Figure 25.1. This application uses OpenMP, and has characteristics that highlight the influence of thread distribution (i.e., affinity) upon the applications' power performance, and demonstrates some measurement and analysis techniques on workload energy behavior. As we will see, fairly simple runtime operation changes can result in considerable application power performance effects.

The NPB are a set of benchmarks targeting performance evaluation of highly parallel supercomputers. They are developed and maintained by the NASA Advanced Supercomputing (NAS) Division. The EP (embarrassingly parallel) benchmark is a compute intensive "CPU-bound" workload. The EP benchmark highlights modern CPU power management influence while varying runtime application behavior. Non-CPU bound applications will have additional power consumption influences from memory access and I/O patterns.

We will illustrate the effect and importance of measuring power-performance both on an Intel Xeon E5 v2 (Ivy Bridge) based server and on an Intel Xeon Phi 7120A coprocessor. Our Intel Xeon system is dual processor, with each processor having eight cores with the capability of having two hardware threads per core (i.e., does hyperthreading). The result is that our test system has 32 logical CPUs. The Intel Xeon Phi coprocessor is hosted on an Intel Xeon E5 v2 (Ivy Bridge) based server. The coprocessor has 61 cores, with 4 threads per core, giving 244 hardware threads. The Intel Xeon Phi coprocessor's massive parallelism is particularly well suited to illustrate the influence of affinity upon power performance.

Coprocessor power measurements are taken by using the performance and status virtual file system under /sys, specifically /sys/class/micras/power. Processor power measurements are taken by reading /dev/cpu/0/msr based upon a program obtained from Vince Weaver's RAPL project page. See Section "For more information."

(There are a variety of other tools that can be used to measure power and energy. For example, the Intel Energy Checker SDK, and the "micmsc" host application that comes with the Intel® Xeon Phi™ coprocessor's Intel Manycore Platform Software Stack (Intel MPSS) distribution.)

METHODOLOGY

Below, we illustrate the methodology, in detail, on an Intel® Xeon Phi™ coprocessor consisting of 61 cores and 244 logical processors. We also show the data from Intel Xeon processor experiments. Processor data collection follows the same methodology—a benefit of the tight relationship and

(1) Download the NAS Parallel Benchmarks (reference at the end of this chapter). I found these directions a little cryptic and misleading.

   a. Click on the "NAS software download site" link. You'll find it underneath the "Summary of source code releases" table.

   b. Click on the "Software Request Form". Though the implication is that you need to submit a form and will likely hear back from some official agency in a few days, it is actually a click through download wizard.

   c. Select "NPB- NAS Parallel Benchmarks" and then "Next".

   d. The rest of the processes are bureaucratic and excessive, but eventually you'll be able to download the version you want. We will assume you downloaded NPB3.3.1.tar for our instructions.

(2) Untar. Note that you may find that even though the file is labeled tar.gz, it is in fact just a tar file

```
tar xfv NPB3.3.1.tar
```

(3) Use the OpenMP version

```
cd NPB3.3.1/NPB3.3-OMP/
```

(4) Use the make.def_intel template under config/NAS.samples

```
cd config
cp NAS.samples/make.def_intel ./make.def
```

BUILD FOR THE INTEL® XEON® PROCESSOR

(5) Build the EP benchmark for the Intel Xeon processor. The binary is in NPB3.3.1/NPB3.3-OMP/bin and is called ep.C. Rename it to ep.C.x to distinguish it from the coprocessor version.

```
# From the directory NPB3.3.1/NPB3.3-OMP/
make EP CLASS=C VERSION=VEC
mv bin/ep.C bin/ep.C.x
```

BUILD FOR THE INTEL XEON PHI COPROCESSOR

(6) Modify the make.def to cross compile for the Intel Xeon Phi coprocessor by modifying the following lines within make.def

```
FFLAGS    = -O3 -openmp -mmic
FLINKFLAGS = -O3 -openmp -mmic
CFLAGS    = -O3 -openmp -mmic
CLINKFLAGS = -O3 -openmp -mmic
```

(7) Build the EP benchmark for the Intel Xeon Phi coprocessor. The binary is in NPB3.3.1/NPB3.3-OMP/bin and is called ep.C. Rename it to ep.C.knc to distinguish it from the processor version.

```
# From the directory NPB3.3.1/NPB3.3-OMP/
make EP CLASS=C VERSION=VEC
mv bin/ep.C bin/ep.C.knc
```

FIGURE 25.1

Building the NAS Parallel Benchmark EP for a Class C problem size for both the Intel Xeon processor and the Intel Xeon Phi coprocessor.

compatibility between the Intel Xeon Phi coprocessors and Intel processors. We did our Intel Xeon processor experiments and analysis on an RHEL (Redhat Enterprise Linux) distribution using a 3.10.0 Linux Kernel. Our kernel did not have the proper PAPI (Performance Application Programming Interface) kernel modifications for measuring RAPL (Runtime Average Power Limit) performance events, and needed to be patched.

We measure the computational performance per watt for different types of OpenMP affinity, specifically compact and scatter. As described above, "compact" affinity packs consecutive threads together, in order, on the same core and then continues packing them on adjacent cores to best allow resource sharing (such as cache). In contrast, "scatter" affinity spreads consecutive threads on different cores and is useful in environments where there is little sharing or synchronization between threads.

Keep the granularity "fine." There are three types of granularity, "core," "fine," and "thread". Using "core" granularity binds an OpenMP thread to a specific core, meaning only one particular core, e.g., core25, will execute a given OpenMP thread; though that thread can move to any of the four different thread contexts executing on that core. Use of "fine" or "thread" granularity are the same, causing an OpenMP thread to be bound to only one thread context within that core. The default OpenMP granularity is "core." You can use the KMP_AFFINITY environmental variable to set the granularity at runtime,

```
export KMP_AFFINITY='scatter,granularity=fine'
```

Use a Class C problem size. This is so the runtime of each data collection is performed in a reasonable amount of time. Each collection of 244 runs will take roughly 45 min, requiring around 3 h to collect all four sets of data. Depending how fast your processor is and the time available for your experiments, you may want to set the problem size to smaller (CLASS = B) or larger (CLASS = D). You set the size of the problem through the CLASS operand in your "make."

Vary the threads from one to the maximum number the coprocessor can execute simultaneously, i.e., 244. You can do this in a few different ways. We choose to use the OpenMP runtime environmental variable, OMP_NUM_THREADS. Since affinity affects thread distribution across the cores, its effect is tied to the number of application threads.

To reduce the amount of data collected, increment the number of threads each sample uses by four threads, e.g., use one thread for sample 1, five threads for sample 2, nine threads for sample 3, and so on. In the case of the coprocessor, as each core can execute four threads simultaneously, this is a natural number to use. See Figure 25.2. As long as we are sampling, when the same number of threads are

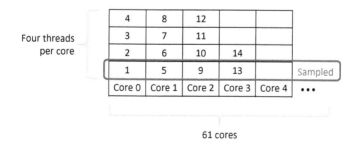

61 cores

FIGURE 25.2

Sampling of every 4th thread on the Intel® Xeon Phi™ coprocessor.

executing per core, the relative difference in power between the samples is maintained and we have like data. If we had instead been comparing a sample ending with three threads per core against another sample ending at one thread per core, we would be comparing unlike data as the core power usage for three threads is going to be greater than that for one thread. Though this is not important when using "scattered" affinity, for compact, we want to use some multiple of the number of threads that can execute on a core. For the Intel® Xeon processor, this is two threads per core. For the Intel® Xeon Phi™ coprocessor, it is four threads per core. Usage of this increment should not affect the data collected or the analysis.

Repeat the entire data collection for each thread number and type of affinity four times and average the results. More statistically rigorous data can be achieved with more collection runs, but for the purposes of this collection, four runs will be enough to illustrate the technique.

DATA COLLECTION

For each data collection, see Figure 25.3, log the default output of NPB EP followed up by a dump of the power information contained within /sys/class/micras/power. You may want to express this script in a more conventional form similar to Figure 25.4 using a script file with arguments. At the Pearls Web site, http://lotsofcores.com, you will find these same scripts but in a more traditional multiline form. The form in Figure 25.5 is convenient because it allows very rapid experimentation and

```
#script to collect the data
export KMP_AFFINITY='scatter,granularity=fine' ; for j in 1 2 3 4 ; do
>&2 echo ; >&2 echo EXPT $j; for i in {1..244..4}; do export
OMP_NUM_THREADS=$i; echo OMP_NUM_THREADS\($OMP_NUM_THREADS\); >&2 echo
-n $OMP_NUM_THREADS; ./ep.C.knc ; echo PWR********; cat
/sys/class/micras/power ; done > epC_1_244_4_scatter_$j.log ; done
```

FIGURE 25.3

Script to collect power and performance data from an Intel Xeon Phi coprocessor.

```
#script to collect the data
export KMP_AFFINITY='scatter,granularity=fine' ; \
for j in 1 2 3 4 ; do \
    >&2 echo ; \
    >&2 echo EXPT $j; \
    for i in {1..244..4}; do \
        export OMP_NUM_THREADS=$i; \
        echo OMP_NUM_THREADS\($OMP_NUM_THREADS\); \
        >&2 echo -n $OMP_NUM_THREADS; \
        ./ep.C.knc ; \
        echo PWR********; \
        cat /sys/class/micras/power ; \
    done \
    > epC_1_244_4_scatter_$j.log ; \
done
```

FIGURE 25.4

A more conventional view of the script to collect power and performance data from an Intel Xeon Phi coprocessor.

```
#Script to reduce the data
$ sed -n '/^OMP/ p; /Completed/{N;N;N;N;N;N; p;}; /Mop/ p; /^PWR/
{N;N;p}' epC_1_244_4_scatter_1.log > epC_1_244_4_scatter_reducedA.log
#strip out unused lines
$ sed -n '/Time/{s/[^0-9.]*/\n/; p}; /threads/{s/[^0-9.]*//g; p};
/Mop/{s/[^0-9.]*//g; p}; /^PWR/{N;N;s/^PWR[*]*\n//;p}'
epC_1_244_4_scatter_reducedA.log > epC_1_244_4_scatter_reducedB.csv
#strip out unwanted text
$ sed -n '/^$/{N;N;N;N;N;N;N; s/\n/,/g; p}'
epC_1_244_4_scatter_reducedB.csv > epC_1_244_4_scatter_reducedC.csv
#put in csv format using ",".
```

FIGURE 25.5

Script to extract desired performance power data and delete unneeded data.

customization without the need to edit and validate each time. Figures 25.6 and 25.7 are examples of both outputs. Perform this data collection for both

KMP_AFFINITY = 'scatter,granularity=fine' and
KMP_AFFINITY = 'compact,granularity=fine'.

Use another script, such as that shown in Figure 25.7, to extract the data. The sed (Stream EDitor) script in Figure 25.7 extracts the Number of available threads, CPU time, Mop/s total, Mop/s/thread, Total power for win 0, and Total power for win 1. It then places the result in a CSV data format.

(For the coprocessor, there is little documentation for the format of the data output of /sys/class/micras/power outside of the source code, and even that poorly defines what exactly "win 0" and "win 1" are other than that they are power averages over some interval. See the article, https://software.intel.com/en-us/articles/measuring-power-on-intel-xeon-phi-product-family-devices. Try using one versus the other to see if there are any significant differences.)

Use your own favorite tool to plot the result. We used Microsoft Excel to import, reduce, and plot the data.

Obtain two plots for this data, Performance/Power, and Power/Thread Number. Both provide insight into how affinity can influence application power consumption. Your plots should be very similar to Figures 25.8 and 25.9. Figure 25.8 shows the performance per watt (Mops/s/W) as a function of the number of OpenMP threads used. Figure 25.9 shows power (watts) by itself as a function of the number of threads.

ANALYSIS

We will first look at the power and performance of the Intel Xeon Phi coprocessor, and then at the Intel Xeon processor. We can point to some of the key features of the plots and deduce their origin. You should compare these plots to your own and see if you can identify similar features. Figure 25.8 shows performance (Mega operations/sec) per power consumed or Mops/s/W. This plot of performance per watt is perhaps the most dramatic evidence of the influence of OpenMP affinity on the power consumed by an application.

What is the largest difference you see between the scattered affinity results verses compact? Figure 25.8 shows that at points, scattered affinity has a more than two Mop/s greater performance per watt than if compact affinity were used instead. As a sanity check, verify that the two plots converge

```
NAS Parallel Benchmarks (NPB3.3-OMP) - EP Benchmark

Number of random numbers generated:      8589934592
Number of available threads:                      1

EP Benchmark Results:

CPU Time = 1096.0997
N = 2^    32
No. Gaussian Pairs =      3373275903.
Sums =      4.764367927994402D+04    -8.084072988036997D+04
Counts:
   0    1572172634.
   1    1501108549.
   2     281805648.
   3      17761221.
   4        424017.
   5          3821.
   6            13.
   7             0.
   8             0.
   9             0.


EP Benchmark Completed.
Class             =                      C
Size              =             8589934592
Iterations        =                      0
Time in seconds   =                1096.10
Total threads     =                      1
Avail threads     =                      1
Mop/s total       =                   7.84
Mop/s/thread      =                   7.84
Operation type    = Random numbers generated
Verification      =             SUCCESSFUL
Version           =                  3.3.1
Compile date      =            10 Mar 2015

Compile options:
    F77              = ifort
```

FIGURE 25.6

Output from the NPB EP run on an Intel Xeon Phi coprocessor.

(Continued)

```
FLINK           = $(F77)
F_LIB           = (none)
F_INC           = (none)
FFLAGS          = -O3 -openmp -mmic
FLINKFLAGS      = -O3 -openmp -mmic
RAND            = randi8


Please send all errors/feedbacks to:

NPB Development Team
npb@nas.nasa.gov
```

FIGURE 25.6, Cont'd

```
119000000    #Total power for running average Window 0
118000000    #Total power for running average Window 1
121000000    #power for current 5 msec sample (Instantaneous power)
189000000    #Max Instantaneous power over some sampling period
34000000     #PCI-E connector power
33000000     #power delivered by 2x3 power connector
54000000     #power delivered by 2x4 power connector
38000000 0 869000     #Core rail (Power, Current, Voltage)
32000000 0 1000000    #Non-core rail (Power, Current, Voltage)
33000000 0 1501000    #Memory subsystem rail (Power, Current, Voltage)
```

FIGURE 25.7

Output from a sampling of /sys/class/micras/power on an Intel Xeon Phi coprocessor.

at 1 and 244 threads. These are trivial cases that should have the same thread distribution across the cores no matter the affinity. (You may see a slight difference due to the operating system executing on the last core and, depending upon the OpenMP implementation, the threading policy avoiding allocating threads on that core.)

Look more closely at the plots. Are there any correlations between the notable features and thread distribution across cores? There is a whole host of information that you can obtain from this figure. Notice that some of the features on the "scatter" plot correspond to when all the cores are filled with the same number of executing threads, say 2 cores/thread, and your samples start filling up the next number of threads, say 3 cores/thread. For example, in Figure 25.8, at 61 threads, there is a significant drop in performance per watt. Also, the implication is that for an application (or part of an application) that is CPU bound, using affinity="scatter" may provide better performance.

Look at the drop in performance at 61 threads. Every added thread increases the application's performance by increasing the amount of parallelism until each of the cores is filled with a given rank, in this case, one thread per core. After every core is executing one thread, and the next rank of threads start, there is a drop in performance as the first few cores fill with the additional threads and experience

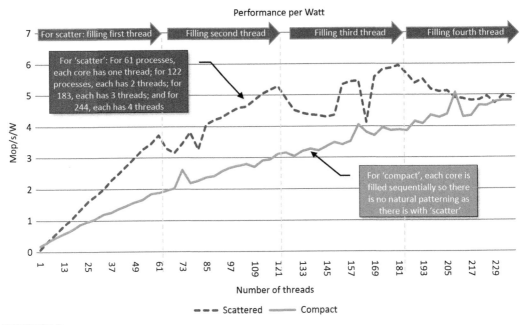

FIGURE 25.8

A comparison of the performance per watt (Mop/s/W) on an Intel Xeon Phi coprocessor.

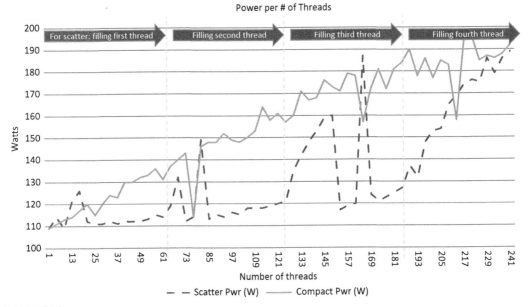

FIGURE 25.9

A comparison of the power performance of NPB EP for scatter and compact affinities on an Intel Xeon Phi coprocessor.

more contention than when there was with only one thread per core. At a certain point, the number of threads increases enough so that even with the per core drop in the performance, the increase in the number of executing threads results in a net increase. Another interesting feature of this plot is the continuous degradation in performance after there are three threads being executed on all three cores. This is because executing four threads per core results in so much contention within and between cores that the increased number of threads executing is not able to compensate for the loss in performance per thread, for this application.

The Xeon data, though different in some ways, are very similar, see Figures 25.10 and 25.11. There is a distinct difference between the affinities. Scatter affinity gives a better performance per watt. Compact is more linear. There are some evocative features that imply something about the nature of either the algorithm, the hardware, or both.

Let's look at some of the major features of the plots.

Plot character: The most obvious feature in the plots is the change in character at the transition from 16 to 17 cores. Interestingly, these features are from very different causes. For compact, the change means that the workload is starting to use the second socket. For scatter, this is the point where the workload starts using two threads per core. Another is when, for scatter affinity, the second socket starts to be used.

Power limiting: Unlike the coprocessor, the power consumed appears to be limited at 90 W. Without further investigation, it looks as if there is some type of thermal throttling happening. This may be an area of concern if the throttling results in a decrease in performance due to the enforced use of a higher (lower performance) P-state.

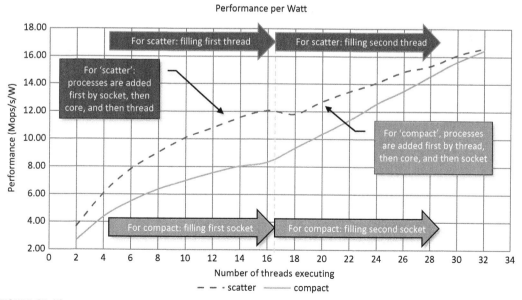

FIGURE 25.10

A comparison of the performance per watt (Mop/s/W) on an Intel Xeon processor.

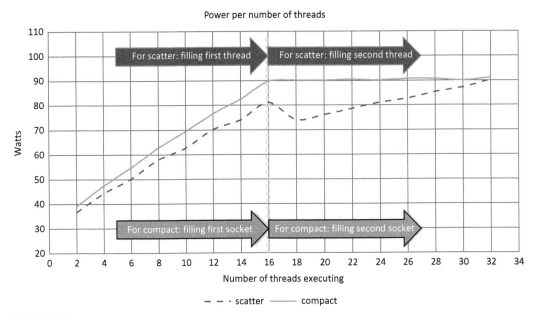

FIGURE 25.11

A comparison of the power performance of NPB EP for scatter and compact affinities on an Intel Xeon processor.

Power scaling: There is a difference in scale between the watts used. The Intel Xeon processor uses from 35 to 90 W, whereas the coprocessor, between 110 and 190 W. This is probably the result of the different ways what the hardware measures power and energy. The coprocessor and processor are of substantially different design and from different silicon generations—e.g., the coprocessor is a unique 22 nm architecture, whereas the processor is a 22 nm shrink of the 32 nm Sandy Bridge architecture. Even so, notice that the change between the minimum and maximum power are similar, 80 W for the coprocessor and 55 W for the processor. This difference is even less if some type of power limiting is taking place on the processor, limiting the maximum wattage.

Volatility: There is also a distinct difference in the volatility of the plots. This is much more difficult to quantify as there are too many factors: difference and maturity of architecture, different ways of measuring power, and different software and hardware operating environments, to name a few.

DATA CENTER: INTERPRETATION VIA WATERFALL POWER DATA CHARTS

In this section, we look at system resource utilization, and power data collection and visualization tools for effective cluster management over time. A wealth of information can be gathered and observed about system performance and power utilization; the data, along with the means to view it at a cluster level, allows users and administrators to detect inefficiencies that lead to unintended power consumption.

Many cluster setups today collect system data to detect reliability issues and, to some extent, effective utilization of the system. What we propose here is to collect power consumption data along with performance metrics, as well as using visualization tools to observe consumption in the cluster as a whole. The premise is that effective utilization of the compute capacity should yield the most effective power consumption attainable (and power consumption data should generally agree with performance data); and visualization tools allow you to quickly assess, at-a-glance, what is happening in the entire cluster.

Collection of power statistics is growing in importance, as cluster administrators are responsible for assessing the Power usage effectiveness of their datacenters for governmental reporting purposes.

The correlation of seemingly disparate events, or information about jobs run, allows you to pinpoint the root cause of performance degradation, to observe and tune the performance and power efficiency of software, and to scope future cluster hardware (and software) needs. To accomplish this, it is necessary to employ a data collection mechanism capable of minimizing its impact on overall system usage, capable of collecting enough useful detail, and capable of reliably storing the data in a centralized location for later consumption. There are several collection and profiling software options available today. For the purposes of this pearl, we will use and discuss the NWPerf data collection and profiling mechanism, as it satisfies the aforementioned requirements.

Beyond the data collection mechanism, we need to employ visualization software to display the data meaningfully and actionably; we'll choose CView to meet these needs. Both NWPerf and CView software packages are currently used in the Pacific Northwest National Labs' (PNNL) Linux-based cluster environment: throughout this section we describe a reference environment that mirrors what is used at PNNL to provide you with a practical example of how data collection and visualization can be configured.

NWPerf

NWPerf is freely available software that collects performance data for every job run on a supercomputer or compute cluster. The software was designed (and can be configured) for minimal impact on application performance while gathering required performance data. The historical record created by NWPerf has proven to be invaluable for software vendors, scientists, programmers, and analysts evaluating balance metrics for future procurements. Succinctly, the performance behavior of any run or sets of runs can be accessed via a Web interface, which means that silent performance regressions from vendor and programmer updates can be identified—even months—after the software changes are pushed into production. Workload assessments and balance metrics can be built from NWPerf database queries.

NWPerf collects performance and power consumption using the Intelligent Platform Management Interface (IPMI) for Intel Xeon Processor systems, and the libmicmgmt API for the Intel Xeon Phi Coprocessor. The libmicmgmt API comes with the Intel® Manycore Platform Software Stack (Intel® MPSS).

Once clients, collectors, and an object store are configured, data collection can commence at 1-min (or longer) intervals. From here, we can employ data extraction mechanisms, such as monitoring and visualization scripts. Please note that in some circumstances, you may need to use a different monitoring system, with a more frequent sample rate to be more frequent: Intel used a 500 ms sample rate to observe power spikes occurring at various points during the DGEMM VPU phase of the Linpack benchmark while micro-tuning for a Green500 submission; to do this, Intel employed a specific process (not discussed at length here) that used power meters for node measurement and calibration, the micsmc utility for coprocessor power measurement, and IPMI for automated node measurement.

WATERFALL CHARTS GENERATED WITH CVIEW FROM NWPERF DATA

NWPerf collects performance utilization data (processor and I/O subsystems) as well as power consumption data, and stores it in a centralized database. Two user interactive systems are available to display the data:

1. NWPerf provides a user web service for displaying their jobs, allowing display and comparison with 2D graph views. This provides cluster users a personalized view of where and how their jobs are running. NWPerf is built and designed to work on linux.
2. The other tool is CView; it provides the 3D waterfall charts shown in this chapter. Waterfall charts allow for a more extensive representation of in-progress work across multiple dimensions (e.g., time, power consumption, resource consumption, and systems to name a few). CView is developed primarily on Ubuntu linux systems, but Redhat, Microsoft Windows, and OS X build environments work as well.

The waterfall charts generated shown in this chapter are created using the CView tool.

Overall, at a high level, the following ingredients are used for data collection, integration and viewing; these are described in greater detail below:

1. A data collection mechanism (collectd or ganglia) is installed on all compute nodes.
2. A cluster-collectd node receives the data from compute nodes and funnels it into a NWPerf "service."
3. An NWperf instance subscribes to this data service and stores the data in a ceph object store (storage).
4. The gen_cview tool runs every minute to collect 2 hours of ceph data; creating data-sets for CView.
5. CView is run on endpoint (client) systems.

The aforementioned functions 2-4 could technically all reside on the same server in a small cluster environment. For larger clusters, we recommend separating where cluster-collectd, NWperf, and gen_cview are run.

INSTALLING AND CONFIGURING NWPerf AND CView

In order to deploy a full NWPerf to CView visualization system, you need to start by deploying a data collection tool in the cluster itself. For this example, we will use the collectd tool, though similar steps can be taken when using ganglia for data collection.

1. Install collectd on all cluster compute nodes. Direct all nodes to channel data to a centralized collectd node, setting the hostname as appropriate, and configuring the Intel MIC plugin to collect additional data for the coprocessors; changes to collectd.conf are shown in Figure 25.12.
2. Install collectd and NWPerf on the central "cluster-collectd" node. The configuration allows for data to be accepted from the network, and then published as an nwperf service. The nwcollectd

```
LoadPlugin network
LoadPlugin mic

<Plugin network>
Server "cluster-collectd" "25826"
ReportStats false
</Plugin>
<Plugin mic>
    ShowCPU true
    ShowCPUCores false
    ShowMemory true
    ShowTemperatures true
    ShowPower true
</Plugin>
```

FIGURE 25.12

collectd.conf snippet showing network data send and a plugin for the coprocessor.

```
<LoadPlugin python>
  Globals true
</LoadPlugin>
LoadPlugin Network
<Plugin network>
Listen "cluster-collectd" "25826"
ReportStats false
</Plugin>

<Plugin python>
ModulePath "/usr/lib/python2.6/site-packages/nwperf"
Import nwcollectd
            <Module nwcollectd>
                NameServer "tcp://nwperf-ns:6967"
                ClusterName "cascade"
                IP "192.168.1.1"
            </Module>
</Plugin>
```

FIGURE 25.13

collectd.conf snippet showing network data send.

python plugin will register with the nwperf nameservice defined in the config file. In Figure 25.13, we show that a cluster name and an IP address for external connection need to be specified. We will use the cluster name "cascade" throughout this example.

3. Configure long-term storage. In order for NWPerf to gather and collect the data in long-term storage, in this example, we use a ceph object store pool. This assumes you have ceph running and can create a new pool according to the instructions on the NWPerf Website. Once nwperf is installed on the server that will be processing data, we run a few configuration commands to modify some of the defaults in the /etc/nwperf.conf file (see Figure 25.14).

The default assumes the hostname "nwperf-ns" is setup in /etc/hosts or DNS, so that all services can talk to the NWPerf nameservice. Once you have started the nwperf services and have

```
#Specify a cluster name
nwperfconfig -a cluster -v <cluster name>
#Setup a periodic data set dump.
nwperfconfig -a gen_cview.command -v "gen_cview -c %(cluster) -o
/dev/shm/%(cluster)7 -r 60 "
#Specify which nwperf workers to start
nwperfconfig -a services -v gen_cview,nwperf-ceph-store,nwperf-ns
#start Services
restart nwperf
```

FIGURE 25.14

nwperf configuration commands to setup services based on the installed defaults.

collectd running a nameservice query is possible: as an example "nwperf-nsq.py tcp://nwperf-ns:6967 listServices," should return "cascade.allpoints." The ceph processing program subscribes to this service to store data in the ceph pool.

4. Install CView. Download the CView source, compile and install it according to the README instructions, using cmake.

5. Create a CView configuration file.

First, create a basic CView file by running the cviewall tool:

```
cviewall -url http://lotsofcores.com/power/cview1/ -metrics '(mic-0/cpu-user,mic-1/
cpu-user)'
```

This is one sample data set we provided. Please visit http://lotsofcores.com/power for more tips, and information on several different collections of data and how to view them using cviewall. You are encouraged to take cviewall for a spin!

To interact with CView, use the keys w, a, s, d, arrow keys, pgup, pgdown, and mouse buttons to move the graphics around and view them. If you have the AntTweakBar library installed, you can press "t" to get access to various control windows. Once you have a configuration that meets your needs, you can press "z" for a screenshot, or "~" to dump the configuration to a file. This config text file, defaults to the name "cviewall.cview," uses the Apple plist format, and can be modified to suit your specific needs. Once you have a config file, you can run "cview -c <config file>" to start up CView using the saved configuration. Many modifications can be done to this file to split the window into multiple areas, or to do data calculations. A sample config file showing multiple clusters, with calculations, is available on the http://lotsofcores.com site as part of the downloads for this chapter.

The gen_cview tool is run regularly to dump the most recent 2 h CView to /dev/shm/<cluster name>, using the data in ceph as configured and described above. This same tool can be used to generate data sets using historical data using the selection and summation options on the command line.

The data in /dev/shm/<cluster name> data can be provided to a Web server, or directly accessed by the CView program. A wsgi python module for the Web server can also pull this data as needed and is included in the NWPerf codebase. Once a Web server is configured to serve these files, we can then access this data with CView from any client (Figure 25.15).

In a production environment, you can set up and configure kiosks to support the interactive consumption of this pre-configured data for administrators and users. These kiosks can display a waterfall graph of time series performance metrics. They can also support the inclusion of text, images, bar

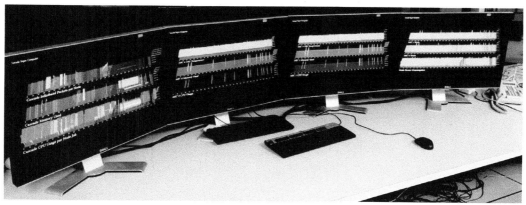

FIGURE 25.15

Cluster usage data visualization on multiple screens.

graphs, InfiniBand cable maps, etc. Data for the waterfall chart can be input from a defined `CView` data set, or from streaming command line data. `CView` supports continuous reloads so that waterfall graphs can offer up-to-the-minute data for real-time analysis. The 3D views represented through waterfall charts in `CView` can be manipulated and navigated using mouse and keyboard commands, as previously described.

Multiple waterfall charts can be displayed on a single screen using a grid-like layout system, for example, one can put different data on each screen of a multiple-monitor system to correlate various aspects of a cluster's resource consumption as seen in Figure 25.15.

INTERPRETING THE WATERFALL CHARTS

Each waterfall plot can display multiple dimensions of data. A typical use case is to plot data for each node in a cluster, over a period of time, with the third dimension representing resource consumption such as power or memory use. The consumption can be represented like a heat map, so the eye can easily decipher where problem spots exist. Thus, as seen in Figure 25.16, the X axis in a waterfall plot may be cluster nodes; the Y axis is time; and the Z axis is power consumption (in watts). Color-coding the resource consumption (in this case, power) where the color blue represents a "cooler" temperature, and yellow to red represents continuously "hotter" temperatures allows fast interpretation of cluster node power consumption. In gray scale, the waterfall charts represent the highest resource consumption in lighter shades (toward white) plus greater height across the Y axis. The color versions of these waterfall charts are available on http://lotsofcores.com as part of download of figures from this book. Correlating power data with separate graphs showing jobs run by different users, and with charts representing CPU and I/O consumption, we can determine which jobs make inefficient resource use and/or which jobs may have changed in behavior over time. A change in behavior might be an indication of modifications resulting in worse power consumption and performance compared to historical measurements.

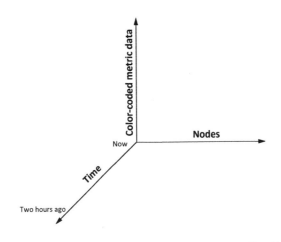

FIGURE 25.16

CView waterfall graph axis.

As an example of what waterfall plots may look like for a sample NWChem run, Figure 25.17 shows multiple waterfall graphs depicting CPU utilizations across two Intel Xeon Phi coprocessors, and one Intel Xeon processor.

The two graphs on the left represent CPU use by the two coprocessors installed in the system. On the left side of each graph, a color-map line shows a legend for the scale. In this graph, the number of jiffies is used. A jiffy in Linux terms is the amount of time in one tick; on most Linux systems there are 100 ticks per second, each jiffy counted falls into one of many buckets, such as system time, user time, idle time, etc.

The bottom right chart represents power consumption, as reported by IPMI, on the host server. The red color indicates when the server reached 1500 W consumption.

The upper right chart represents the CPU consumption on the Intel Xeon processor-based host measured in jiffies.

The data represented in the visualization charts that follow was collected and supplied by the Pacific Northwest National Laboratory (PNNL).

The following are additional data representations showing what can be done when NWPerf and CView are combined, as described in the aforementioned steps. Figure 25.18 shows poor CPU usage across a set of nodes resulting from memory bandwidth issues (will show as cooler colors on a color chart and darker shades on a gray scale chart).

Similarly, you can represent power, CPU, and memory consumption, down to the coprocessor level for each individual node, as seen in the following two figures (Figures 25.19 and 25.20).

These waterfall graphs can be quickly created to compare different metrics simultaneously.

In our experience, the mere act of showing waterfall graphs to users has proven beneficial because they can now see when their jobs are running and what they are doing and can take charge of addressing inefficiencies in their software. Administrators can also monitor these waterfall graphs for behavior changes: in one instance, we found jobs that collectively were not using systems to their fullest extent because of a global synchronization issue; in another case, we found recurrent jobs were taking longer than usual to complete and root-caused the problem to a compile-time issue. The waterfall graphs

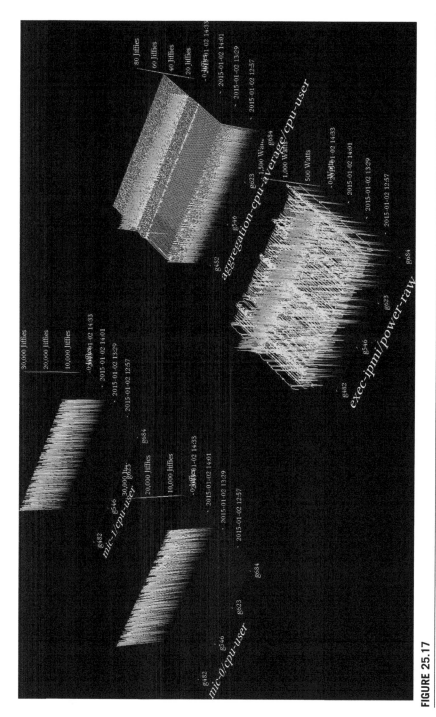

FIGURE 25.17

CPU consumption across two Intel Xeon Phi coprocessors, an Intel Xeon processor-based host, and IPMI power.

FIGURE 25.18

CPU, Memory and InfiniBand usage across a cluster.

FIGURE 25.19

Power consumption on host and coprocessor (watts).

FIGURE 25.20

CPU, memory, and temperature readings on a single coprocessor over time.

provide a powerful means to assess cluster utilization "at a glance"—which is easier for the eye to parse than raw data or individual system alerts.

So what would the "ideal" performance and power consumption of a cluster look like? In theory, the coprocessors' host CPUs would run at 80% or greater utilization, and we would have balanced general consumption across the cluster. This would mean that jobs are spread across the cluster and operating as efficiently as possible, which inherently minimizes runtime and power consumption. On an Intel Xeon Phi coprocessor, the ideal state would be to have either all the cores fully engaged in computation, with a minimal amount of I/O work being performed, or a subset of the cores being fully utilized while the remaining cores are idled (in power conservation mode). When visualizing consumption data, it is important to look at both system resource consumption and power consumption together to tell the whole story—looking at only one of these components will likely not provide insights on what improvements can be made.

Processor manufacturers will continue to push the envelope by increasing performance and reducing power of future processors. Collecting historical data across a cluster during its lifetime will prove useful when evaluating future system platforms: investigators and administrators can quickly determine the performance and power benefits from running their applications on these new platforms, relative to their installed base, and derive a return-on-investment analysis on whether to invest in upgrading or augmenting their installed base with the new platforms thanks to the historical data captured.

SUMMARY

In Section "Introduction to measuring and saving power", we discussed the ever-growing importance of power efficiency and the need for a holistic approach that employs the most power efficient hardware combined with efforts to insure power efficient applications. By studying how applications are making effective use of the hardware, at both the scale of the cluster (nodes) and individual systems (cores), we can improve the hardware utilization and reduce the power footprint of their application.

In Section "Application: Power measurement and analysis", we looked at how an application is designed, particularly, how application thread distribution can have a significant impact on its performance per watt. By looking at the impact upon both a high core count Intel Xeon processor and the Intel® Xeon Phi™ coprocessor, we illustrated the importance of such measurements and analysis, and how it will become increasingly significant as the core count continues to increase. In the NPB EP example, changing the OpenMP threads runtime distribution, through setting runtime environment variables KMP_AFFINITY and OMP_NUM_THREADS, resulted in a difference in performance per watt of up to 2 Mops/s/W. The impact of such savings in a data center could be significant. Though we only looked at OpenMP, this same result would have occurred no matter the threading model used. In addition, plots of power and performance per number of threads can reveal notable application design and execution features. These features in turn provide insights into application internals, allowing the developer to change the application's design to improve performance per watt.

Finally, in Section "Data center: Interpretation via waterfall power data charts", we explored how space, power, cooling and infrastructure are all important considerations when building and maintaining large data centers. As such, the collection of system performance and power utilization data is important for both users and administrators of large clusters. Just as important, the monitoring of consumption data with graphical rendering so correlations (e.g., between multiple subsystems or over time) is possible. Waterfall plots are an effective method to easily scan usage across a large cluster, and then decide how to drill down to specifics. It is also important to note that no single waterfall chart tells the entire story; correlations between multiple data views are necessary to ascertain the situation and course of action for any identified problems. We invite you to try viewing data by visiting http://lotsofcores.com/power for updated information on example data files we have provided and how to view them with cview—it is very educational to try it "hands on."

FOR MORE INFORMATION

Here are some additional reading materials we recommend related to this chapter.

- NAS Parallel Benchmarks, Downloaded, March 16, 2015 from http://www.nas.nasa.gov/publications/npb.html.
- Lawson, G., Sosonkina, M., Yuzhong, S., 2014. Energy evaluation for applications with different thread affinities on the Intel Xeon Phi, In: Computer Architecture and High Performance Computing Workshop (SBAC-PADW), 2014 International Symposium on Paris: IEEE.
- Intel Corporation, Intel® Xeon Phi™ Coprocessor Software Developers Guide, March 2014, downloaded March 16, 2015 from https://software.intel.com/mic-developer.
- Farber, Rob and Taylor Kidd, Measuring Power on Intel® Xeon Phi™ Product Family Devices, March 6, 2015. Downloaded March 16, 2015 from https://software.intel.com/en-us/articles/measuring-power-on-intel-xeon-phi-product-family-devices.
- Reinders, J., Jeffers, J., 2014. High Performance Parallelism Pearls. Morgan Kaufmann, Burlington, Massachusetts.
- Intel Corporation, User and Reference Guide for the Intel® C++ Compiler 15.0. Downloaded March 27, 2015 from https://software.intel.com/en-us/compiler_15.0_ug_c.
- Intel Corporation, Intel® Energy Checker SDK. Downloaded April 2015 from https://software.intel.com/en-us/articles/intel-energy-checker-sdk/.
- Collectd—The system statistics collection daemon—https://collectd.org/.
- The NWPerf software can be downloaded from https://github.com/EMSL-MSC/NWPerf and is developed and maintained by the Pacific Northwest National Laboratory (PNNL).
- CView engine is freely available from https://github.com/EMSL-MSC/cview.
- Weaver, Vince, "Reading RAPL energy measurements from Linux", http://web.eece.maine.edu/~vweaver/projects/rapl/.
- Anttweakbar library: http://anttweakbar.sourceforge.net/doc/.
- Goodell, J., 2006. Big Coal: The Dirty Secret Behind America's Energy. Houghton Mifflin Harcourt.
- "Energy Aware Computing"—Power Approaches for Green System Design. Steigerwald et al. Intel Press, ISBN 13 978010934053-41-6.
- View information on data sets, and how to view them with cview, at http://lotsofcores.com/power.
- Download the code from this, and other chapters, http://lotsofcores.com.

Author Index

511

Subject Index

Note: Page numbers followed by *f* indicate figures.